The Feminist Encyclopedia of French Literature

The Feminist Encyclopedia of French Literature

Eva Martin Sartori, Editor-in-Chief

Editors

Middle Ages
Eva Martin Sartori

Sixteenth Century
Colette H. Winn

Seventeenth Century
Perry Gethner

Eighteenth Century
Samia I. Spencer

Nineteenth Century
Juliette Parnell-Smith and Mary Rice-DeFosse

Twentieth Century
Susan Ireland and Patrice J. Proulx

Greenwood Press
Westport, Connecticut • London

Library of Congress Cataloging-in-Publication Data

The feminist encyclopedia of French literature / Eva Martin Sartori,
  editor-in-chief.
    p. cm.
  Includes bibliographical references and index.
  ISBN 0–313–29651–0 (alk. paper)
    1. French literature—Women authors—Encyclopedias. 2. French
literature—Encyclopedias. 3. Women authors, French—Biography—
Encyclopedias. 4. Feminism and literature—Encyclopedias.
5. Women in literature—Encyclopedias. I. Sartori, Eva Martin.
PQ149.F47   1999
840.9'9287'03—dc21   98–44595

British Library Cataloguing in Publication Data is available.

Library of Congress Catalog Card Number: 98–44595
ISBN: 0–313–29651–0

First published in 1999

Greenwood Press, 88 Post Road West, Westport, CT 06881
An imprint of Greenwood Publishing Group, Inc.
www.greenwood.com

Printed in the United States of America

The paper used in this book complies with the
Permanent Paper Standard issued by the National
Information Standards Organization (Z39.48–1984).

10 9 8 7 6 5 4 3 2 1

Contents

Preface

In the seventeenth century, the popular novelist Madeleine de Scudéry lamented the fate of women writers: "Among the infinite number of beautiful women who doubtless lived during the centuries preceding our own, we have barely heard of only two or three: and during those same centuries, we can see the glory of men solidly established by the written works they have left us."[1] More than three hundred years later, Scudéry's descendants are reclaiming women writers from obscurity. *The Feminist Encyclopedia of French Literature*, together with other recent reference works, brings to public attention the works and world of French women writers, past and present.

Our current state of historical knowledge allows us to state with some degree of certainty that the earliest known literary productions by women living in Europe were by French women. As far back as the twelfth century, women troubadours in the south of France were writing poems in Occitan, a gallo-roman language. French women continued writing through the ages, their number increasing as education became more available to women of all classes. And yet, of the great numbers of works by women writers who preceded the current feminist movement, very few survived. My own education in French literature, first as an undergraduate at a women's college that can be fairly qualified as "feminist," and later in graduate school, included but a small number of women writers. A few had been "canonized": Marie de France, Marguerite de Navarre, Madeleine de Scudéry, Mme de Lafayette, Mme de Sévigné, Mme de Staël, George Sand, Marceline Desbordes-Valmore, Colette, Simone de Beauvoir, Nathalie Sarraute, and Marguerite Duras. Critics, mostly male, had judged the works of only these few women writers worthy of recognition.

As part of the feminist move to reclaim women writers and to rethink literary history, scholars in French literature began to take a new look at women writers who had been popular during their lifetime but who had not been admitted into the canon. These women numbered in the hundreds, if not the thousands, thus surpassing the number we could realistically include in one volume.

Our intention in producing *The Feminist Encyclopedia of French Literature* was to provide a compendium of information about women writers and the world in which they lived. Space limitations forced us to make choices. Our first decision was to limit the women authors included to those writers who lived and worked mainly in France. Among those are writers who are well known, such as Lafayette and Sand, but many more who are not, partly because they practiced genres, such as diaries, journals, memoirs, and popular and travel literature, that were not considered part of high culture. In addition to women writers, there are entries on important women who wielded political power but were not themselves writers. The actions of Diane de Poitiers, Marie and Catherine de Medici, Madame du Barry, and Madame de Châteauroux and the ways in which the public perceived them directly or indirectly affected the lot of less visible women.

The only writer included who was neither French nor lived in France is Isabelle de Charrière, who was born and reared in Holland and spent her adult life in Switzerland. However, French was her language of choice, her literary affiliations were with French literature, and her work has become part of the French canon.

The entries on individual women are complemented by essays on broad literary, historical, political, and sociological topics. The reader will find information on literary genres, such as the novel, poetry, and the short story; literary movements, such as classicism, realism, and surrealism; life-cycle events particular to women, such as menstruation and menopause; institutions and events that affected women differently than men, such as laws on marriage, divorce, and education; and lists of important organizations and archives. Such information is often difficult to come by, and by compiling it in one volume we hope to give the reader access to the many dimensions of a writer's life and work. Thus, someone interested in the novels of George Sand, for example, can refer to the entries on marriage and divorce laws, on women's access to education, on the Revolution of 1848, and on the development of the novel, as well as bibliographic references for further exploration.

The individual entries are followed by a general bibliography (Appendix A), a chronology of the women writers included (Appendix B), and a subject index. A list of the contributors concludes the volume. For the reader's convenience, we have placed an asterisk after the first mention in an entry of a name or a subject for which a separate entry exists in the *Encyclopedia*.

The alphabetical organization sometimes makes for strange bedfellows but avoids the imposition of a value system and provides the reader with the most convenient access to information on a writer or a subject. Alphabetization here takes into account blank spaces: La Vigne comes before Labé. Women's names often present problems since a writer may use a maiden name, a married name, or a pseudonym. We have used the most common form whenever possible. Pseudonyms are used when a writer is known primarily by that name, as in the case of George Sand or Gyp, but not when, in our judgment, the pseudonym is less well known than the family name, as in the case of Marie d'Agoult. Cross-references are listed in the subject index.

In terms of our methodological approach, we asked the contributing scholars to focus on the development of a "feminist" consciousness, on each writer's awareness of the ways in which her gender shaped her outlook and her opportunities, and to reflect on the way categorizations, structures, and terms used to describe literary works have been defined for women and the ways in which women writers have responded to these definitions.

"Times have changed," observed one scholar in response to a questionnaire on the inclusion of women writers in college and university curricula. Course offerings now include many more women authors, and many institutions offer programs in gender and women's studies, or, as some respondents noted, under the banner of multiculturalism. The presence of women in administrative positions in institutions of higher education, as department chairs, deans, and presidents, also encourages scholars to present the works of women writers to their students. The pace of dissertations on women writing in French has accelerated. While between 1963 and 1980, in the United States, only seven dissertations had been written on French women writers, the number jumps to thirty-six for the period between 1981 and 1997—more than five times as many. The number of scholars contributing to this volume is another indication of the vitality of the field.

The publication of modern anthologies and editions of works by French women writers has greatly facilitated the inclusion of these writers in the curriculum. We hope *The Feminist Encyclopedia of French Literature* will contribute to a greater awareness and appreciation of women writing in French, and we eagerly await the publication of new editions and anthologies.

I wish to thank the period editors, who assembled a group of expert and enthusiastic scholars to write the entries in this volume, wrote many of the entries themselves, and edited them with the exigencies of a reference work in mind. I am especially grateful to Perry Gethner, whose sharp eye and keen mind, generously volunteered in the final editing phase of the project, have made this a much more polished work than it would have been without his help. Of course the editors' collective gratitude goes to the scholars who contributed their expertise and their time and made possible this compendium of information about women writers in France, their lives, their works, and the conditions under which they lived.

In addition, the editors would like to acknowledge the following sources of support for *The Feminist Encyclopedia of French Literature*: Susan Ireland: the Grant Board of Grinnell College; Patrice J. Proulx: the University Committee on Research of the University of Nebraska at Omaha; Samia I. Spencer: the College of Liberal Arts at Auburn University for a Faculty Development Grant; Eva M. Sartori: The University of Nebraska-Lincoln for a Faculty Development Leave.

NOTE

1. Madeleine de Scudéry, quoted in Faith E. Beasley, *Revising Memory: Women's Fiction and Memoirs in Seventeenth-Century France* (New Brunswick, NJ: Rutgers University Press, 1990), 55.

A Feminist History of French Literature

THE MIDDLE AGES

The history of women authors throughout the French Middle Ages, that is from the Merovingian period (c. 475) through the fifteenth century, is framed by the proscriptions of Church Fathers against women writing. Most influential in denying women the right to teach—whether *viva voce* or in writing—were the letters of Paul (d. A.D. 67), who specifically silences woman and forbids her to engage in preaching or didactic activity because of the double transgression her mother Eve committed in the Fall: "Let a woman learn in silence with all submissiveness. I permit no woman to teach or to have authority over men; she is to keep silent. For Adam was formed first, then Eve; and Adam was not deceived, but the woman was deceived and became a transgressor" (1 Timothy 2: 11–14). Paul's view of the doubly disobedient nature of woman became a tenet of Christian theology, and Church Fathers of the third and fourth centuries, for example, Tertullian and Jerome, retrospectively link her sins of disobedience to her sexuality, concluding, as does the latter: "As long as woman is for birth and children, she is different from man as body from soul. But if she wishes to serve Christ more than the world, then she will cease to be a woman and will be called man."[1] Logically, then, only religious women who by their devotion to Christ transcend their sexual identity are permitted to write. Indeed, in the Merovingian and Carolingian period, Frankish women writers whose works have been preserved are most often religious. The interdiction against female teaching is made even more powerful by the Church's suspicion of secular literary activity, whatever the writer's sex, as it leads to the creation of *fabulas*, which at the least distract human attention from spiritual and moral concerns or, worse, provoke sinful thoughts and activity.

Several consequences follow from the above and apply to the entire period: First, few women venture into writing, since it is seen as a gendered (male) activity, and those who do so most easily, that is, with Church blessing, are religious women whose sex, according to Jerome's thinking, does not therefore taint their compositions. Such writing nuns, whose language is, of course, Latin, are best exemplified in McNamara's important collection of seventeen Frankish female saints' lives and documents from the Merovingian period, which includes a letter of monastic advice from Caesaria II, abbess of Saint Jean d'Arles (c. 550), to Saint Radegund, abbess of Poitiers and Frankish queen (525–587), whose own *vita* was written by both a male and a female hagiographer, Fortunatus and Baudonivia; in addition, the *vita* of Saint Austreberta (650–703) appears from its preface to have been composed at the behest of a later abbess by a younger nun. In the later Middle Ages, religious women write about their own mystical experiences. Petroff shows that for Marguerite d'Oingt (d. 1310), prioress of a Carthusian house near Lyons, who wrote in both Latin and Franco-Provençal, authorial self-consciousness is so important that she conceives of her visions of Christ, whose wounds are inscribed on his body as a text, as scripted in her own heart, and that her role is to transfer these inscriptions into her book. In addition to mediating the visionary experience, writing can be used against the mystic, as in the case of Marguerite Porete (d. 1310), extracts of whose *Mirouer des simples ames* were condemned as heretical by the Inquisition in Paris. Interestingly, not all French mystics write their own visions: for example, the life of Marie d'Oignies (1177–1213), the first Béguine, whose example of a spiritual, charitable life led in the world rather than the cloister influenced the explosive growth of the movement around Liège, was written by the influential churchman Jacques de Vitry, who abandoned the professoriate in Paris to become her disciple. As Petroff shows, the theologically conservative Jacques de Vitry's authorship ironically enhanced the authority of Marie, whose ideas of reform and extra-monastic practices were regarded with suspicion by the Church and whose visions, recounted by her amanuensis, often contain erotic love imagery.

A second consequence is that even fewer secular women wrote texts. Patristic distrust of women's learning or teaching and the association between divine (male) creativity and language (''In the beginning was the Word, and the Word was with God, and the Word was God''—John 1:1) made it especially difficult for women outside monasticism to establish their *auctoritas*, that is, their right to create texts equally credible as those of male authors. That difficulty can be seen in the importance they attach to constructing elaborate prefaces wherein they justify their taking up the pen. In three prefatory sections, Dhuoda, a Carolingian noblewoman writing in 842, consistently invokes the humility *topos* as she regrets her stylistic inability, yet she simultaneously proclaims her right as the mother of an absent son to write a handbook that will literally embody her counsel and represent her to the boy held hostage far away. In other words, she divests *auctoritas* of its male-gendered implications and transforms it into maternal authority. Furthermore, she subtly turns her putative lack of rhetorical skill into a guarantee of her text's moral and spiritual authenticity. The task of establishing authority is even more difficult for women writing in the vernacular, for example, the late twelfth-century author Marie de France*, whose *Lais* carry the double obstacle to credibility of being written not in Latin, the language of truth, but Anglo-Norman dialect, and of memorializing popular oral Celtic tales rather than serious philosophical or theological subjects. As Freeman, Foulet and Uitti, and others have shown, Marie carefully constructs her General Prologue not only to emphasize her own participation in the transmission of knowledge by glossing meanings encoded by earlier authors but also to highlight the value of her undertaking both as a moral corrective to idleness and as a historical contribution to the perpetuation of cultural (Celtic) memory. She further invests the *Lais* with authority when she dedicates them to the king of England, thus implying a close enough association to warrant further credibility. The importance of establishing authority even toward the end of the French Middle Ages is exemplified by Christine de Pizan*, a prolific author (thirty-six books and letters) who, early in her career as a public author addressing public concerns (after she wrote poetry* of a more private nature about her widowhood), devises an even more elaborate strategy in her *Livre de la Cité des Dames* (1404–5): by fragmenting her authorial voice among her *personae*, the naive young scholar Christine who tends to believe male misogyny, and the three daughters of God who consistently debunk it, Christine de Pizan focuses her readers' attention on an antimisogynist authority of divine origin, which inexorably constructs a defense of female virtue and excellence. The foregrounding of a pro-female divine authority is made even more powerful by Christine's choice of a vision to frame her attack on misogyny, thus using an important element of religious women's writing to undermine male, often Church-sponsored criticism of women.

While Patristic distrust of writing women is probably the most important element to be considered, other factors contributed to their limited numbers. First, education* was usually available to noble women and daughters of wealthy or powerful families only, and only in the cloister or at the hands of a learned clerk hired by her family, since cathedral schools and universities were not open to women. In the second half of the twelfth century, Marie, countess of Champagne, and her sister Alix, daughters of King Louis VII of France by his first wife, Eleanor of Aquitaine, received their education at the royal court from the nun Alix de Mareuil. Alix read Latin well enough to have a correspondence with the churchman Adam de Perseigne; Marie's patronage of translations* of Latin texts into French may suggest her greater comfort in the vernacular. In any case, no writing by either woman survives, although the absence may be due to their use of clerkly secretaries in the important Champenois chancelry. At a much less grand level in the first half of the twelfth century, if we believe the authenticity of the *Historia calamitatum* and the lovers' correspondence (a vexed issue), Héloïse* was first educated by her uncle, the canon Fulbert. Even before she was tutored by Abelard, who had been given lodgings by her uncle in exchange for his supervision of her, "the breadth of her learning made her an exceptional woman. Literary knowledge is so rare in persons of the female sex that she exerted an irresistible attraction, and her reputation," states Abelard, "was already well-known in the kingdom." One of the three lengthy and learned letters of the correspondence is attributed to Héloïse. Christine de Pizan's excellent education in the fourteenth century was the result not only of her intellectual father's oversight but also of his important position at the court of King Charles V, which gave her access to the court library. Recent scholarship suggests, however, that rudimentary education in writing and calculating was given to most noble women from the late twelfth century on so that they could better manage their household and keep accounts. Confirmation comes from Marie de France's *lai Milun*, in which a woman of noble birth but of no special power writes letters to accompany her abandoned child and to carry on a love affair with its father. Given this wider spread of rudimentary literacy than originally acknowledged by scholars, the fact that more medieval French women did not write is curious. While the fragility of letters and manuscripts, the cost in time and money of reproducing the latter, and the difficulty of conserving them (e.g., only five manuscripts of Marie de France's *Lais* survive, of which only two are complete or nearly complete) undoubtedly contribute to the relatively small corpus of medieval French women's writings, the discouraging effect of misogynist pronouncements cannot be underestimated. In addition to the accessibility of other writers' manuscripts and writing materials, the availability of sufficient leisure time to indulge the writing habit or the financial resources to support that habit would have been crucial. It is not clear, for example, whether Marie de France's dedication of her *Lais* to the English king and her *Fables* to Count William were intended only to assure their protective enhancement of her reputation or to encourage their financial patronage as well. Christine de Pizan, widowed early and beset by her husband's and father's debts, solved her financial problems by actively cultivating royal patronage and earning her living from her writing, thus becoming the first professional French woman writer.

It is interesting that the one exception to the relative scarcity of secular medieval women writers—the eighteen or nineteen *trobairitz**, poetesses who wrote in Provençal between 1170 and 1260, among them the Comtessa de Dia*, Castelloza*, Tibors, and Azalaïs—is associated with a different geographical area, southern France, and with different conditions of composition. The *trobairitz* appear to have formed a network of women writers in communication with each other or conscious of each other's and the male troubadours' work. Some of the poetesses were clearly wealthy patrons as well, for example, Ermengarde, comtesse de Narbonne. In contrast, the best-known northern French patroness, Marie de France, seems only to have underwritten the works of male authors: Chrétien de Troyes, Gautier d'Arras, Gace Brûlé, Evrat, and the translator of the *Eructavit*. And it is not Eleanor of Aquitaine, queen of England, whose patronage of the troubadours was known, to whom Marie de France dedicates her *Lais*, but rather to Eleanor's husband, Henry II. In addition to forming a nucleus, which probably promoted their authorial self-consciousness, the *trobairitz*'s role as writers was acknowledged at large in society by their inclusion in the semiofficial *vidas*, of which one hundred have been preserved. This acknowledgment, coupled with the absence of self-deprecation about their writing (although they do typically deprecate the unrequited love which they suffer), suggests that these women writing in the *langue d'oc* did not encounter the same obstacles—that is, suspicion of their *auctoritas*, isolation from other women authors, and the physical and financial limitations noted above—as did their northern French counterparts writing in dialects of the *langue d'oïl*. Indeed, the survival in Occitania of Roman law, which allowed southern French women to inherit wealth and thus attain a greater degree of economic and legal independence, as well as the looser economic and political organization, with fewer large cities, more generalized impoverishment, less rigid class distinctions, and greater emphasis on kinship rather than feudal ties may all have contributed to creating the special conditions in which these poetesses thrived.

Grace M. Armstrong

NOTE

1. *Comm. in Epist. ad Ephes.* III, 5, quoted in M. Warner, *Alone of All Her Sex: The Myth and the Cult of the Virgin Mary* (New York, 1976), 73.

BIBLIOGRAPHY

Secondary Texts

Duby, Georges, et al., eds. *Femmes et histoire*. Paris: Plon, 1993.
Erler, M., and M., Kowaleski, eds. *Women and Power in the Middle Ages*. Athens: University of Georgia Press, 1988.
Foulet, A., and K. D. Uitti. "The Prologue to the *Lais* of Marie de France: A Reconsideration." *Romance Philology* 35 (1981–1982): 242–249.
Freeman, M. "Marie de France's Poetics of Silence: The Implications of a Feminine *Translatio*." *PMLA* 99 (1984): 860–883.
Gaunt, S. *Gender and Genre in Medieval French Literature*. Cambridge: Cambridge University Press, 1995.
Krueger, R. L. *Women Readers and the Ideology of Gender in Old French Verse Romance*. Cambridge: Cambridge University Press, 1993.
McNamara, J., and J. E. Halborg, eds. and trans. *Sainted Women of the Dark Ages*. Durham: Duke University Press, 1992.
Paden, W. D., ed. *The Voice of the Trobairitz: Perspectives on the Women Troubadours*. Philadelphia: University of Pennsylvania Press, 1989.
Petroff, E. A. *Medieval Women's Visionary Literature*. New York: Oxford University Press, 1986.
Riché, P. *Education et culture dans l'Occident médiéval*. London: Variorum Reprints, 1993.
Shahar, S. *The Fourth Estate: A History of Women in the Middle Ages*. London: Methuen, 1983.

SIXTEENTH CENTURY

Until recently Burkhardt's view that the Renaissance was an era of great opportunities for women went unchallenged. Some claim today that the Middle Ages was a golden age for women and the Renaissance a period of decline. Others, taking a more moderate position, envision the Renaissance as a period of paradoxes and ambiguities for French women, marked by an increase in educational opportunities on the one hand and a decrease in economic power and an expansion of legal and moral restrictions on the other. The loss by tradeswomen of the guild privileges and rights they had previously enjoyed is frequently taken as a case in point. Women's access to learning was certainly greatly facilitated by the advent of the printed word and by humanists and reformers as well. While the former placed new emphasis on education, believing that it led to virtue, the latter supported the opening of vernacular schools to enable individuals to read the Bible* and works of piety. Mentalities, however, did not change suddenly, and attitudes toward the educability of women and the worth of education for women remained generally ambivalent. Humanists sought to reconcile women's education with conventional norms of sex-stereotyped behavior and the social ideal of the family*. They considered learning useless to women of the middle class and thought that it should be limited to the daughters of royalty and nobility who might be forced into public service. While these received an education comparable to that of males of equal social status, women who did not fall in these categories generally remained illiterate. Hence contemporary writers' conflicting statements. On the one hand, Madeleine Neveu (alias des Roches*) celebrates the new educational opportunities the Renaissance offers women of the upper class: "You seem inclined toward the Muses . . . Well born and living at a propitious time for learning" (*Epître à ma Fille*, in *Oeuvres*, 1578). On the other hand, Louise Labé* begins her dedicatory letter to Clémence de Bourges, a powerful feminist manifesto, by presenting the Renaissance as a progressive era, temporarily denying the problem she is about to address. Irony enables her to accuse without assuming responsibility: "The time having come, Mademoiselle, when the stern laws of men no longer bar women from devoting themselves to the sciences and disciplines" (*A.M.C.D.B.L.*, in *Oeuvres*, 1555). Others of a more combative spirit, for example, Hélisenne de Crenne*, Marie de Romieu*, and Marie de Gournay*, the last two active participants in the so-called *Querelle des femmes**, express bravely their indignation against the prevailing sexism of their time.

From this two conclusions can be drawn: (1) Early modern French women, except for a small percentage, did not significantly benefit from the humanists' special interest in education. As Madeleine Lazard rightly stresses (97), women's education does not become a social reality before the turn of the century, with the spread of female teaching orders, in particular the Ursulines, the Compagnie de Marie-Notre-Dame founded in 1607 by Jeanne de Lestonnac (Montaigne's niece), the Visitation founded in 1610 by François de Sales and Jeanne de Chantal*, and the Filles de la Charité founded in 1633 by Vincent de Paul and Louise de Marillac. (2) In early modern France, more women wrote than ever before. La Croix-du-Maine and Du Verdier's *Bibliothèques* include some forty names. It is important to remember, however, that these women were truly exceptional. Those who made a living by their pen—Catherine des Roches* and Marie de Gournay—were extreme rarities in their time.

Some of these women are well known to us today for having spent much of their lives in the public eye. Although they may not have been the main actors on the political scene of their time, queens, regents, and princesses actively participated in the political, religious, and cultural life of the Renaissance and contributed in many ways to the process of change. Marguerite de Navarre*, known to her contemporaries as a skilled diplomat and negotiator, was dispatched to negotiate King François I's release after his defeat at Pavia (1525). She assumed a preponderant role, through her own works and through her encouragement and patronage, in the spread of Platonic philosophy and the development of controversial ideas and early Protestantism in France. She also deserves credit for supporting the foundation of the Royal Readers (the future Collège de France) in 1530 and for turning Nérac, her residence in Navarre, into a radiant center of humanist cultural activity. When her Protestant husband was accused of treason, Marguerite de Valois* courageously took his defense in her *Mémoire justificatif*. Exiled in Usson after her divorce* from Henri IV, she directed her energies toward the creation of an academy, pursuing her youthful interest in poetry and philosophy. Upon her return to Paris after an exile of nineteen years, she founded the famous academy on the rue de Seine, directly opposite the Louvre, which gathered together all the surviving friends of her youth during the last ten years of her life (1605–15). Anne de Bretagne* is remembered today for her generous patronage of the leading writers of her day and for inaugurating the custom of ladies-in-waiting. This practice was continued by Louise de Savoie*, who displayed as well an interest in the education of young noblewomen, and by Anne de Beaujeu, who summarized her views on the subject in her *Enseignements* (1504–1505), which was to be presented to her daughter Suzanne de Bourbon on her marriage.

The remaining women fall into three categories: (1) women of the nobility or the upper bourgeoisie, for example, Catherine des Roches or Marie Le Gendre*, who received an education far above the norm for their sex, and those raised in an intellectual and literary community (e.g., the Morel daughters who had ample opportunity to become acquainted with the leading humanists of their day in their own drawing room, and Gabrielle de Coignard*, whose father was *Maître ès jeux floraux* for more than thirty years); (2) women who were related to literary men, for example, Pernette du Guillet* (Maurice Scève), Madeleine de l'Aubespine* (Ronsard), Marie de Gournay (Montaigne), and Marie Le Gendre (François Le Poulchre). The so-called *amours d'alliance* became so common in the sixteenth century that the term and the practice itself were soon ridiculed (Rabelais, *Quart Livre*, ch. IX); and (3) daughters of the bourgeoisie (e.g., Louise Labé) whose enlightened fathers saw to it that they received an excellent humanist education. They are sometimes thought to have the most authentic and individual voices.

Little is known of the lives of most of these women and the circumstances of their writing and publication. While elogia, panegyrics, and poetic tributes written in their honor tell us a great deal about their relation to contemporary male writers and the way they were perceived in the literary arena, little is known about their relation to each other. Nevertheless, addresses to female readership and dedications to female patrons attest to the crucial role female literary friendship* played in legitimizing women's publication. The lists of women worthies often found in these works reflect, paradoxically, women's attempts to construct their own *auctoritates* and to establish an authority of origin, as well as their effort to singularize their own experience, hence the tendency to praise erudite women from the past or from abroad rather than their own contemporaries. The same could be said of literary influence. Seldom do women acknowledge their familiarity with another woman's work. However, critics have recently shown the impact Louise Labé's works had on Catherine des Roches, Gabrielle de Coignard, and Marie Le Gendre. Detailed scrutiny of contemporary documents concerning literary circles presided over by women (e.g., the salon* of Marie de Pierrevive in Lyons, the salon of the Morels, the Dames des Roches, the Villeroys, Claude-Catherine de Clermont, known as Mme de Retz, the academy of Marguerite de Valois [see C. Keating]) or frequented by women (e.g., the Floral Games, the Palace Academy [see R. J. Sealy]), study of the intellectual settings sympathetic to women's literary pursuits such as the Lyonese milieu, accounts of women's personal libraries, as well as examination of women's epistolary exchanges, would tell us a great deal more about learned women, their relation to each other, and their preponderant role in women's destinies as patrons, protectors, sponsors, and mentors.

The body of works produced by early modern French women is astonishing in size and range. They applied their talents to nearly all genres—conduct books and marriage* manuals (Anne de Beaujeu), journals (Louise de Savoie), letters (Catherine de Bourbon*, Jeanne d'Albret*, Anne de Rohan*, the Dames des Roches), memoirs* (Jeanne d'Albret, Marguerite de Valois), pamphlets (Marie de Gournay), *discours* (Marie de Romieu, Gabrielle de Coignard, Marie Le Gendre), sonnets and elegies (Louise Labé, Pernette du Guillet, the Dames des Roches, Gabrielle de Coignard), devotional poetry (Katherine d'Amboise*, Gabrielle de Coignard, Anne de Marquets*), ballets (Catherine de Parthenay*), pastoral (Catherine des Roches), epics (Gabrielle de Coignard), and so on—and excelled or composed pioneer works in many of them. Hélisenne de Crenne wrote the first sentimental novel* in France (*Les Angoysses douloureuses qui procedent d'amours*, 1538). Georgette de Montenay* composed the first book of Christian emblems ever written in any language by a woman (*Emblèmes ou devises chrestiennes*, 1566). The Dames des Roches produced the first collection of private letters by women in France (*Les Missives*, 1586). Marguerite de Va-

lois's *Mémoires* (composed prior to 1600) is the first autobiographical work
known to have been written by a woman in the French language. Louise Bourgeois* not only contributed to the advancement of midwifery but also initiated
the tradition of "women's secrets" in putting into writing her own professional
knowledge for women who would follow in her footsteps.

Writing within the literary traditions in vogue (e.g., Petrarchism, Neoplatonism, Pleiade and penitential poetry, Neostoicism, etc.), they often challenged the
assumptions encoded in the genres they employed. These appropriation maneuvers resulted in perpetual tension, which reflects the tension of writing as a
woman. While some followed in the footsteps of their immediate predecessors,
writing *chansons* (e.g., Pernette du Guillet, Madeleine de l'Aubespine), *débat*
(e.g., Louise Labé), or *novellas* (e.g., Marguerite de Navarre), others turned to
more scholarly endeavors. Marguerite de Navarre, Catherine des Roches, and
Marie Le Gendre wrote dialogues, a genre that enjoyed enormous success with
the humanists. Hélisenne de Crenne, Catherine des Roches, and Catherine de
Parthenay took an active part in the large humanist project of translating classical
works into the vernacular. A vibrant advocate of woman's rights, Marie de
Gournay also won fame for her pioneer work in translation, linguistics, editorial
practices, and poetic theories. Women's growing interest in scientific subjects
is attested by Marie de Cotteblanche's* translation of the *Trois Dialogues* of
the cosmographer Pierre Messie (1579). Others undertook the translation of
Scriptural texts (e.g., Catherine des Roches and Gabrielle de Coignard), a task
thought to be best suited to their sex.

Early modern women wrote on everything from politics to aesthetics, from
laws and customs to religion and education, from female experience to women's
rights. Aside from their literary worth, their works stand today as important
documents for both the history and culture of early modern France and women's
history. Not only do they provide fascinating accounts of events of great historical significance, but they give us valuable insight into court intrigues, contemporary debates, and women's social and personal experiences. Early modern
women tell of the oppression and constraints of their existence, their misfortunes
in love and marriage, their sorrows over the death of relatives and friends, the
difficulties they encountered in their intellectual pursuits, and so on.

This sourcebook is part of the larger enterprise to restore the record of early
modern women writers. In the last two decades, the status and condition of
women in early modern France have generated exciting new research and interdisciplinary inquiry. A host of critical studies have shown the merits of various authors and single works. The notion of genre has been revisited in light
of women's texts. Some texts are finally accessible in modern editions and
English translations. Excerpts of women's writing are now included in anthologies and literary histories in an effort to counterbalance the male-centered
canon. And yet we still have far to go to dispel the mystery surrounding the
lives and works of those omitted here for lack of information: Madeleine de
Bourdeille, Marguerite Cambis, the Clèves sisters, Jeanne Gaillarde, Anne de

Graville, Mme de Lignolles, Jacqueline de Miremont, Suzanne de Nervèze, Anne Picardet, Hélène de Surgères, and many others who protected themselves by anonymity and by avoidance of publication. How much unpublished writing have we lost? How much more remains uncovered in private and municipal archives? It is our hope that this important task will be pursued by the new generation of scholars.

Colette H. Winn

BIBLIOGRAPHY

Primary Texts

Labé, Louise. *Oeuvres complètes*. Ed. François Rigolot. Paris: Flammarion, 1986.
Roches, Dames des. *Les Oeuvres*. Ed. Anne R. Larsen. Geneva: Droz, 1993.

Secondary Texts

Berriot-Salvadore, Evelyne. *La Femme dans la société française de la Renaissance*. Geneva: Droz, 1990.
Burkhardt, Jacob. *Civilisation de la Renaissance en Italie*. 3 vols. Trans. H. Schmitt, reviewed and corrected by Robert Klein. Paris: Librairie Plon et Club du meilleur livre, 1958. 2: 343–51.
Davis, Natalie Zemon. *Society and Culture in Early Modern France*. Stanford: Stanford University Press, 1979.
Keating, Clark L. *Studies on the Literary Salon in France (1550–1615)*. Cambridge, MA: Harvard University Press, 1941.
Kelly-Gadol, Joan. "Did Women Have a Renaissance?" In *Becoming Visible: Women in European History*. Ed. Renate Bridenthal and Claudia Koonz. Boston: Houghton Mifflin, 1977. 138–164.
Larsen, Anne R. " 'Un Honneste Passetems': Strategies of Legitimation in French Renaissance Women's Prefaces." In *Ecrire au féminin à la Renaissance: Problèmes et perspectives*. Ed. François Rigolot. *L'Esprit Créateur* 30, no. 4 (1990): 11–22.
Lazard, Madeleine. *Images littéraires de la femme à la Renaissance*. Paris: PUF, 1985.
Lerner, Gerda. *The Creation of Feminist Consciousness from the Middle Ages to Eighteen-Seventy*. New York: Oxford University Press, 1986.
Maclean, Ian. *The Renaissance Notion of Woman: A Study in the Fortunes of Scholasticism and Medical Science in European Intellectual Life*. Cambridge: Cambridge University Press, 1980.
Rose, Mary-Beth, ed. *Women in the Middle Ages and the Renaissance*. Syracuse, NY: Syracuse University Press, 1986.
Sealy, Robert J. *The Palace Academy of Henry III*. Geneva: Droz, 1981.
Wiesner, Merry E. *Women and Gender in Early Modern Europe*. Cambridge: Cambridge University Press, 1994.

SEVENTEENTH CENTURY

The seventeenth century saw a substantial increase in the number of women writing and an even greater increase in the number of women publishing* their work. The development of the salons integrated women to an unprecedented extent into the literary life of the times and made "women's taste" a factor to be reckoned with for writers of both genders. Not all women authors intended their works for publication, especially those composing in forms that were highly personal (letters or memoirs), and/or women who wanted their writings to be circulated only within their limited circle. A significant percentage of those who published did so under their own name; women of the nobility who published were more likely to prefer anonymity. The seventeenth century also marked the first cases of (middle-class) women who succeeded in supporting themselves by their writing, with fiction proving the most lucrative branch of literature.

Public recognition of the talents of women authors became more common. Although excluded from the ranks of the Académie Française, they were eligible to compete for its annual poetry prize, and women frequently won it. Several were elected to the academies of Arles and Padua, which admitted women from the outset. Works by women were reviewed, often favorably, in gazettes and were cited in historical or theoretical treatises. Nevertheless, attacks against women writers likewise multiplied in the same period. The most successful were accused of lending their names* to male ghost writers, even though everyone at the time knew the charge to be false. Detractors often tried to discredit a woman author by taxing her life or her works, or both, with immorality.

Women of the seventeenth century cultivated nearly every type of literary form and were often pioneers in the introduction of new forms or in the transformation of older ones. Within the area of fiction, women helped to initiate the vogue of the gallant heroic novel, the psychological novel, the picaresque novel, the epistolary novel, the *nouvelle historique*, and the literary fairy tale*. Madeleine de Scudéry's* *Le Grand Cyrus* and *Clélie* were among the century's bestsellers, and her major innovations (detailed psychological analysis, greater emphasis on conversation than on action, the attempt to merge figures of ancient history with the author's contemporaries, the suggestion that the private lives of famous people played a decisive, though hidden, role in their public lives) would be adopted by numerous later novelists. Lafayette's* *La Princesse de Clèves*, long acknowledged as the first canonical masterpiece in the history of the French novel, combines purity of style, psychological depth, and social critique. The heroine's concern for her integrity and independence led to unconventional passages (the avowal to her husband, her refusal to marry the hero at the end) that scandalized many of the original readers. An even more daring role model was the heroine of Villedieu's* *Henriette-Sylvie de Molière*, who enjoys adopting male dress and behavior, and who in the course of her picaresque-like adventures repeatedly flouts society's norms for respectable women.

A substantial quantity of poetry flowed from the pens of seventeenth-century women. Apart from epic and satire, women cultivated virtually every poetic form known to the age, from the lighthearted to the serious. To be sure, most of the salon verse was intended as a refined game, designed to be circulated only among friends, though by the final third of the century a number of women were getting poems accepted by the principal literary gazette, the *Mercure ga-*

lant. La Suze* was apparently the first to have a collection of her poems published during her lifetime, but she was to be the first of many.

Perhaps the most visible breakthrough occurred in the theater.* Around the middle of the century women playwrights first succeeded in getting their works staged by professional companies. Several of their plays were popular enough to be revived, and there was even a command performance at court of Villedieu's *Le Favori*. Women tried their hand at all available dramatic forms, from full-length tragedy and tragicomedy to the one-act farce, as well as the opera libretto, and the majority of the extant plays are known to have been performed. Also, some women wrote for private theatricals or for use by schoolgirls.

The influence of the salons contributed to the introduction of a number of short forms in which women were among the leading practitioners, such as the portrait, the maxim, the conversation, and the dramatic proverb. The salons also exerted a major impact on literary style and taste, which affected male and female authors alike. The emphasis on such qualities as elegance and clarity in writing, a preference for wit and badinage, as well as insistence on respectful behavior toward women, both in real life and in fiction, all impacted on the emerging national style. The salons, in addition to encouraging writers of both sexes, served as a kind of substitute university for women and made its female members feel directly involved in the creative process as readers and critics. By awakening women's interest in science and philosophy, they helped create a market for nontechnical works on these subjects written in French. They likewise contributed to the renewed interest in such issues as women's education, the equality of the sexes, and the relation between public and private realms (which led to questioning traditional definitions of history and gave impetus to writers of memoirs and historical novels).

Women were similarly active in the religious sphere. New religious orders were created in this period, including the abbey of Port Royal, and some of them were favorable to literary activity. A sizable number of women composed religious poetry or devotional works. Some of them maintained extensive correspondences which were published posthumously. While theology remained an exclusively male bastion, women could and sometimes did record their inner lives. Women were leading participants in the Jansenist movement around the middle of the century, while Jeanne Guyon* was the leading voice in an influential, if controversial, mystical movement known as quietism. Other women published books of moral and spiritual advice, usually addressed to girls. Even if their views on the role of women in society remained conventional, they were seriously committed to the education of their own sex.

Throughout the century the bluestocking was singled out for merciless ridicule. But despite caricatures such as those found in Molière's *Les Femmes savantes*, the small number of women who devoted themselves to serious labors of scholarship were neither inept nor silly. Several women published works of great distinction, such as Marie de Gournay, who edited and annotated the final version of Montaigne's *Essais*; Marguerite Buffet*, who composed a significant treatise on the French language; and Anne Dacier*, a leading expert on Greek literature.

The way women were portrayed in literature showed significant change, with a greater percentage of dramatic and fictional protagonists displaying heroic traits, self-reliance, and a strong sense of self-worth. This was especially frequent in works of female writers, but not necessarily limited to them. On the one hand, the highly visible activity of women in the political sphere (notably during the two regencies and in the Fronde*, as well as the influence of women at Louis XIV's court) was a major contributing factor in the prominence of the *femme forte* in print. On the other hand, women were also praised for their naturalness and spontaneity in expressing their personal feelings, especially in the letter form. Sévigné* was the greatest, but hardly the only, able female letter writer of the age.

Perry Gethner

BIBLIOGRAPHY

Secondary Texts

Backer, Dorothy. *Precious Women*. New York: Basic Books, 1974.
Beasley, Faith. *Revising Memory: Women's Fiction and Memoirs in Seventeenth-Century France*. New Brunswick, N.J.: Rutgers University Press, 1990.
DeJean, Joan. *Tender Geographies: Women and the Origins of the Novel in France*. New York: Columbia University Press, 1991.
Lougee, Carolyn. *Le Paradis des femmes: Women, Salons, and Social Stratification in Seventeenth-Century France*. Princeton: Princeton University Press, 1976.
Maclean, Ian. *Woman Triumphant: Feminism in French Literature, 1610–1652*. Oxford: Clarendon Press, 1977.
Magendie, Maurice. *La Politesse mondaine et les théories de l'honnêteté en France au XVIIe siècle, de 1600 à 1660*. Paris: F. Alcan, 1932.
Pelous, Jean-Michel. *Amour précieux, amour galant (1654–1675)*. Paris: Klincksieck, 1980.
Reynaud, Gustave. *La Femme au XVIIe siècle: Ses Ennemis et ses défenseurs*. Paris, 1929.

EIGHTEENTH CENTURY

At no other time except our own were French women as influential and as visible as they were in the eighteenth century. Their reign, acknowledged throughout the continent, was epitomized by three royal mistresses—the duchesse de Châteauroux* (1717–1744), the marquise de Pompadour* (1721–1764), and the duchesse du Barry* (1743–1793)—who left their mark on the private and public spheres. From the pinnacle of the court and the lodestone of salons to the streets of Paris and the market alleys of Les Halles, women's involvement in social, political, cultural, literary, and economic activities was, undoubtedly, France's most striking and unique distinction. That peculiarity did not escape the attention of Montesquieu's astute observer, Rica, who noted, in the *Lettres persanes*, that it is impossible to fathom the inner workings of France without understanding the women who govern its mighty. Early on, rulers of Europe realized the importance of befriending the king's favorites and *salonnières*. Frederick the Great of Prussia acknowledged his country's debt to Châteauroux, although he was unable to preserve similarly cordial relations with her more powerful successor, Pompadour, whose pro-Austrian leanings were instrumental in the diplomatic revolution known as the *renversement des alliances*. By mid-century and for two decades, the much-vilified Pompadour was a force to be reckoned with, in the signing of treaties, the appointment of ministers and ambassadors, the development of industrial and architectural projects, and nominations to the French Academy. She was, however, universally credited for her patronage of arts and literature, especially for her backing of the century's most ambitious and controversial publishing endeavor, the *Encyclopédie**.

Traditionally praised for their support of the *philosophes*—long considered true founders of the Enlightenment*—*salonnières* such as Mme de Lambert*, Mme du Deffand, Mme d'Epinay*, Mme Geoffrin*, and Mlle de Lespinasse*, were probably the only eighteenth-century French women whose role, though often underestimated, was never overlooked. Recently, the gracious hostesses have been returned to the forefront, where their contributions have been recognized to be on a par with those of their more famous guests. Convincingly, Dena Goodman has demonstrated that equality among the sexes, the polite discourse of sociability, and the values imparted by *salonnières* were crucial elements in the development of modern Western civilization and its republican model of government. According to her, the French Enlightenment was grounded in a female-centered mixed-gender sociability that imprinted French culture, the Enlightenment, and civilization itself as feminine.

Literary scholars are also focusing more attention on the *salonnières'* own writings, while uncovering a wealth of literature by women. For the stage alone, Cecilia Beach discovered hundreds of comedies, tragedies, tales, and ballet-operas penned by more than seventy female playwrights, including Empress Catherine the Great of Russia, author of several volumes of plays in French. Undaunted by the indignities suffered at the hands of theaters—detailed in two pamphlets by Olympe de Gouges* and summarized by Montanclos's* famous lamentation—"O la cruelle chose d'être auteur femelle!" (O what a cruel fate to be a female author!)—women dramatists persevered, nevertheless, and saw their work performed on the most prestigious Parisian stages. Plays by Barbier*, Benoist*, Beauharnais*, Favart*, Falconnet*, Gomez*, and du Bocage*, among others, were produced at the Comédie Française, Théâtre Français, Comédie Italienne, and Théâtre Italien.

Women contributed generously to other genres as well. While novelists such as Graffigny*, Charrière*, and Riccoboni* have been recognized among the century's most notable fiction writers, some of that era's best-selling authors, whose works were translated and read throughout the continent—for example, Cottin*, Benoist, and Montolieu*—have since fallen into near oblivion; today, their novels are difficult to find. It is not only the quantity of women's writing that is remarkable, but also its quality. Although excluded from membership in the Académie Française until 1980, females were, nevertheless, occasionally recognized by that august body. Mme d'Epinay's *Conversations d'Emilie* was the recipient of the Académie's first Prix d'Utilité, while Adélaïde Dufrénoy* was the first woman to win its coveted prize for poetry. In the less sexist provincial academies, women not only participated in competitions and were recipients of prizes, but also served as full-fledged members.

Topics treated in women's literature spanned the entire gamut of human interests. Du Bocage wrote travel letters; Caylus* described life at the court; Huber* advocated the use of reason in religious matters and offered a liberal interpretation of the Protestant faith, passionately engaged in discussions of moral and philosophical issues, disagreed with Rousseau's view of the natural man, and translated Johnson, Fielding, and Hume; Jodin* was a social reformer who also advocated civil rights for women; Lézardière*, a political scientist, published several volumes on political theory; while Thiroux d'Arconville*, who lived to be eighty, devoted her life to research on physics, anatomy, natural history, agriculture, botany, and chemistry, publishing seventy volumes, including sixteen medical publications. Most often, however, women reflected on matters of private life, family relations, and, especially, their own status. Campan*, Genlis*, Miremont*, and Leprince de Beaumont* denounced prejudice against their sex, deplored the quality of the education they received, set out to propose new pedagogical methods and programs, wrote textbooks and literature for children, and became distinguished educators. Women's thirst for knowledge and information eventually led to the creation of a press of their own. *Le Journal des dames* reflected their concerns, offered advice for their daily lives, and provided a forum for exchange of ideas, thus contributing to the nascent feminist consciousness.

By the late 1780s, Enlightenment thought had spread beyond the elite, giving rise to claims for civil and political rights. Energized by the ideals of the French Revolution*, women sought to become full citizens and engaged passionately in revolutionary activities. They submitted petitions and grievance lists, made pleas and delivered eloquent speeches before the Legislative Assembly, formed revolutionary clubs and societies, led bread riots, and demanded justice and equal rights. Undoubtedly the most articulate and most fearless of revolutionary women, Olympe de Gouges drafted a *Declaration of the Rights of Woman* and published scores of political pamphlets. Indefatigable, this foresighted social reformer and sharp political analyst pleaded for moderation, advocated national unity, and warned against the execution of Louis XVI. Her unabashed hatred for Robespierre eventually led to the guillotine* in 1793, thus silencing the most powerful voice for women's rights.

Perhaps emblematic of the hopes of women in eighteenth-century France was the fate of the duchesse du Barry. Rising from the *petit peuple*, Louis XV's favorite reached the status of pseudo-queen before falling under the forceful edge of the guillotine. Illegitimately, like her, since deprived of legal rights, women gained new strength and assertiveness throughout the Age of Enlightenment and achieved rare prominence and visibility. Their progress came, however, to a crashing halt as the Revolution turned into Terror: women's political gatherings and clubs were outlawed, and militant feminists derided and beheaded. In short, to use Vigée-Lebrun's* words, women reigned, the Revolution dethroned them.

Samia I. Spencer

BIBLIOGRAPHY

Secondary Texts

Abensour, Léon. *La Femme et le féminisme avant la Révolution*. Paris: Ernest Leroux, 1923.

Beach, Cecilia. *French Women Playwrights before the Twentieth Century: A Checklist*. Westport, CT: Greenwood Press, 1994.

Bonnel, Roland, and Catherine Rubinger, eds. *Femmes Savantes et Femmes d'Esprit: Women Intellectuals of the French Eighteenth Century*. New York: Peter Lang, 1994.

Goncourt, Edmond de le, and Jules Goncourt. *The Woman of the Eighteenth Century*. Trans. Jacques Le Clercq and Ralph Roeder. New York: Minton, Balch and Co., 1927.

Goodman, Dena. *The Republic of Letters: A Cultural History of the French Enlightenment*. Ithaca, NY: Cornell University Press, 1994.

Gouges, Olympe de. *Adresse aux représentants de la nation*. Paris: N.p., 1790.

———. *Les Comédiens démasqués ou madame de Gouges ruinée par la Comédie Française pour se faire jouer*. Paris: Imprimerie de la Comédie Française, 1790.

Lee, Vera. *The Reign of Women in Eighteenth-Century France*. Cambridge, MA: Schenken, 1975.

Levy, Darline Gay, Harriett Branson Applewhite, and Mary Durham Johnson. *Women in Revolutionary Paris, 1789–1795*. Urbana: University of Illinois Press, 1979.

Spencer, Samia I., ed. *French Women and the Age of Enlightenment*. Bloomington: Indiana University Press, 1984.

NINETEENTH CENTURY

In France, the nineteenth century can be said to begin with the Revolution of 1789. The Revolution profoundly destabilized the traditional social order, and with it the categories that organized human experience under the Ancien Régime, not least among them gender. In this century, the history of France was alternately marked by revolution and reaction, with women benefiting from periods of greater liberalization, only to lose ground in periods of repression. Later in the century, the progress of the industrial revolution in France slowly transformed the material conditions of existence, with a significant impact on literary production.

In the aftermath of the first Revolution, French women of the nineteenth century found themselves increasingly restricted in their activities. According to certain Enlightenment ideas frequently associated with Jean-Jacques Rousseau, women belonged to the sex that was both physically weaker and morally stronger. The private sphere of the home and family was considered woman's "proper" place, and her essential role was the nurturing of children, while man's role lay in the public sphere of activity. The political, economic, and social rise of the bourgeoisie served to reinforce this division of gender roles. The Napoleonic Code* made women legal minors for the entire span of their lives, under the control of fathers and husbands. Women, confined to the spaces of the home, boudoir, and salon, wrote from within the private domain. Yet the move to publish was an incursion into the public sphere of masculine activity. The woman who aspired to authorship was viewed as a bluestocking—a bas-bleu*—who was attempting to deny her femininity* by adopting masculine dress and pursuits. Worse yet, she might be accused of prostituting herself by making public thoughts and desires that should have remained private. Despite legal and social restrictions placed on their gender during the post-revolutionary period, women continued to write, although many were forced to assume a masculine pseudonym in order to publish.

In the face of increasing repression under Napoleon early in the century, Germaine de Staël* continued to exercise her prerogative to think, to theorize, and to question the patriarchal order and women's place in it. Mme de Staël wrote openly from a position of resistance, and suffered the consequence: exile. Nonetheless, Staël provided a model for women writers in the following generations. Like her artist heroine, Corinne, she embodied the quest to articulate the feminine experience in an authentic voice despite the constraints imposed upon her.

It is difficult to define women's writing according to the literary movements and genres used to trace masculine literary history. In order to give voice to their own specificity, women writers often subverted or transformed masculine models, producing hybrid genres or inventing entirely new ones, adapted to meet their own artistic needs.

The search for self-expression is clearly discernible in the Romantic period, when women had to define themselves against an androgynous masculine model which subsumed the feminine within itself, ostensibly reducing women to silent objects (e.g., Lamartine's Elvire). This did not prevent women from adopting the position of speaking subjects, however. Thus, the poet Marceline Desbordes-Valmore* employed the personal lyric as did her male contemporaries, yet the self that emerges in her poetry is distinctive. Hers is a rich, sonorous corpus that draws on Desbordes-Valmore's experience as a mother, her sensuality, and her affinity with nature. Such topoi continued in women's writing into the twentieth century, seen, for example, in the poetry of Anna de Noailles*.

Other women poets were not as successful at reconciling the tension between their feminine identity and the poet's creative agency, almost always cast as masculine. Louise Ackermann* wrote highly acclaimed philosophical poetry, but found it necessary to divorce herself from her female body in order to do so. Louise Colet* and Louisa Siefert* were applauded for the aesthetic and political force of their works when judged according to the masculine norm, but they were denigrated as women. While Maria Krysinska*, originator of *vers libre*, was the author of both Symbolist* and decadent poetry in which the self is problematized, by the end of the century the sapphic verses of Renée Vivien* spoke of a self well outside the role defined for her gender.

Like male novelists, women often used the serialized form of the *roman feuilleton*. The novel or novella, short story*, and other narrative genres often demonstrated women's capacity as speaking subjects, in the role of narrator. However, women novelists rarely used the mimetic techniques characteristic of realism* and naturalism*. Instead, they employed less direct forms such as the sentimental or social novel, or even the *roman champêtre* in order to represent and critique social oppression, encoded within melodramatic or idealist plots. Women writers not only invented new genres, they often employed multiple genres. Chief among them was George Sand*, who rivaled Victor Hugo in popularity, output, and versatility. Her enormous oeuvre encompasses many of the political, philosophical, and artistic tendencies of the century. Meanwhile, at the end of the century, the works of Rachilde* test the limits of gender construction with their exploration of gender role inversion, cross-dressing*, androgyny*, and many dimensions of eroticism.

Among the genres most closely tied to women's established role were works on the philosophy of education, didactic literature, and children's literature*. Although some women wrote for the theater with success, this was a literary arena considered too public for their gender. Exceptions included Marie-Adélaïde Barthélémy Hadot*, Delphine Gay de Girardin*, George Sand, and Judith Gautier*, writers whose personal connections made their entry into the theater less difficult. Actresses who frequented the salons and established friendships with women authors strengthened these ties.

Autobiography* was perhaps the single most important genre practiced by women of all classes, from the aristocratic Marie d'Agoult*, to the working-class Suzanne Voilquin*, to the courtesan Liane de Pougy*, to name only three. Women's autobiographies combined the memorialist's desire to record significant events and observations and the more self-revealing confessional mode. The autobiographical novel and *roman à clé* were often used as well to present a thinly disguised version of personal experience. Such is the case with Agoult's *Nélida*, Sand's *Elle et lui*, or Colet's *Lui*. Travel literature*, grounded in autobiographical writing, achieved the status of an accepted literary genre. Writers like Flora Tristan* incorporated travel writing, autobiography, and social documentary into powerful calls for social reform. Women like Judith Gautier and Christine Belgiojoso* also reworked the orientalism* of their male counterparts, sometimes undercutting the fantasmatic masculine vision with critiques of women's oppression in other societies and cultures.

As the century unfolded, women moved increasingly out of the private space of the salons, sometimes from economic necessity as much as by choice. Journalism offered important opportunities for women to claim a role in the political life of the nation. This was especially true as readership grew. The move into the public sphere was accelerated under more liberal regimes. At such moments women's clubs and newspapers were reestablished. In the 1830s and 1840s the polemic literature of figures like Pauline Roland*, Eugénie Niboyet*, Claire Démar*, and Suzanne Voilquin, many of them nourished by utopian socialism, sought to liberate women from patriarchal oppression.

Some used journalism, essay, and exposé to further the cause of movements like Saint-Simonianism*, but soon asserted their own increasingly political "feminist" voices, although the term "feminist" came into use only later in the century. In times of political crisis or revolution, women claimed the rights denied to them in the press and sometimes in the streets. Women's political engagement through the written word reached a zenith in 1848 when Sand virtually served as minister of propaganda. Agoult produced her *Lettres républicaine*, and the women of *La voix des femmes* translated their writings into public action. Such activity was short-lived, however, crushed by political censure and the women's own internal divisions and disillusionment.

After the 1848 revolution*, women's clubs were closed, feminist newspapers were shut down, and feminist leaders were either scattered in exile, imprisoned, or otherwise silenced. The climate of the Second Empire was less open, but women like Jenny d'Héricourt* and Juliette Adam* responded to the pervasive misogyny of nineteenth-century French thought and letters, and to specific thinkers like Michelet and Proudhon. Realist, naturalist, and decadent writers were notorious in their negative depiction of women. Women in the latter half of the century are often portrayed as demons, as vampires, or, as in Villiers de l'Isle-Adam's novel *L'Eve future*, as androids.

The Paris Commune* saw a strong resurgence of women's political activism despite the hostile climate. The women of Paris were the first to take revolutionary action in the Commune of 1871. They continued to demand their right to fight alongside their brothers in this period. Later, Louise Michel* would write the history of the Commune in a radically new form, giving voice to women in a move quite different from Agoult's history of 1848, which had been written from an outsider's "objective" perspective and which reinforced the masculine tradition of the historical genre.

Oddly enough, the regime that crushed the Commune was responsible for slowly improving women's socioeconomic conditions during the last quarter of the nineteenth century. During these years, freedom of the press was reestablished, allowing a resurgence in the feminist movement. Feminism* was then dominated by bourgeois liberal feminists such as Maria Deraismes* and Hubertine Auclert*. The main struggle was to give women the same political rights as men.

One critical dimension in women's struggle was the need for better education and training as growing numbers of women entered the work force. The 1880 Camille Sée law instituted the first lycées for girls, although their curriculum was not the same as boys'. In this same period, French industries turned to a cheaper labor force composed mainly of women, thus creating a rivalry with male workers. These new socioeconomic conditions partly explain the misogynistic undercurrent of the French left.

In spite of Barbey d'Aurevilly's scathing satire *Les bas-bleus*, women wrote extensively. The nineteenth century saw an explosion in the number of women writers. By 1894, 1,200 female authors were registered in the Société des gens de lettres, while 32 women were members of the Société des auteurs dramatiques.

Unlike the beginning of the nineteenth century, when women of the upper classes had greater access to the literary profession, the late nineteenth century saw many more working-class and middle-class authors, including such diverse authors as Marguerite Audoux*, Augustine Blanchecotte*, Gyp*, and Jeanne Marni*, whose literary productions were often their main source of income.

If gender bias often constrained women in the nineteenth century, they nevertheless produced a vast body of written texts. In recent years, scholars have begun to acknowledge women's struggles for political and social equality and their key contributions to reformist movements. Nevertheless, their literary accomplishments have often been obscured by the gender bias of the twentieth century. Only a handful of nineteenth-century women have regained a place in the contemporary literary canon. Although there is much ongoing feminist scholarship aimed at reevaluating women's literature in this period and reaffirming its significance, in the final analysis, the literary history of women's writing has yet to be written.

Mary Rice-DeFosse and Juliette Parnell-Smith

BIBLIOGRAPHY

Secondary Texts

Abensour, Léon. *Le Féminisme sous le règne de Louis-Philippe et en 1848*. Paris: Plon, 1913.
Albistur, Maïté, and Daniel Armogathe. *Histoire du féminisme français du moyen âge à nos jours*. 2 vols. Paris: Des femmes, 1977.
Aron, Jean-Paul. *Misérable et glorieuse: la femme au XIXe siècle*. Paris: Fayard, 1980.
Ataud, Claire. *Lire les Femmes de lettre*. Paris: Dunod, 1993.
Moses, Claire Goldberg. *French Feminism in the Nineteenth Century*. Albany: State University of New York Press, 1984.

TWENTIETH CENTURY

The twentieth century is a period in which France has participated in two world wars, witnessed the independence of most of its colonies, experienced mass immigration, and confronted the internal tensions that have arisen from the Occupation and the Algerian War. In terms of literary and philosophical movements, the same century has moved from surrealism* and existentialism* through the Nouveau Roman*, the Theater of the Absurd, and the Nouvelle Vague to, in recent times, postmodern and postcolonial literature and thought. The twentieth century has also seen the emergence of large numbers of women writers who have expressed themselves in fictional and nonfictional forms on topics ranging from a questioning of women's role in society to the significance for women of reclaiming voices, bodies, and identities.

In the social and political spheres, a series of important reforms have allowed women greater freedom to shape their own lives. In the early part of the century, women were still seeking to affirm their political and civil rights. It was only in 1938 that married women became legal majors; the Constitution of 1946, while guaranteeing women the same rights as men, did not question the unequal position of the married woman in relation to her husband as defined by the Napoleonic Code*. While women obtained the right to vote* in 1944, not until 1965 did they have the right to engage in a career or to control their own bank accounts without the consent of their spouse.

Significant gains were made in education and the workplace during the twentieth century. In 1900 there were 624 women university students in the whole of France as compared to 27,000 men. With the institution in 1924 of a secondary school program which would be the same for both sexes, the number of women in higher education grew steadily, equaling that of men in 1971 and surpassing it by 70,000 in 1990. In the workplace, women have entered an increasingly large number of professions. As early as 1922, writer and activist Colette Yver* addressed the difficulties of balancing a career with domestic duties, and commented on women's participation in traditionally male-dominated professions, especially the sciences. Gains made during the interwar period suffered a setback, however, under the Vichy government, which, with its emphasis on family and traditional values, prohibited married women from working in the public sector. While protection for women working outside the home began at the end of the nineteenth century, the most important legislation was introduced after World War II* and focused on three main areas: maternity* leave, night work, and sexual harassment. Subsequent legislation mandated equal pay for equal work (1972), prohibited gender-based discrimination (1975), and guaranteed equal rights in the workplace (Roudy* law of 1983). However, although women are protected by law, factors related to gender still affect their employment—for the most part, women remain concentrated in lower-paying or part-time jobs and receive fewer promotions.

In terms of reproductive rights, women were legally prevented from obtaining contraceptives until the passage of the Neuwirth Law in 1967, and from having abortions* until new legislation was introduced in 1974 and adopted in its final form in 1980. Early in the century, activists such as Nelly Roussel* argued against "forced" maternity, claiming that the government's natalist policies posed a threat to women's autonomy and equality. Subsequently, in reaction to the 1920 law banning the sale of contraceptives, several movements were founded—the Movement for Family Planning (1956) and Choisir (1971) are two of the most noteworthy. Activists such as Gisèle Halimi*, a lawyer and one of the founders of Choisir, played a major role in the struggle for reproductive rights and for increased legal protection against sexual assault. In *La Cause des femmes* (1973), Halimi describes her involvement in the famous Bobigny trial, a case that led to the liberalization of legislation on abortion.

Although literary histories of the early years of the century suggest the relative absence of women writers, an examination of their literary production indicates that a large number of women were, in fact, writing, and points to the patriarchal biases inherent in canon formation. A prominent group of Parisian-based writers raised provocative questions relating to female sexuality—Renée Vivien and Natalie Barney*, in particular, focused on lesbian identity. Lesser-known writers of the Belle Epoque, including Louise-Marie Compain*, Gabrielle Reval*, and Hélène Brion*, addressed issues of women's suffrage, labor laws, and pacifism in their essays and treatises, and portrayed independent women in their fictional work. Many of the women writers at this time were still from the middle and upper classes; some depended on male patrons, and either attributed their works to male authorship (as Colette* did in her early works), had recourse to pseudonyms (Harlor*, Rachilde, Gérard d'Houville*), or published their works anonymously (the autobiography of Catherine Pozzi*, for example). In addition, women faced difficulties in the production and distribution of their texts, given that men controlled all aspects of publishing. It was not until 1968 that a woman first owned her own publishing house—when Régine Deforges* founded L'Or du Temps. The renowned Editions des femmes was established in 1973.

The impression of a small number of women writers was reinforced by the literary production of the two world wars—the fact that war writing is a traditionally male genre further contributed to the androcentric canon. Contrary to popular belief, however, women did in fact have much to say about the war. Writers such as Marcelle Tinayre*, Marcelle Capy, Lucie Delarue-Mardrus*, and Camille Mayran produced a variety of texts that portray a wide range of positions in relation to the war. As regards World War II, the best-known writers were again male; the role of women has been sorely neglected until recently, both in relation to the World War II Resistance* and the Holocaust*.

Elsa Triolet*, active in the Resistance, was the first woman to receive the Prix Goncourt. Her prize-winning collection of short stories, *Le Premier Accroc coûte deux cents francs* (1945), explores the position of women in the Occupation years. Other women who were active members of the Resistance (Marguerite Duras*, Clara Malraux*, Edith Thomas*, and Lucie Aubrac*) have described their experiences in memoirs and in fictional form. While Elie Wiesel remains the most well known writer on the Holocaust, women writers, too, evoked the horrors of the camps in a variety of genres: novels (Anna Langfus*), autobiographical narratives (Charlotte Delbo*, Fania Fénelon), plays (Delbo, Langfus, Liliane Atlan*), and poetry (Micheline Maurel*). These writers, like their Belle Epoque counterparts, are currently being revisited as scholars seek to reevaluate the role of women during the two world wars.

Despite the ground-breaking work of numerous early twentieth-century women writers, two women in particular found their way into the canon and profoundly influenced later generations of feminists—Colette and Simone de Beauvoir*. With her focus on women as subjects of their own desire and her revalorization of the maternal, Colette is one of the most important precursors to contemporary feminism. Both her life as a music-hall performer and her literary work raise questions about women's sexuality and their role in society. Unlike Colette, Beauvoir favored a more intellectual approach with an emphasis on philosophy and sociopolitical issues. Her revolutionary work, *Le Deuxième Sexe* (1949), theorized the concept of a socially constructed female identity and provided a critique of the institution of marriage and the notion of maternity* as woman's biological goal.

The postwar period saw the publication of a series of novels that dealt with gender roles and adolescent sexuality, as the teenager made her appearance on the literary scene. The most acclaimed of these, Françoise Sagan's* *Bonjour Tristesse* (1954), challenges traditional representations of adolescent love, while *Le Rempart des béguines* (1951, Françoise Mallet-Joris*), and *Les Petits Enfants du siècle* (1961, Christiane Rochefort*) depict, respectively, a violent sexual relation between a young girl and an older woman, and the sexual initiation of a young teenager living in a housing project. The works of these and other writers reflect the social and economic changes taking place in the 1950s and 1960s, changes documented in Geneviève Gennari's* *Le Dossier de la femme* (1965), a historical study that examines the status of women between 1889 and 1964.

The events of May 1968 constitute a pivotal point in regard to the condition of women in the twentieth century. The women's liberation movement (MLF) was one of the most significant movements to emerge from 1968. Writers such as Sophie Chauveau* have chronicled the consciousness-raising, demonstrations, and general sense of vitality that characterized this period, which saw the creation of numerous women's groups—Féminin et masculin futur, Psychanalyse et Politique*, Féminisme révolutionnaire, and Féminisme et Marxisme, for example. As these groups began to address the different forms of women's oppression, whether social, political, or linguistic, a series of journals devoted to women's issues appeared and became a center of intellectual debate—*Questions féministes* (later *Nouvelles Questions féministes*), *F-Magazine*, and *Sorcières*, for example.

Sexual difference, one of the most important issues to be raised in the 1970s, was the focus of numerous texts ranging from the highly theoretical to the very popular. Hélène Cixous*, Luce Irigaray*, and Julia Kristeva*, the three best-known theorists of sexual difference, examined this issue in psychoanalytic, philosophical, and linguistic terms. Cixous's "Le Rire de la Méduse," with its emphasis on language, identity, and the body, challenges traditional representations of women. Irigaray's *Spéculum de l'autre femme* (1974) provides a critique of the patriarchal Western philosophic tradition from Plato to Hegel, and

Kristeva, in many of her works, associates the feminine with the pre-Oedipal and underscores the revolutionary potential of language.

The question of women's relation to language and the body posed by these theoretical texts is echoed in popular works by writers such as Annie Leclerc*, Marie Cardinal*, and Benoîte Groult*. Leclerc's *Parole de femme* (1974), a lyrical exploration of women's bodily experiences, equates giving birth with creating a new language. In *Les Mots pour le dire* (1975), Cardinal critically examines the crucial role of language in the construction of female identity, while Groult's *Ainsi soit-elle* (1975) focuses on the social construction of identity.

With its focus on thinking and writing "otherwise" and on finding a voice for women, feminism led to an explosion in women's writing in the 1970s that continued through the 1990s. The impact was felt in two main areas: formal experimentation and themes. Building on the earlier work of Nathalie Sarraute* and Marguerite Duras, writers who had rejected linear narrative structures in order to express previously unexplored emotional states, the *écriture féminine** that emerged in the mid-1970s challenged patriarchal language and traditional forms. This avant-garde experimental style associated with writers such as Hélène Cixous and Chantal Chawaf* stressed the corporeality of language and the role of subversive word play. The search for innovative literary forms has in recent years been expressed in the poetry of Anne-Marie Albiach* and Marie Etienne*, for example, whose work is often characterized by minimalism and typographical experimentation. Women also sought to convey the female experience through revisionist mythmaking strategies (Cixous, Michèle Sarde*) and the reworking of the structures and themes of fairy tales and legends (Pierrette Fleutiaux*, Sylvie Germain*, Marie Redonnet*).

Both the experimental and the more conventionally written texts have given voice to women's concerns on the thematic level. In addition to the continued focus on the body expressed through the themes of aging, maternity, menstruation*, and sexuality, these works also explore the social dimensions of issues relating to abortion (Annie Ernaux*); incest (Christine Angot*), mother-daughter relations (Dominique Rolin*), and madness (Jeanne Hyvrard)* are also receiving increased attention. In the theater, an unprecedented number of women playwrights are staging works related to women's lives, in particular mother-daughter relationships (Denise Chalem*), surrogate motherhood (Denise Bonal*), and marriage (Josiane Balasko*). In these and other texts, women writers are examining the complex intersections of race, class, and gender. At the same time, more new voices continue to emerge, suggesting paths to be followed in the future. In particular, writers of immigrant descent are examining issues related to immigration, integration, and racism, and especially their implications for women from diverse cultural traditions (Farida Belghoul*, Calixthe Beyala*, Kim Lefèvre*, and Leïla Sebbar*, for example).

As the century draws to a close, women's literary production continues to branch out in new directions and to raise important questions for the future. It is our hope that *The Feminist Encyclopedia of French Literature* will enhance our understanding of women's literary presence in France and will encourage further explorations of their work.

Susan Ireland and Patrice J. Proulx

BIBLIOGRAPHY

Secondary Texts

Albistur, Maïté, and Daniel Armogathe. *Histoire du féminisme français.* 2 vols. Paris: Editions des femmes, 1977.

Atack, Margaret, and Phil Powrie. *Contemporary French Fiction by Women: Feminist Perspectives.* New York: Manchester University Press, 1990.

Bishop, Michael. *Contemporary French Women Poets.* 2 vols. Amsterdam: Rodopi, 1995.

Cordero, Christiane. *Le Travail des femmes.* Paris: Le Monde-Editions, 1994.

Duchen, Claire. *Feminism in France: From May '68 to Mitterand.* Boston: Routledge and Kegan Paul, 1986.

Holmes, Diana. *French Women's Writing, 1848–1994.* Atlantic Highlands, NJ: Athlone Press, 1996.

Lamar, Celita. *Our Voices, Ourselves: Women Writing for the French Theatre.* New York: Peter Lang, 1991.

Marks, Elaine, and Isabelle de Courtivron. *New French Feminisms: An Anthology.* New York: Shocken Books, 1981.

Milligan, Jennifer E. *The Forgotten Generation: French Women Writers of the Inter-war Period.* New York: Berg, 1996.

Montreynaud, Florence, ed. *Le Vingtième Siècle des femmes.* Paris: Nathan, 1995.

Sartori, Eva M., and Dorothy W. Zimmerman, eds. *French Women Writers: A Bio-Bibliographical Source Book.* Westport, CT: Greenwood Press, 1991.

Waelti-Walters, Jennifer, and Stephen C. Hause, eds. *Feminisms of the Belle Epoque: A Historical and Literary Anthology.* Lincoln: University of Nebraska Press, 1994.

The Feminist Encyclopedia of
French Literature

A

Abortion. Abortion and abortifacient techniques have had a unique history in France and are the subject of an extensive and varied literature. Abortion was officially criminalized in 1556 when Henri II's edict declared that a woman who had had an abortion was guilty of murder. Although literary representations of the practice were generally indirect before the nineteenth century, references to abortion can be found in Montesquieu's *L'Esprit des lois* (1748), Rousseau's *Emile* (1762), and Sade's *La Philosophie dans le boudoir* (1795). In 1791 the Revolutionary Penal Code partially decriminalized abortion by shifting the culpability to the abortionist. Article 317 of the 1810 Napoleonic Code* reinstated severe punishment for patient and practitioner alike (also relevant was Article 340, which prohibited any legal basis for determining the paternity of illegitimate children). In 1852 the French Academy of Medicine voted to adopt the principle that abortion was an acceptable procedure if the pregnancy endangered the life of the mother. Abortion in nineteenth-century France was less and less limited to the working and marginal classes and increasingly a recourse for middle- and upper-class women, as represented in Dumas fils's play *La Femme de Claude* (1873). However, it was not until the late nineteenth century that abortion, in the context of the 1890s depopulationist debate, became a widely articulated social and literary issue. The politically and socially conservative depopulationists saw abortion as a veritable crime against the nation, a selfish, anti-patriotic act. Neo-Malthusians, whose desire to control population growth and ameliorate society expressed itself in their support of working-class and women's issues, championed the legalization of abortion and the woman's right to choose. A myriad of literary works during this period represent abortion, including Alexandre Boutique's *Les Malthusiennes* (1893), Daniel Riche's *Stérile* (1898), Emile Zola's *Fécondité* (1899), Lucien Décaves's *La Clarière* (1900), Paul Bru's *Le Droit d'être mère* (1901), Michel Corday's *Sésame ou la maternité consentie* (1903), André Couvreur's *La Graine* (1903), Jeanne Caruchet's *L'Ensemencée* (1904), Ferdinand Kolney's *Le Salon de Madame Tru-phot* (1905), Camille Pert's *Le Bonheur conjugal* (1905), Edouard Lepage's *Avortée* (1907), and Gaston Tournier's *La Fabrique des anges* (1907). Also during this period, abortion, which previously had been performed primarily by midwives, became the property of institutionalized medicine. World War I* and the heavy French casualties intervened and halted any further consideration of liberalizing abortion laws. The reality of legalized abortion would have to wait until 1973, when the Veil law decriminalized the procedure.

Leonard R. Koos

BIBLIOGRAPHY

Donovan, James M. "Abortion, the Law, and the Juries in France, 1825–1923." *Criminal Justice History* 9 (1988): 157–158.

Fuchs, Rachel. *Poor and Pregnant in Paris: Strategies for Survival in the Nineteenth Century.* New Brunswick, NJ: Rutgers University Press, 1992.

Kopaczynski, Germain. "Simone de Beauvoir's *The Second Sex*: Laying the Groundwork for Abortion." *Cithara* 33 (1994): 648–676.

Pelletier, Madeleine. "Feminism and the Family: The Right to Abortion." Trans. Marilyn J. Boxee. *French-American Review* 6 (1982): 3–26.

Ronsin, Francis. *La Grève des ventres. Propagande néo-malthusienne et baisse de la natalité française (XIXe–XXe siècles).* Paris: Aubier Montaigne, 1980.

Shorter, Edward L. *A History of Women's Bodies.* New York: Basic Books, 1982.

Ackermann, Louise Victorine Choquet (1813–1890). Known for her erudition and considered one of the best poets of the century. Born in Paris, Louise spent a solitary and melancholy childhood in the country, near Montdidier. Her philosophical poetry has its roots in the literary education* guided by her father, who exposed her to freethinkers such as Molière and Voltaire. Ackermann's mother countered with religious instruction. Louise nonetheless cultivated her poetic impulse in verse that was not published, however, until 1863. Meeting Paul Ackermann in Berlin in 1838 redirected her attention to philology and the mastery of yet other foreign languages, among them Sanskrit, Chinese, and German. Despite her initial reserve, her marriage to Ackermann in 1843 was indeed happy, yet short-lived because of his death in 1846. Devastated, she retreated to Nice, where she lived alone and spent her days gardening, reading, and writing. Her pessimism, motivated by her personal loss, takes a philosophical turn in her writing that shifts from personal lyricism to impersonal expression. Ackermann's published works, including short stories*, elegies, and the *Poésies philosophiques*, expressed her view of the human condition. Our quest for knowledge, she believed, culminates in tormenting doubt. Her originality lies in the careful prosodic treatment she gives to the profound moral and spiritual crisis of the fin de siècle. Ackermann's privileged place in French poetic and intellectual history provides strong evidence of women's capacity for creative thought. Yet she also promotes a domestic role for women, from whom she holds herself apart. Her literary achievements were praised by critics even as they were baffled by her. Barbey d'Aurevilly, for example, admired her work but considered her a monster. To keep the literary ground she had gained, Ackermann may have pretended to believe that women should return to *their* domestic place. The feminist ambivalence in Ackermann more likely inscribes the difference that she perceived from the literary self she had become through her writing.

Adrianna M. Paliyenko

BIBLIOGRAPHY

Primary Texts

Contes en vers. Paris: Garnier Frères, 1855.
Contes et poésies. Paris: Hachette, 1863.
Poésies philosophiques. Paris: Lemerre, 1871.
Poésies. Premières poésies. Poésies philosophiques. Paris: Lemerre, 1874.
Ma vie. Paris: Lemerre, 1885.
Pensées d'une solitaire. Paris: Lemerre, 1903.

Secondary Texts

Aulard, François Victor Alphonse. ''Mme Ackermann.'' *Revue bleue* 20 (1890): 620–623.
Caro, Elme. ''La Poésie philosophique dans les nouvelles écoles: Madame Ackermann.'' *Revue des deux mondes* 3 (1874): 241–263.
Grenier, Edouard. ''Souvenirs littéraires.'' *Revue bleue* 52 (1893): 107–117.
Haussonville, [Gabriel Paul Othenin de Cléron] Comte de. ''Mme Ackermann d'après des lettres et des papiers inédits.'' *Revue des deux mondes* 106 (November 1891): 318–353.
Jenson, Deborah. ''Gender and the Aesthetic of 'le Mal': Louise Ackermann's *Poésies philosophiques, 1871.'' Nineteenth-Century French Studies* 23, nos. 1 and 2 (Fall-Winter 1994–95): 175–193.

Adam, Juliette (née Juliette Lambert, also known as Juliette Lamber) (1836–1936). An autodidact, her literary career began with articles and novels* defending women's rights. In her fight for women's emancipation, she specifically denounced the inequality between men and women in such matters as divorce* and access to the learned professions and public affairs (see, for instance, *Le Mandarin* and *Education de Laure*). For twenty years (1879–1899) she headed the *Nouvelle Revue*. The review focused on social and political developments and strove to educate the masses about such concerns. Reflecting the prestige of this publication, Adam had exclusive publication rights for the works of famous writers such as Pierre Loti and Paul Bourget.

Politically active, she was concerned with foreign affairs, especially the fight against isolationist policies, as well as with domestic politics, where she worked for the defense of the Republic. Under the pseudonym Paul Vasili, she also published a series of social analyses including *La Société de Londres, La Société de Vienne*, and *La Société de Saint-Pétersbourg*. Her salon*, thanks to her Egeria, George Sand*, was one of the most brilliant of the time. It was the center of Parisian elite life between 1879 and 1903. Although essentially literary at first, it became a political haven often frequented by the famous French statesman Gambetta, Adam's longtime friend. Known as the "Grande Française" because of her patriotism, she is also remembered as an important contributor to literature. The Académie Française awarded her several prizes, one of which was awarded in 1927 for the entirety of her literary work.

Frédérique Van de Poel-Knottnerus

BIBLIOGRAPHY

Primary Texts

Le Mandarin. Paris: Michel Lévy, 1860.
Mon Village. Paris: Michel Lévy, 1860.
Récits d'une paysanne. Paris: Librairie Claye, 1863.
L'Education de Laure. Paris: Michel Lévy, 1868.
Laide. Paris: Calmann-Lévy et Librairie Nouvelle, 1878.
Vasili, Paul. *La Société de Paris. Le Grand Monde*. Paris: Nouvelle Revue, 1887.
Mes Illusions et nos souffrances pendant le siège de Paris. Paris: A. Lemerre, 1906.
Mes Angoisses et nos luttes, 1871–1873. Paris: A. Lemerre, 1907.

Secondary Texts

Blanc-Péridier, Adrienne. *Une Princesse de la Troisième République. Juliette Adam*. Paris: Edition "Education Intégrale," 1936.
Daudet, Ernest. *Les Coulisses de la société parisienne*. Paris: P. Ollendorf, 1893.
Gambetta, Léon. *Lettres de Gambetta*. 1868–1882. Ed. Daniel Halévy and Emile Pilias. Paris: B. Grasset, 1938.
Morcos, Saad. *Juliette Adam*. Beirut: Dar Al-Maaref, 1962.

Adultery. The theme of adultery appears as one of the founding motifs in French literature. The twelfth-century romance of Tristan and Yseult sets the tone and establishes the dominant triangle, that in which the wife is the adulterous partner. The adulterous couple of courtly literature may be seen as a comment on the lack of affection between spouses in arranged marriages*. Indeed, it is the adulterous couple who experience true love, although they rarely, if ever, meet a happy end. If the narrative does not end with one or the other or both of them dead, they are separated and, usually, repentant. The trope of the repentant lovers reminds the reader that adultery, like marriage, was not a civil matter. Rather, it fell to the jurisdiction of the Church, which prescribed penance for the wayward spouse.

Parodies of this conjugal triangle soon appeared in the comic literature of the thirteenth century, most particularly in the fabliaux*. Love among members of the nobility is downgraded to adulterous affairs in which the culpable male is most frequently a priest or a young student. The husband in this triangle becomes a new literary type, the "cocu battu et content" (the battered but happy cuckold). This figure also makes his appearance on the stage in the medieval farce. Unlike the fabliau, where the adulterous wife is rarely if ever punished, the farce frequently stages correctional performances that may be seen as cautionary exemplars for "loose" wives.

In the sixteenth century, the Rabelaisian question of whether or not Panurge should marry, since marriage by definition leads to unhappiness and *cocuage*, remains closely linked to the themes of the farce and fabliau. The tales and commentary in Marguerite de Navarre's* *Heptaméron*, on the other hand, deftly combine both the comic tradition with the serious side of the courtly ideal and overlay both with Renaissance and Neoplatonic values. Perhaps because of the Platonic alternative, the emphasis placed on questions of women's fidelity and virtue becomes more pronounced. The *Heptaméron* offers models of women who reject adulterous liaisons in favor of preserving their honor.

Among the most striking articulations of this theme is *La Princesse de Clèves*. Madame de Lafayette's* heroine incarnates the biblical interpretation of adultery where the psychological supersedes the physical. It matters little what the Princesse does; her guilt is established a priori. That this version of the adulterous woman remains fixed in French literature is evident from the variant on this scenario played out nearly two hundred years later in Marguerite Duras's* *Moderato cantabile*: a series of conversations in a café brands Anne Desbardes as an adulterous woman.

Despite the proto-feminism of an Olympe de Gouges*, neither the Enlightenment* nor the French Revolution* brought about any serious changes in the overarching attitudes toward adultery. Thus, in *Les Liaisons dangereuses*, Laclos's Présidente, a paragon of virtue, dies of the chagrin of betrayal in her adulterous affair. Nevertheless, the death of Valmont, her seducer, does in some sense maintain the traditional "courtly" paradigm. While the social shifts inherent in the fall of the *Ancien Régime* would facilitate similar shifts in the class of the characters regularly portrayed in French literature, the image of the adulterous woman crystallizes in Flaubert's Emma Bovary. Adultery, albeit an escape from the ennui of the bourgeoisie, cannot truly be condoned. However sympathetic Flaubert may have been toward Emma, it is she who dies at the end of the novel.

Despite the fact that at the end of the twentieth century, feminist thought may have somewhat modified the view of the adulterous woman as a guilt-ridden/guilty literary figure, the long-standing acceptance in French society of the husband's right to have a mistress continues to inform the literary motif of adultery and to represent it through *la femme adultère*. Exceptions to this rule, nonetheless, have begun to appear as the volume of texts authored by women increases.

Edith J. Benkov

BIBLIOGRAPHY

Armstrong, Nancy, and Leonard Tennehouse, eds. *The Ideology of Conduct: Essays on Literature and the History of Sexuality*. New York: Methuen, 1987.

Buschinger, Danielle, ed. *Amour, mariage et transgressions au Moyen-Age*. Actes du Colloque d'Amiens, March 1983. Göppingen: Kümmerle, 1984.

Coulon, Henri. *Le Divorce et l'adultère*. Paris: Marchal et Billard, 1982.

Duby, Georges. *Le Chevalier, la femme et le prêtre*. Paris: Hachette, 1981.

Tanner, Tony. *Adultery and the Novel*. Baltimore: Johns Hopkins University Press, 1979.

Agoult, Marie d' (née Marie-Catherine-Sophie), comtesse de Flavigny (1805–1876). Marie d'Agoult is viewed as one of the greatest feminists of her time. Even before her *Essai sur la Liberté* (1847), in which she denounces women's lack of freedom and argues for their rights, she led a very untraditional life for a woman of her era and class. Although a wife and a mother, she left her household to live with her lover, Franz Liszt, to whom she bore three children. Her fight for women's equality was probably enhanced not only by the fact that a divorce* was unthinkable but because, once her relationship with Liszt ended, she had no rights to her own children since she had not married their father.

As was the case for many women of her social rank who did not submit to the marital rules of her time, she would have been banned forever from her society had not her intelligence prevailed. Writing under the pseudonym Daniel Stern, she began her literary career as an art critic for *La Presse*, and throughout her life she never stopped contributing articles on art and literature to newspapers. But her interests extended beyond art and literature. She became a member of the editorial board of *Le Temps*, for which she wrote historical as well as political pieces. She also wrote short stories* and a novel*, *Nélida* (1846).

Although *Nélida* generated a great deal of attention, she did not see herself as a fiction writer. Rather, she focused on becoming a historian, an essayist and a critic. Her reputation followed quickly with her *Lettres républicaines* (1848) and *Esquisses morales et politiques* (1849). She received much acclaim for her *Histoire de la Révolution de 1848* (1850–1853), which was followed by a successful play, *Jeanne d'Arc* (1857), staged both in France and Italy.

Born of a French father and a German mother, she longed for strong ties between the two countries. She regularly contributed articles on German art and literature to the *Revue Germanique*. The war of 1870 affected her greatly, but as a fervent republican she remained faithful to France.

Leading a very social life, she attracted lawyers, scientists, historians, and politicians to her famous salon*. Among her notorious friends, she counted Lamennais, Sainte-Beuve, Michelet, and George Sand*, with whom she had a (sometimes difficult) lifetime relationship and who immortalized her liaison with Liszt in *Horace*.

Marie d'Agoult left two autobiographical works: *Mes Souvenirs, 1806–1833* (1877) and *Mémoires, 1833–1854* (1927), the latter of which she was unable to complete. Her letters to Franz Liszt have for the most part been destroyed. His correspondence with her, however, is practically intact and has been published in two volumes under the title *Correspondance de Liszt et de la comtesse d'Agoult, 1833–1864* (1933).

Frédérique Van de Poel-Knottnerus

BIBLIOGRAPHY

Primary Texts

Nélida. Paris: Calmann-Lévy, 1846.
Essai sur la Liberté. Paris: Calmann-Lévy, 1847.
Lettres républicaines. Paris: Calmann-Lévy, 1848.
Esquisses morales et politiques. Paris: Chez Pagnerre, Libraire, 1849.
Histoire de la Révolution de 1848. Paris: Gustave André, 1850–1853.
Jeanne d'Arc, drame historique. Paris: Calmann-Lévy, 1857.
Stern, Daniel. *Mes Souvenirs, 1806–1833*. Paris: Calmann-Lévy, 1877.
Mémoires, 1833–1854. Paris: Calmann-Lévy, 1927.

Secondary Texts

Aragonnès, Claude. *Marie d'Agoult*. Paris: Hachette, 1938.
Ollivier, Daniel. *Correspondance de Liszt et de la comtesse d'Agoult, 1833–1864*. Paris: Grasset, 1933.
Sand, George. *Horace*. Paris: Editions de l'Aurore, 1982.
Vier, Jacques. *Daniel Stern, Lettres républicaines du Second-Empire*. Paris: Editions du Cèdre, 1951.
———. *La Comtesse d'Agoult et son temps*. Paris: Armand Colin, 1959.

Aïssé, Charlotte Elisabeth (c. 1694–1733). Born in the Caucasian Mountains and captured by the Turks, she was sold at age four to the Comte de Ferriol, the French ambassador to Constantinople, for 1,500 pounds. In France she was brought up in the genteel ways of her times and mingled with the great literary figures of the Enlightenment*. Aside from her exotic origin and renowned beauty, the main event of her life was her love for the libertine Chevalier Blaise Marie d'Aydie. For some unknown reason, she refused to marry him, although she bore him a child. Aïssé befriended Julie Calandrini, a deeply religious woman who tried to convince her either to marry or to renounce Aydie and to return to the Church. Aïssé died prematurely from tuberculosis in 1733. It has often been remarked that the extraordinary circumstances of her life appear to be inspired by the eighteenth-century novel*.

Aïssé's letters to Julie Calandrini were first published in 1787, with a romanticized biography and notes by Voltaire, one of her literary admirers. The letters are a masterpiece of the genre, not only because they present the dilemma of a young woman trying to choose between love and religion, but also because of their style and their description of the Regency period. However, there is some question whether Aïssé is the author of these letters.

Valérie Lastinger

BIBLIOGRAPHY

Primary Text

Lettres de Mademoiselle Aïssé à Madame Calandrini qui contiennent plusieurs anecdotes de l'histoire du temps, depuis l'année 1726 jusqu'en 1733. Précédées d'un narre très-court de l'histoire de mademoiselle Aïssé, pour servir à l'intelligence de ses lettres. Avec des notes, dont quelques-unes sont de M. de Voltaire. Paris: La Grange, 1787.

Secondary Texts

Curtis, Judith. "The Epistolières." In *French Women and the Age of Enlightenment.* Ed. Samia I. Spencer. Bloomington: Indiana University Press, 1984. 126–141.
Wall, Glenda. "Aïssé." In *An Encyclopedia of Continental Women Writers.* Ed. Katharina M. Wilson. New York: Garland, 1991. Vol. 1: 12–13.

Albiach, Anne-Marie (1937–). Of Catalan origin, Albiach is a poet who cofounded *Siècle à mains,* collaborates on a number of journals, and is a recognized translator (notably of Louis Zukofsky). In her work, near-blank pages dominate and geometrical images abound in a rarefied atmosphere offering sober, abstract lines. Her poetry* originates in personal experience pared down to appear impersonal, and privileges memory, the body, and desire, themes that are clearly observable in the eroticism of her first poems. Although Albiach does not directly address gender issues, the syntactic conjunctions she creates between linguistic and typographical elements and blank spaces represent dialogue and relationship, and this "geometry of gesture" includes an exploration of the uncharted terrain separating the masculine and the feminine.

Karen Bouwer

BIBLIOGRAPHY

Primary Texts

Flammigère. London: Siècle à mains, 1967.
Etat. Paris: Mercure de France, 1971.
"H II" linéaires. Paris: Le Collet de Buffle, 1974.
Césure: Le Corps. Paris: Orange Export Ltd., 1975.
Objet. Paris: Orange Export Ltd., 1976.
Mezza voce. Paris: Flammarion, 1984.
Anawratha. Paris: Spectres Familiers, 1984.
Figure vocative. Paris: Lettres de Casse, 1985.
Le Chemin de l'ermitage. Pointe-à-Pitre: Première Saline, 1986.
Travail vertical et blanc. Paris: Spectres Familiers, 1989.

Secondary Texts

Bishop, Michael. "Anne-Marie Albiach." In *Contemporary French Poets.* Vol. 2. Amsterdam: Rodopi, 1995. 134–154.
Gleize, Jean-Marie. *Le Théâtre du poème: Vers Anne-Marie Albiach.* Paris: Belin, 1995.

Albret, Jeanne d' (1528–1572). Queen of Navarre, Protestant leader, author of *Mémoires* and letters. The daughter and only child of Marguerite de Navarre* and Henri d'Albret, king of Navarre, she received a thorough education* in the care of her mother's friend Aymée de Lafayette but did not spend much time with either of her parents and is only rarely mentioned in her mother's letters.

In 1537 her father and her uncle, François I, began to consider rival marriage*
alliances for her, and in 1541, as part of his political maneuvering against
Charles V, François I arranged her marriage with the duke of Cleves. D'Albret,
who had to be carried to the altar, prepared a written protest in which she
claimed that her mother threatened to beat her if she did not obey. But Marguerite de Navarre's role was ambiguous, and she was caught between her
brother's and her husband's ambitions. She delayed sending her daughter to live
with the duke until François no longer needed the alliance, and the marriage
was annulled. D'Albret was married in 1548 to Antoine de Bourbon, a match
that pleased her, at least initially, and two children lived to adulthood, Henri
(the future Henri IV), born in 1553 and Catherine, born in 1559.

Jeanne d'Albret publicly adopted the Reformed faith in 1560. Antoine de
Bourbon also converted, but abjured in 1562 under pressure from Catherine de
Medici* and other nobles. When he died in 1562, she was left to administer the
Kingdom of Navarre on her own, as widowed regent for her son. She established
Calvinism there, and was active politically and in the military defense of the
territory during the first two Wars of Religion, until she sought refuge with other
Huguenot families in La Rochelle. Her reign and the edicts she promulgated
were marked by religious tolerance, and she insisted that Catholics should have
their right to worship protected in her lands. With Gaspard de Coligny, she was
one of the two acknowledged leaders of the Huguenot cause. She encouraged
and was a model for many Huguenot women, including Charlotte de Bourbon*,
Louise de Coligny, and Georgette de Montenay*. She died in June 1572, after
having agreed to the marriage of her son to Marguerite de Valois*, daughter of
Catherine de Medici.

Jeanne d'Albret's letters deal with her political and religious activities and
her relationships with her husband and her son. Her *Mémoires* (written in 1568)
are an intellectual and spiritual autobiography* for the period from 1560 to 1568,
carefully designed to refute critics who referred to her ''imbecility'' as a woman,
to justify her actions as queen of Navarre and leader of the Huguenot resistance,
and to protest the Huguenots' and her own loyalty to the crown, in the hopes
of convincing the king and the queen mother to put an end to the Wars of
Religion and to maintain and increase the tolerance for the Huguenots that had
been sketched out in the Edict of January in 1562 and echoed in her own edict
on religious liberty in 1564. While she failed in her lifetime, the impact of her
work can be seen in the Edict of Nantes, promulgated by her son in 1598.

Jane Couchman

BIBLIOGRAPHY

Primary Texts

Lettres d'Antoine de Bourbon et de Jehanne d'Albret. Ed. de Rochambeau. Paris: Renouard, 1877.
Mémoires et poésies. Ed. Alphonse de Ruble. Paris, 1893. Geneva: Slatkine, 1970.

Secondary Texts

Bainton, Roland H. "Jeanne d'Albret." In *Women of the Reformation in France and England.* Boston: Beacon Press, 1973. 43–73.
Roelker, Nancy L. "The Appeal of Calvinism to French Noblewomen in the Sixteenth Century." *Journal of Interdisciplinary History* 2 (Spring 1972): 391–418.
———. *Queen of Navarre: Jeanne d'Albret.* Cambridge, MA: Belknap Press, 1968.

Alia, Josette (1936–). Journalist for *Jeune Afrique* (1960–1962) and foreign correspondent for *Le Monde* (1962–1967), Alia is currently an associate editing director for the *Nouvel Observateur.* Since 1985 she has covered Africa and the Middle East, analyzing in particular the destiny of minority groups. She makes this same topic the focus of her fictional work *Quand le soleil était chaud.* In this novel*, Alia emphasizes the role of women—Jewish, Muslim, or Christian—who transcend their ethnic and religious differences to find love and meaning in the Middle East, where peace is constantly jeopardized by man's intolerance of others.

                                                              Sylvaine Egron-Sparrow

BIBLIOGRAPHY

Primary Texts

La Guerre de Mitterrand: La Dernière Grande Illusion. Paris: Orban, 1991.
Quand le soleil était chaud. Paris: Grasset, 1993.
Au coeur de la voyance. Paris: Plon, 1995.

Allart, Hortense (1801–1879). Novelist, essayist, literary critic, and historian. Allart's culminating work, *Les Enchantements de Prudence*, was published in 1872 when she was seventy-one. The semi-fictionalized autobiography* contains an unusual potpourri of period Romanticism*, personal experiences, commentaries describing the horrors that many women were forced to endure, and a call for social awareness and action. Much of the novel's* force lies in Allart's poignant descriptions of her own unhappy marriage*, which lasted a scant year.

She produced nine other novels, including *Gertrude* (1828), *Jérome ou le jeune prélat* (1829), *Sextus ou le Romain des Maremmes* (1832), *L'Indienne* (1832), *Settimia* (1836), *Clémence* (1865), and her three *Petits Livres* (1850–1851). Her heroines are typically intelligent young women who strive for a happy marriage but hold fast to their individuality, independence, and self-respect. She also wrote historical works and essays. In *La Femme et la démocratie de nos temps* (1836), one of her best-known essays, she declares that the equality of the sexes cannot be denied, asserts that society should create a new governmental hierarchy that includes gifted, educated women as well as men, calls for better education* for women, and urges legalized divorce*, forbidden at the time. Herself the devoted mother of two out-of-wedlock sons, she sought throughout her life to better the situation of unwed mothers.

In 1836 Allart wrote several articles on women's issues for the short-lived

(1836–1837) publication *La Gazette des femmes*, and participated in the feminist movement led by Flora Tristan*. Allart also carried on an interesting correspondence, somewhat adversarial, mostly cordial, with George Sand* for more than forty years.

Helynne H. Hansen

BIBLIOGRAPHY

Primary Texts

Allart, Hortense. *La Femme et la démocratie de nos temps*. Paris: Delaunay et A. Pinard, 1836.
———. *Settimia*. 2 vols. Paris: Arthus Bertrand, 1836.
———. *Lettres inédites à Sainte-Beuve (1841–1848)*. Paris: Mercure de France, 1908.
———. *Nouvelles Lettres à Sainte-Beuve*. Geneva: Droz, 1965.
Allart de Thérèse, Madame Hortense. *Gertrude*. 4 vols. Paris: Ambroise Dupont et Cie., 1828.
———. *Sextus ou Le Romain des Maremmes*. Paris: Heidelhoff et Campe, 1832.
———. *L'Indienne*. Paris: Ch. Vimont, 1832.
——— [anonymous]. *Jérome ou le jeune prélat*. Paris: Chez Ladvocat, 1829.
Méritens, Hortense de. *Clémence*. Paris: Sceaux: Typographie de E. Dépée, 1865.
Saman, Madame P. de. *Les Derniers Enchantements, Gertrude, Harold, Le Jeune Comte Henri, Lettres de Béranger*. Paris: Michel Lévy frères, 1874.
———. *Les Nouveaux Enchantements*. Paris: Calmann-Lévy, 1882.
Saman l'Esbatx, Madame P. [Hortense Allart de Méritens]. *Les Enchantements de Prudence*. Paris: Typographie de E. Dépée, 1872.

Amar, Marlène (1949–). Cinema critic and novelist. Born in Algeria to a Sephardic Jewish family, Amar now lives and works in Paris. Her two novels* recount the exile and fragmentation of her family after they are forced to move to France during the Algerian War. The interrelated themes of loss, memory, nostalgia, and the erasure of the family's Algerian cultural identity recur in both texts, making them examples of what is often called *nostalgérie*. Both novels focus on the experiences of the women in the family. In particular, *La Femme sans tête* uses images related to the female body to raise questions about assimilation and difference and to propose a new form of writing the body.

Susan Ireland

BIBLIOGRAPHY

Primary Texts

La Femme sans tête. Paris: Gallimard, 1993.
Des Gens infréquentables. Paris: Gallimard, 1996.

Amazons. The ancient Greek myth* of the Amazons, fierce warrior women who lived without men in their own country ruled by a queen, inspired many French writers in all eras. They enter French literature in the twelfth century, especially in Benoit de Sainte-Maure's *Roman de Troie*, dedicated to Aliénor d'Aquitaine, where they are transformed into courtly knights. The most original early treatment of the Amazon motif was that of Christine de Pizan* (c. 1364–c. 1431). Pizan was an explicit feminist who wrote extensively defending women from the misogyny of her time. In several works, especially in *Le Livre de la cité des dames* (1405), she cites Amazons to argue that women are capable of great physical feats and nobility, and makes of them the foundation for her city. Pizan calculates that their nation lasted 800 years and concludes that no male-led country had more noble or capable leaders.

The image of the beautiful Amazon queen became a staple of French literature through the sixteenth and seventeenth centuries, but usually as a minor character. The eighteenth century saw a renewal of feminism*, and Anne-Marie du Bocage's* play *La Tragédie des Amazones* (1749) asserts the Amazons' love of liberty.

The association of Amazons with lesbians is primarily a twentieth-century phenomenon, though one can find scattered references earlier (e.g., Brântome's *Les Dames galantes*, 1586, fifth discourse). Natalie Clifford Barney* took on the persona of "*l'Amazone*" in her lesbian circle and writings. Monique Wittig* wrote an influential feminist novel, *Les Guérillères* (1969), in which Amazonian women defeat the patriarchy and create a new world with new language. Wittig and Sande Zeig continued to explore the relations between Amazons and modern lesbians in *Brouillon pour un dictionnaire des amantes* (1975). The motif has inspired important works by Louky Bersianik, Hélène Cixous*, Françoise d'Eaubonne, Richard Demarcy, and others.

Diane Griffin Crowder

BIBLIOGRAPHY

Secondary Texts

Jay, Karla. *The Amazon and the Page: Natalie Clifford Barney and Renée Vivien*. Bloomington: Indiana University Press, 1988.
Kleinbaum, Abby Wettan. *The War against the Amazons*. New York: McGraw-Hill, 1983.
Petit, Aimé. "Le Traitement courtois du thème des Amazones d'après trois romans antiques: Enéas, Troie, et Alexandre." *Le Moyen Age* 89 (1983): 63–84.
Salmonson, Jessica A. *The Encyclopedia of Amazons: Women Warriors from Antiquity to the Modern Era*. New York: Paragon House, 1991.

Amboise, Katherine d' (?–1550). Daughter of Charles II d'Amboise, seigneur de Chaumont, and niece of Cardinal Georges d'Amboise, she was married three times: first to Christophe de Tournon, seigneur de Beauchastel, who left her widowed at age twenty; then for nearly forty years to Philibert de Beaujeu; and lastly, at age sixty-five, to Louis de Clèves. Her personal sorrows inspired her to write the *Livre des prudens* and a *Complainte*, both in prose, and the *Devotes Epistres*, in verse. The *Livre des prudens*, dated July 1, 1509, offers a catalogue of men and women from history, mythology, and the Bible* who were notable for their prudence or lack thereof. It is dedicated to Dame Prudence, who asserts that by recalling her personal tragedies (the loss of both her parents, her first husband, and their only child), the author will overcome her sorrow. Katherine apologizes for her inexperience in writing but also contends that since women have more limited access to learning than men, their work is more deserving of charitable reception. The plaintive disclaimer of her ignorance and fear of prolixity which concludes almost every chapter leads her to name sources where readers can find more details: Boccaccio, Vincent de Beauvais, Orosius, Lucan, the Bible, chronicles, and Roman history. If her honor as a woman exempts her from speaking at greater length about such villains as Nero, her interest in women is justified by her own gender. God has given her intelligence and reason, so she will use them to relate the good that has come from women. Organizing her examples according to the six ages of history, she identifies six prudent and six imprudent figures per age, praising eight women (Isis, Minerva, Deborah, etc.) and reproving five others (Eve, Jezebel, Brunehaut, etc.).

Given Katherine's declaration that she regularly retires to her study to compose "lamentations and feminine regrets," it is not surprising that her second prose work is a *Complainte de la dame pasmee contre fortune*. After fainting at sad news, the author is resuscitated by Dame Reason, who instructs her as to the causes of misery in the world. She advises her not to accuse Fortune but to recognize adversity as part of God's order and to seek Patience brought by Christ. Reason accompanies Katherine to the Park of Divine Love, where she finds Patience seated at the foot of the Tree of the Cross.

Katherine's final work seems to have grown from this allegorical journey: the *Devotes Epistres* announces the sinner's reconciliation with Christ, affirmed in the text and depicted in the miniatures, where an angel brings a ring from heaven to the kneeling author. Christ accepts Katherine's request for pardon and responds with the assurance that she will find repose at the Manor of Prayer in the company of Charity and Reason.

Although her works survive in few manuscripts (three for the *Complainte*, one each for the *Prudens* and *Epistres*), they are noteworthy for their numerous miniatures as well as the text. Each source clearly identifies the author by name and coat of arms and portrays her, at times, accompanied by a younger girl who is probably her niece and heir, Antoinette d'Amboise. The seventy-four miniatures of the *Prudens* manuscript depict, often with Katherine herself, the famous men and women she evokes.

Mary Beth Winn

BIBLIOGRAPHY

Primary Texts

La Complainte de la dame pasmee contre fortune. Paris, BN MS. n.a.fr. 19738 and two
    MSS. in private hands.
Le Livre des prudens. Paris, Bibliothèque de l'Arsenal MS. 2037.
Les Devotes Epistres de Katherine d'Amboise. Ed. J.-J. Bourasse. Tours, 1861 (BN MS.
    fr. 282).

Secondary Texts

Berriot-Salvadore, Evelyne. *Les Femmes dans la société française de la Renaissance.*
    Geneva: Droz, 1990. 417–420.
Souchal, G. "Le Mécénat de la famille d'Amboise." *Bulletin de la Société des anti-
    quaires de l'Ouest et des Musées de Poitiers* 13, no. 4 (1976): 567–612.

Amrouche, Marie-Louise Taos (1913–1976). Born in Tunis of an Algerian
immigrant family and later naturalized French, Amrouche was the first well-
known Algerian woman writer. Besides publishing novels*, short stories*, and
poems, Amrouche also gave recitals of Berber chants and hosted radio programs
in Kabyle. Her autobiographical works depict a fragmented female self torn
between her French, Algerian, and Berber identities. The main themes of her
work focus on personal identity, confession, sexual phantasms, and her marginalization as a woman and a writer. Her writing marks the beginning of a
women's literature in Algeria.

Armelle Crouzières-Ingenthron

BIBLIOGRAPHY

Primary Texts

Jacynthe noire. 1947. Paris: Joëlle Losfeld, 1996.
Rue des Tambourins. Paris: La Table ronde, 1960.
Le Grain magique, contes, poèmes et proverbes berbères de Kabylie. Paris: Maspéro,
    1966.
L'Amant imaginaire. Paris: Nouvelle Société Morel, 1975.
Solitude ma mère. Paris: Joëlle Losfeld, 1995.

Secondary Texts

Brahimi, Denise. *Taos Amrouche, romancière.* Paris: Joëlle Losfeld, 1995.
Déjeux, Jean. *La Littérature féminine de langue française au Maghreb.* Paris: Karthala,
    1994.
———. *Maghreb. Littératures de langue française.* Paris: Arcantère, 1993.
Giono, Jean. *Entretiens avec Jean Amrouche et Taos Amrouche.* Paris: Gallimard, 1990.

Anarchism. Pierre Joseph Proudhon's social theories started the anarchist movement. In 1871 Mikhail Boukanine created the first anarchist group, after his
secession from the Marxists. After Bakounine's death in 1876, Prince Kropot-
kine took over. Under his direction, anarchism went through various transformations. At first, anarchists rejected any form of authority. Then in the 1880s
and 1890s, influenced by nihilism, they advocated the destruction of authority
by any means, including terrorism. By the 1900s, anarchists had changed their
focus to anarcho-syndicalism.

Earlier on, women had an uneasy relationship with anarchism because of
Proudhon's misogynistic and antifeminist legacy. This attitude later changed in
the 1880s when anarchists proclaimed that the family* unit was a space of
oppression for women and also demanded better education* for women. Women

often wrote in anarchist newspapers such as *Le Libertaire* or even founded their own, like Anna Mahé's *L'Anarchie*. However, Louise Michel* achieved a rare feat in becoming an anarchist leader.

Leading feminists such as Nelly Roussel*, Madeleine Pelletier*, Séverine*, and Marguerite Durand* had contacts with anarchists mainly through Paul Robin's neo-Malthusian movement. They helped him to promote contraception to give back to women control of their own bodies and fertility, thus liberating them from poverty and unwanted maternity*.

Juliette Parnell-Smith

BIBLIOGRAPHY

Dhavernas, Marie-Jo. "Anarchisme et féminisme à la Belle Epoque." *La Revue d'en face*, no. 2 (Autumn 1982): 49–61, and no. 13 (Winter 1983): 61–80.
Mahé, Anna. *L'Hérédité et l'éducation*. Paris: Ed. de l'Anarchie, 1908.
Maitron, Jean. *Le mouvement anarchiste en France*. 2 vols. Paris: Maspéro, 1975.
Michel, Louise. *Prise de possession*. Saint-Denis: Publication du groupe anarchiste de Saint-Denis, 1890.
———. *Souvenirs et aventures de ma vie*. Ed. Daniel Armogathe. Paris: Maspéro, 1983.
Rabaut, Jean. *Histoires des féminismes*. Paris: Stock, 1978.
Ronsin, Francis. *La Grève des ventres. Propagande néo-malthusienne et baisse de la natalité en France, XIXe–XXe siècle*. Paris: Aubier, 1980.
Rowbotham, Sheila. *Women in Movement: Feminism and Social Action*. New York: Routledge, 1992.

Androgyny (1800–1900). In classical mythology, the androgyne was a unified being composed of two bodies, male and female, later split in two by Zeus. The androgyne thus represented an original unity later torn asunder. In nineteenth-century French literature, in the turbulent and unstable years after the Revolution* when ''unity'' and continuity of social identity were lost, androgynes and androgyny often are used to figure not only the threats to unity brought about by general social changes, but also more specifically by changes in gender identities and roles.

One of the main transformations in the understanding of identity that occurs during this time is the dim but growing realization that social and gender identities are in large part constructed and not innate. Honoré de Balzac's works, such as *Le Colonel Chabert*, reveal that the identity created by social rules and customs is more important even than one's literal, physical presence. When Chabert returns to Paris after recovering from amnesia, he learns that society has deemed him dead and that he cannot, in fact, live in society as himself. This growing consciousness of the social construction of identity holds true especially for gender, and it is here that androgyny, in its mixing of male and female, can show how gender is not a simple anatomical fact but rather a complex construction of social codes. Balzac's *Séraphîta* centers on an androgyne, an angel, whose gender identity depends upon the person who sees her and not on anatomical givens. Many of Balzac's texts have androgynous characters, or characters who in some way call into question gender identity and gender roles: Vautrin, Paquita, Zambinella, Gillette, Fœdora, to name a few well-known ones.

It is perhaps George Sand* who in her life and her works makes this artificial, social nature of the limits placed on women by their gender most visible by creating an androgynous identity for herself in real life and by representing androgynous characters in her works. When Sand dressed as a man and roamed about Paris, she found the physical and social freedom she lacked when wearing female garb, and thereby made visible the artificial social limits placed on women. This same emphasis on gender codes arises in her novels* in both specific examples of androgynous characters and in narratological issues of gender.

Many other canonical nineteenth-century writers touch on themes of androgyny in their texts. In Stendhal, androgyny comes to figure changing social roles, particularly those relating to class and notions of superiority. Théophile Gautier's *Mademoiselle de Maupin* centers androgyny on the question of the possibility of unity, at once aesthetic and social. Gustave Flaubert's Emma, labeled an androgyne by Baudelaire, taps into the Flaubertian question of the clichéd nature of language. There, the coded and artificial nature of gender figures the coded nature of all meaning and identity.

The works of Rachilde* at the end of the nineteenth and well into the twentieth century most clearly focus on the constructed nature of gender identity and show its artificiality. Through the creation of androgynous characters whose social gender identity is the reverse of their biological sexual identity, Rachilde, in such texts as *Monsieur Vénus*, makes the constructed nature of gender the very substance of her decadent texts.

Dorothy Kelly

BIBLIOGRAPHY

Primary Texts

Balzac, Honoré de. *Séraphîta* Paris: Bureau de la Revue de Paris, 1834.
———. *Le Colonel Chabert*. Paris: George Barrie et fils, 1836.
Flaubert, Gustave. *Madame Bovary*. Paris: Lévy, 1857.
Gautier, Théophile. *Mademoiselle de Maupin*. 2 vols. Paris: Renduel, 1835–1836.
Rachilde. *Monsieur Vénus*. Paris: F. Brosser, 1889.
Sand, George. *Lélia*. 2 vols. Paris: H. Dupuy, 1833.
Stendhal [Marie-Henri Beyle]. *Le Rouge et le noir*. Paris: Librairie Larousse 1830.

Secondary Texts

Heilbrun, Carolyn G. *Toward a Recognition of Androgyny*. New York: Knopf, 1973.
Kelly, Dorothy. *Fictional Genders: Role and Representation in Nineteenth-Century French Narrative*. Lincoln: University of Nebraska Press, 1989.
Naginski, Isabelle. *George Sand: Writing for Her Life*. New Brunswick, NJ: Rutgers University Press, 1991.
Schor, Naomi. *Breaking the Chain: Women, Theory, and French Realist Fiction*. New York: Columbia University Press, 1985.

Weil, Kari. *Androgyny and the Denial of Difference*. Charlottesville: University Press of Virginia, 1992.
Women's Studies: An Interdisciplinary Journal. Special Issue on Androgyny. Vol. 2, no. 2 (1974): 139–271.

Angeville, Henriette d' (1794–1871). Angeville was a mountain climber and the second woman to reach the top of Mont Blanc, in 1838, a feat she described in *Mon Excursion au Mont Blanc*. Henriette d'Angeville's narrative underscores the physical and ideological obstacles she overcame. Her descriptions of physical hardship are combined with comments on the process of writing about an experience located outside the norms of feminine behavior. Her narrative features a conversation with Marie Paradis, a peasant who was the first woman to reach the top of Mont Blanc, which introduces the issue of class in the genre of travel literature*.

Bénédicte Monicat

BIBLIOGRAPHY

Primary Text

Mon Excursion au Mont Blanc, 1839. Paris: Editions Arthaud, 1987.

Secondary Text

Monicat, Bénédicte. *Itinéraires de l'écriture au féminin: Voyageuses du 19e siècle*. Amsterdam: Rodopi, 1996.

Angot, Christine (?–). Angot's plays and novels* are inspired by her experience of father-daughter incest from the age of thirteen to twenty-six. The novel *Interview* (1995), for example, juxtaposes descriptions of an unpublished interview about incest with memories of a trip to Sicily with her husband and daughter. The intrusive questions and comments of a journalist run throughout the text as Angot evokes the physical and psychological effects of the incest, the silence surrounding it in her family, and her relationship with her mother and her own daughter. In the play *Corps plongés dans un liquide*, Angot's explicit—often crude—language describes the forms and violence of a father's sexual relations with his daughter, a relationship symbolized by bodily fluids. Angot's second play, *Nouvelle vague*, again deals with the topics of sexual violence and perverted male sexuality by giving voice to a psychopath who reveals his fantasies and troubled attitudes toward women.

Susan Ireland

BIBLIOGRAPHY

Primary Texts

Vu du ciel. Paris: L'Arpenteur-Gallimard, 1990.
Not to Be. Paris: L'Arpenteur-Gallimard, 1991.
Corps plongés dans un liquide. Paris: Editions Comp'Act, 1993.
Nouvelle vague. Paris: Editions Comp'Act, 1993.

Léonore, toujours. Paris: L'Arpenteur-Gallimard, 1994.
Interview. Paris: Fayard, 1995.

Anissimov, Myriam (1943–). Novelist and biographer of Primo Levi. Born in a Swiss refugee camp, Anissimov immigrated to France with her family. A strong Jewish identity permeates her work, in which guilt, anguish, self-deprecation, and a search for appeasement and wholeness define the authorial voice. In *Le Resquise* and *Le Marida*, Anissimov's gift for comedy and satire lightens the tragic undertones of her family epics, while tragedy is more in evidence in the meditative, autobiographical *Dans la plus stricte intimité*. In *Rue de nuit*, she explores the allegorical narrative form, imagining an innocent victim persecuted for unstated crimes in a Kafkaesque world. In her work, Anissimov raises the question of a Jewish woman's difficult quest for self and her role in the contemporary world.

Madeleine Cottenet-Hage

BIBLIOGRAPHY

Primary Texts

Comment va Rachel? Paris: Denoël, 1973.
Le Resquise. Paris: Denoël, 1975.
Rue de nuit. Paris: Julliard, 1977.
L'Homme rouge des Tuileries. Paris: Julliard, 1979.
Le Marida. Paris: Julliard, 1982.
Le Bal des Puces. Paris: Julliard, 1985.
La Soie et les cendres. Paris: Payot, 1989.
Dans la plus stricte intimité. Paris: Editions de l'Olivier, 1992.
Primo Levi. Le Suicide d'un optimiste. Paris: Lattès, 1996.

Recordings

Myriam Anissimov chante Albertine Sarrazin. Disques Polydor, 1969.

Anne, Catherine (?–). Actress, director, and playwright. Anne directs many of her own plays, and created the Compagnie A Brôle Pourpoint. Female characters seeking to affirm their identities are often set up in pairs, revealing relationships between sisters or friends, as in *Eclats, Tita-Lou*, and *Ah! Annabelle*. In the case of *Agnès*, the fractured identity of an incest victim is portrayed by three actresses who represent the randomness of memories drawn from Agnès's childhood, adolescence, and adulthood. By interweaving different moments in time, Anne illustrates the complex web of emotions expressed in Agnès's relationships with family members, a gynecologist, lawyers, and her male friend and confidant.

Jan Berkowitz Gross

BIBLIOGRAPHY

Primary Texts

Une Année sans été. Paris: Actes Sud-Papiers, 1987.
Combien de nuits faudra-t-il marcher dans la ville. Paris: Actes Sud-Papiers, 1988.

Eclats. Paris: Actes Sud-Papiers, 1989.
Tita-Lou. Paris: Actes Sud-Papiers, 1991.
Le Temps turbulent. Paris: Actes Sud-Papiers, 1993.
Agnès suivi de Ah! Anabelle. Paris: Actes Sud-Papiers, 1994.
Ah la la! Quelle histoire. Paris: Actes Sud-Papiers, 1995.
Surprise. Paris: Actes Sud-Papiers, 1995.

Secondary Texts

Martinez, Manuel Garcia. "*Agnès*, directed by Catherine Anne." *Western European Stages* 7, no. 2 (1995): 55–58.
"Paroles de femmes au théâtre." Discussion. *Les Cahiers des Lundis*. Paris: Association Théâtrales, 1993–94. 21–30.
Schäfer, Renate. "Ecrire l'inceste: Confidence et contre-attaque." *Etudes Théâtrales* 8 (1995): 19–20.
Servin, Micheline. "Aujourd'hui, quels théâtres? Pour quoi?" *Les Temps modernes* 572 (March 1994): 180–184.
Surel-Turpin, Monique. "Catherine Anne et la dénonciation de l'inceste." *Etudes Théâtrales* 8 (1995): 72–73.

Anne de Bretagne. *See* Bretagne, Anne de.

Arnaud, Angélique (née Bassin) (1799–1884). Novelist and journalist. An unhappily married provincial mother of two, Angelique Arnaud struggled to educate her children and write before moving with them to Paris in 1848. An initial attraction to Saint-Simonianism* and social questions in the 1830s emboldened her to devote herself, not without financial difficulty and emotional cost, to writing, feminism*, and social renovation. The large gaps in her literary publication—three social novels* in the July Monarchy and several works in the Third Republic—are filled by articles in periodicals such as Fanny Richomme's *Le Journal des femmes*, *La Gazette de Nice* (in which she reviewed Proudhon's *De l'amour*), and Léon Richer's *Le Droit des femmes*, later named *L'Avenir des femmes*. Maria Deraismes* spoke at the burial of this lesser-known figure who contributed to the century's major feminist movements.

Cheryl A. Morgan

BIBLIOGRAPHY

Primary texts

Une Correspondance d'enfants. Gannat: Impr. de Goninfaure-Arthaud, 1834.
Une Correspondance saint-simonienne. Angélique Arnaud et Caroline Simon (1833–1838). Ed. Bernadette Louis. Paris: Côté-femmes, 1990.
La Comtesse de Sergy. Paris: Charpentier, 1838.
Clémence. Paris: Berquet et Pétion, 1841.
Coralie l'inconstante. Paris: Berquet et Pétion, 1843.
Une Tendre Dévote. Paris: Sartorius, 1874.
La Cousine Adèle. Paris: E. Dentu, 1879.

François Del Sarte, ses découvertes en esthétique, sa science, sa méthode. Paris: C. Delagrave, 1882.

Secondary Text

Cohen, Margaret. "In Lieu of a Chapter on French Women Realists." In *Spectacles of Realism: Body, Gender, Genre.* Ed. Margaret Cohen and Christopher Prendergast. Minneapolis: University of Minnesota Press, 1995. 90–119.

Arnothy, Christine (1930–). Novelist, playwright, and journalist, Arnothy, born in Hungary, published her first and most acclaimed work, *J'ai quinze ans et je ne veux pas mourir,* in 1954. This autobiographical novel* is based on the diary she kept during the German siege of Budapest (1944–1945). She continued to write autobiography* in *Il n'est pas si facile de vivre* (1957), in which she describes her arrival in France, and in *Jeux de mémoire* (1981), which recounts her childhood. Arnothy has also written historical novels, such as *Le Cardinal prisonnier* (1962), and thrillers, including *Vent africain* (1989) and *Voyage de noces* (1994).

Ana M. de Medeiros

BIBLIOGRAPHY

Primary Texts

J'ai quinze ans et je ne veux pas mourir. Paris: Fayard, 1954.
Il n'est pas si facile de vivre. Paris: Fayard, 1957.
Le Cardinal prisonnier. Paris: Julliard, 1962.
J'aime la vie. Paris: Grasset, 1976.
Jeux de mémoire. Paris: Fayard, 1981.
Vent africain. Paris: Grasset, 1989.
Voyage de noces. Paris: Plon, 1994.

Atlan, Liliane Cohen (1932–). Hidden during World War II* in the south of France (1939–1945), she grew obsessed by the genocide of 6 million Jews. Following her baccalaureate, Atlan was hospitalized for anorexia. She later enrolled at the Ecole Gilbert Bloch d'Orsay and was married in 1952.

Atlan's poetic theater*, *Monsieur Fugue* (1967), focuses on the fantasies of children led to the crematorium. *Les Messies* (1968) features irreverent galactic beings. With *La Petite Voiture de flammes et de voix* (1971), Atlan begins fleshing out problems of women in society, plunging audiences into the world of a soul divided—a woman split in two, attempting to heal her torments through eroticism, drugs, knowledge, and revolt. Panic, a video-play character (*Elle a peur,* 1976) stemming from work with drug-addicted youth, probes a woman's inability to cope. *Leçons de bonheur* (1982) dramatizes the healing process of a love gone sour. *Opéra pour Térézin* (1989), based on fiber optic systems, dramatizes the heroism of starving musicians, painters, and writers imprisoned in the concentration camp of Térézin.

Bettina L. Knapp

BIBLIOGRAPHY

Primary Texts

Monsieur Fugue. Paris: Seuil, 1967.
Les Messies. Paris: Seuil, 1969.
La Petite Voiture de flammes et de voix. Paris: Seuil, 1971.
Leçons de bonheur. Paris: Théâtre Ouvert, 1982.
L'Amour élémentaire. Toulouse: L'Ether Vague, 1985.
Le Rêve des animaux rongeurs. Toulouse: L'Ether Vague, 1985.
Les Passants. Paris: Payot, 1988.
Les Musiciens, les émigrants. Paris: Editions des quatre-vents, 1992.
Opéra pour Térézin. Montpellier production, Radio France, 1989.
Theater Pieces: An Anthology. Trans. Marguerite Feitlowitz. Greenwood, FL: Penkevill,
    1985.

Secondary Texts

Knapp, Bettina L. *Liliane Atlan.* Amsterdam: Rodopi, 1988.
''Mal-Etre: L'Oeuvre scénique et poétique de Liliane Atlan.'' *Les Nouveaux Cahiers*
    (Summer 1995).

Aubespine, Madeleine de l' (Dame de Villeroy) (1546–1596). Madeleine de
l'Aubespine wrote under the pseudonym Callianthe at the court of Catherine de
Medici*. She is one of the few women poets celebrated by the poets of the
Pléiade. She and Ronsard exchanged sonnets: Ronsard praises her poetic talent;
she addresses Ronsard as her mentor. Madeleine de l'Aubespine is also recognized by Belleau in one of his *Pierres precieuses*, and she appears in the verse
of Jamyn and Passerat. Her known works demonstrate a broad range of genres:
sonnet, epigram, debate, poetic dialogue, religious lyric, chanson, translation*.
Her poetry* is not thought to have been published during her lifetime, although
several of her works were published posthumously in the *Cabinet satyrique*
(1618). Much of her work remained either unattributed or misattributed until
Roger Sorg's publication of her works in 1926. Sorg's research also identified
her as ''Rosette'' in Philippe Desportes's love sonnets. Her three-year alliance
with Desportes began in 1570 while he was serving as *secrétaire de la chambre*
for her husband, Nicolas de Neufville. The poems she exchanged with Desportes
during this time explore Petrarchan conventions from a personalized, feminine
subject. In her ''Sonnets d'amour,'' she focuses primarily on the Neoplatonic
ideals of equality and freedom in love. Two ''Sonnets chrestiens'' reflect a
transition to religious lyric. Included among her known work is also a translation
of the second of Ovid's *Epistles*. Madeleine de l'Aubespine's versatility as a
poet and her association with the Pléiade circle distinguish her among women
Renaissance poets.

Martha Nichols-Pecceu

BIBLIOGRAPHY

Primary Text

Les Chansons de Callianthe: fille de Ronsard (Madeleine de l'Aubespine, Dame de Villeroy). Introduction by Roger Sorg. Paris: Chez l'imprimeur Léon Pichon, 1926.

Aubrac, Lucie (1912–). In the early days of the German Occupation, Aubrac played an exceptional role in the World War II French Resistance*. She helped found the movement Libération-Sud, which published *Libération*, a clandestine paper urging opposition to Pétain's regime as well as to the Nazis. Aubrac assumed the multiple tasks of *lycée* teacher, homemaker, mother, and member of the Resistance. On three occasions she rescued her husband from French and German prisons. In *Ils partiront dans l'ivresse* (1984), she recounts nine months of her resistance activities—a period that coincided with the nine months of her second pregnancy. Named to the Consultative Assembly in Algiers, she became France's first woman parliamentarian.

Margaret Collins Weitz

BIBLIOGRAPHY

Primary Text

Ils partiront dans l'ivresse. Paris: Seuil, 1984.

Secondary Texts

Weitz, Margaret Collins. "Lucie Aubrac: Femme Engagée." *Contemporary French Civilization* 15, no. 1 (1991): 93–99.
———. *Sisters in the Resistance: How Women Fought to Free France.* Ed. Margaret Collins Weitz. New York: Wiley, 1995.

Films

Boulevard des Hirondelles. Dir. Josée Yanne. M.J.N. Productions, 1992.
Lucie Aubrac. Dir. Claude Berri, 1997.

Auclert, Hubertine (1848–1914). Auclert is a key figure of French feminism*. Born in the Allier, when she arrived in Paris in 1873 she collaborated on the women's rights association led by Léon Richer and Maria Deraismes*. She proceeded to found her own society, Droit des femmes, in 1876 in order to focus on women's political rights and equality. A steadfast republican, Auclert allied herself at various times with the workers' movement and socialist politics. She was often a controversial figure because of her militantism and intervention tactics. She brought feminist issues into the public sphere as a tireless demonstrator and petition-writer. She led the first campaign for women's right to vote* in 1881 and 1885, and she created her own feminist newspaper, *La Citoyenne* (1881–1891), which she used to promote women's rights. She was also one of the first to use the term *féminisme*. She started the organization Suffrage des femmes in 1883. In 1888 she followed her lover Antonin Lévrier to Algeria, where she married him and stayed until his death in 1892. While there, Auclert traveled and met Algerian women. She wrote articles about them and about colonial politics, collected in *Femmes arabes en Algérie* (1900), and she wrote petitions in support of (French) education* for Algerian girls. Upon her return to Paris, she went back to her feminist writing and campaigning, speaking at several political congresses and raising public consciousness about women's right to vote. In 1908 her views finally prevailed among French feminists.

Joëlle Vitiello

BIBLIOGRAPHY

Primary Texts

Historique de la société Le Droit des femmes, 1876–1880. Paris: 1881.
Les Femmes arabes en Algérie. Paris: Société d'éditions littéraires, 1900.
L'Argent de la femme. Paris: Pedone, 1904.
Le Nom de la femme. Paris: Société du livre à l'auteur, 1905.
Le Vote des femmes. Paris: V. Giard and E Brière, 1908.
Les Femmes au gouvernail. Paris: Marcel Giard, 1923.
La Citoyenne: Articles de 1881 à 1891. Ed. Edith Taïeb. Paris: Syros, 1982.

Secondary Texts

Brahimi, Denise. *Femmes arabes et soeurs musulmanes.* Paris: Editions Tierce, 1984.
Hause, Steven C. *Hubertine Auclert: The French Suffragette.* New Haven: Yale University Press, 1987.
Li Dzeh-Djen. *La Presse féministe en France de 1869 à 1914.* Paris: Librairie L. Rodstein, 1934.
Misme, Jane. "Les Grandes Figures du féminisme: Hubertine Auclert." *Minerva* 19 (October 1930).
Scott, Joan Wallach. *Only Paradoxes to Offer: French Feminists and the Rights of Man.* Cambridge, MA: Harvard University Press, 1996.

Audouard, Olympe (1830–1890). One of the most prominent bourgeois feminist writers of her time and also one of the most avid women travelers of her generation. A feminist activist who ardently defended women's right to divorce*, she separated from her husband and moved to the south of France to lead an independent life. She launched several newspapers and became the target of legal actions for her public advocacy of women's rights (as a woman she could not publish a political newspaper, and her speeches were quickly declared a threat to the public order and forbidden as subversive acts). Audouard's involvement in feminist movements permeates her writings but is voiced with particular force in her travel literature*. When she explores Egypt, Turkey, Russia, or North America, she does so with the same set of concerns she has in France: the social and legal status of women. In Russia she praises women's access to higher education*, while in the United States she notes women's relative independence, even asserting that the Mormons' institution of polygamy ultimately offered women less hypocritical and more economically just treatment than the wife-plus-mistress practice that prevailed in France. In Turkey Audouard admires the respect and protection accorded to women and presents an idyllic vision of the harem while acknowledging the less than pleasant condition in which lower-class women live. Audouard's fierce defense of French colonial undertakings, in particular of the Suez Canal, adds further complexity to her narratives, in which feminism*, colonialism*, and bourgeois ideology intersect.

Bénédicte Monicat

BIBLIOGRAPHY

Primary Texts

Voyage à travers mes souvenirs: ceux que j'ai connus, ce que j'ai vu. Paris: E. Dentu, 1884.
Le Canal de Suez. Paris: E. Dentu, 1864.
Les Mystères de l'Egypte dévoilés. Paris: E. Dentu, 1866.
Les Mystères du sérail et des harems turcs. Paris: E. Dentu, 1866.
L'Orient et ses peuplades. Paris: E. Dentu, 1867.

Secondary Text

Monicat, Bénédicte. *Itinéraires de l'écriture au féminin: Voyageuses du 19e siècle.* Amsterdam: Rodopi, 1996.

Audoux, Marguerite (pseudonym of Marguerite Donquichotte) (1863–1937). Novelist and short story* writer. She was only five when her mother—whose name she would later adopt—died and her father, a poor carpenter, abandoned her. After a stay in the Bourges orphanage, she became a farm servant in Sologne. In 1881 she moved to Paris where, despite her poor eyesight, she worked as a seamstress and devoted what free time she had to writing. Impressed by her talent, Octave Mirbeau found a publisher for her first novel* and wrote an enthusiastic preface. *Marie-Claire* (1910) became a best-seller and won the Femina Prize.

The first-person narrator of the novel recounts the experiences she had as an orphan and farm servant. Using a movingly understated language, she restricts herself to her point of view as a child and depicts a world marked by poverty, silence, and death. It is a world in which traditional social forces—from the Catholic Church to the bourgeoisie—deny little Marie-Claire independence and self-respect. It is also a world from which escape seems impossible. Throughout the novel, however, the protagonist finds solace in reading and the world of the imagination. She slowly learns that language can be a source of love and that narrative can prolong memory and communicate truth. By the time she becomes a young woman, she is strong enough to assert her freedom and go to Paris.

Audoux continued to write until her death. She published *L'Atelier de Marie-Claire* (1920), which lacked the powerful simplicity of her first novel and elicited mixed reviews. She also published two other novels—*De la Ville au moulin* (1926) and *Douce Lumière*, (1937)—as well as a collection of stories, *La Fiancée* (1932), many of which had already appeared in *Le Chaland de la reine* (1910). Though these works are not without interest, they fail to match the purity and poignancy of *Marie-Claire*. The latter is a masterpiece, both a technical tour de force and a touching portrait of the plight of working-class girls in the second half of the nineteenth century.

Gerald Prince

BIBLIOGRAPHY

Primary Texts

Le Chaland de la reine. Nevers: Les cahiers nivernais, 1910.
Marie-Claire. Paris: E. Fasquelle, 1910.
L'Atelier de Marie-Claire. Paris: E. Fasquelle, 1920.
De la Ville au moulin. Paris: E. Fasquelle, 1926.
La Fiancée. Paris: Flammarion, 1932.
Douce Lumière. Paris: Grasset, 1937.

Secondary Texts

Garreau, Bernard-Marie. *Marguerite Audoux*. Paris: Tallandier, 1991.
Lanoizelée, Louis. *Marguerite Audoux: Sa Vie, son oeuvre*. Paris: Maurice Pernette, 1954.
Reyer, Georges. *Marguerite Audoux. Un Coeur pur*. Paris: Grasset, 1942.

Aulnoy, Marie-Catherine Le Jumel de Barneville, baronne d' (also known as comtesse) (1650 or 1651–1705). What is known of her life suggests that it was turbulent. After marriage* at age fifteen or sixteen to a man more than twice her age, she was accused of having conspired with her mother to have her husband denounced for *lèse-majesté*. Forced to flee, she traveled widely with her mother (to Flanders, England, and possibly Spain), but eventually returned to Paris. Later, she was implicated in a plot to have a friend's husband murdered, and only narrowly escaped punishment. Sometime after 1685 she began a sa-lon*, and she published her first novel*, *Histoire d'Hypolite, comte de Duglas*, in 1690. Enormously successful in France and abroad, d'Aulnoy's oeuvre is as vast as it is diverse, consisting of historical novels, memoirs*, devotional po-etry*, travel literature*, and fairy tales*. Although many of her works conform to late seventeenth-century French literary trends, several of them also blaze new paths. In her historical fiction (*Mémoires de la cour d'Espagne*, 1690; *Histoire de Jean de Bourbon*, 1692; *Nouvelles espagnolles*, 1692; *Nouvelles ou mémoires historiques*, 1693; *Mémoires de la cour d'Angleterre*, 1695; *Le Comte de Warwick*, 1703), d'Aulnoy continues an earlier female literary tradition, best represented by Villedieu* and Lafayette*, to which she adds the pronounced taste of late seventeenth-century France for exotic adventures. Her travel nar-rative *Relation du voyage d'Espagne* (1691) is often cited as an innovative account of late seventeenth-century Spain. However, it is with her collections of fairy tales (*Les Contes des fées*, 1696–97, and *Contes nouveaux ou les fées à la mode*, 1697) that she made her most original and enduring contribution. Besides coining the term *conte de fées* (which was imported into English as "fairy tale" in 1698), d'Aulnoy incorporated into her twenty-five stories an extraordinarily broad knowledge of oral folklore, which she melded with motifs from chivalric romance. In terms of gender and sexuality, her tales are noteworthy, among other things, for highlighting heroines' roles and for including many plots with animal brides or grooms ("Serpentin vert," "Prince Marcassin," "La Biche au bois," "L'Oiseau bleu," "Le Mouton," and "Chatte blanche"). Through numerous reprints and translations, d'Aulnoy's fairy tales had a significant influence on later writers, particularly in Germany, and in the eighteenth and nineteenth centuries became favorites of children's literature*.

Lewis C. Seifert

BIBLIOGRAPHY

Primary Texts

Contes. 2 vols. Ed. Jacques Barchilon and Philippe Hourcade. Paris: Société des textes français modernes, 1997.

Secondary Texts

Defrance, Anne. "Ecriture féminine et dénégation de l'autorité: Les *Contes de fées* de Madame d'Aulnoy et leur récit-cadre." *Revue des sciences humaines* 238 (1995): 111–126.
DeGraff, Amy. *The Tower and the Well: A Psychological Interpretation of the Fairy Tales of Madame d'Aulnoy*. Birmingham, AL: Summa Publications, 1984.
Hannon, Patricia. "Feminine Voice and the Motivated Text: Mme d'Aulnoy and the Chevalier de Mailly." *Marvels and Tales* 2, no. 1 (1988): 13–24.
Mitchell, Jane Tucker. *A Thematic Analysis of Madame d'Aulnoy's Contes de fées*. University, MI: Romance Monographs, 1978.
Welch, Marcelle Maistre. "Les Jeux de l'écriture dans les contes de fées de Mme d'Aulnoy." *Romanische Forschungen* 101, no.1 (1989): 131–142.

Autobiography. Autobiography, defined broadly as the account of one's personal history, includes various subgenres, such as memoirs*, confessions, letters, diaries, personal essays, and autobiographical novels*. Personal elements in women's writing are evident as early as the laments of the *trobairitz** in southern France. The most significant medieval texts are Christine de Pizan's* semi-autobiographical *Chemin de long estude* (1403) and *L'Avision Christine* (1405). Women's autobiographical writing in the early periods often reflects imitation of male models. At the same time, women also managed to inscribe subtly their own agendas into their life stories.

It is difficult to separate autobiography from the various subgenres, especially that of the memoir. In general, however, we can say that autobiography is characterized by greater introspection and a focus on the development of one's inner life, whereas memoirs often stress the individual's achievements and to some extent public events and contemporary personages. Memoirs and letters were popular female forms in the seventeenth and eighteenth centuries, and often reveal personal perspectives on history.

The long tradition of spiritual autobiography, including the *Vie* of Antoinette

Bourgignon (1683) and the autobiography of Madame de Guyon* (published posthumously in 1720), measures the development of the subject in relation to God. "Modern autobiography," beginning with Rousseau's *Confessions* (1767–1769), broke from the spiritual model and offered a secular focus—a study of the development of the individual and his/her personality, including the impact of childhood and intimate experiences. Madame Roland*, influenced by Rousseau's frankness, wrote her life story while in prison in 1793. Her unassuming tone, however, characteristic of women's autobiography of the time, has nothing of Rousseau's "Moi seul!"

Female autobiographical production increased in the nineteenth century, when women of diverse classes took up the pen. Many still felt pressure to write under male pen names*, however, such as George Sand* and Daniel Stern (Marie d'Agoult*, *Mémoires*, 1833–1855). During this period, a changing society, an evolving sense of history, and new roles for women impacted the female autobiographical subject. Several women's life stories, for example, share elements with the *Bildungsroman*, or novel of self-discovery and development. For example, prostitute turned actress (and later countess) Céleste Mogador* sifts through her questionable past and traces her social evolution in her life story. Sand's monumental *Histoire de ma vie* (1847–1855) offers a personal portrait against the backdrop of French history and follows traditional autobiographical form in many ways. She refutes the male model established by Rousseau, however, by refusing to reveal intimate details of her sexual life (obviously dangerous territory for women) and by excluding compromising information about people who were still alive.

Because of greater mobility in the nineteenth century, women experimented with travel literature*, which in the Romantic period shared many elements with autobiography. They situated the autobiographical subject in a broader context—woman as foreigner, missionary, social reformer. Germaine de Staël's* *De l'Allemagne* appeared in 1810, Flora Tristan's* *Pérégrinations d'une pariah* in 1838, and Cristina di Belgiojoso's* *Souvenirs dans l'exil* in 1850.

In the second half of the century, women autobiographers are greatly influenced by social and political changes. Memorialists such as Tristan, Suzanne Voilquin*, and Louise Michel* (*Mémoires*, 1886) explored labor reform and socialist and communist themes. The popular autobiographical novel of the nineteenth century, such as Staël's *Corinne ou l'Italie* (1807) and Sand's *Lélia* (1833), also led the way for twentieth-century texts which fuse fictional and autobiographial elements.

In the twentieth century, debates surrounding the possibility of a unified self, the validity of memory, and the notion of "truth" challenged the autobiographical project. Many of these issues also paralleled the emergence of autobiographical criticism, particularly after World War II*. Critics argued whether autobiography was a branch of history or a literary genre. James Olney posited that autobiography was neither fiction nor history, but each individual's "metaphor of self." Whereas noted critic Philippe Lejeune conceptualized the notion of an "autobiographical pact," a contract between writer and reader, Nancy Miller argued the need to "read for difference" when approaching women's texts, positing the idea that women's writing is nuanced because of public expectations and limitations on female expression. Miller's "personal criticism" often includes autobiographical anecdotes, blurring distinctions between objective criticism and self-portraiture.

The New Novel, or *Nouveau Roman**, which sparked such textual innovation as the play of truth and fiction, resistance to chronological plots, and narrative experimentation (fluctuating subject positions, temporal shifts), greatly influenced autobiographical writing, including that of Nathalie Sarraute* (*Enfance*, 1983). Marguerite Duras's* practice of self-quotation led to the rewriting/revising of material from the autobiographical novel *Un Barrage contre le Pacifique* (1950) in later texts: *L'Amant* (1984) and *L'Amant de la Chine du nord* (1991). Duras's "intergeneric rewritings" (novel rewritten as autobiography, play recast as film scenario) have emphasized the gap between the past of experience and the present of writing, as well as the contextual nature of events. Raylene L. Ramsay situates "new autobiographies" somewhere between autobiography and fiction, story and history.

The evolution of women's roles and feminist consciousness have also been integral to twentieth-century autobiography, evident in Simone de Beauvoir's* *Mémoires d'une jeune fille rangée* (1958), *La Force de l'âge* (1960), and *La Force des choses* (1963). Women have sought innovative forms and language in order to inscribe their modern realities and their own subjectivity. They have also expressed their sexuality more freely, particularly in the contemporary period. Women have also explored lesbian identity (Violette Leduc*, Monique Wittig*) in their life writing. The feminist movement also influenced women's autobiography, especially from the 1970s onward. Discussions of womanhood, the maternal, and the body remain crucial today. The mother-daughter relationship, for example, is central to Marguerite Yourcenar's* *Souvenirs pieux* (1974) (the first volume in her autobiographical trilogy), Cardinal's* *Les Mots pour le dire* (1975), and Annie Ernaux's* autobiographical/biographical *Une Femme* (1987) and *Je ne suis pas sortie de ma nuit* (1997). Hélène Cixous* and Luce Irigaray* continue to be influenced by psychoanalysis and deconstruction, and have explored the notion of an *écriture féminine**. Issues of liberation also emerge in feminist essays and "autobiographical essays" such as Cixous's utopian "Le Rire de la Méduse" (1975). Julia Kristeva's* essays have treated personal experiences within the context of the feminist movement and political/ cultural happenings in France.

Claire Marrone

BIBLIOGRAPHY

Secondary Texts

Beasley, Faith E. *Revising Memory: Women's Fiction and Memoirs in Seventeenth-Century France*. New Brunswick, NJ: Rutgers University Press, 1990.

Hewitt, Leah. *Autobiographical Tightropes*. Lincoln: University of Nebraska Press, 1990.

Jelinek, Estelle. *The Tradition of Women's Autobiography: From Antiquity to the Present*. Boston: Twayne, 1986.

May, Georges. *L'Autobiographie*. Paris: Presses Universitaires de France, 1979.

Miller, Nancy. "Women's Autobiography in France." In *Subject to Change: Reading Feminist Writing*. New York: Columbia University Press, 1988.

Ramsay, Raylene L. *The French New Autobiographies: Sarraute, Duras and Robbe-Grillet*. Gainsville: University Press of Florida, 1996.

Sheringham, Michael. *French Autobiography: Devices and Desires: Rousseau to Perec*. Oxford: Clarendon Press, 1993.

Autriche, Marguerite d' (1480–1530). Regent, patron, and poet. Born on January 10, 1480, to Marie de Bourgogne and Emperor Maximilian of Austria, Marguerite was betrothed in 1482 to the thirteen-year-old dauphin of France, the future Charles VIII. Arriving in France in 1483, she spent her childhood there as the "petite reine," only to suffer a humiliating rejection when Charles married Anne de Bretagne* in 1491. Marguerite's subsequent marriage* in April 1497 to Don Juan of Spain ended with his untimely death six months later. In 1501 she married Philibert de Savoie, brother of Louise de Savoie*. After his death in 1504, Marguerite, once again a widow, assumed the famous motto "Fortune infortune fort une." When her brother Philippe le Beau died in 1506, Marguerite was appointed regent of the Netherlands and guardian of her nieces and nephew, the future Charles Quint. Taking up residence in Malines, she fulfilled her political and familial roles to the great admiration of her contemporaries. Among her last significant acts was the signing of the Ladies' Peace in 1529. She died in 1530.

Best known for her enlightened patronage of artists (Jean Perréal, Michel Colombe, Conrad Meyt), musicians (Pierre de La Rue, Josquin des Prés), scholars (Erasmus, Vives, Agrippa), and poets at her court of Malines, her library was one of the richest of the time. Her court historiographer, Jean Lemaire de Belges, wrote the *Epîtres de l'Amant Vert* for Marguerite as well as the *Couronne Margaritique* and the *Regretz de la Dame infortunée*; Jean Molinet, Octovien de Saint-Gelais, Michel Riccio, and other poets dedicated works to her, many dealing with her personal experience. Lemaire praises Marguerite's literary talents, but her total creative output, difficult to identify with certainty, may not have exceeded 700 lines: four *complaintes* and several lyric pieces. Her earliest *complainte* concerns her misfortunes in France; her outrage at repudiation by Charles VIII provokes a cry for vengeance, and in one revelatory stanza she calls on all women to read her words, heed her example, and reject faithless men. Her lament "Se je souspire" on the death of her brother (1506), set to music in an anonymous motet using Latin and French text, preceded the lament on her father's death (1519). A *Complainte d'amour*, found in a lavishly illustrated manuscript (Vienna HB 2584), reveals Marguerite's sorrow at having to abandon her beloved to save her honor. In these texts Marguerite speaks in the first person, but nothing in the sources necessarily identifies the *persona* with the author. Similarly, while many poems of her three celebrated chanson albums use a female voice, the convention was not limited to women writers. Extratextual elements offer additional signs of authorship: manuscript decoration (the "marguerite" or daisy), script, and titles suggest that at least five lyric poems can be attributed to her, including the autograph (?) "C'est pour james que regret me demeure."

Marguerite's poetry* is inextricably tied to her own life. Regret and sorrow set the tone of most of her literary work, but her correspondence attests to her astute political sense and keen mind. Although she lamented her fate as a victim of Fortune, she also accepted the obligations of her social and political position and used her experience both to develop her own moral fortitude and to advise others. Ill-fated in love and marriage, she cautioned women against the duplicity of men while appealing to their sense of honor. In some *rondeaux* this advice seems lighthearted, if caustic, but elsewhere, especially in her *Complainte d'amour*, she reveals the painful conflict between honor and true affection, ruefully concluding that women must value their honor above love and even life.

Mary Beth Winn

BIBLIOGRAPHY

Primary Texts

La Complainte de dame Marguerite d'Autrice, fille de Maximilian, roy des Romains. Ed. Max Bruchet. In *Marguerite d'Autriche, duchesse de Savoie.* Lille: Danel, 1927. 314–317.

"Gedichten op Margaretha van Oostenryk en Philips den Schoonen." Ed. J. F. Willems. In *Belgisch Museum voor den Nederduitsche Tael-en-Letterkunde* 9 (January 1845): 141–145.

La Complainte de Marguerite d'Autriche. Ed. Josef Strelka. In *Gedichte Margarethes von Osterreich, die Handschrift 2584 der Wiener National bibliothek.* Vienna, 1954 (= *Complainte d'amour*).

La Complainte que faict la fille unicque de Maximilien Empereur depuis son douloureux trespas. In *Albums poétiques de Marguerite d'Autriche.* Ed. Marcel Françon. Cambridge, MA: Harvard University Press, 1934. 256–259.

" 'Se je souspire' and Lyric pieces." In *Albums poétiques de Marguerite d' Autriche.* Ed. Marcel Françon. Cambridge, MA: Harvard University Press, 1934.

The Chanson Albums of Marguerite of Austria: Mss. 228 and 11239 of the Bibliothèque royale de Belgique, Brussels. A Critical Edition and Commentary. Ed. Martin Picker. Berkeley: University of California Press, 1965.

Album de Marguerite d'Autriche (MS. 228). Peer: Facsimile Musica Alamire, 1986.

Correspondance de Marguerite d'Autriche. Ed. L.Ph. C. Van den Bergh. Leiden, 1845.

Correspondance de l'Empereur Maximilien Ier et de Marguerite d'Autriche, sa fille, Gouvernante des Pays-Bas. Paris, 1839. Ed. André Glay. New York: Johnson Reprint, 1966.

Secondary Texts

De Boom, Ghislaine. *Marguerite d'Autriche-Savoie et la Pré-Renaissance.* Paris: Droz, 1935.

De Boom, Ghislaine, and Marcel Françon. "Les Poésies de Marguerite d'Autriche." *Romanic Review* 25 (1934): 207–219.

Gachet, Emile. *Albums et oeuvres poétiques de Marguerite d'Autriche.* Brussels: Librairie scientifique et littéraire, 1849.

B

Babois, Marguerite Victoire (1760–1839). She achieved literary fame with her elegiac poems. In her first collection of poems, *Elégies maternelles*, she expressed her grief after the premature death of her daughter in 1792. Literary critics were moved by the depth of her feelings and love for her daughter. She also published another collection of poems, *Elégies nationales*, which were inspired by the turbulent history and politics of France in 1815. She received a great deal of encouragement and numerous accolades from contemporary authors and poets such as Jean-François Ducis and Marie-Joseph Chénier.

Juliette Parnell-Smith

BIBLIOGRAPHY

Primary Texts

Elégies et poésies diverses de Marguerite Victoire Babois. 2 vols. Paris: Nepveu, 1838.
Elégies. Nice: Edition du Centaure, 1973.

Badinter, Elisabeth (1944–). A philosopher and the first female professor at the Ecole Polytechnique in Paris, Badinter is the author of numerous sociohistorical essays, some of which are published under the title *L'Amour en plus* (1980). In this work, she argues that it is not instinct but societal conditioning that instills maternal love. Although she describes herself as a feminist, clearly indebted to Simone de Beauvoir*, she acknowledges that militant feminists— who see her as a privileged woman—question her commitment to their cause. In her more recent works, *L'Un est l'Autre* (1986) and *Qu'est-ce qu'une femme?* (1989), she warns of the dangers for women of emphasizing gender-based differences—these differences may be used to maintain a patriarchal society in which women are judged to be inferior. After working with her husband on a biography of Condorcet, Badinter addressed the question of what defines a man in today's society in *X Y: De l'identité masculine* (1992). Badinter's work proposes a revolution in family relationships, one that will take into consideration both men's paternal love and women's role as members of the work force.

Ana M. de Medeiros

BIBLIOGRAPHY

Primary Texts

L'Amour en plus. Paris: Flammarion, 1980.
Emilie, Emilie: L'Ambition féminine au 18ème siècle. Paris: Flammarion, 1983.
L'Un est l'Autre. Paris: Odile Jacob, 1986.
Condorcet (1743–1794). Paris: Fayard, 1988.
Correspondance inédite de Condorcet et Madame Suard, 1771–1791. Paris: Fayard, 1988.
Qu'est-ce qu'une femme. Paris: P.O.L., 1989.
X Y: De l'identité masculine. Paris: Odile Jacob, 1992.

Secondary Texts

Lindsay, Cécile. "*L'Un e(s)t l'Autre*: The Future of Difference in French Feminism." *L'Esprit Créateur* 29, no. 3 (Fall 1989): 21–35.
Rodgers, Catherine. "Elisabeth Badinter and the Second Sex: An Interview." *Signs: Journal of Women in Culture and Society* 21, no. 1 (Autumn 1995): 147–162.

Balasko, Josiane (1950–). Actress, playwright, and director of theater* and film, Balasko began her career in the comedy format of the one-woman show in the 1970s. After collaborating with the Splendid troupe in the 1980s, she achieved international celebrity for her creation of a lesbian love triangle in the 1995 film *Gazon maudit* (French Twist). Balasko's unconventional women, such as the pregnant ex-wife who shows up unannounced in *L'Ex-Femme de ma vie*, or the bitter woman in a train station in *Nuit d'ivresse*, expose male hypocrisy and forge mutually satisfying relationships. A committed feminist, Balasko creates original female roles as a means of combating stereotypes.

Jan Berkowitz Gross

BIBLIOGRAPHY

Primary Texts

L'Ex-Femme de ma vie. Paris: Actes Sud-Papiers, 1989.
Nuit d'ivresse. Paris: Actes Sud-Papiers, 1990.
Balasko, Josiane, et al. *Le Père Noël est une ordure*. Paris: Actes Sud-Papiers, 1986.

Film

Gazon maudit. Performance by Josiane Balasko. 1995. Videocassette. Miramax, 1996.

Bancquart, Marie-Claire (1932–). Professor of French literature, literary critic, poet, and novelist. Best known for her poetry*, Bancquart has also published several novels* and has written on Anatole France, Guy de Maupassant, and surrealism*. In her novels, Bancquart uses traditional narrative plots to explore the loneliness of the long-married couple, as seen through the woman's eyes.

Her female—and male—characters come to a better understanding of themselves and each other after the trying experience of separation (*Elise en automne, La Saveur du sel*). In her poetry—a spiritual and ethical meditation on existence—Bancquart focuses on mortality and the fragility of the body as well as on the notions of alienation and belonging.

Martine Motard-Noar

BIBLIOGRAPHY

  Primary Texts

Mémoire d'abolie. Paris: Belfond, 1978.
Partition. Paris: Belfond, 1981.
Opportunité des oiseaux. Paris: Belfond, 1986.
Opéra des limites. Paris: José Corti, 1988.
Végétales. Montereau: Les Cahiers du Confluent, 1988.
Elise en automne. Paris: Bourin, 1991.
Sans lieu sinon l'attente. Paris: Obsidiane, 1991.
La Saveur du sel. Paris: Bourin/Julliard, 1993.
Dans le feuilletage de la terre. Paris: Belfond, 1994.
Enigmatiques. Paris: Obsidiane, 1995.

  Secondary Texts

Bishop, Michael. "L'Année poétique: De Césaire et Glissant à Broda et Bancquart."
      French Review 68, no. 5 (May 1995): 933–946.
———. "Marie-Claire Bancquart." In *Contemporary French Women Poets*. Vol. 1. Amsterdam: Rodopi, 1995. 128–144.

Barbier, Marie-Anne (1670–1745). Born in Orléans to a respectable and moderately prosperous family, she moved to Paris by 1700, where the respected playwright Edme Boursault became her mentor. She had all eight of her stage works performed at the Comédie Française or the Opéra, with her first two tragedies achieving the most success. Her published works include four tragedies, a one-act comedy, three opera libretti (two of them apparently in collaboration), and several volumes of miscellany containing short poems, novellas, and literary criticism. Her tragedies, especially *Arrie et Pétus* (1702) and *Cornélie mère des Gracques* (1703), are well constructed works with vigorous portrayals of heroic women. But she did not deliberately debase the male characters in her plays in order to exalt the women unduly, as her critics allege. The preface to *Arrie et Pétus* is noteworthy because Barbier explicitly situates herself within a distinguished and ongoing tradition of women authors in France (being one of the first to view women writers as having a distinct history), and because she fearlessly attacks the standard misogynist view according to which, since women lack creative ability, anything outstanding they produce must really be the work of male ghost writers. Barbier's main achievement was to prove both that women writers could achieve distinction in the branch of literature most esteemed in her day (tragedy), and that a genre so burdened with conventions could still serve to proclaim the glory of remarkable women from the past.

Perry Gethner

BIBLIOGRAPHY

Primary Text

Barbier, Marie-Anne. *Arrie et Pétus.* In *Femmes dramaturges en France (1650–1750).* Ed. Perry Gethner. Seattle: Biblio 17, 1993.

Secondary Text

Michau, Charles. ''Le Théâtre de Mlle Barbier.'' *Mémoires de la Société d'Agriculture, Sciences, Belles-lettres et Arts d'Orléans* 75 (1906): 117–138.

Barney, Natalie Clifford (1877–1972). Born into a wealthy American family, Barney frequently visited Paris with her mother, who studied painting there with Whistler. Attracted by the relatively tolerant atmosphere of Paris, which allowed her to move openly in lesbian circles, Barney settled there permanently in 1900 and established a fashionable salon* on rue Jacob, which she hosted for over fifty years. She is particularly well known for the central role she played in the Parisian lesbian community, which was largely made up of expatriate artists and writers. A generous and supportive friend, Barney cultivated connections between women and established an Academy of Women as a forum for literary exchange among French, American, and British women. She was notorious for her numerous women lovers, among them the poet Renée Vivien*, the courtesan Liane de Pougy*, and the artist Romaine Brooks. Many of her contemporaries portrayed the vivacious Barney in their novels*, where she appears under many names*, such as Valerie Seymour in Radclyffe Hall's *The Well of Loneliness* (1928), Laurette Wells in Lucie Delarue-Mardrus's* *L'Ange et les pervers* (1930), and Vally in Vivien's *Une Femme m'apparut* (1904). Considered something of a dilettante who declared that her life was her greatest work of art, Barney wrote plays, poetry*, and several novels in French, all of them inspired by her love for women and the cult of Sappho, which she and Renée Vivien hoped to revive. She is best known today for her perceptive memoirs* and witty volumes of epigrams.

Tama Lea Engelking

BIBLIOGRAPHY

Primary Texts

Eparpillements. 1910. Paris: Persona, 1982.
Pensées d'une amazone. Paris: Emile-Paul, 1920.
Aventures de l'esprit. 1928. Paris: Persona, 1982.
Nouvelles Pensées d'une amazone. Paris: Mercure de France, 1939.
Souvenirs indiscrets. Paris: Flammarion, 1960.
Traits et portraits. 1963. New York: Arno, 1975.

Secondary Texts

Benstock, Shari. *Women of the Left Bank: Paris, 1900–1940*. Austin: University of Texas Press, 1986.
Causse, Michèle, and Berthe Cleyrergue. *Berthe ou un demi-siècle auprès de l'amazone*. Paris: Editions Tierce, 1980.
Jay, Karla. *The Amazon and the Page: Natalie Clifford Barney and Renée Vivien*. Bloomington: University of Indiana Press, 1988.
Orenstein, Gloria. "Natalie Barney's Parisian Salon: The Savoir Faire and Joie de Vivre of a Life of Love and Letters." *Thirteenth Moon* 5, nos. 1 and 2 (1980): 77–95.
Wickes, George. *The Amazon of Letters: The Life and Loves of Natalie Clifford Barney*. New York: Putnam, 1976.

Baroche, Christiane (?–). Novelist, author of short stories*, poet, journalist, and researcher at the Institut Curie. Baroche's short stories—from *Les Feux du large* (1975) and *Chambres, avec vue sur le passé* (1978), for which she won the Prix Dakar and the Goncourt, to the more recent *Bonjour, gens heureux . . .* (1993)—focus on the themes of solitude, aging, memory, and the search for happiness. Her story "Si j'étais l'homme que tu dis . . ." is a parodic response to *La Maison Tellier* in which she rewrites Maupassant's patriarchal tale of love and marriage*. The highly acclaimed *La Rage au bois dormant* (1995) recounts the intersecting lives of two women friends during and after World War II*. Both women, who are characterized by their inner strength and self-determination, play an active role in the Resistance, one of them as the leader of the local Resistance group. *L'Hiver de beauté* (1987) was inspired by Choderlos de Laclos's *Les Liaisons dangereuses*, a novel that infuriated Baroche because of its treatment of the Marquise de Merteuil. Baroche's playful feminist rewriting of Laclos presents her own vision of Madame de Merteuil, criticizes the fact that women are judged on external appearances, and, as in her other novels, challenges stereotypical gender roles and the character traits traditionally labeled masculine and feminine.

Susan Ireland and Patrice J. Proulx

BIBLIOGRAPHY

Primary Texts

Les Feux du large. Paris: Gallimard, 1975.
Chambres, avec vue sur le passé. Paris: Gallimard, 1978.
L'Ecorce indéchiffrable. Marseille: Actes Sud, 1978.
Pas d'autre intempérie que la solitude. Paris: Gallimard, 1980.
Perdre le souffle. Gallimard, 1983.
Un Soir, j'inventerai le soir. Marseille: Actes Sud, 1983.
Plaisirs amers. Marseille: Actes Sud, 1984.
L'Hiver de beauté. Paris: Gallimard, 1987.
Et il ventait devant ma porte. Paris: Gallimard, 1989.
Les Ports du silence. Paris: Grasset, 1992.

Bonjour, gens heureux. . . . Paris: Julliard, 1993.
La Rage au bois dormant. Paris: Grasset, 1995.

Barry, Marie Jeanne Bécu du (1743–1793). The illegitimate daughter of a seamstress, she was educated in a Parisian convent* and became the last of Louis XV's mistresses. Ravishingly beautiful at age fifteen, she worked as a hairdresser, a governess, and an apprentice in a fashion house until she was taken up by Jean du Barry, an aristocratic gambler who specialized in the trade of women. He introduced her to society and arranged a nominal marriage* with his brother, making her the comtesse du Barry and allowing her to be accepted at court. Jeanne's influence as the proclaimed official mistress unleashed a campaign of defamation led by the minister Choiseul and his sister, the duchesse de Gramont, who commissioned libels disclosing Jeanne's plebeian origins and her past as a prostitute. Although considered a ruling power in France, instrumental in exiling Choiseul and supporting the Triumvirate of ministers (d'Aiguillon, Maupéou, and Terray), Barry was more interested in neoclassical art for her Versailles apartments and, later, for her Château de Louveciennes, a gift from Louis XV. Confined to a nunnery for months after the king's death in 1774, Barry returned to her estates to continue her liaison with the duc de Brissac and to help royalists during the Revolution*. Financial aid to French émigrés in London and an attempt to recover her legendary jewelry cost her her life. Accused by the Committee of Public Safety of having conspired against the Republic, Barry was tried before the Tribunal of Paris and forced up the steps of the guillotine*.

Karyna Szmurlo

BIBLIOGRAPHY

Secondary Texts

Castelot, André. *Madame du Barry.* Paris: Perrin, 1989.
Haslip, Joan. *Madame du Barry: The Wages of Beauty.* London: Weidenfeld, 1991.

Barthélémy-Hadot, Marie-Adélaïde (1763–1821). Dramatist and novelist. A schoolteacher by profession, Barthélémy-Hadot was widowed at a young age and lived by her pen thereafter. The most prolific French woman writer of her time, she published close to thirty historical novels* in three to five volumes and several works of adolescent literature. She is also the author of a dozen melodramas* produced on Parisian stages between 1804 and 1816. Women characters play a predominant role in all her writings. They are frequently portrayed as victims of society, but glorified for their moral superiority, their devotion as mothers and wives, and their heroism.

Marie-Pierre Le Hir

BIBLIOGRAPHY

Primary Text

Clarice, ou la femme précepteur. Paris: Barba, 1812.

Secondary Text

Le Hir, Marie-Pierre. "Le Mélodrame de Madame Hadot, ou le poison de la différence."
     French Review 63 (May 1990): 950–958.

Bas-bleu. The term *bas-bleu*, a translation of the eighteenth-century English
"bluestocking," became current in France in the early nineteenth century. The
word "bluestocking" was derived from a joke made in 1756 about an eccentric
scholar, Benjamin Stillingfleet, who liked to wear blue stockings instead of the
customary white hose. He frequented gatherings of both men and women who
shared intellectual interests in the 1750s as members of the bluestocking circle.
The publications of women writers who attended these gatherings, including
Elizabeth Carter, Elizabeth Montagu, and Hester Chapone, made them famous.
Remembering the prejudice that associated learned women with sexual license
in antiquity and beyond, these eminently respectable English women writers
aimed to show that learning in women could be united with virtue, friendship*,
and mutual support in the life of the mind. In England, by the 1780s, the French
word *bas-bleu* was sometimes used instead of bluestocking. Chapone alluded to
"bas-bleu" ladies. People spoke of going to a "bas-bleu" party. Hannah More
published her poem, "The Bas-Bleu; or Conversation," in 1786. However, feelings about the so-called bluestockings could be ambivalent: some regarded them
with esteem; others saw them as objects of ridicule and satire. It was difficult
for women to elude the fact that the intellect was widely conceived as a masculine attribute: therefore, to show signs of intellect was necessarily to risk being
judged "unfeminine." Hence the agonized attempts of many women writers,
including Mme de Staël* and George Sand*, to avoid being considered *bas-
bleus*. In a series of caricatures, *Les Bas-Bleus*, printed in *Le Charivari* in 1844,
the artist Honoré Daumier satirized the literary woman, always unattractive and
selfish, like the one who departs for her publishers, leaving her husband to care
for their infant. A virulent attack was launched by the conservative Catholic
writer Jules Barbey d'Aurevilly in *Les Bas-bleus* (1878). For him, the *bas-bleu*
is the professional literary woman who thinks that she is man's intellectual
equal: acceptance of her claim is yet another disastrous legacy of the French
Revolution*. Today, what remains of the term "bluestocking"/*bas-bleu* in English, as in French, lies far from the noble aspirations and endeavors of the
original bluestocking circle. The underlying meaning of the word is now largely
derogatory: it denotes an unprepossessing intellectual or literary female pedant,
and it should be consigned to history.

Renee Winegarten

BIBLIOGRAPHY

Secondary Texts

Barbey d'Aurevilly, Jules. *Les Bas-bleus. Les Oeuvres et les hommes au XIXe siècle.*
     Vol. 5. Paris: Palmé, 1878.
Myers, Sylvia Harcstark. *The Bluestocking Circle.* Oxford: Clarendon Press, 1990.

Beauharnais, Fanny de (1737–1813). Born in Paris, Marie-Anne-Françoise Mouchard de Chaban became a countess by her 1753 marriage* to Claude de Beauharnais. After it ended in an amicable separation, she opened her salon*, where guests included Sebastien Mercier, Cazotte, Baculard d'Arnaud, Restif de la Bretonne, and her lover, the poet Claude Dorat. She was obliging and controversial, and, because of Dorat, some contemporaries disputed her authorship of the considerable number of works of prose and verse bearing her name. The themes of her novels* testify to the literary tastes of the late eighteenth century: frenetic sensibility, the gothic, orientalism*. The heroine of *L'Aveugle par amour* blinds herself as an expression of love for a blind man, while *Les Noeuds enchantés* is replete with fairies, genies, and *aventures galantes*. Florizène, the cynical protagonist of the *Lettres de Stéphanie*, is a precursor of Laclos's Mme de Merteuil. In *L'Abailard supposé*, the young widow of a cruel older man intends never to rewed, until duped by a handsome young suitor whom she believes (erroneously) to have been castrated. The author knew something about conjugal imbalance, having been married in her teens to a man twenty years older than she, and found out about violence and resilience when she was imprisoned during the Terror. She survived it to reopen her salon.

Joan Hinde Stewart

BIBLIOGRAPHY

Primary Texts

Mélanges de poésies fugitives et de proses sans conséquence. Amsterdam and Paris: Delalain, 1776.
Lettres de Stéphanie. Paris: Deriaux, 1778.
L'Abailard supposé ou le sentiment à l'épreuve. Amsterdam and Paris: P.-F. Gueffier, 1780.
L'Aveugle par amour. Paris and Amsterdam: P.-F. Gueffier, 1781.
La Fausse Inconstance ou le triomphe de l'honnêteté, pièce en cinq actes. Paris: Lesclapart, 1787.
Les Noeuds enchantés. Paris: De l'Imprimerie papale, 1789.

Secondary Texts

Arnauld, A. V., A. Jay, E. Jouy, and J. Norvins. *Bibliographie nouvelle des contemporains, ou dictionnaire historique et raisonné*. Paris: Librairie Historique, 1821.
Desnoiresterres, Gustave. *Le Chevalier Dorat et les poètes légers au XVIIIe siècle*. Paris: Perrin, 1887.
Marquiset, Alfred. *Les Bas-Bleus du Premier Empire*. Paris: Honoré Champion, 1913.
Versini, Laurent. *Laclos et la tradition*. Paris: Klincksieck, 1968.

Beaumer, Madame de (eighteenth century). No birth or death dates are known for this assertive feminist and pacifist, the first female editor of the *Journal des dames*, who assumed the leadership of that paper in 1761, transformed it from a benign bagatelle to a reformist publication, then disappeared in 1763 as mysteriously as she had materialized. She was briefly under the protection of the prince de Conti and the Jaucourt family, who shared her Huguenot loyalties, and she had strong connections with Holland. She championed women, but also the poor, crusading for social justice, religious toleration, Freemasonry, republican liberty, international peace, and equality. The royal censors distrusted her, and she knew her days as editor were numbered, so she filled each issue of her newspaper with her claim that the subjugation of women was a universal tragedy. She called for a "revolution" in female consciousness, vowing to be one of the first to precipitate it. Respect between the sexes would lead to the same between social classes and nations and would eliminate war. Styling herself *autrice* and *éditrice*, she assured her readers that she loved her sex and would always vindicate its honor. Mme de Beaumer dressed like a man when she conducted business with the booktrade authorities, who, when they finally suspended her paper, ordered her to write a fashion magazine instead. She responded in a fierce diatribe that she could not repudiate the principles of a lifetime and relinquished the paper to a tamer woman whom the censors approved.

Nina Rattner Gelbart

BIBLIOGRAPHY

Primary Texts

Journal des dames. 1759–1778 (intermittent).

Secondary Texts

Gelbart, Nina Rattner. "Female Journalists." In *A History of Women in the West*. Ed. Georges Duby and Michelle Perrot. Vol. 3. *Renaissance and Enlightenment Paradoxes*. Ed. Natalie Zemon Davis and Arlette Farge. Cambridge, MA: Harvard University Press, 1993. 420–435.
———. *Feminine and Opposition Journalism in Old Regime France: Le Journal des dames, 1759–1778*. Berkeley: University of California Press, 1987.
———. "The *Journal des dames* and Its Female Editors: Politics, Censorship and Feminism in the Old Regime Press." In *Press and Politics in Pre-Revolutionary France*. Ed. Jack Censer and Jeremy Popkin. Berkeley: University of California Press, 1987. 24–74.
Van Dijk, Suzanna. *Traces des femmes. Présences féminines dans le journalisme français du XVIIIe siècle*. Amsterdam: AOA-Holland University Press, 1988.

Beaumont, Marie Le Prince de. *See* Leprince de Beaumont, Jeanne-Marie.

Beauvoir, Simone de (1908–1986). Beauvoir's carefully crafted memoirs* reveal an individual determined to prove to the world and to herself that a woman can be as intelligent, accomplished, and independent as any man. In the first volume of her autobiography*, *Mémoires d'une jeune fille rangée*, Beauvoir describes her early sensual closeness to her mother, her rejection of the Catholic religion and of God, and her determination to avoid the repetitive household chores performed by her mother. She also traces her gradual achievement of independence through education*, her relationship with Jean-Paul Sartre, and her break from the bourgeois conditioning which she blamed for the premature death of her best friend, Zaza (Mabille) Lacoin.

Beauvoir's realization that she needed to understand what difference the fact of being born a woman had made in her development resulted in the 1949 publication of *Le Deuxième Sexe*, a book that encouraged all women to look at the limitations societal conditioning had placed on their lives and to seek independence and liberation. Reluctant at first to accept the label "feminist" out of the conviction that the triumph of socialism would mean automatic equality for women, Beauvoir gradually became disenchanted with the secondary roles to which women were relegated in socialist circles, and in the 1970s she began to participate actively in meetings, demonstrations, and publications championing feminist causes and women's rights. She campaigned for the legalization of abortion* in France and gave moral and sometimes financial support to individual women who appealed to her for help. Beauvoir's correspondence, donated to the Bibliothèque Nationale, reveals the extent to which she became a mentor, psychological counselor, political support system, and patient reader of manuscripts for grateful and devoted correspondents, the vast majority of them women.

Beauvoir's early philosophical essays incorporate existentialist ideas into her view of society. *Pyrrhus et Cinéas* examines the value of human activity, while *Pour une morale de l'ambiguïté* stresses the importance of individual transcendence, suggesting that the freedom of each individual depends on the freedom of others. Finally, *L'Existentialisme et la sagesse des nations* highlights the inevitable connection Beauvoir sees between politics and morality.

While the philosophical essays concentrate on the general human condition, Beauvoir uses her fictional characters to examine a multitude of options in women's lives. *Quand prime le spirituel* portrays adolescent girls on the brink of maturity and contains an ironic portrait of a fictional Zaza driven to death by a domineering and controlling mother. Beauvoir weaves into her first published work, *L'Invitée*, the story of her attempt with Sartre to replace the traditional couple relationship with a trio, posing the philosophical problem of woman as Other. Her 1945 play, *Les Bouches inutiles*, emphasizes the importance of men and women working together to achieve mutually beneficial political ends. Several of Beauvoir's novels* underscore the problems of balancing career and family: *Les Mandarins* (Prix Goncourt, 1954) presents the postwar Parisian intellectual milieu partially from the point of view of a woman psychiatrist trying to balance work, marriage*, and motherhood, while the protagonist of *Les Belles Images* rebels against societal expectations as she loses her tenuous hold on juggling her commitments to an advertising career, husband, children, and lover. The three stories in *La Femme rompue* explore the problems of aging, divorce*, and lack of individuality and self-esteem through the female protagonists.

Beauvoir's autobiographical works provide a privileged insight into the way in which one of the most influential women of the twentieth century reacted to events, pressures, and day-to-day existence. Her wartime journals and unedited letters to Sartre, published posthumously, reveal previously unknown aspects of Beauvoir. The worldwide renown of *Le Deuxième Sexe*, the extensive range of her work, and, perhaps most important, the energy and commitment of a woman determined to help other women examine their lives and achieve some degree of liberation have made Beauvoir, despite her conscious choice not to have children of her own, a maternal figure and a powerful role model for generations of women throughout the world.

Yolanda Astarita Patterson

BIBLIOGRAPHY

Primary Texts

L'Invitée. Paris: Gallimard, 1943.
Le Deuxième Sexe. Paris: Gallimard, 1949.
Mémoires d'une jeune fille rangée. Paris: Gallimard, 1958.
Les Mandarins. Paris: Gallimard, 1954.
Les Belles Images. Paris: Gallimard, 1966.
La Femme rompue. Paris: Gallimard, 1967.
Quand prime le spirituel. Paris: Gallimard, 1980.
Lettres à Sartre. 2 vols. Paris: Gallimard, 1990.

Secondary Texts

Bair, Deirdre. *Simone de Beauvoir: A Biography*. New York: Summit Books, 1990.
Moi, Toril. *Feminist Theory and Simone de Beauvoir*. Oxford: Basil Blackwell, 1990.
Patterson, Yolanda Astarita. *Simone de Beauvoir and the Demystification of Motherhood*. Ann Arbor: UMI Research Press, 1989.
Simons, Margaret A., ed. *Feminist Interpretations of Simone de Beauvoir*. University Park: Pennsylvania State University Press, 1995.

Beccary, Madame (also known as Beccari) (eighteenth century). Little is known about the life of this novelist born in Italy to a family of poets. She anglicized her name to Beccary and published four works presented as translations of English novels*, imitating the popular novels of Mme Riccoboni* and capitalizing on the Anglomania of the second half of the eighteenth century. Beccary's novels are highly moralistic tales. She exults in the sentimentality of her staunchly virtuous heroines without questioning or decrying the sexual double standards of her day as did Riccoboni. Most of Beccary's female protagonists triumph, as in *Lettres de Milady Bedfort* (1769), *Mémoires de Lucie d'Olbery* (1770), and *Milord d'Ambi* (1778), but in her last work, *Mémoires de Fanny Spingler* (1781), Beccary demonstrates that not all virtue is rewarded.

Aurora Wolfgang

BIBLIOGRAPHY

Primary Texts

Lettres de Milady Bedfort, traduites de l'anglais par Mme B . . . G . . . Paris: N.p., 1769.
Mémoires de Fanny Spingler. Neuchâtel: Impr. de la Société Typographique, 1781.

Mémoires de Lucie d'Olbery, traduits de l'anglais par Mme B . . . G . . . Paris: N.p., 1770.
Milord d'Ambi, histoire anglaise par Mme B. Paris: Gaugery, 1778.

Secondary Texts

Stewart, Joan Hinde. *Gynographs: French Novels by Women of the Late Eighteenth Century.* Lincoln: University of Nebraska Press, 1993.
Versini, Laurent. *Laclos et la tradition.* Paris: Klincksieck, 1968.

Beck, Béatrix (1914–). Swiss-born, Beck has spent most of her life in France, where her fate has been repeatedly marked by tragedy: she was two when her father (Belgian writer Christian Beck) died, and a young adult when her mother committed suicide. She later married a stateless Jew who died prematurely in 1940 after being drafted by the French army. To survive in Nazi-occupied France as the single parent of a three-year-old daughter, Beck worked odd jobs and wrote in her spare time. After winning the Goncourt Prize for *Léon Morin, prêtre* (1952), she devoted herself entirely to writing. From her first novels* centering on the autobiographical character of Barny, to her more recent fantastic tales, her texts explore the destinies of unconventional women. Whether homeless, widows, midgets, prostitutes, lunatics, or fairies, Beck's female characters are assertive, freethinking women whose independence enables them to survive.

Frédérique Chevillot

BIBLIOGRAPHY

Primary Texts

Barny. Paris: Gallimard, 1948.
Une Mort irrégulière. Paris: Gallimard, 1950.
Léon Morin, prêtre. Paris: Gallimard, 1952.
Cou coupé court toujours. Paris: Gallimard, 1967.
L'Epouvante, l'émerveillement. Paris: Le Sagittaire, 1977.
Noli. Paris: Le Sagittaire, 1978.
La Décharge. 1979. Paris: Grasset, 1980.
Josée dite Nancy. Paris: Grasset, 1981.
L'Enfant chat. Paris: Grasset, 1984.
Un(e). Paris: Grasset, 1989.
Une Lilliputienne. Paris: Grasset, 1993.
Moi ou autres. Paris: Grasset, 1994.

Bédacier, Catherine Durand, dame. *See* Durand, Catherine, Dame Bédacier.

Belghoul, Farida (1958–). Born in Paris, where her Kabyle (Algerian) parents had immigrated, she has played an important part in the anti-racist struggle, through her forceful interventions in immigration debates and her co-leadership of the second national march for equality in France, Convergence '84 pour l'égalité. Belghoul has made two films, *C'est Madame la France que tu préfères?* and *Le Départ du père.* She is best known for her critically acclaimed novel*, *Georgette!,* which uses a stream-of-consciousness technique and whose narrator is a young girl. In *Georgette!*, Belghoul courageously critiques the intersecting forces of racism and sexism.

Mark McKinney

BIBLIOGRAPHY

Primary Texts

"La Différence entre dominant et dominé." *Bulletin de l'agence IM'média* (May-June 1984): 19–21.
Georgette! Paris: Bernard Barrault, 1986.

Secondary Texts

Delvaux, Martine. "L'Ironie du sort: Le tiers Espace de la littérature beure." *French Review* 68, no. 4 (March 1995): 681–693.
Hargreaves, Alec G. *La Littérature beur: Un Guide bio-bibliographique.* New Orleans: CELFAN Edition Monographs, 1992.
———. *Voices from the North African Immigrant Community in France: Immigration and Identity in Beur Fiction.* Providence, RI: Berg, 1991.
Rosello, Mireille. "*Georgette!* de Farida Belghoul: Télévision et départenance." *L'Esprit Créateur* 33, no. 2 (Summer 1993): 35–46.

Belgiojoso (or Belgioioso), Cristina Trivulzio di, "la Bellejoyeuse" (1808–1871). An Italian activist influential in Italy's unification movement. She wrote extensively in French and Italian. Her prominent Parisian salon* (1835–1842) attracted ex-patriots and intellectuals, including George Sand*, Marie d'Agoult*, Frédéric Chopin, and General Lafayette. She was instrumental in the popular uprisings of the 1840s in Italy. During the "Roman revolutions," she directed military hospitals and oversaw some 300 nurses. In Locate, near Milan, and in Turkey, she bought property and founded agricultural communities and schools. Her travels to the Near East to regions little known to Western women led to her *Souvenirs dans l'exil* (1850) and *La Vie intime et la vie nomade en Orient* (1855). Belgiojoso also founded newspapers and wrote on history, religion, and women's issues. "Della presente condizione delle donne e del loro avvenire" (On the present circumstances of women and their future) appeared in 1866.

Claire Marrone

BIBLIOGRAPHY

Primary Texts

Essai sur la formation du dogme catholique. 4 vols. Paris: Jules Renouard aud Cie., 1842–43.
L'Italia e la rivoluzione italiana nel 1848. Torina: Tip. artistica sociale, 1849.
Scènes de la vie turque. Paris: Molévy frères, 1858.

Secondary Texts

Archer Brombert, Beth. *Cristina: Portraits of a Princess.* New York: Alfred A. Knopf, 1977.
Crémieux, Benjamin. *Une Conspiratrice en 1830, ou le Souper sans la Belgiojoso.* Paris: Editions Pierre Lafitte, 1928.

Knibiehler, Yvonne. "Du nouveau sur la Princesse de Belgiojoso." *Rassegna storica del Risorgimento.* Rome, 1971.
Spinosa, Antonio. *Italiane: Il lato segreto del Risorgimento.* Milan: Arnoldo Editors, 1994.

Bellon, Loleh (1925–). Formed by the avant-garde director Charles Dullin, Bellon has pursued an acting career—celebrated for its nuances and wit—in both contemporary drama (Genet's *Le Balcon*) and classics (Corneille's *L'Illusion comique*). She began writing plays in the late 1970s to create challenging roles for women, notably Suzanne Flon. Her eight social comedies foreground with irony and tenderness the complicated ties that bind contemporary women. In *Les Dames du jeudi* (1976) and *De si tendres liens* (1995), in particular, her women characters, through flashbacks and dream sequences, play out a life's worth of intense competition with and ferocious love for each other.

Judith G. Miller

BIBLIOGRAPHY

Primary Texts

De si tendres liens. Paris: Gallimard, 1984.
Les Dames du jeudi, Changement à vue, Le Coeur sur la main. Paris: Gallimard, 1986.
L'Eloignement. Arles: Actes Sud-Papiers, 1987.
Une Absence. Arles: Actes Sud-Papiers, 1988.
La Chambre d'amis followed by *L'Une et l'Autre.* Arles: Actes Sud-Papiers, 1995.

Belot (or Bellot), Octavie Guichard, Présidente Durey de Meynières (1719–1804). Essayist and translator, Belot was declared the Sévigné* of her century by Voltaire. Her short but productive literary career spanned 1758–1765, the years of her two marriages. After her first husband's death, Belot spent her meager annuity to learn English and became a successful translator. She secured a pension from the king for her much admired translations of Johnson's *Histoire de Rasselas*, Sarah Fielding's *Ophélie* (1763), and Hume's sixteen-volume *Histoire de l'Angleterre* (1763–1765). Through her translations, combative prefaces, and essays, Belot passionately engaged moral and philosophical questions. In *Réflexions d'une provinciale sur le discours de J.-J. Rousseau* (1756), Belot critcized Rousseau's discourse on equality, rejecting his notion of natural, solitary man. In *Observations sur la noblesse et le tiers-état* (1758), Belot argued that the nobility should remain military and eschew commerce. After she remarried, Belot expressed her talents in private letters.

Aurora Wolfgang

BIBLIOGRAPHY

Primary Texts

Réfléxions d'une provinciale sur le discours de J.-J. Rousseau touchant l'inégalité des conditions, par Madame B***. London: N.p., 1756.

Observations sur la noblesse et le tiers-état, par Madame B***. Amsterdam: Arkstée
and Merkus, 1758.
Mélanges de littérature anglaise, traduits par Madame B***. The Hague: Prault fils,
1759.
*Histoire de Rasselas, prince d'Abyssinie de Samuel Johnson, traduite de l'anglais par
Octavie Belot*. 1760. Reprint. Paris: Desjonquères, 1994.
Ophélie. Roman traduit de l'anglais. 2 vols. Amsterdam: N.p., 1763.

Secondary Text

Swiderski, Marie-Laure Girou. "Mme Belot: Une Tâcheronne des lettres?" *Studies on
Voltaire and the Eighteenth Century* 304 (1992): 816–817.

Belvo (or Bellevaux), Marquise de (1728–?). Little is known about this novelist except that she was the aunt of Mme de Genlis* and a friend of Marmontel.
In 1761 she published a first version of her monophonic epistolary novel*,
*Quelques lettres écrites en 1743 et 1744 par une jeune veuve au chevalier de
Luzeincour*. In the 1769 edition she expanded the novel's twenty-seven letters
to fifty-three, reportedly with the assistance of Gautier de Montdorge, and replaced the hopeful anticipation of the first ending with the young widow's demise. Belvo's unnamed heroine models her letters after those of Madame de
Sévigné*. Not only does the heroine admire "her" Sévigné, she is an
eighteenth-century version: her letters exude charm and wit; she visits the court
at Versailles, frequents authors, loves her daughter, and even temporarily resides
at Les Rochers, making this work a true homage to the seventeenth-century
letter writer.

Aurora Wolfgang

BIBLIOGRAPHY

Primary Texts

Quelques lettres écrites en 1743 et 1744 par une jeune veuve au chevalier de Luzeincour.
London: Gautier de Montdorge, 1761.
Lettres au chevalier de Luzeincour par une jeune veuve. London: N.p., 1796.

Secondary Texts

Genlis, Stéphanie-Félicité, comtesse de. *Mémoires inédits de Mme la comtesse de Genlis
sur le dix-huitième siècle et la Révolution française 1766–1814*. Paris: Librairie
de Ladvocat, 1825.
Stewart, Joan Hind. *Gynographs: French Novels by Women of the Late Eighteenth Century*. Lincoln: University of Nebraska Press, 1993.
Versini, Laurent. *Laclos et la tradition*. Paris: Klincksieck, 1968.

Benmussa, Simone (?–). Author, director, novelist, and editor of the *Cahiers
Renaud-Barrault*, Benmussa is well known for her innovative approach to stage
adaptation. Choosing prose texts in which reality, memory, dream, and fantasy
intersect, Benmussa creates fluid plays that are unfettered by the conventions of
the traditional dramatic text. When retelling George Moore's novella about a
woman disguised as a man (*La Vie singulière d'Albert Nobbs*, 1978), Benmussa
reconstructs the story from a woman's perspective, relegating Moore's narrative

presence to a "voice off." Feminist criticism has focused on Benmussa's unusual presentation of women characters, especially her portrayal of Freud's famous patient, Dora, which Benmussa adapted from Hélène Cixous's* *Le Portrait de Dora*. Benmussa's interest in other authors has also led to a critical work on Ionesco, a film on Nathalie Sarraute*, and stage adaptations of Sarraute's *Enfance* and of works by Henry James, Gertrude Stein, and Edith Wharton.

Jan Berkowitz Gross

BIBLIOGRAPHY

Primary Texts

Eugène Ionesco. Paris: Seghers, 1966.
La Traversée du temps perdu. Paris: Des femmes, 1978.
La Vie singulière d'Albert Nobbs. Paris: Des femmes, 1978.
Apparences. Paris: Des femmes, 1979.
Le Prince répète le prince. Paris: Seuil, 1984.
Nathalie Sarraute. Lyons: La Manufacture, 1987.

Film

Benmussa, Simone, dir. *Portrait d'écrivain: Nathalie Sarraute*. Production Centre Pompidou, 1977.

Secondary Texts

Diamond, Elin. "Benmussa's Adaptations: Unauthorized Texts from Elsewhere." In *Feminine Focus*. Ed. Enoch Brater. London: Oxford University Press, 1989. 64–78.
Savona, Jeannette Laillou. "In Search of a Feminist Theatre: *Portrait of Dora*." In *Feminine Focus*. Ed. Enoch Brater. London: Oxford University Press, 1989. 94–108.

Benoist (or Benoît), Françoise Albine (1724–1809). Born in Lyons, she married a draftsman; as a widow, she set up residence in Paris. Her short-lived *Journal en forme de lettres, mêlé de critiques et d'anecdotes* (1757) contains a moving defense of women authors, cited by her contemporaries. Benoist also wrote plays, including *Le Triomphe de la probité* (after Goldoni) and *La Supercherie réciproque*, but she is best known for her novels*: *Mes Principes ou la vertu raisonnée, Elisabeth, Célianne ou les amants séduits par leurs vertus, Lettres du colonel Talbert, Agathe et Isidore, L'Erreur des désirs, Sophronie ou leçon prétendue d'une mère à sa fille, Folie de la prudence humaine*, and *Les Erreurs d'une jolie femme ou l'Aspasie française*. Her production of novels is notable both for its quantity and its variety of tone and form. In texts often running to several volumes, packed with misadventures and aphorisms, and where the protagonists may bear oriental-sounding names (e.g., Falzor, Zalais, and Mozime), Benoist treats an unusually rich panoply of subjects and themes, touching on the condition of women in mid-eighteenth-century France: the ravages of male jealousy, the ambiguities of female virtue and conjugal fidelity, secret marriages*, profligacy, parental tyranny, maternal love, desire, and the aging woman.

Joan Hinde Stewart

BIBLIOGRAPHY

Primary Texts

Mes Principes ou la vertu raisonnée. Paris: Cuissart, 1759–1760.
Célianne ou les Amants séduits par leurs vertus. Paris: Lacombe, 1766.
Elisabeth. Amsterdam: Arkstée and Merkus, 1766.
Lettres du colonel Talbert. Amsterdam and Paris: Durand, 1767.
Agathe et Isidore. Amsterdam and Paris: Durand, 1768.
La Supercherie réciproque. Amsterdam and Paris: Durand, 1768.
Le Triomphe de la probité. Paris: Le Jay, 1768.
Sophronie ou leçon prétendue d'une mère à sa fille. London and Paris: Duchesne, 1769.
L'Erreur des désirs. Paris: Regnard and Demonville; Lyons: Cellier; Rouen: Lucas, 1770.
Folie de la prudence humaine. Amsterdam and Paris: Chez la veuve Regnard et Demonville, 1771.
Les Erreurs d'une jolie femme ou l'Aspasie française. Brussels and Paris: Duchesne, 1781.

Secondary Text

La Porte, Joseph de (Abbé). "Madame Benoit." In *Histoire littéraire des femmes françaises.* Paris: Lacombe, 1769. Vol. 5: 309–379.

Bernard, Catherine (1663–1712?). Born in Rouen to a comfortable Huguenot family, she moved to Paris to pursue her literary interests. Shortly before the revocation of the Edict of Nantes (1685), she converted to Catholicism, which alienated her from her family. She appears to have been a close friend of Fontenelle, who is sometimes said to have collaborated with her. Bernard excelled in poetry* and prose as well as drama. Her occasional verse won prizes from the Académie Française and the Jeux floraux de Toulouse, and was anthologized well into the eighteenth century. She also earned honorary membership in the Accademia dei Ricovrati of Padua. Bernard's historical novels* (*Fédéric de Sicile*, 1680; *Eléonore d'Yvrée*, 1687; *Le Comte d'Amboise*, 1689; *Inès de Cardoue*, 1696) and short story* (*Histoire de la rupture d'Abenamar et de Fatime*, 1696) were well received in her time and praised for their stylistic qualities. In these novels, she demonstrates a keen grasp of psychological description and gives a resolutely pessimistic portrayal of love. Her novel *Inès de Cardoue* features two fairy tales*, including a version of "Riquet à la houppe" that preceded Perrault's more famous version. Bernard's tale, unlike Perrault's, does not condemn the heroine's imagination but rather women's confinement in marriage*. In addition, Bernard wrote two plays, both of which were staged. *Laodamie* (1689) holds the distinction of being the first full-length play by a woman to be performed at the Comédie Française. *Brutus* (1691) was performed some forty-three times and was remembered long enough to receive favorable comparison to Voltaire's tragedy on the same subject (1730). Bernard, who was plagued by poverty, eventually received financial support from the austere Chancelière de Pontchartrain. However, this support came at a price: Bernard was obliged to abandon the theater* and eventually stopped publishing altogether.

Lewis C. Seifert

BIBLIOGRAPHY

Primary Texts

Oeuvres I: Romans et nouvelles. Ed. Franco Piva. Paris: Nizet, 1993.
Laodamie reine d'Epire. In *Femmes dramaturges en France (1650–1750), Pièces choisies.* Ed. Perry Gethner. Seattle: Biblio 17, 1993. 181–242.

Bernheim, Cathy (1948–). Writer, translator, television scriptwriter, literary critic for *Libération* and *Femme actuelle*, and film critic for *Libération*. A militant feminist, Bernheim participated in every major feminist event and demonstration of the 1970s, signed the ''Manifeste des 343'' in favor of the legalization of abortion*, and collaborated on several important collective works, including the well-known *Les Femmes s'entêtent* and *Le Sexisme ordinaire*. She discusses the beginning of the women's movement in *Perturbation, ma soeur* (1983), and in her autobiography*, *L'Amour presque parfait* (1991), she explores the meaning of love, particularly between women, while continuing her sociohistorical study of the women's movement.

Joëlle Vitiello

BIBLIOGRAPHY

Primary Texts

Perturbation, ma soeur. Naissance d'un mouvement de femmes. Paris: Seuil, 1983.
Qui êtes-vous, Mary Shelley? Paris: La Manufacture, 1987.
Cobaye Baby. Paris: La Manufacture, 1987.
Valentine Hugo. Paris: Presses de la Renaissance, 1989.
Côte d'Azur. Paris: Gallimard, 1989.
Quel Cinéma! Paris: L'Ecole des Loisirs, 1990.
L'Amour presque parfait. Paris: Editions du Félin, 1991.

Bernheim, Emmanuèle (1956–). Author of novels* and short stories*, Bernheim also adapts books for television. Her minimalist style, which has been compared to that of Annie Ernaux*, reveals her female protagonists' most intimate fears, desires, and fantasies with surgical precision. In her first novel, *Le Cran d'arrêt* (1985), Bernheim depicts a woman who, driven to commit an act of violence, later seeks out and seduces her victim. Her focus on the habits, cruelty, vulnerability, and perversity of ordinary yet autonomous women is designed both to engage and to disquiet the reader.

Joëlle Vitiello

BIBLIOGRAPHY

Primary Texts

Le Cran d'arrêt. Paris: Denoël, 1985.
Un Couple. Paris: Gallimard, 1988.
Sa Femme. Paris: Gallimard, 1993.

The *Beur* Novel. The term *Beur*, which first appeared in the working-class suburbs of Paris in the 1970s, was coined by young people of Maghrebi origin as an epithet describing themselves, and is a *verlan* (backslang) expression involving a double inversion of the syllables of the word *arabe (arabe >rebeu>beur)*. The epithet became widely used in the 1980s when the media devoted much attention to the *Beurs* and events related to them—the creation of Radio Beur (1981), the Marche des Beurs (the 1983 Marche pour l'égalité et contre le racisme), and the emergence of SOS Racisme (1984). Although the expression *Beur* was originally created as a means of rejecting the negative connotations bestowed on the term *arabe*, and of designating an identity that is both Arab *and* French, many second- and third-generation Maghrebi now dislike the expression, fearing it has been co-opted by the media and is being used in the same pejorative sense as *arabe*. This is particularly true of the feminine form *beurette*, which is found primarily in the media.

The *Beur* novel was first defined by Alec Hargreaves as the body of texts written by the French-born children of North African immigrant workers. Others, following the example of Michel Laronde, prefer a broader definition, which includes novels that deal with issues related to the *Beurs*, but which are not necessarily written by them. The women whose novels are most often described as *Beur* include Farida Belghoul*, Aïcha Benaïssa, Antoinette Ben Kerroum-Covlet, Sakinna Boukhedenna*, Djura*, Tassadit Imache*, Ferrudja Kessas, Soraya Nini, and Leïla Sebbar*. Most *Beur* novels are autobiographical in nature and address social and political questions such as the Algerian War, racism, integration, and living conditions in suburban areas. Besides these general themes, the novels written by women focus on the female protagonists' double marginalization as women and as members of an ethnic minority. In their search for an identity, the characters reject arranged marriages and the traditional gender roles prescribed by their Maghrebi families, enter into conflictual relationships with their fathers and brothers, and demand a voice and a place for themselves in contemporary France.

Susan Ireland

BIBLIOGRAPHY

Primary Texts

Belghoul, Farida. *Georgette!* Paris: Barrault, 1986.
Ben Kerroum-Covlet. *Gardien du seuil.* Paris: Harmattan, 1988.
Benaïssa, Aïcha. *Née en France: Histoire d'une jeune beur.* Paris: Payot, 1990.
Boukhedenna, Sakinna. *Journal. Nationalité: "immigré(e)."* Paris: Harmattan, 1987.
Kessas, Ferrudja. *Beur's Story.* Paris: Harmattan, 1990.
Nini, Soraya. *Ils disent que je suis une beurette.* Paris: Fixot, 1993.

Secondary Texts

Hargreaves, Alec G. "History, Gender and Ethnicity in Writing by Women Authors of Maghrebian Origin in France." *L'Esprit Créateur* 33, no. 2 (Summer 1993): 23–34.

———. *La Littérature beur: Un Guide bio-bibliographique.* New Orleans: CELFAN Edition Monographs, 1992.

———. *Voices from the North African Immigrant Community in France: Immigration and Identity in Beur Fiction.* Oxford: Berg, 1991.

Ireland, Susan. "Writing at the Crossroads: Cultural Conflict in the Work of *Beur* Women Writers." *French Review* 68, no. 6 (May 1995): 1022–1034.

Laronde, Michel. *Autour du roman beur: Immigration et identité.* Paris: Harmattan, 1993.

Rosello, Mireille. "The 'Beur Nation': Toward a Theory of 'Departenance.' " *Research in African Literatures* 24, no. 3 (Fall 1993): 13–24.

Beyala, Calixthe (1961–). Born in Cameroon, Beyala is a self-proclaimed radical feminist. Since 1987 she has written seven novels* and a feminist essay. Most of her fiction depicts women struggling to find their identity and the dispossessed searching for their voice in a hostile world. Her style is often surrealistic, combining poetic and street language. Beyala's first two novels are perhaps her most original works—the first, *C'est le soleil qui m'a brûlée* (1987), portrays the awakening of a young African girl to the plight of women victimized by a brutal, corrupt, postcolonial patriarchal system, while the second, *Tu t'appelleras Tanga* (1988), deals with the taboo topics of incest, child prostitution*, and the loss of parental love. Its unconventional narrative highlights the transmission of a life story from one woman to another, and the emphasis on female bonding in these two novels has led some critics to characterize Beyala's characters as lesbians, an assertion denied by the author. While her most popular novel, *Le Petit Prince de Belleville* (1992), and its sequel, *Maman a un amant* (1993), focus on immigration, racism, and interracial relationships, her most recent fictional works portray African female protagonists and their quest for identity when they settle in France. The always controversial Beyala has also written a feminist manifesto, *Lettre d'une Africaine à ses soeurs occidentales* (1995), which uses strong words and images to upbraid Western women for abandoning feminism* and failing to support African women in their struggles.

Joëlle Vitiello

BIBLIOGRAPHY

Primary Texts

C'est le soleil qui m'a brûlée. Paris: Stock, 1987.

Tu t'appelleras Tanga. Paris: Stock, 1988.

Seul le Diable le savait. Paris: Le Pré aux Clercs, 1990.

Le Petit Prince de Belleville. Paris: Albin Michel, 1992.

Maman a un amant. Paris: Albin Michel, 1993.

Assèze l'Africaine. Paris: Albin Michel, 1994.

Lettre d'une Africaine à ses soeurs occidentales. Paris: Spengler, 1995.

Les Honneurs perdus. Paris: Albin Michel, 1996.

Secondary Texts

Almeida, Irène Assiba d'. *Francophone African Women Writers: Destroying the Emptiness of Silence.* Gainesville: University Press of Florida, 1994.

Brière, Eloise. *Le Roman camerounais et ses discours*. Ivry: Editions Nouvelles du Sud, 1993.

Cazenave, Odile. *Femmes rebelles*. Paris: L'Harmattan, 1996.

Volet, Jean-Marie. "Calixthe Beyala or the Literary Success of a Cameroonian Woman Living in Paris." *World Literature Today* 67, no. 2 (1993): 309–314.

Bible. In an interesting essay, Marguerite Soulié addresses the involvement of three great noblewomen in the Reform movement and their relation to the Bible. Marguerite de Navarre* (1492–1549), duchess of Alençon and queen of Navarre, wrote letters, religious plays, and spiritual songs that express the joy and mystical communion that she derived from reading the Bible. In this, Marguerite resembled the Christian woman upheld in the Protestant pamphlets of the 1540s to the 1560s for her devotion to the reading of Scripture. Marguerite de Navarre, however, never broke with the Roman Catholic Church even though many of her proteges were active in the new religious circles marked by *évangélisme*. In her meditations on the Bible, she affirms the centrality of Christ's redemption and the free gift of grace apart from works. Her religious perspective is nurtured by her readings of Scripture and her humanist culture: she had Greek texts translated, read Latin philosophers, and encouraged vernacular translations of Scripture.

The daughter of Marguerite de Navarre, Jeanne d'Albret* (1528–1572), was also endowed with a rare energy in regard to the Reform as well as other aspects of her personal life. Risking excommunication by the pope and repudiation by her husband, Jeanne d'Albret proclaimed her loyalty to the Reform. She used Scripture to back her politically based decisions, citing as her model King Josias, who renewed the faith of Israel through his rediscovery of the book of the law. Reform poets admiringly gave her the name of the biblical prophetess and military leader Deborah, symbolizing her heroic courage in the face of adversity. In her correspondence and then in her memoirs written in La Rochelle in 1568, she defends her loyalty to God, king, and country, as well as her commitment to the education* of her son, the future Henry IV. As Evelyne Berriot-Salvadore states, D'Albret used writing as a political weapon to legitimize her conversion in 1560 to the Protestant cause (410). The third woman, Charlotte Arbaleste, a young widowed mother, found herself at the heart of the St. Bartholomew's Day Massacre in Paris in 1572. Saved from death, she found refuge at Sedan, where she met Philippe de Mornay, seigneur du Plessis, a Protestant warrior, who married her. Her *Mémoires*, dedicated to her eldest son, retrace a half century of familial and political history. Undertaken as a mother's spiritual guide for her son, in it she reveals her strong faith in God's protection and her obedience to Scripture, which she cites throughout.

Nancy Roelker has shown that the Reformed cause was a way for these already strong and independent noblewomen to enhance their numerous political, familial, and social activities. What about city women and the learned women of the urban elite? Natalie Z. Davis concludes that most Huguenot city women came from families of craftsmen, merchants, and professional men and that many were widows or with employ of their own (80–81). As with noble-women, commitment to the Reform complemented the scope that these women's lives already had in the public sphere. Few learned women, however, joined the Reform: Calvinist women did not publish (Davis, 85).

Among Catholic women who published extensively and for whom Scripture formed an integral part of their writing identity are Madeleine (1520–1587) and Catherine des Roches* (1542–1587). The Catholicism of the Dames des Roches is closely linked to their devotion to the monarchy. Together with the humanist professionals who attended their salon* in their hometown of Poitiers, they formed part of the newly emerging class of the *noblesse de robe* that sought to strengthen a national consciousness founded on the Gallican formula "To live under one God, one King, one faith, one law." Both mother and daughter were outspoken critics of the Reform movement, due in great part to the disorders of the civil wars that destroyed half of Poitiers in 1562 and again in 1569. Made-leine frequently cites Scripture on the necessary union of works and faith in her denunciation of Reformed ministers who preach peace but incite to war. Her syncretism leads her to find moral consolation for her difficulties in both Scrip-ture and Neoplatonic thought. Catherine's use of the Bible is marked by a fem-inist consciousness that led her to justify her choice to remain unmarried so as to pursue a life of learning and writing with her mother. Her *Un Acte de la Tragicomédie de Tobie*, published in the 1579 edition of *Les Oeuvres*, is a daring adaptation of the Apocryphal Book of Tobit: Sarah and her mother, minor char-acters in the original, become protagonists who express deep ambivalence con-cerning the norms governing female conduct and the necessary separation from the mother upon the daughter's marriage.* Catherine thus uses the virginal her-oine of Neoplatonic and biblical texts to resist sociosexual norms imposed on the women of her time.

Anne R. Larsen

BIBLIOGRAPHY

Primary Texts

Des Roches, Madeleine and Catherine. *Les Oeuvres*. Ed. Anne R. Larsen. Geneva: Droz, 1993.
Jeanne d'Albret. *Mémoires et poésies de Jeanne d'Albret*. Ed. Baron Alphonse de Ruble. Paris: E. Paul, Huart and Guillemin, 1893.
Mornay, Charlotte Arbaleste, Dame de. *Mémoires de Madame de Mornay*. 2 vols. Ed. Mme de Witt. Paris: Mme Veuve J. Renouard, 1868.

Secondary Texts

Berriot-Salvadore, Evelyne. *Les Femmes dans la société française de la Renaissance*. Geneva: Droz, 1990.
Davis, Natalie Zemon. *Society and Culture in Early Modern France*. Stanford: Stanford University Press, 1965.
Larsen, Anne R. "Chastity and the Mother-Daughter Bond: Odet de Turnèbe's Response

to Catherine des Roches.'' In *Renaissance Women Writers: French Texts/American Contexts*. Ed. Anne R. Larsen and Colette H. Winn. Detroit: Wayne State University Press, 1994. 172–188.

Roelker, Nancy. ''The Appeal of Calvinism to French Noble Women in the Sixteenth Century.''*Journal of Interdisciplinary History* 2 (1972): 391–418.

Soulié, Marguerite. ''Les Femmes et la Bible aux temps de la Réforme.'' *Bulletin de la Société de l'histoire du protestantisme français* 39 (1983): 269–275.

Billetdoux, Raphaële (1951–). Novelist and filmmaker. Billetdoux's writing is primarily concerned with the awakening and fulfillment of women's desires, both sexual and other. She depicts a society in mutation, using a variety of female perspectives (mothers, single and married women), and shows a particular predilection for the dilemmas and rebellions of young women attempting to attain womanhood from within bourgeois, patriarchal contexts. In her portrayal of women's struggles, Billetdoux focuses on society's fear of women's will, doubts, and desires, as well as its resistance to accepting them as independent beings.

Joëlle Vitiello

BIBLIOGRAPHY

Primary Texts

Jeune Fille en silence. Paris: Seuil, 1971.
L'Ouverture des bras de l'homme. Paris: Seuil, 1973.
Prends garde à la douceur des choses. Paris: Seuil, 1976.
La Lettre d'excuse. Paris: Seuil, 1981.
Mes Nuits sont plus belles que vos jours. Paris: Grasset, 1985.
Entrez et fermez la porte. Paris: Grasset, 1990.
Mélanie dans un vent terrible. Paris: Grasset, 1994.

Birth control. Birth control has always existed, but it was the fall in the French birthrate during the second half of the eighteenth century (preceding that in other Western countries) that first suggests its widespread use. Official hostility to contraception appeared during the nineteenth century when it became feared that the continuing demographic decline would threaten France's world position. This, however, did not deter those who saw a small family* as necessary to personal fulfillment from choosing to use birth control. Coitus interruptus, the oldest form of contraception, was still the most widely used during this period, although abortion* was often resorted to as a contingency measure.

Birth control became an issue of national debate at the end of the nineteenth century thanks to the neo-Malthusian Paul Robin. His Ligue de la régénération humaine sold condoms, pessaries, vaginal douches, and birth control literature, but was opposed by a powerful pronatalist lobby, led by Dr. Jacques Bertillon's Alliance nationale pour l'accroissement de la population française. Feminists such as Marie Huot, Marguerite Durand*, Nelly Roussel*, and Madeleine Pelletier* also began to discuss birth control in the women's press, although not all feminists supported their claim for women to have the right to control their own bodies.

Heavy losses during World War I* heightened an already present demographic panic, resulting in the 1920 law banning the sale or distribution of contraceptives and propaganda in favor of contraception or abortion. Somewhat ironically, the law did not make contraception itself illegal. It also excluded condoms as necessary in the fight against venereal disease. A woman's duty, according to those in power, was to have many children, a result the 1920 law failed to produce.

The notion of family planning and responsible parenthood gained momentum in the 1950s and 1960s thanks to the work of Dr. Marie-Andrée Lagroua Weill-Hallé and her Mouvement français pour le planning familial. Her motivation was a concern for women's health, not feminism* or neo-Malthusianism*, although revoking the 1920 law was one of the main demands of feminist campaigners of the second postwar period. It was also the early 1960s that saw the introduction of oral contraceptives (the pill) in France.

The Neuwirth Law, adopted in 1967, revoked the law of 1920. It allowed the manufacture, import, and sale of contraceptives under state control and the setting up of centers for family planning and education*. In spite of this, women's reproductive rights remained a major focus of feminist campaigners in the 1970s as they sought to obtain the legalization of abortion and improvements to the Neuwirth Law. Further legislation in 1974 introduced reimbursement for the cost of contraceptives by social security, although only a number of first and second generation pills (and no third generation ones) are reimbursed today.

Since the 1970s, there has been a steady increase in contraceptive use, and France now has the highest use of modern methods of birth control in the world (Spirra, 10). The pill is the most popular form, taken by 36.8 percent of women between the ages of 20 and 49, followed by intrauterine devices (IUDs), used by 16.1 percent of women (INSEE, 85). The use of condoms has, however, significantly increased since the late 1980s, and three-quarters of 15–18-year-olds now use a condom for their first sexual encounter (Krémer).

Unlike a century ago, the issue of birth control is, today, intimately linked to the question of women's emancipation in the public mind. A 1991 survey confirmed that 78 percent of adults were in total agreement with the statement that contraception has led to the true emancipation of women (Secrétariat d'Etat, 14).

Victoria B. Korzeniowska

BIBLIOGRAPHY

Mouvement français pour le planning familial. *D'Une Révolte à une lutte: 25 ans d'histoire du planning familial.* Paris: Tierce, 1982.

Netter, Albert, and Henri Rozenbaum. *Histoire illustrée de la contraception de l'Antiquité à nos jours.* Paris: Les Editions Roger Dacosta, 1985.

Ronsin, Francis. *La Grève des ventres: propagande néo-malthusienne et baisse de la natalité française (XIXe–XXe siècles).* Paris: Aubier Montaigne, 1980.

INSEE/Service des Droits des Femmes. *Les Femmes*. Paris: INSEE, 1995.
Krémer, Pascale. "Le Recours à la pilule contraceptive stagne chez les adolescents." *Le Monde*, May 28, 1996.
Spirra, Alfred, ed. *Contraceptifs oraux remboursés et non remboursés*. Paris: INSERM/ La Documentation Française, 1993.
Serfaty, David. *La Contraception*. Paris: Doin, 1992.
Secrétariat d'Etat aux droits des femmes et à la vie quotidienne. *Les Français et la contraception*. Paris: IFOP, 1991.

Blanc, Thérèse (1840–1907). Novelist, translator, literary critic, and travel writer, Blanc also wrote under the pseudonym Thérèse Bentzon. As the major female contributor to the *Revue des deux mondes*, she was especially productive in the domain of British and American literature as a critic and a translator. Supported by important male critics, including Ferdinand Brunetière, she published many novels* that explore issues of concern to women, such as divorce* and the status of women in relation to the institution of marriage*. Blanc was also a successful writer of travel literature* and focused on women's lives in places such as Russia and North America.

Bénédicte Monicat

BIBLIOGRAPHY

Primary Texts

Choses et gens d'Amérique. Paris: Calmann-Lévy, 1891.
Constance. Paris: Calmann-Lévy, 1891.
Notes et voyages. Nouvelle-France et Nouvelle Angleterre. Paris: Calmann-Lévy, 1899.
Promenades en Russie. Paris: Hachette, 1903.

Blanchecotte, Augustine-Adolphine-Malvina Souville (1830–1897). Born into poverty, and a seamstress by trade, Blanchecotte achieved literary fame with her poetry*. *Rêves et réalités*, her first published work, was crowned by the Académie Française. The critic Sainte-Beuve and the poet Alphonse de Lamartine also praised her poetry. In her 1868 essay, *Impressions d'une femme*, she questioned the restrictions and stereotypes imposed on her gender by society. Nonetheless, writing empowered her to overcome her initial marginalization and brought her public recognition. Blanchecotte continued to publish poetry, novels*, and essays during her lifetime. She became a teacher in her last years.

Juliette Parnell-Smith

BIBLIOGRAPHY

Primary Texts

Rêves et réalités. Paris: Le Doyen, Lacroix-Comon, 1856.
Impressions d'une femme. Paris: Didier, 1868.
Tablettes d'une femme pendant la Commune. Paris: Didier, 1872.

Blémur, Jacqueline Bouette de (1618–1698). The productive historian of the Benedictines, Jacqueline Bouette de Blémur claimed links to the powerful Montmorency clan as well as to Pierre-Daniel Huet. Her family ties gained her entry when only five years of age to La Trinité in Caen, Normandy, where she received all her schooling under the guidance of her aunt. Jacqueline served as *chapelaine* and secretary to the Abbess Laurence de Budos; she did not welcome Laurence's successor, Marie-Eléonore de Rohan*, as abbess, and they maintained only those relations required by civility.

Huet urged Jacqueline to publish her writings, especially her ongoing series of biographies of the outstanding nuns of her order, *L'Année Bénédictine*, which appeared in six volumes between 1667 and 1673. In 1679 she reworked some of this material to reappear in the *Eloges de plusieurs personnes illustres de l'ordre de St. Benoît*. Her biographies of Charlotte Le Sergent (1685) and Pierre Fourrier (1678) were reissued often. In 1677 Jacqueline published an *Exercice de la mort* designed to edify both religious and lay readers. She also rewrote and adapted a play or series of pious tableaux by Father Poiré, "Les Grandeurs de la mère de Dieu." She published four folio volumes of *Vie des Saints*, a compendium of both ancient and modern saints' stories. Dedicated to powerful people in the world and the monastery, the *Vies* recast the biblical imagery in *précieux* rhetoric. The author's naive tone accepts all aspects of the "Christian marvelous," but she handles her intricate tales with novelistic skill. Her work was noticed and approved by Jean Mabillon, originator of the science of diplomatics.

Jacqueline left Caen for the center of the Blessed Sacrament of Catherine de Bar, and then was appointed prioress of Châtillon-sur-Loing. Exhausted by her labors, she became blind, and her studious life ended at the monastery of the Rue Cassette in Paris, where she died in 1698.

Mary Rowan

BIBLIOGRAPHY

Secondary Texts

Bremond, Henri. *Histoire littéraire du sentiment religieux en France depuis la fin des guerres de religion*. Paris: Armand Colin, 1967.
Chaussy, Yves. *Les Bénédictines et la réforme catholique en France au XVIIe siècle*. Paris: Editions de la Source, 1975.
Huet, Pierre-Daniel. *Mémoires*. Ed. Philippe-Joseph Salazar. Paris: Société de Littératures Classiques, Klincksieck, 1993.

Bocage, Anne-Marie Fiquet. *See* Du Bocage, Anne-Marie Fiquet.

Bonal, Denise (?–   ). Actress, playwright, and professor of theater*. Born in Algeria, Bonal first wrote for radio and was awarded the Prix Arletty for her theater in 1989. Her plays take a cynical look at the bonds between mothers and their children. In *Légère en août*, for example, five surrogate mothers discuss the market value of their babies in a chic clinic where issues of class and race take precedence over maternal instincts. In *Portrait de famille* (1983) and *Passions et prairie* (1988), aging mothers look to outsiders for the care and companionship their ungrateful children seem unwilling to provide.

Jan Berkowitz Gross

BIBLIOGRAPHY

Primary Texts

Honorée par un petit monument. Paris: EDILIG, Théâtrales, 1982.
Portrait de famille. Paris: EDILIG, Théâtreales, 1983.
Passions et prairie; Légère en août. Paris: EDILIG, Théâtrales, 1988.
Turbulences et petits détails suivi de J'ai joué à la marelle, figure-toi . . . . Paris: Editions Théâtrales, 1994.

Secondary Texts

Bonal, Denise. "Il m'arriverait plus tard quelque chose d'important." *Les Cahiers de Prospero* 7 (1996): 60–69.
Lamar, Celita. "Usurping Center Stage—Women Interacting." In *Our Voices, Ourselves.* New York: Peter Lang, 1991. 56–82.

Boukhedenna, Sakinna (1959–). Born in Mulhouse to Algerian parents, Boukhedenna had a turbulent adolescence marked by problems at school, unemployment, and conflict with her parents. At age twenty-one she went to Algeria in search of a better future and a clearer sense of her identity, but soon returned to France, where she believes she has more freedom as a woman. Boukhedenna's polemical autobiographical text, *Journal. "Nationalité: immigré(e),"* describes her problems and condemns the marginalization of women of Maghrebi descent who are rejected by both France and Algeria. At once feminist and anticolonialist, the journal examines the intersections of sexism and racism, and demands a voice, a place, and an identity for women of Maghrebi origin living in France today.

Susan Ireland

BIBLIOGRAPHY

Primary Text

Journal. "Nationalité: immigré(e)." Paris: L'Harmattan, 1987.

Secondary Texts

Hargreaves, Alec G. "History, Gender and Ethnicity in Writing by Women Authors of Maghrebian Origin in France." *L'Esprit Créateur* 33, no. 2 (Summer 1993): 23–34.
———. "Resistance and Identity in *Beur* Narratives." *Modern Fiction Studies* 35, no. 1 (Spring 1989): 87–102.
———. *Voices from the North African Immigrant Community in France.* New York: Berg, 1991.

Ireland, Susan. "Writing at the Crossroads: Cultural Conflict in the Work of *Beur* Women
     Writers." *French Review* 68, no. 6 (May 1995): 1022–1034.
Laronde, Michel. *Autour du roman beur*. Paris: L'Harmattan, 1993.

Bouraoui, Nina (1967–   ). Born of a French mother and an Algerian father,
Bouraoui spent her first fourteen years in Algiers. She won the Prix Inter-Livre
in 1991 for her first novel*, *La Voyeuse interdite*. Although she claims not to
be a feminist, she denounces the oppression of women in patriarchal Arabo-
Muslim society, unveils sexual taboos, speaks about puberty, desire, neurosis,
and incest, and describes obsessive relationships with the mother. Her marginal
characters, whether male or female, rely on imagination and masochism to survive in a suffocating world where they try desperately to fit in, searching for an
identity. Her introspective, stream-of-consciousness style expresses both poetic
violence and an almost obscene sensuality in a world that oscillates between
phantasms and harsh reality. She has proven to be one of the most original
writers of the present generation.

Armelle Crouzières-Ingenthron

BIBLIOGRAPHY

   Primary Texts

La Voyeuse interdite. Paris: Gallimard, 1991.
Poing Mort. Paris: Gallimard, 1992.
Le Bal des murènes. Paris: Fayard, 1996.

   Secondary Texts

Crouzières-Ingenthron, Armelle. "Naissance du moi, naissance d'une écriture: Parole
     baudelairienne dans *La Voyeuse interdite* de Nina Bouraoui." *Journal of Magh-
     rebi Studies* 1 (1993): 63–71.
———. "Paroles d'eau: Les Tourbillons du moi et de l'écriture dans *La Voyeuse inter-
     dite* et *Poing Mort* de Nina Bouraoui." In *Histoire d'eaux, émergence d'une
     écriture dans les textes d'écrivaines francophones*. New York: Peter Lang, 1995.
     9–27.

Bourbon, Catherine de, princess of France, duchess of Bar (1559–1604).
Daughter of Jeanne d'Albret* and granddaughter of Marguerite de Navarre*,
Bourbon was to follow in a long line of strong women figures. Obstinately
proclaiming her devotion to the Protestant faith, she brought about her own
exclusion from the court of her brother, Henri IV. Throughout her life, she met
with one misfortune after another: the loss of her parents in early adolescence;
a forced renunciation of her beloved, Charles de Bourbon; an unhappy marriage*
to Henri de Lorraine which ended by papal annulment; interminable financial
strains and illnesses. She died at the age of forty-five, most likely of tuberculosis.
   The story of Bourbon's life is captured in what remains of her correspondence, which spans the years 1570 to 1603. There are 224 letters published in
Ritter's edition of 1927. These letters serve as historical documents as well as

intimate accounts of the challenges that Bourbon endured as a woman struggling to survive in a world that rejected her independence of spirit. She corresponded with many prominent figures of her time, addressing issues ranging from the political to the personal, skillfully balancing an innate assertiveness with discretion and humility. Her style is graced with feminine subtleties, her expression enhanced by its spontaneous simplicity.

Her correspondence reveals an inability to fully escape the solitude that plagued her daily existence, as well as a profound need to verbalize her experience. Among Bourbon's letters were discovered a number of poems in which she expresses this struggle more intensely. The few noteworthy compositions that remain are five religious poems (three sonnets, two stances) written in 1595, during a particularly trying period of her life. Struck with sickness and spiritual anxiety, she turned to the writing of religious verse for consolation.

Bourbon's letters and poems reflect persistent efforts to free herself from silence and marginalization, highlighting at the same time an audacious refusal to submit to royal pressures that deny her chosen faith. Unfailingly, she continued upon the path of difference, honoring the women who had traveled it before her. Her life, in all its drama, exemplifies the endeavors of many Renaissance women to achieve recognition and autonomy.

Melanie E. Gregg

BIBLIOGRAPHY

Primary Text

Lettres et poésies de Catherine de Bourbon (1570–1603). Ed. Raymond Ritter. Paris: Champion, 1927.

Secondary Texts

Armaille, Marie Celestine Amélie, Comtesse de. *Catherine de Bourbon: soeur d'Henri IV*. Paris: Didier et Cie., 1865.

Caumont La Force, Charlotte-Rose de. *Anecdote galante, ou histoire secrette de Catherine de Bourbon duchesse de Bar, et soeur de Henry le grand roy de France et de Navarre. Avec les intrigues de la cour durant les regnes de Henry III et de Henry IV*. Ed. A. Nancy, 1703.

Ritter, Raymond. *Catherine de Bourbon 1559–1604: La Soeur d'Henri IV*. Paris: J. Touzot, 1985.

Bourbon, Charlotte de Montpensier, princesse d'Orange (1546 or 1547–1582). French Huguenot. Her extensive correspondence relates to her marriage* to William the Silent, Prince of Orange and Stadtholder of the Netherlands, her political role, and her family network, including Henry of Navarre. Daughter of the Catholic Louis de Bourbon, Duke of Montpensier, and the Protestant sympathizer Jacqueline de Longwy, she was placed in the Convent of Jouarre as an infant, professed as a nun, and made abbess at the age of twelve or thirteen. In 1571 she fled the convent* and the country with the help of her sister Françoise de Bourbon-Montpensier, Duchess of Bouillon, and Jeanne d'Albret*, Queen of

Navarre, and sought refuge with the Prince Palatine. In 1575 she married William the Silent and worked actively with him and as his delegate to strengthen his precarious position in his struggle against the Spanish Catholic forces in the Netherlands. She nursed him back to health after an assassination attempt in the spring of 1582, soon after the birth of their sixth daughter, but died herself a few weeks later.

She was one of a remarkable group of French Protestant women who contributed to the development and defense of their faith in the sixteenth century, and whose writing was part of their public role. Many of her letters are reproduced in Jules Delaborde's biography. On one level, they can be read as exemplifying the roles of dutiful daughter and equally dutiful companionate wife. Although she defied her father's wishes by fleeing the convent and converting to Protestantism, her letters to him are couched in terms of respect and submission, and she never abandoned her hope of being reconciled with him. Her letters to her husband, who was frequently absent on political and military ventures, reveal the increasing importance of her advice and her activities on his behalf, and show her gradually making a more or less stable home for him and for his numerous children, including five by previous marriages. A closer reading of her letters reveals that she skillfully used the conventions of the epistolary genre to negotiate her own emancipation while at the same time preparing the ground for a reconciliation with her family in France. This included the restoration of her property and a significant contribution to the alliance between her husband and the French crown under Henri III and Catherine de Medici* and, after her death, under Henri IV.

Jane Couchman

BIBLIOGRAPHY

Secondary Texts

Anderson, James. *Ladies of the Reformation*. London: Blackie, 1855. 634–665.

Bainton, Roland H. "Charlotte de Bourbon." In *Women of the Reformation in France and England*. Boston: Beacon Press, 1973. 89–111.

Couchman, Jane. "Charlotte de Bourbon's Correspondence: Using Words to Implement Emancipation." In *Women Writers in Pre-Revolutionary France*. Ed. Colette H. Winn and Donna Kuizenga. New York: Garland, 1997.

Delaborde, Jules. *Charlotte de Bourbon, Princesse d'Orange*. Paris: Fischbacher, 1888.

Walker, Frances M. C. *Cloister to Court: Scenes from the Life of Charlotte de Bourbon*. London: Longmans, Green, 1909.

Wedgwood, Cecily V. *William the Silent: William of Nassau, Prince of Orange, 1533–1584*. New Haven: Yale University Press, 1944.

Bourdic-Viot, Marie-Anne Payan de l'Estang, marquise d'Antremont (also known as Mme de Bourdie) (1746–1802). In 1770 Bourdic-Viot published her *Poésies*, a collection of dedicatory epistles, elegies, madrigals, quatrains, epigrams, and letters. The letters are particularly interesting, not only for their treatment of love and friendship*, but also for their commentary on her literary and social position as a writer. Unpretentiously, she frequently claimed to write for pleasure rather than glory and often minimized the value of her own work, claiming that writing came naturally, almost instinctively. She celebrated the serenity of her retreat, which allowed her to remain independent from worldly cares, yet she actively cultivated literary and musical interests and solicited judgments on her poetry* from prominent writers, notably Voltaire. She composed the *Eloge de Montaigne* (1782) for her reception as a member of the Nîmes Academy; in it she credited him with inspiring Enlightenment* thought. She authored several unpublished works, including the poem ''Le Monde tel qu'il est''—a celebration of modern times and an expression of her unequivocal embrace of the world.

Marie-Pascale Pieretti

BIBLIOGRAPHY

Primary Texts

Eloge de Montaigne. Paris: Pugens, An VIII (1800).
Poésies de Mme la marquise d'Antremont. Amsterdam: N.p., 1770.

Bourette, Charlotte Reynier (1714–1784). ''La muse limonadière,'' as she was known, held a salon* for some thirty-six years at which she welcomed scholars and writers and at which plays were occasionally performed. Bourette composed verse celebrating important events and people, and even ordinary aspects of Parisian life—the last a subject for which she has been criticized. Some forty examples of her work are housed at the Bibliothèque Nationale. She published a collection of her works, *La Muse limonadière ou recueil d'ouvrages en vers et en prose* in 1785, and a one-act comedy, *La Coquette punie*, which was performed at the Théâtre Français.

Jennifer L. Gardner

BIBLIOGRAPHY

Primary Texts

La Coquette punie. Paris: J. F. Bastien, 1779.
La Muse limonadière ou recueil d'ouvrages en vers et prose. Paris: S. Jorry, 1755.

Secondary Texts

Grimm, Frederick Melchior. *Correspondance littéraire, philosophique et critique*. Ed. Maurice Tourneux. Paris: Garnier Frères, 1877. Vol. 3: 59.
Voltaire. ''Correspondance.'' *Oeuvres complètes*. Paris: Garnier Frères, 1880. Vol. 8: 537; Vol. 42: 129.

Bourgeois, Louise (also known as Boursier) (1563–1636), midwife and writer. Born at Faubourg, near Paris, to a middle-class family, she married the barber surgeon Martin Boursier. Adversity and the encouragement of her midwife led her to turn to midwifery to support her family. Well read in classical sources as well as current medical theories, with a natural aptitude for midwifery, she benefited from the teachings of her husband, who had studied many years under Ambroise Paré. She began to practice midwifery among the poor of Paris but soon gained recognition among ladies of quality and was called to attend members of the French court and the royal family. Her rapid success was frowned upon by other midwives, who resented competition from a "surgeon's wife."

Louise Boursier is remembered today for having delivered all Marie de Medici's* children as well as for being the first midwife to write a book on obstetrics, combining theory and the analysis of actual cases. First published in 1609, her *Observations diverses, sur la sterilité, perte de fruict, foecondité, accouchements, et maladies des femmes, et enfants nouveaux-naiz* enjoyed great popularity until the early part of the eighteenth century, with numerous editions and translations into Latin, English, German, and Dutch. The 1626 edition, considerably enlarged, includes the *Recit veritable de la naissance de messeigneurs et dames les enfans de France, avec les particularitez qui y ont esté*, which provides a vivid account of the birth of the future Louis XIII, and the *Instruction à ma Fille*, a manual on childbirth for the enlightenment of her daughter as well as midwives and mothers. Louise Boursier had gained wide renown as a midwife when, on June 5, 1627, the death in childbirth of Marie de Bourbon-Montpensier (sister-in-law to Louis XIII) tarnished her reputation forever. Although the autopsy report prepared by "ten learned physicians" did not implicate her directly, Louise Boursier felt compelled to write an *Apologie* in which she violently denounced the incompetence and lack of integrity of the signatories. This tragic incident put an end to her career. At the age of sixty-four she devoted herself to writing her recollections and her *Recueil des Secrets* (published in 1634). In the latter she outlines the treatment of various diseases, diseases of women, and cosmetic procedures to beautify the face and the hands, remove smallpox pits, and do away with warts, moles, and freckles.

Louise Boursier lived in a fascinating age, memorable for its fundamental discoveries in human anatomy and the anatomy of female genitalia, and its major advances in gynecology and obstetrics (although the genuine scientific revolution occurs in the last third of the seventeenth century with Regnier de Graff's description of the ovary [1672] and Ludwig von Hammen's, Antony van Leeuwenhoek's, and Johann Ham's studies of the configuration of the spermatozoa [1677]). Among the ablest practitioners of this period were Ambroise Paré (1510–1590) and Jacques Guillemeau (1550–1612); they are credited with the development of two important procedures, the podalic version and the caesarean section. Medical humanists participated in the general spread of knowledge made possible by printing, by providing complete editions, translations, and revisions of classical sources as well as medical manuals in the vernacular (e.g., Paré's *Livre de la generation*, 1575) in an attempt to dispel old concepts and erroneous beliefs (e.g., L. Joubert's *Erreurs populaires touchant la medecine . . .*, 1578) and put an end to the obsolete practices of ignorant and reckless midwives. The humanist campaign stands at the root of the inevitable clash between tradition and advancing science, theory and practice, which soon took the shape of a long and ferocious battle between the sexes (as evidenced by the 1627 conflict). It is commonly believed that Louis XIV inaugurated "the man-midwife trend" by calling the obstetrician Julien Clément to Mlle de La Vallière's childbed (1663). Yet the irruption of men into the art of midwifery, till then a monopoly of women, aroused much suspicion and controversy until the beginning of the eighteenth century.

Louise Boursier, no doubt, contributed to the advancement of French midwifery (as Jean Astruc notes in his *L'Art d'accoucher réduit à ses principes* [1766] and more recently midwife Françoise Olive in her introduction to the *Observations* [1992]) but, above all, she "served as an elevating influence among female midwives" (Cutter & Viets, 76–77) by advocating the necessity for midwives to acquire theoretical knowledge together with practical expertise. To Louise Boursier belongs the honor of dignifying the art of midwifery and inaugurating with her *Instruction à ma Fille* the female written tradition of passing down women's *secrets*. Her initiative was followed by Marguerite de la Marche, a reputable practitioner of the Hôtel-Dieu (the first school of midwifery, founded in the early 1600s), who published her *Instructions familières & tres faciles par questions et réponses, touchant toutes choses qu'une femme doit savoir* in 1677, and by the renowned Mme Le Boursier du Coudray, who authored *Abrégé de l'Art des accouchements* in 1754.

Colette H. Winn

BIBLIOGRAPHY

Primary Texts

Observations diverses, sur la sterilité, perte de fruict, foecondité, accouchements, et maladies des femmes, et enfants nouveaux naiz Amplement traittées, et heureusement practiquées par L. Bourgeois dite Boursier sage femme de la Roine Oeuvre util et necessaire à toutes personnes Dedié à la Royne. Paris: A. Saugrain, 1609. (Mazarine 38511)

Observations diverses, sur la sterilité, perte de fruict, foecondité, accouchements, et maladies des femmes, et enfants nouveaux naiz Amplement traictées et heureusement praticquées par L. Bourgeois dite Boursier sage femme de la Roine Oeuvre util et necessaire à toutes personnes Dedié à la Royne [followed by *Recit veritable de la naissance de Messeigneurs et Dames les enfans de France. Avec les particularitez qui y ont esté, & pouvoient estre remarquees* and *Instruction à ma Fille*]. Paris: Melchior Mondiere, 1626. (Arsenal 80. S. 10896)

Apologie de Louyse Bourgeois dite Bourcier sage femme de la Royne Mere du Roy, & de feu Madame. Contre le Rapport des Medecins. Paris: Melchior Mondiere, 1627. (Bibliotheque Mazarine 33569)

Recueil des Secrets, de Louyse Bourgeois dite Boursier, sage-femme de la Royne Mere du Roy, Auquel sont contenues ses plus rares experiences pour diverses maladies, principalement des femmes avec leurs embelissemens. Paris: Melchior Mondiere, 1635. (Bibliothèque de l'Arsenal 8. S. 10896)

Observations diverses, sur la sterilité, perte de fruict, foecondité, accouchements, et maladies des femmes, et enfants nouveaux naiz Amplement traictées et heureusement praticquées par L. Bourgeois dite Boursier sage femme de la Roine Oeuvre util et necessaire à toutes personnes Dedié à la Royne. Paris: Jean Dehoury, 1652 [the second book, the *Recit veritable*, and the third are published the same year by Henri Ruffin]. (St. Louis, Becker Library, 610.9 B776 1652)

Recueil des Secrets de Louyse Bourgeois dite Boursier, sage-femme de la Royne Mere du Roy . . . Paris: Jean Dehoury, 1653. (St. Louis, Becker Library, 610.9 B776 1653)

Observations diverses sur la stérilité, perte de fruits, fécondité, accouchements et maladies des femmes et enfants nouveau-nés, suivi de *Instruction à ma fille* [1652]. Preface by Françoise Olive. Paris: Côté-Femmes, 1992.

Secondary Texts

Berriot-Salvadore, Evelyne. *Un Corps, un destin—La femme dans la médecine de la Renaissance*. Paris: Champion, 1993.

Cutter, Irving S., and Henry R. Viets. *A Short History of Midwifery*. Philadelphia: W. B. Saunders, 1964.

Donnison, Jean. *Midwives and Medical Men: A History of Interprofessional Rivalries and Women's Rights*. London: Heinemann Educational, 1977.

Kalisch, P. A., M. Scobey, and B. J. Kalisch. "Louyse Bourgeois and the Emergence of Modern Midwifery." *Journal of Nurse Midwifery* 26, no. 4 (1981): 3–17.

Perkins, W. "Midwives versus Doctors: The Case of Louise Bourgeois." *Seventeenth Century* 3 (1988): 135–157.

———. "The Relationship Between Midwife and Client in the Works of Louise Bourgeois." *Seventeenth-Century French Studies* 11 (1989): 28–45.

Petrelli, R. L. "The Regulation of French Midwifery during the *ancien régime*." *Journal of the History of Medicine* 26 (1971): 276–292.

Winn, Colette H. "De sage (-) femme à sage (-) fille: Louise Boursier, *Instruction à ma Fille* (1626)." *Papers on French Seventeenth-Century Literature* 24, no. 46 (1997): 61–83.

Boursier, Louise. *See* Bourgeois, Louise.

Breast-feeding. The practice of breast-feeding is in itself an act that generates little controversy. But since feeding a child is a task that can be performed quite efficiently by another woman (a wet-nurse) or by substituting alternative foods, it is one of the oldest examples of delegation of maternal duties. For centuries, mothers have been the target of discourses, often not their own, that promote either maternal breast-feeding or wet-nursing.

Discussions of this issue reached a peak during the Enlightenment*, when the *philosophes* joined the Church and physicians in advocating maternal nursing, a practice that fitted well with the new domestic definition of women. Jean-Jacques Rousseau was the most articulate of the maternal breast-feeding advocates, and, for a few years following the publication of his *Emile* (1762), a nursing renewal took place among educated women. But the use of wet-nurses continued and took such proportions that the city of Paris felt it necessary to regulate it. Wet-nursing disappeared only after World War I*, when pasteurized cow's milk became widely available and replaced breast-feeding in general. So, in effect, maternal nursing has never been a widespread practice in France.

It is easy to understand why all campaigns failed to establish the practice of maternal breast-feeding: whereas the moral and health-related arguments in its favor were admirable, none addressed the financial need for a family to resort to the use of wet-nursing. A working-class mother's wages surpassed the fee paid to a wet-nurse, which explains why working-class families made up the bulk of the wet-nurse clientele.

Within the intimate setting of the nuclear family*, mothers were caught in a bind: if they did not nurse the child, they were bad mothers; it they did, the husband was seen as unjustly deprived of his sexual rights (physicians and the Church prescribed abstinence during lactation). Such anxiety is already apparent in the novels written in the few years after the publication of *Emile*. One of Isabelle de Charrière's* heroines summarizes why Rousseau's rhetoric failed to speak *to* rather than *about* mothers: "Of me, of my health, of my pleasure, not a word: the only concern was this child that did not yet exist" (*Letters of Mistress Henley Published by Her Friend.* New York: MLA Texts and Translation, 1993, 38). As in other practices related to both families and children, mothers were burdened with a decision that in effect was not entirely theirs and with arguments not their own.

Valérie Lastinger

BIBLIOGRAPHY

Secondary Texts

Fox-Genovese, Elizabeth. "Women and Work." In *French Women and the Age of Enlightenment.* Ed. Samia Spencer. Bloomington: Indiana University Press, 1984. 111–127.

Knibiehler, Yvonne, and Catherine Fouquet. *L'Histoire des mères du moyen-âge à nos jours.* Paris: Montalba, 1981.

Sussman, George D. *Selling Mother's Milk: The Wet-Nursing Business in France, 1715–1914.* Urbana: University of Illinois Press, 1982.

Brégy (or Brégis), Charlotte Saumaise de Chazan, comtesse de (1619–1693). One of the more influential *précieuses*, she spent most of her life in the service of Queen Anne d'Autriche, eventually attaining the rank of *dame d'honneur* and confidante. In 1637 she married the comte de Brégy, to whom she had already borne a daughter. She used her court connections to launch her husband in a diplomatic career. The marriage* was not happy, due primarily to her frustration with her numerous pregnancies. She obtained a financial separation in 1651, and, after a long series of lawsuits, a definitive separation. To her protectress, however, she remained staunchly loyal, even refusing an offer to join the entourage of Queen Christina of Sweden. In 1666 and 1667 she published collections of her letters, poems, and portraits, including an especially popular set of *questions d'amour*. Her wit, both oral and written, made her a favorite in literary circles and earned her the praise of such leading male writers as Benserade and Quinault. She was apparently the first to object openly to the social obligation placed upon women to marry and bear children. She complained that repeated pregnancies could ruin the looks of a beautiful woman (as happened to her), while interfering with cultivation of intellectual pursuits and with a woman's sense of self-worth. It is believed that Molière used her as the model for the foolish Bélise in *Les Femmes savantes*, perhaps because her salon* included several of his leading enemies.

Perry Gethner

BIBLIOGRAPHY

Secondary Text

Backer, Dorothy. *Precious Women*. New York: Basic Books, 1974.

Bretagne, Anne de (1476–1514). Duchess of Brittany, queen, regent, writer. Although her fortune was certainly a factor in both of her marriages*, Anne de Bretagne retained a certain amount of power over both her fortune and her province. She served as queen while Charles VIII was in Naples, and Louis XII allowed her to retain responsibility for governing and protecting Brittany. Brantôme asserts in his *Vies des dames illustres* that she was the first queen to keep a court of women, including many of the most prominent noblemen's daughters, thus initiating one of the earliest "schools" for noblewomen. This interest in women's education* must in part stem from her experience in the court of Anne de Beaujeu (1441–1552). Beaujeu served as regent during the minority of her brother (Charles VIII), and her interest in noblewomen's education is evidenced by *L'Enseignement des filles* (1503/4?), which she wrote for her daughter. Both Anne de Bretagne and Louise de Savoie*, another powerful noblewoman of the same generation, continued this tradition of education for women at court.

Velvet Pearson

BIBLIOGRAPHY

Secondary Text

Gabory, Emile. *Anne de Bretagne*. Paris: Plon, 1941.

Brion, Hélène (1882–1962). Hélène Brion was an elementary schoolteacher and a feminist and socialist activist. Well known both during the Belle Epoque and after World War I* for her activities in labor organizations and women's suffrage groups, she was imprisoned for three years (1918–1921) for speaking publicly against the war. Simultaneously aligned with socialist and feminist groups, she recognized the inequities that women faced in mainstream political organizations, gave speeches on this topic, and wrote the political brochure "La Voie feministe" (1916). At the end of her life, Brion wrote the 5,000-entry "Encyclopédie féministe," which remains unpublished and can be consulted at the Marguerite Durand Library* in Paris.

Juliette M. Rogers

BIBLIOGRAPHY

Primary Texts

La Voie féministe. 1916. Ed. Huguette Bouchardeau. Paris: Syros, 1978.
"Encyclopédie féministe." Manuscript, Marguerite Durand Library, Paris.

Brisac, Geneviève (1951–). Novelist, journalist, translator, and author of children's stories. Brisac's tragicomic novels recount the lonely, often cruel, childhood of young girls and adolescents. The adolescents' eating disorders and their relationships with their mothers form the main themes of Brisac's work. Feeling persecuted and abandoned, sisters join forces in a fierce struggle against the various types of disorder that threaten their lives—death, war, adults, madness, the Holocaust*. Their fight to survive and to control their lives takes a variety of forms and is most strikingly represented by the protagonist's anorexia in *Les Filles* (1987) and *Petite* (1994). Brisac's unsentimental chronicle of the stages of the illness and the ensuing treatment and cure constitutes a powerful picture of family relations and of the psychology of the female adolescent. Brisac is also the author of an essay on the American writer Flannery O'Connor, and her most recent novel, *Week-end de chasse à la mère* (1996), presents an ironic account of the relationship between a divorced mother and her young son.

Susan Ireland

BIBLIOGRAPHY

Primary Texts

Les Filles. Paris: Gallimard, 1987.
Madame Placard. Paris: Gallimard, 1989.
Loin du Paradis, Flannery O'Connor. Paris: Gallimard, 1991.
Petite. Paris: L'Olivier, 1994.
Week-end de chasse à la mère. Paris: L'Olivier, 1996.

Brohon, Jacqueline-Aimée (1737?–1778). Brohon achieved early literary success: her first novel*, *Les Amans philosophes* (1755), was published when she was barely eighteen, followed soon after by *Les Graces de l'ingénuité* in *Le Mercure de France* (1756), later adapted as a play. Brohon then apparently underwent a religious conversion and produced mystical works that were published posthumously: *Instructions édifiantes sur le jeûne de Jésus-Christ au désert* (1791) and *Réflexions édifiantes* (1791). These works, meditations on the supremacy of heart over reason, have been compared to those of Swedenborg. Her religious visions are at times prophetic, describing a future when victims would come to power; this suggests why the later works enjoyed a resurgence of popularity in 1790–1793, when they were read as politically meaningful by some Jacobins. Brohon's mysticism has not yet been adequately situated in relation to the tradition of European female mystics from the Middle Ages onward.

Sally O'Driscoll

BIBLIOGRAPHY

Primary Texts

Les Amans philosophes, ou le triomphe de la raison. Amsterdam: Hochereau l'aîné, 1755.
Les Graces de l'ingénuité. In *Le Mercure de France,* February 1756.
Instructions édifiantes sur le jeûne de Jésus-Christ au désert. Paris: Didot l'aîné, 1791;
      Paris: Mme. Lesclapart, 1791.
Réflexions édifiantes. Paris: Didot l'aîné, 1791.

Secondary Texts

Briquet, Fortunée B. *Dictionnaire historique, littéraire, et bibliographique des françaises.*
      Paris: Gille, 1804.
La Porte, Joseph de. *Histoire littéraire des femmes françaises.* Paris: Lacombe, 1769.
Viatte, Auguste. "Une Visionnaire au siècle de Jean-Jacques." *Revue des questions his-*
      toriques 98 (1923): 336–344.

Buffet, Marguerite (seventeenth century). Nothing is known of her life. In 1668 she published *Nouvelles Observations sur la langue française, avec les Eloges des illustres scavantes, tant anciennes que modernes.* In the preface she argues that women are, by nature at least, men's equals, if not their superiors. For Buffet, power for women lies in being able to speak or write well. The first half of this hybrid text is a French grammar addressed primarily to women. The ultimate arbiters of correct usage are the members of polite society, male and female, as opposed to the all-male French Academy. The second half is a portrait gallery of illustrious women past and present, chosen for their linguistic excellence. Buffet includes women who published their writings, as well as those whose works circulated in manuscript, and those known for their conversational brilliance. She extends the definition of *savante* to include women who speak or write well, not simply those who were learned in the traditional sense of the term. Little has been written about her.

Faith E. Beasley

BIBLIOGRAPHY

Secondary Texts

DeJean, Joan. *Tender Geographies.* New York: Columbia University Press, 1991.
Reiss, Timothy. *The Meaning of Literature.* Ithaca, NY: Cornell University Press, 1992.
Timmermans, Linda. *L'Accès des femmes à la culture (1598–1715).* Paris: Nizet, 1993.

C

Calages, Marie Pech (or Puech) de (1630–1661). Writer. Born in the region of Ancenis, the Pech family was forced to move to the Languedoc as the result of a duel in which her father fought. As a young woman she showed a talent for poetry* and submitted a number of entries to the Jeux Floraux of Toulouse, for which she won several prizes. In 1649 she married Henri de Calages, an educated person who possessed a taste for learning and a substantial library. The couple shared an interest in writing, and both composed poetry, Henri's favorite subject being the joys of family life, while the only surviving work of Marie is the more public, epic poem *Judith, ou la Délivrance de Béthulie, poème saint*, published in 1660 to honor the new queen of France, Marie-Thérèse. Both Louis XIV and his bride were so impressed with Calages's work that they accorded her a pension and named Calages, who was pregnant at the time, as wet-nurse of their first child. Although there is no evidence that Calages knew the poem *Imitation de la victoire de Judich* (1594) by Gabrielle de Coignard*, she does acknowledge her indebtedness to Du Bartas's *Judit* (1574). She continued to work through her pregnancy, revising *Judith* and composing new work, including a poem on the presentation of the Virgin in the Temple; both the revision and the new work are lost. Marie died in childbirth on October 8, 1661.

Hannah Fournier

BIBLIOGRAPHY

Primary Text

Judith, ou la Délivrance de Béthulie, poème saint dédié à la Reyne par Mademoiselle de Calages. Toulouse: Par Arnaud Colomiez, 1660.

Secondary Texts

Lahondès, J. de. "Une Poétesse épique toulousaine." *Revue des Pyrénées* 15 (1903): 583–603.

Sayce, R. A. *The French Biblical Epic in the Seventeenth Century.* Oxford: Clarendon
    Press, 1955.

Campan, Jeanne Louise Henriette Genest (1752–1822). Best known for her
memoirs* of Marie-Antoinette* and Old Regime France, Mme Campan was a
leader in early nineteenth-century women's education*. Born into a wealthy
family, she received an excellent education in literature, music, and languages,
and was known for her impeccable diction. At age fifteen she became a reader/
tutor to the daughters of Louis XV, and in 1770 she joined Marie-Antoinette's
staff.

According to her memoirs, her relationship with the queen was intimate, in
spite of her more liberal views on politics and education. While Campan's relationship with the crown did not bring her personal injury during the riots of
1792, her house was burned and she was ruined. After the Jacobins were removed from power, Campan decided to spend the last of her resources to open
an institution for the education of girls at St. Germain, where the daughters of
James Monroe, Thomas Pinckney, and Joséphine de Beauharnais were enrolled.
After the creation of the Legion of Honor by Napoleon, Campan headed the
Imperial School at Ecouen, which was designed according to the Emperor's
wishes.

A product of the mid-eighteenth century, Campan had long criticized convent* education and the sequestering of young elite daughters. She preferred
instead a more liberal education less led by formula. Under Napoleon's patronage, however, she partially conformed to his wishes concerning female education, that is, that curricula be restricted to practical domestic activities, with
some attention to fine arts. Campan, however, went beyond Napoleonic dictates,
adding domestic economy and foreign languages, reducing religious observance,
and including male instructors on her teaching staff. Her letters to Napoleon's
step-daughter Hortense, published after her death in 1834, are the best statement
of her educational policy.

Susan P. Conner

BIBLIOGRAPHY

Primary Texts

Lettres de deux jeunes amies. Paris: N.p., 1811.
Mémoires sur la vie privée de Marie-Antoinette, reine de France et de Navarre. Paris:
    Baudouin frères, 1823.
De L'Education. Paris: Baudouin frères, 1824.
Correspondance inédite de Madame Campan avec la Reine Hortense. Paris: Levasseur,
    1835.

Secondary Texts

Marsangy, Bonneville de. *Madame Campan à Ecouen.* Paris: H. Champion, 1879.
Scott, Barbara. "Madame Campan, 1752–1822." *History Today* 23 (October 1973): 683–
    690.

Cardinal, Marie (1929–). Born in Algiers to a French colonial family, Cardinal was forced to leave the country soon after the outbreak of the Algerian War. Algeria is present in many of Cardinal's texts, as she attempts to come to terms with her exilic experience and to reconcile her French and Algerian origins. She currently divides her time between Montreal and southern France.

Throughout her works, Cardinal addresses issues of race, class, and gender-based discrimination. Her preface to *Nous, Noirs Américains évadés du ghetto* . . . (1978), for example, demonstrates her support for the anti-racist struggle of African Americans. Early in her career, Cardinal worked with feminist lawyer and activist Gisèle Halimi*, turning Halimi's reflections on women's reproductive rights into *La Cause des femmes* (1973). Another collaborative work, consisting of a series of interviews with writer Annie Leclerc* (*Autrement Dit*, 1977), exemplifies Cardinal's commitment to critically examining such significant issues for women as the complexities of the mother-daughter relationship, the dangers of sexual stereotypes that reduce women to objects, and the crucial role of language in the construction of female identity. These themes—along with a critique of the repressive institutions of church and state—appear in *Les Mots pour le dire* (1975), a fictionalized rendering of the author's descent into madness and her subsequent rebirth through psychoanalytic treatment.

Later texts illustrate Cardinal's use of revisionist mythmaking strategies to reconceptualize marginalized female figures. In *Le Passé empiété*, Cardinal depicts a subversive protagonist who recreates the story of Clytemnestra—the mythological figure assassinated by her son for having killed her husband—and inscribes her within a framework that emphasizes female bonding and the essential function of storytelling. Similarly, in her translation* of Euripides's *Medea* (*La Médée d'Euripide*, 1987), Cardinal seeks to resituate the extraneous figure of Medea, accused of infanticide, by theorizing a connection between her status as outsider and her violent impulses. All of Cardinal's texts question the socio-political construction of woman in a patriarchal society and attest to her continuing desire to explore the revolutionary implications of writing women into myth* and history.

Patrice J. Proulx

BIBLIOGRAPHY

Primary Texts

Les Mots pour le dire. Paris: Editions Grasset et Fasquelle, 1975.
Autrement dit. Paris: Editions Grasset et Fasquelle, 1977.
Preface to *Nous, Noirs Américains évadés du ghetto.* . . . by Jean McNair et al. Paris: Seuil, 1978.
Au Pays de mes racines. Paris: Editions Grasset et Fasquelle, 1980.
Le Passé empiété. Paris: Editions Grasset et Fasquelle, 1983.
La Médée d'Euripide. Paris: Editions Grasset et Fasquelle, 1987.
Cardinal, Marie, and Gisèle Halimi. *La Cause des femmes.* Paris: Editions Grasset et Fasquelle, 1973.

Secondary Texts

Donadey, Anne. "Répétition, maternité, et transgression dans trois oeuvres de Marie
    Cardinal." *French Review* 65, no. 4 (March 1992): 567–577.
Durham, Carolyn. *The Contexture of Feminism: Marie Cardinal and Multicultural Diver-
    sity.* Urbana: University of Illinois Press, 1992.
Hall, Colette. *Marie Cardinal.* Amsterdam: Rodopi, 1994.
Lionnet, Françoise. "Métissage, Emancipation and Female Textuality in Two Franco-
    phone Creole Writers." In *Life/Lines: Theorizing Women's Autobiography.* Ed.
    Bella Brodzki and Celeste Schenck. Ithaca: Cornell University Press, 1988.
Proulx, Patrice J. "Revision and Revolution: Writing Women into Myth and History."
    Women in French Studies 3 (Fall 1995): 100–111.

Caro, Pauline (1835–1901). Little has been written about this prolific author
who published twelve novels* and a book of short stories* between 1865 and
1901. She was married to Académie Française member Elme-Marie Caro (1826–
1887), whose scholarly production focused on a critique of positivism. While
he wrote laudatory articles on Mme de Staël*, Louise Ackermann*, and George
Sand*, Elme-Marie never mentioned the works of his own wife. Nor did Pauline
attach an author's preface or introduction to any of her writings. In 1890 Marius
Topin included Caro among the four female and twenty male novelists examined
in his *Romanciers contemporains*, deeming Caro's novels praiseworthy for their
"héroïsme sublime de l'immolation" (319). Given the silence surrounding Caro
the person, it is perhaps not surprising that Topin misread what Caro the author
was communicating via her prose, namely, that when women become the subject
of their own textual production, apparent self-obliteration is transformed into
self-expression. The psychological realism characterizing Caro's oeuvre provides a space for the frank, often naturalist description of woman's mistreatment
at the hands of those male figures to whom she is legally bound. But Caro also
writes of the happiness woman might attain once her status as desiring subject
is acknowledged. For Caro, this happiness is achieved not through marriage*,
as the norms of society would have it, but through true love for which marriage
is often not the vehicle.

Michelle Chilcoat

BIBLIOGRAPHY

Primary Texts

Le Péché de Madeleine. In *Revue des Deux Mondes* (15 March 1864).
Flamen. Paris: Lévy, 1866.
Histoire de Souci. Paris: Lévy, 1868.
Les Nouvelles amours de Hermann et Dorothée. In *Revue des Deux Mondes* (15 Novem-
    ber 1870).
La Fausse Route. Paris: Plon, 1890.
Amour de jeune fille. Paris: Lévy, 1891.
Fruits amers. Paris: Lévy, 1892.
Après la moisson. In *Revue Parisienne* 3 (1894): 136–160.

Les Lendemains. Paris: Lévy, 1895.
Pas à pas. Paris: Lévy, 1898.
Aimer, c'est vaincre. Paris: Hachette, 1900.

Secondary Text

Topin, Marius. "Mme Benzton. Mme Caro. Mme Craven." In *Romanciers contemporains*. Paris: Librairie Académique, 1890. 301–319.

Carpe diem. The *carpe diem* ("pluck the day") motif, whose onomastic origins can be traced to Horace, permeates not only classical Greek and Latin poetry* but also lyric poetry from fifteenth-century Italy to sixteenth-century Spain to seventeenth-century England. Revealing an obsession with the passage of time, the *carpe diem* motif reaches its apogee in early modern France, not only in the celebrated Pléiade poets, but also in Marot, Scève, Saint-Gelais, Des Périers, and Pasquier. As both topos and literary technique, the *carpe diem* motif provides a veritable gold mine for examining questions of gender and what might be called "temporal ideology." Women figure in the motif in two important ways: first, as addressees of male poets' verses, and second, as writers formulating their own versions of this temporal topos.

Construed traditionally as a compliment and an invitation, and more recently as an instrument of seduction, *carpe diem* has received much critical mention, but little sustained attention. Perhaps this comparative dearth of scholarly scrutiny results from what appears to be a too obvious functioning of the literary motif. Even the most casual reader notes that in *carpe diem* poems the (older) male poet—with distinctly erotic designs—exhorts the (younger) female addressee to take advantage of the present moment. Should she resist his plea to love him while the time is ripe, the poet warns, her beauty will fade (like that of an ephemeral rose) without her ever having contributed it to a good cause (such as himself). But what is the nature of this tactic? How does it function, both rhetorically and psychologically? While at first glance one might see in these poems an Epicurean exhortation to "gather [ye] rosebuds while ye may," other rhetorical elements in the poems often obfuscate that univocal reading, revealing a complex dynamic between speaker and addressee.

Consider Ronsard's "Mignonne, allons voir si la rose" (1550), "Jeune beauté, mais trop outrecuidée" (1550), and "Je vous envoye un bouquet que ma main" (1555). In this prototypical form of the motif, the image of the withered rose suggests the declining, aging body of the addressee after she has rejected the poet's advances (representing the menacing future), just as the budding, fresh rose evokes the presently glowing, youthful body of the addressee (incarnating the Epicurean present). Aging, depicted as more terrible than death, is a fate from which the poet himself is excluded within the space of the poems. Since elsewhere Ronsard betrays his anxiety about the decline of his own body ("Quand je suis vingt ou trente mois" [1555], "Celuy qui est mort aujourdhuy" [1556], and "Voicy le temps, Hurault, qui joyeux nous convie" [1578]), the *carpe diem* poems appear to constitute a projection of the poet's own fear of aging onto the Other, incarnated textually in the female body.

The *carpe diem* motif assumes an even more vituperative tone in Ronsard's *Sonnets pour Hélène* (1578), where the threat of the addressee's physical deterioration becomes more explicit. In "Je ne veux point la mort de celle qui arreste," the poet vengefully wishes not death but gray hair and aging upon his spurning lady. In "Quand vous serez bien vieille," the dead poet is paradoxically depicted as more alive (his *corpus* still has the ability to affect) than the aging Hélène (who slowly winds down her life at the spinning wheel). Ronsard thereby deftly reverses their life cycles. Thus subtending the didactic message of these *carpe diem* poems urging the addressee to "pluck the roses of life" is the male poet's desire to gain mastery over both time (through his projections into the future) and the female body (through his ability to cause its premature aging). The poems develop on an if/then axis, unfolding in a mercilessly linear time frame.

At the pinnacle of the *carpe diem* motif's popularity, a number of women poets proffer their distinct visions of this temporal topos, initiating a kind of poetic dialogue with male colleagues. In a series of forty-five poems entitled "Responses" in her *Secondes Oeuvres* (1583), Catherine des Roches* formulates both philosophical and psychological objections to the temporal ideology inherent in the *carpe diem* motif, often within the context of her rejection of the rhetorical aim of that motif (the woman's seduction). She continually subverts the power both of bodily deterioration itself and of the poets who use it as a threat by minimizing the importance of physical beauty in comparison with the nobler qualities of the soul and of "vertu," exemplified, as evidenced in her "Dialogue d'Iris et Pasithée," by the practices of reading and writing.

While Catherine des Roches explicitly repudiates the *carpe diem* motif, other sixteenth-century women poets more implicitly counter the temporal ideology underlying the topos. Pernette du Guillet's* *Rymes* (1545) reveal a radically different attitude toward time from that of her editor Antoine Du Moulin and of her fellow poet Maurice Scève. Nowhere in her work does a hint of anxiety about the inexorable passage of time surface, and she never uses the words "immortalité" or "éternité." An analysis of Pernettian temporal vocabulary (the notions of "contentement durable" and the search for fulfillment in the present) evinces the complete absence of anxiety about the future and the poet's insistence upon the present moment. Louise Labé's* *Oeuvres* (1555) also privilege a kind of circular temporality, as evidenced in both the preface and the sonnets. As the poet notes in her preface, by reading one's own past writing, one rediscovers previous thoughts while simultaneously bringing new judgments to them. Indeed, for Labé the pleasures of writing reside not in the promise of poetic immortality, but in the enjoyment of the present fused with the past.

While it is tempting to see in the women poets' embrace of the present a circular notion of time, anatomically female in its cyclical repetition as distinguished from male poets' phallic, linear projections, such a division would be deceptively tidy. Male poets of course depict circular or lyric time, replete with images of Ixion, wheels, and rings (as seen especially in Tyard's Neoplatonic verses), and female poets are not entirely immune to the notion of poetic immortality (as Catherine des Roches's work illustrates). Yet ultimately, the ubiquity of the *carpe diem* motif in male poets and the concomitant rejection or avoidance of it by female poets suggest that sins of omission in traditional analyses of the motif have led to errors of commission. An examination of women poets' responses to *carpe diem* forces us to rethink our reading of the motif and expands our understanding of both gender and temporal ideology in early modern France.

Catherine Yandell

BIBLIOGRAPHY

Primary Texts

Des Roches, Catherine. *Oeuvres*. 1579. Ed. Anne R. Larsen. Geneva: Droz, 1993.
――――. *Les Secondes Oeuvres*. Poitiers: Nicolas Courtoys, 1583.
Du Guillet, Pernette. *Rymes*. 1545. Ed. Victor Graham. Geneva: Droz, 1968.
Labé, Louise. *Oeuvres complètes*. 1555. Ed. François Rigolot. Paris: Flammarion, 1986.
Ronsard, Pierre de. *Oeuvres complètes*. 1550–1584. Ed. Jean Céard, Daniel Ménager, and Michel Simonin. Paris: Gallimard, 1993.
Tyard, Pontus de. *Erreurs amoureuses*. 1549. Ed. John McClellan. Geneva: Droz, 1967.

Secondary Texts

Berg, Elizabeth. "Iconoclastic Moments: Reading the *Sonnets for Helene*, Writing the Portuguese Letters." In *The Poetics of Gender*. Ed. Nancy K. Miller. New York: Columbia University Press, 1986. 208–221.
Jones, Ann Rosalind. *The Currency of Eros: Women's Love Lyric in Europe, 1540–1620*. Bloomington: Indiana University Press, 1990.
Lesko Baker, Deborah. "Entering the Literary Stage: The Epistre à Mlle Clemence de Bourges lyonnaise." In *The Subject of Desire: Poetics and Intersubjectivity in the Works of Louise Labé*. Lafayette: Purdue University Press, 1997.
Mathieu-Castellani, Gisèle. "Les Marques du féminin dans la parole amoureuse de Louise Labé." In *Louise Labé: Les voix du lyrisme*. Ed. Guy Demerson. Paris: Editions du CNRS, 1990. 189–205.
Read, Kirk. "Louise Labé in Search of Time Past: Prefatory Strategies and Rhetorical Transformations." *Critical Matrix* 5 (1990): 63–86.
Weber, Henri. *La Création poétique au seizième siècle en France*. Paris: Nizet, 1955. 333–356.
Yandell, Cathy. "Carpe Diem, Poetic Immortality, and the Gendered Ideology of Time." In *Renaissance Women Writers: French Texts/American Contexts*. Ed. Anne R. Larsen and Colette H. Winn. Detroit: Wayne State University Press, 1994. 115–129.

Castelloza (second half of twelfth century? first half of thirteenth century?). According to the *vida* (biography) included in a number of thirteenth-century song manuscripts, Castelloza was a noblewoman from Auvergne, the wife of

Turc de Mairon, who loved Arman de Breon and sang of him in her songs. Intertextual evidence provided by her three (possibly four) extant love songs indicates that she had poetic relations with the court of Dalfin d'Alvernha, Count of Clermont (c. 1155–1235). An envoi at the end of one song suggests that she maintained a poetic exchange with another *trobairitz** (woman troubadour), Almuc de Castelnou. Although the conventional portrait offered in the *vida* describes her as beautiful, learned, and very happy, the persona she develops in her songs is consistently in the mode of suffering lover who finds comfort only in memories, words, and dreams. Experimenting with different roles, she sets up a series of double reversals within the normally reversed hierarchy of the humble troubadour lover and his superior lady. Assuming the subject position despite the criticism she anticipates from those who do not expect a lady to speak of love, Castelloza evokes and rejects the image of the haughty *domna* (lady), projecting it instead on her cruel beloved. Like the troubadour lover, she maintains her loyalty and faithfulness in love, threatens death if her beloved fails to respond, and expects only joy from him. The subordinate position she thus assumes replicates the subordination of women in medieval society but projects it through the typical stance of the poet lover, empowered by poetry and song.

Matilda Tomaryn Bruckner

BIBLIOGRAPHY

Primary Texts

Bruckner, Matilda Tomaryn, Laurie Shepard, and Sarah White, eds. *Songs of the Women Troubadours*. New York: Garland, 1995.

Secondary Texts

Bossy, Michel-André, and Nancy Jones. ''Gender and Compilational Patterns in Troubadour Lyric: The Case of Manuscript N.'' *French Forum* 21 (1996): 261–280.
Bruckner, Matilda Tomaryn. ''Na Castelloza, Troibaritz, and Troubadour Lyric.'' *Romance Notes* 25, no. 3 (1985): 239–253.
Dronke, Peter. ''The Provençal Trobairitz Castelloza,'' In *Medieval Women Writers*. Ed. Katharina Wilson. Athens: University of Georgia Press, 1984. 131–152.
Gaunt, Simon. *Gender and Genre in Medieval French Literature*. Cambridge: Cambridge University Press, 1993. 158–179.

Caumont de La Force. *See* La Force, Charlotte-Rose Caumont de.

Caylus, Marthe-Marguerite de Villette de Murcay, marquise de (1673–1729). In her *Souvenirs*, she presents an eyewitness account of the game of intrigue and passion played by the courtiers, princes, and mistresses surrounding Louis XIV. Her contemporaries described her as a woman of rare beauty, charm, intelligence, and wit. Born into a Protestant family, she was a great-granddaughter of the poet Théodore Agrippa d'Aubigné and a niece of Madame de Maintenon* who took her away from home at an early age in order to convert her to Catholicism. She was brought up at court and given a superior education*. At thirteen, she married an inadequate husband, the drunkard comte de Caylus, and entered into a lifelong relationship with the duc de Villeroi. Racine wrote the prologue to *Esther* for her to recite. She was twice exiled from court—once as punishment for a mocking remark, and once for her relationship with Villeroi—but was readmitted in order to prevent her from falling under Jansenist influence. The king found her too outspoken, but she had considerable influence because of her closeness to her aunt. At the urging of the elder of her two sons, she dictated the *Souvenirs* toward the end of her life. They were published by Voltaire as one of the most faithful descriptions of the inner life of the court. Written with classical restraint and clarity, the *Souvenirs* emphasizes the role of women, and the pain and humiliation they pay for their power. Her affectionate letters to Mme de Maintenon and to her son reveal details of life at court, the channels of influence, and the reversals that followed the death of Louis XIV.

Pauline Kra

BIBLIOGRAPHY

Primary Texts

Souvenirs de Madame de Caylus. Amsterdam: L. J. Robert, 1779.
Souvenirs et correspondance de Madame de Caylus. Ed. Emile Raunié. Paris: G. Charpentier, 1881.

Secondary Texts

Lettres de Madame de Maintenon. Maestricht: J.-E. Dufour, 1789. Vol. 6.
Saint-Simon. *Mémoires.* Paris: Gallimard, 1983–1988. Vol. 2 and passim.

Cerf, Muriel (1950–). Cerf published her first autobiographical travel novel, *L'Antivoyage*, at the age of twenty-four. She has since written more than a dozen books in which she explores women's sexual freedom and desires. She portrays contemporary *femmes fatales* and *ingénues libertines* who toy with men while attempting to redefine their own identity and to heal painful emotional wounds. Her female protagonists, some of whom recur in several novels, are always resourceful and witty. Interested in new technology, Cerf has her own Web site where she displays excerpts—in both English and French—from her latest works.

Joëlle Vitiello

BIBLIOGRAPHY

Primary Texts

L'Antivoyage. Paris: Mercure de France, 1974.
Le Diable vert. Paris: Mercure de France, 1975.
Les Rois et les voleurs. Paris: Mercure de France, 1975.
Hiéroglyphes de nos fins dernières. Paris: Mercure de France, 1977.
Le Lignage du serpent. Paris: Mercure de France, 1978.
Les Seigneurs du Ponant. Paris: Mercure de France, 1979.

Amérindiennes. Paris: Stock, 1979.
Une Passion. Paris: J.-C. Lattès, 1981.
Maria Tiefenthaler. Paris: Albin Michel, 1982.
Une Pâle Beauté. Paris: Albin Michel, 1984.
Julia M. ou le premier regard. Paris: Laffont, 1991.
Une Rêverie florentine. Paris: Laffont, 1991.

Certain, Marie-Françoise (?–?). Little is known of this poet. Her name appears on a collection of *Nouvelles Poésies ou Diverses pièces choisies tant en vers qu'en prose*, dated 1665. There is also an opuscule, printed separately as an entertainment perhaps to be performed as a ballet, entitled *L'Elève d'Erato, Idille mise en musique* (n.d.). In it, a choir of Muses invites authors and musicians to draw near to Apollo in a laurel grove. Diana, the victorious huntress, is the heroine of this delicate item. She is against love, the domain of the Muse Erato, and calls it the tyrant of hearts and ravisher of freedom's empire. Curiously, her brother Apollo agrees with her, while the Muses, especially Calliope, Euterpe, Melpomene, and Thalia, admire her. If anything, this short piece, in elevating Diana above her brother, even above the Muses, shows a *précieux* partisanship, and a mistrust of love that is of the period.

Dorothy Backer

BIBLIOGRAPHY

Secondary Text

Jal, A. *Dictionnaire critique de biographie et d'histoire*. Paris: H. Plon, 1867.

Chaix, Marie (1942–). Chaix's life was indelibly marked by her father's collaboration with the Vichy régime during World War II*, recounted in *Les Lauriers du lac de Constance: Chronique d'une collaboration* (1974). This was followed by three other autobiographical novels: *Les Silences ou la Vie d'une femme* (1976), *L'Age du tendre* (1979), and *Juliette, chemin des Cérisiers* (1985), which tells the stories of her mother and of the Chaix family's lifelong servant Juliette. The most remarkable feature of Chaix's novels is how she consistently situates her protagonists within a genealogy of women. While this genealogy traces with devastating clarity the destructive effects of the legacy of perceived female difference, inferiority, and submission that women pass down unquestioned from generation to generation, it nonetheless also serves as homage to the women unable to break out of this heritage, women strongly influenced by their times, who cared for and shaped their children in the only way they knew how.

Katherine Stephenson

BIBLIOGRAPHY

Primary Texts

Les Lauriers du lac de Constance: Chronique d'une collaboration. Paris: Seuil, 1974.
Les Silences ou la Vie d'une femme. Paris: Seuil, 1976.

L'Age du tendre. Paris: Seuil, 1979.
Le Salon des anges. Paris: Seuil, 1982.
Juliette, Chemin des cérisiers. Paris: Seuil, 1985.
Barbara. Paris: Calmann-Lévy, 1986.
Un 21 Avril à New York: Journal 1980–1982. Paris: Seuil, 1986.
Le Fils de Marthe. Paris: Calmann-Lévy, 1990.

Secondary Text

Guers-Villate, Yvonne. "Two Responses to a Mother's Death: Simone de Beauvoir's *Une Mort très douce* and Marie Chaix's *Les Silences ou la Vie d'une femme.*" *West Virginia University Philological Papers* 31 (1986): 111–115.

Chalem, Denise (1952–). Actress and playwright. Born in Egypt of Jewish ancestry, Chalem explores the roots of female identity in relation to the mother. In her first play, *A cinquante ans elle découvrait la mer,* the daughter as writer—played by Chalem—confronts the death of her mother. Through the creative process of pinning pages on a clothesline, the daughter reconstructs memories of time spent with her mother, from arguments over marriage* to tender moments at Hanukkah. Speaking alternately to herself and to her absent mother, the daughter intermingles feelings of grief, guilt, anger, and love as she relives scenes involving her mother.

Jan Berkowitz Gross

BIBLIOGRAPHY

Primary Texts

A cinquante ans elle découvrait la mer. Paris: Actes Sud-Papiers, 1985.
Selon toute ressemblance. Paris: Actes Sud-Papiers, 1986.
Couki et Louki sont sur un bateau. Paris: Actes Sud-Papiers, 1987.

Secondary Text

Lamar, Celita. "Mothers and Daughters." In *Our Voices, Ourselves.* New York: Peter Lang, 1991. 25–47.

Chansons de geste. The *chansons de geste,* epic poems which were first performed orally and then written down from the end of the eleventh century through the fourteenth, celebrated the heroic deeds of male figures as they fought for their king and/or God. Since, as a late twelfth-century romance of Chrétien de Troyes observes, "Fame ne set porter escu / Ne ne set de lance ferir" (Woman does not know how to carry a shield / Or strike with a lance) (*Le Chevalier au lion.* Ed. D. Hult, 2098–2099), it is not surprising that women rarely play more than a marginal role in French epic cycles—those of the Emperor Charles, William, and the rebel barons—through the end of the twelfth century. The virtual exclusion of women from this genre at its height stems not only from its martial character, which is perhaps best illustrated by the fact that a version of the earliest such poem, the *Chanson de Roland,* was sung to excite the courage of William the Conqueror's troops as they went into the Battle of

Hastings (1066). The marginalization is a result as well of the ethos of these poems, which, according to Kohler, celebrate for a warrior audience either their own communal military undertakings or those of their ancestors. The community's identity is thus memorialized in its members' uniting to fight an adversary, and questions of difference—for example, social stratification among warriors themselves, or, although absent from Kohler's analysis, sexual roles—are downplayed unless they threaten the community's or the nation's harmony.

It is perfectly logical, then, that when women are mentioned in the "classic" *chansons de geste*, it is usually in their role as adjuncts, that is, faithful wives or wives-to-be who cement the bond between the hero and another male and then oversee their absent husbands' domains, or as war trophies attesting to heroes' valor. The first role is perhaps best exemplified by Aude, the fiancée of the eponymous hero of the *Chanson de Roland*, whose 4,002 verses contain only two references to her for a total of 21 verses. In the first, her brother Olivier berates Roland for refusing to inform Charlemagne of the infidel's attack against them by threatening to stop the marriage*, a threat that elicits from Roland no reference to Aude but only a query about the reasons for Olivier's anger. The second reference occurs when Aude asks for news of her fiancé from the returning Charlemagne, who, grief-stricken at Roland's loss, announces his death and immediately proposes to replace her dead fiancé with his own son. After expressing her consternation at this "strange" offer, Aude falls down dead and is mourned by the remaining barons. The lack of importance accorded her affection, which is so strong that she dies rather than take another husband, stands in stark contrast to Roland's failure to even think of her as, dying, he speaks instead of the beauty of his sword, which has allowed him to increase Charles's empire. Aude's marginalization is symptomatic of the lack of importance a sentimental relationship with women holds for the male audience, who, according to Gaunt, are more interested in male bonding. Confirmation comes from the same poem, which pays significantly more attention to Bramimonde, widow of the pagan leader Marsile. Her greater prominence can be explained by the fact that her voluntary conversion to Christianity* represents the greatest victory a male epic audience could conceive: by renouncing paganism, she is a living witness of the superiority of the Christian warriors, their faith, and their God; furthermore, as a converted woman, she enters the Emperor's marriage gift and can thus be used to begin a new lineage, thus swelling the Christian ranks.

In the few poems where women play a more central role, their roles as converts, surrogates for the absent warrior husband, and/or objects of exchange who strengthen the bond between the men who possess them still predominate. In the *Chanson de Guillaume* (at the turn of the twelfth century), for example, William's wife Guiborc—a pagan until her capture by him—actively encourages her husband when his resolve to conquer pagans flags, claiming to prefer that he die rather than humiliate his lineage. Shortly after, she supports her husband by putting together an army to reinforce his troops. In William's absence, she and the women left behind in Orange are twice shown to be the city's only defenders, once decked out in male armor and able to make the opposing pagan army believe they are men. It is important to note that her activities strengthen the male order by forcing William to become a more effective representative of it. In the few poems where women actively criticize that order, Kay shows that they are ignored or punished.

Later *chansons de geste*, dating from the thirteenth century on, for example, *Huon de Bordeaux*, *Berthe au grand pied*, and *Florence de Rome*, often accord greater importance to the woman as object of the hero's love. The attention to the male-female bond as well as to the *merveilleux* probably suggests cross-pollination between epic poetry and metric romance, whose audience was at least half and possibly predominantly female.

Grace M. Armstrong

BIBLIOGRAPHY

Secondary Texts

Campbell, Kimberlee. "Fighting Back: A Survey of Patterns of Female Aggressiveness in the Old French *Chanson de Geste*," In *Charlemagne in the North: Proceedings of the Twelfth International Conference of the Société Roncesvals*, Edinburgh: Société Roncesvals British Branch, 1993.

Combarieu du Grès, Micheline de. *L'Idéal humain et l'expérience morale chez les héros des chansons de geste des origines à 1250*. Aix-en-Provence: Université Provence, 1979.

Gaunt, Simon. *Gender and Genre in Medieval French Literature*. Cambridge: Cambridge University Press, 1995.

Kay, Sarah. "La Représentation de la fémininité dans les chansons de geste." In *Charlemagne in the North: Proceedings of the Twelfth International Conference of the Société Roncesvals*. Edinburgh: Société Roncesvals, British Branch, 1993.

Kohler, Erich. *L'Aventure chevaleresque: Idéal et réalité dans le roman courtois*. Trans. E. Kaufholz. Paris: Gallimard, 1984.

Chansons de toile, or "spinning songs," dating for the most part from the second half of the twelfth century, are anonymous lyric poems that present the point of view of a female persona and in many cases offer the early Middle Ages' most direct expression of female desire. Some of the *chansons de toile* have the woman speak of her feelings while sewing or spinning (whence the name of the genre), whereas others may take place in a more public place such as a fountain or beside a stream. Most often identified by the name of the female character—Bele ("Fair") Aye, Doette, Erembor, Aiglentine, and others—the poems speak of a love that is passionate and frequently defiant of opposition, and the language is rhetorically simpler and less ornamented than the usual courtly lyrics of the time. The *chanson de toile* may end happily, with a marriage*, reunion, or reconciliation, or unhappily, with the woman rejected or abandoned.

Norris J. Lacy

BIBLIOGRAPHY

Primary Text

Zink, Michel. *Belle: Essai sur les chansons de toile, suivi d'une édition et d'une traduction*. Paris: Champion, 1978.

Secondary Text

Bec, Pierre. *La Lyrique française au moyen âge*. Paris: Picard, 1977.

Chantal, Jeanne-Françoise Frémyot (or Frémiot), later Baronesse Rabutin de (1572–1641). Canonized 1767. The second of three children, Chantal was educated in the humanities by her widower father and in ''feminine'' arts by a maternal aunt. Widowed at age twenty-seven, Chantal was left with four young children. Her intelligence, managerial skills, large-scale devotion to charitable work, and strong will enabled her to survive the ensuing difficult years under her father-in-law's dominance. Chantal's encounter in 1604 with François de Sales, bishop of Geneva, resulted in an intimate spiritual friendship* and the shared foundation in Annecy of the Visitation Sainte-Marie (1610), which would become a cloistered order eight years later and which would encompass eighty houses by the time of Chantal's death. Designed for women not strong enough for a life of physical hardship, as well as for usual postulants, the order stressed strict inner ascesis, physical simplicity, and active obedience to the promptings of the divine will. An emphasis on development of the individual human spirit and on the unpretentious sacrality of daily life, differentiated this commonsense order of *honnêteté* from the heroic self-abnegation of more extreme contemplative houses, such as the Carmelites or Port-Royal*. Chantal's writings, consisting primarily of thousands of brief letters that address administrative and spiritual problems in newly established houses, or that address family concerns, bear witness to her great task of organization and training, and to the extent of her celebrity and influence. Her prose is concrete, yet vivid and lively, with an emphasis on realistic detail and illustrative anecdote; it is without affectation or pious generalization. According to Sainte-Beuve, there had never been a portrait better than her formal deposition written in 1627 for the canonization of François de Sales. Chantal's son was the father of Madame de Sévigné*.

Roberta S. Brown

BIBLIOGRAPHY

Primary Texts

Chantal, Ste Jeanne-Françoise Frémyot de. *Sa Vie et ses oeuvres*. Edition authentique publiée par les soins des Religieuses du Premier Monastère de la Visitation Sainte-Marie d'Annecy. 8 vols. Paris: Plon, 1874–1879.
———. *Correspondance*. Ed. Marie-Patricia Burns. 6 vols. Paris: Les Editions du Cerf, 1986–1996.

Secondary Text

Stopp, Elisabeth. *Madame de Chantal: Portrait of a Saint*. Westminster, MD: The Newman Press, 1963.

Chapsal, Madeleine (1925–). Chapsal began her writing career working for *L'Express* in 1953; her two best-known books draw on her work as a journalist. *Envoyez la petite musique* (1984) is a collection of interviews featuring writers such as Jean-Paul Sartre, Claude Mauriac, Louis-Ferdinand Céline, Henri de Montherlant, and Jacques Lacan; *La Jalousie* (1977) comprises a series of dialogues with six French women on the topic of jealousy, including Jeanne Moreau, Régine Deforges*, and Pauline Réage. Since writing her first novel*, *Un Eté sans histoires* (1973), Chapsal has produced several best-sellers, including *La Maison de jade* (1986) and *Suzanne et la province* (1993). She attributes their popularity to her ability to write about situations, dilemmas, and challenges typical of most women's lives. Chapsal's work is often linked to her personal experiences: divorce*, sibling rivalry, mental depression, and the anguish of infertility. Her novels feature contemporary heroines not bound by old stereotypes—independent career women who solve family and romantic problems by using their own resources. The themes in Chapsal's texts point to a feminist consciousness in which women's everyday concerns as mothers, daughters, and wives rise to the forefront.

Julia Lauer-Chéenne

BIBLIOGRAPHY

Primary Texts

Un Eté sans histoire. Paris: Mercure de France, 1973.
La Jalousie. Paris: Fayard, 1977.
Envoyez la petite musique. Paris: Grasset, 1984.
La Maison de jade. Paris: Grasset, 1986.
Une Saison de feuilles. Paris: Fayard, 1988.
La Chair de la robe. Paris: Fayard, 1989.
Si aimée, si seule. Paris: Fayard, 1990.
Le Retour du bonheur. Paris: Fayard, 1990.
La Femme abandonnée. Paris: Fayard, 1992.
Oser écrire. Paris: Fayard, 1993.
Suzanne et la province. Paris: Fayard, 1993.
L'Inventaire. Paris: Fayard, 1994.

Charrière, Isabelle de (1740–1805). Born Isabella van Tuyll van Serooskerken, Belle de Zuylen was not bound by the conventions of her country, her social station, or her sex. Dutch, she felt bonded to the French and wrote in their language. Her first novel*, *Le Noble* (1763), satirized her aristocratic class (and her scandalized family withdrew it from publication). She did not try to hide her intelligence, her sensuality, or her desire for autonomy. These qualities made finding a husband problematic, although she had many suitors, including Boswell. At the age of thirty she chose Charles-Emmanuel de Charrière, a Swiss nobleman and her brothers' former tutor, who would, she felt, respect her autonomy, the intellectual freedom she prized. The couple settled in a quiet Swiss village where she spent the next thirty years writing, reading, and receiving guests.

Charrière prolifically wrote fiction, plays, verses, and musical compositions, and, as the Revolution* approached, polemical and philosophical works. Her letters form six of the ten volumes of her complete works. Her longest epistolary exchange was her correspondence of almost twenty years with the (libertine and married) Swiss army officer Constant d'Hermenches; her most celebrated, with his nephew, Benjamin Constant, with whom she was romantically involved.

Always interested in the status of women, she focuses on female issues, especially in her novels. Her four early ones, *Lettres neuchâteloises* (1784), *Lettres de Mistriss Henley publiées par son amie* (1784), *Lettres écrites de Lausanne* (1785), and *Caliste, ou Suite des lettres écrites de Lausanne* (1787), use the epistolary convention with its emphasis on the affective and intimate to portray women in their different stages of life, and their various relationships and roles. Her characters, traditional or marginal—the provincial aristocrats, but also the seamstress who bears a child out of wedlock—experience love, *courtship, marriage*, pregnancy, and maternity*, and, like those of Jane Austen, with whom she is often compared, within the context of their daily existence and among the seemingly trivial objects of domestic life. Unidealized, her picture is also unromanticized. Marriageable young women wait for suitors who cannot commit; marriage disappointments bring disillusion and loss of self; and sentimental considerations are never very far from economic ones. Reason, virtue, and happiness are not moral but social constructs which stifle and oppress, but which women must adopt in order to survive. The inconclusive endings of most of her early novels underscore her reluctance to enclose her heroines in the traditional female patterns. Charrière's later novels do not neglect women but link their stories with moral, ethical, and philosophical considerations (the notion of duty in *Trois femmes* [1796], the question of faith and the consequences of its loss in *Honorine d'Userche* [1798]). Wary of dogma, and a partisan of moderation and compromise, this "revolutionary aristocrat" does not preach revolution or revolt. To inform is to reform. Like Mistriss Henley, Charrière would simply like to put everything in its proper place and have people see themselves as they really are.

Ruth P. Thomas

BIBLIOGRAPHY

Primary Text

Oeuvres complètes. 10 vols. Ed. Jean-Daniel Candaux et al. Amsterdam: Van Oorschot, 1979–1984.

Secondary Texts

Fink, Beatrice, ed. *Isabelle de Charrière/Belle Van Zuylen*. Special Issue of *Eighteenth-
    Century Life* 13, no. 1 (February 1989).
Jackson, Susan K. "The Novels of Isabelle de Charrière, or A Woman's Work Is Never
    Done." *Studies in Eighteenth-Century Culture* 14 (1985): 299–306.
Trousson, Raymond. *Isabelle de Charrière*. Paris: Hachette, 1994.

**Chastenay de Lanty, Louise Marie Victoire (called Victorine), comtesse de
(1771–1855).** She received a classical education* and published wide-ranging
historical studies and literary translations* from the English (Oliver Goldsmith's
Le Village abandonné and Ann Radcliffe's *Les Mystères d'Udolphe*, both 1797).
She is best remembered, however, for her memoirs*, which provide a perceptive,
not unsympathetic view of the Revolution*, despite her brief imprisonment and
that of her family. Her scholarly works are in intellectual history: *Du Génie des
peuples anciens* (1808) surveys writings from the Middle East, the West, India,
and China, for twenty centuries before Christianity*; *De l'Asie* (1832) focuses
on the thought of Asia; and *Les Chevaliers normands* (1816) discusses the chivalric tradition's capacity to produce major historical figures. *Calendrier de
Flore, ou Etudes de fleurs d'après nature* (1802–1803) is a descriptive botanical
study. Her work gained her a place in contemporary intellectual circles, but, as
she comments trenchantly in her memoirs*, her contribution was not (and has
not yet been) fully acknowledged.

Sally O'Driscoll

BIBLIOGRAPHY

Primary Texts

Calendrier de Flore, ou Etudes de fleurs d'après nature. Paris: Maradan, 1802–1803.
Les Chevaliers normands, en Italie et en Sicile. Paris: Maradan, 1816.
De l'Asie, ou considérations religieuses, philosophiques, et littéraires sur l'Asie. Paris:
    Jules Renouard, 1832.
Du Génie des peuples anciens, ou tableau historique et littéraire. Paris: Maradan, 1808.
Mémoires de Madame de Chastenay, 1771–1815. 2 vols. Paris: E. Plon, Nourrit et Com-
    pagnie, 1896.

Translations by Mme de Chastenay

Les Mystères d'Udolphe, by Oliver Goldsmith. Paris: Maradan, 1797.
Le Village abandonné, by Ann Radcliffe. Paris: Maradan, 1797.

Secondary Text

Kastener, J. "La Dernière Chanoinesse d'Epinal: Madame de Chastenay (1771–1855)."
    Révolution dans les Vosges: Revue d'histoire moderne 19, no. 2 (1930): 49–58,
    and 19, no. 3 (1931): 132–140.

Châteauroux, Marie-Anne de Mailly-Nesle, duchesse de (1717–1744).
Though blamed for the decline of the monarchy's prestige, the ablest of the four
Nesle sisters—who all shared Louis XV's bed—upgraded the status of *maîtresse*

en titre (official mistress) to an institution of state, setting the stage for her successors. The widow of the marquis de Tournelle, she made use of her charms under the tutelage of the duc de Richelieu, her cousin and counselor in the game for power. She requested financial allowances, legitimation of any children she might bear the king, and the dismissal from the royal court of her eldest sister, Mme de Mailly. In 1743 the title of duchesse and the estate of Châteauroux sealed her success. Châteauroux's growing ambitions made her instrumental in Richelieu's martial politics. Frederick the Great considered her a stabilizing agent in Franco-Prussian relations. At the summit of her brief career, she persuaded the lethargic king to lead the army into the War of the Austrian Succession against Austria, a move that won him the surname "Well-Beloved." When Châteauroux followed the successful king into the Austrian Netherlands, he became suddenly ill. Influenced by his religious and political advisors, the penitent Louis XV dismissed her in Metz. She died shortly thereafter. Although many, including Richelieu, accused the minister Maurepas, her longtime opponent, of a crime, peritonitis, rather than a poison, caused her early death.

Karyna Szmurlo

BIBLIOGRAPHY

Secondary Texts

Conner, Susan. "Women and Politics." In *French Women and the Age of Enlightenment.* Ed. Samia I. Spencer. Bloomington: Indiana University Press, 1984. 49–63.
Good, G. P. *Louis XV: The Monarchy in Decline.* London: Longmans, Green, 1956.

Châtelet, Gabrielle Emilie le Tonnelier de Breteuil, marquise de (1706–1749). Châtelet was born in Paris into well-connected aristocracy. Gifted in mathematics, physics, philosophy, and languages, she received an excellent education* with the most distinguished scholars of the day and became an eminent scientist as well as an accomplished musician and singer. She married Marquis Florent Claude du Chastellet-Lomont in 1725, and met Voltaire in 1733, joining him in her husband's chateau at Cirey. Their subsequent collaboration and friendship* lasted until her death.

Critics have recently focused on her fame as a *femme savante* (an intellectual woman), not just Voltaire's mistress. A translator and interpreter of Newton's works, she was among the first to make him accessible in France, establishing her scholarly reputation in the intellectual battle between Newtonians and Cartesians. She also wrote one of the first accounts of the works of Christian Wolff. Among her scientific works are a discussion of Leibnitz's metaphysics in *Institutions de physique* (1740), a treatise on the nature of fire in *Dissertation sur la nature et la propagation du feu* (1744) and, perhaps her most important work, the 1749 translation* from Latin of Newton's *Principia Mathematica* (1687), with commentary. A philosophical treatise on happiness is her personal view of a popular topic in the eighteenth century.

Châtelet's passionate participation in the social and cultural life of her day is balanced by her dedication to the pursuit of truth and knowledge. A lifelong proponent of women's rights, her feminist ideas are best expressed in her preface to a commentary on Mandeville's *The Fable of the Bees* (1705). One of the most learned women of her century, Châtelet firmly believed in the education of women, blaming social barriers and prejudices for women's apparent lack of achievement in the arts and sciences. She also wrote numerous letters, an unpublished commentary on the Bible*, as well as three chapters of an unpublished *Grammaire raisonnée*. Châtelet died giving birth to the child of her lover, Jean-François de Saint-Lambert.

Felicia B. Sturzer

BIBLIOGRAPHY

Primary Texts

Institutions de physique. Paris: Prault, 1740.
Dissertation sur la nature et la propagation du feu. Paris: Prault, 1744.
Principes mathématiques de la philosophie naturelle de Newton. Trans. Mme du Châtelet. Paris: Desaint et Saillant, 1759.
Lettres de la Marquise du Châtelet. Intro. T. Besterman. Geneva: Institut et Musée Voltaire, 1958.
Discours sur le bonheur. Intro. Robert Mauzi. Paris: Les Belles-Lettres, 1961.

Secondary Texts

Badinter, Elisabeth. *Emilie, Emilie. L'ambition féminine au 18e siècle*. Paris: Flammarion, 1983.
Edwards, Samuel. *The Divine Marquise*. London: Cassell, 1971.
Ehrman, Esther. *Mme du Châtelet*. Leamington Spa: Berg, 1986.
Hamel, F. *An Eighteenth-Century Marquise. A Study of Emilie du Châtelet and Her Times*. London: Stanley Paul and Co., 1910.
Maurel, A. *La Marquise du Châtelet, amie de Voltaire*. Paris: Hachette, 1930.
Vaillot, René. *Madame du Châtelet*. Paris: Albin Michel, 1978.

Chauveau, Sophie (1953–). Novelist, journalist, essayist, and scriptwriter. Throughout her work, Chauveau focuses on strong women, be they fictional characters, historical or mythical figures, or the real women who influenced her life—her grandmother, Christiane Rochefort*, Simone de Beauvoir*, Kate Millett, and other militant feminists of the 1970s. Her autobiographical texts, from *Débandade* to *Eloge de l'amour au temps du SIDA*, propose a philosophy of love and life based on equality between the sexes and chronicle her participation in the women's movement and her discovery of lesbianism* and of women's friendship*. In *Débandade*, Chauveau blames the men of her generation for the failure of the sexual revolution and calls for a new ''art of seduction,'' a contemporary version of the seventeenth-century ''Carte du Tendre'' described by Madeleine de Scudéry*. Here, as in *Eloge de l'amour au temps du SIDA*, Chauveau emphasizes women's desire, bemoaning the decline of passion and refusing to see feminism* and sensuality as mutually exclusive. In *Mémoires d'Hélène*, her Helen of Troy is a fictional version of such a sensual feminist—

beautiful, passionate, and an astute politician. Chauveau's revisionist rewriting of the Trojan War is presented from the perspective of Helen, who recounts her life, the war, and her utopian vision of a new civilization in which men and women are equal.

Susan Ireland

BIBLIOGRAPHY

Primary Texts

Débandade. Paris: Alésia, 1982.
Carnet d'adresses. Paris: Jean-Jacques Pauvert, 1985.
Mémoires d'Hélène. Paris: Robert Laffont/Jean-Jacques Pauvert, 1988.
Patience on va mourir. Paris: Robert Laffont, 1990.
Les Belles Menteuses. Paris: Robert Laffont, 1992.
Eloge de l'amour au temps du SIDA. Paris: Flammarion, 1995.

Secondary Text

Gouvernet, Gérard. "*Débandade* de Sophie Chauveau: Une Nouvelle Préciosité?" In *Continental, Latin-American and Francophone Women Writers*. Vol. 2. Ed. Ginette Adamson and Eunice Myers. Lanham, MD: University Press of America, 1990. 137–143.

Chawaf, Chantal (1943–). Born of a dying mother during a bombardment in Paris which killed both of her parents, Chawaf was told of the circumstances of her birth when she was an adult. Chawaf weaves this traumatic experience into all of her eighteen books by exploring the themes of inner oppression, solitude, abandonment, and the craving for love and for a return to the womb. Her sensuous and poetic style, characterized by metaphors uniting anatomy and nature, expresses her desire for life. Her first published text, *Rétable*, followed by *La Rêverie* (1974), written in stream-of-consciousness form with long, lyrical sentences interspersed with dialogues, is in part autobiographical; like all Chawaf's texts, it tells of anguish and the search for the mother. In her early books, *Cercoeur* (1975), *Blé de semences* (1976), and *Le Soleil et la terre* (1977), Chawaf expresses the maternal metaphor by way of a plethora of food images, for her definition of maternity* is linked to universal nurturing in the broad sense of giving life, as opposed to destroying it. Her most recent text, *Vers la lumière* (1993), offers a solution to her quest for the dead mother. She transforms a loss (her mother) into creation (a new language). The book illustrates her theory, expounded in a 1992 theoretical essay, *Le Corps et le verbe: La Langue en sens inverse*, in which she objects to the opposition between body and mind. She calls for a "regressive" writing which posits the return to the maternal as the source of life by introducing the feminine into the masculine, the body into the mind. *Vers la lumière* depicts a woman who ends her quest by plunging into the sea (*mer*) in order to be reunited with her dead mother (*mère*), a metaphor for the writing of the body, which will open communication between men and women. In her attempt to spiritualize the biological, Chawaf creates a literature of resistance by calling for a language of the flesh and of the affect, and by adopting a poetic style of writing which merges body and mind.

Monique Saigal

BIBLIOGRAPHY

Primary Texts

Rétable; La Rêverie. Paris: Editions des femmes, 1974.
Cercoeur. Paris: Mercure de France, 1975.
Blé de semences. Paris: Mercure de France, 1976.
Le Soleil et la terre. Paris: Pauvert, 1977.
Le Corps et le verbe: La Langue en sens inverse. Paris: Presses de la Renaissance, 1992.
Vers la lumière. Paris: Editions des femmes, 1993.

Secondary Texts

Bosshard, Marianne. "Le Mythème de la femme comme initiatrice à la spiritualisation de la chair." In *Mythes dans la littérature contemporaine d'expression française.* Ed. Metka Zupančič. Ottawa: Le Nordir, 1994. 146–155.
Hannagan, Valérie. "Reading as a Daughter: Chantal Chawaf Revisited." In *Contemporary French Fiction by Women.* Manchester: Manchester University Press, 1970. 177–191.
Jardine, Alice A., and Anne M. Menke, eds. "Chantal Chawaf." Trans. Christine Laennec. In *Shifting Scenes: Interviews on Women, Writing, and Politics in Post-68 France.* New York: Columbia University Press, 1991. 17–31.
Powrie, Phil. "A Womb of One's Own: The Metaphor of the Womb-Room as a Reading-Effect in Texts by Contemporary French Women Writers." *Paragraph* 12 (1989): 197–211.
Saigal, Monique. "Comment peut-on créer un nouveau langage féminin aujourd'hui?" In *Thirty Voices in the Feminine.* Ed. Michael Bishop. Amsterdam: Rodopi, 1996. 65–76.

Chedid, Andrée (1920–). Poet, novelist, short-story writer, and playwright. Born in Cairo to a Lebanese family who had emigrated to Egypt during the mid-nineteenth century, Chedid studied in England, in France, and at the American University in Cairo. After publishing her first volume of poetry* in English, *On the Trails of My Fancy* (1943), she moved to Paris in 1946 and began to write in French. A prolific author, Chedid has written nearly thirty books of poetry, ten novels*, six plays, four volumes of short stories*, and an autobiographical text, *Saisons de passage* (1996), as well as a book on Lebanon and several essays on poets and painters. She has received numerous literary awards and prizes, among them the Prix Hassan II des Quatre Jurys (1994), and the recent Grand Prix de Littérature Paul Morand (1994), bestowed by the Académie Française for the totality of her work. Chedid is considered the leading figure in the *unanimiste* poetical movement. Her poetry, while addressing preoccupations common to both men and women, often asserts a woman's perspective, as in "La Femme des longues patiences" (*Fraternité de la parole*, 1976). Her poems are intimate and focus on peace and war, love and loss, and the intersections of West and East. These same themes appear in her novels, short stories, and plays. Her fiction remains deeply anchored in the Middle East, particularly in the landscapes of Lebanon and Egypt—the Nile is central to her imagery—even when events take place in Paris. While she would not proclaim herself a feminist but rather a humanist, Chedid's first novel, *Le Sommeil délivré* (1952), describes a community of strong women in a Middle Eastern country who create bonds beyond age, class, and religious differences. This pattern of overcoming differences of all kinds is a hallmark of Chedid's work and applies especially to women characters in *Les Marches de sable* (1981) and *La Maison sans racines* (1985). In Chedid's texts, women are often at the forefront of movements for change—be they individual or collective—as are children and the disabled.

Joëlle Vitiello

BIBLIOGRAPHY

   Primary Texts

On the Trails of My Fancy. Cairo: Horns, 1943.
Le Sommeil délivré. Paris: Stock, 1952.
Le Sixième Jour. Paris: Julliard, 1960.
Fraternité de la parole. Paris: Flammarion, 1976.
La Femme en rouge et autres nouvelles. Paris: Flammarion, 1978.
Les Marches de sable. Paris: Flammarion, 1981.
La Maison sans racines. Paris: Flammarion, 1985.
L'Enfant multiple. Paris: Flammarion, 1989.
Poèmes pour un texte (1970–1991). Paris: Flammarion, 1991.
Saisons de passage. Paris: Flammarion, 1996.

   Secondary Texts

Knapp, Bettina. *Andrée Chedid*. Amsterdam: Rodopi, 1984.
Villani, Sergio, ed. *Andrée Chedid: Chantiers de l'écrit*. Woodbridge, Ont.: Les Editions
      Albion Press, 1996.
Vitiello, Joëlle. "Friendship in the Novels of Andrée Chedid." *Symposium* 49, no. 1
      (Spring 1995): 65–80.

Chéron, Elisabeth Sophie (1647–1711). Born to a Huguenot father and a Catholic mother, Sophie was brought up a Protestant but became a convert to the Roman Catholic faith in 1668 after painting the portrait of Henriette de Lorraine, mother superior of the Abbey of Jouarre. She learned the elementary principles of drawing and painting from her father and gracefully executed the portraits of many famous people. She may well have been the first woman admitted into the Royal Academy of Painting at Paris in 1672, where her works were considered to be outstanding and exceeding the ordinary strength of a woman.

   The talents of Sophie Chéron were multiple: she was at the same time an accomplished painter, engraver, musician, and poet, and she became a member of the famous Academy of Ricovrati in Padua in 1699. If she is indeed the author of "La Coupe du Val de Grâce" (1669), a poem of some 800 lines in answer to the poem Molière wrote to the glory of Pierre Mignard and which criticizes Mignard's famous fresco, she exhibited her literary skill at an early age. Indeed, Sophie was the student of Charles Lebrun and may well have taken sides in the rivalry which opposed Lebrun (first painter of Louis XIV, in charge of the decoration of Versailles, director of the Gobelins factory, and chancellor of the Academy of Painting) to Mignard. She is remembered for her powerful and graceful paraphrase of the Book of Psalms, published in 1694, and she proved with her heroicomic poem "Les Cerises renversées," which relates an incident in which she was involved, that she felt equally at ease dealing with light topics.

She married, at a rather late age, Jacques Le Hay, an engineer in the king's court, and died in Paris.

                                                                    Marie-France Hilgar

BIBLIOGRAPHY

Primary Text

Essay de Pseaumes et Cantiques mis en vers, et enrichis de figures. Paris: Michel Brunet, 1694.

Secondary Texts

Fidière, Octave. *Les Femmes artistes.* Paris: Charavay frères, 1885.
Gréder, Léon. *Elisabeth-Sophie Chéron.* Paris: Henri Jouve, 1909.
Roujon, Henri. *Dames d'autrefois.* Paris: Hachette, 1911.

Children's literature. The relatively new field of children's literature has offered female creativity a privileged domain of expression usually condoned and even encouraged by the most conservative authorities. Early on, many anonymous storytellers passed on their lore and wisdom to their female charges (family or apprentices) in the form of folktales. Mireille Piarotas in *Des Contes et des femmes* (1996) tracks down the remnants of these female oral narratives in the folktales' literate versions, noting that strong female characterization and symbols appear in the less adulterated tales. During the seventeenth and eighteenth century, using these texts as palimpsests, educated women such as Madame d'Aulnoy* (1650–1705) produced courtly fairy tales*, some of which would become part of the literary canon for children. Whereas fairy tales as art form had been appropriated by male writers, for example Charles Perrault (1628–1703), their female contemporaries presented a literary feminized version of the fairy tales, influenced by aesthetics and the *précieuses'* taste for elaborate courtship, platonic love, and independence.

Madame de Genlis* (1746–1830) broke with the fairy tale tradition and created more realistic tales and fables specifically for the purpose of enlightening youth. Her stories focused on young characters who reform their weaknesses through discipline, physical exercise, and sensible diets; girls were advised against fancy costumes and idleness and instructed in history, writing, reading, botany, and other fields. Genlis concluded the collection of stories with an apology for great women artists and a demand for equality between men and women made possible through a solid education* for girls. Madame Guizot* (1773–1827) gave a different version of didactic literature with moralistic stories and novels* aimed at edifying readers and teaching them their Christian and social duties. Guizot's novels portrayed numerous female characters who controlled their household through persuasive sweetness and silent but clear expectations. This strong pedagogical trend, which responded to the new demands for abstraction and literacy imposed by the beginning of education for girls, was also represented by Zénaïde Fleuriot* (1829–1899) and Julie Gouraud d'Aulnay (1832–1891), two of the most famous writer-educators from a group often referred to as "the governesses."

Eugénie Foa* (1796–1853) deserves special mention for her creation of the didactic magazine for children *Le Journal des enfants* (1833), and for her own novels in which female ambition was justified for moral purposes. Madame Alfred Fouillée, under the pseudonym G. Bruno, influenced several generations of schoolchildren with her still famous fictionalized textbook *Le Tour de France par deux enfants* (1877).

Set apart from the more didactic writers, Sophie de Ségur* (1799–1874) earned canonical status because of her innovative narrative techniques, imaginative plots and characters, and realistic settings. She introduced children, and girls in particular, to reading for entertainment and presented them with a seditious view of the adult world through comedy.

These authors cannot be labeled feminist at first glance, the moralistic framing of their writings favoring a social status quo that did not promote the advancement of women. Yet, these writers preached by example rather than words, earning a living by the pen and depicting young girls in simple attire gardening, building log cabins with boys, and writing their memoirs*. A more subtle analysis shows the subversive powers of these stories where boys were shaped by a female code of ethics that could give girls the upper hand if they played by its rules.

By the turn of the century, children's literature reflected the social changes that slowly promoted women's and children's emancipation. Gyp's* (Sybille Gabrielle de Mirabeau, 1849–1932) novels for children, for instance, introduced mischievous and imaginative girls who sought personal happiness, but without breaking away from their social structure. Mme Mesureur, Mme Cazin, Mme de Witt, and Magdeleine du Genestoux, among many other prolific women writers of the time, played on the same ambivalence while describing lively, witty girls who conformed to the prevalent idealized cultural images of children and women as redeemers of society. The blatant conventionality of these writings allowed their authors to be published and become models for young readers who would not have had access to female writers if not for them. From testimonies of later feminists (among them Beauvoir*) it can be argued that girls were more sensitive to the murmur of dissent represented by these early works than to their conformity.

After World War I*, literary production for children accelerated and diversified, while authors specialized in the many topics newly accepted in children's literature. Literature for children still offered women a way to protest or counteract the effects of a patriarchal society on their environment, their cultures, language and regions, their animals, and their children without confronting it openly. Some women writers renewed the oral tradition of old, collecting, rewriting, and preserving the folktales endangered by aggressive linguistic and cultural national policies on centralization. Others adapted historical narratives for children, preserving the past or exhuming forgotten women from it. Still others produced mysteries, adventure stories, or domestic dramas featuring young female protagonists as heroines.

Two major mid-century writers deserve to be cited by name: Lucie Rauzier-Fontagne (1895–1986), whose fictional girls overcome adversity with courage, wit, and compassion, and Colette Vivier (1898–1974) whose novels depict serious themes such as collaboration and resistance or the role of the girl within her family from the point of view of the child, thereby launching the narrative "I" in children's literature.

In the latter part of the twentieth century many women who write for children (Hélène Ray, Claude-Rose Touati, Marie-Aude Murail) do so from a feminist perspective, advocating the rights of children as well as girls and women.

In the twentieth century children's literature developed its own canon and critical standards. Literary scholars such as Marie-Thérèse Lazarus, Luce Fillol, Mathilde Leriche, Martha Caputo, and Claire Huchet helped the field gain recognition. Now women writers of children's literature can claim it as their field of choice.

Christine Lac

BIBLIOGRAPHY

Secondary Texts

Diament, Nic. *Dictionnaire des écrivains pour la jeunesse 1914–1991.* Paris: L'Ecole des Loisirs, 1993.

Ottevaere-van Praag, Ganna. *La Littérature pour la jeunesse en Europe occidentale (1750–1925).* Bern: Peter Lang, 1987.

Perrot, Jean, and Véronique Hadengue. *Ecriture féminine et littérature de jeunesse.* Paris: La Nacelle, 1994.

Piarotas, Mireille. *Des contes et des femmes. Le Vrai Visage de Margot.* Paris: Imago, 1996.

Bookstores

Bibliothèque L'Heure Joyeuse. 6–12, rue des Prêtres Saint-Severin. 75005 Paris.

Centre National du Livre pour Enfants. La Joie par les Livres. 8, rue Saint-Bon, 75004 Paris.

Christianity. The beliefs and practices of the Christian religion had a heterogeneous impact on the lives of French women. The established Christian Church of the early medieval period inherited traditions that both empowered and subordinated women. The teachings of Jesus assembled in the four gospels had the potential to provide women with a new, more elevated status in society. Jesus preached the equality of all his believers in his doctrine. He spoke directly to women and accepted them as his followers along with men. He allowed women a role outside the family* and their relationships to men. In later centuries, Christian women repeatedly cited these ideas of Jesus as the basis for claiming the right to learn, preach, and create a life outside the confines of marriage* and motherhood. Furthermore, the Virgin Mary and other prominent women in the early writings of the Church served as new role models and key sources of authority to which women might appeal.

Yet the New Testament and the writings of the early Christian theologians also contained potent misogynistic ideas that helped to limit woman's role in society and to subordinate her to male authority inside and outside the Church. The writings of Peter, Paul, Timothy, and Christian fathers like Jerome, Tertullian, and Augustine emphasized the inferiority of women and denied them a place in the priesthood. Furthermore, the Old Testament image of Eve as the source of original sin continued to portray women as a source of corruption to men. Christian writers, connecting all sexuality with sin, also insisted that intercourse should take place only within marriage for the purpose of procreation. With this double legacy of empowerment and subordination, the Christian religion in France experienced periods of enthusiasm and reform that led to increased opportunities for women, soon followed, however, by long periods of consolidation and conservatism that ultimately restricted women's lives.

After Clovis, King of the Franks, was converted to Christianity by his wife Clothilde in the sixth century, bishoprics and monastic orders, including religious communities for women, following the authority of the popes and Church councils, spread all over the major cities of central France. Pledging a life of obedience, poverty, and chastity, women could make a life outside of marriage and the family in these monasteries, convents*, abbeys, and priories. A woman who chose to live as a nun was not seen as equal in power or nature to a monk, but she could share equal access to divine favor, knowledge, and spiritual authority on earth. The nun's principal responsibility was to pray in order to exculpate the sins of others and herself. Since religious women were not ordained, they could not preach or administer the sacraments as the male clergy could. Yet the cloistered and sanctified life of the monastery and convent did provide women with educational opportunities usually reserved for men. In these protected shelters, women were taught to read and given the opportunity to study important texts of antiquity and the early Church. They also wrote their own words and thoughts.

From the seventh to the tenth centuries, many of these religious communities consisted of adjoining foundations for men and women now referred to as double monasteries. As abbesses and foundresses of double monasteries, women could assume powers reserved only for bishops, abbots, and the ordained male clergy. They wielded both religious and secular power. In the secular arena, the abbess was responsible for maintaining the lands held in the name of the order. She directed the collection of tithes and the choice of the village clergy and oversaw the religious lives of those living on the monastery lands. The abbess was also responsible for the religious life of the nuns and monks of her order.

By the end of the thirteenth century many double monasteries were disbanded when popes and bishops decided to segregate male and female ecclesiastics, as part of a larger process of reform and centralization that led to greater control of all aspects of the religious life by a male hierarchy. The abbesses and nuns then lost their claims to male privileges and powers. Restrictions against women avowing novices, hearing confession, preaching, and singing the Gospel were instituted by Pope Innocent III at the beginning of the thirteenth century. The Emperor Charlemagne confirmed the superior authority of bishops over abbesses and forbade women even to assist in the administration of the sacraments. Prohibitions against joint houses, against nuns teaching boys, and against any extraneous contacts between religious women and their male confessors gained wide acceptance at this time. Church laws also insisted that women must remain cloistered at all times.

Despite the restrictions of the cloistered convent, noble and propertied women attempted to create a full life. Through prayer and meditation, some women mystics claimed direct visions from God. They often engaged in acts of suffering and sacrifice in imitation of Christ and envisioned a union with Jesus that was highly erotic. The ecstatic power of the mystic was understood as a gift from God. Religious women like the Belgian mystic Julian of Cornillon were accorded status and respect that few other women won. Women were thought to be especially receptive to this mode of spirituality because of their less rational and more credulous natures. In the twelfth and thirteenth centuries, female mystics in the cloister gained status, recognition, and authority within the reformed Church, but at a price, because male clerics usually emphasized the mystic's irrational nature and always claimed that she was an exception, to be admired but not imitated.

Outside the institutional Church, some female visionaries without an affiliation to any established order became important religious figures, and thousands of women, in numbers far beyond what the older and new orders could accept, responded to the religious zeal of the period by creating a religious life outside the cloistered convent. Calling themselves Beguines, these women took no formal vows but wanted nonetheless to emulate Jesus by adopting lives of chastity, penitence, prayer, poverty, and physical labor. From the thirteenth to the fifteenth centuries, the Beguine movement spread throughout northern France and Belgium and to the south of France. Gradually, these women began to congregate in houses, called beguinages, where they lived a regulated life of prayer, charity, and work under the supervision of an appointed mother of the house. But the Beguines never lived by a uniform rule or under a general supervisory system. Without any institutional organization, they lived lives with more individualism and freedom than nuns or married women did.

Their piety was seen as exemplary, and their desire to work was acceptable. Some Beguines, like Marie d'Oignies, became influential figures. However, the lack of institutional organization also created situations that brought the Beguines into conflict with the Church. Some Beguines engaged in translating Holy Scripture into French and composed exegeses, which was prohibited by the Church. They even debated questions of faith after reading translations of theological works. Marguerite Porete, a Beguine from Hainaut, preached in Valenciennes, Chalons, Tournai, and Paris. She composed a mystical work, *Le Mirouer des simples âmes*, which was denounced as heretical, and she was burned at the stake in 1310. By the fifteenth century, Church authorities had turned their houses into simple shelters for women.

Women also took part in other heretical movements that emerged in southern France in the thirteenth century. The Albigensians, or Cathars, rejected not only the Church and its rituals as the work of the devil, but also the material world. They believed that a woman, through baptism and study, could become the equal of male believers and achieve ultimate purity, becoming a *perfecta*. French noblewomen played an instrumental role in maintaining the Cathar religion after the king of France and the Church launched a crusade to eradicate the heresy. They hid other Cathars and directed the defense of their castles during the crusade. The Cathars eventually surrendered, and the 200 believers were burned to death.

By the fifteenth century, the French Church had effectively subdued and restricted most forms of female religiosity that challenged male Church authority. However, the sixteenth century experienced a new wave of religious enthusiasm that challenged all established Church dogma—including traditional gender relations—that came to be known as the Protestant Reformation*. Protesting against a corrupt and hierarchical Church, Jean Calvin called for a "priesthood of all believers," implying that the chosen, whether male or female, were of equal status. His message appealed to women who longed for a more active role in Church life. Calvin's followers became known as the Huguenots in France. While Protestantism remained a minority religion in France, it ripped apart the country in bloody conflict for more than a century. Noble and royal women played a significant role in these wars of religion. Urban women of the middle ranks of society also embraced Protestantism because it offered a sense of equality in the religious realm that they were already experiencing in the economic realm as the helpmates and partners of their husbands. The new faith insisted that women be literate so they too could read and interpret the Bible*, and it also called for men and women to participate in church by singing hymns and praying together. Yet the new Protestant preaching never challenged male patriarchy, for while Huguenots preached that men and women were equal in faith, they also maintained that there was still rank and gender hierarchy in society. Protestants not only renounced the celibate life of the cloister, they also gave up the worship of the saints and the cult of the Virgin Mary. However, a majority of peasant women and noble women remained Catholic. Peasant women continued to rely on the Virgin Mary and the saints to negotiate the hardships of life, while many noble women did not want to surrender their exclusive world of the convent, where education* and visionary experience were allowed.

The Church fathers responded by making concessions during the Counter-Reformation. The Church allowed new groups of nuns to be organized: avowed women who could teach and serve the needs of the sick and the poor outside the cloistered convent. Angela Mérici's Ursuline sisters took on the job of educating young Catholic girls outside the convent. By the seventeenth century the Ursulines were the principal teachers of Catholic girls in France. Other orders such as the Order of the Visitation and the Sisters of Charity took on more public functions like nursing the sick and caring for the poor in public settings in the seventeenth century. Their numbers and activities increased in the nineteenth century as they began to nurse in prisons and military wards.

By the early eighteenth century the secular ideas of the new science and the Enlightenment* were becoming dominant in urban France among the middle classes and the elite. Following the Revolution* of 1789, revolutionaries tried to enact the Enlightenment into law by outlawing Catholicism and replacing it with forms of civic religion. While this civic religion was embraced by the people of the cities, especially men who saw it as part of the new social contract, it did little for women. In fact, women were the principal protesters against the outlawing of Catholicism. In provincial towns and villages, ordinary women led riots to reclaim the right to practice their religion and rejected the new worship. They often hid priests and held lay masses in their own homes. For these French women, the Church constituted a vital source of charity and support for the family. The Revolution's offer of representative government and free trade meant little to women who could not feed their families. Ironically, women now became the defenders of the Church and its traditional role in French society.

Women's counterrevolutionary activities labeled them as conservative, upholders of the status quo, while men were seen as the champions of modern political democracy. Throughout the nineteenth century women outnumbered men in almost every aspect of religious life: regular church attendance; participation in revivals, pilgrimages, new confraternities, and educational and social welfare organizations; and also in commitment to religious orders. The Church now actively encouraged nuns to work in hospitals, schools, and a whole range of public missions.

The Church also actively promoted a softer, more sentimental form of Catholicism by endorsing popular religious devotions like the cult of the Sacred Heart of Jesus and accepting as authentic several apparitions of the Virgin Mary. Bernadette Soubirous of Lourdes became the most famous of these modern French visionaries. Lay women found that the Church spoke to their special needs as mothers and wives. The Church valued domestic virtues like resignation, morality, inwardness, forgiveness, patience, and charity. French middle-class women used the Church to engage in an array of charitable activities and thus entered the public sphere to reform a godless world. Working-class women were often the beneficiaries of such charitable activities. Historians have connected this feminization of Catholicism in France to the ascendancy of a bourgeois ideology of separate spheres that designated religion to be part of women's sphere of activity while men took care of politics and economic activity in the public sphere.

This feminization of Catholic experience in nineteenth-century France had a mixed impact on women's lives. On the one hand, women were able to create vital and productive lives for themselves as nuns, charity workers, and reformers; women entered the public sphere to work and spread their moral influence. On the other hand, women's close ties to the Catholic Church resulted in them being labeled politically conservative and hyperreligious. At worst, women were seen as superstitious, ignorant, and anti-modern. This view allowed republican politicians to continually deny women the vote in France. Republicans reasoned that women would use the vote to return the Catholic Church to power and usher in monarchical rule. This argument had such power in France that women did not gain the vote until after World War II*.

Throughout the twentieth century the Catholic Church in France continued to promote this vision of female religious life. The Church endorsed only two roles for women: wife and mother within the family or nun within a religious order. The continued presence of the Catholic Church in women's lives meant that modern feminism* made little impact in France until the late 1960s. By providing women with a specific female religious world of support and security and allowing little room for dissent, the Catholic Church in France allowed women to cultivate their talents and abilities within a circumscribed space.

Suzanne Kaufman

BIBLIOGRAPHY

Secondary Texts

Bainton, Roland. *Women of the Reformation in France and England.* Boston: Beacon Press, 1975.

Barber, M. C. "Women and Catharism." *Reading Medieval Studies* 3 (1977): 45–58.

Davis, Natalie Zemon. "City Women and Religious Change." In *Society and Culture in Early Modern France.* Stanford: Stanford University Press, 1975.

Desan, Suzanne. *Reclaiming the Sacred: Lay Religion and Popular Politics in Revolutionary France.* Ithaca: Cornell University Press, 1990.

Gold, Penny Schine. *The Lady and the Virgin: Image, Attitude and Experience in Twelfth-Century France.* Chicago: University of Chicago Press, 1985.

Johnson, Penelope. *Equal in Monastic Profession: Religious Women in Medieval France.* Chicago: University of Chicago Press, 1991.

Langlois, Claude. *Le Catholicisme au féminin: Les Congrégations françaises à supérieure générale au XIXe siècle.* Paris: Cerf, 1984.

Neel, Carol. "The Origin of the Beguines." *Signs* 14 (1989): 321–341.

Petroff, Elizabeth A. *Medieval Women's Visionary Literature.* New York: Oxford University Press, 1986.

Pope, Barbara Corrado. "Immaculate and Powerful: The Marian Revival in the Nineteenth Century." In *Immaculate and Powerful: The Female in Sacred Image and Social Reality*. Ed. Clarrissa W. Atkinson, Constance H. Buchanan, and Margaret R. Miles. Boston: Beacon Press, 1985. 173–200.

Rapley, Elizabeth. *The Dévotes: Women and the Church in Seventeenth-Century France*. Montreal; Buffalo: McGill-Queen's University Press, 1990.

Roelker, Nancy L. "The Appeal of Calvinism to French Noble Women in the Sixteenth Century." *Journal of Interdisciplinary History* 2, no. 4 (Spring 1972): 391–418.

Smith, Bonnie. *Ladies of the Leisure Class: The Bourgeoises of Northern France in the Nineteenth Century*. Princeton: Princeton University Press, 1981.

Wemple, Suzanne Fonay. *Women in Frankish Society: Marriage and the Cloister, 500–900*. Philadelphia: University of Pennsylvania Press, 1981.

Christine de Pizan (c. 1364–c. 1431) was the first woman in Europe to earn her living by her pen. She was born in Venice and came to France at the age of four. Her father, Thomas, had been appointed court physician and astrologer to the French king Charles V. Pizan married Etienne de Castel in 1379 and had three children with him. The family's fortunes had begun to decline in 1380 with the death of Charles V, and things got worse when Pizan's father died without making provision for his family. In 1389 Pizan's husband died, leaving his financial affairs in disarray. She now was a twenty-five-year-old widow with her children, her mother, and a niece to support. Fortunately her father had given her an education* that was unusual for girls at that time, and after her husband's death she resumed her study of learned works and began to write. Soon she found wealthy patrons and began to write lyric poetry* for them. But her real love was learned treatises, often in the form of allegory. She succeeded in making a good living from her writing and produced twenty-five major works, ranging from love poetry to mythographic texts, from allegories to biographies and religious texts. Her last work, finished shortly before her death, was a poem in praise of Joan of Arc, a heroine who combined all the aspirations Pizan had harbored for women: a divinely inspired young girl showed the French what military prowess could accomplish for the cause of French unity and defense against the English. Pizan probably did not live to see Joan's tragic end in 1431.

Already in her first collection of poetry, the *Cent Balades* (1390s), Pizan introduced a theme that had not been part of the repertory of lyrical topics until then: widowhood. She created the moving voice of a bereaved woman who reflects on her status in the world and rings the changes on the theme of solitude. In later texts, such as *Le Livre des trois vertus* and *Lavision-Christine* (both 1405), she returned to this topic, this time highlighting the social and economic consequences of losing one's husband. She exhorted widows to be strong and assertive (not "cowering dogs") and to use legal means to lay claim to what is owed them. Another theme that appeared in the *Cent Balades* was a critique of courtly conventions that Pizan believed devalued women. In *L'Epistre au Dieu d'Amour* (1399) Cupid addresses himself to all lovers in the French realm and tells them that women feel betrayed by them through their continuous slander and defamation. Pizan saw courtly love* not as a tribute to women but as a male commodification of women and their love. Pizan elaborated on this theme in her *Dit de la pastoure* (1403), which, using conventions of the established lyric genre of the *pastourelle*, shows the effect a nobleman's courting and eventual abandonment of a simple shepherdess has on the innocent girl. In *Cent Balades d'amant et de dame* (1405–1410), Pizan adopted a dialogic form and, through the voices of a lover and the lady he finally abandons to a death of grief, we hear the power play that underlay gender relations in the Middle Ages.

Around 1400, Pizan became involved in a literary debate on the merits of the thirteenth-century *Roman de la Rose*, a love allegory by Guillaume de Lorris that was later expanded to a work of encyclopedic proportions by Jean de Meun. A lover's quest for a rose and her love becomes the pretext for lengthy speeches by various characters, of which several are openly misogynistic. When the well-known intellectual Jean de Montreuil circulated a treatise in praise of the *Rose*, Pizan felt compelled to respond and to make her point that because of its misogynism the *Rose* should not be read, let alone praised. She defined herself here as a woman intellectual who has every right to participate in a public debate and whose obligation it is to point to the potential harm that can come to women from misogynistic literary works.

In *L'Epistre au Dieu d'Amours* Pizan had Cupid remark that if women had written books the literary tradition would look quite different. Pizan's *Livre de la cité des dames*, finished c. 1405, seems to be a response to that complaint. This book creates a utopian city as a refuge for all women who have been slandered in literature and historiography, promising them eternal protection. Pizan begins the book by showing herself in her library and study, perusing various volumes. Unexpectedly she comes upon a book by Matheolus, the quintessential misogynist treatise, written in the late thirteenth century. She is instantly plunged into a deep melancholy, despising herself and her feminine nature. Suddenly, three ladies appear to her and identify themselves as Reason, Rectitude, and Justice. Their task is to open Pizan's eyes to the true worth of women and help her construct an allegorical city where every stone is a woman of achievement and virtue. Pizan offers a revisionist version of Western culture here, one that emphasizes women's contributions in the fields of letters, military arts, agriculture, and other areas. Pizan makes a strong case for the education of girls, who, she claims, will show that they are just as talented as boys as soon as they are given access to equal educational opportunities. Her own story testifies to the advantages women can reap from a thorough education. In the last book of the *Cité* Pizan turns to female saints (almost all of them martyrs) and shows how the virtues of strength, loyalty, and solidarity that she advocates for all women were particularly visible in these saints. Throughout the book she uses the same strategy to refute the misogynists. Modeling her work on the scholastic dialogue between a master and a pupil, she addresses herself to the three ladies and repeats all the misogynist commonplaces and prejudices of her time. The ladies then list examples that show how wrong the misogynists are.

In the continuation of the *Cité, Le Livre des trois vertus*, Pizan leaves the utopian world and returns to the real world of late medieval France. In turn addressing queens, princesses, noble ladies, merchants' and peasants' wives, the poor, and prostitutes, Pizan develops a handbook for a virtuous and productive life in the midst of the treacheries and dangers of her society. Prudence and foresight, discretion and humility, will enable these women to navigate a society marked by deep class divisions and the ravages of the Hundred Years War.

It is this war and the French civil war that erupted after the assassination of the Duke of Orléans on the orders of the Duke of Burgundy in 1407 that dominate much of Pizan's remaining works. The role of women in society she sought to improve with the two works just discussed no longer preoccupied her. In later texts, such as the *Lamentacion sur les maux de la guerre civile* (1410) or *L'Epitre de la prison de vie humaine* (1418), women appear mostly as bereaved widows who should rise up against the folly of war or who should resign themselves to the unhappiness of life on earth and look toward the next life for consolation. Her last work on Joan of Arc (1429) reflects the hope that this valiant young girl brought to the French nation, occupied by the English and led by a weak dauphin.

With the publication of E. J. Richards's translation of *Le Livre de la cité des dames* (New York: Persea, 1982), Christine de Pizan studies in the United States began to flourish. Though this work was not a big success in her lifetime, for modern critics it seems to be the most interesting because it fits into current feminist research interests. Some groundwork still needs to be done: not all of Pizan's works exist in critical or accessible editions. One of the important currents in criticism has been to show how Pizan constructs a new female authority in a male-dominated clerical world. Her relationship to her authoritative sources, and her voice, as it changes from lyrical poet to feminist and political writer, have generated many studies, as has her place in the didactic tradition of her time. A number of international conferences have focused on Christine de Pizan and the *Newsletter of the Christine de Pizan Society* constantly updates readers on the large and varied output by Christine de Pizan scholars.

Renate Blumenfeld-Kosinski

BIBLIOGRAPHY

Primary Texts

Oeuvres poétiques. 3 vols. Ed. Maurice Roy. Paris: Firmin Didot, 1886–1896.
Lavision-Christine. Ed. Mary Louis Towner. Washington, DC: Catholic University Press, 1932.
Le Livre de la cité des dames. 2 vols. Ed. Maureen Curnow. Diss., Vanderbilt University, 1975.
Cent Ballades d'amant et de dame. Ed. Jacqueline Cerquiglini. Paris: Union Générale d'Editions, 1982.
The Epistle of the Prison of Human Life and the Lament on the Evils of Civil War. Ed. and trans. Josette A. Wisman. New York: Garland, 1984.

Le Livre des trois vertus. Ed. Charity Cannon Willard and Eric Hicks. Paris: Champion, 1989.

Secondary Texts

Blumenfeld-Kosinski, Renate. "Christine de Pizan and the Misogynistic Tradition." In *The Selected Writings of Christine de Pizan.* New York; London: W. W. Norton, 1997. 297–311.

Brownlee, Kevin. "Widowhood, Sexuality, and Gender in Christine de Pizan." *Romanic Review* 86 (1995): 339–353.

Gottlieb, Beatrice. "The Problem of Feminism in the Fifteenth Century." In *The Selected Writings of Christine de Pizan.* Ed. Renate Blumenfeld-Kosinski. New York; London: W. W. Norton, 1997. 274–297.

Kelly, Joan. "Early Feminist Theory and the *Querelle des Femmes,* 1400–1789." In *Women, History, and Theory: The Essays of Joan Kelly.* Chicago: University of Chicago Press, 1984. 65–109.

Kennedy, Angus J. *Christine de Pizan: A Bibliographical Guide.* London: Grant and Cutler, 1984. [Updated to 1987 in E. J. Richards, ed., *Reinterpreting Christine de Pizan* (Athens: University of Georgia Press, 1992)].

Quilligan, Maureen. *The Allegory of Female Authority: Christine de Pizan's "Cité des Dames."* Ithaca: Cornell University Press, 1991.

Richards, Earl Jeffrey. "Christine de Pizan and the Question of Feminist Rhetoric." *Teaching Language through Literature* 22 (1983): 15–24.

Schibanoff, Susan. "Taking the Gold Out of Egypt: The Art of Reading as a Woman." In *Gender and Reading.* Ed. Elizabeth A. Flynn and Patrocinio P. Schweickart. Baltimore: Johns Hopkins University Press, 1986. 83–106.

Sullivan, Karen. "At the Limit of Feminist Theory: An Architectonics of the *Querelle de la Rose.*" *Exemplaria* 3 (1991): 435–466.

Willard, Charity Cannon. *Christine de Pizan: Her Life and Works.* New York: Persea, 1984.

Yenal, Edith. *Christine de Pizan: A Bibliography.* 2nd ed. Metuchen, NJ: Scarecrow Press, 1989.

Cinema. French women have directed films from the beginning of cinema: Alice Guy, who directed the first fiction film ever made—*La Fée aux choux* (1896)—also made numerous one-reelers in France and America. She used cinema to tell realistic tales of people—especially women—through poetic images. Another pioneer, feminist critic Germaine Dulac, developed her own aesthetic theory of "musically constructed films" (for example, her *Disque 927* on Chopin's music) to make impressionistic (*La Souriante Madame Beudet,* 1923) or surrealistic movies (*La Coquille et le clergyman,* 1927). Of the early women directors, only Marie Epstein made the transition to sound. Her first movies, codirected with her brother Jean Epstein, had an avant-garde flavor (*Finis Terrae*), while her later work with Jean Benoît-Lévy explored daily life (*Ames d'enfants,* 1924), portrayed women as central characters (*La Maternelle,* 1933; *La Mort du cygne,* 1937), and exemplified poetic realism with its lyrical treatment of populist subjects.

Women directors abandoned poetic realism after the horrors of World War

II*, turning to either sociohistorical or fictional subjects. Nicole Védrès adopted a reporter's objective style (*La Vie commence demain*, 1949), while Jacqueline Audry celebrated women writers by adapting their novels*: Mme de Ségur's* *Les Malheurs de Sophie* (1946), Colette's* *Gigi* (1949) and *Mitsou* (1956), and her sister Colette Audry's *Soledad, fruits amers* (1967). Some women authors turned their own novels into intellectual films—Marguerite Duras's* *Nathalie Granger* (1973), *India Song* (1975), *Baxter, Vera Baxter* (1977)—or films designed for the general public on topics ranging from romance (Françoise Sagan's* *Les Fougères bleues*, 1977) to a young girl's coming of age (Catherine Breillat's *36 Fillette*, 1988).

Other directors, including Yannick Bellon and Agnès Varda, used the documentary genre to portray reality from a woman's perspective. Bellon gave a voice to ordinary islanders—*Goémons* (1946)—and to those who have been silenced—*Varsovie quand même* (1953), *Brésiliens d'Afrique, Africains du Brésil* (1973)—before going on to make controversial fiction films on women that deal with issues of rape*, incest, and drugs. Varda, too, filmed documentaries that focus on individual subjects or groups (*Black Panthers*, 1968). Her fiction films focus on women and their search for personal freedom. *L'Une chante, l'autre pas* (1976) narrates the parallel yet distinct journeys to independence of two female friends empowered by solidarity between women. Her work, a mixture of *cinéma-vérité* and fictional creation (*Sans toit ni loi*, 1985), mirrors the fluidity of her *cinécriture*.

Women directors of the 1970s such as Paula Delsol, Charlotte Dubreuil, Dolorès Grassian, Nelly Kaplan, Jeanne Moreau, and Michèle Rosier were feminist both in their choice of topics and in their representation of women, asking questions about the role and position of women in society. In Coline Serreau's *Mais qu'est-ce qu'elles veulent?* (1975–1978), for example, answers about the rights and the desires of women are provided by dozens of women in the work force.

In the 1980s, most films made by women reinterpret women's shifting roles in personal, political, and social relationships. Serreau pokes fun at role reversal (*Trois Hommes et un couffin*, 1985) and revises traditional tales (*Romuald et Juliette*, 1989); Diane Kurys portrays her adolescence (*Diabolo Menthe*, 1977) and women's intimacy (*Coup de foudre*, 1983); Vera Belmont expresses her disillusionment with communism in *Prisonniers de Mao* (1979) and *Rouge Baiser* (1985), as does Camille de Casablanca (*Pékin Central*, 1986; *Après la pluie*, 1989). During the same period, Belgian director Chantal Akerman radically deconstructs traditional linear cinematic narratives and replaces them with fragmented stories in cyclical sequences (*Toute une nuit*, 1982). Similarly, other women directors, such as Aline Isserman, Jeanne Labrune, and Patricia Mazuy, experiment with new cinematic storytelling techniques, as does 1990s director Pascale Ferran (*Petits Arrangements avec les morts*).

In the 1990s, women directors are filming diverse, marginalized characters— colonized Africans (Claire Denis, *Chocolat*, 1988), a serial killer (Denis, *J'ai *pas sommeil*, 1994), a homosexual brother (Catherine Corsini, *Les Amoureux*, 1993), and lesbian lovers (Josiane Balasko*, *Gazon maudit*, 1994).

Through their creative languages and visions, women directors have profoundly marked the evolution of French cinema. Thus, it is fitting that two women's films celebrate its 100-year anniversary: Varda's *Les Cent et Une Nuits*, and Anne-Marie Miéville's *2 × 50 Ans de cinéma français*.

Florence Martin

BIBLIOGRAPHY

Secondary Texts

Colvile, Georgiana. "Mais qu'est-ce qu'elles voient? Regards des Françaises à la caméra." *French Review* 67, no. 1 (October 1993): 73–81.

Erens, Patricia, ed. *Issues in Feminist Film Criticism*. Bloomington: Indiana University Press, 1991.

Flitterman-Lewis, Sandy. *To Desire Differently*. Chicago: University of Illinois Press, 1990.

Forbes, Jill. *The Cinema in France after the New Wave*. Bloomington: Indiana University Press, 1992.

Gillain, Anne. "L'Imaginaire féminin au cinéma." *French Review* 70, no. 2 (December 1996): 259–270.

Guy-Blache, Alice. *Autobiographie d'une pionnière du cinéma (1873–1968)*. Paris: Denoël-Gonthier, 1976.

Lauretis, Teresa de. *Feminism, Semiotics, Cinema*. Bloomington: Indiana University Press, 1984.

Lejeune, Paule. *Le Cinéma des femmes*. Paris: Atlas Lhermier, 1989.

Mayne, Judith. *The Woman at the Keyhole: Feminism and Women's Cinema*. Bloomington: Indiana University Press, 1990.

Penley, Constance, ed. *Feminism and Film Theory*. New York: Routledge, 1988.

Silverman, Kaja. *The Acoustic Mirror: The Female Voice in Psychoanalysis and Cinema*. Bloomington: Indiana University Press, 1988.

Varda, Agnès. *Varda par Agnès*. Paris: Cahiers du Cinéma, 1994.

Cixous, Hélène (1937–   ). Novelist, essayist, playwright, professor of literature, and founder and director of the Paris Centre de Recherches en Etudes Féminines. Born in Algeria to an Austro-German mother and a French father, Cixous is a Sephardic Jewish author of French expression whose poetic style has philosophical underpinnings. By means of her writing, she seeks to free herself from repressive, masculine discourses that devalue women, other cultures, and nature. Cixous's trajectory intersects with the deconstructive project critiquing Western metaphysics, which, since Plato but especially since Descartes, turns differences into oppositions and hierarchies. Discarding the term "feminist" along with its metaphysical residue, Cixous replaces it with the expression *écriture féminine**. For Cixous, "feminine"—as opposed to "masculine"—has to do with giving and generosity rather than retentiveness; women are more likely to be generous because of their subalternate position in society. Cixous uses "writing" in the strong sense of inscription in and on the body. Far from being an essence, the body, caught in historical configurations, is always encoded; inscriptions of pain and pleasure in the flesh translate themselves into spoken words and writing on the page.

Throughout her career, Cixous has championed the cause of women—and of humanity in general—in their quest for truth. Through her redemptive project, she continually searches for new ways out (*sorties*) of a world dominated by a masculine metaphysics. A feminist project that aims at a simple reversal of power would, she argues, merely be more of the same.

Cixous writes at the intersection of her own story and of history. In building her critical and creative works, she collaborates with writers, playwrights, painters, and political figures who combat power and denounce the global equivalence of cultural goods, natural goods, and money. In 1969 Cixous was awarded the Médicis Prize for her autobiographical narrative *Dedans* (1969), in which, following the death of her father, she traces her way out of the family and into the world. Her birth is, paradoxically, first a death. To give birth to oneself—a dominant metaphor in Cixous's work—is an active process, continually to be begun again. Her search for other discursive possibilities and other modes of exchange leads her from her thesis on the paradoxes of creation in James Joyce to a critique of Hegel's dialectic of recognition (*Prénoms de personne*).

In the 1970s, Cixous began to concern herself more directly with the cause of women. In "Le Rire de la Méduse" (1975), she urges women to use laughter to shatter the meaning of masculine discourse that passes for the law. *La Jeune Née* (1975), a text co-authored with Catherine Clément*, again foregrounds the struggle of women, especially when read in light of Freud's study of hysteria. Using certain elements of psychoanalysis—the unconscious, dreams, and the subversion of sexual identities—Cixous exhorts women to break their silence and write themselves in order to create new forms of the imaginary. She replaces the forces of death at work in master/slave scenarios with scenes of life and nourishment in which partners give themselves freely to each other. Cixous creates different approaches to the Other through a rereading of Heidegger's meditations on thinking, dwelling, and the poet. Heidegger inspired much of Cixous's feminist fiction as well as her texts on Clarice Lispector, all published by the Editions Des Femmes in the late 1970s. In the 1980s, Cixous's interest in epic theater* was strengthened by her encounter with Ariane Mnouchkine*. This type of theater provided her with an opportunity to explore the inscription of "feminine" styles—of women and of men—in other cultures. After writing her plays on Cambodia and India, she engaged in a poetic meditation on apartheid and the gulag (*Manne*, 1988). Other local and global dilemmas continue to provide an impetus for her writing, from the corruption of politicians to the scandal of blood contaminated by the AIDS virus.

Cixous makes a distinction between her writerly endeavors and direct militancy that elicits protest in the streets. Her feminine writing (*écriture féminine*) seeks to express new forms and other languages, breaking away from "death-laden'' discourses whose only aim is profit. Such writing opens up a dialogue with others and allows them to speak. For Cixous, the struggle of women goes hand in hand with the constant search for new, ever-elusive forms of democracy and community.

Verena Andermatt Conley

BIBLIOGRAPHY

Primary Texts

L'Exil de James Joyce ou l'art du remplacement. Paris: Grasset, 1968.
Dedans. Paris: Grasset, 1969.
Prénoms de personne. Paris: Seuil, 1974.
''Le Rire de la Méduse.'' *L'Arc* 61 (1975): 39–54.
Le Livre de Promethea. Paris: Gallimard, 1984.
L'Histoire terrible mais inachevée de Norodom Sihanouk, roi du Cambodge. Paris: Théâ-
	tre du Soleil, 1985.
Manne. Paris: Des Femmes, 1988.
L'Histoire (qu'on ne connaîtra jamais). Paris: Théâtre du Soleil, 1994.
La Ville parjure ou le réveil des Erynies. Paris: Théâtre du Soleil, 1994.
Cixous, Hélène, and Catherine Clément. *La Jeune Née.* Paris: Union Générale d'Editions,
	1975.

Secondary Texts

Conley, Verena Andermatt. *Hélène Cixous: Writing the Feminine.* 1984. Lincoln: Uni-
	versity of Nebraska Press, 1992.
Sihach, Morag. *Hélène Cixous: The Politics of Writing.* London: Routledge, 1992.

Clairon, Claire Josèphe Hyppolyte Leris de la Tude (1723–1803) was the illegitimate daughter of a Flemish mother and a French soldier. La Clairon, as she was known, gained fame as a tragic actress, starring in the plays of Marmontel and Voltaire, among others; her love life was reputedly scandalous and her conversation witty. She left the Comédie Française and her career in 1766 in a dispute between the actors and the theater management. Clairon also wrote: she published a short collection of poetry* and prose (*Morceaux choisis du portefeuille de Mlle Clairon,* 1762) and her combined memoirs* and manual of acting technique, *Mémoires d'Hyppolite Clairon, et réflexions sur l'art dramatique* (1798); she also left some of her prolific correspondence, short dialogues, and novellas. A scurrilous early biography (of ''Cronel'') and Goncourt's 1890 biography concentrated on her personality, notoriety, and famous friends such as Diderot, Garrick, and the Baron de Staël. Only in recent criticism has Clairon's writing been appreciated for its stylistic innovations.

Sally O'Driscoll

BIBLIOGRAPHY

Primary Texts

Morceaux choisis du portefeuille de Mlle Clairon. Amsterdam: Veuve de J. F. Jolly,
	1762.

Mémoires d'Hyppolite Clairon, et réflexions sur l'art dramatique. Paris: F. Buisson, 1798.

Poésies de Mademoiselle Clairon, publiées pour la première fois en France. Paris: Imprimerie de l'armorial français, 1898.

Secondary Texts

Courteault, Paul. "Mlle Clairon et Lekain à Bordeaux." *Actes de l'Académie de Bordeaux* 1 (1914): 237–256.

Dussane, Béatrix. "Quelques Reines du théâtre: Clairon." *Revue hébdomadaire* 47, no. 4 (1938): 7–36.

Feuillère, Edwige. *Moi, la Clairon.* Paris: Albin Michel, 1984.

Gaillard de la Bataille, Pierre-Alexandre. *Histoire de la vie et moeurs de Mlle Cronel, dite Fretillon, actrice de la Comédie de Rouen, écrite par elle-même.* The Hague: Aux dépens de la Compagnie, 1741.

Goncourt, Edmond de. *Les Actrices du XVIIIe siècle: Mademoiselle Clairon. D'après ses correspondances et les rapports de police du temps.* 1890. Reprint. Paris: Flammarion/Fasquelle, 1927.

Haussonville, Othenin, comte d'. "Mlle Clairon et le Baron de Staël." *Revue hébdomadaire* 19, no. 4 (1910): 5–33.

Spink, John Stephenson. "Mlle Clairon à Ferney." *Bulletin de la Société des historiens du théâtre* 3 (1935): 65–74.

Classicism. This term, which has played a dominant role in French literary history, was imposed retroactively by critics, and upon a group of writers most of whom would not have viewed themselves as belonging to a movement or school. Chronologically, the word usually covers a number of influential critics and authors from the reigns of Louis XIII and Louis XIV, though some would restrict the classical period to a mere quarter of a century (1660–1685). Definitions vary, but typically include the following: belief in the need to impose regulations on the French language and on literary composition, which included the founding of the Académie Française; insistence on elegance, clarity, and simplicity of expression; in-depth analysis of human passions; endorsement of absolutist monarchy and of conservative views in the religious, moral, and social spheres; concern for preserving but modernizing the heritage of Greco-Roman antiquity; eagerness to please a highly cultivated public, drawn from the nobility and the upper bourgeoisie, requiring refinement that transcends mechanical rules.

There are at least three major ways in which classicism affected or was affected by women. First of all, theorists of the time recognized that women comprised a major portion of the readership for literary works and of the theater-going public, and that any writer hoping for success could not ignore women's taste. This last was usually understood to mean an emphasis on love plots in drama and fiction, the revival of the chivalric ideal in which a proper hero always showed absolute respect and devotion to his ladylove, a rejection of crudity of language and thought, and the promotion of non-Aristotelian literary genres (such as novels*, letters, memoirs*, fairy tales*, operas, etc). During the celebrated *Querelle des anciens et des modernes** (which can be seen as a split within the ideology of classicism itself), women and their male supporters championed the Modern cause, often claiming that women's taste had helped to improve the overall quality of French literature. The Ancients, on the other hand, held that women's taste was having a harmful effect.

A second type of impact involved the growing number and increased acceptance of women writers. By deemphasizing the role of erudition in the formation of an author, and by proposing recent French writers, alongside (or even in place of) Greek or Latin, as models for imitation, classicism made literary composition more feasible for women, most of whom did not have access to the type of education* available to men. Many women writers saw themselves as active participants in a great ongoing French cultural enterprise.

The third impact, about which it is harder to generalize, is the shift in how authors of the classical period, whether male or female, depicted their female characters. Although negative portrayals were by no means uncommon, including satires on learned ladies, prudes, and coquettes, a large percentage of writers presented the women they depicted with respect and sensitivity. The era of Louis XIII saw an explosion of works that glorified heroic women, many of them warriors or reigning queens. The second half of the century saw the rise of psychological novels where articulate and introspective heroines wrestle with moral dilemmas and social stereotypes. Authors of tragedies presented numerous female protagonists who display remarkable energy and moral integrity, even though they rarely enjoy the same freedom of action as their male counterparts. The emphasis on analysis of the passions contributed to the trend toward more complex female characters throughout this period.

Perry Gethner

BIBLIOGRAPHY

Secondary Texts

Bénichou, Paul. *Morales du grand siècle*. Paris: Gallimard, 1948.
Borgerhoff, E.B.O. *The Freedom of French Classicism*. Princeton: Princeton University Press, 1950.
Bray, René. *La Formation de la doctrine classique en France*. Paris: Hachette, 1927.
Peyre, Henri. *Qu'est-ce que le classicisme?* Paris: Nizet, 1965.
Viala, Alain, ed. *Qu'est-ce qu'un classique? Littératures classiques* 19 (1993): special issue.

Clément, Catherine (1939–). Clément's varied career includes positions such as professor of philosophy, journalist for *Le Matin*, co-editor of *L'Arc*, and diplomat at the Ministère des Relations Extérieures. She was a controversial figure in the women's movement of the 1970s, much criticized by certain women's liberation groups for her adoption of a Marxist perspective. At this time, Clément privileged the class struggle over the gender struggle, and called for an alliance between intellectuals and the working class. This theoretical stance is evident in "Enclave Esclave" (1975), written after the discussion on women and sexuality during the "Week of Marxist Thought" in Paris.

Clément is best known for her work in *La Jeune Née*, which she co-authored with Cixous*. The opening essay, "The Guilty One," focuses on repressed and alienated female subjects. Clément revisits the archetypal figures of the hysteric and the sorceress, and reexamines Freud's discussion of seduction and guilt in the family romance. In the final section of *La Jeune Née*, she engages in a dialogue with Cixous which takes as its subject the ambiguity of the hysteric, and asks whether Freud's Dora is a resisting heroine or a victim.

Clément, who participated in the seminars of Jacques Lacan, is also the author of several important studies of psychoanalysts: *Les Fils de Freud sont fatigués* (1978) and *Vies et légendes de Jacques Lacan* (1981). Her work on Lacan, which attempts to clarify the complex arguments presented in *Ecrits*, illustrates Clément's belief that the categories of "male" and "female" are sociolinguistic constructs.

Another significant study, *L'Opéra ou la défaite des femmes* (1979), examines how culture has defined the female opera singer, analyzes famous librettos from a feminist perspective, and discusses why the death of female protagonists is a recurrent plot motif in operas which place them in the role of heroine. In *La Syncope: Philosophie du ravissement*, Clément examines the phenomenon of swooning, which is traditionally associated with women—especially as a manifestation of hysteria. Clément's fictional works reflect her theoretical concerns. Her most recent novel, *La Putain du Diable*, is at once an irreverent account of French intellectual life since 1945 and a spirited defense of reason.

Susan Ireland and Patrice J. Proulx

BIBLIOGRAPHY

Primary Texts

La Syncope: Philosophie du ravissement. Paris: Grasset, 1970.
Les Fils de Freud sont fatigués. Paris: Grasset, 1978.
L'Opéra ou la défaite des femmes. Paris: Grasset, 1979.
La Sultane. Paris: Grasset, 1981.
Vies et légendes de Jacques Lacan. Paris: Grasset, 1981.
La Putain du Diable. Paris: Flammarion, 1996.
Cixous, Hélène and Catherine Clément. *La Jeune Née*. Paris: Union Générale d'Editions, 1975.

Secondary Text

Jardine, Alice A., and Anne Menke, eds. *Shifting Scenes: Interviews on Women, Writing, and Politics in Post-68 France*. New York: Columbia University Press, 1991.

Coicy, madame de (eighteenth century). Little is known about her except that she wrote two feminist works during the years preceding the French Revolution* about the equality of the sexes in the eyes of nature. Because the only physical difference between the sexes is the organs necessary for reproduction, which have no effect on the mind, men and women are mentally and physically equal. Their natural equality is deformed by society through the different standards in education*. It is the duty of the government to establish the principles by which its citizens are educated; consequently the government is responsible for this inequity. Coicy states that women, although lacking in the knowledge that men possess, participate in the affairs of men and are necessary to them. She illustrates the important role women have played despite their disadvantaged upbringing through anecdotes of famous women throughout history, from the ancient Greeks, Romans, Germanic peoples, and the Gauls up to the present. Coicy believes that women should have the same rights as men to display their prowess and contends that accomplished men owe much to their wives and female relations. Women should have the right to wear medals for their participation.

Antoinette Marie Sol

BIBLIOGRAPHY

Primary Texts

Les Femmes comme il convient de les voir; ou, Aperçu de ce que les femmes ont été, de ce qu'elles sont, et de ce qu'elles pourroient être. London and Paris: Bacot, 1785.
Demandes des femmes aux Etats Généraux; par l'auteur des Femmes comme il convient de les voir. N.p., n.d. [1789?].

Coignard, Gabrielle de (c. 1550–c. 1586), devotional poet. Little is known of Gabrielle de Coignard's early life. She belongs by birth and marriage* to the parliamentary *élite* of Toulouse. Her father, Jean de Coignard, Maître ès jeux floraux, for more than thirty years, was extremely influential in cultivated circles. Coignard was given a good education* and raised in the Catholic faith. In 1570 she married Pierre de Mansencal, a noted lawyer who soon after their marriage became president in the Parliament of Toulouse. He died in 1573, leaving her with two young daughters to raise alone. To honor her memory, Jeanne and Catherine de Mansencal published the *Oeuvres chrestiennes* their mother composed during her widowhood. First published in 1594 in Toulouse, then in Avignon (1595) and Lyons (1613), the *Oeuvres chrestiennes* consists of two parts: the first part contains 129 sonnets, and the second 21 poems of different length, among which are some *Noëlz, complaintes, stances,* hymns, *discours,* three narrative poems, and a short epic celebrating the victory of the biblical heroine Judith.

Gabrielle de Coignard was unknown to literary historians up to the 1860s. Since then, modest samplings of her poetry* have appeared in a few anthologies. The *Oeuvres chrestiennes* clearly grows out of the devotional production connected with the devotional revival in the last third of the sixteenth century. Among the most significant phenomena of this period are (1) the advent of Henri III, who led his whole nation to penitence and devotion, hoping to appease God's wrath and put an end to civil wars; (2) the publication of two major works which stand at the root of the vast movement to disseminate devotional practice throughout Europe, Ignace de Loyola's *Exercitia spiritualia* (1548) and Luis de Granada's *Libro de la oración y meditatíon* (1566), translated into French by François de Belleforest in 1575 under the title *Le Vray Chemin*; and (3) the overall effort to popularize devotion in an attempt to meet "the Calvinist challenge," the Marot-Bèze psalter with its direct, vernacular appeal.

The *Oeuvres chrestiennes* traces the successive phases of the poet's spiritual quest. In the first part, the contemplation of this world's beauty leaves the soul burning with desire for celestial things. Spiritual ascent requires renunciation—renunciation of worldly pleasures and glory for the promise of eternal reward, of profane love for sacred love, of the sophistication of profane rhetoric for a more humble, sober, anti-pagan approach—and thus generates contradictory emotions. Torn between the conflicting demands of flesh and spirit, the poet moves throughout phases of anguish, doubt, lamentation, and despair. She reflects on the fragility of human life, vanity, human pain (symbolic of sin), man's corruption and *aveuglement* as well as her own sins before passing on (in the second part of the collection) to the contemplation of Christ's redemptive act. The *vanitas* imagery, the imagery of the *ars moriendi*, and that of the Bible* dominate the sonnets.

The second part of the collection concerns the poet's meditation together with the reflections it arouses in her mind. Characterized by painful reflection on sin, death, and the Last Judgment, the Christian virtues of charity and continence, and various events in the life of Christ (the Nativity, Passion, crucifixion, descent into hell, resurrection), the meditation ends in joyful reconciliation with Christ. Of particular interest are the Passion poems in which Gabrielle de Coignard follows closely the phases of meditation (prayer, meditation, contemplation) delineated by Granada in *Le Vray Chemin*. She seems to delight in elaborate and vivid description of Christ's suffering body, and such scenes as the nailing to the cross, the stretching of Christ's body to make it fit the cross, and the painful removal of the nails. Special attention is also given to the depiction of the spiritual agony of the Virgin Mary over Christ's physical agony and his impending death. The techniques used by Gabrielle de Coignard, the interest in narrative detail of gesture and action, together with an inclination to pathos, are typical of the devotional tradition.

Colette H. Winn

BIBLIOGRAPHY

Primary Texts

Oeuvres chrestiennes. Toulouse: Pierre Jagourt et Bernard Carles, 1594.

Oeuvres chrestiennes. Tournon: Pour Jacques Faure, libraire en Avignon, 1595.

Oeuvres chrestiennes. Lyons: Abraham Cloquemin, 1613.

Oeuvres chrestiennes. Ed. Colette H. Winn. Geneva: Droz, 1995.

Secondary Texts

Berriot-Salvadore, Evelyne. *Les Femmes dans la société française de la Renaissance*. Geneva: Droz, 1990. 434–443.

————. "Les Héritières de Louise Labé." In *Louise Labé: les voix du lyrisme*. Ed. Guy Démerson. Saint-Etienne: Publications de l'Université de Saint-Etienne, Editions du CNRS, 1990. 93–106.

Cave, Terence. *Devotional Poetry in France c. 1570–1630*. Cambridge: Cambridge University Press, 1969.

Salies, Pierre. "Gabrielle de Coignard: Poétesse toulousaine du XVIe siècle." *Archistra* 79 (March-April 1987): 33–43.

Winn, Colette H. "Une Lecture au féminin: *L'Imitation de la victoire de Judich* par Gabrielle de Coignard (1594)." In *L'Exégèse biblique au seizième siècle. Oeuvres & Critiques* Ed. Colette H. Winn. 20, no. 2 (1995): 123–142.

Colet, Louise (1810–1876). Best known perhaps for her intimate and literary correspondence with Gustave Flaubert, Colet wrote numerous works with feminist themes, notably her *Poème de la femme* (1853–1856). Because she was the mistress of some famous contemporaries—Victor Cousin, Alfred de Musset, Alfred de Vigny, and Flaubert—Colet's work was often overshadowed by that of her more famous lovers. She participated more actively, nonetheless, than simply as muse in the literary and political activities of her day: she published collections of poems, novels*, and novellas, and deserves recognition as one of the more important literary feminist writers of the time.

Her 1836 collection of poems, *Les Fleurs du midi*, attracted the friendship of the poet and songwriter Béranger. When, in 1839, the Académie Française set as the topic for its annual poetry prize the inauguration of the Musée de Versailles where the recently deceased Marie d'Orléans's statue of Jeanne d'Arc was the central display, Colet's poem on Jeanne d'Arc won. Colet thus became only the fifth woman medallist since the prize had been established in 1671. Among those impressed were Victor Cousin, who soon became her protector and later acknowledged paternity of her daughter, Henriette. Four years later she won the prize for "le Monument de Molière." In 1852, the year of her friendship with Musset, she received the prize for "La Colonie de Mettray," dedicated to Victor Hugo, then in exile. In 1854, the year Alfred de Vigny became her lover, she won the Académie's prize for "L'Acropole d'Athènes," which she dedicated to him. Colet won this prize more often than any other woman in French history.

In 1846 Colet met Flaubert and soon became his mistress. Their liaison was interrupted in 1848, resumed in 1851, and terminated in 1854. In the latter period, Flaubert had become a more successful writer (he was working on *Madame Bovary*) and helped Colet revise and edit her work. He appeared to appreciate her passionate love, energy, and generosity. After their definitive separation, Colet published a novel featuring Flaubert and several of his friends in a rather obvious roman à clef, *Une Histoire de soldat*.

Lui, roman contemporain treats the subject of the relationship between Musset and George Sand*, which is the subject of both Sand's *Elle et lui* and Paul de Musset's *Lui et elle*. Colet's novel shifts between the frame novel (the account of the friendship between Stéphanie de Rostan [Colet] and Albert de Lincel [Musset] and the embedded first-person narration of his affair with Antonia Back (Sand). The novel dramatizes the personal and professional dilemmas of two literary women and shows the accommodations women make to men. Many Colet works can be understood as protofeminist texts in which female characters seek their individual voices within the limited male-dominated context of their time.

E. Nicole Meyer

BIBLIOGRAPHY

Primary Texts

Fleurs du midi, poésies. Paris: Dumont, 1836.
Folles et saintes. 2 vols. Paris: Pétion, 1844.
Les Chants des vaincus, poésies nouvelles. Paris: A. René et Cie., 1846.
Poème de la femme. 3 vols. La Paysannne, 1853. La Servante, 1854. La Religieuse. Paris: Perrotin, 1853–1856.
Quatre Poèmes couronnés par l'Académie française. Paris: Librairie nouvelle, 1855.
Une Histoire de soldat. Paris: A. Cadot, 1856.
Lui, roman contemporain. Paris: Librairie nouvelle, 1860. Geneva: Slatkine Reprint, 1873.

Secondary Texts

Beizer, Janet. Ventriloquized Bodies: Narratives of Hysteria in Nineteenth-Century France. Ithaca: Cornell University Press, 1994.
Gray, Francine DuPlessix. Rage and Fire: A Life of Louise Colet, Pioneer Feminist, Literary Star, Flaubert's Muse. New York: Simon and Schuster, 1994.

Colette, Sidonie-Gabrielle (1873–1954). After a privileged childhood in Burgundy, where her mother inspired in her a reverence for nature, Colette married Henri Gauthier-Villars in 1893 and moved to Paris. Her husband, ''Willy,'' introduced her to literary and musical salons* and published her early novels* under his name (the Claudine series). After her divorce*, she earned a living first as a music-hall artist—a profession considered scandalous at the time— then as a reporter. She signed her novels ''Colette Willy'' until 1923; after this, she wrote her best-known works under the name ''Colette'' and eventually made a living from her writing.

Although Colette disliked politics and did not belong to any feminist organizations, her writings illustrate, from a female perspective, the many changes in women's personal lives from the Belle Epoque to the 1950s. Claudine à l'école offers a view of the education* of women in late nineteenth-century France, while La Maison de Claudine is a poetic evocation of the life of a provincial, middle-class, female adolescent. L'Envers du Music-Hall describes the living conditions and dilemmas of impoverished women artists. Colette also explores the ''demimonde'' at the turn of the century (Chéri, Gigi), and portrays the waiting and suffering of women in wartime (La Chambre éclairée, L'Etoile Vesper). Finally, she depicts the clash of the sexes and social classes after World War I* (La Fin de Chéri, La Chatte).

By focusing on the marginalized (women, adolescents, homosexuals), Colette challenges commonly accepted literary standards of morality, definitions of identity, and visions of aging. In *Le Pur et l'impur*, she provides her own perspective on female sexuality and lesbianism*, while her novels and short stories* subvert stereotypes of femininity* (moral weakness, duplicity, submissiveness), underlining the experiences common to all relationships: sexual awakening, vulnerability, inauthenticity, jealousy, fear of solitude (*Le Blé en herbe, La Femme cachée*). Colette's characters are often resilient women who learn how to distinguish between sexual desire and love, to survive difficult relationships, and to find refuge in sisterhood (*Duo, Le Toutounier*). Her texts propose a reworking of the themes of marriage* and motherhood: examining with humor the conventions that bind couples, she creates androgynous characters and an inspiring, nonconformist model of maternity*. At the same time, she demystifies love, emphasizes role-playing, and explores role reversal and relationships traditionally considered scandalous (for instance, between a young man and an older women in *Chéri* and *Le Blé en herbe*). Colette proposes new paradigms of female independence, friendship*, and solidarity (*La Seconde*). *La Vagabonde* recounts the experiences of a music-hall actress who chooses independence and integrity over the security of marriage and finds self-knowledge through writing. In *La Naissance du jour* and *Sido*, Colette paints the fictional self-portrait of a writer who turns to her mother as a model of creativity, wisdom, and reconciliation with oneself, while also engaging in a debate on men's appropriation of the female voice and on readers' expectations of women writers. This discussion of writing, gender, and genre continues throughout her later works (*L'Etoile Vesper, Le Fanal bleu*).

In her time, Colette was popular with a public attracted by the seemingly confessional aspect of her works. Even though her style was admired for its sensuousness, critics often lamented her indifference to political and metaphysical issues, finding her milieus, her marginal characters, and her focus on sexual relationships to be trivial. In the 1970s, however, her writing was celebrated for recognizing women's resistance to imposed roles and the multiplicity of their desires. Recent feminist critics interested in theories of subjectivity and the constructedness of gender have highlighted the tensions between reading Colette's work as the *inscription* of her own experience, and reading it as the complex *construction* of a self in writing. Colette's modernity resides in her blurring of genres and categories of gender. By resisting her readers' assumptions about women writing in a masculinist literary tradition, she has played a pioneering role in claiming a space for female voices.

Catherine Slawy-Sutton

BIBLIOGRAPHY

Primary Texts

La Vagabonde. Paris: Ollendorf, 1911.
Chéri. Paris: Fayard, 1920.
La Maison de Claudine. Paris: Ferenczi, 1922.

La Femme cachée. Paris: Flammarion, 1924.
La Naissance du jour. Paris: Flammarion, 1928.

Secondary Texts

Eisinger, Erica, and Mari McCarthy, eds. *Colette: The Woman, the Writer*. University
        Park: Pennsylvania State University Press, 1981.
Evans, Martha Noel. "Colette: The Vagabond." In *Masks of Tradition: Women and the
        Politics of Writing in Twentieth-Century France*. Ithaca: Cornell University Press,
        1987.
Huffer, Lynn. *Another Colette: The Question of Gendered Writing*. Ann Arbor: Univer-
        sity of Michigan Press, 1992.
Jouve, Nicole Ward. *Colette*. Bloomington: Indiana University Press, 1987.
King, Adèle. *French Women Novelists: Defining a Female Style*. New York: St. Martin's
        Press, 1989.
Resch, Yannick. *Corps féminin, corps textuel*. Paris: Klincksieck, 1973.
Strand, Dana. *Colette: A Study of the Short Fiction*. New York: Twayne, 1995.

Collaboration. *See* World War II: Collaboration.

Colleville, Anne Hyacinthe de Saint-Leger, dame de (1761–1824). Parisian
novelist and dramatist. Her works often deal with independent women, such as
in the novels* *Mme de M***, ou la Rentière* (1802) and its sequel, *Victor de
Martiques, ou Suite de la rentière* (1804). Her first novel, *Lettres du chevalier
de Saint-Alme et de la mademoiselle de Melcourt* (1781), published one year
before Laclos's *Les Liaisons dangereuses*, uses the same epistolary genre that
dominated the middle of the eighteenth century and helped place many female
authors on the literary map. She followed this novel with *Alexandrine, ou
l'amour est une vertu* (1783) and later spoke to husbands in *Salut à MM. les
maris ou, Rose et d'Orsinval* (1806). Her last novel, *Coralie, ou le danger de
se fier*, appeared in 1816. Of the three one-act plays that she produced, the best-
received, *Les Deux Soeurs*, was presented for the first time at the Théâtre des
Variétés Amusantes in Paris in June 1783. This play appears in several collections of French plays such as the *Petite Bibliothèque des théâtres* (vol. 12, 1785)
and the *Collection de pièces françaises* (vol. 21, 1790). A play about a victim
of the Revolution*, *Le Porteur d'eau*, was evidently burned by the author.

Sarah Harrell DeSmet

BIBLIOGRAPHY

Primary Texts

Lettres du chevalier de Saint-Alme et de la mademoiselle de Melcourt. Amsterdam and
        Paris: De Lormel, 1781.
Alexandrine, ou l'amour est une vertu. Amsterdam and Paris: De Lormel, 1783.
Les Deux Soeurs. Paris: Cailleau, 1783.
Mme de M***, ou la Rentière. Paris: Maradan, 1802.
Victor de Martiques, ou Suite de la rentière. Paris: Privately published, 1804.
Salut à MM. les maris, ou Rose et d'Orsinval. Paris: Borniche, 1806.

Secondary Text

Buck, Claire, ed. *The Bloomsbury Guide to Women's Literature*. New York: Prentice Hall, 1992.

Collin, Françoise (1928–). Philosopher, novelist, essayist, and professor of feminist theory*. Since the publication of her essay on Maurice Blanchot, Collin has been particularly interested in questions of writing and language, especially as they relate to women and patriarchal systems. In 1973 Collin founded *Les Cahiers du GRIF*, a Brussels-based magazine which expresses the views of the GRIF (Groupe de Recherche d'Information Féministes). In its reassessment of Beauvoir's* views on *fémininitude* and on the need for women to emulate men in order to succeed, this interdisciplinary group emphasizes the specificity of women's own experiences and values. It also rejects the psychoanalytically oriented and primarily Paris-based feminist organizations of the early seventies, proposing instead a new definition of female identity based on sorority. Collin contributed many prefaces, introductory statements, and essays on language (*langage-femme*), the body, feminist ethics, and maternity* to *Les Cahiers du GRIF*.

In her work, Collin stresses the need to overcome male domination through dialogue and sharing which must begin among women themselves. By reclaiming their bodies, women can cease to be objects created by the male gaze. Collin believes that the creative use of language can lead to empowering new possibilities for men and women.

Metka Zupančič

BIBLIOGRAPHY

Primary Texts

Rose qui peut. Paris: Seuil, 1962.
Maurice Blanchot et la question de l'écriture. 1971. Paris: Gallimard, 1986.
Ed. *Le Sexe des sciences: Les Femmes en plus*. Paris: Autrement, 1992.
Collin, Françoise et al., eds. *Le Corps des femmes. Les Cahiers du GRIF*. Brussels: Complexe, 1992.
———. *Le Langage des femmes. Les Cahiers du GRIF*. Brussels: Complexe, 1992.
———. *Les Enfants des femmes. Les Cahiers du GRIF*. Brussels: Complexe, 1992.
———. *La Société des femmes. Les Cahiers du GRIF*. Brussels: Complexe, 1992.

Secondary Texts

Jardine, Alice A., and Anne M. Menke, eds. *Shifting Scenes: Interviews on Women, Writing, and Politics in Post-68 France*. New York: Columbia University Press, 1991.
Rémy, Monique. *Histoire de mouvements de femmes. De l'utopie à l'intégration*. Paris: L'Harmattan, 1990.

Colonialism. The nineteenth century in France was a time of renewed territorial, cultural, and economic colonial conquest. Women were part of this enterprise in two main areas: as producers (and reproducers) of the myths and phantasms that served to legitimize French expansion, and as participants in the very process of the conquest. Most often, women's very colonial discourse suggests their questioning of a colonial ideology in which women writers' status was problematic within the dominant system. As fiction writers, many women used the colonial context in novels* situated in exotic places whose stories feature servants (and sometimes, but rarely, heroines) from "savage" tribes. Although not as systematically associated with conquest as were British women, French women writers often took on the roles of witnesses and defenders of the colonial enterprise in their nonfictional texts. They came to embody "Civilization." As colonial ideology had feminized the "other" lands in order to give itself a sense of possession, it feminized colonization itself and empowered women as key providers of culture. The substantial body of travel literature* written by women throughout the century testifies to the colonial responsibility assumed by its authors, from the Saint-Simonians to the uniquely programmatic, systematic studies of colonial strategies written by Isabelle Massieu at the end of the century. Because of their status within French society and other limitations placed on their writings, many women writers question (if indirectly) the justifications for and implementation of the colonial enterprise. In the case of Algeria, poor policies and impossible goals are criticized by some and even characterized by others as unjustifiable. In many cases, the evocation of women of other cultures by French women writers leads to a complex dialectic between the notions of possession of self and possession of the other.

Bénédicte Monicat

BIBLIOGRAPHY

Primary Texts

Auclert, Hubertine. *Les Femmes arabes en Algérie*. Paris: Société d'Editions Littéraires, 1900.
Bonnetain, Raymonde. *Une Française au Soudan: Sur la route de Tombouctou, du Sénégal au Niger*. Paris: Librairies-Imprimeries réunies, 1894.
Girault, Augustine. *En Algérie*. Paris: Librairie Centrale des Publications Populaires, 1881.
Lemire, Fanny. *Voyage à travers le Binh-dinh*. Lille: Imprimerie de L. Danel, 1889.
Massieu, Isabelle. *Les Anglais en Birmanie*. Conférence. Rouen: E. Cagniard, 1899.
———. *Comment j'ai parcouru l'Indo-Chine: Birmanie, Etats Shans, Siam, Tonkin, Laos*. Paris: Plon, 1901.
———. *Népal et les pays hymalayens*. Paris: Félix Alcan, 1914.
Voilquin, Suzanne. *Souvenirs d'une fille du peuple: La Saint-Simonienne en Egypte, 1834–1836*. Reprint. Paris: Maspéro, 1978.

Secondary Text

Kniebiehler, Yvonne, and Régine Goulatier. *La Femme au temps des colonies*. Paris: Stock, 1985.

Commune, The Paris. The Paris Commune lasted from March 18 to May 28, 1871. While it received different interpretations, one fact remains indisputable: the massive participation of women in this event, which was started by Montmartre women when they prevented Thiers's soldiers from seizing Parisian cannons.

Despite women's enthusiasm and willingness to serve and fight for the Commune, they were put aside and mistrusted. However, the Commune passed several favorable laws regarding free compulsory lay education* for all, equal pay for female and male teachers, and recognizing women and children of free unions as legitimate family*.

Some women rose to fame during the Commune. Louise Michel*, a celebrated orator, organized the "vigilance" committees. She also demanded vocational schools for women. Paule Mink opened a school free to all. Elizabeth Dmitrieff and Nathalie Lemel headed a group known as L'Union des femmes pour la défense de Paris et les soins aux blessés. They devoted their energies to the defense of Paris and the care of the wounded. They also raised issues about women's work and education. Most Communard women belonged to the working class, while their leaders came from the middle class. Their fight for the Commune was linked with their own emancipation. The communard Benoit Malon declared that it was the first time in history when women became politically active, mostly in revolutionary clubs. André Léo* was a well-known woman journalist who regularly denounced the antifeminism of the Commune, which assigned to women only the traditional tasks of field nurses or water carriers.

Women's fierce courage in combat prompted the Versaillais to invent the "pétroleuse" stories about women incendiaries in order to prevent other women from joining their ranks. Many women were summarily executed after the Commune, and several hundred were deported or imprisoned for their first attempt in history to exert their political rights.

Juliette Parnell-Smith

BIBLIOGRAPHY

"André Léo (1824–1900) une journaliste de la Commune." *Le Lérot rêveur*, no. 44 (March 1987): 9–60.
Blanchecotte, Augustine. *Tablettes d'une femme pendant la Commune.* Paris: Didier, 1872.
Gullickson, Gay L. *Unruly Women of Paris: Images of the Commune.* Ithaca: Cornell University Press, 1996.
Lissagaray, Prosper-Olivier. *Histoire de la Commune de 1871.* Paris: Petite collection Maspéro, 1982.
Michel, Louise. *La Commune.* Paris: P. V. Stock, 1898.
Minck, Paule. *Communarde et féministe, 1839–1901: Les mouches et les araignées, Le travail des femmes, et autres textes.* Préface, notes et commentaires par Alain Dalotel. Paris: Syros, 1981.

Moses, Claire Goldberg. *French Feminism in the Nineteenth Century*. Albany: State University of New York Press, 1984.

Schulkind, Eugène W. "Le Rôle des femmes dans la Commune de 1871." *1848—Revue des révolutions contemporaines*. 425 no. 185, (February 1950).

Thomas, Edith. *Les "Pétroleuses."* Paris: Gallimard, 1963.

Compagnonnage. In the nineteenth century, compagnonnage was the part of the guild system that survived in France from the Middle Ages. The journeyman artisans, or *compagnons*, who formed the membership of the secret societies in this system were exclusively male, although the word *compagnonne* was sometimes applied to women workers. The only woman involved was the so-called Mother who kept the local chapter house of the society. The compagnonnage, despite its masculine character, became an important motif for women writers such as George Sand* and Flora Tristan,* who used it as a metaphor for working-class and even national solidarity. The latter embarked on her own *tour de France*, the traditional journeyman's circuit around the country, in an effort to organize workers. Her journal of her travels appeared posthumously.

Mary Rice-DeFosse

BIBLIOGRAPHY

Primary Texts

Perdiguier, Agricol. *Le Livre du compagnonnage*. 2 vols. Paris: Pagnerre, 1841.

Sand, George. *Le Compagnon du tour de France*. Ed. Jean Courrier. Intro. René Bourgeois. Grenoble: Presses Universitaires de Grenoble, 1988.

Tristan, Flora. *Le Tour de France*. 2 vols. Ed. Jules Puech. Intro. Stéphane Michaud. Paris: Seuil, 1980.

Secondary Texts

Bouvier-Ajam, Maurice. "George Sand et le compagnonnage." *Europe* 587 (March 1978): 117–119.

Briquet, Jean. *Agricol Perdiguier: Compagnon du tour de France et représentant du peuple, 1805–1875*. Paris: Ed. de la Butte aux Cailles, 1981.

Goodwin-Jones, Robert. *Romantic Vision: The Novels of George Sand*. Birmingham, AL: Summa, 1995.

Lane, Brigitte. "Mystique ouvrière et utopie sociale dans *Le Compagnon du tour de France*: Le Mariage du Christ et la (recon)naissance du 'peuple roi'." *George Sand Studies* 14 (Spring 1996):45–58.

Rice-DeFosse, Mary. "George Sand, Flora Tristan, and the Tour de France." In *The Traveler in the Life and Works of George Sand*. Ed. Tamara Alvarez-Detrell and Michael G. Paulson. Troy, NY: Whitston, 1994.

Schor, Naomi. *George Sand and Idealism*. New York: Columbia University Press, 1993.

Sivert, Eileen Boyd. "Flora Tristan: The Joining of Essay, Journal, Autobiography." In *Women's Essays: Genre Crossings*. Ed. Ruth Ellen Boetcher Joeres and Elizabeth Mittman. Bloomington: Indiana University Press, 1993. 52–72.

Compain, Louise-Marie (?–?). Novelist, journalist, and author of political and feminist treatises. Among Compain's most famous political works are *Les*

Femmes dans les organisations ouvrières (1910) and ''Les Conséquences du travail de la femme'' (1913). In marked contrast to the working-class women of her socialist political texts, the female protagonists of Compain's novels*, though they are strong and independent, ultimately seek a protected life in a bourgeois setting. *L'Un vers l'autre* (1903), for example, explores the changing dynamics of the male-female relationship, presenting a female protagonist who leaves her husband to seek financial independence. Compain was also an activist who spoke publicly on socialism, women, and labor law, and who served as a delegate at the International Women's Suffrage Convention in Stockholm in 1911.

Juliette M. Rogers

BIBLIOGRAPHY

Primary Texts

L'Un vers l'autre. Paris: Stock, 1903.
L'Opprobre. Paris: Stock, 1905.
''En feuilletant les Catalogues.'' Paris: L'Union pour la Vérité, 1910.
Les Femmes dans les organisations ouvrières. Paris: Giard et Brière, 1910.
''L'Action sociale des femmes.'' Paris: Union Française pour le Suffrage des Femmes, 1912.
La Vie tragique de Geneviève. Paris: Calmann-Lévy, 1912.
L'Amour de Claire. Paris: Calmann-Lévy, 1912.

Secondary Text

Waelti-Walters, Jennifer. *Feminist Novelists of the Belle Epoque: Love as a Lifestyle*. Bloomington: Indiana University Press, 1990.

Condorcet, Sophie de Grouchy de (1764–1822). Sophie de Grouchy was born into a close-knit family of the nobility. As a girl, she spent a year and a half as a lay canoness in a priory, where she read voraciously, especially Voltaire and Rousseau, and from which she emerged devoted to the ideals of the Enlightenment*. In 1786 she married the mathematician and philosopher Condorcet; they had one daughter. It was probably Sophie who inspired Condorcet to write, soon after their marriage*, the remarkable essays in which he argued that women were no less endowed than men with feelings, conscience, and reason, and advocated equal civil rights for them.

Sophie opened a salon* in 1787, frequented by figures such as the marquis de La Fayette, Thomas Jefferson, Thomas Paine, and Adam Smith, that became a locus of republicanism. Condorcet was a maker of the Revolution* and also its victim: condemned by the Convention, he escaped the guillotine* only to die by suicide. Sophie survived the Terror by courage, ingenuity, and skill as a portrait painter. Throughout the era of the Napoleonic empire and religious monarchical reaction, she remained loyal to her republican and philosophical beliefs, and spent her last years producing an edition of her husband's writings.

Her own chief work was a commentary, *Lettres sur la sympathie*, accompanying her translation* of Adam Smith's *Theory of Moral Sentiments*. Her essay argues that every person is endowed with a natural sympathy with the pleasures and pains of others that is the source of our moral sentiments, and with a capacity for reflection from which come our ideas of morality and justice. The obstacle to virtue and happiness lies not in human nature, but in corrupt social institutions; and those, Sophie believes, can be reformed. Written in 1793, this treatise is an act of faith in the Enlightenment made in the very face of the Terror.

Janet Whatley

BIBLIOGRAPHY

Primary Texts

Théorie des sentiments moraux. Suivi d'une dissertation sur l'origine des langues. Par Adam Smith. Trans. S. Grouchy Veuve Condorcet. Paris: F. Buisson, 1978.
Avertissement. Oeuvres complètes de Condorcet. Paris: Heinrichs, 1804.
Préface. Esquisse d'un tableau historique des progrès de l'esprit humain (1795, 1822). Paris: Garnier-Flammarion, 1988.
Lettres sur la sympathie, suivies des lettres d'amour. Ed. Jean-Paul de Lagrave. Montreal and Paris: L'Etincelle Editeur, 1994.

Secondary Texts

Badinter, Elisabeth, et Robert Badinter. *Condorcet, un intellectuel en politique.* Paris: Fayard, 1988.
Boissel, Thierry. *Sophie de Condorcet, femme des Lumières.* Paris: Presses de la Renaissance, 1988.
Brookes, Barbara. "The Feminism of Condorcet and Sophie de Grouchy." *Studies on Voltaire and the Eighteenth Century* 189 (1980): 297–361.
Lagrave, Jean-Paul de. "L'Influence de Sophie de Grouchy sur la pensée de Condorcet." *Condorcet, mathématicien, économiste, philosophe, homme politique: Colloque International.* Ed. Pierre Crepel and Christian Gilain. Paris: Minerve, 1989.
Valentino, Henri. *Madame de Condorcet, ses amis et ses amours.* Paris: Perrin, 1950.

Constant, Paule (1944–). Constant spent her childhood in various French colonies where her father was a doctor for the military; she is currently a professor of French literature at the University of Aix-Marseille. *Ouregano* (1979), a story set in Africa, launched her career as a postcolonial novelist; its sequel, *Propriété privée* (1981), introduces the theme of girls' education* as a major focus of her work. Constant's analysis of the relationships between a young girl who returns to France from the colonies, her grandmother, and a nun at the convent* school reveals a keen understanding of female psychology, of matriarchal hierarchies of power, and of female survival rituals—themselves oppressive at times. The author further explores these topics in a long essay—*Un Monde à l'usage des demoiselles* (1987)—which describes the institution of the convent school from the Middle Ages to the nineteenth century as a haven created by women for the initiation of girls. In *Le Grand Ghâpal* (1991), she depicts powerful, self-reliant female characters who live in an abbey. In these works, Constant provides a provocative analysis of female culture as both empowering and debilitating.

Christine Lac

BIBLIOGRAPHY

Primary Texts

Ouregano. Paris: Gallimard, 1979.
Propriété privée. Paris: Gallimard, 1981.
Balta. Paris: Gallimard, 1983.
Un Monde à l'usage des demoiselles. Paris: Gallimard, 1987.
White Spirit. Paris: Gallimard, 1989.
Le Grand Ghâpal. Paris: Gallimard, 1991.
La Fille du Gobernator. Paris: Gallimard, 1994.

Convents. A convent is an institution in which nuns, women who have taken religious vows, live and perform a series of daily liturgical tasks. Nuns live according to various rules, presided over by an abbess or mother superior. The medieval Catholic Church put forth life in the convent as the most laudable choice for women. In theory, by renouncing the world and devoting her life to prayer, a woman might come closer to God and to spritual perfection. In the Middle Ages, convents offered women who did not wish to marry or who had been widowed secure places in which to live and work. They provided education* in Latin and religious literature and were one of the few places in which women became actively literate. Convent life was, however, mostly available to the upper classes, and class differences often remained important inside the convent walls.

The Church attempted many times to make consecrated women submit to total, unrelieved enclosure inside convent walls. Ecclesiastical writers argued that nuns had to be confined, both to protect them from men and to protect men from uncontrollable female sexuality. In the high Middle Ages, many women chose the newer and less structured Franciscan and Dominican orders over the strictly conventual Cluniacs and Cisterians. Their attempts to work outside the convent, however, were unsuccessful, and the Church hierarchy soon succeeded in enclosing many of the reformed orders. The educational system in convents also suffered as medieval universities, now centers for training theologians, excluded women from the study of Latin; from this period on, female writers would write in the vernacular. During the thirteenth century many women who longed for a religious life but did not wish to be enclosed chose to take moderate vows while remaining at home. These women were known as Beguines.

The same battles continued throughout the late Middle Ages and the early modern period, but changing social needs helped nuns to find ways to work outside the convent. A 1545 edict of the Council of Trent, responding to allegations made by Protestant reformers, decreed strict enclosure for all nuns. Orders dedicated to ministry outside the convent, such as the French Visitandines founded by Jeanne Frémyot, baronesse de Chantal*, were forced to submit to enclosure. The first order to be free of the convent was the Daughters of Charity, founded by Vincent de Paul in 1634, which gradually became entrusted with the administration of hospitals and other institutions. They began a trend away from convent life which would continue throughout the modern period. In the meantime, however, monasticism continued to be an activity primarily for the upper class. Convents often functioned as places of retirement for noble women, such as Louise de La Vallière, mistress of Louis XIV.

This tendency toward exclusivity caused the French monastic system to suffer greatly during the Revolution*. In 1790 the Constituent Assembly declared all religious houses closed and suppressed all orders that were not devoted to teaching or nursing. The last enclosed convent was suppressed in August 1792, and many nuns who refused to leave were executed. Post-revolutionary France, however, experienced a resurgence of interest in the monastic life, particularly for women. Many orders already dedicated to direct ministry expanded their activities to include active missionary work in French-controlled territories, but the orders which preferred the convent and enclosure also prospered. During the Vatican II Council (1962–1965), the Church officially recognized the importance of the work done by nuns outside the convent and raised active social work to the same status as that of enclosed contemplation.

Belle Stoddard Tuten

BIBLIOGRAPHY

Johnson, Penelope D. *Equal in Monastic Profession: Religious Women in Medieval France*. Chicago: University of Chicago Press, 1991.
McNamara, Jo Ann. *Sisters in Arms: Catholic Nuns through Two Millenia*. Cambridge, MA: Harvard University Press, 1996.
Les Religieuses dans le cloître et dans le monde des origines à nos jours: Actes du deuxième Colloque International du C.E.R.C.O.R. Poitiers: Université de Saint-Etienne, 1994.

Corday, Charlotte (1768–1793). Known primarily as the young woman from Caen who murdered the radical journalist Marat in his bathtub, Corday was a revolutionary in her own right, well educated and courageous. Although the Jacobins defamed her as a monstrous, crazed "femme-homme," she was proud of her womanliness and saw it as entirely compatible with intelligent, decisive political action. Above all else, she meant to be "useful," to save her country from a destructive tyrant. The night before the murder, she composed her "Adresse aux Français," explaining to the nation her intentions to liberate France and urging others to complete the job should she fail. Then, during the four days between her killing of Marat and her own execution, she composed six letters from prison, to the Committee of Public Safety, to the Girondin Barbaroux, and to her father, in which she quoted from Voltaire, Rousseau, Corneille, and Plutarch. She compared herself to Brutus, simply doing her duty. The Revolutionary Tribunal refused to believe that a mere woman could conceive and execute such an act alone, but the idea was exclusively hers. Anticipating the calumnies of Marat's supporters, she requested that her portrait be painted, to show her strength, beauty, and composure, and to safeguard her reputation for posterity. Her self-presentation in her letters as a patriot and a woman was stunning in its unwavering righteousness, but she also interjected some humor. The effect was that she disarmed her detractors and came across as a sensible, sympathetic person who has never ceased to fascinate.

Nina Rattner Gelbart

BIBLIOGRAPHY

Primary Texts

Archives Nationales. Series W 277 dossier 82, and W293.
Oeuvres politiques. Caen: Le Gost, 1863–1864.

Secondary Texts

Bonnet, Jean-Claude. *La mort de Marat.* Paris: Flammarion, 1986.
Defrance, Eugène. *Charlotte Corday et la mort de Marat. Documents inédits sur l'histoire de la Terreur.* Paris: Mercure de France, 1909.
Montfort, Catherine R. ''For the Defence: Charlotte Corday's *Letters from Prison.''* *Studies on Voltaire and the Eighteenth Century* 329 (1995): 235–247.
Vatel, Charles. Fond Vatel at Bibliothèque de Versailles, F656–682.
Walter, Gérard. *Actes du Tribunal Révolutionnaire.* Paris: Mercure de France, 1968.

Cosmopolitism. Cosmopolitism was not only an ideal of the Enlightenment*, it was a way of life for many enlightened individuals in the eighteenth century. With its belief in the universality of human values and in the necessity of transcending parochial boundaries, cosmopolitism finds its correlative in the international journals, correspondence, visits, and travels linking educated individuals in America, England, Holland, France, Prussia, Austria, Switzerland, and elsewhere.

Cosmopolitism is closely linked to clubs and academies, the cafés and parlors where well-known international figures such as Hume, Franklin, Jefferson, Grimm, Goethe, and Beccaria shared ideas with their French counterparts: Montesquieu, Voltaire, Diderot, d'Alembert, Helvétius, Condorcet, and others. In France the salons* of Mesdames Geoffrin*, Helvétius, and Condorcet* were among the gathering places for such exchanges. The influential activity of the salons was recognized by Franklin, who credited Madame Helvétius with providing a significant link in the international discourse on religion, politics, and ethics. If wit was required of participants, he noted, it was wit applied to social issues. D'Alembert praised the salon for supporting the election of cosmopolitans to the Académie Française, and Hume applauded the mutual respect between foreign emissaries and local intellectuals. In the years prior to the French Revolution*, the salon of Sophie Condorcet would join those of Mme de Boufflers and Mme Helvétius in the dissemination of radical ideas. Besides providing a cosmopolitan venue, educated women maintained extensive correspondence with foreign intellectuals and dignitaries. Geoffrin's letters to the crowned heads of Europe and Mme du Deffand's* letters to Horace Walpole are illustrative.

Attitudes toward women intellectuals and salon life were not without ambiguity. Hume and Voltaire worried about the chameleon-like behavior that characterized salon life with its requirements that participants be pleasing in the eyes of the women hosts. Morellet praised Mme d'Holbach, who played a passive role in her husband's gatherings, unlike Mme Helvétius, who played a defining role in hers. Dinner parties at d'Holbach's were praised by Voltaire, Hume, Morellet, and Franklin alike, as sites of "virile" cosmopolitism, in contrast to the salon's genteel tone.

The *Encyclopédie*'s* definition of cosmopolitism illustrates the tension in Enlightenment thinking between an ideal community of like-minded individuals, with its inherent exclusivity, and the principle of universal equality, with its acceptance of differences. The definition sends readers to the word "philosophe," considered a synonym for the cosmopolitan ideal, and clearly a community of men. Indeed, it could be argued that in its emphasis on discovery of other lands, travels in the known world, and participation in clubs and academies, cosmopolitism was less easily lived by women, whose freedom of movement was limited by social conventions.

Caryl L. Lloyd

BIBLIOGRAPHY

Schlereth, Thomas J. *The Cosmopolitan Ideal in Enlightenment Thought*. Notre Dame: University of Notre Dame Press, 1977.

Cosnard, Marthe (1614–after 1659). Marthe Cosnard was born in Séez, Normandy, the daughter of Thomas Cosnard and Catherine Du Frische. The family circle, composed of cultivated professionals, who counted the poet and bishop Jean Bertaut among their friends, brought Cosnard into contact with Pierre Corneille, who dedicated a laudatory poem to her. Her intellectual accomplishments were acknowledged during her lifetime, and she is included by her contemporary, Jean de La Forge, in his *Cercle des femmes savantes*, where he cites her precious pseudonym, Candace. Apart from her works, little is known of her life beyond her lifelong decision to remain unmarried, which earned her the title of the "virgin of Séez." She is certainly the author of the three-act play *Les Chastes Martirs* (1651); other plays have been attributed to her, probably incorrectly: *Les Filles généreuses* (n.d.), *Le Martyre de Saint Eustache* (1643), and *Le Martyre de Sainte Catherine* (1649). However there is reason to believe that she is the author of *La Grande Bible renouvelée*, a collection of short plays presenting various personages of the Bible*, a work that has been falsely attributed to Françoise Pascal* despite the fact that the title page attributes it to M.V.V.C.D.S. (Marthe Vierge [adj.] Cosnard de Séez).

Hannah Fournier

BIBLIOGRAPHY

Primary Text

Cosnard, Marthe. *La Tragédie des chastes martyrs*. Ed. L. de La Sicotière. Rouen: Société des Bibliophiles Normands, 1888.

Secondary Text

Lancaster, Henry Carrington. *A History of French Dramatic Literature in the Seventeenth Century*. Baltimore: Johns Hopkins University Press, 1929–1942. Vol. 2: 672–674.

Cotteblanche, Marie de (sixteenth century). Translator. Daughter of Guy de Cotteblanche, a lawyer at the Parlement de Paris, and Catherine Hesselin, whom he married in 1517, Marie de Cotteblanche came from a bourgeois family of Mayenne. The only information available on her comes from the *Bibliothèques* (1584) of La Croix du Maine and Du Verdier, who note that she is a ''Demoiselle Parisienne'' gifted in philosophy and mathematics, and still living in 1566 (I, 88).

Marie de Cotteblanche's only known work, the French translation* of three Spanish *Coloquios* or *Diálogos* by the cosmographer Pierre Messie (Pero Mexía or Mejía, 1497–1551), was published in 1566 in Paris by Frédéric Morel and reissued five times between 1566 and 1593. Following Du Verdier, critics thought that Marie used Claude Grujet's French translation of these dialogues, which he included in the same volume as his translation of the *Diverses Lessons de Pierre Messie* (1566). However, it is Grujet who used Marie's version verbatim without stating its provenance.

The three dialogues that Marie de Cotteblanche translates are concerned with geophysics and cosmography. Four reasons may explain her interest. First, the flexibility and freedom of the genre of the dialogue likely attracted her. Second, the dialogue, a favorite humanist genre, helped make learning more accessible to a wider readership eager to expand its knowledge. In her preface, Cotteblanche states her great love of books, study, and learning. Third, Pierre Messie's preference for the vernacular was of particular appeal to women, who were denied the school study of Latin. Women, moreover, were allowed to translate, especially books of piety; and translation afforded them the possibility of writing and publishing. Finally, Cotteblanche states her great interest in the scientific subject matter of these dialogues. She was no exception. During her lifetime, numerous scientific works were dedicated to women. Many well-known women of the nobility were versed in the sciences. Catherine de Medici* was keenly interested in astronomy and the natural sciences, Marguerite de Navarre* and Diane de Poitiers* in medical treatises, and Catherine de Clermont, maréchale de Retz, in philosophy and mathematics. Women of the learned gentry also read scientific literature. Educators such as Guillaume de La Tayssonnière recommended a scientific training for young girls.

Despite this changing cultural expectation, women who wrote on scientific matters were subject to criticism. To avoid judgment, Cotteblanche refused to have her name printed on the title page of her translation, signing instead with her initials. Her purpose, she states, is to please her readers, not to draw attention to herself. She dedicated her translation to her friend and guardian Marguerite de Saluces, maréchale de Termes, as a gift of thanks for having taught her Italian and for encouraging her to write.

Anne R. Larsen

BIBLIOGRAPHY

Primary Text

Trois Dialogues de M. Pierre Messie, touchant la nature du Soleil, de la Terre, et de toutes les choses qui se font et apparoissent en l'air. Paris: Frédéric Morel, 1579.

Secondary Texts

Berriot-Salvadore, Evelyne. *Les Femmes dans la société française de la Renaissance.* Geneva: Droz, 1990.
———. "Les Femmes et les pratiques de l'écriture de Christine de Pisan à Marie de Gournay." *Réforme, Humanisme, Renaissance* 16 (1983): 52–69.
La Croix du Maine et Du Verdier. *Les Bibliothèques françoises.* 6 vols. Ed. Rigoley de Juvigny, 1772–1773. Reprint. Graz: Academische Druck, 1969.
Larsen, Anne R. "Marie de Cotteblanche: Préfacière et traductrice de trois dialogues de Pierre Messie." *Etudes Littéraires* 27, no. 2 (1994): 111– 119.
Mexia, Pedro. *Les Diverses Lessons de Pierre Messie [. . .].* Trans. Claude Grujet. Paris: M. Prevost, 1566. (BN Z. 32322)
———. *Dialoghi di Pietro Messia, tradotti nuovamente di spagnuolo in volgare da Alfonso d'Ulloa.* Trans. Alfonso Ulloa. Venice: Plinio Pietrasanta, 1557. (BN Z. 3444)
———. *Diálogos o Coloquios of Pedro Mejía.* Ed. Margaret Mulroney. Iowa City: University of Iowa Studies in Spanish Language and Literature, 1930.

Cottin, Sophie Risteau (1770–1807). Born into a family of Protestant merchants, she grew up in Bordeaux, then returned to Paris after her marriage* to banker Paul Cottin in 1789. Their happiness was short-lived because of Paul's health and the political turmoil that was to follow. Widowed at twenty-three, Cottin experienced tragedy and financial hardship.

Her literary production included five novels*, *Claire d'Albe* (1799), *Malvina* (1801), *Amélie Mansfield* (1802), *Mathilde* (1805), and *Elisabeth ou les exilés de Sibérie* (1806); a short piece inspired by the Bible*, *Jéricho ou la pécheresse convertie*; and a collection of letters. Her first and most popular novel, *Claire d'Albe*, met with unprecedented success, and her talent as a gifted writer was recognized by Chateaubriand, Hugo, Lamartine, and Stendhal. Soon, her works were translated into more than a half-dozen languages and adapted for the stage. Her novels survived in France for several decades after her death; however, her Anglo-Saxon readership seemed to have an insatiable appetite for the English translations, especially in the United States, where *Elisabeth* appears to have been used in French classes through the early twentieth century.

Female characters occupy center stage in Cottin's novels and bear remarkable resemblance to their author: sensitive to the beauty of nature, prone to experience acute sadness, and likely to find comfort in friendship* and religion. However, behind their delicate and romantic beauty, these passionate and confident "women of fire" live life to the fullest, challenge authority, and defy the social order.

Samia I. Spencer

BIBLIOGRAPHY

Primary Texts

Claire d'Albe. 1799. Paris Régine Deforges, 1976.
Malvina. Paris: Maradan, 1801.
Amélie Mansfield. Paris: Giguet et Michaud, 1802.
Elisabeth ou les exilés de Sibérie. Paris: Giguet et Michaud, 1806.
Oeuvres complètes. Ed. J. Michaud. Paris: Corbet, 1820.

Secondary Texts

Gaulmier, Jean. "Roman et connotations sociales: *Mathilde* de Mme Cottin." *Roman et société*. Ed. Michel Raimond. Paris: Collin, 1973. 7–17.
Marquiset, Alfred. "Madame Cottin." In *Les Bas-Bleus du Premier Empire*. Paris: Champion, 1914. 15–16.
Spencer, Samia I. "Sophie Cottin." In *French Women Writers: A Bio-Bibliographical Source Book*. Ed. Eva M. Sartori and Dorothy W. Zimmerman. Westport, CT: Greenwood Press, 1991. 90–98.
Stewart, Joan Hinde. *Gynographs: French Novels by Women of the Late Eighteenth Century*. Lincoln: University of Nebraska Press, 1993.
Sykes, L. C. *Madame Cottin*. Oxford: Basil Blackwell, 1949.

Courtly love. Frequently assumed to be a medieval concept, the term "courtly love" (*amour courtois*) was in fact first introduced in 1883 by French medievalist Gaston Paris to describe the adulterous passion between Lancelot and Queen Guenevere in Chrétien de Troyes's twelfth-century verse romance, *Le Chevalier de la Charrète*. Where other knights strive to strike a balance between love and the vocation of arms, Lancelot willingly compromises his chivalric reputation for his love, adoring strands of her golden hair as if they were holy relics and throwing battles at her command. Dedicated to Countess Marie de Champagne, the *Charrète* belonged, it is assumed, to the milieu described in Andreas Capellanus's *De arte honeste amandi*, in which the countess presided over courts of love—ludic parallels to the feudal courts being established by Henry II of England and other contemporary princes—rendering decisions over the proper conduct of affairs of the heart. The taxonomic impulse evident in the rhetorical prescriptions of Book One—how a nobleman's speech to a bourgeois woman should differ from his speech to a noblewoman, and so on—together with the preemptive tone of the judgments rendered by the countess and her friends, creates an impression of social consensus around the practice of love and other chivalric pursuits. Assuming courtly love to be a fixed and definable code, however, raises as many problems as it solves when we turn to contemporary literary texts. For example, while the countess's pronouncement that love (as something that must be freely given) is necessarily incompatible with marriage* (a constrained social relation) coincides with the adulterous passion of a Tristan and Iseut or Lancelot and Guenevere, it fails to account for the image of conjugal love drawn in Chrétien de Troyes's romances *Erec et Enide*, *Le Chevalier au Lion*, or his "anti-Tristan," *Cligée*.

In fact, rather than serving as the stable reference point which helps us understand medieval culture, courtly love has come to function as the aporia around which all our critical debates—those due to lacunae in our historical knowledge as well as those deriving from theoretical or ideological differences—seem to turn. What was its status: historical reality or pure literary convention? What was its function in medieval society? Was it a subversive counterdiscourse, the revenge of the disenfranchised knight and the unhappily married woman (the *mal-mariée*) against the feudal patriarch? Or was it, in contrast, a normalizing discourse aimed at disciplining the passions of the young knight—his love service to the lady functioning as a displaced enactment of his devotion to his feudal lord? Was courtly love feminist? Did the exaltation of the courtly lady signal the "femininization" of feudal society, an advance over the violence of the masculinist, warrior ethos of the *chanson de geste** (exemplified by the *Chanson de Roland*)? Or was it antifeminist, reifying all women in the distant, often forbidding figure of the *domna* who was merely the flip side of the abject woman of the discourses of medieval misogyny? These are some of the questions surrounding the term "courtly love."

What are we left with? Recent work on the history of French medieval studies reveals how the institutionalization of the discipline from the 1870s through World War I* (manifested, for example, in the endowment of chairs and the founding of professional journals) inaugurated a notion of professionalism linked to a positivist ideal of scientific objectivity itself predicated on the repression of romantic passion and a homosocial exclusion of the feminine. If that was the milieu in which Gaston Paris elaborated his notion of courtly love, the modern critical conjuncture, with its emphasis on questions of agency and textuality, has produced a distinct set of issues and questions, one which makes more apparent the extent to which discussions of courtly love participate in the ideological complexities of assessing the role of women in medieval society. Deconstructing the universalist claims implicit in the founding discourses of nineteenth-century medievalism unsettles the possibility of taking courtly love as a codified practice with unambiguous meaning. Feminist critics, reclaiming the physicality which in the misogynist tradition is taken as a mark of women's inferiority, have lately devoted much attention to the female body: as the subject as well as the object of desire; as the producer of an alternative discourse that contests that of patriarchal authority; as the object of a sexual violence often indistinguishable from the plot of romance; as the site of the inscription of differences of race and class previously effaced in the totalizing image of the courtly *domna*, but central to women's biological role in the dynastic politics that played an increasingly important role in the transmission of power in the high Middle Ages. Historical practice or literary convention, adulterous or conjugal, subversive or accommodationist, feminist or misogynist: the complex history of courtly love shows that to analyze representations of love in the French Middle Ages is inevitably to find them inflected by the social and theoretical concerns of our own historical moment. It is perhaps this which explains why the purportedly medieval phenomenon of courtly love has remained so consistently the center of controversy and critical excitement.

Sharon Kinoshita

BIBLIOGRAPHY

Secondary Texts

Bloch, R. Howard. 'Mieux vaut jamais que tard': Romance, Philology, and Old French Letters." *Representations* 36 (1991): 64–86.

Burns, E. Jane, et al. "Feminism and the Discipline of Old French Studies: *Une Bele Disjointure.*" In *Medievalism and the Modernist Temper.* Ed. R. Howard Bloch and Stephen G. Nichols. Baltimore: Johns Hopkins University Press, 1996. 225–266.

Duby, Georges. *Love and Marriage in the Middle Ages.* Trans. Jane Dunnett. Chicago: University of Chicago Press, 1991.

Kelly, Henry Ansgar. "The Varieties of Love in Medieval Literature According to Gaston Paris." *Romance Philology* 40 (1987): 301–327.

Lomperis, Linda, and Sarah Stanbury, eds. *Feminist Approaches to the Body in Medieval Literature.* Philadelphia: University of Pennsylvania Press, 1993.

Moi, Toril. "Desire in Language: Andreas Capellanus and the Controversy of Courtly Love." In *Medieval Literature: Criticism, Ideology, and History.* Ed. David Aers. New York: Saint Martin's Press, 1986. 11–33.

Craven de la Ferronays, Pauline (1808–1891). Prominent author of religious writings known in France and abroad mostly for her best-selling narrative, *Récit d'une soeur.* She started writing late in life, partly to secure her family's financial situation. Her writings are deeply defined by her Catholicism, as demonstrated by her many narratives of exemplary lives and her best-selling text. The latter consists of a compilation of correspondence between her brother and his wife, interspersed with editorial comments and narratives by Craven herself. Such was her success that she became one of the few nineteenth-century authors to receive an annuity from her publisher.

Bénédicte Monicat

BIBLIOGRAPHY

Primary Texts

Récit d'une soeur. Paris: Imprimerie de J. Claye, 1866.
Le Comte de Montalembert. Paris: Didier, 1873.

Le Mot de l'énigme. Paris: Didier, 1874.
Réminiscences, souvenirs d'Angleterre et d'Italie. Paris: Didier, 1879.

Crenne, Hélisenne de (literary pseudonym of Marguerite Briet) (1510?–1560?), novelist, epistolary writer, and translator. Very few details are known about the life of Crenne, except for what readers extrapolate, often too much so, from her first work, the semi-autobiographical novel *Les Angoysses douloureuses qui procèdent d'amours* (1538, considered France's first sentimental novel*), and from her second work, the *Epistres familieres et invectives* (1539). Both of these are works of autobiographical fiction and relate the development of a remarkable feminist consciousness, one ideologically connected to the debate on women in the sixteenth century—the *Querelle des femmes**. They also relate the emerging awareness of the specific conditions under which women lived in France in the 1530s. These conditions are always described from the point of view of the woman. Hélisenne, the narrator and protagonist in these two works, is responding to the misogynist prejudice and slander, indeed the physical harm and mental anguish, inflicted on her and women in general by an extremely abusive husband, and by others of his persuasion. Hélisenne is also countering, especially in her *Epistres*, traditional accusations (contemporary, classical, Judeo-Christian) made against women, just as Christine de Pizan* (*Livre de la cité des dames*, 1405), an important source model for Crenne, had done before her.

The resounding theme of Crenne's works is Hélisenne's insistence on the literary, writerly autonomy of women and on women as morally, intellectually, and thus socially the equal of men, both in the private and public domains. This liberating theme of female autonomy, competence, and achievement is crystallized in particular in the eighth personal letter in the striking image of woman as ''Virago,'' that is, as ''she who performs *manly* tasks.'' Equality feminism* broadly defined is thus the hallmark of Crenne's literary endeavors.

Crenne also published two other works: a philosophical allegory pitting reason against passion (*Le Songe*, 1540) and a fictionally oriented translation* of the first four books of Virgil's *Aeneid* (*Les Quatre Premiers Livres des Eneydes du treselegant poete Virgile*, 1541).

Research trends on Crenne have only recently begun to take her *Epistres* into account, thanks in great part to the English translation and the insightful introduction by Mustacchi and Archambault. Though critical inquiry into the *Angoysses* continues to dominate studies on Crenne, the tide has begun to turn. Two recent critical editions of Crenne's epistolary work should help renew and sustain interest in this monument of early modern feminist consciousness and female accomplishment.

Jerry C. Nash

BIBLIOGRAPHY

Primary Texts

Les Oeuvres de ma dame Hélisenne de Crenne. Facsimile reproduction of the 1560 last
     edition. Geneva: Slatkine Reprints, 1977.

Les Angoysses douloureuses qui procèdent d'amours, Première partie. Ed. Jérôme Vercruysse. Paris: Lettres Modernes, 1968.
Les Epistres familières et invectives de ma dame Hélisenne. Ed. Jean-Philippe Beaulieu, with Hannah Fournier. Montreal: Les Presses de l'Université de Montréal, 1995.
Les Epistres familières et invectives. Ed. Jerry C. Nash. Paris: Champion, 1996.

Secondary Texts

Baker, M. J. "France's First Sentimental Novel and the Novels of Chivalry." *Bibliothèque d'Humanisme et Renaissance* 36 (1974): 33–45.
Jensen, Katharine Ann. "Writing Out of the Double Bind: Female Plot and Hélisenne de Crenne's *Angoysses douloureuses qui procèdent d'amours.*" *Oeuvres & Critiques* 19 (1994): 61–67.
Nash, Jerry C. " 'Exerçant oeuvres viriles': Feminine Anger and Feminist (Re)Writing in Hélisenne de Crenne." *L'Esprit Créateur* 30 (1990): 38–48.
———. "The Fury of the Pen: Crenne, the Bible, and Letter Writing." In *Women Writers in Pre-Revolutionary France: Strategies of Emancipation.* Ed. Colette H. Winn and Donna Kuizenga. New York: Garland, 1997. 207–225.
———. "Renaissance Misogyny, Biblical Feminism, and Hélisenne de Crenne's *Epistres familières et invectives.*" *Renaissance Quarterly* 50, no. 2 (1997): 379–410.
———. "The Rhetoric of Scorn in Hélisenne de Crenne." *French Literature Series* 19 (1992): 1–9.
Winn, Colette H. "R-écrire le féminin: *Les Angoysses douloureuses qui procèdent d'amours* d'Hélisenne de Crenne (1 ère partie): Autour des notions de transgression et de 'jouyssance.' " *Renaissance and Reformation* 28 (1992): 39–55.
Wood, Diane S. "The Evolution of Hélisenne de Crenne's Persona." *Symposium* 45 (1991): 140–151.

Cross-dressing. Women have dressed as men throughout French literary and cultural history. Categorizing their acts as mere practicality may seem logical, but it is much more interesting—and more accurate—to read cross-dressing as a space in which women have reinvented Woman for centuries.

Early examples of cross-dressing include women who were praised for passing as men to study in monasteries; Joan of Arc, who was burned at the stake for specifically refusing to give up male dress; and heroines of medieval romances whose authors commend them for reshaping their destinies while they critique the social conditions that made their strategy necessary.

In the early modern period, many women warriors excelled in military exercise and wore male dress. Saint-Balmon*, and later Montpensier* and La Guette* during the Fronde*, all exceeded expectations for women; most important, they wrote about it. They certainly influenced later writers, such as Villedieu*, Murat*, d'Aulnoy*, and L'Héritier*, whose respective novels* and fairy tales* use cross-dressers to interrogate issues of identity and social status. As such, they contrast greatly with the already stereotypical representations found in texts by d'Urfé and Scarron and in numerous dramatic works where cross-dressed women are apparently expected to produce laughs even as they raise anxieties.

In the nineteenth century, women like George Sand* and Sarah Bernhardt did indeed wear male dress, but the female cross-dresser as literary figure became increasingly entrapped in the erotic imagination of male authors, for example Théophile Gautier's *Mademoiselle de Maupin* (1835). Currently, the cross-dresser is almost an icon in feminist and cultural studies theories, but, ironically, cross-dressed women rarely show up in literature. One explanation for their absence may be that Freud's work on the fetish, and the importance it places on the phallus, has animated most early twentieth-century ideas about cross-dressing and transvestism, including those of Magnus Hirshfeld and Havelock Ellis. Consequently, if a woman has no phallus to fetishize, the fact that she wears men's clothes seems to be considered insignificant, at least to psychoanalysts, and cross-dressing is a site of male privilege.

Margaret Wise

BIBLIOGRAPHY

Primary Texts

Aucassin et Nicolette. Ed. Mario Roques. Paris: Champion, 1969.

Aulnoy, Comtesse de. "Belle-Belle." In *Les Contes nouveaux*. Paris: Librairie des bibliophiles, 1881.

La Guette, Madame de. *Mémoires*. Paris: Mercure de France, 1982.

L'Héritier de Villandon, Marie-Jeanne. "Marmoisan." In *Oeuvres meslées*. Paris: Guignard, 1696. 26–96.

Montpensier, duchesse de. *Mémoires*. Paris: Foucault, 1824.

Murat, comtesse de. "Le Sauvage." In *Histoires sublimes*. Paris: Florentin, 1699.

Villedieu, Madame de. *Mémoires de la vie de Henriette Sylvie de Molière*. Tours: Université François Rabelais, 1977.

Secondary Texts

Boullough, Vern L., and Bonnie Bullough. *Cross-Dressing, Sex and Gender*. Philadelphia: University of Pennsylvania Press, 1993.

Gaber, Marjorie. *Vested Interests*. New York: Harpers, 1993.

D

Dacier, Anne Le Fèvre (1654–1721). Born into a financially comfortable and intellectually driven family, she married André Dacier, a classical scholar in his own right. Dacier was schooled in languages, became fluent in Greek and Latin, and demonstrated an affinity for the classics and translation*. With her husband and other linguists, she translated and edited works by Callimachus, Dictys, and Aurelius and was also responsible for translations of Terence's comedies, the poetry* of Anacreon and Sappho, and Plato's *Phaedo*. Dacier offers insightful remarks on these editions. Her own critical work includes *Homère défendu contre l'Apologie du R. P. Hardoüin ou suite des causes de la corruption du goust*. In a most clear display of feminist consciousness and resistance, Dacier tackles the well-respected and celebrated classical critic Hardoüin for his critiques of detractors and defenders of Homer and his *Iliad*. She felt it most pressing to redress Hardoüin's misreadings and to rearticulate her positions on the classical poet. While Hardoüin does not explicitly name Dacier, a fact which, she argues, subtends a sexist dimension, she explicitly names him and dissects his observations of Homer. In a quasi-battle over Homeric interpretations, a face-off between a polished woman erudite and a male critic, Dacier challenges specifically Hardoüin's supposition that he alone knows the true subject of the *Iliad*, as well as a broader legacy of French male scholars as keepers of knowledge and authorities on matters of literary import.

T. Denean Sharpley-Whiting

BIBLIOGRAPHY

Primary Text

Homère défendu contre l'Apologie du R. P. Hardoüin ou suite des causes de la corruption du goust. Paris: Chez Jean-Baptiste Coignard, 1716.

Translations by Dacier

La Poésie d'Anacréon et de Sapho avec des remarques par Madame Dacier. Amsterdam: Chez la veuve de Paul Marret, 1716.

Les Comédies de Térence avec des remarques de Madame Dacier. Amsterdam: Chez J.
  Ollier, 1691.

Secondary Texts

Farnham, Fern. *Madame Dacier: Scholar and Humanist.* Monterey, CA: Angel Press,
  1976.
Mazon, Paul. *Madame Dacier et les traductions d'Homère en France.* Oxford: Clarendon
  Press, 1936.

Dada. The short-lived Dada movement, born in Zurich's Cabaret Voltaire in
1916 and ending in Paris in 1923, with additional groups in Berlin, New York,
Hanover, and Cologne, was unique among European avant-gardes for its inter-
nationalism and extremism. The movement's name—arbitrarily chosen from a
dictionary, according to Tristan Tzara—embodies the subversive referentiality
that would characterize Dada performance. In addition, due perhaps to the cabaret setting of its activities, women played a significant role in Dada. Artists
and writers such as Céline Arnaud, Gabrielle Buffet-Picabia, Suzanne Duchamp,
Emmy Hennings, Hannah Höch, and Sophie Taeuber-Arp contributed to Dada
performances, exhibitions, and publications. The media used by these women
included both the traditional (poetry* and painting) and the nontraditional (tex-
tiles, photomontage, masks, and marionettes). Despite the frequently nonrefer-
ential nature of dadaist representation, critiques of traditional conceptions of
gender found their way into the dadaist gesture of revolt, particularly in the
work of Marcel Duchamp. His *Nu descendant un escalier No. 2* (1912), *La
Mariée mise à nu par ses célibataires, même* (1912–1923), and *L.H.O.O.Q.*
(1919) subvert the Western pictorial tradition of an idealized feminine beauty,
and his own transvestite alter ego Rose Sélavy parodied contemporary gender
expectations. When Dada disappeared in 1923, its inheritor, surrealism*, re-
verted to more traditional figurations of women, often with misogynistic overtones.

Leonard R. Koos

BIBLIOGRAPHY

Ball, Hugo. *Flight out of Time: A Dada Story.* Trans. Ann Raimes. Ed. John Elderfield.
  New York: Viking, 1974.
Béhar, Henri, and Michel Carassou. *Dada, histoire d'une subversion.* Paris: Fayard, 1990.
Dachy, Marc. *The Dada Movement, 1915–1923.* New York: Editions d'Art Albert Skira,
  1990.
Hedges, Inez. *Languages of Revolt: Dada and Surrealist Literature and Film.* Durham:
  Duke University Press, 1983.
Lanchner, Carolyn. *Sophie Taeuber-Arp.* New York: Museum of Modern Art, 1981.
Richter, Hans. *Dada, Art and Anti-Art.* Trans. David Britt. London: Thames and Hudson,
  1965.
Sanouillet, Michel. *Dada à Paris.* Paris: Jean-Jacques Pauvert, 1965.

Dalibard de Saint-Phalier. *See* Saint-Phalier Dalibard, Françoise-Thérèse Aumerle de.

Daubié, Julie Victoire (1824–1874). Pioneered the study of the economic and educational plight of nineteenth-century French women. A Saint-Simonian economist, she became an early crusader for women's suffrage, after being the first woman to earn a higher degree (the *baccalauréat*) and a master's degree in letters in the French university system (Lyons, 1861 and Paris, 1871). She died on the eve of receiving her Ph.D.

Raymonde A. Saliou Bulger

BIBLIOGRAPHY

Primary Texts

Du progrès dans l'enseignement primaire. Justice et liberté! Paris: Impr. de Mme Clay, 1862.
L'Émancipation de la femme. Paris: Ernest Thorin, 1871.
Le Manuel du jeune homme. Paris: Ed. Silvio Pellico, 1872.
La Tolérance du vice. Paris: L'Association pour l'émancipation progressive de la femme, 1872.
La Femme pauvre au XIXe siècle. Pref. Agnès Thiercé. Vol. 1. Paris: Côté-femmes, 1992.

Secondary Texts

Bulger, Raymonde A. Saliou. *Lettres à Julie Victoire Daubié (1824–1874): La Première bachelière de France et son temps.* New York: Peter Lang, 1992.
Bulletin du Centre Pierre Léon d'histoire économique et sociale 2–3 (1993).

Decadence (c. 1884–1914). The French literary movement of Art for Art's Sake, led by Théophile Gautier, glorified the aesthetic object as the inspiration for pure contemplation divorced from moral, social, or personal meanings. Decadence, anticipated by the pessimistic philosophy of Schopenhauer, and inaugurated by Joris-Karl Huysmans's *A rebours* (1884) and the poetry* of Jules Laforgue (1885–1887), adds to the religion of art a cult of sensuality and a contempt for life. Thus one finds in decadence four major subjects: society is corrupt and unworthy of our commitment; possession of the rare and precious object—material or human—can offer us a contemplative joy; suicide, murder, or infanticide is justifiable if it removes an ugly or inconvenient human object from our lives, or even if it merely affords us an ecstatic thrill; one's choice of a mode of sexual gratification should be completely free, and sharply distinguished from procreation—heterosexual vaginal intercourse between two married consenting adults is the least worthy and least desirable of all forms of *jouissance.*

Decadent authors generally dissociate themselves from these extreme positions in their conclusions, which typically show a protagonist caught in an impasse, or destroyed. But they share with their protagonists the symptoms of "spilt aristocracy" (an allusion to T. E. Hulme's sarcastic definition of Romanticism as "spilt religion") In a post-revolutionary world, birth as a member of the nobility no longer automatically endows one with authority and privilege, and writers must appeal to a mass public rather than to royal or noble patrons. Distinction must then derive (or so the decadents seem to believe) from being daringly immoral even to the point of self-degradation, to prove one's courage and independence.

For a woman, decadent values could offer freedom from a conventional marriage* and the imperative of reproduction, and the possibility of cultivating oneself rather than being devoted solely to others. Marie Bashkirtseff (1858–1884) exemplified such aims, and thus helped found the myth* of a female *culte du moi*. A brilliant musician and painter, killed prematurely by tuberculosis, she wrote a *Journal* published in 1888 in bowdlerized form. An unexpurgated version appeared in 1901, and her correspondence in 1891. These works had great influence at the time.

Rachilde* (pseudonym of Marguerite Eymery, 1860–1953) was the leading female decadent writer. The *Mercure de France* (1890–1965), which she co-founded with her husband Alfred Vallette, was the most prestigious organ of the decadent movement during La Belle Epoque. Her writings are distinct from those of the male decadents in several ways. She avoids digressive descriptions of the aesthetic object or decor—the male decadents are much more homemakers than she. She does not treat murder for thrills, but instead innovates more widely than do her male colleagues in elaborating fictions concerning nonconventional sexual behavior such as necrophilia (*La Tour d'amour*), fetishism (*Monsieur Vénus*), or bestiality (hinted at in *L'Animale*). And she blurs genders more aggressively than do male writers, not only with scenes of cross-dressing*, but also with explicit titles of novels* published in the 1890s—*Monsieur Vénus*, *La Marquise de Sade*, and *Madame Adonis*. Rachilde, however, proclaimed woman's irremediable biological and emotional inferiority in her *Pourquoi je ne suis pas féministe* (1928). She finds women sensualistic, capricious, envious, jealous, and unfit for public affairs.

The feminist social center of decadence was Natalie Barney's* prominent Paris literary salon*. Barney openly defended lesbianism* in her writings while the circle of male writers associated with the famous decadent journal *Le Chat noir* (1882–1895) was defending homosexuality. She inspired at least three lesbian novels, notably Liliane de Pougy's* *Idylle-sapphique* (1901). Colette* describes this circle in *Le Pur et l'impur* (1931).

Laurence M. Porter

BIBLIOGRAPHY

Benstock, Shari. *Women of the Left Bank: Paris, 1900–1940*. Austin: University of Texas Press, 1986.

Bronfen, Elisabeth. *Over Her Dead Body: Death, Femininity and the Aesthetic*. Manchester, UK: Manchester University Press, 1992.

Carter, A. E. *The Idea of Decadence in French Literature, 1830–1900*. Toronto: University of Toronto Press, 1958.

Dijkstra, Bram. *Idols of Perversity: Fantasies of Female Evil in Fin-de-siècle Culture.* New York: Oxford University Press, 1986.

Offen, Karen M. "First Wave Feminism in France. Network and Resources." *Women's Studies International Forum* 5 (1982): 685–689.

Porter, Laurence M. "Decadence and the *Fin-de-Siècle* Novel." In *The Cambridge Companion to the Modern French Novel from 1800 to the Present.* Ed. Timothy Unwin. Cambridge: Cambridge University Press, 1997.

Waelti-Walters, Jennifer. *Feminist Novelists of the Belle Epoque: Love as a Lifestyle.* Bloomington: Indiana University Press, 1990.

Deforges, Régine (1935–). Deforges has been involved in various aspects of French cultural life: publishing*, cinema*, and literature. In 1968 she became the first woman to own a publishing house, L'Or du Temps. Her first publication, an erotic text attributed to Louis Aragon, was confiscated shortly after its appearance. This early association with erotic writing was continued in her interviews with the author of *L'Histoire d'O*, Pauline Réage (1975), and her two volumes of erotic stories, *Lola et quelques autres* (1979) and *Contes pervers* (1980). She has written several novels*, most of them historical. The best known are those in the *Bicyclette bleue* trilogy, set during the Occupation and characterized, as are many of her novels, by a preoccupation with female sensuality, but which do not fundamentally challenge patriarchal values.

Angela Kimyongür

BIBLIOGRAPHY

Primary Texts

O m'a dit. Entretiens avec Pauline Réage. Paris: J.-J. Pauvert, 1975.
Blanche et Lucie. Paris: Fayard, 1977.
Le Cahier volé. Paris: Fayard, 1978.
Lola et quelques autres. Paris: Jean Goujon, 1979.
Contes pervers. Paris: Fayard, 1980.
La Révolte des nonnes. Paris: La Table ronde, 1980.
La Bicyclette bleue. Paris: Ramsay, 1981.
101 Avenue Henri Martin. Paris: Ramsay, 1983.
Le Diable en rit encore. Paris: Ramsay, 1985.
Noir Tango. Paris: Fayard, 1991.

Secondary Text

Richard, Anne. "Régine Deforges." In *Dictionnaire littéraire des femmes de langue française.* Paris: Karthala, 1996. 179–182.

Delarue-Mardrus, Lucie (1874–1945). Artist, musician, and prolific writer, Delarue-Mardrus produced over thirty novels*, twelve volumes of poetry*, several plays, biographies, and numerous articles ranging from her impressions of the Middle East to beauty tips. The youngest of six daughters, she was born and raised in Normandy, a major theme in her poetry and the focus of several novels. Her novels were popular, but she identified herself primarily as a poet even though her carefully crafted poems drew criticism for their original use of language, sensual imagery, and aversion to maternity*, a theme also found in her novels. Her writing contains essentialist elements, as well as a feminist concern for social injustices toward women. Married for a time to the Egyptian translator Joseph Charles Mardrus, she also had relationships with women such as Natalie Barney*, who inspired a collection of love poems. Delarue-Mardrus died forgotten and impoverished after suffering from rheumatism for many years.

Tama Lea Engelking

BIBLIOGRAPHY

Primary Texts

Occident. Paris: Fasquelle, 1901.
Marie, fille-mère. Paris: Fasquelle, 1908.
Le Roman de six petites filles. Paris: Fasquelle, 1909.
L'ex-voto. Paris: Fasquelle, 1922.
L'Ange et les pervers. Paris: Ferenczi, 1930.
Mes Mémoires. Paris: Gallimard, 1938.
Nos Secrètes Amours. Paris: Les Isles, 1957.

Secondary Texts

Engelking, Tama Lea. *"L'Ange et les pervers*: Lucie Delarue-Mardrus' Ambivalent Poetic Identity.'' *Romance Quarterly* 39, no. 4 (November 1992): 451–466.
Harry, Myriam. *Mon Amie, Lucie Delarue-Mardrus*. Paris: Ariane, 1946.
Newman-Gordon, Pauline. "Lucie Delarue-Mardrus." In *French Women Writers: A Bio-Bibliographical Source Book*. Ed. Eva Martin Sartori and Dorothy Wynne Zimmerman. Westport, CT: Greenwood Press, 1991. 109–120.
Plat, Hélène. *Lucie Delarue-Mardrus: Une Femme de lettres des années folles*. Paris: Grasset, 1994.
Waelti-Walters, Jennifer. *Feminist Novelists of the Belle Epoque*. Bloomington: Indiana University Press, 1990.

Delbée, Anne (1946–). Delbée has led an energetic, multi-faceted career as actress, director, author, and administrator. Her early creations include a montage of texts by Victor Hugo and stunning productions of Schiller's *Les Brigands* (1971) and Claudel's *L'Echange* (1975). Along with Racine, the latter two authors have dominated her tenure as one of the rare women named to head state-subsidized theaters (Angers, 1981–1985, and Nancy, 1986–1991). Fascinated by strong temperaments and impossible situations, Delbée delved into the life of nineteenth-century sculptress Camille Claudel and brought her tragic internment to light in a fiery and much-praised production, *Une Femme*, which explores the artist's exploitation by her mentor Auguste Rodin and her brother Paul Claudel.

Judith G. Miller

BIBLIOGRAPHY

Primary Texts

Une Femme, Camille Claudel. Paris: Presses de la Renaissance, 1982.
Elle qui traversa le monde. Paris: Presses de la Renaissance, 1985.

Delbo, Charlotte (1913–1985). Arrested with her husband, Georges Dudach, for their involvement in the Resistance, Delbo became one of the 230 female political prisoners deported to Auschwitz-Birkenau on January 24, 1943. She evokes the lives of each of these women in *Le Convoi du 24 janvier* (1965), and most of her other work is inspired by her experience as a woman in a concentration camp. In her emotionally charged vignettes and prose poems, Delbo depicts her fellow prisoners as sisters, daughters, and mothers who express themselves through the written and spoken word, and who empower each other through their solidarity and communal presence. Although the Holocaust* was the main inspiration for her narratives and plays, Delbo also denounced the political atrocities that have taken place in Spain, Algeria, Greece, and Argentina. Throughout her work, Delbo emphasizes the need for survivors to bear witness to human suffering in the name of freedom.

Frédérique Chevillot

BIBLIOGRAPHY

Primary Texts

Le Convoi du 24 janvier. Paris: Minuit, 1965.
Auschwitz et après. 3 vols. Paris: Minuit, 1970–1971.
La Sentence. Honfleur: P. J. Oswald, 1972.
Qui rapportera ces paroles? Paris: P. J. Oswald, 1974.
Maria Lusitania. Le Coup d'état. Paris: P. J. Oswald, 1975.
Spectres, mes compagnons. 1977. Paris: Berg International, 1995.
La Mémoire et les jours. 1985. Paris: Berg International, 1995.

Secondary Texts

Bracher, Nathan. ''Humanisme, violence et métaphysique: La Thématique du visage chez Charlotte Delbo.'' *Symposium* (Winter 1992): 255–272.
Lamont, Rosette. ''Charlotte Delbo: A Woman/Book.'' In *Faith of a (Woman) Writer.* Ed. Alice Kessler-Harris and William McBrien. Westport, CT: Greenwood Press, 1988. 247–252.
Rittner, Carol, and John K. Roth. *Women and the Holocaust.* New York: Paragon House, 1993.

Delphy, Christine (1941–   ). Well known for her essays on socialist feminist theory*, Delphy was once described by Simone de Beauvoir* as France's most exciting theorist. In 1977 she and Beauvoir co-founded the review *Nouvelles questions féministes*, which is devoted to feminist theory and focuses on the social and historical aspects of woman's experience. *The Main Enemy* (1977), the first English translation of her work, contains the article in which Delphy criticizes Annie Leclerc's* *Parole de femme* and its essentialist and idealist arguments. Her work analyzes gender relations, in particular the economic oppression of women within a patriarchal society. In *Close to Home* (1984), the author offers the reader a materialist analysis of women's oppression, using Marxist precepts in her analysis of the patriarchy. In Delphy's works, materialist feminism* often serves to express her opposition to notions of biology and psychology as a means of explaining women's subordination in contemporary society. Her most recent work, *Familiar Exploitation* (1992), continues her examination of the ways in which women are exploited within the family*, offering a new analysis of marriage* in modern Western societies.

Ana M. de Medeiros

BIBLIOGRAPHY

Primary Texts

"Le Patrimoine et la double circulation des biens dans l'espace économique et le temps familial." *Revue Française de Sociologie* 10 (1969): 664–686.
"Proto-féminisme et anti-féminisme." *Les Temps Modernes* 346 (May 1976): 1469–1500.
Delphy, Christine, and Diana Leonard. *Familiar Exploitation: A New Analysis of Marriage in Contemporary Western Societies*. Oxford: Polity Press, 1992.

Secondary Text

Jackson, Stevi. *Christine Delphy*. London: Sage Publications, 1996.

Démar, Claire (1800?–1833). Not much is known of Claire Démar's life. A marginal member of the Saint-Simonian family*, she developed her own theory on women, the state, and society. Démar committed suicide in 1833, leaving behind articles, letters, and two pamphlets of particular interest to feminists: *Appel d'une femme au peuple sur l'affranchissement de la femme* (1833) and *Ma Loi d'avenir* (published posthumously in 1834 by the *Tribune des femmes*). Outside of the Saint-Simonian family, the pamphlets did not reach a great audience and were received with little interest.

Démar's contribution to feminism* lies both in her critique of bourgeois capitalist institutions and in bringing to the fore questions of women's voice, subjectivity, and sexuality. At the heart of Démar's project is moral reform, especially the reform of laws governing legitimacy and marital fidelity. In both pamphlets, Démar outlines a radical restructuring of French society and its ideological underpinnings based on a redefinition of women's—particularly the mother's—role in the polis. *Appel d'une femme* prefigures *Ma Loi d'avenir* in that it presents not a law of the future, but rather a scathing critique of both the Civil Code of 1804 and traditional Christian and bourgeois values. As she catalogues the injustices of the Civil Code, Démar exposes the inherent unfairness of a legal system that is based not on equality, but on domination and exclusion.

If we consider the Code of 1804 as securing paternal authority (*puissance paternelle*) and female minority, then Démar's future law seeks to rewrite the social/sexual contract in order to accommodate women's experience. And if in *Appel d'une femme* Démar calls for women's rights to sexual and social equality, in *Ma Loi d'avenir* she examines the linguistic, sexual, social, and economic power codes that regulate women's sexuality. Stemming from Saint-Simonian beliefs in a noncapitalist society (or *association*) and in sexual freedom, the future law would first abolish laws governing inheritance and legitimacy and then establish a new morality based on mystery and mobility. "Mystery" refers not to bourgeois modesty, but rather to the protected secrecy of intimate relations. Démar held that whereas bourgeois society, through the mechanisms of public opinion and monogamy, protects a father's right to know who his "own" children are, the law of the future would herald women's status as citizens and protect female desire. This is indeed the bone Démar picks with the *Tribune des femmes*: the more orthodox Saint-Simonian view was to advocate a public morality (*moralité publique*). Démar rejects this traditional mechanism of the bourgeois public sphere, and opts for a law of mystery, which would protect sexual freedom and lend a new interpretation of legitimacy. According to Démar, all pregnant women are divinely pregnant; God is the only certain father, and thus all children are legitimate. Structuring the new society around the signs of conception and sexual pleasure, Démar effectively dislodges a sociolinguistic order based on the law of the father and the primacy of the phallus. Démar's final reform would be in the makeup of the family. In *Ma Loi d'avenir*, she calls for the end of the "laws of blood" in favor of a truly social family, and proposes a sort of social day-care system.

Démar's frankness and originality shocked her contemporaries. Her style possesses the same mobility and kinetic energy as her ideas. Démar's work is important not only for those interested in a woman's response to the Civil Code, but also for those interested in a nineteenth-century treatment of what are often considered twentieth-century questions of difference, experience, and sexuality/subjectivity.

Annie Smart

BIBLIOGRAPHY

Primary Texts

Appel d'une femme au peuple sur l'affranchissement de la femme. Paris: Privately printed, 1833.

Ma Loi d'avenir. Intro. by Suzanne Voilquin. Paris: Tribune des femmes, 1834.

Secondary Texts

Bulciolu, Maria Teresa. *L'Ecole Saint-Simonienne et la femme*. Pisa: Goliardica, 1980.

Moses, Claire Goldberg, and Leslie Wahl Rabine. *Feminism, Socialism, and French Romanticism*. Bloomington: Indiana University Press, 1993.

Dentière (or D'Ennetières), Marie (d. 1561). Activist reformer and writer. An Augustinian nun in Tournai, she left her convent* in 1521 and joined reformers in Strasbourg, marrying Simon Robert, a former priest. The couple moved to Aigle, where Robert was pastor, and had several children. Widowed, in 1533 Dentière married Antoine Froment (1509–1581), young pastor and supporter of Guillaume Farel. In 1535 the family arrived in Geneva and quickly entered the struggle to win the city for the reformed religion. The earliest work now attributed to Dentière is *La Guerre et deslivrance de la ville de Genesve [composée et publiée en 1536 par Marie Dentière de Tournay, ancienne abbesse et femme d'Antoine]* (1536), a colorful narrative history of the Catholic Duke of Savoy's defeat by a Protestant army.

When the Protestant Council of 200 exiled Farel and Jean Calvin in 1538, Dentière wrote a letter to Marguerite de Navarre*, the *Epistre tres utile faicte et composée par une femme Chrestienne de Tornay, Envoyée à la Royne de Navarre seur du Roy de France* . . . (1539). The salutation identifies the author by the initials M.D. and calls the Council members "false apostles, cowards in battle, enemies of truth, and bold as slugs." The edition was quickly confiscated, and only two copies are known to have survived.

The *Epistre* consists of three parts. The first part is a cover letter to Marguerite de Navarre which deplores the state of the Geneva church and the general corruption of the times. Dentière asks Marguerite to implore her brother, François I, to intervene. She insists on the right of women to interpret and teach the Bible* and addresses her letter also to "other women held in captivity" and "poor little women desiring to know and understand the truth." The second part is a "Defense of Women." These pages belong to the tradition of the *Querelle des femmes*. Dentière presents a litany of strong and eloquent women from both the Old and New Testaments. She attacks the notion that women are the source of evil and insists that women are capable and entitled to interpret Scripture and teach one another. The third part is the epistle proper. Although Dentière specifically attacks the Council, this section presents her eclectic reflections on some of the most sharply debated theological questions of the Reformation*. She reveals her Augustinian formation, as well as affinities with the evangelical reformers whom Marguerite followed and protected.

Nothing indicates that Marguerite either received the letter or answered it. The years following its publication have left us few traces of Dentière. Contemporary documents suggest that she and Froment fell out of favor with Calvin and Farel. A 1546 letter from Calvin to Farel gives a scathing portrait of Dentière moving about Geneva, daring to preach in such public places as street corners and inns.

One last record of Dentière's teaching dates from 1561, the presumed year of her death. A pirated edition of one of Calvin's sermons on Paul's Epistle to Timothy, *Sermon de M. J. Calvin ou il est montré qu'elle doit estre la modestie des femmes en leurs habillemens* includes a preface, "To the Christian Reader," again indicating the author only by the initials, M.D. Both works preach modesty in dress and reflect the sumptuary laws passed in Geneva in the 1550s.

Dentière conveys her own position on doctrine as well as on women's apparel, jewels, and cosmetics.

Mary B. McKinley

BIBLIOGRAPHY

Primary Texts

La Guerre et deslivrance de la ville de Genesve [composée et publiée en 1536 par Marie Dentière de Tournay, ancienne abbesse et femme d'Antoine]. Edited, with an introduction and notes, by Albert Rilliet. In *Mémoires de la Société d'Histoire et d'Archéologie de Genève.* Vol. 20. Geneva: Imprimerie Charles Schuchardt, 1881.

Epistre tres utile faicte et composée par une femme Chrestienne de Tornay, Envoyée à la Royne de Navarre seur du Roy de France, Contre Les Turcz, Iuifz, Infideles, Faulx chrestiens, Anabaptistes, et Lutheriens [à Anvers, chez Martin l'Empereur]. Geneva: Jean Gérard, 1539.

Un Sermon de M. J. Calvin ou il est montré qu'elle doit estre la modestie des femmes en leurs habillemens. N.p., 1561.

Herminjard, A.-L. *Correspondance des Réformateurs dans les pays de langue française. Recueillie et publiée avec d'autres lettres relatives à la Réforme et des notes historiques et biographiques.* 9 vols. Geneva: H. Georg, 1866–1897. Reprint. Nieuwkoop: B. De Graaf, 1965. Vol. 5, # 785, 295–304.

Secondary Texts

Backus, Irena. "Marie Dentière: Un Cas de féminisme théologique à l'époque de la Réforme?" *Bulletin de la Société de l'Histoire du Protestantisme Français* 137 (1991): 177–195.

Head, Thomas. "The Religion of the *Femmelettes*: Ideals and Experience among Women in Fifteenth- and Sixteenth-Century France." In *That Gentle Strength: Historical Perspectives on Women in Christianity.* Ed. Lynda Coon, Katherine Haldane, and Elisabeth Sommer. Charlottesville: University Press of Virginia, 1991. 149–175.

McKinley, Mary. "The Absent Ellipsis: The Edition and Suppression of Marie Dentière in the Sixteenth and the Nineteenth Centuries." In *Women Writers in Pre-Revolutionary France: Strategies of Emancipation.* Ed. Colette H. Winn and Donna Kuizenga. New York: Garland, 1997. 85–99.

Thompson, John Lee. "Calvin and Marie Dentière." In *John Calvin and the Sarah: Women in Regular and Exceptional Roles in the Exegesis of Calvin, His Predecessors, and His Contemporaries.* Geneva: Droz, 1992. 40–45.

Deraismes, Maria (1828–1894). Playwright, author, journalist, and a leading feminist. She rejected marriage* to preserve her own socioeconomic independence. In 1863 she published a collection of plays with feminist overtones, *Théâtre chez soi.* In the late 1860s, Deraismes promoted feminist issues in her articles and well-attended public lectures, which were later published in *Eve dans l'humanité.* In 1869 she co-founded, with Léon Richer, the feminist weekly *Le Droit des femmes.* A year later, she created the feminist organization, L'Association pour le droit des femmes.

In the 1870s Deraismes became involved in a controversy over Barbey d'Aurevilly's infamous *Nain Jaune* article, "Les Bas bleus." She attacked his criticisms of women's intellectual abilities with her own series of articles. She denounced as well Alexandre Dumas fils's depiction of women's natural inferiorities in *Eve contre Monsieur Dumas fils*. She continued her attacks against misogynist authors in *Le Théâtre de Monsieur Sardou*.

By the 1880s Deraismes had recognized the necessity of allying herself with the Liberal Republicans because of their common agendas. She thus adopted a specific strategy for the feminist movement: "La politique de la brèche." Fearing the Church's influence over women, Deraismes became very active in the anticlerical movement. In her writings, she demanded equal education* and pay for women and saw in prostitution* a by-product of patriarchy. Influenced by Fourier, and unlike her contemporaries, she thought that sexual passion and fulfillment should be a goal for every woman.

In the 1890s Deraismes fought for the inclusion of women in the Freemasonry. A member in 1882, she created the first mixed lodge in 1893. When she died a year later, the Republican feminist movement lost its principal leader, who had greatly advanced women's rights with her relentless intellectual and political activism.

Juliette Parnell-Smith

BIBLIOGRAPHY

Primary Texts

Le Théâtre chez soi. Paris: Amyot, 1863.
Nos Principes et nos moeurs. Paris: Michel Lévy frères, 1868.
Eve contre Monsieur Dumas fils. Paris: E. Dentu, 1872.
France et progrès. Paris: Librairie de la Société des gens de lettres, 1873.
Le Théâtre de Monsieur Sardou. Paris: E. Dentu, 1875.
Les Droits de l'enfant. Paris: E. Dentu, 1887.
Epidémie naturaliste. Paris: E. Dentu, 1888.
Eve dans l'humanité. Paris: L. Sauvaitre, 1891. Rpt. Paris: Coté-femmes, 1990.
Oeuvres complètes. 2 vols. Paris: Alcan, 1895–1896.
Ce que veulent les femmes. Articles et conférences de 1869 à 1891. Paris: Syros, 1980.

Deroin, Jeanne (1805–1894). Feminist, teacher, labor organizer, journalist, and pamphleteer. The Parisian laundress Jeanne Deroin sent her "profession of faith" to the Saint-Simonian newspaper the *Globe* in the early 1830s, in which she expressed distrust of Enfantin's religious hierarchy and her conviction that women must have equal rights. Deroin collaborated on the *Femme libre*, published by working-class Saint-Simonian women, and in 1832 married Desroches, a fellow socialist with whom she had three children. During the 1840s she passed her schoolteaching exam with difficulty and resurfaced as a political activist and journalist in 1848. Deroin, Eugénie Niboyet*, Désirée Gay, and Adèle Esquiros founded the Club for the Emancipation of Women in February 1848 and campaigned for women's right to vote* in the 1848 elections. In May, when Niboyet launched the daily newspaper *La Voix des femmes*, the club was renamed La Société pour la voix des femmes. Deroin started her own short-lived weekly, *La Politique des femmes*, followed by the monthly *L'Opinion des femmes*, in which she urged republican support of women's suffrage and political participation. To make her point, she ran as the first woman candidate for the Legislative Assembly in 1849. In 1849 Deroin and Niboyet were both among the founding members of the Fraternal Association of Socialist Male and Female Teachers and Professors. Niboyet also helped Deroin organize women in trade associations and founded the Union of Workers' Associations in 1850. For their subversive associationist activities both women served six months in prison in 1851. Deroin left for England in 1852, where she tutored and published the *Almanach des femmes* (in French and English) from 1852 to 1854. After the 1859 amnesty, Deroin remained in England but corresponded with Hubertine Auclert* and Léon Richer, who published some of her letters in his periodical *Le Droit des femmes*.

Cheryl A. Morgan

BIBLIOGRAPHY

Primary Texts

Association fraternelle des Démocrates Socialistes des deux sexes pour l'affranchissement politique et social des femmes. Paris: Imprimerie Lacour, 1849.
Du Célibat. Paris: Les Marchands des nouveautés, 1851.
Almanach des femmes/The Women's Almanack. London: J. Watson, 1853, 1854.
"Profession de foi de Melle Jenny de Roin." In *De la liberté des femmes: Lettres des dames au Globe (1831–1832)*. Textes recueillis et présentés par Michèle Riot-Sarcey. Paris: Côté-femmes, 1992.
Aux lecteurs du departement de la Seine. Paris: Imprimerie Lacour, n.d.
Campagne électorale de la citoyenne Jeanne Deroin et pétition des femmes au peuple (16 mars 1848). Paris: Imprimerie Lacour, n.d.

Secondary Texts

Fraisse, Geneviève. "Les Femmes libres de 48: Moralisme et féminisme." *Les Révoltes logiques* 1 (1975).
Gordon, Felicia, and Marie Cross. *Early French Feminisms, 1830–1940: A Passion for Liberty*. Cheltenham and Brookfield: Edward Elgar, 1996.
Moses, Claire Goldberg. *French Feminism in the Nineteenth Century*. Albany: State University of New York Press, 1984.
Riot-Sarcey, Michèle. *La Démocratie à l'épreuve des femmes: Trois figures critiques du pouvoir, 1830–1848*. Paris: Albin Michel, 1994.
Scott, Joan Wallach. *Only Paradoxes to Offer. French Feminists and the Rights of Man*. Cambridge: Harvard University Press, 1996.
Thomas, Edith. *Les Femmes de 1848*. Paris: P.U.F., 1948.

Desbordes-Valmore, Marceline (1786–1859). Actress and singer, freelance lyricist for musical romances, author of children's stories and tales for children in both verse and prose, novelist, and poet. In an era that privileged male education* and writing, she was primarily self-taught. Because her family had been impoverished by the upheavals of the French Revolution*, she became a stage actress at the age of eleven. After her mother's death during their visit to Guadeloupe, Marceline returned to Europe, where she played and sang in Rouen, Lille, Brussels, and Paris. She yearned to write, and eventually published various pieces in prose and in verse. One can say that her life shaped her first volumes, because she published *Elégies, maries, et romances* (1817) as well as *Poésies* (1820) while working as an actress. *Les Veillées des Antilles* (1820) consists of short stories* mostly in prose, reminiscent of Desbordes-Valmore's time in Guadeloupe. They illustrate the unique sense of place that characterizes her writing. She also wrote for children while she was raising her own single-handedly because her husband, actor Prosper Valmore, was often on the road in the provinces. She had two children out of wedlock who died before her 1817 marriage*, then lost her first child by Valmore within a month of the birth. Years later, her two grown daughters also predeceased her, so that only one son survived her. *Contes en vers, Contes en prose*, and *Le Livre des mères et des enfants* were all published in 1840. *Les Anges de la famille* (1849) and *Jeunes Têtes et jeunes coeurs* (1855) continue her cycle of tales, which ends with the posthumous *Contes et scènes de la vie de famille* (1865), which appeared in fifteen editions.

Because Desbordes-Valmore wrote from a position of social marginalization, personal experience informs her writing, unfettered by literary convention. Indeed, nature's opposition to culture is a significant motif in her works. Desbordes-Valmore freely expresses a mother's grief, the joys of feminine intimacy, and the fullness of woman's sensuality. While the feminine experience shapes her works, writing itself increasingly molded her life, for she became a prolific author and eventually gave up singing and performing to devote herself to literature. *Elégies et poésies nouvelles* (1825), *Poésies* (1830), *Les Pleurs* (1833), *Pauvres Fleurs* (1839), and *Bouquets et prières* (1843) are cycles of poems which end with the posthumous *Poésies inédites* (1860), the volume Desbordes-Valmore was editing right before she died. She also published more short stories, including the "Salon de Lady Betty" (1836), "Huit femmes" (1845), and three novels: *Une Raillerie de l'amour* (1833), the autobiographical *L'Atelier d'un peintre* (1833), which evokes her artisan father and his milieu, and *Violette* (1839).

While all of her works are being reedited, more attention has been given to Desbordes-Valmore's poetry*, acknowledged even in her own day for its distinctive qualities. Although critics attempted to praise Desbordes-Valmore's poetic voice, they fell short of appreciating the Romantic feminine difference evident in it. Writing from outside the academy, Desbordes-Valmore can explore her musical talent with freer forms than poets trained in strict classical metrics. If her rhythmic patterns are original, it is in the sense that they open up the musicality of poetry and broaden poetic possibilities. She uses maternity* and childbearing metaphors for creativity: these are for her dynamic processes which emphasize metamorphosis and difference as positive values. Thus Desbordes-Valmore criticizes misogynist ideologies that relegate women's writing to second-class status. Likewise, she uses her pen to fight against social injustice, such as industry's exploitation of child labor or working conditions in France or Belgium.

When writing about poetry itself, she expresses her feminine difference by addressing her muse as a sister who listens and who can create a peaceful relationship which, while not devoid of grief or suffering, is never tense or antagonistic. She often sets up dialogic situations in her poems. The intersubjective patterns displace the traditional persona-centered single voice and engage the reader as another subject of the poetic experience. Desbordes-Valmore's exclamatory style, apparent in her nature metaphors, evokes sisterhood in the context of a series of alternately happy and sad experiences: friendship*, love, mourning, remembrance, and hope. Her landscapes have an engaging sensual dimension. Unlike the poetic images of her male contemporaries, they are distinct products of the imagination, based on bonding rather than on isolation.

Brigitte Roussel

BIBLIOGRAPHY

Primary Texts

Oeuvres poétiques complètes. 2 vols. Grenoble: PUG, 1973.
Vingt-Deux Lettres. Paris: Arbre, 1986.
Contes. Lyons: PUL, 1989.
Les Petits Flamands. Geneva: Droz, 1991.
L'Atelier d'un peintre. Paris: Miroirs, 1993.

Secondary Texts

Ambrière, Francis. *Le Siècle des Valmore.* 2 vols. Paris: Seuil, 1987.
Bonnefoy, Yves. Préface to *Poésies,* by Marceline Desbordes-Valmore. Paris: Gallimard, 1983.
Danahy, Michael. ''Desbordes-Valmore, Marceline.'' In *A New History of French Literature.* Ed. Denis Hollier. Cambridge, MA: Harvard University Press, 1989.
———. ''Marceline Desbordes-Valmore et la fraternité des poètes.'' *Nineteenth Century French Studies* 19, no. 3 (Spring 1991): 386–393.
Ferguson, Simone. ''Marceline Desbordes-Valmore: Une voix féminine au milieu du carnage des révolutions.'' *Revue francophone de Louisiane* 6, no. 2 (Winter 1991): 27–35.
Haxell, Nichola-Anne. ''Childbirth and the Mine: A Reading of the Gaea-Myth in Zola's *Germinal* and the poetry of Marceline Desbordes-Valmore.'' *Neophilologus* 73, no. 4 (October 1989): 522–531.
Johnson, Barbara, Joan Dejean, and Nancy K. Miller, eds. *Displacements: Women, Tradition, Literature in French.* Baltimore: Johns Hopkins University Press, 1991.
Plante, Christine. ''Marceline Desbordes-Valmore: Ni poésie féminine, ni poésie féministe.'' *French Literature Series* 16 (1989): 78–93.
Wartelle, André. ''La Poésie de Marceline Desbordes-Valmore et Chateaubriand.'' *Les Etudes Classiques* 56, no. 3 (July 1988): 265–271.

Deshoulières, Antoinette du Ligier de la Garde, madame (1637–1694). The daughter of a *maître d'hôtel* to Marie de Medici* and Anne d'Autriche, she received an exceptional education*, which included several languages, poetry*, music, and dance. After marrying, she followed her husband to Brussels, where she was briefly imprisoned for protesting against the nonpayment of his pension as governor. Shortly thereafter, she returned to Paris, where she became acquainted with many of the most prominent figures of the social and literary scene, including Corneille, La Rochefoucauld, Pellisson, and Quinault. Far from being a passive observer, she actively participated in several literary quarrels. In 1677, for instance, she supported Pradon's *Phèdre et Hippolyte* against Racine's *Phèdre*. More decisively, she was known to be an advocate of the "modern" side of the ongoing Quarrel of the Ancients and the Moderns. This explains in part the caustic allusions made by Boileau, chief proponent of the Ancients, in his misogynistic *Satire X*, known as "Against Women." Although Deshoulières wrote two tragedies (*Genséric* and *Jules Antoine*), she is best known for her poetry, which she published in two collections, in 1688 and 1695. Although she used several poetic forms popular in salon* circles (verse epistles, madrigals, songs), the bulk of her *oeuvre* is composed of more prestigious (and more "masculine") genres, including eclogues, elegies, and idylls. Some of Deshoulières's earliest poems reflect her interest in Gassendi's anti-metaphysical and Epicurean philosophy, but the vast majority of her poems weave traditional pastoral topoi with descriptions of nature and animals that in some respects prefigure a later Romantic consciousness (e.g., her famous idyll, "Les Moutons"). Like many women writers of her day, she portrays an extremely skeptical vision of love. Unlike them, however, she depicts an acute consciousness of her own authorial persona and the challenges of authorship generally (e.g., the epigram "Au Père Bouhours" and "Epître chagrine, à Mlle de La Force"). Although recognized by the Académie d'Arles and the Accademia dei Ricovrati of Padua and often praised in her own time, Deshoulières has subsequently been neglected or received generally unfavorable critical attention.

Lewis C. Seifert

BIBLIOGRAPHY

Primary Texts

Anthologie poétique française, XVIIe siècle. Ed. Maurice Allem. Paris: Garnier-Flammarion, 1966. 2:343–352.
Anthologie de la poésie française du XVIIe siècle. Ed. Jean-Pierre Chauveau. Paris: Poésie/Gallimard, 1987. 386–388.

Desjardins, Marie-Catherine. *See* Villedieu, Marie-Catherine Desjardins.

Dia, Comtessa de (second half of twelfth century?). Among the best and most well known of the women troubadours (*trobairitz**), the Comtessa de Dia has frequently (though not definitively) been identified as Beatrice, wife of William II of Poitiers, count of Valentinois—which would make her a contemporary of the troubadour Raimbaut d'Aurenga (c. 1144–1173). A short *vida* (biography) that appears in a number of thirteenth-century song manuscripts describes her as a beautiful and good lady, the wife of William of Poitiers who fell in love with Raimbaut d'Aurenga and made many good songs about him (a claim that has sometimes led to identifying her as the anonymous lady debating in a *tenso* with Raimbaut). Based on intertextual evidence, she participated in a circle of poets that included Azalais de Porcairgues, Raimbaut, and Bernart de Ventadorn. Working with and against the constraints of troubadour lyric, the Comtessa develops a variety of personal tones and moods in her four extant cansos (love songs), one of which ("A chantar m'er de so q'ieu no volria") was preserved with its music and is frequently included in anthologies as well as in recorded and live performances. With considerable rhetorical skill, she combines the sensual voice that typifies the female speaker of woman's song, the *domna*'s image of beauty and worth as projected by the troubadour lover, and the troubadour's own lyric "I" cast in the role of complaining suppplicant, to produce a distinctive and lively poetic voice unafraid to confess desire, dismiss gossips, threaten her beloved, and claim a lady's right to sing of love.

Matilda Tomaryn Bruckner

BIBLIOGRAPHY

Primary Text

Bruckner, Matilda Tomaryn, Laurie Shepard, and Sarah White, eds. *Songs of the Women Troubadours*. New York: Garland, 1995.

Secondary Texts

Bruckner, Matilda Tomaryn. "Fictions of the Female Voice: The Women Troubadours." *Speculum* 76 (1992): 865–891.
Finke, Laura A. "The Rhetoric of Desire." In *Feminist Theory: A Woman's Writing*. Ithaca: Cornell University Press, 1992. 29–74.
Kay, Sarah. "Derivation, Derived Rhyme, and the Trobairitz." In *The Voice of the Trobairitz*. Ed. William D. Paden. Philadelphia: University of Pennsylvania Press, 1989.

Didactic literature. The French Revolution* gave a high priority to the task of reforming education*, improving literacy rates, and providing public instruction for the new citizenry. Though no one contested women's equal right to education, debates concerning the content of their instruction reined in certain freedoms women had gained through revolution. The curriculum for women came under the scrutiny of legal and social arbiters seeking to balance intellectual and moral development with women's domestic and civic function.

The development of a *morale laïque* through the secularization of education required the adaptation of religious training to the changing political and social life in France. Moral instruction was central to women's education and informed the construction of domestic woman. Madame Campan* was instrumental in getting the Institut National des Jeunes Filles recognized as an imperial establishment and set about codifying a program for girls that included both practical and intellectual study. Madame de Genlis* was a noted pedagogue whose *Théâtre à l'usage des jeunes personnes*, written in 1780, was destined for a young female readership of all classes.

Young women were instructed in the classics of French literature, and there was a predilection for the Christian moralizing literature of the seventeenth century: Bossuet, Fénelon, Madame de Maintenon*, Pascal, Racine, Jean-Baptiste Rousseau, and Madame de Sévigné* for the prose writers; Corneille, the dramatist; La Fontaine, for his moral tales; and l'Abbé de Lhomond, for the first Latin grammar published in French (*Eléments de la grammaire latine*, 1780). These texts formed the canon of women's education in the nineteenth century. The literature of the eighteenth century was ignored. Women were introduced to contemporary poets such as the very orthodox Victor de Laprade (*Poèmes évangéliques*) and Joseph Autran. The Romantics were rejected as authors of vain and misguided literature, harmful to a girl's innocence.

Historical narratives featuring elevated moral subjects were also used as instructional texts and offered both lessons in rhetoric and exemplary spiritual virtues. Moral lessons abounded in the tales of Joan of Arc's execution, the death of Saint Louis, the baptism of Saint Augustine. Parables of female virtue told through stories of a solitary flower, an hour at the windowsill, or a nocturnal contemplation of the heavens were also incorporated into the curriculum for women. Literary creation through tales of love and fantasy was never encouraged, as they were considered dangerous for a girl's moral upbringing.

Yet as women authors and poets, including George Sand*, Juliette Lamber, and Marie d'Agoult* came onto the scene, female authorship became the subject of a handful of novels* that promoted the talent of women writers yet did not abandon the theme of women's domestic role. *L'Espérance et la charité*, written in 1850 by the comtesse de Bassanville, tells the story of a young female poet, Fermina, who goes to Paris to seek fame as a writer. In Paris, she happens on success, fortune, a husband, and motherhood. Once she gives birth, Fermina abandons her literary career to devote herself to her children.

Women's preoccupation with the theory and practice of education is pervasive in the nineteenth century. It can be seen in the works of numerous women writers, among them Madame de Rémusat*, the comtesse de Ségur*, Eugénie de Guérin*, Clémence Royer, Marguerite Tinayre, and Henriette de Witt.

Constance Sherak

BIBLIOGRAPHY

Primary Texts

Campan, Jeanne de. *De l'éducation, suivi des conseils aux jeunes filles, d'un théâtre pour les jeunes personnes et de quelques essais de morale*. Paris: Baudouin Frères, 1824.

Dupanloup, Felix. *Lettres sur l'éducation des filles et sur les études qui conviennent aux femmes dans le monde*. Paris: J. Gervais, 1879.

Genlis, Stéphanie Félicité, comtesse de. *Mémoires inédits de Madame la Comtesse de Genlis, sur le dix-huitième siècle et la rèvolution française, depuis 1756 jusqu'à nos jours*. Paris: Ladvocat, 1825.

――――. *Théâtre à l'usage des jeunes personnes*. Paris: Panckoucke, 1779–1780.

Lhomond, Abbé Charles-François. *Eléments de la grammaire latine*. Paris: Calas, 1780.

Secondary Texts

Bicard, Isabelle. *Saintes ou pouliches: l'éducation des jeunes filles au XIXe siècle*. Paris: Albin Michel, 1985.

Constant, Paule. *Un Monde à l'usage des demoiselles*. Paris: Gallimard, 1987.

Lévy, Marie-Françoise. *De mères en filles: L'Education des Françaises, 1850–1880*. Paris: Calmann-Lévy, 1984.

Mali, Millicent S. *Madame Campan: Educator of Women, Confidante of Queens*. Washington, DC: University Press of America, 1979.

Mayeur, Françoise, *L'Education des filles en France au XIXe siècle*. Paris: Hachette, 1979.

――――. ''L'Education des filles: Le Modèle laïque.'' In *Histoire de la vie privée*, vol. 4. Ed. Philippe Ariès and Georges Duby. Paris: Seuil, 1987.

Dieulafoy, Jane (1851–1916). Author of numerous travel narratives, historical studies, novels*, and plays, Dieulafoy was one of the most respected women intellectuals of her time (although she is sometimes singled out for the pants she wore rather than for her books). As was the case for many women authors of travel literature*, her own writing career was closely tied to her husband's profession. When Marcel Dieulafoy went to Persia, first as an engineer and later as an archeologist in charge of digging around the Susa site, Jane accompanied him as his collaborator. She considered his mission hers and did not emphasize her spousal status in her writings, except when she complained that it prevented her from fully participating in the archeological mission. She became the official photographer of the expeditions and took extensive notes which would form the basis of her narratives. Dieulafoy's works are of a decidedly scientific and scholarly nature as opposed to the often impressionistic writings of many women travelers. Her scientific bent may partly explain why she received the approval of the intellectual community despite, or perhaps because of, the unusual position she held both as a woman and a writer.

Bénédicte Monicat

BIBLIOGRAPHY

Primary Texts

La Perse, la Chaldée et la Susiane. Paris: Hachette, 1887.
A Suse, journal des fouilles, 1884–1885. Paris: Hachette, 1888.
Aragon et Valence. Paris: Hachette, 1901.
Castille et Andalousie. Paris: Hachette, 1908.

Secondary Texts

Gran-Aymeric, Eve, and Jean Gran-Aymeric. *Jane Dieulafoy: Une Vie d'homme*. Parris: Perrin, 1991.

Monicat, Bénédicte. *Itinéraires de l'écriture au féminin: Voyageuses du 19e siècle*. Atlanta: Rodopi, 1996.

Divorce. Until the end of the Ancien Regime, despite the prominence of civil jurists, commandments of the Church continued to prevail in French legislation. Marriage* could not be broken but only annulled in rare cases, following long and costly trials in ecclesiastical courts. These ecclesiastical bodies alone could temporarily loosen marital bonds by recommending separation. Such exceptions were granted when the wife was adulterous, or when cohabitation endangered the life of a spouse—generally the wife. According to the law, physical abuse was the only reason for a wife to seek separation; furthermore, the ill treatment had to be life-threatening. Even infectious diseases were not sufficient grounds for separation. However, sometimes, but not always, judges took mental or venereal disease into consideration. On the eve of the Revolution*, the *philosophes*, with the exception of Voltaire, were reluctant to oppose the indissolubility of marriage; but in 1789–1790 at least twenty books and pamphlets on divorce were circulating.

Given the important role of the clergy during the early stage of the Revolution and the persistent loyalty to the monarchy and the Church, democratic leaders sought to avoid a confrontation and so delayed action on divorce. The Constitution of 1791 recognized marriage as a civil contract but remained silent on divorce. However, a few rebellious citizens decided to divorce before a *notaire* and then remarry their spouse in city hall. Nevertheless, a much larger number of people submitted petitions in favor of divorce. In 1792 the deputies received a list of demands by women, divorce being foremost among them. Shortly after the events of August 10, 1792, when the Revolution broke all ties with the Ancien Régime, divorce was legalized. In the heat of the moment no deputy voted against it, the only objections being procedural. The Napoleonic Code* of 1803 reestablished judicial separation, but divorce remained very difficult to obtain. Following the Restoration in 1816 and the empowerment of the clergy, divorce was prohibited.

However, following the Revolution of 1830, reestablishment of divorce seemed imminent, since its repeal in 1816 had symbolized a radical and ecclesiastical reaction. Four times the deputies voted resoundingly in favor of divorce, but the upper chamber rejected it and proposed instead to reform judicial separation—a suggestion the lower chamber categorically refused. In 1834 deputies gave up trying. With the Revolution of 1848*, divorce once again seemed unavoidable. But, after the initial revolutionary fervor had passed, a powerful drive was mounted against such "enemies of families and property" as "communists" and feminists. Gathered in "Le Club des femmes" and around Eugénie Niboyet* (the publisher of *La Voix des Femmes*), feminists were ruthlessly berated and derided and their demands confused with those in favor of divorce. The granting of universal suffrage had resulted in the election of an ultraconservative majority, so when Crémieux proposed the reestablishment of divorce, fellow deputies burst into laughter. The commission in charge of studying the matter decided to cancel or postpone the project. Nor had partisans of divorce any reason to rejoice following the coup d'état of 1851, since Louis Napoléon, who was ruling with the support of the Church and the conservatives, continued to evade the subject. However, the reformers triumphed briefly, when the Commune*—just four days before its fall—proposed to reestablish divorce.

Under the Third Republic, as early as 1872, the movement in favor of divorce gained unprecedented momentum, thanks to three leaders: Aléxandre Dumas; Léon Richer, publisher of *L'Avenir des femmes* and head of an important feminist group; and, especially Alfred Naquet, a young left-wing deputy. Under the influence of Léon Richer, Naquet gradually softened his extremely radical views against marriage and family*, and crisscrossed the country for ten years, lecturing and trying, tirelessly, to galvanize public opinion and the press. At last, he became the "apostle" and "father" of divorce when the third and most moderate of his proposed bills was passed in 1884.

On the one hand, judges who applied the new legislation were generally understanding. They rarely rejected requests when husband and wife agreed to divorce, thus stretching the law to allow divorce by mutual consent. Public opinion, on the other hand, continued to view divorcés, especially women, with suspicion and aversion. Opponents of divorce fueled this attitude of rejection, denounced the failure of justice, opposed attempts to ease legislation, and awaited an opportunity to launch their counterattack. That moment arrived with the extraordinary rise of the extreme right on the eve of World War II* and the advent of the Vichy government. Although the National Revolution did not dare to abolish divorce, it provided limited victories to opponents of divorce with the adoption of the 1941 legislation. Henceforth, divorce was banned during the first three years of marriage, the notion of "abuse" was narrowly defined, and advertisement by divorce agencies offering to provide this service on credit was prohibited. Following the Liberation, all but the first of these measures remained.

Until the 1970s, divorce laws had not changed much from those passed in 1884, which were largely inspired by the Civil Code of 1804. However, on every level—social, ideological, economic, and religious—the France of 1970 had nothing in common with that of 1884. No longer was divorce stigmatized, and public opinion demanded more relaxed divorce procedures, similar to those of other countries. The most notable innovations of the new 1975 law were the reestablishment of divorce by mutual consent and the granting of divorce under new circumstances: mutual acknowledgment of failure, mental illness, and separation for more than six years; furthermore, the notion of "failure" replaced that of "fault."

Francis Ronsin and Samia I. Spencer

BIBLIOGRAPHY

Secondary Texts

Naquet, Alfred. *Le Divorce*. Paris: E. Dentu, 1877.
Phillips, Roderick. *Family Breakdown in Late Eighteenth-Century France: Divorces in Rouen, 1792–1803*. London: Clarendon Press, 1980.

Riot-Sarcey, Michele. *La Démocratie à l'épreuve des femmes*. Paris: Albin Michel, 1994.

Ronsin, Francis. *Le Contrat sentimental. Débats sur le mariage, l'amour, le divorce, de l'Ancien Régime à la Restauration*. Paris: Aubier, 1990.

————. *Les Divorciaires. Affrontements politiques et conceptions du mariage dans la France du XIXe siècle*. Paris: Aubier, 1992.

Schamber, Ellie Nower. *The Artist as Politician: The Relation Between the Art and Politics of French Romantics*. Lanham, MD: University Press of America, 1984.

Thibault-Laurent, Gérard. *La Première Introduction du divorce en France sous la Révolution et l'Empire (1792–1816)*. Clermont-Ferrand: Imprimerie Moderne, 1938.

Djebar, Assia (1936–). Djebar was born in Cherchell, Algeria, of Algerian parents. Her father was a schoolteacher for the French school system in Algeria. The first Algerian woman ever to enter the elite Ecole Normale Supérieure de Sèvres, Djebar has taught history and literature at different universities in several countries and currently lives in Paris. She identifies herself as an Algerian woman who writes in French only because she went to French schools and never mastered written Arabic.

Djebar wrote her first novel*, *La Soif* (1957), in two months and was simultaneously hailed as an Algerian Françoise Sagan* and harshly criticized for writing about a narcissistic, selfish, and bourgeois young woman instead of concentrating on the Algerian War of Liberation, which was raging at the time. Her next two novels both showcased the war and presented sexual politics within the couple and the nation as the next struggle to be faced. At the time, she emphasized the couple (as opposed to life within the extended family* network) as a potential site of positive change in the condition of Algerian women. In 1969 she stopped publishing* books for a period of about ten years. She directed her first feature film, *La Nouba des femmes du Mont Chenoua*, in 1977–1978. Part documentary and part fiction, the film focuses on Lila, a woman who returns to her village to interview her female relatives about their lives during the war of liberation. *La Nouba* was followed by *La Zerda ou les chants de l'oubli*, a 1982 documentary about Maghrebian history between 1912 and 1942.

Djebar's experience as a filmmaker enabled her to return to writing. In 1980 she published a collection of short stories*, *Femmes d'Alger dans leur appartement*, in which she shifted away from her former focus on the couple and moved toward the need for female solidarity in the struggle for women's liberation. In *L'Amour, la fantasia* (1985), she wrote in the autobiographical mode for the first time. This book, the first of a projected quartet (of which three volumes have been published to date), rewrites the history of Algeria from the beginning of French colonization in 1830 to the present. In it, Djebar foregrounds both the role of Algerian women in the anticolonial struggles of the nineteenth and twentieth centuries and the violence done to them. *L'Amour, la fantasia* is also her most thorough attempt at dealing with her relationship to the French language: going to school enabled her to escape female confinement, but at the cost of linguistic colonization and separation from other women.

In her writing, Djebar does violence to the French language in order to bring out both the history of her people and the voices of silenced Algerian women. Her style has evolved from the relatively simple chronological *La Soif* to a complex, polyphonic, and architectural form of writing, with tightly structured organization and fragmented narrative. *Ombre sultane* (1987) and *Vaste est la prison* (1995), the next two books of the quartet, pick up the themes of the challenges of and need for female solidarity, the importance of female genealogy, and the remembrance of war. The latter novel is the most openly autobiographical of her entire work. Finally, Djebar is also famous for her retelling of the stories of historically important female Islamic figures, in *Loin de Médine* (1991). Her latest book, the haunting *Blanc de l'Algérie* (1996), is a personal meditation on the recent assassinations of many Algerian intellectuals and writers.

Assia Djebar is the foremost woman writer from the Maghreb. Her oeuvre, deeply feminist without being didactic, is among the very best written in the French language.

Anne Donadey

BIBLIOGRAPHY

Primary Texts

La Soif. Paris: Julliard, 1957.
Les Impatients. Paris: Julliard, 1958.
Les Enfants du nouveau monde. Paris: Julliard, 1962.
Les Alouettes naïves. Paris: Julliard, 1967.
Femmes d'Alger dans leur appartement. Paris: Des femmes, 1980.
L'Amour, la fantasia. Paris: J. C. Lattès, 1985.
Ombre sultane. Paris: J. C. Lattès, 1987.
Loin de Médine: Filles d'Ismaël. Paris: Albin Michel, 1991.
Vaste est la prison. Paris: Albin Michel, 1995.
Le Blanc de l'Algérie. Paris: Albin Michel, 1996.

Films

Djebar, Assia, dir. *La Nouba des femmes du Mont Chenoua*. 1978.
———. *La Zerda ou les chants de l'oubli*. 1982.

Djura (1949–). Singer and writer. The second of thirteen children, Djura moved to Paris with her parents in 1954. Her first text, the autobiographical *Le Voile du silence* (1990), recounts the main events of her life, from her childhood in Kabylia to fame in France. She describes in particular the frequent beatings at the hands of her alcoholic father, his refusal to allow her to pursue an acting career, her eldest brother's imprisoning of her in Algeria, and her brother and niece's attempt to kill her, her Breton husband, and their unborn child. A second text, *La Saison des Narcisses* (1993), interweaves reflections on her own life with anecdotes drawn from the lives of a wide range of other Algerian women. Djura is best known as the lead singer of Djurdjura, the musical group she founded, which mixes Western and Berber instruments and musical traditions. A self-proclaimed feminist, she speaks out against the oppression of Algerian women and sees herself as part of a long line of rebellious women—including Shéhérazade and the legendary Berber warrior Kahina—who have transgressed the patriarchal order. Djura has also made a prize-winning film (*Ali au pays des merveilles*) about the lives of North Africans working in France.

Susan Ireland

BIBLIOGRAPHY

  Primary Texts

Le Voile du silence. Paris: Michel Lafon, 1990.
La Saison des Narcisses. Paris: Michel Lafon, 1993.

Dormann, Geneviève (1933–). Journalist and author of novels* and fictional biographies, Dormann has received numerous literary prizes that testify to the quality and popularity of her work. She neither advocates feminism* nor describes herself as a feminist, but voices feminist concerns in *Le Roman de Sophie Trébuchet* and *Amoureuse Colette*. In her novels, heroines embrace life with energy and audacity, challenging the conventions of their milieu through such gestures as discarding their wedding rings. Male characters, on the contrary, are portrayed as weak, cowardly, and self-centered—just means to an end in the female protagonists' search for fulfillment. For Dormann, a successful woman chooses her fate in spite of familial or temporal constraints. Dormann's irreverent style, with its mixture of colloquial expressions, unexpected metaphors, and pastiches, satirizes bourgeois values and hypocrisy.

Marie Liénard

BIBLIOGRAPHY

  Primary Texts

La Fanfaronne. Paris: Seuil, 1959.
Le Chemin des dames. Paris: Seuil, 1964.
La Passion selon saint Jules. Paris: Seuil, 1969.
Je t'apporterai des Orages. Paris: Seuil, 1971.
Le Bateau du courrier. Paris: Seuil, 1974.
Mickey l'ange. Paris: Seuil, 1977.
Fleur de péché. Paris: Seuil, 1980.
Le Roman de Sophie Trébuchet. Paris: Albin Michel, 1982.
Amoureuse Colette. Paris: Herscher, 1984.
Le Bal du dodo. Paris: Albin Michel, 1989.
La Petite Main. Paris: Albin Michel, 1993.
La Gourmandise de Guillaume Apollinaire. Paris: Albin Michel, 1994.

Dorval, Marie (1798–1849). Born to a family of itinerant stage artists, she became the foremost actress of the Parisian Boulevard. Fully identifying onstage with the passionate characters she portrayed, she triumphed in Dumas's *Antony*

(1831), Hugo's *Marion Delorme* (1831), and Alfred de Vigny's *Chatterton* (1835). Dorval used her keen knowledge of stage choreography to breathe theatrical life into the Romantics' texts. She ended a heady affair with Vigny in order to support, through grueling theatrical touring, her children and her husband. Her unwavering friendship* with George Sand* led to a woman-centered project, *Cosima* (1840), which garnered only critical scorn.

Judith G. Miller

BIBLIOGRAPHY

Primary Texts

Lettres à Alfred de Vigny. Paris: Gallimard, 1942.
Sand, George. *Correspondance inédite de George Sand et Marie Dorval, publiée avec une introduction et des notes*. Ed. Simone Cavaillet-Maurois. Paris: Gallimard, 1953.

Secondary Texts

Ambrière, Francis. *Mademoiselle Mars et Marie Dorval au théâtre et dans la vie*. Paris: Seuil, 1992.
Arland, Marcel. *Une Passion romantique: Alfred de Vigny et Marie Dorval*. Brussels: Editions de la Nouvelle Revue Belgique, 1945.
Coupy, Emile. *Marie Dorval, documents inédits, biographie, critique et bibliographie*. Paris and Brussels: Librairie Internationale A. Lacroix, Verboeckhoven et Cie., 1868.
Gaylor, Anna. *Marie Dorval: Grandeur et misère d'une actrice romantique*. Paris: Flammarion, 1989.
Hagenauer, Paul. *La Vie douloureuse de Marie Dorval*. Paris: Editions de Navarre, 1972.

Doutreligne, Louise (1948–). Nom de plume of Claudine Fiévet. Actress, director, and playwright, Doutreligne uses theater* to explore women's sensuality. In *Petit' Pièces intérieures* and *Femme à la porte cochère*, provocative, erotic encounters reveal the force of women's desire, while in *Teresada'* Doutreligne compares all-consuming desire to the ecstasy of mystics through her portrayal of the mind-body torment of Theresa of Avila. In Doutreligne's presentation of Saint Theresa's struggle for transcendence, Theresa's relationship to the written word plays a major role in fulfilling her unsatisfied desire and leading her to salvation. In *Conversations sur l'infinité des passions*, Doutreligne adapts for the stage intimate conversations between couples from different periods of the past in order to illustrate the protean forms of women's passion and desire.

Jan Berkowitz Gross

BIBLIOGRAPHY

Primary Texts

Détruire l'Image. Paris: Théâtre ouvert, Tapuscrit, 1979.
Quand Speedoux s'endort; Qui est Lucie Syn'? Paris: EDILIG Théâtrales, 1983.
Croq. D'amour. Paris: Actes Sud-Papiers, 1985.
Petit' Pièces intérieures. Paris: Actes Sud-Papiers, 1986.

Teresada'. L'Avant-Scène 808 (1987).
Femme à la porte cochère. Paris: Actes Sud-Papiers, 1988.
Conversations sur l'infinité des passions. Paris: Editions des Quatre Vents, 1990.
Carmen, la nouvelle. L'Avant-Scène 937/938 (1993).

Secondary Text

"Paroles de femmes au théâtre." Discussion. *Les Cahiers des Lundis.* Paris: Association
    THEATRALES, 1993–1994. 21–30.

Droit du seigneur (droit de cuissage). Historical documents of early medieval
times confirm the rights of lords over the bodies of female serfs. On her wedding
night, the bride was deflowered by the master before being intimate with her
husband. Gradually, and as early as 1409, parliaments attempted to abolish the
practice and replace it with a tax. However, the custom was deeply rooted and,
despite the abolition of serfdom, it continued to exist well into the eighteenth
century, as evidenced by Voltaire's *Le Droit du seigneur ou l'écueil du sage*
(1762) and Beaumarchais's *Le Mariage de Figaro* (1784). It also left enduring
scars throughout the industrial age.

As females entered the labor force in greater numbers, they were often expected to provide sexual favors in the workplace, the lords having been replaced
by employers and foremen. Domestic help and farm workers did not fare better,
as they often had to fulfill the needs of male employers and their growing sons.
This new form of "droit du seigneur" was no longer a formal right since, in
principle, women were free to accept or refuse the unsolicited advances. On a
practical level, however, they feared the anger of the seducer, the loss of their
jobs, and humiliation by authorities if they reported the crime.

One of the most notorious cases of sexual harassment occurred in 1905, provoked by a supervisor in a Limoges porcelain factory. Initially the employer
and authorities protected the man because of his status and gender. However,
after a bitter strike that divided the city, and thanks to the support of labor
unions, women prevailed and the aggressor was removed. In 1992, after nearly
a century of struggle, sexual harassment in the workplace was finally recognized
as a crime, following the enactment of laws protecting women against abuse of
power and demands for sexual favors.

Samia I. Spencer

BIBLIOGRAPHY

Bouthors, André. *Coutumes locales du baillage d'Amiens, redigées en 1507.* Amiens:
    Imprimerie Duval et Hermant, 1845.
De l'Abus du pouvoir sexuel. Le Harcèlement sexuel au travail. Paris and Montreal:
    Editions La Découverte/Le Boréal, 1990.
Fugier, Anne-Marie. *La Place des bonnes. La Domesticité féminine à Paris en 1900.*
    Paris: Grasset, 1979.
Louis, Marie-Victoire. *Le Droit de cuissage. France, 1860–1930.* Paris: Les Editions de
    l'Atelier, 1994.

Merriman, John M. *Limoges, la ville rouge. Portrait d'une ville révolutionnaire.* Paris: Belin, 1990.

Sullerot, Evelyne. *Histoire et sociologie du travail féminin.* Paris: Editions Gonthier, 1968.

Du Bocage (or Du Boccage), Anne-Marie Fiquet (1710–1802). Born into a family that recognized her talent for writing, Bocage received a solid education* in an exclusive Parisian convent*—an unusual practice for a daughter of the rich bourgeoisie. At seventeen, she married a poet and translator, settled in Rouen, and established a renowned provincial salon*. The couple traveled extensively throughout Europe.

At first, her literary talent was recognized in private circles where her travel letters—especially those addressed to her sister—delighted readers. Public fame came later with publication of her favorite genre, poetry* adapted from or inspired by the likes of Milton and Pope. In 1746 she received the First Prize of the Academy of Rouen for a poem entitled "De l'influence mutuelle des beaux-arts et des sciences."

Today, however, Bocage is best known for *Les Amazones* (1749), a play that originally met with moderate success. Contemporary critics are particularly interested in Bocage's recurrent theme of power, echoed throughout her works through female characters. Sometimes the theme is also treated through male characters, such as Columbus in *La Colombiade* (1756). In the latter part of her life, Bocage, by then a wealthy and independent widow, devoted herself to the art form she enjoyed most—writing in the style of other poets.

Valérie Lastinger

BIBLIOGRAPHY

Primary Texts

Les Amazones. Tragédie en cinq actes. Paris: F. Mérigot, 1749.

Recueil des oeuvres de Madame du Bocage. Lyons: Les Frères Périsse, 1762, 1764, 1770.

Lettres de Madame du Bocage contenant ses voyages en France, en Angleterre, en Hollande et en Italie pendant les années 1750, 1757 & 1757. Dresden: G. C. Walther, 1771.

Secondary Texts

Gill-Mark, Grace. "Anne-Marie du Bocage: Une Femme de lettres au XVIII siècle." *Bibliothèque de la Revue de littérature comparée* 41 (1927).

Mulvihill, Maureen E. "Anne-Marie Fiquet du Bocage née Le Page." In *An Encyclopedia of Continental Women Writers.* Ed. Katharina M. Wilson. New York: Garland, 1991. Vol. 1:141–143.

Virolle, Roland. "Types sociaux en Normandie au XVIIIe siècle: Anne-Marie du Bocage, la dixième muse." *Etudes normandes* (1979): 66–80.

Du Deffand, Marie de Vichy-Chamrond, marquise (1697–1780). Born into Burgundian nobility, she married the marquis du Deffand in 1718 but eventually separated from him. Witty and cultured, du Deffand soon embraced the brilliant society of the Regency, met Voltaire, with whom she carried on an extensive correspondence, and had several liaisons, notably with the regent. Her salon*, opened in 1730, hosted the aristocratic and intellectual celebrities of the day, including the duchesses du Maine and du Luxembourg, the ducs de Choiseul and de Lauzun, the marquises de Boufflers and du Châtelet*, as well as Fontenelle, Voltaire, Montesquieu, Marivaux, d'Alembert, and Condorcet. It was in her salon that the Enlightenment* movement began to manifest itself more openly. Having gone blind by 1754, she took on as companion and reader the impecunious Julie de Lespinasse*, her brother's illegitimate daughter. Lespinasse's ten-year subservience to the increasingly cantankerous du Deffand came to an abrupt end when the latter found that some of her habitués, notably d'Alembert, Turgot, and Marmontel, preferred the company of the younger woman. Late in life, du Deffand formed a passionate attachment to Horace Walpole, as attested by her voluminous correspondence with him. Her main claim to fame is her legacy as a prolific and gifted *épistolière*. On the whole, she remained attuned to the skeptical, witty spirit of Voltaire and unresponsive to the pre-Romantic stirrings of Rousseau's generation.

Gita May

BIBLIOGRAPHY

Primary Texts

Correspondance complète de la marquise du Deffand avec ses amis, le Président Hénault, Montesquieu, d'Alembert, Voltaire, Horace Walpole. Ed. M. de Lescure. Paris: Plon, 1865.
Correspondance de Mme du Deffand avec la duchesse de Choiseul, l'abbé Barthélémy et M. Craufurt. Ed. le marquis de Sainte-Aulaire. Paris: Michel Levy, 1866.
Letters to and from Madame du Deffand and Julie de Lespinasse. Ed. Warren Hunting Smith. New Haven: Yale University Press, 1938.
Lettres de la marquise du Deffand à Horace Walpole. Ed. Mrs. Paget Toynbee. London: Methuen, 1912.
Madame du Deffand: lettres à Voltaire. Ed. Joseph Trabucco. Paris: Bossard, 1922.

Secondary Texts

Craveri, Benedetta. *Madame du Deffand et son monde.* Trans. Sibylle Zavriew. Paris: Le Seuil, 1987. Also trans. Teresa Waugh. *Madame du Deffand and Her World.* Boston: David R. Godine, 1994.
Curtis, Judith. ''The Epistolières.'' In *French Women and the Age of Enlightenment.* Ed. Samia I. Spencer. Bloomington: Indiana University Press, 1984. 226–241.
Duisit, Lionel. *Madame du Deffand, épistolière.* Geneva: Droz, 1963.
Goodman, Dena. *The Republic of Letters. A Cultural History of the French Enlightenment.* Ithaca, NY: Cornell University Press, 1994.
Lloyd, Caryl L. ''Marquise du Deffand.'' In *French Women Writers.* Ed. Eva Martin Sartori and Dorothy Wynne Zimmerman. Westport, CT: Greenwood Press, 1991. 134–142.
May, Gita. ''Salons littéraires au XVIIIe siècle.'' *Dictionnaire Universel des littératures.* Ed. Béatrice Didier. Paris: Presses Universitaires de France, 1994.

Dufrénoy, Adélaïde-Gillette Billet (1765–1825). A prolific writer who published in a wide variety of genres, this daughter of a Parisian jeweler owes her fame to her poetic works. Well educated and versed in Latin, Dufrénoy married a wealthy lawyer at fifteen. After the loss of her husband's fortune during the Revolution*, she supported the family* by working as a copyist until awarded a pension by Napoleon. Her most popular collection of poems, *Elégies* (1807), earned her the nickname "the French Sappho." In 1812 Dufrénoy published an autobiographical novel*, *La Femme Auteur ou les inconvénients de la célébrité,* in which she asserts that becoming an author ruins a woman socially. Three years later, she became the first woman to win the French Academy's prize for poetry*, awarded for the best poem on "La Mort de Bayard."

Dufrènoy collaborated on various literary collections for women, including *Bibliothèque choisie pour les femmes* (1818–1821). She also published numerous pedagogical works, the most notable being *Biographie des jeunes demoiselles ou vies des femmes célèbres* (1816). In a preface to this collection of sketches, Dufrénoy explains that she attempted to limit her selection to virtuous role models for her young female readership. However, Dufrénoy's main goal is to extol her subjects' achievements as artists and/or public figures. In the same vein, *Françaises* (1818) is a collection of historical short stories* portraying episodes in the lives of famous women.

Mary McAlpin

BIBLIOGRAPHY

Primary Texts

La Femme Auteur ou les inconvénients de la célébrité. Paris: Béchet, 1812.
Biographies des jeunes demoiselles ou vies des femmes célébres depuis les Hébreux jusqu'à nos jours. Paris: Eymery, 1816.
Les Françaises. Nouvelles. Paris: Eymery, 1818.
Oeuvres poétiques de Mme Dufrénoy précédées d'observations sur sa vie et ses ouvrages. Paris: Moutardier, 1827.

Secondary Text

Brécourt-Villars, Claudine. *Ecrire d'amour: Anthologie de textes érotiques féminins, 1799–1984*. Paris: Ramsay, 1985.

Du Noyer, Anne-Marguerite Petit, dame (1663–1719). Born in Nîmes, she lost her mother shortly after her birth and was raised by her maternal aunt in the Protestant faith. After the revocation of the Edict of Nantes in 1685, she fled Nîmes, disguised in cook's attire, and sought refuge in Holland and then in London in order to escape forced conversion. In 1688 she returned to Paris to live with her aunt and uncle, who had both abjured their Protestant beliefs to save his wealth. Since she was the sole inheritor of her uncle's vast fortune, he attempted to make her renounce Protestantism and found her a Catholic suitor. Guillaume du Noyer promised never to constrain her in matters of religion so long as she raised their children in the Catholic faith. They married in 1688, and her inheritance allowed him to buy a government post in the Languedoc region. A compulsive gambler and womanizer, he squandered her fortune. In 1701 she decided to escape France with her two daughters and join her coreligionists in Holland.

Her situation as a politico-religious exile in the "Refuge" prompted her to seize upon writing as her vocation. She supported herself and her daughters through journalism and gazetteering. From 1704 to 1717 she published *Lettres historiques et galantes* (111 letters in seven volumes) in Cologne. The first few volumes appeared under the pseudonym Mme de C***. These letters attained extreme popularity. Under the guise of a correspondence between two lady friends, one in Paris and the other in the provinces, Mme du Noyer described political, historical, religious, and mundane events of the era. The anecdotal material is spiced with biting polemical remarks. In 1710 she published her *Mémoires* in hopes of clearing her reputation. Viewing her own persecution and the general persecution of the Huguenots as a human rights violation, she lent a unique twist to women's memoirs* of the period. Between 1711 and 1719 she also contributed to the periodic press, in a well-known gazette, the *Quintessence*. She died in Voorburg on May 28, 1719.

Henriette Goldwyn

BIBLIOGRAPHY

Primary Texts

*Lettres historiques et galantes par Madame C***, ouvrage curieux*. New ed. London: Jean Nourse, 1733.
Mémoires de Mme du Noyer, écrits par elle-même pour servir de suite à ses lettres. Vol. 6. London: Jean Nourse, 1739.

Secondary Texts

Goldwyn, Henriette. "Mme du Noyer: Dissident Memorialist of the Huguenot Diaspora." In *Women Writers in Pre-Revolutionary France: Strategies of Emancipation*. Ed. Colette H. Winn and Donna Kuizenga. New York: Garland Press, 1996. 117–126.
Nabarra, Alain. "Mme du Noyer et la *Quintessence*: La Rencontre d'une journaliste et d'un journal." In *Femmes savantes et femmes d'ésprit*. Ed. Roland Bonnel and Catherine Rubinger. New York: Peter Lang, 1994. 45–77.
Sgard, Jean, ed. *Dictionnaire des journaux 1600–1789*. Vol. 2. Paris: Universitas, 1991.
Van Dijk, Suzanna. *Traces de femmes. Présence féminine dans le journalisme français du XVIIIe siècle*. Amsterdam and Maarssen: Academic Publishers Associated, 1988.

Durand, Catherine, Dame Bédacier (?–1736?). Virtually nothing is known of her life. Since a volume of her posthumous writings appeared in January 1737, it is presumed that she died the preceding year. Other scholars have given her date of death as 1712–1715. She is listed on the title pages of her works as

Madame D* or Madame Durand, even after her death; she never used her married name of Bédacier. The only certain date is 1701, when she won the poetry* prize of the Académie Française. Her novels*, which stress plot more than psychological depth, consist mainly of love stories with conventional plots, such as *La Comtesse de Mortane* and *Le Comte de Cardonne*, or historical fiction in the *galant* style, such as *Mémoires secrets de la cour de Charles VII*. More original are *Les Petits Soupers de l'été* (1702), which makes an attempt to portray the mores of the cultured aristocracy of the author's day, including its taste for fairy tales*, and *Les Belles Grecques* (1712), a study of four courtesans of antiquity in which sexual license is deemphasized in order to focus on the ladies' intelligence, refinement, and (in some cases) fidelity. She was the first to publish comedy-proverbs (playlets that illustrate a well-known proverb, which is not mentioned in the text; the audience is supposed to guess it), which were to become a popular salon* entertainment in the eighteenth century. While she was not the originator of this subgenre, her charming playlets certainly contributed to its popularity.

Perry Gethner

BIBLIOGRAPHY

Storer, Mary Elizabeth. *La Mode des contes de fées, 1685–1700.* Geneva: Slatkine Reprints, 1972.

Durand, Marguerite (1864–1936). Durand began her career in the theater* and performed at the Comédie Française. In 1888 she and her husband Georges Laguerre launched *La Presse*, the official mouthpiece of Général Boulanger. Durand later initiated *Le Courrier du Figaro* (1891), a weekly supplement to *Le Figaro*. She subsequently created and presided over the daily *La Fronde* (1897), the first feminist newspaper entirely administered and written by women. The paper eventually became the property of its contributors. *La Fronde* published articles on such feminist issues as women's education* and labor rights. It also highlighted women authors and treated political debates such as the Dreyfus affair. Durand also launched an international colloquium on women's rights with Maria Pognon and others in 1900, a conference of women's labor and an Office du Travail féminin in 1907, a conference on civil rights and female suffrage with Jeanne Oddo-Deflou and Madame Vincent in 1908, and an exhibit on famous women of the nineteenth-century in 1922. In 1927 the Maison des Journalists admitted Durand and Sévérine*. The extensive collection of materials on women's issues and feminism* which Durand donated to the city of Paris became the basis of the Marguerite Durand Library*, the first French library of feminist documentation.

Claire Marrone

BIBLIOGRAPHY

Secondary Texts

Albistur, Maïté, and Daniel Armogathe. *Histoire du féminisme français*. Paris: Editions des femmes, 1977.
Dizier-Metz, Annie. *La Bibliothèque Marguerite Durand: Histoire d'une femmme, mémoire des femmes*. Paris: Mairie de Paris-Agence culturelle de Paris, 1992.

Duras, Claire de (1777–1828). Born in Brest to an admiral in the royal navy and a woman raised in Martinique, Duras had a happy childhood until her parents' separation in 1792, and her father's execution with the Girondins in 1793. While in exile in London, she married another Breton, the duc de Duras, and had two daughters before returning to France in 1808. With the restoration of Louis XVIII, the duc de Duras became chamberlain, and the family moved into the royal palace. There, the duchess held a salon* that included Chateaubriand and other outstanding intellectuals of the period.

Duras did not become a novelist until her friends urged her to write down the stories she told in her salon*. Her three published novels* relate in a very modern way the psychological anguish of people who are excluded from high society, marriage*, and happiness by no fault of their own. Ourika is black; Edouard is a middle-class lawyer in love with an aristocrat; Olivier is impotent. Chantal Bertrand-Jennings sees in the social exclusion of Edouard and Olivier (feminized heroes), and especially that of Ourika, a metaphor for the feminine condition. Michèle Bissière has studied the revolt against the father in *Ourika* (1824) and *Edouard* (1825), concluding that the results are far more devastating for Ourika.

Duras was aware of the injustice of society in its unequal treatment of people of different races and genders. Her novels protest against this injustice and portray social deviants with warmth and sympathy.

Lucy M. Schwartz

BIBLIOGRAPHY

Primary Texts

Pensées de Louis XIV, extraites de ses ouvrages et de ses lettres manuscrites. Paris: Firmin-Didot, 1827.
Réflexions et prières inédites. Paris: Débécourt, 1839.
Edouard. Ed. Claudine Herrmann. Paris: Mercure de France, 1983.
Ourika. Ed. Joan DeJean and Margaret Waller. New York: MLA, 1994.

Secondary Texts

Bardoux, Agénor. *La Duchesse de Duras*. Paris: C. Lévy, 1898.
Bertrand-Jennings, Chantal. "Condition féminine et impuissance sociale." *Romantisme* 63 (1989): 39–50.
Bissière, Michèle. "Union et désunion avec le père dans *Ourika* et *Edouard*." *Nineteenth-Century French Studies* 23 (1995): 316–323.

Crichfield, Grant. *Three Novels of Madame de Duras: "Ourika," "Edouard," "Olivier."* The Hague: Mouton, 1975.

Decreus-Van Liefland, Juliette. *Sainte-Beuve et la critique des auteurs féminins.* Paris: Boivin, 1949. 91–107.

Merlant, Joachim. "Le Roman d'analyse de 1804 à 1830: Mme de Duras." In *Le Roman personnel de Rousseau à Fromentin.* Paris: Hachette, 1905. 301–315.

Pailhès, Gabriel. *Mme de Duras et Chateaubriand d'après des documents inédits.* Paris: Perrin, 1910.

Riberette, Pierre. "Le Modèle d'*Olivier.*" *Bulletin de la Société Chateaubriand* 28 (1985): 93–100.

Sainte-Beuve, Charles Augustin. "Madame de Duras." In *Oeuvres.* 2 vols. Paris: Gallimard, 1951. 2: 1042–1058.

Duras, Marguerite (1914–1996). Novelist, playwright, essayist, and filmmaker. Born Marguerite Donnadieu at Gia Dinh in former French Indochina, Duras moved to Paris in 1932 to study law and political science. She was a member of the Resistance during World War II*, and recounts her war experiences in *La Douleur* (1985), a series of autobiographical and fictional texts. In the 1970s she participated in the French women's liberation movement in campaigns such as the struggle for the right to abortion*. She contributed to the feminist journal *Sorcières*, but she did not like to be categorized as a feminist. Although Duras is now recognized as one of the most creative minds of the second half of the twentieth century, her work remained marginal until the publication of *L'Amant* in 1984.

The world of Duras's first novels* is already a female universe in which the protagonists are often women, but the narrators are mostly men. These texts announce the themes that recur throughout her oeuvre: madness, desire, and the split female subject. These early realist texts are characterized by psychological analysis, the use of familiar language, and explicit political commentary.

Duras abandoned traditional novelistic forms in the late 1950s. Although she denied any relationship with the Nouveau Roman* group, she is frequently associated with it. Her experimentation with novelistic form led her to adopt a minimalist style, which has been linked to *l'écriture féminine** and even to feminist aesthetics. Critics have viewed the minimalism of her style as a textual inscription of the unconscious and an illustration of women's absence and silence in a phallocentric world. The distinctive "blanks" in her work that deny textual closure have also been interpreted as reflecting the theme of unfulfilled desire that pervades her work.

Desire is indeed central to Duras's writing, where it is usually associated with the story of an impossible, passionate love, and is manifested in the split of the female subject. Sometimes expressed as lack and negation in the early novels, female desire becomes a more positive force in the later works. Silence and madness—which characterize Durassian women more than men—also function as an effective weapon against male narrators, who are denied rational explanations and the appropriation of their story by female characters. Women thus manage to resist being reduced to the status of objects, though their transformation into subjects has not yet occurred in early novels such as *Moderato Cantabile* (1958) and *Le Ravissement de Lol V. Stein* (1964).

Duras's representations of female protagonists remain ambivalent, however, as they often position women in such conventional roles as silent and mad women, whores and femmes fatales—the objects of male discourse and desire. Nonetheless, these women characters paradoxically contribute to the deconstruction of traditional modes of thinking related to the categories man/woman: masculine/feminine, subject/object, spectator/spectacle, active/passive, colonizer/colonized. Duras's texts set in Indochina, for example, destabilize the relation of colonizer/colonized through her portrayal of a diseased colonial society.

In her novels and films, Duras creates a complex, ambiguous fictional world; her representations of gender and race have been variously interpreted as essentialist and constructionist. She polarized her critics even more with the publication of her erotic/pornographic texts in the 1980s. One of her main achievements is no doubt the fact that her work, which often subverts accepted gender roles, continues to challenge our conceptions of women.

S. Pascale Bécel

BIBLIOGRAPHY

Primary Texts

Moderato Cantabile. Paris: Minuit, 1958.
Hiroshima mon amour. Paris: Gallimard, 1960.
Le Ravissement de Lol V. Stein. Paris: Gallimard, 1964.
Le Vice-Consul. Paris: Gallimard, 1965.
La Maladie de la mort. Paris: Minuit, 1982.
L'Amant. Paris: Minuit, 1984.
Duras, Marguerite, and Xavière Gauthier. *Les Parleuses*. Paris: Minuit, 1974.
Duras, Marguerite, and Michelle Porte. *Les Lieux de Marguerite Duras*. Paris: Minuit, 1977.

Secondary Texts

Cohen, Susan D. *Women and Discourse in the Fiction of Marguerite Duras: Love, Legends, Language*. Amherst: University of Massachusetts Press, 1993.
Marini, Marcelle. *Territoires du féminin*. Paris: Minuit, 1977.
Selous, Trista. *The Other Woman: Feminism and Femininity in the Works of Marguerite Duras*. New Haven: Yale University Press, 1988.
Willis, Sharon. *Marguerite Duras: Writing on the Body*. Chicago: University of Chicago Press, 1987.

E

Eaubonne, Françoise d' (1920–). Essayist, novelist, poet, literary critic, and editor. Eaubonne has been active in the group Ecologie et féminisme since 1972 and in the militant feminist SOS Sexisme since 1988. Her work includes numerous essays on feminism*, mainly from the 1970s; in such texts as *Le Féminisme: histoire et actualité* (1972), *Le Féminisme ou la mort* (1974), and *Les Femmes avant le patriarcat* (1976), she finds possible models for new human relationships in social structures of the past in which women played influential roles. In *Ecologie-Féminisme* (1979), Eaubonne links the exploitation of women and that of the earth, stressing the need to prevent their further destruction and domination by phallocentric systems. She has also written a feminist utopian novel as well as essays and fiction on artists and public figures, including Verlaine and Rimbaud, Madame de Staël*, Simone de Beauvoir*, Qiu Jin, and Isabelle Eberhardt.

With her frank, provocative style, Eaubonne uses literature as a weapon in the struggle to make humanity as a whole more equitable; men's freedom, she argues, depends on that of women. Although she fights against patriarchal interpretations of history, Eaubonne refuses to confine herself to a notion of gender-based writing.

Metka Zupančič

BIBLIOGRAPHY

Primary Texts

Verlaine et Rimbaud. Paris: A. Michel, 1960.
Une Femme témoin de son siècle: Germaine de Staël. Paris: Flammarion, 1966.
Le Féminisme, histoire et actualité. Paris: A. Moreau, 1972.
Le Féminisme ou la mort. Paris: P. Horay, 1974.
Les Femmes avant le patriarcat. Paris: Payot, 1976.

Ecologie-Féminisme. Paris: Ed. Actualité Temps Présent, 1979.
Une Femme nommée Castor: Mon Amie Simone de Beauvoir. Paris: Encre, 1986.

Ecole lyonnaise. Although the *Ecole lyonnaise* was never in any real sense a poetic school but rather a random group of poets who happened to exercise their craft in Lyons at approximately the same historical moment, those associated with it do form a sufficiently coherent intellectual and literary community to justify the use of this term, even in the absence of an official poetic manifesto. The most important part of this label is in fact the adjective, because poets writing in the city of Lyons in the first half of the sixteenth century were nurtured and inspired by the exceptional concomitance of intellectual and commercial currents that made Lyons the most prominent and most progressive city in France. As Saulnier has pointed out, it was the first major city in France to be truly bourgeois (that is, under the control of bourgeois leaders, rather than of aristocrats or of royal appointees). It also played an important role in the commercial life of France, situated as it was at the crossroads of Western Europe, on highways leading to Germany and Italy and bordered by the then independent Duchy of Savoy. Removed from the conservative influence of the Sorbonne, it was a city whose population included a large number of families of Italian origin, so that it was very much attuned not only to Italian trade but also to Italian intellectual and cultural movements. Lyons was extremely receptive to Neopetrarchan poetry*, to Ficinian Neoplatonism, and to the new codes of love propagated by authors such as Sperone Speroni and Leone Ebreo. It is no coincidence that the event that propelled Maurice Scève, the principal poet of the *Ecole lyonnaise*, to prominence on the international humanist stage was the "discovery" of the tomb of Petrarch's Laura in Avignon. The strong Italian influence on Lyonese poetry is also shown not only in the themes and vocabulary of Pernette du Guillet's* verse (appropriately entitled *Rymes*, after Petrarch's work), but also in the fact that the very first sonnet of Louise Labé's* collection is in Italian. Of course, their contemporary male colleagues also exhibit the same influences.

It has become conventional wisdom to state, after Joan Kelly Gadol, that the condition of women did not improve at all during the Renaissance and that in fact women lost certain of the gains they had made during the Middle Ages. While a cursory reading of the laws passed in the sixteenth century concerning women may appear to confirm this, in fact, the way these laws were interpreted shows that the situation was much less dire than is often stated. Danielle Haase-Dubosc is undertaking some very interesting research in this area, and Natalie Zemon Davis has shown that women played a much larger role both inside and outside the home than might be suggested by contemporary courtesy books. Davis reports on a document from Lyons in which a shoemaker confesses that his family's prosperity was due less to his own commercial efforts than to the successful linen trade plied by his wife (Davis, 70). Lyons was probably the most advanced (or the least retarded, depending on one's point of view) city of

France as a favorable setting for women's gains in the intellectual, commercial, and social sphere. So much so that there was a debate between the women of Paris and Lyons, called the *Querelle des rescriptions*, in which the Lyonese women are presented as worshiping at the shrine of Lust, Pride, and Venality and of being unhealthily partial to imported Italian makeup (see Saulnier, *Scève*, 24). Lyonese intellectuals also tended to take up the defense of women in the *Querelle des femmes**, as is evidenced by Symphorien Champier's *Nef des Dames vertueuses* in 1503. In the first part of the sixteenth century, the city also saw the creation of literary salons* in which women played a leading role. It is scarcely surprising that it was in this relatively liberal milieu, rather than in the more dogmatic and traditional Paris, that du Guillet and Labé were able to pursue their poetic activity. Although in the preface she wrote for her work Labé suggests that writing can bring social stigma to a woman who engages in this activity (this is ostensibly why she invites Clémence de Bourges to support her as she makes her own writing public), it is obvious from the unusually large number of poems written in praise of her work (see Rigolot's edition) that she was highly respected by the male poets of the Lyons circle. This esteem is confirmed by the fact that both Scève and Magny saw fit to engage in poetic dialogue with du Guillet and Labé, respectively. A further indication of the openness of Lyonese society to women writing is the fact that, even though her poetry celebrates her (relatively) chaste love for Maurice Scève, it was at the urging of her husband that du Guillet's verse was published shortly after her death.

Lyons was the milieu that allowed the two most important female poets of the French Renaissance to flourish. Both because of the city's social structure (the major role played by its bourgeoisie is perhaps one of the answers to the puzzle of how Louise Labé, a ropemaker's daughter, received an excellent humanist education* and how she came in contact with the aristocrat Clémence de Bourges) and thanks to its intellectual climate, inspired by Italian Neoplatonic thought, Lyons provided the appropriate environment for the *Ecole lyonnaise*, a movement which, for its time, was unusually sympathetic to women and to their literary aspirations.

Lance K. Donaldson-Evans

BIBLIOGRAPHY

Primary Texts

Du Guillet, Pernette. *Rymes*. Ed. V. Graham. Geneva: Droz, 1968.
Labé, Louise. *Oeuvres complètes*. Ed. François Rigolot. Paris: Flammarion, 1986.

Secondary Texts

Davis, Natalie Zemon. *Society and Culture in Early Modern France*. Stanford: Stanford University Press, 1975.
Jones, Ann Rosalind. "Assimilation with a Difference: Renaissance Women and Literary Influence." *Yale French Studies* 62 (1981): 135–153.

———. *The Currency of Eros: Women's Love Lyric in Europe*. Bloomington: Indiana University Press, 1990.
Saulnier, V.-L. "Etude sur Pernette du Guillet et ses *Rymes*." *Bibliothèque d'Humanisme et Renaissance* 4 (1944): 7–119.
———. *Maurice Scève*. 2 vols. Paris: Klincksieck, 1984.

Ecriture féminine. This term, for which there is arguably no adequate English equivalent, has sparked theoretical debate among feminists since it appeared in Hélène Cixous's* performative essay-manifesto, "Le Rire de la Méduse" (1975). In this text and in the lengthier *La Jeune Née* (1975), Cixous articulates her utopian desire to see a new form of writing that would express the feminine, defined in feminist psychoanalytic terms as what has historically been repressed by the masculine libidinal economy manifest in dominant patriarchal structures. Positing the inherent bisexuality of the unconscious, Cixous calls for an exploration of feminine drives that would subvert the dominant discourse, through a writing characterized by open-endedness, difference, disruptive wordplay, and revisionary rereadings, and especially by a closer relation to the body as a site where the unconscious finds expression in creative/procreative desires. While claiming that the feminine should not be conflated or confused with the "female," Cixous nonetheless privileges women in her theory, for she believes that their access to language and writing has been inhibited by male authorities, and that it is time they liberated their voices and desires. Cixous's emphasis on maternal metaphors has led many feminist critics to accuse her of essentialism*, for they argue that her theory is grounded in biology and thus reproduces the very reductive stereotypes she attempts to deconstruct. Others argue that Cixous's constantly shifting metaphoric associations constitute a necessary and effective destabilizing strategy. Questions of essentialism still fuel feminist criticism in the United States, which is undoubtedly why, even though she has over twenty novels and several plays to her credit, Cixous is still best known for her early theoretical ideals rather than for her evolving and passionate writing practice.

Miléna Santoro

BIBLIOGRAPHY

Binhammer, Katherine. "Metaphor or Metonymy? The Question of Essentialism in Cixous." *Tessera* 10 (Summer 1991): 65–79.
Cixous, Hélène. *Coming to Writing and Other Essays*. Ed. and trans. Deborah Jensen. Cambridge, MA: Harvard University Press, 1991.
———. "Le Rire de la Méduse." *L'Arc* 61 (1975): 39–54.
Cixous, Hélène, and Catherine Clément. *La Jeune Née*. Paris: Union générale, 1975.
Conley, Verena Andermatt. *Hélène Cixous: Writing the Feminine*. Rev. ed. Lincoln: University of Nebraska Press, 1991.
Crowder, Diane Griffin. "Amazons or Mothers? Monique Wittig, Hélène Cixous and Theories of Women's Writing." *Contemporary Literature* 24, no. 2 (1983): 117–144.

Freeman, Barbara. " 'Plus corps donc plus écriture': Hélène Cixous and the Mind-Body Problem." *Paragraph* 11, no. 1 (March 1988): 58–70.

Garcia, Irma. *Promenade femmilière: Recherches sur l'écriture féminine.* 2 vols. Paris: Des femmes, 1981.

Jones, Ann Rosalind. "Writing and the Body: Toward an Understanding of *L'Ecriture féminine.*" *French Studies* 7 (Summer 1981): 247–263.

Marks, Elaine, and Isabelle de Courtivron, eds. *New French Feminisms.* New York: Schocken, 1981.

Rossum-Guyon, Françoise van, and Myriam Díaz-Diocaretz, eds. *Hélène Cixous, chemins d'une écriture.* Saint-Denis: PUV, 1990.

Sellers, Susan, ed. *The Hélène Cixous Reader.* New York: Routledge, 1994.

Education. Equal access to the same educational opportunities for men and women in France is a very recent phenomenon. For centuries, the education of women lagged behind for ideological and economic reasons. Improvements occurred thanks to the efforts of a few enlightened minds, but were primarily brought about by religious conflicts and, from the Revolution* on, by competition between the Church and the Republican state.

Until the nineteenth century, women's education was limited to a privileged few, and proposals for reform remained theoretical. Ancien Régime aristocratic girls were taught by tutors at home and in convents*, while those less fortunate could acquire only a rudimentary education in parish schools and through the oral tradition. On the eve of the French Revolution, literacy rates averaged 47 percent for men and 27 percent for women, as measured by their ability to sign the marriage* register. These figures, however, are only a partial indicator of formal schooling: instruction in reading, writing, and arithmetic followed three consecutive stages, and many students—especially women—left after the reading stage.

Even though there were many well-educated women in the Middle Ages (Dhuoda, Héloïse*, Eleonore of Aquitaine, Christine de Pizan*, the abbesses of Fontevrault, etc.), most of the moral and didactic literature of the time encouraged females to be modest and self-effacing, to fear God and submit to their husband's authority. The most feminist plea for women's education in that period is Pizan's *Livre de la cité des dames* (1405), which asserts that men and women have the same soul and the same intellectual capacity, and that lack of education alone explains the inferior status of women.

The creation of the all-male university in the thirteenth century would start a process of segregation in education in the higher echelons of society. Women were barred from the medical professions in the fifteenth century and excluded as well from the institutions of secondary learning (*collèges*) that were created during the Renaissance. The publication of catalogues of illustrious women in the sixteenth century and the rise to prominence of such women writers as Marguerite de Navarre*, Pernette du Guillet*, Louise Labé*, the Dames des Roches*, and Marie de Gournay* should not obscure the fact that humanism was a predominantly male phenomenon. The humanists were ambiguous in their pronouncements on women's education, encouraging them to study the sacred texts but not the classics. Protestant thinkers stressed the moral importance of woman as wife and educator and encouraged the development of limited instruction for girls, which became possible after the Edict of Nantes (1598) allowed them to practice their religion and open their own schools. However, evidence from the seventeenth century points to great differences in the literacy levels of Protestant men and women. In the Renaissance context, Cornélius Agrippa's *De la noblesse et préexcellence du sexe féminin* and François de Billon's *Le Fort inexpugnable de l'honneur du sexe féminin* (1555) struck a radical note by advocating the same educational and professional opportunities for the sexes.

The greatest gains for women's education in the Ancien Régime came in the seventeenth century. To fight the spread of Protestantism, the Catholic Church encouraged the development of the teaching orders, more than twenty-five of which specialized in the education of girls. By 1789, the Ursulines had opened over 300 convents in French cities, where they took in paying boarders and educated day students for free. The focus of these female congregations was on educating Christian mothers, and their pedagogy* therefore stressed religious instruction rather than intellectual work. Two institutions for the daughters of the nobility stand out in that period: the convent of Port-Royal*, for its stress on critical thinking in matters of religion, and Saint-Cyr*, for the place it gave the worldly activities of conversation and the theater* in its early years. Educational opportunities for women improved in the cities in the seventeenth century, but they remained inadequate in the country because of a poor economy and a Church decree in 1640 forbidding mixed schools. The Royal Declaration of December 13, 1698, which encouraged each parish to hire a schoolmaster and a schoolmistress, did little to combat rural ignorance, as it was implemented only in areas with a strong Protestant population to be converted.

In the seventeenth century, interest in women's education went beyond moralists and theologians and entered the public realm of the salon*. The *précieux* invoked Descartes's distinction of mind and body to claim the intellectual equality of the sexes. Lecture societies were created to educate middle-class women. Poullain de la Barre's avant-garde *De l'égalité des deux sexes* (1673) would have a great influence on later theoretical discussions. But the most influential treatise on women's education up until 1914 was Fénelon's *De l'éducation des filles* (1687), which limited women's instruction to their future role in society as Christian wives and mothers.

With the dissemination of Locke's ideas on the formation of the mind, the growing attack on religion, and the Enlightenment* belief in progress, education became a central issue of the eighteenth century. But most *philosophes* and social reformers were ambiguous about women's right to extensive knowledge. Only Riballier and Condorcet went beyond the traditional argument that a woman needs to be educated to change society from within the domestic sphere. In his first memoir on public instruction, Condorcet argues that women are entitled to education and to civic and political rights; and he calls for primary and *secondary* instruction for them in *mixed* public institutions. In practice, the number of schools and their programs of study remained basically the same as a century earlier, and indictments of women's inferior education became a staple of female novels*. According to Martine Sonnet, Parisian women received on average one year of formal instruction outside the home to prepare for communion as opposed to four or five for boys, who studied grammar and mathematics as well as religion. Lack of civic or professional outlets explains why the women who wrote about female education (Lambert*, Puisieux*, d'Epinay*, Leprince de Beaumont*, Genlis*, etc.) stressed the personal benefits of instruction as consolation for life's adversities. They suggested extensive programs of readings in history, philosophy, literature, and even the sciences that appear utopian next to the actual religious selections of contemporary female institutions.

With the attacks on the convents mounting in the second half of the century and the new emphasis on domesticity appearing in the wake of Rousseau's *Emile* (1762), more middle- and upper-class women were educated at home. Women were ignored in the proposals for the establishment of a state educational system that multiplied with the expulsion of the Jesuits from France in 1762 and culminated with the Revolution. The Convention bypassed Condorcet's radical ideas and voted instead for the Lakanal decree of October 25, 1795, which called for separate primary instruction with different programs for boys and girls, to be paid for by parents.

Women had much to gain from the competition between church and state over the education of French children in the nineteenth century. Except for the creation under Napoleon of the House of the Legion of Honor for daughters of decorated soldiers (which devoted three-fourths of the day to sewing and housekeeping), the state remained unconcerned by women's education for over fifty years, focusing instead on the establishment of primary and secondary education for men. The Falloux Law (1850) encouraged the creation of separate primary schools for girls in towns of over 800 inhabitants if they could afford the financial strain. The Duruy Law (1867) made these schools compulsory in towns of 500 inhabitants and instituted fee-based municipal secondary courses for women. Primary education itself became free and compulsory for all with the Ferry Laws of 1881–1882. In its early years, the Third Republic (1870–1940) also created normal schools to train lay female teachers in each department as well as state secondary institutions for women (1880 Camille Sée Law). In keeping with the idea that "the Republic instructs virgins, future mothers of men," this law provided five years of general instruction with no outlet in higher education or in the professional world. Secondary programs for boys, by comparison, lasted seven years, included Latin and math, and prepared them for the *baccalauréat* and university studies. Pressure from the lower middle class, a ravaged economy after World War I*, and competition from private schools would lead to the opening up of male secondary schools to women (decree of March 25, 1924).

In the twentieth century, coeducation gradually spread at all levels, though at first for merely economic reasons, since localities often found it difficult to support separate schools. In 1982, for the first time, the Ministry of Education encouraged coeducation for ideological reasons, stating that it would "ensure full equality of chances" and help society to "erase all discrimination against women" (Official Bulletin #29). In the 1990s a higher percentage of women than men successfully pass the baccalaureate and pursue university studies. Recent government action in favor of women's education has focused on fighting sexist representations of women in textbooks, encouraging more women to enter the technical and scientific fields, and ensuring that superior results in the classroom translate into more prestigious careers for women.

Michèle Bissière

BIBLIOGRAPHY

Albistur, Maïté, and Daniel Armogathe. *Histoire du féminisme français*. Paris: Des femmes, 1977.
Berriot-Salvadore, Evelyne. *Les Femmes dans la société française de la Renaissance*. Geneva: Droz, 1990.
Clark, Linda. *Schooling the Daughters of Marianne: Textbooks and the Socialization of Girls in Modern French Primary Schools*. Albany: State University of New York Press, 1984.
Condorcet. Excerpts from *Premier Mémoire sur l'instruction publique. Paroles d'hommes*. Ed. Elizabeth Badinter. Paris: P.O.L., 1989. 89–98.
Constant, Paule. *Un Monde à l'usage des demoiselles*. Paris: Gallimard, 1987.
Delhomme, D., N. Gault, and J. Gouthier. *Les Premières Institutrices laïques*. Paris: Mercure de France, 1980.
Gréard, Octave. *L'Education des femmes par les femmes*. Paris: Hachette, 1886.
Julia, Dominique. *Les Trois Couleurs du tableau noir. La Révolution*. Paris: Blin, 1981. Chapter 9: "Les Lumières sont-elles féministes." 310–331.
Lelièvre, Françoise, and Claude Lelièvre. *Histoire de la scolarisation des filles*. Paris: Nathan, 1991.
Mayeur, Françoise. *L'Education des filles en France au XIXe siècle*. Paris: Hachette, 1979.
Rousselot, Paul. *Histoire de l'éducation des femmes en France*. 2 vols. Paris: Didier, 1883.
Sonnet, Martine. *L'Education des filles au temps des Lumières*. Paris: Cerf, 1987.

Elie de Beaumont, Anne Louise (1729 or 1730–1783). Born in Caen, Anne Louise Morin Dumesnil was married in 1750 to lawyer Jean Baptiste Elie de Beaumont (who, like Voltaire, defended the Calas family), in whose writings she may have collaborated. She became engaged while her family was poor; after her fortunes changed, her relations would have liked her to make a better match, but she insisted on keeping her faith. Her husband's obesity and quasi-impotence are documented in his medical dossier, which sheds light on their style of life. She is the author of the last part of a historical novel* left unfinished by Claudine de Tencin*, *Anecdotes de la cour et du règne d'Edouard II, roi* *d'Angleterre* (1776). Her principal work is *Lettres du marquis de Roselle* (1764). This substantial letter-novel, in which one may see the influence of Rousseau, tells the story of a young man nearly tricked into marrying a dissembling actress; but thanks to the intervention of discerning women friends, he finally weds a virtuous young noblewoman, while the actress repents and enters a convent*. The women characters are more finely drawn than the men, and the novel invites a feminist reading for its meditation on the education* of girls and its plot about marriageability and appearances. Praised for the way virtue triumphs over vice, it was frequently republished and inspired a sequel by Desfontaines de la Vallée.

Joan Hinde Stewart

BIBLIOGRAPHY

Primary Texts

Lettres du marquis de Roselle. Paris: Cellot, 1764.
Anecdotes de la cour et du règne d'Edouard II, roi d'Angleterre [Books 1 and 2 are by Tencin, Book 3 by Elie de Beaumont.] Paris: Pissot, 1776.
Desfontaines, François Georges Fouques. *Lettres de Sophie et du Chevalier de***, pour servir de supplément aux Lettres du marquis de Roselle.* London and Paris: L'Esclapart, 1765.

Secondary Texts

La Porte, Joseph de. ''Madame Elie de Beaumont.'' *In Histoire littéraire des femmes françaises.* Paris: Lacombe, 1769. Vol. 5: 155–188.
Merland, Joachim. *Le Roman personnel de Rousseau à Fromentin.* Paris: Hachette, 1905.
Stewart, Joan Hinde. *Gynographs: Novels by Women of Late Eighteenth-Century France.* Lincoln: University of Nebraska Press, 1993.
Swain, Virginia E. ''Hidden from View: Women Authors and the Language of Rights, 1727–1792.'' In *Intimate Encounters: Love and Domesticity in Eighteenth-Century France.* Exhibition Catalogue, Hood Museum of Art, Dartmouth College, Hanover, NH, 1997.

Encyclopédie. This ambitious intellectual endeavor produced seventeen volumes of text (1751–1765) and eleven volumes of finely executed plates (1762–1772) covering a wide range of topics. Contributors included prominent Enlightenment* figures as well as lesser-known subject specialists. Only two women, one anonymous, are known to have written articles, and their contributions are marginal to the broader project of the encyclopedists: namely, to present the current state of knowledge of the known world and to lend support to progressive ideas. Obstacles to publication were many, including official censorship and suspension of publishing* rights and the enormous cost of the project. Women were important financial backers of the project. In 1759, when the *Encyclopédie* was under its second official suspension, Madame Geoffrin* contributed generously to its survival.

While the active participation of women was limited, their presence in the text and plates is not without interest. Articles focus on women's physical and emotional natures, and their social roles, particularly within the family*. Major articles indicate the work's primary focus concerning women: childbirth, dowry, love, midwifery, marriage*, nuns, motherhood, menstruation*, Salic law*, wet-nurses, and a four-part article on women (*femmes*). Frequent references to women's vanity, frivolity, and weakness (*rouge, roman, efféminé, règles*) and lengthy descriptions of biologically determined behavior (*mansturpation* [*sic*]) reflect commonly held negative images of women.

Contributors to the article on women accept the role of natural law as the basis of women's inferior status in society. The Chevalier de Jaucourt, however, suggests that men's superiority in civil society is contractual and, therefore, subject to change. While most articles advancing human rights apply only to men, challenges to women's inequality may be found throughout the work in the condemnation of the convent* system, arranged marriages, the horrors of childbirth, the superstitions surrounding women's bodies and the portrayal of "evil" women of myth* (see, for example, *enfantement, mariage, Médée, menstruel*).

Women's work is described in both text and plates. They are best represented in the areas of agriculture, commerce, and crafts, with an emphasis on the more traditional women's spheres of textile work and clothes decoration. The plates show women in support roles in less-traditional manufacturing, such as glass, gold, and silver products. Women are also represented in the plates selling cutlery, jewelry, pastries, and corks in small shops. The article *marchands*, devoted primarily to men in commerce, includes a paragraph qualifying as merchants those women who sell cloth, seeds, fruits, and fish. Individual text entries describe in an objective manner most of the trades exercised by women (see, for example, *poissonnière*), although wet-nurses, midwives, and second-hand merchants are among those trades described in negative, even hostile, terms.

In general, readers of the *Encyclopédie* will find considerable information concerning the actual status of women in the eighteenth century and ample evidence of contradictory attitudes toward them. Diligent readers will find threads of an argument in their favor.

Caryl L. Lloyd

BIBLIOGRAPHY

Primary Text

Encyclopédie ou dictionnaire raisonné des sciences, des arts et des métiers, par une société de gens de lettres. Ed. Denis Diderot and Jean Le Rond d'Alembert. Paris: Briasson, 1751–1765.

Secondary Texts

Dock, Terry Smiley. "Women in the *Encyclopédie*." Dissertation, Vanderbilt University, 1979.
Malueg, Sara Ellen Procious. "Women and the *Encyclopédie*." In *French Women and the Age of Enlightenment.* Ed. Samia I. Spencer. Bloomington: Indiana University Press, 1984.

Enlightenment. Chief philosophic movement in Europe, c. 1715–1800. Immanuel Kant defined enlightenment as the "freedom to make public use of one's reason." He thus stressed Enlightenment's ties to freedom, reason, speech, and public reception. In the wake of Francis Bacon and René Descartes, proponents of objectivity in the presentation of knowledge, all knowers were potentially on equal footing, as rights of speech and access to the public came to be viewed as human rights. Yet, apart from Condorcet, the Enlightenment's male thinkers chose not to view women as separable individuals, hence potential knowers or speakers: rather they continued the tradition envisaging them as a class subordinate, by virtue of nature itself, to men. The paradox of this stance—of a philosophy aggressively challenging Christian authority but accepting its hierarchical subjection of women—became increasingly evident, achieving some public recognition during the French Revolution*.

The stylizations of the prevailing *galanterie* encouraged women to think of themselves as the frivolous sex. The Cartesian Protestant Poulain de la Barre, noting their exclusion from all serious self-development, protested their subjugation in *De l'égalite des deux sexes* (1673) and *De l'education des dames* (1679). But no major Enlightenment figure gave sustained attention to women's status. Montesquieu comes closest in his *Lettres persanes* (1721) as he relativizes women's treatment in Persia to that in Paris, and explores sexual dominance. In Voltaire's *Zaire* (1732), freedom of religion, dear to the Enlightenment, does not apply to the female conscience, which knows only love. Yet Voltaire supported modest improvements in female education*. Diderot's sole sustained discussion is a brief and emotional response to the Abbé Thomas's earnest essay on women (1772). Rousseau, whose influence, particularly upon women, flowered after the publication of *La Nouvelle Héloïse* (1761), preached separation of the sexes into two distinct spheres. Yet no era has been described as often as an "age of women" as the French eighteenth century. So mixed by gender was its society that Rousseau denounced female influence, in *Lettres à d'Alembert sur les spectacles* (1758), as destructive. Salons* dominated the entire Enlightenment, from the Duchess du Maine's court at Sceaux to Germaine de Staël's* at the Revolution's outbreak. Spirited setters of the social scene, the salonnières, Mesdames de Lambert*, du Deffand*, Geoffrin*, Necker*, and Mlle de Lespinasse*, achieved recognition accorded no other class of women. But it was the Rousseauian ideal of woman as mother-wife to a nation of citizens that prevailed with the Revolution's leaders. Valiant attempts, by Olympe de Gouges* with her Declaration of the Rights of Women (1792), by revolutionary clubs, in marches and demonstrations, and by writers of petitions, demanding rights to education, inheritance, divorce*, and employment, to force the Revolution to respect the Enlightenment's heritage as theirs, foundered. After a rush of generosity in its early years, the Revolution and its Napoleonic aftermath wrested away many of women's gains and reinstated their subservience to marriage*. Their status as free beings remained moot.

Madelyn Gutwirth

BIBLIOGRAPHY

Gelbart, Nina Rattner. *Feminine and Opposition Journalism in Old Regime France. "Le Journal des dames."* Berkeley: University of California Press, 1987.

Gutwirth, Madelyn. *The Twilight of the Goddesses: Women and Representation in the French Revolutionary Era.* New Brunswick: Rutgers University Press, 1992.

Harth, Erica. *Cartesian Women: Versions and Subversions of Rational Discourse in the Old Regime.* Ithaca: Cornell University Press, 1992.

Hoffmann, Paul. *La Femme dans la pensée des Lumières.* Paris: Ophrys, 1977.

Poulain de la Barre, François. *De l'Education des dames pour la conduite de l'esprit dans les sciences et dans les moeurs.* Paris: J. Dupuis, 1671.

———. *De l'Egalité des deux sexes, discours physique et moral où l'on voit l'importance de se défaire des préjugés.* Paris: Fayard, 1984.

Rousseau, Jean-Jacques. "Lettre à M. d'Alembert sur son Article 'Genève' dans le septième volume de *L'Encyclopédie*, et particulièrement sur le projet d'établir un théâtre de comédie en cette ville." In *Le Contrat social.* Paris: Garnier, 1962.

Spencer, Samia I., ed. *French Women and the Age of Enlightenment.* Bloomington: Indiana University Press, 1984.

Thomas, Antoine-Léonard. "Essai sur le caractère, les moeurs et l'esprit des femmes dans les différents siècles (1772)." *Qu'est-ce qu'une femme?* Ed. Elisabeth Badinter. Paris P.O.L., 1989.

Tomselli, Silvana. "The Enlightenment Debate on Women." *History Workshop* 5 (1984): 101–124.

Epinay, Louise-Florence Tardieu d' (1726–1783). Rousseau's unjust portrayal of Epinay as an overly demanding hostess at the Hermitage, in the *Confessions*, obscured her intellectual accomplishments for a long time. She was a respected writer, critic, salonnière, and friend of the *philosophes*. Plagued by ill health and an unhappy marriage*, she drew strength from her friendships*, her liaison with Grimm, the education* of her children and grandchildren, and from writing. These aspects of her life are fictionalized in *Histoire de Madame de Montbrillant*, a partly autobiographical epistolary novel* unpublished in her lifetime. An original blend of letters and journal entries, *Montbrillant* not only depicts the heroine's sentimental and intellectual journey, but also documents the legal, economic, and educational sides of female life in the eighteenth century. Epinay's other works are moral and pedagogical, including *Lettres à mon fils* (1759), *Mes Moments heureux* (1763), and her best-known *Conversations d'Emilie* (1774), whose second edition received the *Prix d'utilité* of the French Academy in 1783. This novel is a series of conversations between a mother and her ten-year-old daughter, based on Epinay's own experience with her granddaughter, where she outlines her progressive pedagogical goals and methods. Aiming to foster self-sufficiency, she stresses the development of critical skills and grounding in various subjects, including the sciences.

Epinay also edited and published reviews and articles on literature, politics, and economics for the *Correspondance littéraire*. She maintained an extensive correspondence with the Abbé Galiani, whom she kept informed of social, political, and intellectual developments in Paris. One of her best-known letters (March 14, 1772) includes a critique of Thomas's *Essai sur le caractère, les moeurs et l'esprit des femmes* (1772), in which she refutes his ideas on the natural inferiority of women and argues that their subordinate status is attributable to their inadequate education.

Michèle Bissière

BIBLIOGRAPHY

Primary Texts

Mes Moments heureux. Geneva, de mon imprimerie [Gauffecourt], 1758.
Les Contre-Confessions: Histoire de Madame de Montbrillant. Paris: Mercure de France, 1989.
Lettres à mon fils et morceaux choisis. Ed. Ruth Plaut Weinreb. Concord, MA: Wayside, 1989.
Correspondance. 5 vols. Paris: Desjonquères, 1992–1996.
''Les Conversations d'Emilie.'' Ed. Rosena Davison. *Studies on Voltaire and the Eighteenth Century* 342 (1996).

Secondary Texts

Badinter, Elisabeth. *Emilie, Emilie, ou l'ambition féminine au XVIIIe siècle.* Paris: Flammarion, 1983.
Steegmuller, Francis. *A Woman, a Man, and Two Kingdoms: The Story of Madame d'Epinay and the Abbé Galiani.* New York: Knopf, 1992.
Trouille, Mary. ''Sexual/Textual Politics in the Enlightenment: Diderot and d'Epinay Respond to Thomas's Essay on Women.'' *Romantic Review* 85, no. 2 (1994): 191–210.
Weinreb, Ruth Plaut. *Eagle in a Gauze Cage: Louise d'Epinay, Femme de Lettres.* New York: AMS Press, 1993.

Ernaux, Annie (1940–). Ernaux's childhood and adolescence in Yvetot, Normandy, inform much of her writing: her parents, who ran a modest grocery store and bar, helped her obtain the education* and social status to which they could never aspire, irrevocably alienating their daughter from them. Ernaux painstakingly and lucidly chronicles the life of an ordinary French woman in the latter part of the twentieth century. In *Les Armoires vides* (1974) and *Ce qu'ils disent ou rien* (1977), Ernaux reveals the double standards that girls and women face when pursuing the same sexual, intellectual, and professional goals as their male counterparts, in particular if they belong to the working class. Ernaux is the most militant in the autobiographical *La Femme gelée* (1981), a text in which she critiques phallic metaphors used in academic discourse, and unequal gender roles in marriage* and parenting. *Une Femme* (1987) marks another phase in Ernaux's depiction of women's lives, recounting her reconciliation with the socially oppressed mother who was the model for her daughter's independence, energy, and strength. Similarly, *Passion simple* (1991) portrays the vulnerability of a woman ruled by an adulterous passion, which she analyzes almost clinically, and for which she never apologizes. Ernaux, who refuses all labels—including that of feminist—presents a very individual model of self-assertion, one that has proved liberating to many of the readers who have made this novel a best-seller. Her feminist consciousness is rooted in her awareness of various patterns of socioeconomic oppression, which she explores in depth in all of her novels.

Christine Lac

BIBLIOGRAPHY

Primary Texts

Les Armoires vides. Paris: Gallimard, 1974.
Ce qu'ils disent ou rien. Paris: Gallimard, 1977.
La Femme gelée. Paris: Gallimard, 1981.
La Place. Paris: Gallimard, 1983.
Une Femme. Paris: Gallimard, 1987.
Passion simple. Paris: Gallimard, 1991.
Journal du dehors. Paris: Gallimard, 1993.
La Honte. Paris: Gallimard, 1996.
Je ne suis pas sortie de ma Nuit. Paris: Gallimard, 1996.

Secondary Texts

Day, Loraine. "Class, Sexuality and Subjectivity in Annie Ernaux's *Les Armoires vides*." In *Contemporary French Fiction by Women: Feminist Perspectives*. Ed. Margaret Atack and Phil Powrie. Manchester, UK: Manchester University Press, 1990. 41–55.
Lebrun, Jean-Claude, and Claude Prévost. "Ernaux ou la conquête de la monodie." In *Nouveaux Territoires romanesques*. Paris: Messidor-Editions Sociales, 1990. 51–66.
Tondeur, Claire-Lise. *Annie Ernaux ou l'exil intérieur*. Atlanta: Rodopi, 1996.

Erotic fiction (1799 to the present). Boundaries are not clear-cut between erotic and pornographic literature. Pornography's sole purpose is to be sexually stimulating, but many, more ambitious, erotic novels* retain the basic motifs of commercial pornography: defloration, rape*, masturbation, bisexuality, sodomy, group sex, voyeurism, and power relations. Differences occur, then, more along gender than generic lines. In women's works, defloration is much less painful; the prostitution* of women, glorified as a form of male bonding in men's works, is often condemned, even when eroticized; the vocabulary is less crude (a difference that is on the wane); finally, the depiction of lesbianism* may emphasize feeling and does not lead to the affirmation of phallic superiority quite as often as in male pornography.

In France, the pornographic genre took shape in the seventeenth century, with the development of libertine free-thinking (*L'Ecole des filles*, 1655; *L'Académie des dames*, 1659). Typically, erotica were published anonymously, and the identity of a few authors is still a matter of debate, but not until the years of the French Revolution* is there any record of female authorship. The first

French erotic novel authored by a woman, *Illyrine, ou l'Ecueil de l'inexpérience*, by G . . . de Morency (Suzanne Giroux), appeared in 1799–1800, soon to be followed by the novels of the Countess Félicité de Choiseul-Meuse between 1802 and 1809 (*Julie ou j'ai sauvé ma rose*, 1807). They did not have any successors until the 1880s. After the decadent period, perhaps reflecting censorship laws, women's erotica became infrequent until the years following World War I* (the most noteworthy are by René Dunan, a libertarian anarchist), and again from the late 1930s to the late 1960s, with the memorable exception of *Histoire d'O* (1954). (The latter's authorship, still contested by some, has publicly been claimed by Dominique Aury.) Sustained by ideological and political changes, the prestige of *Histoire d'O* may have belatedly contributed to the recent commercial success and literary standing of erotic fiction by women.

The year 1968 launched the women's movement and an unprecedented upsurge of erotic novels by women, some of them published by major publishers. Many, following *Histoire d'O*, are told from the victim's standpoint, but marked by much greater ambivalence. The prostitutes' movement, itself an offshoot of the women's movement, gave rise to some autobiographical works of violent protest that do not exclude eroticism (Xavière, *La Punition*, 1971; Jeanne Cordelier, *La Dérobade*, 1976). Finally, in the sated atmosphere of the 1980s and 1990s, female eroticism asserts itself confidently and without much conflict. It is the province of some talented women writers. Let us mention, among many others, Françoise Rey* (*La Femme de papier*, 1989) and Alina Reyes* (*Le Boucher*, 1988, *Derrière la porte*, 1994, etc.). They both playfully exploit intertextual allusions and narrative reflexivity in the best eighteenth-century tradition, but their first-person fiction imparts a fresh accent and new erotic inventions to formulaic models. Also new is the humor that accompanies much of their narration. Rey's voice is distinctly gendered female, and Reyes has male and female narrators, but both subvert gender lines in their choice of fantasies. Most striking are the centrality and the multiple attractions those novelists ascribe to the male body. Until the recent past, the female body had remained the central erotic object, and the most daring descriptions in erotica by women did not go much beyond the admiring mention of phallic attributes. Given that the erotic genre mostly responds to prevalent cultural values, this newly found ease suggests that women can now freely voice their erotic fantasies.

Lucienne Frappier-Mazur

BIBLIOGRAPHY

Primary Texts

Brecourt-Villars, Claudine, ed. *Ecrire d'amour. Anthologie de textes érotiques féminins (1799–1984)*. Paris: Ramsay, 1985.
Dunan, René. *Les Caprices du sexe*. Paris: N.p., 1928.
Une Heure de désir. Paris: N.p., 1929.
Pauvert, Jean-Jacques, ed. *Anthologie historique des lectures érotiques*. Paris: Simon, Ramsay, Garnier, 1979, 1980, 1982.

Secondary Texts

Frappier-Mazur, Lucienne. "Marginal Canons: Rewriting the Erotic." *Yale French Studies* 75 (1988): 112–128.
Pia, Pascal, ed. *Dictionnaire des oeuvres érotiques*. Paris: Mercure de France, 1971.

Essentialism. The term designates the concept that women and men have distinct essences associated with their sexed biology. Such a concept has been used historically, as in biological determinism, to identify and maintain "natural" sexually segregated social roles for women and men. Women have also recuperated essentialist notions of "woman" by assigning positive interpretations to women's biology, as in radical feminists' celebration of women's reproductive capacities and related "female" character traits (such as being nurturing), and in French feminists' strategic use of essentialism in the metaphor of "writing the body" to characterize *l'écriture féminine** or to elaborate a philosophy of sexual difference.

In the late 1970s, Marxist materialist critiques of the use of essentialism set off a debate that has polarized feminism* and held back the progress of feminist theory* for over a decade. What began as a productive self-critique to keep feminist theorists aware of the dangers of overgeneralizing, of universalizing a monolithic, ahistorical category of "woman," soon degenerated into an uncritical rejection of any theories dealing with sexual difference. Indeed, charges of essentialism became a standard tool for policing "appropriate" topics for feminist investigation and for covering over legitimate differences in philosophical commitments, especially those between American and continental feminist theorists.

The 1990s have seen a redirection of the essentialist debate, mainly through the efforts of various theorists to recover the work of French feminist philosopher Luce Irigaray*, whose complex elaboration of an ethics of sexual difference had at first drawn harsh criticism for its essentialism. Now a radical new materialism is at the center of feminist theorizing, challenging the sex/gender distinction in its investigations of female specificity and sexuality, of the sexed body as the material base of subjectivity, and of the material effects of discourse in constructing sexed bodies.

Katherine Stephenson

BIBLIOGRAPHY

Braidotti, Rosi. *Nomadic Subjects: Embodiment and Sexual Difference in Contemporary Feminist Theory*. New York: Columbia University Press, 1994.
Burke, Carolyn, Naomi Schor, and Margaret Whitford, eds. *Engaging with Irigaray: Feminist Philosophy and Modern European Thought*. New York: Columbia University Press, 1994.
Butler, Judith. *Bodies that Matter: On the Discursive Limits of "Sex."* New York: Routledge, 1993.

Chanter, Tina. *Ethics of Eros: Irigaray's Rewriting of the Philosophers*. New York: Routledge, 1995.

De Lauretis, Teresa. "Upping the Anti (Sic) in Feminist Theory." In *Conflicts in Feminism*. Ed. Marianne Hirsch and Evelyn Fox Keller. New York: Routledge, 1990. 255–270.

Diprose, Rosalyn. *The Bodies of Women: Ethics, Embodiment and Sexual Difference*. London: Routledge, 1994.

Fuss, Diana. *Essentially Speaking: Feminism, Nature and Difference*. New York: Routledge, 1989.

Gatens, Moira. *Imaginary Bodies: Ethics, Power and Corporeality*. New York: Routledge, 1996.

Grosz, Elizabeth. "Irigaray's Notion of Sexual Morphology." In *Reimagining Women: Representations of Women in Culture*. Ed. Shirley Neuman and Glennis Stephenson. Toronto: Toronto University Press, 1993. 182–195.

———. "Sexual Difference and the Problem of Essentialism." In *Space, Time, and Perversion*. New York: Routledge, 1995. 45–57.

Kirby, Vicki. "*Corpus delicti*: The Body at the Scene of Writing." In *Cartographies: Poststructuralism and the Mapping of Bodies and Spaces*. Ed. Rosalyn Diprose and Robyn Ferrell. Sydney: Allen and Unwin, 1991. 88–100.

Schor, Naomi, and Elizabeth Weed, eds. *The Essential Difference*. Bloomington: Indiana University Press, 1994.

Estienne, Nicole (1545–between 1584 and 1596). Writer. Nicole Estienne was the eldest daughter of Charles Estienne of the great Estienne family of printer-scholars. In 1560 she was courted by and encouraged Jacques Grévin, the playwright and poet who fled France later that year because he was a Huguenot. Given her family's Protestant leanings (her uncle Robert was by then established in Geneva), the match may have been broken off at the instigation of young Nicole herself, who seems to have remained a lifelong Catholic. Her involvement with Grévin is reflected in his sonnet sequence *L'Olimpe*, to which she (like Pernette du Guillet* two decades earlier) wrote a few answering poems. Some of these survive, showing her as a self-aware and modest young woman of considerable accomplishment at the age of fifteen. A few years later, before 1564, she married Jean Liébault, who like her father trained as a physician and who was also an author; in addition to completing Charles Estienne's *Maison rustique* after the latter's death, he also wrote independently on women's problems, notably in *La Santé, foecondité et maladies des femmes* (first published in Latin, Paris, 1582). All this suggests that Estienne grew up in intellectual circles with relatively broad connections and interests where, one suspects, her voice was heard, a habit continued in her poetic responses to Grévin, and less personally, to Desportes' *Stances du mariage*. Du Verdier, who met her, although probably only once, praises the quality of her conversation.

Like many women writers of her time, Estienne apparently published none of her work, with the possible exception of a liminary poem for the *Dévotes Méditations chrestiennes sur la mort et Passion de nostre Seigneur Jésus Christ* (ed. Zinguer, 49). Her work centers on reflections on the conditions society inflicts upon woman. In the *Misères* she cites the account in Genesis, presenting woman in most ways as the equal of man, although she is fully aware that women are rarely treated as though this were so. She remarks that a woman is frequently married, without being consulted, to a much older man who may then treat his wife less well than a criminal. If the husband is a young man he may squander all his wife's wealth without consulting her. Her skill and wisdom in running the household, as well as the pain and risks of childbirth, are unlikely to be recognized or valued. Woman's real hope of happiness, according to the *Misères*, is to remain single in her father's house—not a very realistic solution in sixteenth-century France.

It is tempting, but probably inaccurate, to read this as autobiographical. She speaks of herself in the few sonnets that have survived as being not particularly pretty, but infinitely patient, and striving for virtue (for which the responding poems praise her). That is all we can know. She should be understood to be expressing this jaundiced view of the usual female condition as a female writer responding to a current of misogynist, male-authored anti-marriage poems, Desportes's *Stances du mariage* chief among them, and as a privileged, educated woman who had a voice, albeit one limited to the circles of privately circulated manuscripts, and who chose to write about the afflictions of her silent sisters.

Marian Rothstein

BIBLIOGRAPHY

Primary Texts

Les Misères de la femme mariée où se peuvent voir les peines et tourments qu'elle reçoit durant sa vie. Original edition Paris: P. Menier, n.d. Ed. Ilana Zinguer in *Misères et grandeur de la femme au seizième siècle.* Geneva: Slatkine, 1982. 9–55.

Sonnets in reply to Jacques Grévin's sonnet sequence *Olimpe.* In J. Lavaud, "Quelques Poésies oubliées de Nicole Estienne." *Revue du XVIe siècle* 18 (1931): 341–351.

Stances du mariage (in reply to a misogynist poem of the same title by Philippe Desportes) perhaps preserved in BN 500 Colbert no. 500 fol. 87 but never published (cited by Lavaud, *Desportes*, 68).

Grévin, Jacques. *Théâtre complet et poésies choisies.* Ed. Lucien Pinvert. Paris: Garnier, 1922.

Secondary Texts

Lavaud, J. *Philippe Desportes.* Geneva: Droz, 1936.

———. "Quelques Poésies oubliées de Nicole Estienne." *Revue du XVIe siècle* 18 (1931): 341–351.

Estournelles, Louise de Constant d' (1792–1860). Half-sister of Benjamin Constant, who played a semi-parental role toward her, she frequented Charles Nodier's Parisian circle, the salon* de l'Arsenal, which promoted French Romanticism* in literature and the arts. Her best-known novel*, *Deux Femmes* (1836), reflects her strong ties to the Romantic school and her special interest in representing women's struggles during the early years of the Restoration. Male libertinage*, paternal control, female vulnerability, and fatal passion are among its dominant themes. Her earlier novels include *Alphonse et Mathilde* (1819) and *Pascaline* (1821).

Eva Posfáy

BIBLIOGRAPHY

Primary Texts

Alphonse et Mathilde. 2 vols. Paris: Brissot-Thivars, 1819.
Pascaline. Paris: C. Villet, 1821.
Deux Femmes. Paris: Schwartz et Ganot, 1836.

Secondary Text

Letessier, Fernand. "La Romancière Louise d'Estournelles de Constant (1792–1860) et ses amis." *Bulletin de l'Association Guillaume Budé* 4 (December 1964): 464–478.

Etcherelli, Claire (1934–). Etcherelli, an activist writer from a working-class background, portrays women from this milieu. Her most famous work, *Elise ou la vraie vie* (1967), became a cult novel* of the late sixties and seventies and was turned into a movie by director Michel Drach in 1970. The novel, which explores issues of oppression, racism, and sexism in France at the time of the Algerian War, depicts the relationship between an Algerian auto worker and a young French woman working in a Parisian factory. Informed by her own working-class consciousness and experience, Etcherelli examines the problems faced by the least privileged—poverty, exploitation, and social marginalization. In *L'Arbre voyageur*, two women friends work together to alleviate the constraints of motherhood and to create an unconventional, nonpatriarchal family* that suggests a new economy of relationships based on trust, solidarity, and women's leadership.

Joëlle Vitiello

BIBLIOGRAPHY

Primary Texts

Elise ou la vraie vie. Paris: Denoël, 1967.
A Propos de Clémence. Paris: Denoël, 1971.
L'Arbre voyageur. Paris: Gallimard, 1978.
Etcherelli, Claire, Gilles Manceron, and Bernard Wallon. *Cent Poèmes contre le racisme*. Paris: Le Cherche Midi, 1985.

Secondary Texts

Atack, Margaret. "The Politics of Identity in *Elise ou la vraie vie*." In *Contemporary French Fiction by Women: Feminist Perspectives*. Manchester: Manchester University Press, 1990. 56–70.
Doumazane, Françoise. "De la production d'une oeuvre à sa réception: *Elise ou la vraie vie* de Claire Etcherelli." *Pratiques* 32 (1981): 66–104.

Haxell, Nichola Anne. "Framing the Narrative, Framing the Self: Views from the Window in the Novels of Claire Etcherelli." *French Studies* 49, no. 4 (1995): 410–423.

Ophir, Anne. *Regards féminins: Condition féminine et création littéraire: Simone de Beauvoir, Christiane Rochefort, Claire Etcherelli.* Paris: Denoël, 1976.

Ragon, Michel. *Histoire de la littérature prolétarienne en France.* Paris: Albin Michel, 1974.

Etienne, Marie (1938–). Etienne served as secretary to Antoine Vitez at the Théâtre National de Chaillot, where she was responsible for poetry* readings. She has contributed regularly to *Action Poétique* and *La Quinzaine Littéraire.* Her poetic voice, which has been called indiscreet and vehement, expresses the suffering caused by violence perpetrated against women and men. She strives to present untold stories, both of famous historical figures and ordinary women. Etienne quotes from Joan of Arc's trial, creates an alternative version of Racine's *Bérénice* in the form of letters addressed to Titus, and draws on myths*, chronicles, and contemporary *faits divers* in order to examine the feminine condition, both past and present.

Karen Bouwer

BIBLIOGRAPHY

Primary Texts

Blanc clos. Paris: La Répétition, 1977.
La Longe. Paris: Scandéditions-Temps actuels, 1981.
Lettres d'Idumée; Péage. Paris: Seghers, 1982.
Le Sang du guetteur. Montpellier: Actes du Sud, 1985.
La Face et le lointain. Paris: Ipomée, 1986.
Les Barbares. Paris: Lettres de Casse, 1987.
Eloge de la rupture. Plombière-les-Dijon: Ulysse Fin de Siècle, 1991.
Katana. Paris: Scandéditions-Ed. sociales, 1993.

Secondary Text

Bishop, Michael. *Contemporary French Women Poets.* Vol. 2. Amsterdam: Rodopi, 1995. 119–133.

Evangelism. French evangelicals shared with their Lutheran and Calvinist contemporaries a belief in the importance of Scripture and in the reform of predication, as well as in their criticism of pilgrimages, indulgences, and the veneration of saints, but they did not take the revolutionary step of breaking with papal authority, and they often display a high degree of mystical individualism. The most prominent woman associated with this movement is Marguerite d'Angoulême (1492–1549), sister of King François I and, after her marriage to Henri d'Albret in 1527, queen of Navarre. Sponsorship of evangelicals is reflected in her support for Bishop Guillaume Briçonnet, who exchanged spiritual correspondence with her (1521–1525) and sought to involve her in the reform of the diocese at Meaux. This reform was to serve as a model for the country as a whole, but by 1525 the Meaux experiment had failed. France was increasingly polarized between Protestant reformers and conservative Catholics, leaving no space for the initiatives advocated by evangelicals. The religious policy of François I, moreover, was increasingly determined by his political goals and not by the guidance of his sister. The posting of placards attacking the mass (*l'affaire des placards*) in 1534 initiated a period of repression that forced many evangelicals to flee to Strasbourg, and the movement never fully recovered.

Marguerite de Navarre*, nevertheless, continued to protect members of the Meaux group. Gérard Roussel was to become her confessor and almoner as well as bishop of Oléron. Until 1534 Pierre Caroli served as preacher and curate in her duchy of Alençon. Lefèvre d'Etaples spent his final years in her city of Nérac, where Jean Calvin and the poet Clément Marot also found temporary refuge. She was, however, unable to rescue the publisher Louis de Berquin in 1529, a clear sign that her power outside of her own territories was waning.

In addition to active sponsorship of reform, Marguerite de Navarre contributed to the diffusion of new ideas through her own writing. Her religious poetry* provides a detailed expression of her spirituality. The *Dialogue en forme de vision nocturne* (c. 1525), the *Miroir de l'âme pécheresse* (1531), and the works published in her anthology *Les Marguerites de la Marguerite des princesses* (1547) show a commitment to Fabrist piety and to the Lutheran ideals of scriptural primacy and justification through faith. Indeed, the Sorbonne withdrew its condemnation of the *Miroir* (1533) only at the insistence of François I. The frame story of her *Heptaméron* (published posthumously in different versions and with different titles in 1558 and 1559) showed a similar commitment to Scriptural primacy and a feminist orientation. A group of aristocrats, isolated by spring floods in the Pyrenees, read and discuss biblical passages under the guidance not of monks or learned humanists, but of the pious widow Oisille. The female voice, here as in the poetry, is as capable as the male of proclaiming spiritual truth.

Given her public role in promoting reform through her actions and her writing, the Queen of Navarre was an influential example for other women. Nancy Lyman Roelker mentions the significance of an "entourage factor" for aristocratic women who were often linked by common experience as ladies-in-waiting and who were expected to emulate their patroness. Like Marguerite de Navarre, Louise de Montmorency and Jacqueline de Longwy sought to share a newly revitalized faith with their husbands and children. They employed evangelical tutors and, when they could, offered hospitality and protection to reformist preachers. Protected at court during their youth by Marguerite de Navarre, Renée de Ferrare and Marguerite de France were to display a similar interest in sponsoring reform while maintaining ties with Rome. There were also, according to Roelker, other learned women both in Paris and in the provinces whose enthusiasm for religious reform led to their conversion, among them Michelle de Saubonne, the Picard Anne de La Vacquerie, and Roberte Le Lyeur, wife of the humanist Guillaume Budé.

Natalie Zemon Davis has studied the impact of Protestantism on city women, while Roelker pursues the relationship between the female aristocrat and Calvinism. In both instances, it is thought that the new faith provided a welcome opportunity for intellectual and spiritual liberation. French evangelism might have provided a similar attraction, but since evangelicals after the Meaux period lacked the kind of organization, commitment, and identity that the Protestant cause provided, there were few options for women eager for religious reform other than acceptance of Catholic authority or conversion. What evangelical women achieved, aside from their own spiritual satisfaction, was to prepare the way for acceptance of more radical reform by sons, daughters, friends, servants, and others with whom they came in contact or who were familiar with their views. Marie Dentière* clearly saw Marguerite de Navarre as a sympathetic reader for the *Epistre tres utile faicte et composée par une femme chrestienne de Tornay* in 1539, but Dentière had abandoned her convent* and married a Protestant minister in Geneva. It was there, not in France among the threatened and divided remnant of evangelicals, that she hoped to achieve her spiritual fulfillment as a woman declaring the word of God. Marguerite de Navarre's daughter Jeanne d'Albret* became an ardent Calvinist and mother of the Protestant contender for the throne, Henri de Navarre. Louise de Montmorency's descendants include a Huguenot daughter and granddaughters (Madeleine de Mailly, Eléonore and Charlotte de Roye) and, through a second marriage with the Maréchal de Châtillon, the future Huguenot leader Gaspard de Coligny. Women evangelicals are, therefore, important as the vanguard for a Calvinist reform movement that would depend heavily on feminine tenacity and initiative.

Paula Sommers

BIBLIOGRAPHY

Primary Texts

Briçonnet, Guillaume, and Marguerite d'Angoulême. *Correspondance (1521–1524)*. Ed. Christine Martineau, Michel Veissière, and Henry Heller. 2 vols. Geneva: Droz, 1975, 1979.

Marguerite de Navarre. *Dialogue en forme de vision nocturne*. Ed. Pierre Jourda. *Revue du seizième siècle* 13 (1926): 1–49.

———. *L'Heptaméron*. Ed. Michel François. Paris: Garnier, 1972.

———. *Les Marguerites de la Marguerite des princesses*. 4 vols. Ed. Félix Frank. (Rpt. Geneva: Slatkine, 1970). Paris: Jouaust, 1978.

———. *Le Miroir de l'âme pécheresse*. Ed. Joseph L. Allaire. Munich: Fink, 1972.

———. *Le Miroir de l'âme pécheresse*. Ed. Renja Salminen. Helsinki: Suomalainen Tiedeakatemia, 1979.

Secondary Texts

Davis, Natalie Zemon. *Society and Culture in Early Modern France*. Stanford: Stanford University Press, 1975.

Heller, Henry. "Marguerite de Navarre and the Reformers of Meaux." *Bibliothèque d'Humanisme et Renaissance* 33 (1971): 271–310.

Imbart de La Tour, Pierre. *Les Origines de la Réforme.* Paris: Hachette, 1914. Vol. 3.

Roelker, Nancy Lyman. "The Appeal of Calvinism to French Women of the Aristocracy." *Journal of Interdisciplinary History* 2, no. 3 (Spring 1972): 391–418.

———. "The Role of Noblewomen in the French Reformation." *Archiv für Reformationsgeschichte* 3 (1972): 168–195.

Existentialism. Existentialism became a prevailing and popular philosophy in France immediately following World War II*. Jean-Paul Sartre articulated the basic tenets of atheistic existentialism in 1943 in *L'Etre et le néant*, a work that contains the premise that existence precedes essence. Authenticity, freedom, choice, and commitment (*engagement*) are the main concepts of existentialism. In 1949 Simone de Beauvoir* presented the situation of Western women in existential terms in *Le Deuxième Sexe*.

Beauvoir asserts that one is not born, but rather becomes a woman, implying that women have always been strongly conditioned by societal expectations. She argues that women have allowed themselves to become "the second sex"—the Other—objects to be looked at, desired, judged, and exploited by "the first sex," the authoritarian male. Consequently, she urges women to seek liberation by making their own choices and acting in good faith.

Beauvoir's *L'Invitée* makes use of a fictional setting to explore the implications of existentialist philosophy for two women struggling to establish their identities during the Nazi occupation of Paris. A recent study (see Fullbrook) posits that many of Sartre's theories were borrowed from ideas that were originally explored in this 1943 novel*.

Existentialist analyses of gender relationships focus on the subject and object roles played by the individuals involved. A personal relationship is considered to be in good faith when two people accept each other and themselves as subjects (see Barnes). Rather than defining individuals according to social or biological functions, existentialism champions equality of opportunity and authenticity for both sexes.

Yolanda Astarita Patterson

BIBLIOGRAPHY

Primary Texts

Beauvoir, Simone de. *Le Deuxième Sexe.* Paris: Gallimard, 1949.

———. *L'Existentialisme et la sagesse des nations.* Paris: Les Editions Nagel, 1963.

———. *L'Invitée.* Paris: Gallimard, 1943.

———. *Pour une morale de l'ambiguïté.* Paris: Gallimard, 1947.

———. *Privilèges.* Paris: Gallimard, 1955.

———. *Pyrrhus et Cinéas.* Paris: Gallimard, 1944.

Secondary Texts

Barnes, Hazel E. *An Existentialist Ethics.* Chicago: University of Chicago Press, 1968.

Fullbrook, Kate, and Edward Fullbrook. *Simone de Beauvoir and Jean-Paul Sartre: The Remaking of a Twentieth-Century Legend.* New York: Basic Books, 1994.

Moi, Toril. *Feminist Theory and Simone de Beauvoir*. Oxford: Blackwell, 1990.
————. *Simone de Beauvoir: The Making of an Intellectual Woman*. Oxford: Blackwell, 1994.
Simons, Margaret A., ed. *Feminist Interpretations of Simone de Beauvoir*. University Park: Pennsylvania State University Press, 1995.

F

Fable. A brief allegorical narrative, in verse or in prose, acted out most often by animals and occasionally by vegetables who speak and act like humans while retaining their natural traits. Didactic in purpose, the stories illustrate the exemplary values that are revealed in a moral usually expressed at the beginning or end of the fable. Frequently the subjects are inspired from the fabulists of ancient Greek and Latin times.

Although verse fables have been a flourishing literary genre in France for many centuries, few women writers have achieved recognition in this male-dominated branch of literature. Marie de France*, in the late twelfth century, has the distinction of being the first fabulist of either sex to write in the French language. She specifically challenges the traditional male view that only men had the wisdom and talent to write morally instructive stories. Moreover, in an age when education* was usually reserved for the intelligence of men, she addresses the lesson in ''The Cock and the Gem'' to both men and women, thus dissenting from prevailing notions of difference. A native of France, she lived and wrote at the French-speaking court of the Plantagenet kings of England. She composed her *Fables* for a certain Count William sometime before 1189.

One has to wait five centuries for another woman to break through the gender barrier to write fables. Marie-Catherine Desjardins de Villedieu* (1640?–1683), a well-known and prolific author of the seventeenth century, wrote eight lengthy fables entitled *Fables, ou Histoires allégoriques* as part of the court's gift to King Louis XIV (1670). Mme de Villedieu's originality lies in transposing to the world of animals gallant situations of seventeenth-century aristocratic society in which she inscribes a code of feminine sexuality and conduct constructed for women. At a time when women were treated as objects of exchange in the marriage* contract, Villedieu emphasizes a woman's right to free choice in love.

In the late eighteenth century, Marie-Amable Petitau, marquise de La Férandière (1736–1817), proved that a woman fabulist could achieve distinction. Her elegant and well-constructed fables were published in the *Almanach des Muses* from 1780 to 1798. Early in the nineteenth century, another woman broke through the gender barrier to write fables. The comtesse de Genlis* (1746–1830) was the first woman of relatively modern times to produce a complete collection of fables. Entitled *Herbier moral, ou Recueil de fables nouvelles* (1801), her eighteen fables were composed in free verse. Governess to the duchesse de Chartres's children, who included the future King Louis-Philippe, Madame de Genlis refused to portray revolting scenes of violence such as are found frequently in her male predecessors' dramas of power and ethics. She drew her characters mainly from the vegetable kingdom, such as the botanically inspired Papyrus Plant.

The last French female fabulist to achieve literary distinction was a contemporary of Genlis. Marie-Madeleine-Nicole-Aléxandrine Gehier, Madame Joliveau de Segrais (1756–1830) wrote over 175 fables, publishing several editions of her books entitled *Fables nouvelles en vers, suivies de quelques poèmes* (1801) as well as in the *Almanach des Muses*. Because of the social upheavals due to the Revolution*, Madame Joliveau undertook the education of her five children, writing her charming fables to instruct and illustrate proper conduct. Epigrammatic in nature, the dramatic scenes are frequently brief, with the moral suggested by the dialogue.

Nancy D. Klein

BIBLIOGRAPHY

Primary Texts

Genlis, comtesse (née Caroline-Stéphanie-Félicité Du Crest). *Herbier moral, ou Recueil de fables nouvelles, et autres poèsies fugitives*. Paris: Maradan, An VIII [1801].

Joliveau de Segrais. Madame (née Marie-Madeleine-Nicole-Aléxandrine Gehier). *Fables nouvelles en vers, suivies de quelques poèmes*. Paris: Cordier et Legras, 1801. 2nd ed. Paris: L. Collin, 1807. 3rd rev. ed. Paris: Janet et Cotelle, 1814.

La Férandière, marquise de (née Marie-Amable Petitau). *Oeuvres de madame de la Fer****. 3 vols. in 2. Paris: Colnet, 1806. Reprint. Paris: Janet et Cotelle, 1916.

Marie de France. *Marie de France: Fables*. Edited by Alfred Ewert and Ronald C. Johnson. Oxford: Blackwell, 1942.

Shapiro, Norman R., trans. *The Fabulists French: Verse Fables of Nine Centuries*. Chicago: University of Chicago Press, 1992.

Villedieu, Marie-Catherine Desjardins de. *Oeuvres complètes*. 12 vols. Paris: Compagnie des Libraires, 1720–1721. Facsimile. ed. 3 vols. Geneva: Slatkine Reprints, 1971. *Fables ou Histoires allégoriques*, vol. 1: 90–97.

Secondary Texts

Ashby-Beach, Genette. "Les *Fables* de Marie de France: Essai de grammaire narrative." In *Epopée animale, fable, fabliau*. Actes du IVe Colloque de la Société Internationale Renardienne, Publications de l'Université de Rouen, no. 83: 13–27. Ed. Gabriel Bianciotto and Michel Salvat. Paris: Presses Universitaires de France, 1984.

Klein, Nancy Deighton. *Selected Writings of Madame de Villedieu*. New York: Peter Lang, 1995. 115–123.

Laborde, Alice M. *L'Oeuvre de Madame de Genlis*. Paris: Nizet, 1966.

Lafouge, Jean-Pierre. "Madame de Villedieu dans ses Fables." In *L'image du souverain dans le théâtre de 1600–1650. Actes de Wake Forest*. Ed. Milorad R. Margitic and Byron R. Wells. Paris: Papers on Seventeenth Century French Literature, 1987. 501–510.

Fabliaux. Short, generally comic tales, some 150 in number, from the thirteenth century and the first half of the fourteenth. Written in octosyllabic verse, they vary in length from 18 lines to more than 1,200, the average length being around 200 lines. Most of them are anonymous; others give names of known or unknown authors, all male.

The fabliaux have traditionally, but not entirely accurately, been thought to offer an unrelenting expression of the fundamentally misogynist spirit of the Middle Ages. Misogynist themes are indeed abundant in these compositions. Many fabliaux use a specific example of a lustful, greedy, or stupid woman as a way to generalize about the nature or character of the sex as a whole, and not a few contain interventions or diatribes in which the narrator explicitly condemns women. Still other narrators append antifeminist morals to narratives that may not even be critical of women, or that are equally critical of men. In addition, the stories themselves may dramatize shocking examples of women demeaned or, in a few cases, cruelly mistreated. The most extreme example of this variety is *De la dame escolliee* (The Castrated Lady), in which the male character allies deceit with brutal physical violence in order to teach women their proper place—absolute submissiveness—in a marriage*.

Nonetheless, the traditional assumption that the fabliaux are uniformly misogynist is misleading—as must be any attempt to ascribe a uniform view of women to 150 poems written over 150 years. In a number of the fabliaux, the female character is shown to be strong, resourceful, and far more appealing than her husband, who is likely to be stupid or buffoonish. *Berengier au lonc cul* (Beranger Long-Ass), for example, presents a husband who is an outright coward and a liar; his pretenses of being an outstanding knight are brilliantly exposed by his wife, who both humbles and humiliates him. In one of the better-known fabliaux, *La Borgoise d'Orliens* ("The Bourgeoise of Orléans"), the wife informs the servants that her husband is a would-be seducer. Unable to identify him in the dark, they believe her and beat him soundly; all the while, she is spending the evening, in another room of the house, in happy dalliance with her lover. Moreover, her husband, impressed and reassured by her apparent outrage at overtures from a stranger, is happy to be punished: he is a "beaten and happy cuckold."

These and other examples confirm that the fabliau's attitude toward women mirrors that of other texts and of medieval thought in general: it is predominantly negative but far from monolithic.

Norris J. Lacy

BIBLIOGRAPHY

Primary Text

Noomen, Willem, and Nico van den Boogaard, eds. *Nouveau recueil complet des fab-liaux*. 10 vols. [9 to date]. Assen: Van Gorcum, 1983– .

Secondary Texts

Eichmann, Raymond. "The Antifeminism of the Fabliaux." In *Authors and Philoso-phers*. Ed. A. Maynor Hardee. Columbia: University of South Carolina Press, 1979. 26–34.

Lacy, Norris J. *Reading Fabliaux*. New York: Garland, 1993. 60–77.

Fagnon, Marie-Antoinette (?–c. 1770). Little is known about her. She was born in Paris, where she achieved a certain celebrity through her exotic tales, but, according to Joseph de La Porte, she published little after 1755 when, at the height of her popularity, she retired into obscurity. Her best-known fairy tale*, *Minet-Bleu et Louvette*, was first published in the *Mercure de France* and reprinted at least three times throughout the eighteenth century. It is a compli-cated tale of a double enchantment in which Fagnon stresses that for men and women alike beauty comes from within, and a pretty face means little when one lacks sensibility. Her other works include *Kanor, conte sauvage* (1750), an ex-otic tale that takes place in the Amazon and details the miraculous properties of love, and a novel*, *Miroir des princesses orientales* (1755) in the tradition of the *Mille et une nuits*. A magic mirror is given to a princess which reveals to her the innermost thoughts of those who look into it. The mirror will crack only in the hands of the princess who finds her lover or husband constant, something it takes several generations to accomplish.

Antoinette Marie Sol

BIBLIOGRAPHY

Primary Texts

Kanor, conte traduit du sauvage par Mme***. Amsterdam: N.p., 1750.
Le Miroir des princesses orientales, par Mme F. Paris: N.p., 1755.
Minet-Bleu et Louvette, contes. N.p., 1768.

Fairy tales. The French literary fairy tale has the distinction of being a genre created and developed predominantly by women. Even if literary history has traditionally canonized the tales of Perrault at the expense of those by nearly all others, late seventeenth-century women writers such as d'Aulnoy*, Bernard*, Catherine Durand*, La Force*, Lhéritier*, and Murat* not only inaugurated the genre of the *conte de fées* but also published nearly two-thirds of all the fairy tales that appeared between 1690 and 1715 (74 of 114). Until well into the nineteenth century, the *conte de fées* was associated just as much—if not more— with women writers as it was with Perrault. Consequently, many of the tales by d'Aulnoy, La Force, and Murat, especially, had a significant influence on writers of eighteenth- and nineteenth-century France and Germany.

If women writers dominated the production of *contes de fées* in this period, it is in part because the genre developed from a parlor game of seventeenth-century salons*. But as readers' appetite for the genre extended into the eighteenth century, women writers played a less prominent role than earlier, reflecting women's changing cultural and social roles: not only did men outnumber women writers of fairy tales, but male-authored *contes de fées* account for almost two-thirds of those published between 1722 and 1758. Whereas many of these male authors (who included Cazotte, Crébillon, and Rousseau) experimented with parodic, satirical, and pornographic fairy tales, women such as Lintot, Lubert, and Villeneuve* followed the tradition inaugurated by their female counterparts of the previous century, which is characterized by a loose rewriting of folkloric tale-types or motifs, love plots inspired by pastoral and heroic novels, and protagonists of aristocratic birth. Amid stylistic and thematic differences among seventeenth- and eighteenth-century women's fairy tales, one significant commonality is the importance of the fairy figure, who appears more frequently but also more centrally than in the folkloric tradition. Besides acting as a surrogate mother with supernatural powers, most often for heroines, the fairy has also been interpreted as a figure of the woman writer. In the eighteenth-century women's *contes de fées*, the struggle between good and evil fairies becomes far more pronounced than before, suggesting a less euphoric vision of both this character and the genre.

All of the seventeenth- and eighteenth-century fairy tales were written explicitly for adults, and not children, with the notable exception of the stories by Le prince de beaumont*. Most often remembered today for her famous version of "Beauty and the Beast," Leprince de Beaumont is credited with initiating children's literature* in France. After her fairy tales, the genre was considered to be the domain of children. In the nineteenth century, France did not experience the same fascination with the genre as Romantic Germany and Victorian England. Nonetheless, several women writers, including Sand*, Ségur*, and Desbordes-Valmore*, turned their pens to fairy tales, often to take advantage of the lucrative market for children's literature*. With the birth of institutionalized literary criticism in the late nineteenth century came the canonization of Perrault and the devalorization of women fairy-tale writers. Although the best-known twentieth-century French fairy tales have been authored by men (including Apollinaire, Tournier, and Chamoiseau), feminist critics in both France and the United States have recently begun to devote serious attention to the *contes de fées* by French women writers.

Lewis C. Seifert

BIBLIOGRAPHY

Primary Texts

Le Cabinet des fées. 18 vols. Geneva: Slatkine, 1978.
Nouveau Cabinet des fées. Ed. Elisabeth Lemire. Arles: Picquier Poche, 1994.
Fleutiaux, Pierrette. *Métamorphoses de la reine*. Paris: Folio, 1985.

Sand, George. *Contes d'une grand-mère*. 2 vols. Meylan: Editions de l'Aurore, 1982 and 1985.
Ségur, Comtesse de. *Nouveaux Contes de fées*. Paris: Folio, 1985.

Secondary Texts

Barchilon, Jacques. *Le Conte merveilleux français de 1690 à 1790: Cent Ans de féerie et de poèsie ignorée de l'histoire littéraire*. Paris: Honoré Champion, 1975.
Robert, Raymonde. *Le Conte de fées littéraire en France: De la fin du XVIIe à la fin du XVIIIe siècle*. Nancy: Presses Universitaires de Nancy, 1982.
Seifert, Lewis C. *Fairy Tales, Sexuality and Gender in France, 1690–1715: Nostalgic Utopias*. Cambridge: Cambridge University Press, 1996.
Storer, Mary Elizabeth. *Un Episode littéraire de la fin du XVIIe siècle: La Mode des contes de fées en France*. Paris: Honoré Champion, 1928.
Warner, Marina. *From the Beast to the Blonde: On Fairytales and Their Tellers*. London: Chatto and Windus, 1994.

Falconnet (or Falconet), Françoise-Cécile de Chaumont (1738–1819). Born in Nancy, daughter of a bodyguard to King Stanislas of Poland, Falconnet was married twice, first to a cavalry officer, then to a young lawyer she met in the Antilles in the mid-1760s. After returning to Paris in 1767, she gained a reputation as a woman of wit. She held a salon,* published poems in various magazines, and wrote two plays performed at the Théâtre-Français: *L'Heureuse Rencontre* (1771) and *L'Amour à Tempe* (1773). Both plays criticize the abuse of parental authority. In *L'Heureuse Rencontre*, a one-act comedy co-authored by Mme Rozet, Falconnet ridicules a father's tyrannical behavior toward his family*. Eventually, the daughter succeeds in marrying the man of her choice in spite of her father's initial opposition. Falconnet was imprisoned with her husband during the Revolution* and widowed in 1817, two years before her own death.

Cecilia Beach

BIBLIOGRAPHY

Primary Texts

L'Amour à Tempe. Paris: Veuve Duchesne, 1773.
Falconnet, Cécile de, and Mme Rozet. *L'Heureuse Rencontre*. Paris: Veuve Duchesne, 1771.

Secondary Texts

Dictionnaire de Biographie française. Ed. Roman d'Amat. Paris: Letouzey et Ané, 1975.
Dictionnaire des littératures. Ed. Philippe Van Tieghem. Paris: Presses Universitaires de France, 1968.
Prudhomme, L. *Biographie universelle et historique des femmes célèbres mortes ou vivantes*. Paris: Lebigre, 1830.

Family. The basic structure of the family unit, established in the Middle Ages, is defined as *stem family* (*famille souche*). Typically a stem family consisted of

grandparents, children, and grandchildren. Families operated as a unit of production in which, ideally, all members contributed according to their ability and
received according to their needs. The able-bodied grandfather was at the head
of that unit, but on feudal estates his authority was limited by the power of the
lord of the manor, whose own production requirements took precedence over
those of his tenants. There were, however, many variations on this basic structure, and until the nineteenth century, regional developments in the history of
the family are more important than national developments.

Tenants were also not allowed to marry without the permission of the lord,
a rule that further limited the choice of a spouse, which was already subject to
parental approval; usually the marriage* was arranged by the two sets of parents
without consulting the partners. Among property owners the bride's dowry was
considerable and helps explain the preference for sons, the spinsterhood of
younger daughters, and their placement in nunneries.

A bride moved into the husband's family, where she became an additional
member of the production unit. She not only bore children and could not refuse
her conjugal obligations, but she also helped in the work necessary for the
family's survival. At mealtime the woman served the husband and stood in
attendance; she ate afterwards. Just as the authority of the pater familias was
limited by that of the lord of the manor, the sexual relations of any couple were,
certainly in theory, limited by the Church.

Communal control of the good behavior of neighbors was also a factor. While
a husband beating his wife was not condemned, the scolding wife, if she took
to beating her husband, might subject not only her husband, but also her neighbor, to be exposed to public ridicule. Such women became stock characters in
popular literature. Virtuous women were often the object of male aggressors
who described their conquests in military terms, as revealed in the *Heptaméron*
by Marguerite de Navarre*.

Well into the nineteenth century, France was a rural nation, and this basic
family structure remained dominant. Varieties occurred in the families of aristocrats and the urban families of guild members and their dependents. In both
cases the children were, at the age of about eight, sent to other families to be
trained, for example, as pages or apprentices. In the wealthier of such families
a division of labor, best illustrated by the warrior knight or the legal expert, led
to specialized functions of the family members. In prosperous households the
wife filled the role of housekeeper, and as wealth increased she became the
supervisor whose functions were then divided among a housekeeper, cooks, and
other servants. But in the most prosperous families, her supervisory role fell to
the (male) steward or the butler. By the seventeenth century aristocratic women
and those of the upper bourgeoisie saw themselves reduced to childbearing and
to being pawns in the establishment of family alliances. In the guild families
training in specific crafts was expanded to include the three R's when business
required the keeping of books. Evidence, for example from sixteenth-century
heresy trials, indicates that women were not excluded from this training and

could use their education* to master the issues of the theological debates of the Reformation* era. Famous is the earlier Christine de Pizan*, who became the first woman to earn her living as an author. But she too praised loyal and loving wives. Among the bourgeois the practice of sending newborns to wet-nurses—or importing such nurses—became common. This allowed the woman to return to her duties as wife and producer.

Such major developments in ideas as the Reformation, the scientific revolution, the Enlightenment* and even nineteenth-century socialism had little effect on the role of the woman in the family. Christian thinkers stressed that the man should love his wife as Christ loved his Church, but the man was the head, as Christ was the head of the Church. Moreover, the Catholic Church continued to oppose divorce* and to emphasize the sinful nature of sex, and thus perpetuated the negative image of women. The Church also taught the procreative function of marriage, and means of birth control* were not made legal in France until 1967, so that theoretically women could not regulate the number or frequency of children. Political writers saw the family as a micro-monarchy, while socialists examined the functional relationships of production. None of these allowed the woman to become the equal partner of the man, even if an increasing number of writers denied that women were inherently inferior to men. Women, like the lower classes studied by Jean Jaurès, had no French Revolution*. The great reforms laid down in the Napoleonic Code* made the woman a noncitizen subject to her husband.

It is remarkable that France, unlike the United States, saw no feminist movement, even toward the end of the nineteenth century when such movements became vocal also in England and the Netherlands. Unlike other modern nations, French women did not receive the vote until 1945, partly because their alleged loyalty to the teachings of the Catholic Church would offset the popularity of leftism among the electorate. Laws affecting women directly were handed down from the top without grassroots agitation. A long tradition of preoccupation about demography, especially after World War II*, led the French government to implement a comprehensive family policy that encouraged women to have more children, such as *les allocations familiales*, a system of allowance for every second and subsequent child; as recently as 1986, a two-year parental leave for the third child was instituted.

Though in *The Second Sex* (1949), Simone de Beauvoir* denounced the family as a place of oppression for women, this analysis did not become influential until after 1968, when radical feminists made it a cornerstone of their demands for equality. Through their efforts, but also because the number of working women increased dramatically, women made some gains that allowed them to work and have a family. Under Giscard d'Estaing's government, abortion* was legalized and a sixteen-week paid maternity* leave was put in place. With the socialists in power (1981) and the institution of a *féminisme d'état*, more measures were passed recognizing women as *individuals*, for example, the right to an abortion reimbursed by social security, equal legal rights for mothers and fathers with regard to children and property, and a stronger enforcement of "equal pay for equal work."

Though the image of the French family has changed over the last thirty years with the rise of divorces, single parenthood, and *unions libres*, all the reports on the status of French women indicate that attitudes evolve slowly. Women are still regarded as the primary caretakers; often they are the first ones to be laid off in times of economic crisis. This and the tradition of natalist ideology weigh heavily on the future role and representation of French women in the family.

Colette T. Hall and Derk Visser

BIBLIOGRAPHY

Ariès, Philippe. *L'Enfant et la famille sous l'Ancien Régime*. Paris: Seuil, 1973.

Badinter, Elisabeth. *Mother Love: Myth and Reality*. New York: Macmillan, 1981.

Brémond, Janine, and Marie-Martine Salort, eds. *La Famille en question*. Paris: Hatier, 1986.

Duby, Georges, and Michelle Perrot, eds. *A History of Women in the West*. 5 vols. Cambridge, MA: Harvard University Press, 1993.

Flandrin, Jean-Louis. *Families in Former Times: Kinship, Household and Sexuality*. New York: Cambridge University Press, 1979.

Forster, Robert, and Orest Ranum, eds. *Family and Society: Selections from the Annales E.S.C.* Baltimore: Johns Hopkins University Press, 1976.

Jenson, Jane, and Mariette Sineau. *Mitterrand et les Françaises. Un Rendez-Vous manqué*. Paris: Presses de la Fondation nationale des sciences politiques, 1995.

Le Roy Ladurie, Emmanuel. "Un Phénomène bio-socioculturel: L'Allaitement mercenaire en France au 18e siècle." *Communications* 31 (1978).

Lebrun, François. *La Vie conjugale sous l'Ancien Régime*. Paris: A. Colin, 1975.

Quitard, M. *Proverbes sur les femmes, l'amitié et le mariage*. Paris: Garnier frères, 1861.

Segalen, Martine. *Sociologie de la famille*. Paris: A. Colin, 1981.

Shorter, Edward. *The Making of the Modern Family*. New York: Basic Books, 1975.

Fauques (or Faulques), Marie-Agnès Pillement de (c. 1720–c. 1777). Some confusion persists concerning the actual events of Fauques's life, but sources agree that it originated in the Avignon region and ended sometime after 1777 in London. Historians are divided over the issue of her allegedly forced religious vows and later recantation, although Grimm (2: 44) acknowledges her as a former nun. She may have followed an English lord to London, where she took up residence for the rest of her life, earning a living as a writer. Her many novels*, some of which are exceedingly rare, were written in French and English, and published under a variety of pseudonyms including Fauques de Vaucluse. Among the best known, *The History of the Marchioness de Pompadour* elicited royal disapproval, and the French ambassador to Holland was ordered to suppress its French publication. One copy escaped destruction and the book proliferated in German, French, and English. The complex historical and political allegory envisioned in *La Dernière Guerre des bêtes* evinces a profound understanding of European affairs and testifies to Fauques's acumen and desire to effect change in a sphere forbidden to women in the eighteenth century.

Jennifer L. Gardner

BIBLIOGRAPHY

Primary Texts

La Dernière Guerre des bêtes. Fable pour servir à l'histoire du XVIIIe siècle. London: C. G. Seyffert, 1758.
The History of the Marchioness de Pompadour. London: S. Hooper, 1759.

Secondary Texts

Faucou, Lucien. "Notice." In *L'Histoire de Madame la marquise de Pompadour.* Paris: Le Moniteur du bibliophile, 1879. 5–14.
Grimm, Frédéric Melchior. *Correspondance littéraire, philosophique et critique.* 16 vols. Ed. Maurice Tourneux. Paris: Garnier, 1877.
Tourneux, Maurice. "Notice préliminaire to *Lui et moi.*" In *Oeuvres complètes de Diderot.* 20 vols. Ed. J. Assézat and Maurice Tourneux. Paris: Garnier, 1876. Vol. 17: 477–479.

Favart, Marie Justine Benoîte Cabaret du Ronceray (1727–1772). Daughter of musicians of the court of Stanislas Leczinski, duke of Lorraine and previously king of Poland, Favart was born in Avignon and grew up in Lunéville, where she received an excellent training in the performing arts. She made her début on the Parisian stage in 1745, at the Opéra Comique, directed by Simon Favart, whom she married later that year. Known primarily as an actress, dancer, and singer at the Comédie Italienne, Favart was involved in all aspects of the theater*. She was notably responsible for important costume reforms, favoring verisimilitude over coquetry, and she co-authored a number of comedies and parodies, which were successfully performed at the Comédie Italienne, and in which she played the leading female role.

Cecilia Beach

BIBLIOGRAPHY

Primary Texts

Favart, Justine, and Charles Harny. *Les Amours de Bastien et Bastienne.* Paris: Delormel, Foin et Préault fils, 1753.
Favart, Justine, and Chevalier. *Fêtes d'amour ou Lucas et Colinette.* Paris: Veuve Delormel, 1754.
Favart, Justine, Guérin de Frémicourt, and Charles Harny. *Les Ensorcelés, ou Jeannot et Jeannette.* Paris: Veuve Delormel, 1758.
Favart, Justine, and Lourdet de Santerre. *La Fille mal-gardée ou le pédant amoureux.* Paris: N. B. Duchesne, 1758.
Favart, Justine, and Bertrand. *La Fortune au village.* Paris: Duchesne, 1761.
Favart, Justine, Lourdet de Santerre, and M. Favart. *Annette et Lubin.* Paris: Duchesne, 1762.
Théâtre de M. et Mme Favart. Geneva: Slatkine Reprints, 1971.

Secondary Texts

Dictionnaire de biographie française. Ed. Roman d'Amat. Paris: Letouzey et Ané, 1975.
Pougin, Arthur. *Madame Favart: Etude théâtrale 1727–1772*. Paris: Librairie Fisch-
    bacher, 1912.

Femininity. Over the centuries, dictionary definitions of femininity have remained remarkably constant. Since the twelfth century, "feminine" physical
and behavioral traits, those viewed as proper to women, have been defined in
opposition to "masculine" ones: "masculinity" appears as synonymous with
virility and physical strength, and "femininity" with grace and fragility. Despite
such linguistic constants, traditional notions of femininity and masculinity have
come under attack in the twentieth century, especially by feminists whose work
emphasizes the historically specific nature of these concepts. Visual markers of
femininity and the significance assigned to them have varied widely depending
on social context and larger currents of thought.

In every historical period, intellectual and social developments determined the
form taken by these ideas and the extent to which specific groups felt their
impact. During the Middle Ages, two traditions, Christian and courtly, fashioned
images of femininity. Christianity* viewed women as easily swayed, like Eve,
and perhaps inherently evil. When chaste, however, women represented ultimate
holiness: the mother of God. In secular life, courtly traditions similarly idealized
the "lady" whose purity was exalted. Physically, "femininity" was embodied
in quiet, passive demeanor. Images and dress tended to emphasize small, adolescent breasts and a large, oval abdomen. The two most important goals for
women, chastity and motherhood, contained obvious internal contradictions.
Both Christian and courtly images of femininity set unrealistic ideals for women
of all social groups.

In early modern France, from the fifteenth to the eighteenth centuries, new
constructions of femininity developed in conjunction with broad social and economic changes. With the commercial revolution, the discovery of the "new
world," and the invention of printing, goods and ideas began to circulate with
greater rapidity. "Feminine vanity" had always been ridiculed, but now it was
recognized as a stimulus for the luxury trades. The Reformation* and Counter-
Reformation both provided venues for women to play roles aside from those of
wives, mothers, and lovers. Many wealthy women began to participate in literary
and intellectual movements, and a less idealized image of femininity developed
as men and women socialized more together. Chastity became less central to
femininity, as revealed by women's dress during the period. Corsets were worn
to narrow waists and lift breasts while necklines dropped. This femininity was
more explicitly about seduction than purity.

Eighteenth-century culture was dominated by an explosion of "sentiment,"
a trend that encouraged men as well as women to express their feelings in public.
Rousseau's writings represent both a continuation of this movement and a reaction against it. Though both his male and female characters could be equally

sentimental, he argued for specific roles to be taken by each sex. Most important, he emphasized motherhood and especially breast-feeding*, which came back into style among the upper classes at the end of the eighteenth century, thanks to Rousseau's popularity. Feminine nature fated women to live in subjection and to focus on pleasing their husbands and raising their children. Otherwise, they were going against nature and would thus make themselves and others unhappy.

During the nineteenth century, with the expansion and increased influence of the middle classes, interest in masculinity and femininity broadened and intensified. For the first time, men's dress became significantly less colorful, and extravagant fashions were reserved for women. Economic and social structures also increasingly segregated women from men. This physical separation intensified men's views of women's difference. Sophisticated "scientific" theories about femininity and masculinity followed, most famously in Freud's writings. Women who did not live up to models of femininity would not only be less happy; they had a serious illness.

Twentieth-century views of femininity have been much less unified. Though certain types of behavior and appearance continue to be categorized as "feminine," women have greater freedom in deciding whether or not to obey such notions. As gender categories have grown more flexible, new theories about their origin and significance have emerged. Simone de Beauvoir's* groundbreaking work Le Deuxième Sexe was the first attempt at a genealogy of femininity. In literary studies, many secondary works analyze femininity as it is dealt with by a particular author, but few have attempted to discuss it more broadly. Some of the most important recent work has developed in the area where psychoanalysis and literature overlap, as in the writings of Hélène Cixous* and Luce Irigaray*, and the movement called écriture féminine*.

Most feminists see "femininity" as primarily a cultural construction which has changed depending on its historical setting. Current debates revolve around the extent to which there is a "female" nature and, if so, what it means. Many French feminists have tended to highlight "difference." Rather than say that men and women are the same and therefore equal, they argue that a "feminine" nature exists which needs to be given more, not less, voice in society. Any attempt to erase all traces of femininity and masculinity, they argue, would mean eliminating part of women's nature. Instead, they insist that women should be allowed to express their femininity unrestrainedly and without misogyny to misdirect it.

Denise Z. Davidson

BIBLIOGRAPHY

Beauvoir, Simone de. Le Deuxième Sexe. Paris: Gallimard, 1949.
Geffriaud Rosso, Jeannette. Etudes sur la feminité au XVIIe et XVIIIe siècles. Pisa and Paris: Goliardia and A. G. Nizet, 1984.
Jones, Anne Rosalind. "Inscribing Femininity: French Theories of the Feminine." In

Making a Difference: Feminist Literary Criticism. Ed. Gayle Greene and Coppelia
Kahn. New York: Routledge, 1985.
Ozouf, Mona. *Les Mots des femmes.* Paris: Fayard, 1995.

Feminism. Dating the origin of feminism in France depends on how one defines
"feminism." The word was not adopted until the nineteenth century and signified the overt politicization of women's gendered identity and of political,
social, and cultural fights for their equality and liberty. In this more restricted
sense, feminism acquires the same kind of meaning for those struggling against
gender inequality as socialism did for class inequality. However, many scholars
have chosen to see forms of "feminist" consciousness in far earlier time periods
and texts than those of the first, self-proclaimed nineteenth-century feminists.

In searching for the origins of feminist consciousness, scholars have gone
back to medieval literature and texts like Christine de Pizan's* *La Cité des
dames.* Others contend that during the Protestant Reformation* women who
adopted the new faith, with its emphasis on literacy, began to assert their right
to apply themselves to more than the household. While the Salic law* prohibited
women from acting as rulers and curtailed their political and economic rights,
celebrated women authors like Marguerite de Navarre* defended women against
negative stereotypes, even if they did not challenge inequality. During the later
seventeenth century and into the eighteenth century, some women began to play
an increasingly visible role in public life as salonnières.

The upheavals of the eighteenth century, especially the French Revolution*,
witnessed not only the active participation of women, but the emergence of new
demands for the full rights of citizens and a political voice. Feminist appeals
during the Revolution came from Condorcet, and also, most famously, from
Olympe de Gouges* in her 1791 "Déclaration des droits de la Femme et de la
citoyenne," where she argued that women were entitled to the same rights as
men, including political, economic, and speech freedoms. Women such as Pauline Léon* and Claire Lacombe* led political clubs, protesting the Constitution
of 1793's failure to include woman suffrage. However, as the revolution became
more conservative by the fall of 1793, individual women were attacked (de
Gouges was guillotined for treason in November) and women's organizations
were dissolved. In 1795 the National Assembly declared that women should
return to their homes; those found gathering in the streets would be subject to
military discipline.

After Napoleon's rise and fall, women found themselves excluded from the
category of citizen under the 1804 Civil Code. Equally significant, the Code
restricted married women's rights, assured male authority over children, and
enshrined an unequal relationship between the sexes. This more centralized legal
inequality would form the basis against which feminist protest would emerge in
the nineteenth century. Feminism slowly emerged as both a working-class and
middle-class movement at different moments. Starting in the 1830s, utopian
socialists and followers of Saint-Simonianism* began to articulate a feminist

message. Out of this movement came the first autonomous women's newspaper, *La Tribune des femmes*, linking workers' and women's emancipation and urging women to see common interests across class lines. Women like Suzanne Voilquin*, Pauline Roland*, and Claire Démar* also advocated a new, more liberating sexual morality. As the influence of Saint-Simonianism receded, other women found similar inspiration in the socialist vision of Charles Fourier. By the middle of the century socialist-feminist leaders like Flora Tristan* were trying to put these visions into action, urging that the working class organize itself and understand that its freedom depended on the freedom of women.

In mid-century, feminists took an active part in the Revolution of 1848* and the short-lived Second Republic. The lifting of censorship encouraged the creation of new feminist journals and organizations, some emphasizing motherhood as the cornerstone for women's necessary participation in public, political life. However, as was the case in 1793, the new Republican government not only did not recognize women's right to vote*, but also closed their political associations and, in 1850, arrested and imprisoned several of the movement's leaders, including Jeanne Deroin* and Pauline Roland. Feminists were thus excluded from both right- and left-wing politics until the very end of the Second Empire. At that point, women like Maria Desraismes* began to organize against legal barriers to women's equality, arguing for revisions of the Civil Code, and during the events of 1870–71, women like Louise Michel* played a prominent role in the Paris Commune*. Its defeat and the imprisonment of women like Michel meant that the feminism that emerged in the Third Republic, while deeply Republican, was far less left-wing.

Nonetheless, by the 1880s, a growing feminist movement regularly agitated for woman suffrage, women's rights to their own property, and equal educational and occupational opportunities. Women like Marguerite Durand* started a women's daily newspaper, *La Fronde*, in 1897; Hubertine Auclert* refused to pay taxes as long as she was not allowed to vote. More radical feminists like Nelly Roussel* and Madeleine Pelletier* advocated birth control* and the loosening of restrictions on abortion*; more moderate women like Julie Siegfried and Marguerite de Witt Schlumberger emphasized public hygiene, the danger of alcoholism, and the problem of "degeneracy." Others sought to engage feminism and the struggle for the rights of the working class, among them Louise Saumoneau, co-founder of the Groupe féministe socialiste, who remained skeptical about the possibility of collaboration between working-class women and bourgeois feminists. By the early years of the twentieth century, France boasted several women's rights and suffrage organizations; the largest included the centrist Conseil national des femmes françaises and the Union française pour le suffrage des femmes. In 1907 women finally earned the right to control their earnings, and the movement for women's suffrage continued to expand through the first decade and a half of the century, reaching its zenith in 1914, when over 500,000 women "voted"—that is, signed blank ballots indicating their desire to vote during the regular elections for the Chamber and the Senate.

In July 1914, Paris witnessed the largest demonstration in favor of women's suffrage that had ever been held, but the arrival of World War I* halted the movement's forward momentum. Instead, the majority of feminists, like their fellow citizens male and female, became part of the "union sacrée." Some women—notably Louise Saumoneau and Hélène Brion*—adhered to a prewar pacifist feminism, but they remained a distinct minority. Instead most feminist organizations turned to charitable work and campaigns against a host of social ills that threatened the nation. In the interwar period, while feminism made some gains—obtaining baccalaureate degrees for women in 1919 and the elimination of differences in boys' and girls' education* in 1924—it suffered a number of setbacks, notably the failure to gain women's right to vote, defeated by the Senate in 1922, and the passage of the harsh anticontraceptive law of July 3, 1920. Still one of the images of the period, the "garçonne," came to epitomize the "newly" independent single woman, and after 1938 married women were no longer disabled under Article 215 of the Civil Code.

This would not change under the Vichy government during World War II*, but other laws enacted by this regime strengthened the punishment of those performing abortions and made divorce more difficult to obtain. Nonetheless, women actively participated in the Resistance and in efforts to liberate France. Perhaps ironically, however, French women finally received the right to vote under the auspices of General Charles De Gaulle in 1944. Of greater significance for feminism in the postwar period, in 1949 Simone de Beauvoir* published *Le Deuxième Sexe*, with its fundamental assertion that women are not born but made. This work became a landmark for French feminist thought.

Along with other movements, French feminism resurged in the 1960s following the upheavals of May 1968, responding to the sexual division of labor that persisted within student and left politics. While women in the 1950s and 1960s had continued to work in political pressure groups and voluntary associations, they had not created a separate movement for women's liberation. The first use of the term "Mouvement de Libération des Femmes*" referred to the August 1970 action (and arrest) of a group of women for placing a wreath beneath the Arc de Triomphe to commemorate the Unknown Soldier's wife. Women then began to politicize a number of issues, notably reproductive rights; in 1971, 343 women (including Simone de Beauvoir) signed a manifesto where they admitted having had abortions and demanded free access to them for all women. By the mid-1970s, the women's movement divided into several organizations; some, like Choisir, concentrated on reproductive rights and won a significant victory when abortion was legalized in 1975. Some linked class and gender oppression, working within a socialist-feminist agenda; others focused on lesbianism*. One group, Psychanalyse et Politique* (or Psych et Po), splintered off as it emphasized the symbolic oppression of women, their need to free themselves from an internalized misogyny by celebrating their differences from men. By the 1980s, when under the socialist government elected in 1981 France created its first Ministry of Women's Rights*, feminism had become integrated, however problematically, into the political agenda. French feminism at the century's end remains a multivalent force in political, social, intellectual, and cultural life.

Susan R. Grayzel

BIBLIOGRAPHY

Albistur, Maïté, and Daniel Armogathe. *Histoire du féminisme français.* Paris: Editions des femmes, 1977.

Duchen, Claire. *Feminism in France: From May '68 to Mitterrand.* London: Routledge and Kegan Paul, 1986.

Fraise, Geneviève. *Reason's Muse: Sexual Difference and the Birth of Democracy. [Muse de la raison: La démocratie exclusive et la différence des sexes].* Trans. Jane Marie Todd. 1989. Chicago: University of Chicago Press, 1994.

Hause, Steven C., with Anne R. Kenney. *Women's Suffrage and Social Politics in the French Third Republic.* Princeton: Princeton University Press, 1984.

Klejman, Laurence, and Florence Rochefort. *L'Egalité en marche: Le féminisme sous la Troisième République.* Paris: Presses de la Fondation Nationale des Sciences Politiques, 1989.

Marks, Elaine, and Isabelle de Courtivron, eds. *New French Feminisms: An Anthology.* Amherst: University of Massachusetts Press, 1980.

Moses, Claire Goldberg. *French Feminism in the Nineteenth Century.* Albany: State University of New York Press, 1984.

Offen, Karen. "Defining Feminism." *Signs* 14 (Autumn 1988): 119–157.

Perrot, Michelle, ed. *Writing Women's History. (Une histoire des femmes est-elle possible?)* Trans. Felicia Pheasant. 1984. Oxford: Blackwell, 1992.

Scott, Joan Wallach. *Only Paradoxes to Offer: French Feminists and the Rights of Man.* Cambridge, MA: Harvard University Press, 1996.

Smith, Paul. *Feminism and the Third Republic: Women's Political and Civil Rights in France, 1918–1945.* Oxford: Clarendon Press, 1996.

Sowerwine, Charles. *Les Femmes et le socialisme.* Paris: Presses de la Fondation Nationale des Sciences Politiques, 1978.

Feminist theory, United States. Definitions of feminist theory are widely divergent. At best, what theorists agree on is that women are oppressed and must struggle against their oppression.

Feminist theories are often discipline-specific (political scientists focus on women's relation to the state, philosophers examine epistemological issues, etc.). Feminist theory is often classified into subcategories to help map out the field. Many theorists appropriate extant theoretical models and add a feminist perspective to them: liberal feminism* centers on women's equality to men; Marxist feminism considers women as a sex class; postmodern feminism emphasizes the fluidity of the category "Woman"; ecofeminism places women's issues in the context of ecological balance; and socialist feminism brings together an analysis of gender and class. Other theorists create new experientially based models: radical and cultural feminists foreground women's difference and underscore the value of lesbian history and culture; feminists of color call for an analysis of the intersection of race, class, and gender.

More than any others, theories developed by feminists of color have contributed to a radical redefinition of the field. These critics demand that feminist theory move away from using gender as the sole or primary focus of analysis, and follow instead an integrated model which takes into account the relationships among race, class, and gender, so that feminist theory can be truly representative of all women's concerns. The richest contributions to the field are those that create more complex models of analysis and pay attention to more than one facet of oppression. Gayatri Spivak's work, at the intersection of feminism, Marxism, deconstruction, psychoanalysis, and postcolonialism*, is exemplary in this respect.

Anne Donadey

BIBLIOGRAPHY

Allen, Paula Gunn. *The Sacred Hoop: Recovering the Feminine in American Indian Traditions*. 1986. Boston: Beacon Press, 1992.
Anzaldúa, Gloria, ed. *Making Face, Making Soul. Haciendo Caras: Creative and Critical Perspectives by Feminists of Color*. San Francisco: Aunt Lute Books, 1990.
Collins, Patricia Hill. *Black Feminist Thought: Knowledge, Consciousness, and the Politics of Empowerment*. 1990. New York: Routledge, 1991.
Davis, Angela Y. *Women, Race and Class*. 1981. New York: Vintage Books, 1983.
Jaggar, Alison M, ed. *Feminist Frameworks: Alternative Theoretical Accounts of the Relations between Women and Men*. 1978. New York: McGraw-Hill, 1984.
King, Deborah K. ''Multiple Jeopardy, Multiple Consciousness: The Context of a Black Feminist Ideology.'' In *Feminist Theory in Practice and Process*. Ed. Micheline R. Malson, Jean F. O'Barr, Sarah Westphal-Wihl, and Mary Wyer. Chicago: University of Chicago Press, 1989. 75–105.
Lorde, Audre. *Sister Outsider*. Freedom, CA: Crossing Press, 1984.
Moraga, Cherríe, and Gloria Anzaldúa, eds. *This Bridge Called My Back: Writings by Radical Women of Color*. 1981. New York: Kitchen Table Press, 1983.
Mohanty, Chandra Talpade, Ann Russo, and Lourdes Torres, eds. *Third World Women and the Politics of Feminism*. Bloomington: Indiana University Press, 1991.
Rich, Adrienne. *Blood, Bread, and Poetry: Selected Prose 1979–1985*. New York: Norton, 1986.
Showalter, Elaine, ed. *The New Feminist Criticism: Essays on Women, Literature and Theory*. New York: Pantheon Books, 1985.
Warhol, Robyn R., and Diane Price Herndl, eds. *Feminisms: An Anthology of Literary Theory and Criticism*. New Brunswick, NJ: Rutgers University Press, 1991.

Ferrand, Anne de Bellinzani (1657–1740). Ferrand demonstrated a keen gift for the sciences, which she fervently studied. An early passion for Louis Nicolas le Tonnelier de Breteuil apparently provoked her flight to a convent* and forced her marriage* to Michel Ferrand, lieutenant at the Châtelet, with whom she had three children. Breteuil and Ferrand engaged in a tumultuous affair that lasted several years.

Ferrand's life changed drastically in 1683 with the imprisonment and death of her father, accused of embezzlement in Colbert's minting scandal. Humiliated by the Bellinzani disgrace, Ferrand's husband agreed to a separation in 1686. Their last daughter, Michelle, was passed from convent to convent, unaware of her identity until it was brought to light by a notary. Forced into exile, Ferrand returned to Paris in 1691 and established a successful literary salon* in the rue Saint-Honoré.

Ferrand's *Histoire nouvelle des amours de la jeune Bélise et de Cléante*, published subsequently with her alleged letters as the *Histoire des amours de Cléante et Bélise*, exhibits an unusually realistic analysis of the narrator's state of mind. Most of the factual indices closely correspond to the real-life relationship of Ferrand and Breteuil, leading many of Ferrand's biographers to conflate the two indiscriminately.

Jennifer L. Gardner

BIBLIOGRAPHY

Primary Texts

Histoire des amours de Cléante et de Bélise. Paris: N.p., 1691.
Histoire nouvelle des amours de la jeune Bélise et de Cléante. Paris: N.p, 1689.

Secondary Texts

Syveton, Gabriel. "Une Femme de magistrat sous Louis XIV, la présidente Ferrand."
    La Grande Revue, February 15, 1905, 292–324.
Williams, Charles G. S. "Doubling and Omission in the Text of Anne Ferrand/Bélise."
    In *Convergences: Rhetoric and Poetic in Seventeenth-Century France*. Ed. David
    Lee Rubin and Mary B. McKinley. Columbus: Ohio University Press, 1989. 123–
    139.

Fleuriot, Zénaïde (1829–1889). A most successful and prolific author of children's literature*. Fleuriot's works were popular up to World War II* but have now disappeared from children's reading lists. Fleuriot's work has not survived the test of time, perhaps because of the often heavily moralistic tone of her plots. Fleuriot was one of the few women for whom writing became a very lucrative activity. After her move to Paris from her beloved Brittany, she joined the ranks of successful authors associated with the respectable Hachette publishing* house. She also directed journals devoted to educating France's youth. Most of her works are geared toward girls. Fleuriot's universe is one of tradition: she prefers the country to the modern city and laments the loss of religious values, favoring old provincial aristocracy and earnest bourgeoisie. She asserts conventional gender roles and finds hierarchies beneficial; the image of French society she projects in her books is that of a paternalistic social system where order reigns through rigid class and sex hierarchies. However, she also depicts a society where couples are not necessarily happy, where children must learn how to suffer and deal with death, and where immorality is a constant threat. By default, then, one might learn more from her so-called "idealist" writing than from "realistic" novels.*

Bénédicte Monicat

BIBLIOGRAPHY

Primary Texts

Souvenirs d'une douairière. Paris: Dentu, 1859.
Le Petit Chef de famille. Paris: Hachette, 1874.
Bigarette. Paris: Hachette, 1875.
Grand Coeur. Paris: Hachette, 1879.
Tombée du nid. Paris: Hachette, 1881.
Bouche en coeur. Paris: Hachette, 1882.
Gildas l'intraitable. Paris: Hachette, 1886.
Coeur muet. Paris: Hachette, 1889.
Bengale. Paris: Hachette, 1890.

Secondary Text

Fleuriot-Kérinou, Francis. *Zénaïde Fleuriot, sa vie, ses oeuvres, sa correspondance*. Paris: Hachette, 1897.

Fleutiaux, Pierrette (1941–). Novelist and short story* writer, Fleutiaux won the Prix Fémina for her novel* *Nous sommes éternels* (1990) and the Prix Marie-Claire Femmes for *Histoire du tableau*. In *Métamorphoses de la reine*, winner of the Goncourt, Fleutiaux rewrites such traditional fairy tales* as "Sleeping Beauty" ("La Reine au bois dormant") and "Little Red Riding Hood" ("Petit Pantalon rouge"). Her writing, characterized by its mixture of the fantastic and the postmodern, conveys a constant sense of existential questioning and an intense search for different ways to express women's relationships.

Martine Motard-Noar

BIBLIOGRAPHY

Primary Texts

Histoire du gouffre et de la lunette. Paris: Julliard, 1976.
Histoire du tableau. Paris: Julliard, 1977.
La Forteresse. Paris: Julliard, 1979.
Métamorphoses de la reine. Paris: Gallimard, 1985.
Histoire de la chauve-souris. Paris: Julliard, 1989.
Nous sommes éternels. Paris: Gallimard, 1990.
Sauvée! Paris: Gallimard, 1993.
Allons-nous être heureux? Paris: Gallimard, 1994.

Flore, Jeanne (1537–15??). Jeanne Flore is believed to be a pseudonym for the author or authors of the *Contes amoureux* collection of seven tales, in the tradition of Boccaccio's *Decameron*. Critical opinion is fairly evenly divided as to whether the author was male or female, with each group marshalling a different set of facts about the book to support its views. On the one hand, those who believe Flore to have been female point to the celebration of women's sexuality in the volume, and to its critique of unequal marriages* between old men and young girls. On the other hand, proponents of the theory that Flore represents one or more males cite the exploitation and humiliation of female characters in the tales and in the frame, and the fact that women are ordered, rather than invited, to respond to the advances of men.

The *Contes amoureux* does clearly grow out of an Italianate literary atmosphere in Lyons of the 1530s. Discussions of the nature of love and the nature of women (the *Querelle des femmes**) are obviously germane to its origin. But despite using a female pseudonym, the book often leans toward the *negative* side of the *Querelle*, as it shows smart, assertive women to be punished when they do not yield to the advances of male suitors.

Current research on the mystery of "Jeanne Flore" leans toward a composite authorship for the book. Contemporary male authors such as Etienne Dolet and Clément Marot are believed to have participated in the composition of several tales.

Despite the probable impossibility of ever determining with certainty who Jeanne Flore was, the recent revival of interest in the book and in the problem of its authorship is part of a larger process of renewed evaluation of women writers and women's issues in French Renaissance literature.

Cathleen M. Bauschatz

BIBLIOGRAPHY

Primary Text

Contes amoureux par Madame Jeanne Flore. Ed. Gabriel-A. Pérouse. Lyons: Presses Universitaires de Lyon, 1980.

Secondary Texts

Bauschatz, Cathleen M. "Parodic Didacticism in the *Contes amoureux par Madame Jeanne Flore.*" *French Forum* 20, no. 1 (January 1995): 5–21.

Beaulieu, Jean-Philippe. "L'Ambiguïté didactique dans les *Comptes amoureux de Jeanne Flore.*" *Neophilologus* 71, no. 1 (1988): 1–9.

Lazard, Madeleine. "Protestations et revendications féminines dans la littérature française du XVIe siècle." *Revue d'Histoire Littéraire de la France* (November-December 1991): 859–877.

Losse, Deborah N. "Women Addressing Women: The Differentiated Text." In *Renaissance Women Writers: French Texts/American Contexts*. Ed. Anne R. Larsen and Colette H. Winn. Detroit: Wayne State University Press, 1994. 23–37.

Malenfant, Marie Claude. "Le Discours délibératif dans les *Comptes amoureux de* Jeanne Flore: *Exempla* et visées persuasives." *Atlantis* 19, no. 1 (Fall-Winter 1993): 67–76.

Pérouse, Gabriel-André. "Etienne Dolet conteur en langue vulgaire?" In *Etudes sur Etienne Dolet publiées à la mémoire de Claude Longeon*. Ed. G.-A. Pérouse. Geneva: Droz, 1993. 85–90.

Reynolds-Cornell, Régine. "Madame Jeanne Flore and the *Contes Amoureux*: A Pseudonym and a Paradox." *Bibliothèque d'Humanisme et Renaissance* 51 (1988): 123–133.

Winn, Colette H. "Les *Conptes amoureux* de Jeanne Flore: Un Texte-Echo." *Orbis Litterarum* 45 (1990): 97–112.

Foa, Eugénie (1796–1852). Novelist, journalist, children's book author, and publisher. Foa came from two wealthy Jewish families in Bordeaux, the Gradis and the Rodrigues Henriques families. According to her own words, her literary education* was encouraged by her uncle, the scholar and writer Benjamin Gradis. In 1814 she was married to Joseph Foa. The unhappy marriage* ended in separation. Literary ambition as well as economic necessity motivated her pursuit of a literary career. Early on, Eugénie Foa became active in the bourgeois feminist movement. She started out as a collaborator for the *Journal des femmes* (1832), became a participant of the Club des Femmes during the Revolution of 1848*, and also founded L'Oeuvre de Bon Secours, a charitable organization to help unemployed seamstresses. In her early works, such as *La Juive* and *Rachel*, the Jewish woman is a frequent topic. This changed after Foa's conversion to Catholicism, which might have been motivated by market pressures. Foa became known mainly for her children's literature*, which includes biographies of famous men and women, robinsonades, abolitionist and charitable articles, and depictions of Catholic saints' lives. Feminist consciousness as well as entrepreneurial spirit is displayed in her journal *Le Livre de la jeunesse*, founded in 1843. Foa was one of the few authors of the 1830s and 1840s who depicted the difficult situation of the woman writer in children's and young adult literature. She died impoverished.

Elisabeth-Christine Muelsch

BIBLIOGRAPHY

Primary Texts

La Laide. Paris: Vimont, 1832.
Rachel. Paris: Dupuy, 1833.
La Juive: Histoire du temps de la Régence. 2 vols. Paris: Bertrand, 1835.
Le Petit Robinson de Paris, ou le triomphe de l'industrie. Paris: Ebrard, 1840.
Les Saintes. Paris: Privately printed, 1841.
Contes historiques pour la jeunesse. Paris: Desforges, 1843.
Le Livre de la jeunesse. 5 vols. Paris: Privately printed, 1843–1848.
Six Histoires de jeunes filles. Paris: Janet, n.d. [183?].

Secondary Texts

Ezdinli, Leyla. "Altérité juive, altérité romanesque." *Romantisme* 81 (1993): 29–40.
Lejeune-Resnick, Evelyne. "Les Femmes écrivains sous la monarchie de juillet." Dissertation, University of Paris IV, 1983.
"Mme Eugénie Foa." In *Galerie de la presse de la littérature et des beaux arts*. 3 vols. Paris: Aubert, 1841. 3: N.p.

Fontaines, Marie-Louise-Charlotte de Pelard de Givry, comtesse de (?–1730). She was the daughter of the Marquis de Givry, the commander of Metz, a friend of Voltaire, and a novelist. Fontaines wrote two historical novels* that emphasize the importance of women who, although they do not possess direct power to affect the world, are nevertheless responsible for great events. Voltaire praised her first novel and is said to have drawn upon it for his two tragedies, *Artémire* and *Tancrède* (1726). Her novels were often reissued and collected with those of Mme de Lafayette* and Mme de Tencin*. She fell upon hard times and died in poverty, leaving two children.

Antoinette Marie Sol

BIBLIOGRAPHY

Primary Texts

Histoire d'Aménophis, prince de Libie. The Hague: Pierre Gosse et compagnie, 1725.
Histoire de la Comtesse de Savoie. N.p., 1726.

Fontette de Sommery, Mlle de. *See* Sommery, Mademoiselle Fontette de.

Foucher, Michèle (1941–). Actress and playwright. In the ground-breaking one-woman show *La Table: Parole de femmes* (1978), Foucher created what she calls *la personnage populaire.* Focusing on the dining table as the locus of women's experience, Foucher traveled through Alsace, recording conversations primarily with working-class women; she then reconstituted these dialogues on stage. In her presentation of the daily gestures, language, and emotions of these women, Foucher also communicated unspoken attitudes and feelings—the caged bird on stage, for example, suggests confinement. In all of her work, both on-stage and off, Foucher espouses theater* as an extension of life and seeks to increase its accessibility, especially for women.

Jan Berkowitz Gross

BIBLIOGRAPHY

Primary Texts

La Table: Paroles de femmes. In *L'Avant-Scène Théâtre* 636 (October 1978): 23–30.
"Mon Histoire est toujours liée à celle des autres." *L'Avant-Scène Théâtre* 636 (October 1978): 21.

Secondary Text

Lamar, Celita. "Usurping Center Stage—Women Interacting." In *Our Voices, Ourselves.* New York: Peter Lang, 1991. 68–82.

Fouque, Antoinette (?–). Psychoanalyst Fouque is best known for having organized the women's group Psychanalyse et Politique* in 1968. Jacques Lacan inspired its radical ideology, emphasizing the psychosexual dimension of women's oppression. Periodicals published by the group included *Le Quotidien des femmes* (1974–1976), *Des femmes en mouvements mensuelle* (1977–1980), and *Des femmes en mouvements hebdo* (1979–1982); all were short-lived. The articles were anonymous, signed by "une femme" or "des femmes," and tended to be repetitive and self-congratulatory. The book-publishing arm, Editions des femmes, has survived as a commercial enterprise.

Fouque, the main figure in Psych et Po, exerted a strong influence on her entourage which was often compared to that of a cult leader. In 1979 Psych et Po registered the logo MLF (Mouvement de libération des femmes*) as its own property and trademark, arousing the wrath of many feminists who accused the group of being reactionary. By the mid-1980s, interest in Psych et Po had greatly diminished in France. Fouque subsequently moved to California, where she maintained a following. Currently she holds a seat in the European Parliament and serves as vice president of its Commission on Women.

Samia I. Spencer

BIBLIOGRAPHY

Secondary Texts

Chronique d'une imposture. Paris: Association pour les luttes féministes, 1981.
Duchen, Claire. *Feminism in France: From May '68 to Mitterand*. London: Routledge and Kegan Paul, 1986.
————. *French Connections: Voices from the Women's Movement in France*. Amherst: University of Massachusetts Press, 1987.

Fourqueux, Marie-Louise-Anne Bouvard de (née Auget de Monthyon) (1728–?). She married into (at age twelve) a family of political financial advisers; her husband, Michel, became Contrôleur Général in 1787. Her first work, *Zély* (1775), a moral tale, was published anonymously; her later novels* and her memoirs* were published (also anonymously) years after her death. The memoirs, *Confessions de Mme de**** (1817), combine details of her life with reflections on the relations between the sexes and on her own intellectual self-confidence. For example, an anecdote was circulated when the geometrician Clairaut fell in love with her in Mme Du Châtelet's Cirey salon* (c. 1741); her memoir version of this story indicates that her main interest was not gallantry but rather his opinion of her intellect. The later novels (*Julie de St. Olmont* [1805] and *Amélie de Treville* [1806]) take up, in sentimental realist style, Fourqueux's concern with marriage* as a social institution.

Sally O'Driscoll

BIBLIOGRAPHY

Primary Texts

Zély, ou la difficulté d'être heureux. Amsterdam and Paris: A.-M. Dantu, 1775.
Julie de St. Olmont, ou les premières illusions de l'amour. Paris: Dentu, 1805.
Amélie de Treville. Paris: Dentu, 1806.
Confessions de Mme de***. *Principes de morale pour se conduire dans le monde*. Paris: Maradan, 1817.

François, Jocelyne (1933–). Poet and novelist. *Joue-nous "España"* presents François's formative years in Nancy and her break with her bourgeois roots upon discovering philosophy and falling in love with a female classmate in high school. She did not begin writing novels* until divorcing in her thirties and returning to her high-school love, singer and painter Claire Pichaud, with whom she has lived ever since. In her openly autobiographical novels, François details with a poet's sensitivity to language a specifically female experience of life—focused on relationships, as well as the joys to be found in the simple tasks of attending to one's material existence—in terms of a philosophical investigation into how to remain true to oneself in the face of crushing social restrictions and prohibitions.

Katherine Stephenson

BIBLIOGRAPHY

Primary Texts

Les Bonheurs. 1970. Paris: Mercure de France, 1982.
Machines de paix. Paris: Petits Classiques du Grand Pirate, 1976.
Arpad Szenes. Paris: Musée de Poche, 1977.
Les Amantes. Paris: Mercure de France, 1978.
Joue-nous "España." Paris: Mercure de France, 1980.
Signes d'air. Paris: Mercure de France, 1982.
Histoire de Volubilis. Paris: Mercure de France, 1986.
Maintenant. Paris: Petits Classiques du Grand Pirate, 1988.
Le Cahier vert: Journal 1961–1989. Paris: Mercure de France, 1990.
Le Sel. Paris: Mercure de France, 1992.
La Femme sans tombe. Paris: Mercure de France, 1995.

Secondary Text

Shaw, Nanette. "Interview with Jocelyne François." *Thirteenth Moon: A Feminist Literary Magazine* 8, no. 1–2 (1984): 39–49, 52–60.

French Revolution. *See* Revolution, French.

Freudian literary theory. The theory is based on the work of Sigmund Freud (1856–1939), who posited the unconscious, dream theory, the Oedipal conflict, castration anxiety, and penis envy. Among Freud's neurotic patients in cosmopolitan Vienna were women with nonorganic physical symptoms. After hypnotizing these hysterics, Freud found that the "talking cure"—free association in analysis—lifted unconscious repression. The patient could then reconnect the symptom with its origin and resolve the conflict, which was usually sexual in nature.

Modern detractors, literary or psychoanalytic, find his focus patriarchal and exclusively psychological, largely ignoring the influences of race, class, gender, and socialization. Having wondered what women want, Freud concluded that passivity, receptivity, and motherhood characterize the normal female. Repressed drives create tension, but sexual gratification, socially acceptable for men, is denied women. Hence, women are by definition conflicted and symptomatic in Freud's theory.

Although admitting to a limited understanding of women, Freud nonetheless found males superior in terms of superego, physiology, and emotional clarity, especially with regard to the sense of justice and punishment arising from the resolution of the castration complex. Boys see the mother as castrated and fear her example as a threat to their own genitalia. The boy's terror becomes the man's contempt.

Freudian theory can be applied to literary themes, plot structure, textual symbols, use of language, and aesthetics. Plots, like therapy sessions, comprise individual tales (Chodorow); characters, like analysands, grapple with obstacles that thwart their aspirations. Texts function as case histories, dreams (Skura), fantasies, or manifestations of basic Oedipal themes: loss and mutilation, triangular relationships, generational rivalries, and the power struggles which organize family and community life. Techniques of dream interpretation have been applied to literature too. Metonymy, metaphor, and symbolization enrich literary language as well as dreams. However, psychobiographical explorations of authors or characters, once popular critical tools, are less common today.

Susan Grayson

BIBLIOGRAPHY

Chodorow, Nancy. *Feminism and Psychoanalytic Theory*. New Haven: Yale University Press, 1989.
Freud, Sigmund. *Collected Papers, Vol. I*. Trans. Joan Riviere. London: Hogarth, 1950.
————. *A General Introduction to Psychoanalysis*. Trans. Joan Riviere. New York: Pocket Books, 1975.
————. *Inhibitions, Symptoms and Anxiety*. Ed. James Strachey. Trans. Alix Strachey. New York: Norton, 1959.
————. *The Interpretation of Dreams*. Ed. and trans. James Strachey. New York: Avon, 1965.
————. *New Introductory Lectures on Psychoanalysis*. Ed. and trans. James Strachey. New York: Norton, 1964.
————. *Sexuality and the Psychology of Love*. Ed. Philip Rieff. New York: Collier, 1978.
————. *Three Essays on the Theory of Sexuality*. Ed. and trans. James Strachey. New York: Basic Books, 1962.
Gay, Peter. *Freud: A Life for Our Time*. New York: Norton, 1988.
Skura, Meredith. *The Literary Use of Psychoanalysis*. New Haven: Yale University Press, 1981.

Friendship. Since friendship was conceptualized in Ancient Greece by Aristotle and Plato, women have often been deemed unworthy of it. According to the Greek philosophers, friendship was part and parcel of an economy of relationships closely linked to power and male virtue, to the exclusion of those who did not belong to the right class or gender. Cicero could not agree more in his

De amicitia. Only virtuous and wealthy young men were considered capable of the highest level of friendship. Since it was defined principally by absolute equality and reciprocity, while excluding sexual and familial relationships, only free, rich, and powerful men could share in friendship. The prevalence of this view is sturdy. Even the wise Montaigne, who shared a unique friendship with Etienne La Boétie, and whose text ''De l'amitié'' is so famous, could not bring himself to view Marie de Gournay* as worthy of friendship because of her sex. Several critics, such as René Girard, Janet Todd, and Eve Sedgwick, have demonstrated that in literature, representations of friendship often hide betrayals and are perceived as threatening to and competing with heterosexual relationships. Representations of successful friendships in French literature are few, quasi-inexistent between female protagonists or between women and men until the 1960s.

However, friendships among women have their place in literary history. They are represented essentially in correspondence, as in the letters of Madame Roland*, Suzanne Voilquin*, Flora Tristan*, Louise Michel*, and George Sand*. Friendship is also addressed in treatises on the subject, particularly by Madame Thiroux d'Arconville*, Madame Lambert*, and Madame de Maussion during the eighteenth century. Madame Riccoboni* is perhaps the first woman to portray female friendship in her novels.* The friendship between Marguerite and Madame La Tour in *Paul et Virginie* by Bernardin de Saint-Pierre remains one of the exceptional literary portrayals of female friendship.

In contrast, contemporary literature written by women is rich in depictions of female friendship. Claire Etcherelli* portrays the strong friendship of two women, Anne and Millie, who raise each other's children and share housework and money in *L'Arbre voyageur* (1978). Benoîte Groult* and Flora Groult in *Le Féminin pluriel* (1965), Christiane Rochefort* in *Les Stances à Sophie* (1963), Françoise Dorin in *Les Lits à une place* (1980), and Isabelle Hausser* in *Une Nuit* (1987) place successful, and even vital friendships between female protagonists at the center of their works. Françoise Dorin even explores the issue of heterosexual friendships. The main characteristics of the friendships portrayed include elements that escape the control of the Symbolic/patriarchal order: gossip, confidences, and storytelling, which are important in establishing and maintaining connections; laughter; the acknowledgment of the other's body; sharing and a redefinition of gift and exchange; and friendship and solidarity as a pacifist model for communities. This is particularly true of Andrée Chedid's* novels. From *Le Sommeil délivré* on, Chedid has portrayed strong female friendships that transcend age, class, and religious differences. These bonds unite women against individual and collective hardships and against all forms of systemic violence, to the point that one can speak of an ethic of friendship in her works. Female friendships are also prominent in Calixthe Beyala's* novels, grounded in Cameroonian culture, where they express a politics of friendship as a means of resistance against all forms of oppression, and in Assia Djebar's* novels, where they reflect the problematics of traditional and contemporary relationships between Algerian women. In Hélène Cixous's* novels, friendship between women appears as a new epistemological model where notions of equality, reciprocity, gift, exchange, and specularity are redefined outside of a patriarchal societal frame, providing a theoretical support to the novels aforementioned.

Joëlle Vitiello

BIBLIOGRAPHY

Secondary Texts

Todd, Janet. *Women's Friendship in Literature*. New York: Columbia University Press, 1980.

Vincent-Buffault, Anne. *L'Exercice de l'amitié. Pour une histoire des pratiques amicales aux XIIe et XIXe siècles*. Paris: Seuil, 1995.

The Fronde. From 1648 until 1652 France experienced a period of social unrest known as the Fronde. Historians generally divide this civil war into two periods, the parliamentary Fronde, which began in 1648 when the parliament instituted a series of decrees questioning the power of Mazarin, the regent Anne d'Autriche's prime minister; and the princely Fronde, led by Louis XIV's uncles and cousins, whose primary objective was to replace both the regent and the prime minister with a leader from their own ranks. There were urban and provincial uprisings incited by the various leaders. The primary male figures were Gondi (the future cardinal de Retz), the prince de Condé (Louis XIV's cousin), the prince de Conti (Condé's brother), the duc de Longueville (their brother-in-law), and the duc d'Orléans (Louis XIII's brother). This civil war's hallmark is its confusion and disunity. Each group had its own agenda, which frequently conflicted with that of its supposed allies. Participants often changed factions, or even sides. Eventually the non-frondeur parliament succeeded in ending the civil strife and restored the regency to power.

Recently historians have illuminated the often determining role women played in the rebellion. These ''Amazons*,'' as they were frequently called, were active behind the scenes as well as on the battlefield. When in 1650 Mazarin imprisoned Condé, Conti, and the duc de Longueville, an act that fueled the provincial rebellions and drew the duc d'Orléans to the defense of his relatives, the princely party was led by women. Anne-Geneviève de Longueville organized an uprising in Normandy, and eventually had to flee to Holland, where she joined forces with Spanish troops to oppose the regency. The princesse de Condé directed the opposition in her domain of Bordeaux. The duc d'Orléans's daughter, Anne-Marie-Louise d'Orléans, the princesse de Montpensier*, often replaced her weak and indecisive father. She conquered Orléans for the frondeurs and helped Condé's troops to storm Paris by ordering the cannons of the Bastille to fire upon the royal troops. These women were joined by the duchesse de Chevreuse, the marquise de Sablé*, and Isabelle de Châtillon, among others. While historians have tended to trivialize female participation in the Fronde, many of these women's male contemporaries, including Mazarin, considered them a force to be reckoned with. The war was often waged on the level of personal alliances and intrigue. The Fronde illustrated that the "private" realm of intrigues and passions traditionally associated with women was a decisive force in the public, political sphere. This became a literary theme, especially in women's works, after the Fronde. The heroic acts of the Fronde inspired novels*, especially Madeleine de Scudéry's* *Le Grand Cyrus*. Many of the female participants, such as Montpensier, continued their revolt on a literary level by writing their memoirs*.

Faith E. Beasley

BIBLIOGRAPHY

Secondary Texts

Beasley, Faith E. *Revising Memory: Women's Fiction and Memoirs in Seventeenth-Century France*. New Brunswick, NJ: Rutgers University Press, 1990
DeJean, Joan. *Tender Geographies*. Ithaca, NY: Cornell University Press, 1992.
Lorris, Pierre-Georges. *La Fronde*. Paris: A. Michel, 1961.
Méthivier, Hubert. *La Fronde*. Paris: PUF, 1984.

G

Gacon-Dufour, Marie-Armande Jeanne d'Humières (1753–1835). Novelist, polemicist, agronomist, and expert on court life. Scholars remain uninformed about this versatile writer, known only to have been born in Paris and to have died in Brie-Comte-Robert. Her published works include novels* such as *Les Dangers de la coquetterie* (1788), *La Femme grenadier* (1801), and *L'Héroïne moldave* (1818), with two editions of her first printed novel, *L'Homme errant fixé par la raison, ou Lettres de Célidor et du marquis de Tobers* (1787, 1803). Her political pamphlets and books confront the issue of a woman's right to education* (*Contre le projet de loi de S*** M***, portant défense d'apprendre à lire aux femmes, par une femme qui ne se pique pas d'être femme de lettres* [1801] and *De la nécessité de l'instruction pour les femmes* [1805]). The pamphlet *Mémoire pour le sexe féminin contre le sexe masculin* (1787) accuses men, especially the chevalier de Feucher, of corrupting society and of blaming women for its decline. She edited the correspondence of Mme de Châteauroux* (1717–1744) and wrote tales of the courts of Catherine de Medici* and Louis XIV. Finally, she published numerous manuals detailing the running of the household, perfume and soap-making, and advice on maintaining health.

Sarah Harrell DeSmet

BIBLIOGRAPHY

Primary Texts

L'Homme errant fixé par la raison, ou Lettres de Célidor et du marquis de Tobers. Paris: Royez, 1787.

Mémoire pour le sexe féminin contre le sexe masculin. London and Paris: Royez, 1787.

Contre le projet de loi de S*** M***... Paris: Ouvrier, 1801.

La Femme grenadier. Paris: Ouvrier, 1801.

De la nécessité de l'instruction pour les femmes. Paris: Chez Buisson, 1805.

L'Héroïne moldave. Paris: Cogez, 1818.

Secondary Texts

Buck, Claire, ed. *The Bloomsbury Guide to Women's Literature*. New York: Prentice-Hall, 1992.

Michael, Colette. *Les Tracts féministes en France*. Geneva: Slatkine, 1986.

Sullerot, Evelyne. *Histoire de la presse féminine des origines à 1848*. Paris: A. Colin, 1966.

Wilson, Katharina M., ed. *An Encyclopedia of Continental Women Writers*. New York: Garland Publishing, 1991.

Gagneur, Marie-Louise (1832–1902). Novelist, journalist, polemical writer. A lifelong convert to Fourier's philosophy, she tirelessly promoted his ideas. In 1867 she published *Le Calvaire des femmes* in *Le Siècle*. In it, she focused on female workers and their inability to survive because of the lack of education* and suitable work for women. Gagneur declared that women would always be dolls unless they won their freedom and independence through work. Gagneur also wrote anticlerical novels*, such as *La Croisade noire* (1865), to denounce the clergy's nefarious influence. In 1901 she was gratified to find in Zola's *Travail* the continuation of her own ideals.

Juliette Parnell-Smith

BIBLIOGRAPHY

Primary Texts

La Croisade noire. Paris: A. Faure, 1865.
Les Vierges russes. Paris: Dentu, 1880.
L'Aube. Charles Fourier d'aprés Zola et Jaurès. Paris: Dentu, 1901.

Secondary Text

Colin, René-Pierre. "Marie-Louise Gagneur, feuilletoniste: Anticléricalisme et Fourier-isme." *Femmes de lettres au XIXe siècle autour de Louise Colet*. Sous la direction de Roger Bellet. Lyons: Presses Universitaires de Lyon, 1982. 301–310.

Gallaire, Fatima (1944–). Born in Algeria, playwright Gallaire currently re-sides in Paris. She has won the Prix Arletty (1990) and the Prix de l'Académie Française (1994) for her theater*, which she considers a source of liberation and a catharsis for those who challenge authority. Trapped between two cultures, her characters—often women—struggle against the repressive forces of tradition. Her widely performed play *Princesses* (1988) portrays the tragic conse-quences of an estranged daughter's visit to the Algerian village of her childhood. In *Rimm, la gazelle*, an Algerian woman living in Paris returns to mourn her mother, providing the occasion to reconcile her familial past with her present life. Gallaire's plays often explore painful confrontations over issues such as polygamy and the pressure to bear sons (*Les Co-épouses*), adult circumcision and conversion to Islam* (*La Fête virile*), and the relations between a *pied noir* (Algerian-born French) family and their former Arab neighbors from Algeria (*Au loin, les Caroubiers*).

Jan Berkowitz Gross

BIBLIOGRAPHY

Primary Texts

Témoignage contre un homme stérile. In *L'Avant-Scène* 815 (1987).
Princesses ou Ah! Vous êtes venus . . . Là où il y a quelques tombes. Paris: Editions des
    Quatre-Vents, 1988.
Les Co-épouses. Paris: Editions des Quatre-Vents, 1990.
La Fête virile. Paris: Editions des Quatre-Vents, 1992.
Au loin, les Caroubiers suivi de Rimm, la gazelle. Paris: Editions des Quatre-Vents, 1993.
Au Coeur, la Brûlure. In *L'Avant-Scène* 954 (1994).
Molly des sables. In *L'Avant-Scène* 954 (1994).
Les Richesses de l'hiver. In *L'Avant-Scène* 991 (1996).

Secondary Texts

Brahimi, Denise. ''Les Tragédies algériennes de Fatima Gallaire.'' *Notre Librairie* 118
    (1994): 53–56.
Surel-Turpin, Monique. ''Les Dénonciations de Fatima Gallaire.'' *Etudes Théâtrales* 8
    (1995): 34–35, 40.

Garréta, Anne (1962–). Novelist and professor of literature. Garréta attracted substantial attention with her first novel*, *Sphinx* (1986), a text that contains no grammatical markers of gender, thus making it impossible to determine the gender and sexual identity of the two main protagonists. In this contemporary enigma, which moves between Paris and New York, the only clue provided is that one of the characters is African American. In *Sphinx*, Garréta reframes the question of gender, sexuality, and writing—especially the androgynous quality of writing—and revises traditional definitions of love, desire, and friendship*.

Joëlle Vitiello

BIBLIOGRAPHY

Primary Texts

Sphinx. Paris: Grasset et Fasquelle, 1986.
Ciels liquides. Paris: Grasset et Fasquelle, 1990.

Gauthier, Xavière (1942–). Novelist, essayist, and feminist critic. In 1976, inspired by the growing French feminist movement, Gauthier founded and became the editor of the feminist journal *Sorcières*. In *Les Parleuses* (1974)—a series of free-flowing conversations between Gauthier and Marguerite Duras*— the two writers deal with the specificity of literature written by women. In a special issue of *Magazine Littéraire* (1982), Gauthier discussed the characteristics and political implications of *écriture feminine** as it emerged in the 1970s, exploring women's creativity and their use of language. In *Dire nos sexualités* (1976), Gauthier juxtaposes an analysis of trends in the study of female sexuality with men's and women's frank accounts of their sexual experiences. Throughout her work, Gauthier affirms her feminist position by claiming the right for women to express their own bodies, desires, and sexuality—all of which had been previously ignored by Freudian, male-oriented theories of sexuality.

Metka Zupančič

BIBLIOGRAPHY

Primary Texts

Surréalisme et séxualité. Paris: Gallimard, 1971.
Héliogabale, travestissement. Paris: U.G.E., 1973.
Rose saignée. Paris: Des femmes, 1974.
Dire nos sexualités: Contre la sexologie. Paris: Ed. Galilee, 1976.
L'Etrange métamorphose d'Anais. Paris: Ed. Garance, 1980.
La Hague, ma terre violentée. Paris: Mercure de France, 1981.
"Femmes, une autre écriture?" *Magazine Littéraire* 180 (January 1982): 16–17.
L'Insoumise: Biographie de Louise Michel. Paris: Manya, 1990.
Gauthier, Xavière, and Marguerite Duras. *Les Parleuses.* Paris: Minuit, 1974.

Gautier, Judith (1845–1917). Gautier was born outside of Paris, the daughter of Théophile Gautier and Ernesta Grisi, a singer at the Théâtre des Italiens. She spent her childhood living with a wet-nurse, her grandfather, and elderly aunts, then in a convent*. Current theory attributes the escapist tendencies in her writing to these unhappy early years. As an adolescent, she met the literary masters acquainted with her father, who attended his famous Thursday Evenings at the family home, including Gustave Flaubert, the Dumas father and son, the Goncourt brothers, and Charles Baudelaire. During this time, the nineteenth-century Universal Exhibitions provided her first contacts with East Asian and Middle Eastern cultures, which were to become her primary sources of professional inspiration.

In 1866 Gautier married Catulle Mendès, a founding member of the journal *Le Parnasse contemporain*, associated with the circle of Parnassian poets*. During their marriage of eight years, the couple shared friendships with many influential artists, including Richard Wagner, Victor Hugo, Paul Verlaine, the Goncourt brothers, Stéphane Mallarmé, Flaubert, and Leconte de Lisle. Over the years, Gautier would remain in close professional and personal contact with many of these writers. Gautier began to publish at the age of nineteen, under her own name, as well as under the names Judith Walter and F. Chaulnes. During her career, she published numerous short stories, plays that were performed at the Paris Odéon and in New York, three collections of poetry*, a three-volume (unfinished) autobiography*, eight novels*, and many articles on Asian art and culture.

While Gautier's works depict the perceived exoticism of the Middle Eastern and Asian cultures, as did her Orientalist contemporaries, her oeuvre charts new territory. She learned to read Chinese characters and Persian, and relied on original Eastern texts to sustain her narratives. She removed altogether the West European protagonist in order to incorporate directly more original oral traditions and voices. Most of her works received high critical acclaim, especially her novels, some published in serial form in leading literary journals: *Le Dragon impérial* (1868 serial, 1869 novel), set in China; *Iskender* (1869 serial, 1886 novel), set in Persia, a revision of the mythological accounts of the Shah Nameh; *L'Usurpateur* (1875, republished in 1887 as *La Soeur du soleil*) set in Japan; *La Conquête du paradis* (1887), set in India; *Le Vieux de la montagne* (1893), set in Palestine; *Mémoires d'un éléphant blanc* (1894), set in India and Siam; and *Princesses d'amour (courtisanes japonaises)* (1900), set in Japan.

These novels are significant departures from the West European male narrative tradition that seeks to conquer and appropriate Eastern cultures. Gautier's narrating women, whether princesses, revolutionary warriors, mythical Amazons*, or geishas, portray heroic female characters determined to plot their own destinies. In *Princesses d'amour*, for instance, the geishas voice a wish and describe plans for freedom and happiness distinct from the sexual obligations of their profession. We catch a glimpse of the enclosed space of old Japan and enclosed feminine space, as contrasted with modernization and the movement for female equality.

On the surface, Gautier's Middle Eastern and Asian women mirror nineteenth-century West European male fantasies, yet she delves beneath the European quest to enter the harem and to raise the veil. She questions the view of women as objects of aesthetic pleasure, to be conquered and possessed as their native lands were invaded by Western imperialists. She challenges the notion of woman as a paradox: desirable yet intangible, beautiful yet dangerous, and angelic yet demonic. She juxtaposes the traditional perception of a passive woman with a more active image of an intelligent, capable, and courageous one.

Gautier also committed herself to supporting women writers. Because women were not admitted to prestigious male-dominated literary academies, she joined Madame de Broutelles, editor of the journal *Vie Heureuse*, and other women writers, to establish the Académie des Dames (1904). Today, the Académie still awards its original literary prize, the Prix Fémina. As the result of a remarkable career, Gautier was honored as the first woman member of the Academy in France, elected in 1910 over Paul Claudel to the Académie Goncourt. The following year she received the highest civil honor in France and was named a member of the Légion d'Honneur.

Elizabeth Fisher Goldsmith

BIBLIOGRAPHY

Primary Texts

Le Livre de jade. Paris: Lemerre, 1867.
Le Dragon impérial. Paris: Lemerre, 1869.
L'Usurpateur. Paris: Librairie Internationale Albert Lecroix, 1875.
Iskender. Paris: Frinzinie et Compagnie, 1886.
La Conquête du paradis. Paris: Armand Colin, 1890.
Le Vieux de la montagne. Paris: Bibliothèque de Romans Historiques, 1893.

Mémoires d'un éléphant blanc. Paris: Armand Colin, 1894.
Princesses d'amour (courtisanes japonaises). Paris: Ollendorff, 1900.

Secondary Texts

Brahimi, Denise. *Théophile et Judith vont en Orient.* Paris: La Boîte à documents, 1990.
Danclos, Anne. *La Vie de Judith Gautier.* Paris: Barre et Dayez Editeurs, 1993.
Meyer-Zundel, Suzanne. *Quinze Ans auprès de Judith Gautier.* N.p., 1969.
Richardson, Joanna. *Judith Gautier: A Biography.* London: Quartet Books, 1986.

Gay, Sophie (1776–1852). Novelist, journalist, dramatist, and accomplished musician. Sophie-Marie-Françoise Nichault de la Valette was educated in the same Parisian boarding school as Claire de Duras*. At fifteen, she married a wealthy and older financial broker, Gaspard Liottier, by whom she had three children, losing one to an accident. Among the well-known *merveilleuses* of the Directory, Gay hosted a lively literary and musical salon*. In 1799 she divorced her husband and married Jean-Sigismond Gay, a young financier. Gay published *Laure d'Estell* anonymously and defended Germaine de Staël* and her 1802 novel* *Delphine* in the press. She led an animated salon life, but when her husband lost his post in 1810, Gay settled in Paris and began writing professionally. She maintained her salon, published novels* and plays, and collaborated with Sophie Gail on musical projects.

Sainte-Beuve called *Léonie de Montbreuse* (1813) Gay's best work, its delicacy of sentimental analysis reminding him of Mme Riccoboni* and Mme de Souza. While many of Gay's novels present virtuous and genteel women of the Directory or the Empire questing for love, Gay's oeuvre became more diverse following her husband's untimely death in 1822. She wrote historical novels, a volume for children, salon memoirs*, and witty physiologies, a literary genre popular at the time which described a human reality in an objective fashion. Her novel *Ellénore* (1846) claims to tell the life story of the woman who purportedly inspired Benjamin Constant's *Adolphe* (1816). Gay also published widely in the press and launched her own literary and society review, *Causeries du monde* (1833). Devoted to the literary career of her daughter, Delphine Gay de Girardin*, Sophie Gay never stopped writing and was known for her vivacity and sharp wit up until her death.

Cheryl A. Morgan

BIBLIOGRAPHY

Primary Texts

Laure d'Estell. Par Mme***. Paris: Pougens, 1802.
Anatole. Paris: Chez Amboise Tardieu, 1822.
Un Mariage sous l'Empire. Paris: Viennet, 1832.
Causeries du monde. Revue fondée et dirigée par Sophie Gay (1833–1834).
Souvenirs d'une vieille femme. Paris: Ledoux, 1834.

Salons célèbres. Paris: Dumont, 1837.

Ellénore. Paris: Dumont et Petion, 1844–1846.

Secondary Texts

Malo, Henri. *La Gloire du vicomte de Launay: Delphine Gay de Girardin.* Paris: Emile-Paul Frères, 1925.

———. *Une Muse et sa mère: Delphine Gay de Girardin.* Paris: Emile-Paul Frères, 1924.

Sainte-Beuve, C.-A. ''Madame Sophie Gay.'' In *Causeries du lundi.* 15 vols. Paris: Garnier, 1851–1862. 6: 64–83.

Séché, Léon. *Le Cénacle de la ''Muse française'' 1823–1827.* Paris: Mercure de France, 1908.

Gay de Girardin, Delphine (1804–1855). Poet, novelist, journalist, dramatist. Delphine Gay learned valuable lessons reading poetry* in the salons* of her mother, Sophie Gay*, and those of Claire de Duras* and Juliette Récamier, where she received encouragement from writers such as René de Chateaubriand and Alexandre Soumet. Her early poems are both feminocentric and patriotic. Gay privileges such female figures as Mary Magdalene, Joan of Arc, the black heroine of Claire de Duras's *Ourika*, and Madame de Staël's* eponymous heroine of genius*, Corinne. In her occasional poetry, Gay comments on public events, commemorating, for example, the coronation of Charles X and the French conquest of Algiers. While the literary periodical *La Muse française* dubbed her ''our new Corinne,'' Gay styled herself ''the Muse of the Fatherland.''

After a trip to Italy in 1826–1827, during which she began her friendship* with Lamartine, Gay contributed poetry to the periodicals *La Mode* and *Le Voleur*, edited by Emile de Girardin. After her marriage to Girardin in 1831, she held a salon frequented by Honoré de Balzac, Théophile Gautier, and Eugène Sue. The evolution of her writing at this time is most apparent in *Napoline* (1834), a verse narrative depicting the failed social integration and suicide of a young woman of genius*. *Napoline* anticipates her later success in prose as a shrewd and ironic social portraitist. In the early to mid-1830s, Gay de Girardin published novels* and a volume of children's stories. Her wit and political acumen, evident in the newspaper articles she wrote under the pseudonym Vicomte de Launay, make her the first prominent female journalist of the century.

Gay de Girardin also wrote for the stage during the July Monarchy, but her first comedy, *L'Ecole des journalistes* (1839), was censored for its irreverent portrayal of politics and the press. Her tragedies *Judith* (1843) and *Cléopatre* (1847) met with only partial success despite the presence of Rachel in both lead roles. ''Madame Molière,'' as Hugo called her, fared better with *Lady Tartuffe* (1853) during the Second Empire. The comedies and a vaudeville she wrote in the years just prior to her death proved her talent for comedy and earned her a great deal of money.

Cheryl A. Morgan

BIBLIOGRAPHY

Primary Texts

Nouvelles. Presentées par Arlette Michel. Geneva: Slatkine Reprints, 1979.
La Croix de Berny. Paris: Editions France-Empire, 1980.
Chroniques parisiennes, 1836–1848. Ed. Jean-Louis Vissière. Paris: Des femmes, 1986.
Lettres parisiennes du vicomte de Launay. 2 vols. Texte présenté et annoté par Anne Martin-Fulgier. Paris: Mercure de France, 1986.

Secondary Texts

Ezdinli, Leyla. "La Canne de M. de Balzac: Parody at the Intersection of Politics and Literature." *L'Esprit Créateur* 33, no. 3 (Fall 1993): 95–103.
Kelly, Dorothy. "Delphine Gay de Girardin." In *French Women Writers: A Bio-Bibliographical Source Book*. Ed. Eva Martin Sartori and Dorothy Wynne Zimmerman. Westport, CT: Greenwood Press, 1991.
Morgan, Cheryl A. "Les Chiffons de la M(ed)use: Delphine Gay de Girardin, journaliste." *Romantisme* 85, no. 3 (1994): 57–66.

Genius. The Western concept of "genius" has grown from two distinct Latin roots: *genius* and *ingenium*. The former, denoting a protective or malevolent spirit that guarded the patriarch's household, power, and personality, remained significant especially during the Middle Ages, appearing as an allegorical figure in works by Jean de Meun, Christine de Pizan*, and Alain de Lille. Through these representations, "genius" comes to suggest male reproductive sexuality and paternalism.

Modern connotations derive mostly from the Latin *ingenium*, an innate or natural ability. Great Renaissance artists and inventors possessed such inborn talent, skill, and *virtù*. These highly individual performances of genius remain linked with virility in their mastery of rational rules and doctrines, the result of cultivation and learning lavished on men.

Despite the logical space cleared by Cartesian dualism, isolating the mind from the sexed body, the French classical period hotly debated whether women are capable of genius. Although medical treatises of the time overwhelmingly favored its impossibility, authors including Fénelon, Charles Perrault, Poulain de la Barre, and Madame Dacier* speculated on whether the relative exclusion of women from serious learning was instrumental in prohibiting the appearance of female geniuses. The more popular perspective found women's (pro)creativity to be of the body, men's of the mind.

During the late seventeenth and eighteenth centuries, the French obsession with mastery of aesthetic rules gradually gave way to a more English sense of naturalness and poetic originality. More than reason, the genius possessed expansive imagination and energy. In Saint-Lambert's article "Génie" in the *Encyclopédie**, genius approaches the sublime as it receives and processes its object through heightened sensory and imaginative faculties. In Diderot's *Le Neveu de Rameau*, the passions create the male genius, separating him from his rational self and temporarily granting him shamanistic enthusiasm. This view was challenged by arguments such as Condorcet's and Charles Fourier's favoring women's ability to access such exalted realms.

Skepticism toward reason ultimately alienated genius from the rational faculties entirely, heralding the coming of Romanticism*. The medical testimony of Pierre Cabanis and Julien-Joseph Virey denies the female's intellectual capacity, supporting the configuration of the Romantic genius (Balzac's, Gautier's) as a biological male whose mind possesses stereotypically feminine qualities—intuition, imagination, sensitivity, emotion. As Carl Jung would later reinforce, this androgynous "feminine" male genius has no female counterpart. The tragic demise of Germaine de Staël's* title character in *Corinne ou de l'Italie* illustrates the inadmissibility of genius for the Romantic heroine.

Just as the late nineteenth century defined genius as doomed heir to a degenerative disease, an alternative manifestation to epilepsy or mental retardation, so twentieth-century psychoanalytic theories built on Freud's consider genius a psychic abnormality. As (post)modern genius falls into melancholic decomposition, male authors routinely speak of the realization of their ideas and works through the metaphor of childbirth in order to safeguard their political advantage and assure the immortality of their progeny. However, the female mind has reclaimed its body, devising strategies such as Cixous's* *l'écriture féminine** and Kristeva's* linguistic theories to free the spirit of female genius.

Virginia Marino

BIBLIOGRAPHY

Battersby, Christine. *Gender and Genius: Towards a Feminist Aesthetics*. Bloomington: Indiana University Press, 1989.

Besser, Gretchen R. *Balzac's Concept of Genius: The Theme of Superiority in the "Comédie Humaine."* Geneva: Librairie Droz, 1969.

Condorcet, Nicolat Caritat de. *Lettres d'un bourgeois de Newhaven à un citoyen de Virginie sur l'inutilité de partager le pouvoir législatif en plusieurs corps.* 1788. Reprinted as *Sur les élections*. Paris: Fayard, 1986.

Diderot, Denis. *Neveu de Rameau. Oeuvres romanesques*. Ed. Henri Benac. Paris: Editions Garnier Frères, 1979.

Fraisse, Geneviève. *Reason's Muse: Sexual Difference and the Birth of Democracy*. Trans. Jane Marie Todd. Chicago: University of Chicago Press, 1994.

Friedman, Susan Stanford. "Creativity and the Childbirth Metaphor: Gender Difference in Literary Discourse." In *Speaking of Gender*. Ed. Elaine Showalter. New York: Routledge, Chapman and Hall, 1989. 73–100.

Guerlac, Suzanne. "Transgression in Theory: Genius and the Subject of *La Révolution du langage poètique*." In *Ethics, Politics, and Difference in Julia Kristeva's Writing*. Ed. Kelly Oliver. New York: Routledge, 1993. 238–257.

Marini, Marcelle. "The Creators of Culture in France." Trans. Arthur Goldhammer. In *A History of Women: Toward a Cultural Identity in the Twentieth Century*. Ed. Georges Duby and Michelle Perrot. Cambridge, MA: Harvard University Press, 1994. 297–323.

Murray, Penelope, ed. *Genius: The History of an Idea*. New York: Basil Blackwell, 1989.
Pizan, Christine de. *Livre de la cité des dames*. Paris: Stock, 1986.
Staël, Germaine de. *Corinne ou l'Italie*. 2 vols. Ed. Claudine Herrmann. Paris: Editions
    Des femmes, 1979.

Genlis, Stéphanie Félicité Ducrest de Saint-Aubin, marquise de Sillery, comtesse de (1746–1830). A prolific memorialist of Old Regime and Revolutionary France and a writer of novels* and children's plays, Mme de Genlis was a product of eighteenth-century France and the governess/tutor of the children of Philippe, duc d'Orléans, whose family represented a collateral line to the throne of France.

Born into a noble family in Burgundy, and talented in music and literature, Félicité de Saint-Aubin was married at age sixteen to the Comte de Sillery, who was guillotined during the radical phase of the Revolution*. According to her memoirs*, her introduction to the court of Louis XV made her consider more liberal views of politics and gender. Over-rouged and over-corsetted at her debut, she recognized the artificial and ornamental nature that court society had assigned to her sex.

Traveling within Parisian salon* society of the late eighteenth century, Genlis also became a supporter of constitutional monarchy and fiscal reform. As the tutor of the duc d'Orléans' children, she began to frame her educational philosophy which, while criticizing the immoralities of Old Regime court society and the gendered roles of aristocratic men and women, nonetheless challenged the vulgarization of language, the spread of libelous literature (e.g., *Candide*), and the leveling of society. Writing in a witty, conversational style, filled with piquant anecdotes about her youth within the nobility, her books were immediately popular. Like other writers within her circle, she also condemned cloistering and arranged marriages* for young women.

When the French Revolution moved from constitutional liberalism to republicanism and the guillotine* became a force in social control, Genlis condemned the Revolution for its excesses and emigrated. She returned to France only after the rise of Napoleon, who granted her a substantial pension and provided a residence in Paris so that she might assist in his building a new court society. Later she received an additional pension from Napoleon's sister-in-law, Julie Bonaparte, and carried on a lengthy correspondence with Napoleon's sister Elisa during her betrothal (1812–1813). Her plays and writings on Old Regime society remained popular, and some of her comedies, particularly children's theater, were performed at schools directed by Mme Campan* during the First Empire. Her recommendations for the young (both boys and girls) included a more practical curriculum, while maintaining linguistic discipline, and moral tales and comedies to teach appropriate behavior.

Interestingly, in spite of the volume of her work, she is rarely mentioned in dictionaries of the period. As a critic of Old Regime court society, Genlis has more often been supplanted by men such as Choderlos de Laclos, who also knew the world of the duc d'Orléans. On education*, Mme Campan is more often cited than she. Perhaps Sainte-Beuve described best where Genlis has been placed in history when he noted that she was ''one of the names most cited, the most familiar to the ear, and one of those who leaves the least tidy remembrance among new generations.''

Susan P. Conner

BIBLIOGRAPHY

Primary Texts

Précis de l'histoire des femmes françaises les plus célèbres. Paris: Maradan, 1811.
Mémoires inédits de Mme la comtesse de Genlis sur le XVIIIe siècle et la Révolution française, depuis 1756 jusqu'à nos jours. Paris: Ladvocat, 1825.
Oeuvres. Paris: Lecointe et Durey, 1825–1826.
De l'esprit des étiquettes de l'ancienne cour et des usages du monde de ce temps. Rennes: H. Callière, 1885.

Secondary Texts

Broglie, Gabriel de. *Madame de Genlis.* Paris: Librairie Académique Perrin, 1985.
Wyndham, Violet. *Madame de Genlis: A Biography.* London: A. Deutsch, 1958.

Gennari, Geneviève (1920–). Gennari, born in Italy but raised and educated in France, wrote novels*, essays, short stories*, and literary criticism. Her admiration for Simone de Beauvoir* and her preoccupation with existentialist notions of freedom and responsibility inspired her to publish a biography of Beauvoir. *Le Dossier de la femme* (1965), one of Gennari's most significant works, is a historical study that documents the status of French women between 1889 and 1964. In the introduction, which suggests parallels between Gennari and today's ''essentialist'' feminists, she expresses her belief in the existence of a fundamental feminine nature.

A recurrent theme in Gennari's texts is the alienation suffered by women struggling to transcend the conflict between career ambitions and traditional domestic duties. Unresolved issues in her own role as woman and writer led her to undergo psychoanalysis, an experience she recounts in *La Robe rouge* (1978). A member of the first wave of feminist writers, Gennari laid the groundwork for contemporary explorations of the causes and consequences of women's marginalization in society.

Patrice J. Proulx

BIBLIOGRAPHY

Primary Texts

Les Cousines Muller. Paris: Horay-Flore, 1949.
J'éveillerai l'Aurore. Paris: Horay-Flore, 1952.
Simone de Beauvoir. Paris: Editions Universitaires, 1958.
Journal d'une bourgeoise. Paris: Grasset, 1959.
Nouvelles du temps et de l'espace. Paris: Librairie Académique Perrin, 1964.
Le Dossier de la femme. Paris: Librairie Académique Perrin, 1965.

La Fugue irlandaise. Paris: Julliard, 1973.
Un Mois d'août à Paris. Paris: Tchou, 1977.
La Robe rouge. Paris: Tchou, 1978.

Secondary Texts

Becker, Lucille. *Twentieth Century French Women Novelists*. Boston: Twayne, 1989.
Lamoureux, Agnès. "Comment écrivent les femmes: Geneviève Gennari." *La Revue des Deux Mondes* (August 1, 1964): 384–393.
Robinson, Jean Hardy. *Geneviève Gennari*. Boston: Twayne, 1984.

Geoffrin, Marie-Thérèse Rodet (1699–1777). One of the more famous bourgeois women of the eighteenth century, Mme Geoffrin became a leading salon* hostess, tutor of a future monarch, and promoter of intelligent and talented French women and men. Orphaned and reared by her somewhat unusual and quixotic grandmother, Geoffrin noted early in her childhood the importance of intelligence and sensibility, which could, at least partially, overcome a woman's lack of knowledge. She also believed that reading was among the necessary skills of a successful woman, coupled with a nonconfrontational demeanor and an appreciation for lifelong learning.

Geoffrin's introduction into salon society came through her marriage* at age fourteen, and her apprenticeship in Mme de Tencin's* salon in Paris. While Tencin's salon remained primarily literary, Geoffrin later invited musicians and painters to her salon on the rue St. Honoré. For more than twenty-five years she cultivated young women like Julie de Lespinasse*, ran her salon like a business (even keeping a journal of her guests, activities, and expenses), and turned the career of *salonnière* into an art. Religion was a forbidden topic, and she demanded, through one of her famous maxims, that her guests "give and forgive" in the course of their conversations.

Criticized by Voltaire for her inability to write well, and by Montesquieu for her less than adulatory reception of *L'Esprit des lois*, she found Fontenelle to be among her greatest teachers and admirers. She was reputed to be a remarkable conversationalist with the ability to reduce scientific treatises to common language, and she disliked excess in speech, dress, and behavior. Her guest list was established accordingly. In later years, she was invited to Poland by Stanislas Poniatowski, who had become king of Poland but whose youth had been shaped by her tutelage.

Susan P. Conner

BIBLIOGRAPHY

Secondary Texts

Aldis, Janet. *Madame Geoffrin, Her Salon and Her Times, 1750–1777*. New York: Putnam, 1905.
Clergue, Helen. *The Salon: A Study of French Society and Personalities in the Eighteenth Century*. New York: G. P. Putnam's Sons, 1907.

Sainte-Beuve, Charles Augustin. *Portraits of the Eighteenth Century, Historic and Literary*. New York: Putnam, 1905.

Ségur, Pierre Marie Maurice Henri, comte de. *Le Royaume de la rue Saint-Honoré: Madame Geoffrin et sa fille*. Paris: Calmann-Lévy, 1898.

Stanislaw II, August, King of Poland. *Correspondance inédite du roi Stanislas-Auguste Poniatowski et de madame Geoffrin, 1764–1777*. Paris: Plon, 1875.

Germain, Sylvie (1954–). Novelist and professor of philosophy, Germain taught at the Lycée Français in Prague for seven years. She is best known for her historical and fantastic trilogy: *Jours de colère* (1989), *Le Livre des nuits* (1985), and *Nuit-d'Ambre* (1987). Here, as in the rest of her work, Germain presents the epic themes of life and death, love and war, survival and loss, which are expressed through recurrent metaphors related to night and dawn, birth and rebirth. Her characters—especially those of the trilogy—are crushed under the weight of a history that constantly repeats itself. Throughout her work, Germain juxtaposes the realistic and the supernatural, the historical and the poetic, in order to explore the questions of madness, passion, evil, and redemption. Her lyrical approach to metaphysical questions in *La Pleurante des rues de Prague* (1992) is organized around a female character, a vagabond whose gentle crying stands as a metaphor for universal suffering. The weeping woman figure thus reinforces the image of woman's body as a symbol of voice and pain.

Martine Motard-Noar

BIBLIOGRAPHY

Primary Texts

Le Livre des nuits. Paris: Gallimard, 1985.
Nuit-d'Ambre. Paris: Gallimard, 1987.
Jours de colère. Paris: Gallimard, 1989.
L'Enfant Méduse. Paris: Gallimard, 1991.
La Pleurante des rues de Prague. Paris: Gallimard, 1992.
Immensités. Paris: Gallimard, 1993.
Eclats de sel. Paris: Gallimard, 1995.
Les Echos du silence. Paris: Desclée de Brouwer, 1996.

Gille, Elisabeth (1937–1996). Novelist, essayist, and translator of such American writers as Kate Millett, Mary Gordon, and Alison Lurie. Gille's parents—and most of her family members—were deported from France and perished in concentration camps during World War II*, events that she fictionalizes in several of her works. *Un Paysage de cendres* (1996), which emphasizes the importance of female bonding as a survival strategy for the orphaned Léa Lévy, also critiques French complicity in the fate of the Jews and explores the thematics of memory and forgetting. This text elaborates on themes developed in *Le Mirador* (1992), a fictional autobiography* of Gille's mother, Russian émigré writer Irène Némirovsky. In *Le Crabe sur la banquette arrière* (1994), written as a series of brief dialogues between such generic characters as "the sick woman'' and ''the daughter,'' Gille depicts her own battle with cancer and presents an ironic commentary on the way in which society dehumanizes the chronically ill.

Patrice J. Proulx

BIBLIOGRAPHY

Primary Texts

Le Mirador: Mémoires rêvés. Paris: Presses de la Renaissance, 1992.
Le Crabe sur la banquette arrière. Paris: Mercure de France, 1994.
Un Paysage de cendres. Paris: Seuil, 1996.

Giroud, Françoise (1916–). Born in Geneva, Giroud had to drop out of school at age fourteen to help support her family after her father's death. Her career as a journalist and best-selling author started when she was recruited as a screen-writer and assistant movie director. During World War II*, she wrote short stories* for the press and was active in the Resistance until her arrest and im-prisonment. After the Liberation, she collaborated on the creation of *Elle* (1946) and co-founded *L'Express* (1953), with Jean-Jacques Servan-Schreiber. She served as Secretary of State for Women's Condition (1974–1976), and later as Secretary of State for Cultural Affairs (1976–1977). As a cabinet member in charge of women's issues, she focused on promoting women's access to highly skilled professions, worked with Simone Veil to legalize abortion*, and ensured the passage of legislation relaxing divorce laws.

After her experience in politics, chronicled in *La Comédie du pouvoir* (1977), Giroud resumed her activities as a journalist, screenwriter, novelist, biographer, and essayist. Her penetrating interpretation of world events, her brisk and spir-ited style, and the breadth and diversity of her literary interests have earned her the reputation of ''grande dame'' of journalism.

Samia I. Spencer

BIBLIOGRAPHY

Primary Texts

Si je mens. Paris: Stock, 1972.
La Comédie du pouvoir. Paris: Fayard, 1977.
Ce que je crois. Paris: Grasset, 1978.
Une Femme honorable. Paris: Fayard, 1981.
Le Bon Plaisir. Paris: Mazarine, 1983.
Dior. Paris: Editions du Regard, 1987.
Alma Mahler. Paris: Laffont, 1988.
Leçons particulières. Paris: Fayard, 1990.
Jenny Marx ou la femme du diable. Paris: Laffont, 1992.
Les Hommes et les femmes. Paris: Olivier Orban, 1993.
Journal d'une Parisienne. Paris: Seuil, 1994.
Coeur de tigre. Paris: Plon-Fayard, 1995.

Gomez, Madeleine-Angélique Poisson, Dame Gabriel de (1684–1770) was born in Paris to a long line of actors. Married to a profligate Spanish actor, she lived by the pen and was one of the few women playwrights of her time whose plays were staged at the Comédie Française. She captured the contradictory model of female accomplishments and self-expression when the dominant culture's view of women was profoundly negative. Her first sentimental tragedy, *Habis* (1714), triumphed, and was revived in 1732. However, *Marsidie, reine des Cimbres* (1735), *Sémiramis* (1707), and *Cléarque, tyran d'Héraclée* (1717) failed. These political tragedies focus on the suffering of strong-willed women whose heroism lies in rejecting tyranny. Gomez produced many lengthy volumes of fiction, signing her works Mme de Gomez after she remarried. Her short piece, *Journées amusantes* (1722–1731), enjoyed a European vogue. *La Belle Assemblée* (1750), for which she is mostly remembered, ran eight editions, and *Cent Nouvelles* (1711) eighteen. These two popular collections of romances— pseudo-historical stories and exotic-framed tales—reveal the devices and concerns of earlier baroque heroic romances, and a taste for sensibility in the vein of Richardson and Prévost.

S. Pascale Dewey

BIBLIOGRAPHY

Primary Texts

Habis, tragédie. Paris: Pierre Ribou, 1714.

Histoire secrète de la conquête de Grenade. Paris: C. Le Clerc, 1723.

Les Journées amusantes. Paris: N.p., 1723.

Anecdotes ou histoire de la maison ottomane. Lyons: M. Duplain, 1724.

Anecdotes persanes dédiées au roy. Paris: J. B. Mazuel, 1727.

Cent Nouvelles, nouvelles. The Hague: P. de Hont, 1733–1739.

Marsidie, reine des Cimbres, tragédie. Utrecht: Etienne Neaulme, 1735.

Cléarque, tyran d'Héraclée, tragédie. Utrecht: Etienne Neaulme, 1737.

Histoires du comte d'Oxfort, de Milady d'Herby, d'Eustache de St Pierre et de Béatrix de Guiné au siège de Calais. Paris: De Poilly, 1737.

Sémiramis, tragédie en cinq actes et en vers. Utrecht: Etienne Neaulme, 1737.

Crémentine, reine de Sanga, historie indienne. The Hague: H. Van Beeldaren, 1740.

Secondary Texts

Jones, Shirley. "A Woman Novelist of the 1730s: Madame de Gomez." *Studies on Voltaire and the Eighteenth Century* 304 (1992): 788–791.

Jones-Day, Shirley. "A Woman Writer's Dilemma: Madame de Gomez and the Early Eighteenth-Century Novel." In *Femmes savantes et femmes d'esprit: Women Intellectuals of the French Eighteenth-Century*. Ed. Roland Bonnel and Catherine Rubinger. New York: Peter Lang, 1994.

Lancaster, Henry Carrington. *Sunset: A History of Parisian Drama in the Last Years of Louis XIV, 1701–1715*. Baltimore: Johns Hopkins University Press, 1945.

Mish, Charles C. "Mme de Gomez and *La Belle Assemblée*." *Readings in Literary Criticism* 34 (1960): 213–225.

Pitou, Spire. "Pierre Corneille and Madame de Gomez's *Marsidie*." *Romance Notes* 13 (1972): 492–495.

Gouges, Olympe de (née Marie Gouze) (1748–1793). The illegitimate daughter of Voltaire's nemesis, poet Jean-Jacques Le Franc de Pompignan, Gouze was born and raised in Montauban. Widowed at nineteen, after a short-lived unhappy marriage* to Louis-Yves Aubry and the birth of his son, Pierre, she moved to Paris with Jacques Biétrix de Rozières, whom she refused to marry, preferring, instead, the more independent status of concubine.

After a decade of libertine life, Gouges joined a circle of intellectuals and launched a literary career, this despite being uneducated and having learned to speak French only after arriving in Paris—her native tongue was Occitan. Unable to write, she dictated her works, beginning with *Mémoire de Madame de Valmont contre l'ingratitude et la cruauté de la famille de Flaucourt* (1784), a largely autobiographical novel*, followed by some forty plays of varying length, and scores of political letters and pamphlets.

To date, her best known work remains *The Declaration of the Rights of Woman* (1791), dedicated to Marie-Antoinette* and patterned after *The Declaration of the Rights of Man* (1790). Because of her unflinching feminism* and her political outspokenness, she was viewed by some as lunatic or deranged. However, her social and political opinions reveal a sharp political mind, a judicious analyst, and a foresighted social reformer, who warned against excesses, pleaded against the execution of Louis XVI, advocated national unity, and defended the rights of women and the poor. Indefatigable and undaunted by criticism, she expressed her opinions with uncommon vigor and passion, producing myriads of plays, letters, articles, pamphlets, and memoirs* addressed to the king and his ministers, the queen, the people, the National Convention, and Robespierre—"a cannibal," "a monster" whom she abhorred.

Among her many prophecies was the fate that she and her mortal enemy would share—the guillotine*—her hope being that posterity would render her justice. Although shunned in her times and her proposals generally ignored, she has been vindicated. Many of her ideas on the rights of women, the poor, and children born out of wedlock; on prenuptial agreements and divorce*; on health and welfare programs; and on social, political, and fiscal reform have now become common practice.

Samia I. Spencer

BIBLIOGRAPHY

Primary Texts

Oeuvres de la citoyenne de Gouges en deux volumes formant le recueil de ses ouvrages dramatiques et politiques. Paris: Chez le Jay père et chez les marchands de nouveautés, 1793.
Oeuvres. Paris: Mercure de France, 1986.
Ecrits politiques. Pref. Olivier Blanc. Paris: Côté-femmes, 1993.
Oeuvres complètes. Intro. Félix-Marcel Castan. Montauban: Cocagne, 1993– .
Mémoire de Madame de Valmont. Paris: Côté-femmes, 1995.

Secondary Texts

Blanc, Olivier. *Une Femme de libertés: Olympe de Gouges*. Paris: Syros Alternatives, 1989.

Duhet, Paule-Marie. *Les Femmes et la Révolution, 1789–1794*. Paris: Julliard, 1971.

Gutwirth, Madelyn. "The Rights and Wrongs of Woman: The Defeat of Feminist Rhetoric by Revolutionary Allegory." In *L'Encyclopédie, Diderot, l'esthétique: Mélanges en hommage à Jacques Chouillet (1915–1990)*. Ed. Sylvain Auroux et al. Paris: Presses Universitaires de France, 1991. 150–168.

Lacour, Léopold. *Les Origines du féminisme contemporain. Trois Femmes de la Révolution*. Paris: Plon-Nourrit, 1900.

Lairtullier, E. *Les Femmes célèbres de 1789 à 1795*. Paris: Librairie Politique, 1840.

Michelet, Jules. *Les Femmes de la Révolution*. Ed. Françoise Giroud. Paris: Carrère, 1988.

Noack, Paul. *Olympe de Gouges, courtisane et militante des droits de la femme, 1748–1793*. Trans. Isabelle Duclos. Paris: Editions de Fallois, 1992.

Gournay, Marie Le Jars de (1565–1645). Gournay is one of the few French women of letters of her time who supported herself through her writing. How difficult it was to be a woman, young and alone, clearly appears in the three autobiographical texts she published during her lifetime: *Copie de la Vie de la Demoiselle de Gournay, Peincture de moeurs* (1616), and *Apologie pour celle qui escrit* (1626). She explains how she came to spend her childhood in Gournay-sur-Aronde after her father's untimely death, discovered Montaigne's *Essais* when she was seventeen, had to deal with a family financial crisis, and decided to settle in Paris in 1599, counting on the patronage of "noble ladies."

Before she became the editor of his *Essais*, Marie de Gournay wrote a "roman discourant," *Le Proumenoir de M. de Montaigne*, which was published in 1594. It is the story of Alinda, a Persian princess, torn between duty to her father and her passion for young Leontin, who seduces and then abandons her. The form chosen by the author allows her to insert a few paragraphs on the topic of the lack of equality between men and women, which would become the basis for her later feminist texts.

At the beginning of the seventeenth century Marie de Gournay actively participated in the intellectual life of her time and exchanged letters with well-known male and female scholars. She wrote several treatises on education* and a polemical pamphlet on the assassination of King Henri IV, *Adieu de l'Ame du Roy de France et de Navarre*, in 1610. Her passionate defense of Ronsard and the Pléiade poets against the new theories of Malherbe concerning the necessity of "purging" the French language provoked violent attacks against her. So did her *Egalité des hommes et des femmes* in 1626. Although she supported the idea of the French Academy, renewed the approach to translating classical texts, and developed original ideas on poetry* and philology, Marie de Gournay was often and unfairly portrayed as a conservative "old hag" by her critics. On the contrary, her collected works, *L'Ombre de la Demoiselle de Gournay* (1626) and *Les Advis ou les Presens de la Demoiselle de Gournay* (1641), reveal her to be a shrewd linguist and literary critic, a first-rate translator, an accomplished autobiographer, and an original thinker on the questions of education, ethics, and women's rights—a writer with a work of her own.

Elyane Dezon-Jones

BIBLIOGRAPHY

Primary Texts

Les Advis ou les Presens de la Demoiselle de Gournay. Paris: Jean Du Bray, 1641.
Preface to the 1595 edition of Montaigne's *Essais*, with an introduction by François Rigolot. *Montaigne Studies* 1 (1989).
Le Proumenoir de M. de Montaigne, par sa fille d'alliance. Pref. Patricia Cholakian. Scholars' Facsimile Reprints. New York: Delmar, 1985.

Secondary Texts

Dezon-Jones, Elyane. *Marie de Gournay: Fragments d'un discours féminin.* Paris: Corti, 1988.
Ilsley, Marjorie. *A Daughter of the Renaissance: Marie le Jars de Gournay.* The Hague: Mouton, 1963.
Sankovitch, Tilde A. *French Women Writers and the Book.* Syracuse: Syracuse University Press, 1988.

Graffigny, Françoise d'Issembourg de (1695–1758). Françoise d'Issembourg d'Happoncourt was born into the minor nobility in Nancy. Her 1712 marriage* to an abusive husband, François Huguet de Graffigny, ended in a legal separation after nine years and the birth of three children, all of whom died in infancy. In addition to a single and immensely successful novel*, Graffigny wrote stories (including *La Nouvelle espagnole* and *La Princesse Azerolle*), fables, plays (*Cénie* and *La Fille d'Aristide*), and an abundant correspondence. Some 2,500 letters have survived, mostly addressed to her friend François-Antoine Devaux. They began corresponding around 1733, and over the next few decades she wrote him frequent if not daily letters, chronicling literary, social, and political news, as well as her interminable financial worries, her changes of residence, her health concerns, and the vicissitudes of her fourteen-year liaison with a cavalry officer named Léopold Desmarest. The letters she sent during the winter of 1738–1739 from Cirey, where she was the increasingly unwelcome guest of Voltaire and Emilie du Châtelet*, are full of high drama and are an incomparable source of information on the daily routines of Voltaire. Later letters document the anxious gestation of Graffigny's first play, *Cénie*, which was staged in 1750. Graffigny was a woman of erudition and connections, with exceptional powers of observation. Her correspondence has a double interest: it informs us about the events of the day, while providing unusually frank detail about the intimate organization of a woman's life—all in a spontaneous French laden with genial idiosyncracies of style and spelling.

Her *Lettres d'une Péruvienne*, one of the century's most frequently republished novels, has been recognized in recent years as a boldly feminist work. It recounts in letter form the story of Zilia, an Inca princess kidnapped by the Spaniards during the conquest of Peru. The ship on which she is embarked is overtaken by the French; her French rescuer, Déterville, falls in love with her, but she remains faithful to Aza, the Peruvian fiancé-brother from whom she was separated. Even when she discovers in the end that Aza is about to marry a Spanish woman, Zilia still refuses the hand of Déterville: she offers him friendship* and remains unmarried. Part of Graffigny's originality was to create a woman writing not only—and not even principally—to express her love, but rather to critique cultural and social institutions such as the convent* education* of girls. In order to do so, Zilia acquires a new language (her first letters are composed in *quipos*, an Inca system of writing with knots), a new culture, and a new sense of self. The novel's conclusion (Zilia becomes an independent woman, with a fortune, house, and library of her own) challenged accepted notions of fictional endings and seems to have struck contemporary readers as even more exotic than the Temple of the Sun portrayed at the start: they expected to see a heroine end up either married or dead.

Joan Hinde Stewart

BIBLIOGRAPHY

Primary Texts

"La Nouvelle espagnole." In *Recueil de ces messieurs*. [Caylus, Anne-Claude-Philippe, comte de, et al.] Amsterdam and Paris: Chez les Frères Westein, 1745.
"La Princesse Azerolle." In *Cinq contes de fées*. [Caylus, Anne-Claude-Philippe, comte de.] N.p., 1745.
Cénie. Paris: André Cailleau, 1751.
La Fille d'Aristide. Paris: N. B. Duchesne, 1759.
Correspondance de Madame de Graffigny. 4 vols. to date. Ed. J. A. Dainard, English Showalter, et al. Oxford: Voltaire Foundation, 1985– .
Lettres d'une Péruvienne. Intro. Joan DeJean and Nancy K. Miller. New York: Modern Language Association, 1993.

Secondary Texts

Altman, Janet Gurkin. "Graffigny's Epistemology and the Emergence of Third-World Ideology." In *Writing the Female Voice: Essays on Epistolary Literature*. Ed. Elizabeth C. Goldsmith. Boston: Northeastern University Press, 1989.
———. "A Woman's Place in the Enlightenment Sun: The Case of Françoise de Graffigny." *Romance Quarterly* 38 (August 1991): 261–271.
Grayson, Vera L. "The Genesis and Reception of Mme de Graffigny's *Lettres d'une Péruvienne* and *Cénie*." *Studies on Voltaire and the Eighteenth Century* 336 (1996): 1–152.
Jensen, Katharine Ann. *Writing Love: Letters, Women, and the Novel in France (1605–1776)*. Carbondale: Southern Illinois University Press, 1995.
MacArthur, Elizabeth J. "Devious Narratives: Refusal of Closure in Two Eighteenth-Century Epistolary Novels." *Eighteenth-Century Studies* 21, no. 1 (Fall 1987): 1–20.

Miller, Nancy K. *Subject to Change*. New York: Columbia University Press, 1988.
Robb, Bonnie Arden. "The Easy Virtue of a Peruvian Princess." *French Studies* 46, no. 2 (April 1992): 144–159.
Showalter, English, Jr. "Authorial Self-Consciousness in the Familiar Letter: The Case of Madame de Graffigny." *Yale French Studies* 71 (1986): 113–130.

Groult, Benoîte (1920–). Novelist and essayist. Groult, married at twenty and widowed eight months later, was liberated from her family at an early age. From 1945 to 1953 she worked for French Radio. She had two daughters during a brief remarriage, and a third with her current husband, Paul Guimard, a novelist and journalist. Groult's first work was a translation* of Dorothy Parker's short stories*; this was followed by several books and articles written in collaboration with her sister Flora. In 1972 she published her first novel*, *La Part des choses*. Her next work, *Ainsi soit-elle*, a series of essays on the condition of women, quickly became the "bible" of a new generation of French women. In these essays, which are written with mordant humor, Groult exposes the oppression of women, focusing in particular on issues related to education*, maternity*, and female genital mutilation. Her analysis shows how laws enacted by men reinforce the inequities faced by women. In 1977 she published *Le Féminisme au masculin*, a tribute to the few early men like Condorcet who supported women's issues—and were assumed to be mad. With Claude Servan-Schreiber, she founded *F Magazine* for women (*Femmes*). Groult is the first to acknowledge that she came belatedly to feminism*. Since then, she has been one of the most vehement—and accessible—voices of protest against the second-class treatment of women.

Margaret Collins Weitz

BIBLIOGRAPHY

Primary Texts

La Part des choses. Paris: Grasset, 1972.
Ainsi soit-elle. Paris: Grasset, 1975.
Le Féminisme au masculin. Paris: Denoël-Gonthier, 1977.
Les Vaisseaux du coeur. Paris: Grasset, 1988.
La Moitié de la terre. Paris: Moreau, 1991.
Pauline Roland, ou, Comment la liberté vint aux femmes. Paris: Robert Laffont, 1991.
Cette Mâle Assurance. Paris: Albin Michel, 1993.
Groult, Benoîte, and Flora Groult. *Journal à quatre mains*. Paris: Denoël-Gonthier, 1962.
———. *Le Féminin pluriel*. Paris: Denoël-Gonthier, 1965.
———. *Histoire de Fidèle*. Paris: Editions des femmes, 1976.

Secondary Text

Fouletier-Smith, Nicole. "Benoîte Groult." In *French Women Writers*. Ed. Eva Sartori and Dorothy Zimmerman. Lincoln: University of Nebraska Press, 1991.

Guérin, Eugénie de (1805–1848). Born to an impoverished aristocratic family in a remote area northeast of Toulouse, Guérin spent nearly her entire life in the isolated Château du Cayla. Deeply devoted to her younger brother Maurice, whom she had raised, Guérin exchanged a thoughtful, lively, and extensive correspondence with him when he moved to Paris to further his studies. She, along with George Sand* and Jules Barbey d'Aurévilly, played an instrumental role in the posthumous publication of Maurice de Guérin's highly acclaimed prose poem, *Le Centaure*. Guérin's *Journal*, a series of diary entries from 1834 to 1840, impressive yet unaffected in tone, reveals a complex woman and a gifted writer, frustrated by the limits imposed on her creativity both by her social class and her Catholic faith. The reader is moved by Guérin's tone of profound candor and quiet despair and her use of images from nature as she struggles to find her voice in the silence of her Cayla desert.

Jolene J. Barjasteh

BIBLIOGRAPHY

Primary Texts

Reliquiae. Ed. Jules Barbey-d'Aurévilly and G. S. Trébutien. Caen: Hardel, 1855.
Journal et fragments. Paris: Didier, 1862.
Journal et lettres. Paris: Didier, 1862.
Lettres. Paris: Didier, 1864.

Secondary Texts

Bannour, Wanda. *Eugenie de Guérin, ou une chasteté ardente*. Paris: Albin Michel, 1983.
Smith, Naomi Royde. *The Idol and the Shrine*. London: Hollis and Carter, 1949.

Guesnerie, Charlotte Charbonnière de la. *See* La Guesnerie, Charlotte-Marie-Anne Charbonnier de.

Guibert, Elisabeth (1725–c. 1787). Little is known about her. She published a good amount of occasional poetry* in the *Almanach des Muses*, where it is noted that she received financial support from Louis XV in the form of a pension. In her poetry, Guibert writes from a personal point of view, with resignation and sensitivity. She writes of turning from the frivolous and dangerous pursuits of a young woman to those of maturity and friendship*. She extols the virtues of a simple existence and laments infidelity. She also wrote several stock plays that treat conventional subjects or are inspired by classical themes.

Antoinette Marie Sol

BIBLIOGRAPHY

Primary Texts

Poésies et oeuvres diverses. Amsterdam: N.p., 1764.
La Coquette corrigée, tragédie contre les femmes. N.p., 1764.
Le Sommeil d'Amynthe, par Madame G. Amsterdam: N.p., 1768.
Les Filles à marier, comédie en un acte, en vers, par Mme G. Amsterdam: N.p., 1768.
Pensées détachées. Brussels: N.p., 1770.
Les Philéniens ou le patriotisme. Paris: N.p., 1775.

Guillaumin, Colette (1934–). A sociologist for the Centre National de la Recherche Scientifique, Guillaumin has also taught in Canadian universities. Like Monique Wittig* and Christine Delphy*, she is a longtime member of the materialist feminist collective *Questions féministes*. Guillaumin is the only "French feminist" known first and foremost for her pioneering analysis of racist ideology. She places racist and sexist theories and practices in the context of broader racist and sexist ideologies, analyzing the material and historical conditions of the emergence of racist doctrines. She has worked consistently to deconstruct and denaturalize modern notions of race and gender through meticulous historical analysis. She shows that the idea of natural, biological differences between dominant and dominated groups is a creation of the dominant group to perpetuate social relations of exploitation and oppression. According to Guillaumin, the proof that these distinctions are not natural is the systematic and institutionalized way in which they are constantly enforced through education*, the division of labor, and violence. Throughout her work, Guillaumin emphasizes that, although race and gender do not exist as a natural biological reality, the *ideas* of race and gender function as highly effective political, juridical, and material means of justifying appropriation, subjugation, and murder.

Anne Donadey

BIBLIOGRAPHY

Primary Texts

"Aspects latents du racisme chez Gobineau." *Cahiers Internationaux de Sociologie* 42 (January-June 1967): 145–158.
"Caractères spécifiques de l'idéologie raciste." *Cahiers Internationaux de Sociologie* 53 (July-December 1972): 247–274.
L'Idéologie raciste. Genèse et langage actuel. Paris: Mouton, 1972.
"Sur la notion de minorité." *L'Homme et la société* 77–78 (July-December 1985): 101–109.
Sexe, race et pratique du pouvoir: L'Idée de Nature. Paris: Côté-Femmes Editions, 1992.
Racism, Sexism, Power and Ideology. Ed. Robert Miles. Critical Studies in Racism and Migration. London: Routledge, 1995.

Secondary Text

Juteau-Lee, Danielle. "(Re)Constructing the Categories of 'Race' and 'Sex': The Work of a Precursor." Introduction to *Racism, Sexism, Power and Ideology.* Ed. Robert Miles. Critical Studies in Racism and Migration. London: Routledge, 1995. 1–26.

Guillet, Pernette du (1520?–1545). Poet. In 1536 she met Maurice Scève, who was beginning to write the Petrarchist poems that would assure his fame. She was probably the model for the woman he celebrates in his most famous collection of poems, *Délie*.

Married in 1538 (Guillet is her married name), she died at age twenty-five during an epidemic. To honor her memory, her husband asked Antoine du Moulin to prepare an edition of her poems. The volume was published the same year under the title *Rymes*.

A slender book of about eighty pages, the *Rymes* consists of sixty short epigrams, ten songs, five elegies, and two epistles. Throughout the work, the speaking subject (always female) pitches her voice in two different registers. Working within a poetic tradition in which all writing is essentially a rewriting of canonical texts, Guillet assumes the passive position of adored mistress and muse that Petrarchist, specifically Scevian, poetry* assigned to her. She tells how, prior to meeting Scève (identified simply as ''him''), she existed in a somnolent state that bordered on nonbeing. Then the male poet gazed on her. Illuminated by his presence, she was drawn into the light of day. His gaze had such creative power that it fashioned her into what she has become: his muse, the object of his adoration. Finding her own identity in the eyes of the male Other and becoming what he wishes her to be, she assures us that she is happy.

Gradually, however, the speaking subject shifts into a second register, allowing us to hear fleetingly an angry voice that condemns the Petrarchist model with its reified female idol. Alluding to mythological stories that tell of violence and mutilated female bodies, the female subject evokes, with a persistence that is obsessional, images of nudity, of female rage, of the female body being raped by an all-powerful Other. Such images, however, are distanced by virtue of being set in a mythological context. Then, too, they always appear in the middle of a poem. Nearly all of Guillet's poems end by lowering a veil over the violent scene. The female poet concludes by assuring us that she is content to serve as the male poet's inspiration.

Clearly, Guillet seeks to win plaudits from male Petrarchist poets by assuming the role expected of her. At the same time, expressing an anger that only very recent readers have discerned, she seeks to fashion a place for the female body and for the female subject. Rewriting the Petrarchist scenario (but never so aggressively that it will offend her mentor Scève and like-minded contemporary Petrarchist male poets), Guillet manipulates with tact and cunning the authoritative literary forms handed down to her. In the end, she is able to convey, in a number of strong lyric pieces, her own authorial power as a woman writer.

Robert D. Cottrell

BIBLIOGRAPHY

Primary Texts

Rymes. Ed. Victor Graham. Geneva: Droz, 1968.
Labé, Louise. *Oeuvres poétiques, précédées des Rymes de Pernette du Guillet*. Ed. Françoise Charpentier. Paris: Gallimard, ''Coll. Poésie,'' 1983.

Secondary Texts

Cottrell, Robert D. ''Pernette du Guillet and the Logic of Aggressivity.'' In *Writing the Renaissance*. Ed. Raymond C. La Charité. Lexington, KY: French Forum, 1992. 93–113.

Jones, Ann Rosalind. "Assimilation with a Difference: Renaissance Women and Literary Influence." *Yale French Studies* 62 (1981): 135–153.

———. *The Currency of Eros: Women's Love Lyric in Europe.* Bloomington: Indiana University Press, 1990.

Mathieu-Castellani, Gisèle. "La Parole chétive: Les *Rymes* de Pernette du Guillet." *Littérature* 73 (1989): 47–60.

Saulnier, V.-L. "Etude sur Pernette du Guillet et ses *Rymes.*" *Bibliothèque d'Humanisme et Renaissance* 4 (1944): 7–119.

Winn, Colette H. "Le Chant de la nouvelle née." *Poétique* 78 (1989): 207–217.

Guillotine (1792–1982). Known in Italy as the mannaia, in England as the Halifax gibbet, and in Scotland as the Maiden, the guillotine was inaugurated in France in March 1792 at the height of the Revolutionary era. There it bore a number of names, including the nation's razor, the republican sword, the national axe, the people's avenger, the patriotic shortener, and explicitly gendered titles such as Sainte Guillotine, Dame Guillotine, and the Widow.

Beginning in January 1790, the national government of France approved portions of a plan submitted by Deputy Joseph-Ignace Guillotin (1738–1814) to revise the penal code. Rank and privilege were excluded from consideration in determining punishments, sanctions fell solely on the individual, confiscation of goods was prohibited, and the family retained the right to recover the body. One remaining article was proposed by Guillotin: to create an egalitarian and speedy form of capital punishment.

Of the nearly twenty thousand persons who went to the guillotine during the height of revolutionary executions (1792–1794), one-seventh were women, including aristocrats, nuns, working women, servants, and prostitutes. The famous and infamous, including Marie-Antoinette*, Charlotte Corday*, Manon Roland*, Olympe de Gouges*, and Louis XV's mistress, Mme du Barry*, were among them. Their trials and obituaries bear witness to the virulence of revolutionary misogyny: Marie-Antoinette was voracious sexually, and had tried to emasculate the French nation; Barry was lascivious; Olympe de Gouges and Manon Roland had wanted to be men; Charlotte Corday evidenced unfeminine fanaticism.

There is ample evidence that, while women were the minority of victims of the guillotine during the course of the French Revolution*, the machine itself was clearly gendered: on the simplest level, the word "guillotine" is feminine in the French language, the name being based on the feminine gender of the word "machine." In such a context, the guillotine entered verse, songs and popular language. On a more symbolic level, it became Our Lady of the Carrousel, amputating gangrenous members of the "body politic," or it was given holy attributes for its powers of purification.

The guillotine remained the French form of execution until capital punishment was ended in 1982.

Susan P. Conner

BIBLIOGRAPHY

Arasse, Daniel. *The Guillotine and the Terror.* London: Penguin, 1989.

Cortequisse, Bruno. *La Sainte Guillotine.* Paris: Editions France-Empire, 1988.

Fleischmann, Hector. *La Guillotine en 1793, d'après des documents inédits des Archives nationales.* Paris: Librarie des publications modernes, 1908.

Kershaw, Alister. *A History of the Guillotine.* London: J. Calder, 1965.

Lenotre, G. [Louis Gosselin]. *La Guillotine et les exécuteurs des arrêts criminels pendant la Révolution.* Paris: Perrin et Cie., 1922.

Nash, Camille. *Death Comes to the Maiden: Sex and Execution, 1431–1933.* London: Routledge, 1991.

Guizot, Elisabeth-Charlotte-Pauline de Meulan (1773–1827). Guizot was born into a wealthy family whose salon* welcomed many notable figures of the time. In 1790 her father died, leaving the family's finances in ruin. Pauline took charge and turned to writing to earn money. She wrote two novels*; however, she soon turned to journalism and made her living writing columns for *Le Publiciste.* These often treated moral issues or were pieces of theatrical and literary criticism. Germaine de Staël* and Sainte-Beuve were among her admirers, but others considered her compromised by writing for the public. In 1812 she married the historian and politician François Guizot. During the politically turbulent 1820s, Pauline Guizot once again found herself in the position of having to write to support her family*. This time she wrote moral tales for children which, reedited and translated into many languages, met with great success. They often depict a woman without a husband coping with family finances as well as the education* of her children. Her articles as well as her fiction contain undercurrents of criticism of the limitations imposed on women by society.

Antoinette Marie Sol

BIBLIOGRAPHY

Primary Texts

Les Contradictions ou ce qui peut en arriver. Paris: Marandon, an septième [1799].

La Chapelle d'Ayton, ou Emma Courtney, imitée de l'anglais. 5 vols. Paris: Marandan, an septième [1799].

Essais de littérature et de morale. Paris: N.p., 1802.

Les Enfants: Contes à l'usage de la jeunesse. 2 vols. Paris: Delaunay, 1812.

L'Ecolier: Ou Raoul et Victor. 4 vols. Paris: Didier, 1821.

Nouveaux contes à l'usage de la jeunesse. 2 vols. Paris: Didier, 1823.

Education domestique, ou Lettre de famille sur l'éducation. 2 vols. Paris: A. Leroux et Constant-Chantpie, 1826.

Conseils de morale, ou essais sur l'homme, les moeurs, les caractères, le monde, les femmes, l'éducation, etc. 2 vols. Paris: Pinchon et Didier, 1828.

Guyon, Jeanne-Marie Bouvier de la Mothe, dame (1648–1717). Born in Montargis into an aristocratic family of modest means, she married Jacques Guyon at the age of sixteen. He was the heir of a successful local family and was twenty-two years older than she. The marriage was unhappy, primarily due to Jeanne's mother-in-law's hostility toward her. They had five children. A widow at the age of twenty-eight, she became free to pursue her spiritual vocation, which led her first to Savoie, where she was involved in a religious institution for young women who had recently converted from Protestantism to Catholicism. Following a series of disappointments, travels, and vicissitudes, including a serious sickness, she returned to Paris in 1686. Her teaching of "contemplative orison" and her charismatic presence became a pole of attraction for spiritual seekers. In the context of the anti-quietist campaign against the Spanish mystic Molinos, in 1687, she became the epicenter of a drawn-out theological quarrel and persecution instigated by Madame de Maintenon*. Although initially favorably disposed toward her teachings, Bossuet turned hostile toward her, and after a series of intense interviews would condemn her works and her mores, probably under the influence of Madame de Maintenon. Fénelon, with whom she had been in close spiritual relationship since 1688, would become the standard-bearer of her mystical doctrine in striving to demonstrate its conformity to the spiritual tradition of the Church in his *Explication des maximes des saints*. This work was condemned by Rome in 1699. In the meantime, Jeanne Guyon spent more than seven years in captivity, including five years at the Bastille. Liberated in 1703, she spent the last fourteen years of her life in Blois, surrounded by a group of friends and disciples, such as the Scottish knight Ramsay.

Guyon's life and teachings have been considered by some critics as the major episode in the "twilight of mystics" (Louis Cognet) in the Christian West. In the apologetic and dogmatic context of the Counter-Reformation, her works bear witness to the inward dimension of Christian spirituality. Profoundly distrustful of the presumptions of "rational" autonomy, while totally submissive to the authority of the Church, Guyon emphasized the total surrender of the soul to God's guidance and the inner silence of mere contemplation. Critics such as Françoise Mallet-Joris have shown how she was able to claim the inferior status of women in the social and institutional context of her time in order to use it as a vehicle and a symbol of her whole mystical doctrine. Such is one of the major meanings of her emphasis on spiritual "childlikeness" and "passivity" on the spiritual path.

Patrick Laude

BIBLIOGRAPHY

Primary Texts

Madame Guyon et Fénelon. La Correspondance secrète. Ed. Benjamin Sahler. Paris: Dervy-Livres, 1982.
La Vie de Madame Guyon écrite par elle-même. Ed. Benjamin Sahler. Paris: Dervy-Livres, 1983.
Récits de captivité. Ed. Marie-Louise Gondal. Grenoble: Jérôme Millon, 1992.
Les Torrents et Commentaire au Cantique des cantiques de Salomon. Ed. Claude Morali. Grenoble: Jérôme Millon, 1992.

Secondary Texts

Gondal, Marie-Louise. *Madame Guyon (1648–1717): Un Nouveau Visage*. Paris: Beauchesne, 1989.

Laude, Patrick. *Approches du quiétisme.* Seattle: Biblio 17, 1992.
Mallet-Joris, Françoise. *Jeanne Guyon.* Paris: Flammarion, 1978.

Gyp (Sybille Gabrielle Marie Antoinette de Riquetti de Mirabeau, comtesse de Martel de Janville) (1849–1932). The author of more than sixty novels* and numerous newspaper articles and caricatures, Gyp is remembered as a political activist as well as a woman of letters. Her first book, *Petit Bob* (1882), establishes the style for all her future works. As a chronicler of her era, she denounced what she considered the corruptions of society. Taking sides on every political matter of the time, her literary works are filled with anti-Semitic views, anti-Dreyfusard partisanship, and personal reflections about the war and patriotism. Her association with newspapers such as *La Libre Parole, Le Drapeau,* and *La Tribune française* identified her as an extremist.

Although she did not consider herself a feminist, her life as a woman justifies such a description. Gyp was the sole source of income for her household, supporting a husband, three children, and a demanding lifestyle. She had her own salon* in which she participated in political debates, and she campaigned for various candidates. She was asked to contribute to *La Fronde,* a feminist newspaper headed by Marguerite Durand* which hired only female employees. Her female characters were of an independent nature, strong-willed and opposed to traditional conventions such as marriages* of convenience.

Frédérique Van de Poel-Knottnerus

BIBLIOGRAPHY

Primary Texts

Petit Bob. Paris: Calmann-Lévy, 1882.
La Vertu de la baronne. Paris: Calmann-Lévy, 1882.
Autour du divorce. Paris: Calmann-Lévy, 1886.
Israël. Paris: Flammarion, 1898.
Bijou. Paris: Collection Nelson, 1914.
Les Flanchards. Paris: Fayard, 1917.
Souvenirs d'une petite fille. 2 vols. Paris: Calmann-Lévy, 1927–1928.

Secondary Texts

Bonnefont, Gaston. *Les Parisiennes chez elles: Nos grandes dames—Madame la comtesse de Martel (Gyp).* Paris: Flammarion, 1895.
Lorrain, Jean. *Femmes de 1900.* Paris: Editions de la Madeleine, 1932.
Missoffe, Michel. *Gyp et ses amis.* Paris: Flammarion, 1932.
Mouttet, A. *Une Arrière-Petite-Nièce de Mirabeau.* Aix-en-Provence: Achille Macaire, 1889.
Silverman, Willa Z. *The Notorious Life of Gyp, Right-Wing Anarchist in Fin-de-Siècle France.* New York: Oxford University Press, 1995.

H

Halimi, Gisèle (1927–). Feminist attorney and writer. Born in Tunisia, Halimi witnessed the French colonial repression of April 1938 and the early leadership of Bourguiba. Despite the Pétainist culture and anti-Semitism which prevailed in Tunisia, the Jewish Halimi founded the Union of Tunisian Girls, a political left-wing organization for female Tunisian youth. After World War II*, she went to Paris, where she completed a law degree and established her practice.

During the 1960s and 1970s, Halimi successfully defended women and victims of political repression and wrote about the ideological and social significance of these events. She was involved in some of France's most controversial and historically significant trials: the revelation of the torture inflicted upon a young Algerian woman, Djamila Boupacha, by French colonial authorities; her defense of forty-four Algerians accused of carrying out a massacre and rebellion (*El Halia*, 1955); the Bobigny case, which led to the liberalization of legislation on abortion*; and the famous rape* trial of 1978 challenging lax legislation on sexual assault. In 1971 Halimi was one of the 343 women who signed "Le Manifeste de 343," thereby declaring publicly that they had had abortions. Halimi is currently president of the France-based movement Choisir, La Cause des Femmes (The Right to Choose), an organization co-founded with Beauvoir* in 1971, and remains an active feminist leader and legal counselor.

Betty L. McLane-Iles

BIBLIOGRAPHY

Primary Texts

Djamila Boupacha. Preface by Simone de Beauvoir. Paris: Gallimard, 1961.
Le Procès de Burgos. Preface by J. P. Sartre. Paris: Gallimard, 1971.
Avortement: Une Loi en procès-L'affaire de Bobigny. Paris: Gallimard, 1973.
Viol: Le Procès d'Aix-en-Provence. Paris: Gallimard, 1978.
Le Lait de l'oranger. Paris: Gallimard, 1988.

Femmes: Moitié de la terre, moitié du pouvoir. Paris: Gallimard, 1994.
Une Embellie perdue. Paris: Gallimard, 1995.
Halimi, Gisèle, with Marie Cardinal. *La Cause des femmes*. Paris: Editions Grasset, 1973.

   Secondary Texts

Alleg, Henri. *La Question*. Paris: Editions de Minuit, 1958.
Beauvoir, Simone de. *La Force de l'âge*. Paris: Gallimard, 1963.
Vidal-Naquet, Pierre. *La Torture dans la République*. Paris: Editions de Minuit, 1972.

Harlor (1871–1970). Harlor, a pseudonym for Jeanne Clotilde Désirée Perrot, was a prize-winning novelist, the author of five biographies, as well as an art critic, journalist, and activist. For ten years she was a feature editor of *La Fronde*, a weekly newspaper founded in 1896 by Marguerite Durand*. Under the influence of Léopold Lacour, the author of *L'Humanisme intégral*, Harlor fought for women's civic and social equality. These concerns inform many of her novels*, including *Arielle, fille des champs*, the story of a talented peasant girl deprived of an education*; *Le Pot de réséda*, which recounts the plight of a victim of rape*; and other works in which the protagonists search for their freedom in the midst of discrimination and prejudice.

Pauline Newman-Gordon

BIBLIOGRAPHY

   Primary Texts

Le Triomphe des vaincus. Paris: Bibliothèque des Réformes Sociales, 1908.
Tu es femme. Paris: Plon, 1913.
Léopold Lacour. Paris: Sansot, Les Célébrités d'Aujourd'hui, 1914.
Liberté, Liberté chérie. Paris: Crès, 1916.
Le Pot de réséda. Paris: Albin Michel, 1921.
Benvenuto Cellini. Paris: Editions Nilsson, 1924.
Arielle, fille des champs. Paris: Le Rouge et le Noir, 1930.
Gustave Geffroy. Paris: E. Rey, 1933.
Georges Lecomte. Paris: Champion, 1935.
Pascale ou l'Ecole du bonheur. Paris: Editions du Dauphin, 1955.
Les Enamourés, dix contes. Alfort, Seine: Editions du Manuscrit, n.d.

   Secondary Text

Newman-Gordon, Pauline. ''Elements of Feminist Discourse in Harlor.'' *Simone de Beauvoir Studies* 10 (1993): 63–66.

Hausser, Isabelle (?–). Novelist and translator of Eastern European novels*. Many of Hausser's novels recount women's stories and, as in *Nitchevo* (1993), are often linked to Russia, where she lived for several years. In *Une Nuit* (1987), her most interesting novel from a feminist perspective, a woman gives birth in her country house with the help of her best friend, Anne. The text is structured around the rhythm, contractions, and pain of Florence's pregnant body. Between Florence's contractions, Anne recounts stories about her own life, and at the end of the novel the birth of Florence's baby coincides with Anne's birth as a mature woman.

Joëlle Vitiello

BIBLIOGRAPHY

Primary Texts

Célubée. Paris: Julliard, 1986.
Une Nuit. Paris: Julliard, 1987.
Nitchevo. Paris: Editions de Fallois, 1993.
Les Magiciens de l'âme. Paris: Editions de Fallois, 1996.

Hébert, Anne (1916–). Born in Sainte-Catherine-de-Fossambault, Québec, Hébert has lived in Paris since the mid-1950s and has produced a large, greatly admired body of work. She is a highly esteemed author in Canada and throughout the Francophone world, as indicated by the attention devoted to her work at international colloquia organized by French universities. She has also enjoyed impressive official recognition on both sides of the Atlantic, thrice winning Canada's highest literary award, the Governor-General's, twice Québec's highest literary distinction, the Prix David, and Québec's Prix Alain Grandbois, France's Prix des Libraires and Prix Fémina, Belgium's Prix de l'Académie royale, and Monaco's Prix du Prince Rainier.

Hébert has publicly declared her feminism*. Her work displays keen awareness of the complexities of the feminist problematic. She denounces the oppression women have suffered, and demystifies, ridicules, and condemns many aspects of traditional phallocratic institutions (including the influence of organized religion in Québec), while presenting a richly nuanced, diversified vision of women (far less so of men). Hébert's works depict women's oppression, and their brave, inspiring (but often thwarted) aspirations and efforts to lead happy, fulfilling lives. Her works also include characters such as the ''bad'' or repressive mother, and woman as ''castrator'' (of other women as well as of men); such characters have usually become negative as a result of patriarchal oppression, and often serve to highlight by contrast more positive female characters. In Hébert's first novel, *Les Chambres de bois* (1958), for example, the middle-aged servant, Aline, herself the victim of frequent sexual abuse from age thirteen on, first tends to encourage Catherine's evolution toward liberation; later, however, as Catherine begins to challenge the hierarchical class structure of patriarchal society, Aline, nostalgic for the order of a seigneurial Ancien Régime social structure, seeks to discourage Catherine's efforts to free herself. Catherine thus learns to surmount her dependency on Aline and to pursue her own quest for autonomy.

Hébert's awareness of women's oppression and her commitment to feminist struggle are evident in the short stories* of *Le Torrent* (1950) and in the hell-challenging struggle waged by the female protagonist in her volume of poetry*, *Le Tombeau des rois* (1953). The struggle leads to liberation of the female protagonist in both *Les Chambres de bois* and in *Mystère de la parole* (1960), a volume of poetry. These heartening depictions of women's successful liberation give way, in most of her later novels, to a renewed emphasis on the difficulties faced by women: *Kamouraska* (1970), *Les Enfants du sabbat* (1975), *Les Fous de Bassan* (1982), and *Le Premier Jardin* (1988).

Hébert's theater* also presents a rich feminist vision, from young Lucie's quest for intellectual development and higher education* in *Le Temps sauvage* (1960) to the call for female solidarity between French- and English-speaking women in *La Cage* (1990), a particularly significant gesture in the context of contemporary Québec culture, which is dominated by debates about nationalism and the issue of political independence for Québec. *La Cage* suggests that feminism can transcend ethnic, linguistic, and social class differences among women through its promise of the liberation and thus empowerment of an Anglophone character, Lady Rosalinde Crebessa, by the Francophone female protagonist, La Corriveau. Such action by La Corriveau is reflective of Anne Hébert's admirable work, in several literary genres, as a female Francophone writer.

Neil B. Bishop

BIBLIOGRAPHY

Primary Texts

Le Torrent (suivi de deux nouvelles inédites). 1950. Montreal: HMH, 1963.
Les Chambres de bois. Paris: Seuil, 1958.
Le Temps sauvage. La Mercière assassinée. Les Invités au procès. Montreal: HMH, 1967.
Kamouraska. Paris: Seuil, 1970.
Les Enfants du sabbat. Paris: Seuil, 1975.
Héloïse. Paris: Seuil, 1980.
Les Fous de Bassan. Paris: Seuil, 1982.
Le Premier Jardin. Paris: Seuil, 1988.
La Cage. Suivi de L'île de la demoiselle. Montreal: Boréal; Paris: Seuil, 1990.
L'Enfant chargé de songes. Paris: Seuil, 1992.
Oeuvre poétique 1950–1990. Montreal: Boréal, 1992.
Aurélien, Clara, Mademoiselle et le Lieutenant anglais. Paris: Seuil, 1995.

Hébrard, Frédérique (1927–). Daughter of the art historian Lucie Mazauric and the academician André Chamson, Hébrard grew up surrounded by the ebullient intelligentsia of the 1930s—a milieu she invokes in autobiographical novels* such as *La Citoyenne* (1985). Hébrard's fictional works portray powerful women seeking and achieving balance in their lives—most focus on reconciling the needs of an individual woman with those of others. In *Un Mari c'est un mari* (1976), for example, a woman examines her roles and reaffirms her choice of independence, marriage*, and motherhood, while the female protagonist in the more controversial *Le Harem* (1987) contends with social, sexual, and religious taboos. Several of her works have been serialized on television—*Le Château des Oliviers* (1993), for example—making her a popular author whose humanism and feminism* reach many women.

Christine Lac

BIBLIOGRAPHY

Primary Texts

La Petite Fille modèle. Paris: J'ai Lu, 1974.
Un Mari c'est un mari. Paris: Flammarion, 1976.
La Vie reprendra au printemps. Paris: Flammarion, 1978.
La Chambre de Goethe. Paris: Flammarion, 1981.
Un Visage. Paris: Flammarion, 1982.
La Citoyenne. Paris: Flammarion, 1985.
Le Harem. Paris: Flammarion, 1987.
Le Mari de l'Ambassadeur. Paris: Flammarion, 1990.
Le Château des Oliviers. Paris: Flammarion, 1993.
Félix, fils de Pauline. Paris: Flammarion, 1993.
Hébrard, Frédérique, and Louis Velle. *La Demoiselle d'Avignon.* Paris: J'ai Lu, 1989.

Héloïse (c. 1100–1163). First abbess of the Paraclete. She is best remembered for her celebrated love affair with Peter Abelard and the letters they exchanged. Of unknown parentage, perhaps illegitimate, Héloïse was raised by her uncle Fulbert, a canon of Notre Dame de Paris, and educated at the convent* of Argenteuil. Already famed as a girl for her literary skill and learning, she was about seventeen when she met Abelard, a distinguished philosopher of thirty-eight, whom Fulbert engaged as her tutor. Although Abelard later represented himself as a cold-blooded seducer, Héloïse fell swiftly and passionately in love with him, and the two pursued a clandestine affair until Fulbert caught them *in flagrante delicto*. Soon afterward Héloïse was found to be pregnant, so Abelard spirited her to his sister's estate in Brittany, where she gave birth to a son. The philosopher then proposed a secret marriage* in the hope of appeasing Fulbert, a plan Héloïse opposed on both practical and philosophical grounds. Not only would such a marriage never placate her uncle, she predicted, but she also objected to marriage as a form of slavery and legalized prostitution*, protesting that sexual obligations and the transfer of property corrupted the freedom and purity of love. But Abelard overruled her, and she reluctantly agreed to a private wedding, only to deny it when rumors began to circulate. With Héloïse in hiding at Argenteuil, the outraged Fulbert hired thugs to castrate Abelard as he lay asleep. As the scandal could no longer be hidden, Abelard took refuge in monastic vows at St.-Denis, first compelling his wife to take the veil as a nun.

After their ''conversion'' in 1119, Héloïse soon became prioress at Argenteuil—a testimony to her learning and apparent piety, since she had neither birth nor virginity to recommend her for office. Her contact with Abelard did not resume until 1128, when his former abbot Suger schemed to evict the nuns from Argenteuil in order to claim their property for St.-Denis. In this crisis Abelard came to Héloïse's aid, offering her nuns the oratory of the Paraclete built by his former students. Installed as abbess at the new foundation, Héloïse proved an able administrator, attracting many novices and eventually founding six daughter houses. Around 1132 Abelard, wretched in his abbatial position in Brittany, wrote his apologia, the *Historia calamitatum*, to pave the way for a resumption of his teaching career in Paris. Héloïse received a copy ''by chance,'' or more likely by design, and made it the occasion to begin a correspondence.

In two personal letters, Héloïse presents Abelard with a mercurial and highly rhetorical performance, modeling her persona on Ovid's *Héroides*—a collection of epistolary poems in the voices of seduced and abandoned heroines. By turns she expresses anger at Abelard's neglect and mistrust, rages against divine injustice, protests her unswerving love, revels in nostalgia for lost pleasures, confesses the hypocrisy of her monastic life, voices doubts about her salvation, and begs her husband for consolation and advice. Abelard replies, much cooler and less flamboyant; he rebuffs these erotic appeals by attempting to deflect Héloïse's passion toward her new bridegroom, Christ, even as he asks for prayers for his own deliverance. In her third letter Héloïse, again at Abelard's command, shifts to a more monastic discourse and asks him to compose a rule for her nuns. The dossier continues with numerous religious works written by Abelard at Héloïse's request, including the rule, a proto-feminist tract on the history of nuns, a cycle of hymns, and a series of answers to her scriptural questions (the *Problems of Héloïse*). Dying at forty-two, Abelard was buried at his request at the Paraclete. Héloïse rejoined him in 1163, and their grave has long been a pilgrimage site for lovers.

Héloïse's literary fame rests exclusively on her first two letters. In the thirteenth century Jean de Meun translated the correspondence into French and retold the lovers' tale in his *Roman de la Rose*, praising Héloïse for her sagacity and ideal of free love. The letters were admired by Petrarch and other Renaissance humanists, but spurned by Christine de Pizan* on moral grounds. In the eighteenth and nineteenth centuries, a number of highly embellished, fictionalized translations* appeared, making Héloïse into a heroine of sensibility—as evidenced by Pope's *Eloisa to Abelard* and the title of Rousseau's novel, *La Nouvelle Héloïse*. This romantic appropriation spurred a scholarly backlash in the mid-twentieth century as medievalists like D. W. Robertson and John Benton disputed the authenticity of Héloïse's letters, claiming they had been forged by Abelard as part of an exemplary treaty on conversion. Majority opinion now inclines toward accepting the letters and understanding Héloïse in the context of twelfth-century monastic reform, as well as the construction of new discourses on love.

Barbara Newman

BIBLIOGRAPHY

Secondary Texts

Benton, John. ''Fraud, Fiction and Borrowing in the Correspondence of Abelard and Heloise.'' In *Pierre Abelard—Pierre le Vénérable* Ed. René Louis and Jean Jolivet. Paris: Editions du Centre National de la Recherche Scientifique, 1975. 469–506.

Charrier, Charlotte. *Héloïse dans l'histoire et dans la légende*. Paris: Champion, 1933.
Dronke, Peter. "Heloise." In *Women Writers of the Middle Ages*. Cambridge: Cambridge University Press, 1984. 107–143.
Georgianna, Linda. "Any Corner of Heaven: Heloise's Critique of Monasticism." *Medieval Studies* 49 (1987): 221–253.
Kamuf, Peggy. *Fictions of Feminine Desire: Disclosures of Heloise*. Lincoln: University of Nebraska Press, 1982.
McLeod, Enid. *Héloïse: A Biography*. London: Chatto & Windus, 1938.

Héricourt, Jenny d' **(1809–1875).** Feminist, journalist, polemical writer, and medical practitioner. In the 1840s she was known as the principal feminist opponent to Proudhon, who in 1858 published *De la Justice dans la Révolution et dans l'église*. With the help of a mathematical formula, he demonstrated how women were inferior to men physically, intellectually, and morally. He concluded that the only possible arena for women was the private sphere of the family unit. Such virulent antifeminism could be explained by the nascent industrialization of France, where women were increasingly used as cheap labor, therefore competing with male workers.

In 1858 Jules Michelet published *L'Amour*. While seemingly sympathetic to women, Michelet nonetheless considered them to be inferior creatures, always sickly and often invalids. Women's mission was to create a happy and loving home for their husbands, who in return provided for them financially and morally.

In 1860, encouraged by Juliette Lamber (Adam)*, Jenny d'Héricourt published an influential essay, *La Femme affranchie: Réponse à MM. Michelet, Proudhon, E. de Girardin, A. Comte et autres novateurs modernes*, to first refute and attack Proudhon's and Michelet's theories, and then to offer her own views on women. She had an easy task destroying Proudhon's often irrational and illogical statements about women's natural inferiority, and with clever arguments showed women to be the equals of men. In her second volume, she addressed issues affecting women such as the Napoleonic Code* and the question of divorce*. She believed women should have control of their own property, and should be free to enter any profession and be given the same education* as men.

She spent the years 1863 to 1873 in the United States, where she was active in feminist circles, notably with Elizabeth Cady Stanton and Susan B. Anthony.

Juliette Parnell-Smith

BIBLIOGRAPHY

Primary Text

La Femme affranchie: Réponse à MM. Michelet, Proudhon, E. de Girardin, A. Comte et autres novateurs modernes. 2 vols. Brussels: A. Lacroix, 1860.

Secondary Texts

Moses, Claire Goldberg. *French Feminism in the Nineteenth Century*. Albany: State University of New York Press, 1984.

Offen, Karen. "A Nineteenth-Century French Feminist Rediscovered: Jenny d'Héricourt, 1809–1875." *Signs* 13, no. 1 (Autumn 1987): 144–158.

Herrmann, Claudine (1926–). Lawyer, novelist, and editor at Editions des Femmes, where she wrote numerous introductions to feminist texts. Born in Brussels, Herrmann practiced and taught law in France and Afghanistan, and has taught literature in Paris and in Boston. An early essay called "Those Lady Savages" condemns men's misogynistic depiction of women in literature throughout the centuries. She is best known for her feminist work *Les Voleuses de langue* (1976), published as the women's liberation movement was spreading. This work focuses on defining gender differences. Language holds a central place in her argument as it represents a weapon for women. Playing on the double meaning of the words *langue* and *voler*, Herrmann urges women to reappropriate language/tongue and to steal/fly language from men in order to define themselves as subjects. Although Herrmann's position has not evolved much since the 1970s, she remains a key figure among contemporary feminists.

Armelle Crouzières-Ingenthron

BIBLIOGRAPHY

Primary Texts

L'Etoile de David. Paris: Gallimard, 1958.
Maître Talmon. Paris: Gallimard, 1961.
Le Cavalier des Steppes. Paris: Gallimard, 1963.
Le Rôle judiciaire et politique des femmes sous la République romaine. Brussels: Latomus, 1964.
Le Diplôme. Paris: Gallimard, 1965.
Les Voleuses de langue. Paris: Editions des Femmes, 1976.

Holocaust. Women, Jewish and non-Jewish, have turned to fiction, testimonials, drama, and poetry* to interpret their experience of the Holocaust. However, for reasons of gender, and political and personal priorities, none has attracted the same attention as Elie Wiesel. Some of these women writers—part of a first generation—published soon after World War II*, while others nursed their works in silence for years. The novelist Anna Langfus*, who was born in Poland in 1920 and moved to France in 1946, is perhaps the best known. The fictionalization of her own story in understated prose and the refusal to heroicize her protagonists confer considerable emotional power on her narratives of imprisonment, torture, loss, moral dilemmas, and difficult, if not impossible, survival (*Le Sel et le soufre* [1960], *Les Bagages de sable* [1962]). In a different way, Charlotte Delbo*, a non-Jewish member of the French Resistance, maintained linguistic control over her experience at Auschwitz through the use of lyrical autobiographical narratives that incorporate both prose and poetry. Her personal struggle is always submerged within the collective, "I" becoming one with "We." Thus, in *La Mémoire et les jours* (1985), her memories merge with memories of other collective acts of inhumanity in a moving chant of multiple voices. Delbo offers a poignant testimony of the power of the body and of solidarity as mechanisms of resistance. In Fania Fénelon's *Sursis pour l'orchestre*, inspired by the author's internment as a member of the Birkenau women's orchestra, the privileged status of the narrator and a tendency to self-dramatization, combined with occasional flashes of a wry, detached humor, provide a stark contrast with both Langfus and Delbo. All these texts, although dealing with the gender-blind banality of evil, offer special female insights into existence in concentration camps. They evoke the female body, infertility, menstruation*, maternal relationships, erotic exploitation, and the solidarity found in sharing songs, poetry, recipes, laughter, and fears.

Delbo and Langfus also wrote plays on the Holocaust, as did Liliane Atlan*, whose *Monsieur Fugue ou le mal de terre* (1967) depicts a universe in which the magic of storytelling plays an ambiguous role since it cannot save children who are being herded into a death camp. Among women poets, Denyse Clairouin, Lucienne Laurentie, and Micheline Maurel* deserve special mention.

Finally, a younger generation has written texts derived from their knowledge rather than their direct experience of the Holocaust (Viviane Forrester, Michèle Sarde*, and others). *Rue de nuit* by Myriam Anissimov*, uses a very personal Kafkaesque blend of the real and the fantastic that reinterprets, in a contemporary setting, the horror of the Shoah.

Madeleine Cottenet-Hage

BIBLIOGRAPHY

Primary Texts

Anissimov, Myriam. *Rue de nuit*. Paris: Julliard, 1977.
Atlan, Liliane. *Monsieur Fugue ou le mal de terre*. Paris: Seuil, 1967.
Delbo, Charlotte. *Aucun de nous ne reviendra*. Paris: Minuit, 1970.
———. *La Mémoire et les jours*. Paris: Berg International, 1985.
Fénelon, Fania, and Marcelle Routier. *Sursis pour l'orchestre*. Paris: France Loisirs and Stock-Opera Mundi, 1976.
Langfus, Anna. *Les Bagages de sable*. Paris: Gallimard, 1962.
———. *Saute, Barbara*. Paris: Gallimard, 1965.
———. *Le Sel et le soufre*. Paris: Gallimard, 1960.
Maurel, Micheline. *La Passion selon Ravensbruck*. Paris: Minuit, 1965.

Secondary Texts

DeKoven Ezrahi, Sidra. *By Words Alone: The Holocaust in Literature*. Chicago: University of Chicago Press, 1980.
Haft, Cynthia. *The Theme of Nazi Concentration Camps in French Literature*. The Hague and Paris: Mouton, 1973.
Heinemann, Marlene E. *Gender and Destiny: Women Writers and the Holocaust*. Westport, CT: Greenwood Press, 1986.
Pouzol, Henri. *La Poésie concentrationnaire*. Paris: Seghers, 1975.

Hommaire de Hell, Adèle (1819–?). Travel writer whose works and life illustrate the status of the woman writer primarily defined as a wife. Married very young, she traveled with her husband and child through the Caucasus. As a widow, she interrupted her travels and writings but resumed them when she accompanied her son to the Caribbean islands. In her writings she very consciously articulates her role as a wife and the domains she can legitimately explore as a woman. In *Les Steppes de la mer caspienne* she integrates her work and that of her husband, exemplifying the gender-defined differences between feminine and masculine travel discourses.

Bénédicte Monicat

BIBLIOGRAPHY

Primary Texts

De Constantinople à Trieste. Paris: Imprimerie de E. Martinent, 1865.
A travers le monde: La vie orientale. La Vie Créole. Paris: Didier, 1870.
Hommaire de Hell, Adèle, and Xavier Hommaire de Hell. *Voyages dans les steppes de la mer caspienne et dans la Russie méridionale. Voyage pittoresque, historique, et scientifique*. Paris: P. Bertrand, 1843–1845.

Houville, Gérard d' (1875–1963). Pen name of Marie de Régnier, poet, novelist, and critic. Daughter of the Parnassian* sonneteer José Maria de Heredia, and wife of the Symbolist* poet Henri de Régnier, d'Houville chose to write, under her grandmother's name, from a more personal, woman-centered perspective. She wrote numerous novels*, many of them autobiographical in inspiration, but it was her poetry* that won wide critical acclaim, including two prizes from the French Academy. Although critics considered d'Houville's poetry to be more lady-like than the so-called feminine poetry of her day, her poems are often revisionary as she retells the stories of classical heroines and her own forgotten Creole ancestresses from a woman's point of view.

Tama Lea Engelking

BIBLIOGRAPHY

Primary Texts

L'Inconstante. Paris: Fayard, 1903.
L'Esclave. Paris: Calmann-Lévy, 1905.
Le Temps d'aimer. Paris: Fayard, 1908.
Le Séducteur. Paris: Fayard, 1913.
Les Poésies de Gérard d'Houville. Paris: Grasset, 1931.
"Femmes Écrivains: Leurs Débuts." *Les Nouvelles littéraires*, October 6, 1935.

Secondary Texts

Bona, Dominique. *Les Yeux noirs: Les Vies extraordinaires des soeurs Heredia*. Paris: J. C. Lattès, 1989.
Chizerary-Cuny, Henriette de. *Marie de Régnier (Gérard d'Houville): Propos et souvenirs*. Paris: L'Office Mécanographique D. L., 1969.
Engelking, Tama. "The Secret Rebellion of a Literary Daughter: The Poetry of Gérard d'Houville." *French Literature Series* 16 (1989): 94–109.

Gourmont, Jean de. *Muses d'aujourd'hui: Essai de physiologie poétique*. Paris: Mercure de France, 1910.

Le Dantec, Yves-Gérard. "Gérard d'Houville, poète." *Muse française* (January 10, 1931): 17–30.

Maurras, Charles. "Le Romantisme féminin." In *L'Avenir de l'intelligence*. Paris: Flammarion, 1927. 115–234.

Huber, Marie (1695–1753). The second of fourteen children of a patrician family, Huber was born in Geneva, but spent most of her life near Lyons. Influenced by a pietist uncle, Fatio de Duillier, this accomplished Protestant maiden enthusiastically undertook to combat theological dogma with rare logic and common sense. She rejected predestination and sacraments, and favored an inner and more personal religion fostering mysticism and direct relation with God. Advocating reason as her sole guide, she was described as having "a man's mind in a woman's heart." Her first essay, *Le Monde fou préféré au monde sage* (1731), is a series of discussions between three friends, a philosopher, a lawyer, and a businessman, on the subject of human conscience. Her *Lettres sur la religion essentielle* (1738, 1754) opposes rigid church dogma and precedes the deism of her compatriot, Jean-Jacques Rousseau. Immanuel Kant may owe her more than is generally acknowledged. Forceful and unusually independent in her thinking, she is considered the forerunner of liberal Protestantism. All her works were published anonymously in Amsterdam or London. She devoted her discreet life to good deeds and writing.

S. Pascale Dewey

BIBLIOGRAPHY

Primary Texts

Le Monde fou préféré au monde sage, en 24 promenades de trois amis, Criton philosophe, Philon avocat, Eraste négociant. Amsterdam: N.p., 1731.

Le Système des Anciens et des Modernes concilié par l'exposition des sentiments différents de quelques théologiens sur l'état des âmes séparées des corps, en 14 lettres. London: N.p., 1731.

Lettre sur la religion essentielle à l'homme distinguée de ce qui n'en est que l'accessoire. Amsterdam: N.p., 1738.

Suite à la troisième partie sur la religion essentielle à l'homme. London: N.p., 1739.

Suite du système sur l'état des âmes séparées des corps, servant de réponse au livre intitulé Examen de l'origénisme par le professeur Ruchat. London: N.p., 1739.

Suite sur la religion essentielle à l'homme, servant de réponse aux objections qui ont été faites à l'ouvrage qui porte ce titre. London: N.p., 1739.

Secondary Texts

Courdaveaux, Victor. "Une Aïeule du protestantisme libéral, Mlle Marie Huber." *Supplément trimestriel de la critique philosophique*. Paris: La Critique philosophique, 1879.

Metzger, G. A. *Marie Huber (1695–1753), sa vie, ses oeuvres, sa théologie*. Geneva: Imprimerie Rivera Dubois, 1887.

Monod, Albert. *De Pascal à Chateaubriand. Les Défenseurs français du christianisme de 1670 à 1802.* New York: Burt Franklin, 1971.

Perrochon, Henri. "M. Huber, la Lyonnaise." *Etudes Lettres* 3 (1960): 196–208.

Roches, Fr. de. *Défense du christianisme ou préservatif contre un voyage intitulé Lettres sur la religion essentielle à l'homme.* Lausanne: N.p., 1740.

Sayous, Pierre André. "Marie Huber." *XVIIIe Siècle à l'étranger. Histoire de la littérature française dans les divers pays d'Europe depuis la mort de Louis XIV jusqu'à la Révolution française.* Paris: N.p., 1861. 1: 100–121.

Humbert, Jeanne (1890–1986). Humbert was a pacifist and anarchist whose life was devoted to the fight for sexual freedom and birth control*. As a child, she followed her mother, who left a bourgeois husband to live with a militant anarchist, and throughout her life she associated with well-known anarchists. In 1909 she became Eugène Humbert's partner in his neo-Malthusian struggle for the legalization of contraception and abortion*, expounded on in the publication *Génération consciente.* Following the enactment of a 1920 law designed to outlaw public discussion of contraception and abortion, and to prohibit the dissemination of information on birth control, the Humberts were incarcerated several times. After Eugène's death in prison in 1944, Jeanne continued to devote her life to the principles she and her husband had fought for. In addition to writing numerous articles, pamphlets, and books, she resumed publication of *La Grande Réforme*, a newspaper directed by Eugène between 1931 and 1939.

Francis Ronsin and Samia I. Spencer

BIBLIOGRAPHY

Primary Texts

Le Pourissoir. Paris: Editions Prima, 1932.
Sous la Cagoule. Paris: Editions de Lutèce, 1933.
Eugène Humbert. Paris: Editions de la Grande Réforme, 1947.

Secondary Text

Guerrand, Roger-Henri, and Francis Ronsin. *Le Sexe apprivoisé. Jeanne Humbert et la lutte pour le contrôle des naissances.* Paris: Editions de la Découverte, 1990.

Humbert, Marie-Thérèse (1940–). Born on the island of Mauritius and living in France since 1959, Humbert now teaches literature. Her works include a study of Balzac and five fictional autobiographies centering on her childhood experiences. Her first novel*, *A l'autre bout de moi* (1979), contrasts identical female twins in order to dramatize a woman's need to choose between compliant victimization and rebellious isolation in the intensely color-conscious society of Mauritius.

Le Volkameria (1984) and *Une Robe d'écume et de vent* (1989) are set on an imaginary island near Bermuda. Together, they tell a cautionary tale of an insane, abandoned mistress's delusional enslavement to a hopeless love, and her final realization that she can neither rescue nor be rescued.

Un Fils d'orage (1992), an important regional novel depicting the Camargue, is structured around three alternating women's voices, each from a different generation. The granddaughter, who concludes that loneliness is the price of freedom, ultimately resolves to emulate her grandmother by breeding bulls—a metaphor for controlling reproduction. Humbert's most recent novel, *La Montagne des signaux* (1994), compares a brilliant but unhappy career woman with her stay-at-home sister who achieves self-acceptance, thus avoiding the over-simplified claim that autonomy ensures happiness. Throughout her works, Humbert associates traditional views of womanhood with childlike dependency, and affirms the need for women to seek happiness outside conventional relationships.

Laurence M. Porter

BIBLIOGRAPHY

Primary Texts

A l'autre bout de moi. Paris: Stock, 1979.
Le Volkameria. Paris: Stock, 1984.
Une Robe d'écume et de vent. Paris: Stock, 1989.
Balzac, Saché, ou, le nid de coucou. Saint-Cyr-sur-Loire: Pirot, 1991.
Un Fils d'orage. Paris: Stock, 1992.
La Montagne des signaux. Paris: Stock, 1994.

Secondary Text

Lionnet, Françoise. "*Métissage*, Emancipation, and Female Textuality in Two Francophone Writers." In *Displacements: Women, Tradition, Literatures in French*. Ed. Joan DeJean and Nancy K. Miller. Baltimore: Johns Hopkins University Press, 1991. 254–274.

Huston, Nancy (1953–). Born in Calgary, Alberta, Huston has been living in Paris and writing in French since 1973. She became active in the women's movement in the seventies, publishing essays in such feminist journals as *Cahiers du GRIF* and *Sorcières*. Huston's texts give voice to women's stories and deconstruct myths* in which men seek to usurp women's generative function. In *Mosaïque de la pornographie* (1982), Huston critiques the misogyny of the pornographic text through a study that juxtaposes male-authored narratives of the "fallen woman" with the memoirs of a female prostitute. Huston's analysis privileges a woman's voice, effectively countering the male author-narrator's desire to situate the woman as both object and text. The thematics of contractual love is further explored in *A l'amour comme à la guerre* (1984), in which Huston analyzes the sociocultural and political implications of the historical figuration of woman's body as it relates metaphorically and metonymically to both war and prostitution*.

Huston often incorporates autobiographical elements in her critical studies. A notable example of this is *Journal de la création* (1990), in which fragments of the journal recounting her own pregnancy serve as a springboard for Huston's theorization of the ways in which women writers come to terms with the physical and metaphysical intersections between creation and procreation.

Huston's other published work includes novels*, two children's books (written with her daughter Léa), a literary biography of Romain Gary, and two volumes of correspondence. She received the Prix Contrepoint for *Les Variations Goldberg* (1981) and the Prix du Gouverneur général du Canada for *Cantique des plaines* (1993).

Patrice J. Proulx

BIBLIOGRAPHY

Primary Texts

Jouer au Papa et à l'amant: De l'amour des petites filles. Paris: Editions Ramsay, 1979.
Les Variations Goldberg. Paris: Seuil, 1981.
Mosaïque de la pornographie: Marie-Thérèse et les autres. Paris: Editions Denoël/Gonthier, 1982.
"Mouvements et journaux de femmes." *Magazine Littéraire* 180 (January 1982): 28–31.
Journal de la création. Paris: Seuil, 1990.
"Erotic Literature in Post-War France." *Raritan: A Quarterly Review* 12, no. 1 (Summer 1992): 29–45.
Cantique des plaines. Arles: Actes Sud, 1993.
Tombeau de Romain Gary. Arles: Actes Sud, 1995.
Instruments des ténèbres. Arles: Actes Sud, 1996.
Huston, Nancy, and Sam Kinser. *A l'amour comme à la guerre, correspondance.* Paris: Seuil, 1984.

Secondary Texts

Clerval, Alain. "Nancy Huston: *Les Variations Goldberg.*" *Nouvelle Revue Française* 346 (November 1981): 128–130.
Rivière, Anne, and Xavière Gauthier. "Des femmes et leurs oeuvres." *Magazine Littéraire* 180 (January 1982): 36–41.

Hysteria. The Ancient Greeks and Egyptians considered the womb (*hystera*) a source of female infirmities. The current popular view associates hysteria with overreactions, crying, and loss of emotional control—behavior generally attributed to women. Clinically, however, hysteria can be diagnosed as conversion disorder, marked by the appearance of nonorganic physical symptoms, or as histrionic personality disorder, not accompanied by disease but characterized by a reactive, dramatic, attention-seeking personality with more display and exaggeration than depth. Male hysteria, once termed "battle fatigue," was noted in soldiers during and after the world wars. Now identified as post-traumatic stress disorder, this syndrome includes nervousness, hypersensitivity, an exaggerated startle response, conversion symptoms, and depression.

Freud first noticed such complaints in women during his early neurological training at Charcot's Parisian clinic. He treated patients suffering from sensory or motor impairments without organic cause, particularly fainting, paralysis, visual or auditory complaints, convulsions, and difficulty swallowing. Suspecting these hysterical illnesses to be unconscious and sexual in origin, Freud used Charcot's technique of hypnosis to uncover the repressed trauma which the patients had displaced onto physical problems. Once conscious, the conflict and symptoms could be resolved through psychoanalysis. The talking cure led patients to discuss formerly inaccessible material that had manifested itself in diseases, the signifiers of a distress they could not articulate.

Modern critics concur with Freud that his treatments of the hysterics Dora and Anna O. were incomplete, due to his limited understanding of Dora's homosexual feelings and his own. Further, French feminist writers have criticized both Freudian and Greek views of the uterus. In *Le Speculum de l'autre femme*, Irigaray* rereads and reverses Plato's analysis of the womblike cave; Kristeva*, in *Polylogue*, addresses this hysterically/historically maligned maternal space in her discussions of the *chora* or ''receptacle.''

Susan Grayson

BIBLIOGRAPHY

Beizer, Janet. *Ventriloquized Bodies: Narratives of Hysteria in Nineteenth-Century France*. Ithaca: Cornell University Press, 1994.

Chesler, Phyllis. *Women and Madness*. San Diego: Harvest/HBJ, 1989.

Forrester, John. *The Seductions of Psychoanalysis*. New York: Cambridge University Press, 1990.

Freud, Sigmund. *Collected Papers*. Vols. 1, 3, 5. Trans. Joan Riviere. London: Hogarth Press, 1950.

Gallop, Jane. *The Daughter's Seduction*. Ithaca: Cornell University Press, 1982.

Gay, Peter. *Freud: A Life for Our Time*. New York: Norton, 1988.

———, ed. *The Freud Reader*. New York: Norton, 1989.

Irigaray, Luce. *Speculum of the Other Woman*. Trans. Gillian C. Gill. Ithaca: Cornell University Press, 1985.

Kristeva, Julia. *Desire in Language*. Ed. Léon S. Roudiez. Trans. Thomas Gora, Alice Jardine, and Léon S. Roudiez. New York: Columbia University Press, 1980.

Mazzoni, Cristina. *Saint Hysteria: Neurosis, Mysticism, and Gender in European Culture*. Ithaca: Cornell University Press, 1996.

Micale, Mark S. *Approaching Hysteria: Disease and Its Interpretations*. Princeton: Princeton University Press, 1995.

Hyvrard, Jeanne (1945–). Professor of political economy in a Parisian technical *lycée*, Hyvrard is a prolific writer whose first novel*, *Les Prunes de Cythère* (1975), was a ''report'' on the economic and social state of Martinique. Hyvrard's second book, *Mère la mort* (1976), which, like all of her fourteen books, is a poetic treatise on political economics, introduces the Mother metaphor that runs through all her works in various forms. It is the idealized and metaphysical image of the mother, but also represents any oppressive power. She explains her recent concepts in her philosophical dictionary, *La Pensée corps* (1989), where she develops the idea of ''woman-thought,'' a concept already sketched out in her lyrical and philosophical treatise, *Le Canal de la Toussaint* (1986). "Woman-thought" is a nonlinear mode of thinking, difficult to express because of the limits of our language based on rationality (*logos*). Hyvrard's world, based on chaos, aims at fusion through "contrairation," where words can mean one thing and the opposite at the same time. In *Le Cercan* (1987), a poetic biopolitical text dealing with the colonizing nature of cancer and society, Hyvrard posits her attempts to communicate with her overbearing mother through the cancer that afflicted them both. Hyvrard's last published text, *La Jeune Morte en robe de dentelle* (1990), focuses on an oppressive mother whose daughter finally discovers salvation through writing. Hyvrard insists that she writes in order to survive in a society where the media and the cybernetic revolution are dehumanizing the world.

Monique Saigal

BIBLIOGRAPHY

Primary Texts

Les Prunes de Cythère. Paris: Editions de Minuit, 1975.
Mère la mort. Paris: Editions de Minuit, 1976.
La Meuritritude. Paris: Editions de Minuit, 1977.
Le Canal de la Toussaint. Paris: Editions des femmes, 1986.
Le Cercan. Paris: Editions des femmes, 1987.
La Pensée corps. Paris: Editions des femmes, 1989.
La Jeune Morte en robe de dentelle. Paris: Editions des femmes, 1990.

Secondary Texts

Le Clézio, Marguerite. "Mother and Motherland: The Daughter's Quest for Origins." *Stanford French Review* (Winter 1981): 381–390.
Saigal, Monique. "L'Appropriation du corps dans *Le Cercan* de Jeanne Hyvrard." *Atlantis* 16, no. 2 (Spring 1991): 21–30.
———. "Le Cannibalisme maternel: L'Abjection chez Jeanne Hyvrard et Kristeva." *French Review* 66, no. 3 (February 1993): 412–419.
Waelti-Walters, Jennifer. *Jeanne Hyvrard: Theorist of the Modern World*. Edinburgh: Edinburgh University Press, 1996.

I

Imache, Tassadit (1958–). Born in Argenteuil to a Kabyle (Algerian) father and a French mother, Imache grew up in a working-class milieu. Her first novel*, *Une Fille sans histoire*, and her short story* for children, *Le Rouge à lèvres*, revisit the Algerian War period and trace the history of current French-Maghrebi conflicts. Her second novel, *Le Dromadaire de Bonaparte*, continues her examination of women's madness and writing as responses to sexism, patriarchy, and racism. Imache has also published lucid critical statements in the French press on the "Headscarf Affair," the Gulf War, and the hunt for Khaled Kelkal, a Franco-Algerian executed by French police as a Muslim terrorist.

Mark McKinney

BIBLIOGRAPHY

Primary Texts

Le Rouge à lèvres. Paris: Syros/Alternatives, 1988.
Une Fille sans histoire. Paris: Calmann-Lévy, 1989.
Algérie: Filles et garçons. Illus. Anne Tonnac. Paris: Albin Michel Jeunesse, 1991.
"Nous, après le déluge." *Paysages après la bataille*. *Esprit* 172 (June 1991): 98–101.
"De la chasse à l'homme à celle des hommes." *Libération*, October 1, 1995, 7.
Le Dromadaire de Bonaparte. Arles: Actes Sud, 1995.
Je veux rentrer. Arles: Sud, 1998.

Secondary Texts

Chévillot, Frédérique. "Beurette suis et beurette ne veux pas toujours être: Entretien d'été avec Tassadit Imache." *French Review* 71, no. 4 (March 1998): 632:644.
Hargreaves, Alec G. "History, Gender and Ethnicity in Writing by Women Authors of Maghrebian Origin in France." *L'Esprit Créateur* 33, no. 2 (Summer 1993): 23–34.
———. *La Littérature beur: Un Guide bio-bibliographique*. New Orleans: CELFAN Edition Monographs, 1992.
———. *Voices from the North African Immigrant Community in France: Immigration and Identity in Beur Fiction*. Providence, RI: Berg, 1991.

Ireland, Susan. "Rewriting the Story in Tassadit Imache's *Une Fille sans histoire.*" *Women in French Studies* 3 (Fall 1995): 112–122.

Immigration. France has a long history of foreigners coming to work and settle in the country. Immigration is controversial today because some settlers have been marked as racially different and culturally alien. Indeed, "immigrant" in current popular discourse is virtually synonymous with persons who are Muslim and/or of African descent.

France's historically permeable borders allowed a free flow of people from neighboring countries. The linguistic, cultural, and ethnic diversity of premodern French lands meant that a foreigner was simply a stranger to the locality. Indeed, both meanings are included in the one French word, *étranger.* As elsewhere in medieval and early modern Europe, the emblematic stranger was the Jew, and many French communities harassed or expelled their Jewish residents. New religious divisions between Catholic and Protestant culminated in the expulsion of the calvinist Huguenots in 1685, a milestone in the consolidation of French absolutism. The issue of racial difference came to the fore with the enslavement of black Africans in the colonies. It was not until the French Revolution* in 1789, with royal subjects transformed into citizens and citizenesses of the Republic, that a universalist ideal of the nation took hold. For a brief time (male) foreigners were eligible for citizenship. But with aristocratic emigration, continental war, and the Jacobin drive to homogenize the diverse cultures of France, the naturalization of foreigners ended. The Napoleonic Code* of 1804 specifically excluded foreigners from civil and political rights.

The 1830 conquest of Algeria ushered in an era of renewed colonialism* during which concepts of racial difference and categories of French nationality were formalized. Slavery was finally abolished throughout the French empire in 1848. The labor shortage caused by nineteenth-century industrialization attracted European workers to all parts of France. In the north, for example, Belgian women workers crossed the border daily to labor in French textile factories, and in the south Italian male migrants worked in construction and agriculture.

It was only after the massive losses of World War I* that the government officially recognized the necessity of an immigrant work force to supplement the inadequate French labor supply. There was no juridical distinction between male and female immigrant workers, but most women and children immigrants came into France as dependents following the initial migration of male workers. This process was exemplified by the settlement of an estimated 1 million Italians in the two decades after the war. The exception to this pattern were Polish families, recruited as entire communities to work in mining and agriculture, and refugee families fleeing massacre in Armenia, fascism in Italy and Spain, and anti-Semitism in Central and Eastern Europe.

In the 1930s, however, the depression and the rise of fascism prompted increased xenophobia. Spanish Civil War refugees were interned, many Polish families were sent back, and restrictions on legal immigration tightened. With the onset of World War II* in 1939 all foreigners came under suspicion, and upon France's defeat in 1940 the Vichy regime promulgated anti-Semitic laws and began distinguishing between French and foreign Jews. By the end of 1942 approximately 65,000 foreign Jews had been deported to Germany's labor and concentration camps. Many French Jews were subsequently sent to their deaths.

After 1946, clandestine immigrants from Italy, Spain, and Portugal entered France. Arab migrant labor increased even as bitter war raged in Algeria (1954–1962). Algerian independence led to a flood of refugees including 1 million *pieds noirs*, French citizens descended from Spanish, Italian, Corsican, and Maltese settlers, and 60,000 *Harkis*, Algerians who fought on the French side. The political involvement of foreigners in the May 1968 student and worker revolts led to many expulsions and to stricter regulation of immigrants from France's former colonies. Muslim Algerians in particular faced increased popular hostility and government control. The Mitterrand government halted all immigration in 1974, by which time the total number of immigrants formed 7 percent of France's total population, with 2.5 percent coming from non-European countries. This halt in immigration had the unintended consequence of creating permanent North African communities in France as single male migrants, no longer able to go back and forth easily, were joined by their families. Even after the government imposed limits on political asylum, family reunification, and the acquisition of French nationality, the clandestine migration of mostly female family members continued, placing them in a precarious social and economic position.

In the 1980s and 1990s popular anti-immigrant sentiment was inflamed by the racist demagoguery of Jean-Marie Le Pen's right-wing National Front, which blamed foreigners for French unemployment and accused Muslims of islamicizing France. In response, anti-racist movements brought together immigrants and their children, Jewish and Arab organizations, students and intellectuals in support of an inclusive ideal of France. But the strong right-wing current has shown no signs of abating, and the government continues to increase its surveillance and regulation of immigrants. Recent controversies have focused on the status of children born in France to immigrant parents, the wearing of Islamic headscarves by schoolgirls, the practices of polygamy and female genital mutilation among African immigrants, and the expulsion of long-term residents. It remains to be seen how the unitary national identity still upheld by the state will bend to the manifestly multicultural nature of contemporary French society.

Yaël Simpson Fletcher

BIBLIOGRAPHY

Green, Nancy. *Ready-to-Wear and Ready-to-Work: A Century of Industry and Immigrants in Paris and New York*. Durham: Duke University Press, 1997.
Lequin, Yves, ed. *La Mosaïque France: Histoire des étrangers et de l'immigration*. Paris: Larousse, 1988.
Moch, Leslie Page. *Moving Europeans: Migration in Western Europe since 1650*. Bloomington: Indiana University Press, 1992.

Noiriel, Gérard. *The French Melting Pot: Immigration, Citizenship, and National Identity*. Trans. Geoffroy de Laforcade. Minneapolis: University of Minnesota Press, 1996.

Industrialization (nineteenth century). Industrialization refers to an enormous increase in manufacturing productivity due to technological change, labor restructuring, and expanded markets. In France this transformation was gradual, starting in the eighteenth century and continuing well into the twentieth century. Industrialization dramatically altered women's lives by separating the workplace from the home and contributing to new attitudes toward women as workers, mothers, and consumers.

Before industrialization women contributed to the family economy in several ways—by assisting male family members with agriculture, craftsmanship, or trade; producing food and clothing for immediate family consumption; and keeping house and rearing children. Although industrialization introduced water- and then steam-powered machines, particularly in textile production, that could only be operated in a factory setting by scores or hundreds of workers of both sexes, most women continued to work at home (or in a home), in agriculture, as domestic servants, or in some form of domestic manufacturing like the needle trades. Statistics from 1866 indicate that in France 2 million women worked in agriculture, and 1 million worked in industry, either in factories or at home. However, the trend toward industrial manufacturing outside of the home, and the increased amount of time women had to devote to wage-earning activity because their pay rates were so low caused many people in France to perceive women's paid labor as incompatible with housekeeping and childrearing. This perceived conflict between work and motherhood was enhanced by the idealization of domesticity in the middle class, where a rigid gender division of labor between public, income-earning men and private, home-centered women developed. By the end of the nineteenth century wage-earning women were expected to leave the labor market upon marriage* and especially with motherhood, and low wages and poor working conditions for women were justified on the grounds that female labor was only a temporary, even unnatural, occupation rather than a lifelong career.

Throughout the nineteenth century reformers from a wide range of political perspectives addressed the situation of working-class women due to industrialization. Male intellectuals deplored women's industrial labor, especially in factory settings, as causing moral degeneracy, family breakdown, and the unsexing of women. They advocated a purely domestic role for women as consistent with feminine nature and social order. By contrast, female writers, for example Julie-Victoire Daubié* and Flora Tristan*, acknowledging the need and even desirability of women's work, called for improvements in female education*, higher wages for women, and even, in the case of Tristan, equality of the sexes in work, society, and politics.

While industrialization altered the working lives of poor women, it also created a new, supposedly leisured existence for middle-class women. Increased productivity was contingent upon increased consumption, and urban populations generally increased their consumption of manufactured goods during the nineteenth century. However, middle-class women were publicly acknowledged as important consumers since they had the income, earned by husbands and fathers, and the time, not having to perform productive or wage-earning labor, to purchase clothes and household furnishings for themselves and their families.

Feminist scholarship on French industrialization has delineated how the expansion of industrial manufacturing changed women's work and often diminished their status within the family, since the ideal of a male breadwinner providing for an entire family replaced the family economy of collective contributions of all family members in the middle class and eventually in the working class. The most recent scholarship analyzes how gender informed industrialization, notably in the designation of certain jobs, especially skilled ones involving machine operation, as masculine, and the contestation over this attribution when local economies changed and men sought better-paying positions, or when men tried to maintain their jobs against the introduction of simpler, more efficient technology and the hiring of less skilled, cheaper, and usually female labor.

Whitney Walton

BIBLIOGRAPHY

Daubié, Julie-Victoire. *La Femme pauvre au XIXe siècle*. 1869–1870. 3 vols. Paris: Côté-femmes, 1992–1993.

Frader, Laura Levine. "Women in the Industrial Capitalist Economy." In *Becoming Visible: Women in European History*. Ed. Renate Bridenthal, Claudia Koonz, and Susan Stuard. Boston: Houghton Mifflin, 1987. 309–333.

Grafteaux, Serge. *Mme Santerre, a French Woman of the People*. Trans. Louise A. Tilly and Kathryn L. Tilly. New York: Schocken, 1985.

Gullickson, Gay L. *Spinners and Weavers of Auffay: Rural Industry and Sexual Division of Labor in a French Village, 1750–1850*. New York: Cambridge University Press, 1986.

Leroy-Beaulieu, Paul. *Le Travail des femmes au XIXe siècle*. Paris: Charpentier et Cie., 1873.

Liu, Tessie P. *The Weaver's Knot: The Contradictions of Class Struggle and Family Solidarity in Western France, 1750–1914*. Ithaca: Cornell University Press, 1994.

McBride, Theresa. "Women's Work and Industrialization." In *The Industrial Revolution and Work in Nineteenth-Century Europe*. Ed. Lenard R. Berlanstein. New York: Routledge, 1992. 63–80.

Scott, Joan Wallach. *Gender and the Politics of History*. New York: Columbia University Press, 1988. Especially Part 3.

Smith, Bonnie G. *Ladies of the Leisure Class: The Bourgeoises of Northern France in the Nineteenth Century*. Princeton: Princeton University Press, 1981.

Tilly, Louise A., and Joan W. Scott. *Women, Work, and Family*. New York: Routledge, 1987.

Tristan, Flora. *Union ouvrière*. 1843. Paris: Des femmes, 1986.

Walton, Whitney. *France at the Crystal Palace: Bourgeois Taste and Artisan Manufacture in the Nineteenth Century*. Berkeley: University of California Press, 1992.

Irigaray, Luce (1930–). Writer, psychoanalyst, and philosopher. Irigaray is politically identifiable as a feminist activist devoted to the struggle for women's rights in their most practical form—equal pay and the legalization of contraception and abortion*. Her writings are not easily definable as a thematically cohesive whole because of her refusal of traditional representational codes. While her theoretical commitment to feminist politics remains consistent, Irigaray's unorthodox refusal of narrative theoretical strategies has produced a political, poetic interdisciplinary dialogue engaging primarily the fields of linguistics, psychoanalysis, and philosophy. Irigaray's ambitious attempt to open a space in which sexual difference might be theorized necessarily brings about new ways of reading and writing.

In her first two major collections of essays, *Speculum de l'autre femme* (1974) and *Ce Sexe qui n'en est pas un* (1977), Irigaray lays out the theoretical project that, despite her Belgian origins, has come to represent the school of thought known as "French Feminism," a feminism* associated with Lacanian psychoanalysis, poststructuralism, and post-phenomenology. These essays, contradicting Lacan, work toward the creation of an affirmative concept of femininity, a femininity no longer defined—in relation to masculinity—as negation, mirror image, or excess. Irigaray explicitly takes up and implicitly questions these "feminine" positions in her examination of her psychoanalytic and philosophic forefathers in order to reveal their unconscious desires, to make clear the maternal and material debt that masculine discourse refuses to acknowledge. At the same time, she affirms the necessity for women to speak autonomously from a space outside the masculine imaginary, to *parler femme* (not to be confused with Cixous's* *écriture féminine**), to refuse the logic of masculine discourse and to express themselves in their bodily specificity as women and not as the negatively defined other of man.

In her later works, psychoanalysis becomes more a methodology than an object of inquiry. Choosing as her framework the alchemical elements of pre-Socratic philosophy, Irigaray reevaluates Western philosophies in an attempt to reinstitute a genuine, positive difference between the sexes through an assertion of the material, bodily elements of subjectivity. Irigaray begins her tetrology of elements with the archetypically maternal element of water. In *Amante marine. De Friedrich Nietzsche* (1980), Irigaray, who positions herself as the philosopher's "marine lover," calls into question the absence of fluidity in his texts, arguing that this material deficiency reveals his sexual indifference. In *Passions élémentaires* (1982), Irigaray invokes the element of earth to figure a pre-biblical analysis of sexual union, the ethical coming together of two sexually differentiated subjects. Irigaray's encounter with Heidegger in *L'Oubli de l'air chez Martin Heidegger* (1983) affirms the necessity of thinking transcendence and ascension as constitutive of any notion of Being mindful of the fundamental alterity of the two sexes. Finally, Irigaray's as yet unwritten work on Marx and fire promises to develop her analysis of the unspoken role of women as objects of exchange—sexual difference as an axiomatic force in the marketplace.

Irigaray's rehabilitation of the elements, the revaluation of the feminine, maternal body, does not, however, preclude recourse to the divine as a necessary constituent of an ethics of sexual difference. In fact, Irigaray's entire body of work can be read as an attempt to negotiate the space between bodily immanence and divine transcendence as fundamental to rethinking the place of the ethical other. Irigaray posits an asymmetric relation between self and other rooted in sexual difference and the inevitable inequality of the sexes. This negation of sexual equality has caused a theoretical rift between Irigaray and feminists who view socially constructed *gender* difference as an unnecessary evil and see Irigaray's affirmation of *sexual* difference as a dangerous reversion to a biologic determination of female identity as well as a potential erasure of individual differences *between* women. Irigaray's assertion of a sexually grounded notion of subjectivity, however, denies neither the destructive nature of socialized femininity nor women's infinite multiplicity. Respectful of these sociopolitical realities, Irigaray reaches toward an ethical order figured as a sacred union of two distinct sexes, a marrying of the bodily and the divine. Over the past two decades, her political engagements and theoretical questionings have expanded and enriched our understanding of women's issues and provoked an increased awareness of the fundamental importance of such issues to all disciplines and all facets of our lives.

Lisa Walsh

BIBLIOGRAPHY

Primary Texts

Speculum de l'autre femme. Paris: Minuit, 1974.
Ce Sexe qui n'en est pas un. Paris: Minuit, 1977.
Amante marine. De Friedrich Nietzsche. Paris: Minuit, 1979.
Passions élémentaires. Paris: Minuit, 1982.
L'Oubli de l'air chez Martin Heidegger. Paris: Minuit, 1983.
Ethique de la différence sexuelle. Paris: Minuit, 1984.
Sexes et parentés. Paris: Minuit, 1987.
Je, tu, nous: Pour une culture de la différence. Paris: Grasset, 1990.
J'aime à toi. Paris: Grasset, 1992.

Secondary Texts

Chanter, Tina. *Ethics of Eros: Irigaray's Rewriting of the Philosophers*. New York: Routledge, 1995.
Whitford, Margaret, ed. *The Irigaray Reader*. Oxford: Blackwell, 1991.
———. *Luce Irigaray: Philosophy in the Feminine*. London: Routledge, 1991.

Islam. Catholic France, the great defender of Christendom in the Middle Ages, is home to over 5 million Muslims at the end of the twentieth century. The significance of this Islamic presence is inseparable from France's history of colonialism*, in which representations of Muslim women incarnated the multiple differences between East and West.

A monotheistic religion, Islam recognizes one supreme being, a holy book, and a last judgment. Muslims follow the revelations and teachings of the early seventh-century prophet Mohammed, as recorded in the Qur'an. Islam shared with most cultures in Arabia patriarchal practices such as polygamy, the double sexual standard for men and women, and seclusion for upper-class women. Islamic family law, codified in the eighth century, institutionalized the subordination of women. The rapidly expanding Islamic world eventually reached the borders of Europe with Saracen attacks on southern France. The military danger overcome, the Crusades and confrontation in Spain brought Christians into closer contact with Muslims. Scholars studied Islamic science and debated its theology, and popular writers churned out stories of lascivious women and savage men. With the Enlightenment*, universalist thinkers recognized Islam as a world civilization, although the stereotypes of Muslim women as sensual and subservient did not change.

The extension of the French empire into North Africa and the Middle East inaugurated a new period of fascination with Muslim life. Nineteenth-century Orientalist writers and painters popularized the fantasy of the Arab woman, veiled in public, enticingly nude in private. Arguing that the emancipation of women reflected overall social progress, colonialists used the idea of Muslim oppression of women, signified by veiling and seclusion, as a way of defining Arab society as backward. French women travelers, teachers, wives of colonial officials, and nuns produced nuanced accounts of Islamic women which belied male writers' erotic images. Nevertheless, even feminist writers assumed the superiority of the West. Many women in the Islamic world certainly sought education* and desired reform of the patriarchal family law code, but most Muslim feminists linked their struggles to the nationalist, anticolonial movements, with some looking for change within Islam.

The mass of French people first encountered Muslim Arabs and Africans after 1914 as colonial conscripts and workers. Disdained and exploited, these single men were often depicted as violent barbarians who threatened French womanhood. Not until after World War II* did religious difference become a significant factor in attitudes toward Muslims. The bitter struggle to hold onto Algeria (1954–1962) pitted France once more against an Islamic enemy, albeit in the form of an Arab and Berber nationalist insurgency. The militancy of Algerian women came as a particular shock, challenging the image of veiled passivity so prevalent in colonial representations. In the aftermath of the Algerian war political refugees and economic migrants flowed into France from the poverty-stricken Maghreb. The settlement of North African families in urban neighborhoods in the 1970s made it obvious that their presence was permanent. In the next decade, French attitudes became polarized. While the government called for a French version of Islam, the right-wing National Front coalition condoned violent attacks on the North African community and raised the specter of the 1979 fundamentalist revolution in Iran—all this despite the widespread lack of religiosity among Algerian Muslims and their French-born children.

In the news media the veiled woman became a symbol of Islam in France, particularly after a 1989 incident in which three girls were expelled from their school outside Paris for refusing to remove their headscarves in class. Many saw this refusal as a challenge not just to the secular character of French schools, but also to the founding principles of the Republic and, by extension, French identity itself. The issue severely divided feminists, with most supporting the secularist argument, some accepting the expulsions as a necessary repudiation of the patriarchal values of Islam, and still others defending the girls, even if they adhered to an oppressive tradition, in order that they might receive the benefit of a modern education. A government ruling that the wearing of religious clothes was not in itself enough to justify exclusion only partially resolved the issue, for it was only one aspect of a wider panic about the rise of fundamentalism. The relatively few veiled women are often demonized as the vanguard of an expansionist Islam poised to take over France. It must be said, however, that the veil has various meanings for young Muslim women in France. For those from traditional families, the veil provides an acceptable way of leaving home for French schools and work. For others, putting on the veil represents the affirmation of a desire to be both French and Muslim. Veiling can coexist with a refusal of inequality and polygamy, and does not necessarily signal agreement with fundamentalist ideology. The generalized suspicion of Muslims is particularly upsetting for French-Maghrebine women who, unveiled and acculturated, are trying to negotiate their way between the two traditions. The works of writers like Assia Djebar* and artists like Djura* have articulated the difficulties of North African women who reject Islamic practices but maintain pride in their Muslim and Maghrebine heritage.

Yaël Simpson Fletcher

BIBLIOGRAPHY

Ahmed, Leila. *Women and Gender in Islam*. New Haven: Yale University Press, 1992.
Cesari, Jocelyne. *Etre musulman en France: Associations, militants et mosquées*. Paris: Karthala-IREMEM, 1994.
Gaspard, Françoise, and Farhad Khosrokhavar. *Le Foulard et la République*. Paris: La Découverte, 1995.
Graham-Brown, Sarah. *Images of Women: The Portrayal of Women in Photography of the Middle East, 1860–1950*. New York: Columbia University Press, 1988.

J

Jansenism. A rigorous Augustinianism which arose during the first half of the seventeenth century in opposition to an optimistic form of Counter-Reformation theology known as Molinism that minimized the consequences of original sin. In contrast, Corneille Jansen's *Augustinus* (1640) found favor with groups that refused compromise with worldly values by insisting on the need for efficacious grace to overcome concupiscence.

In France, Jansen's proponent was an old friend, Duvergier de Hauranne, abbé of Saint-Cyran, who had become the spiritual director of Port-Royal*. Jansenism was attacked on two fronts. Jesuits found its penitential spirit and stress on the difficulty of achieving salvation too disheartening for average Christians. Furthermore, Louis XIV saw the Jansenists as an obstacle to his desire to subordinate foreign and domestic policy to the interests of the absolutist state.

Repeated royal and papal condemnation changed the focus of Jansenism over the seventeenth and eighteenth centuries. Jansenists saw themselves as persecuted defenders of the truth, as upholders of the rights of the individual conscience against arbitrary authority. Women played a heroic role in this opposition, as seen in the accounts of captivity by nuns of Port-Royal who, like Angélique de Saint-Jean, were exiled to other convents* in 1664 for their refusal to sign the formulary. Their *relations de captivité* are among the most powerful texts written by nuns at that institution.

Port-Royal's austere devotion attracted the support of numerous sympathizers, not all of whom were, strictly speaking, Jansenists. Noble women such as Anne de Rohan*, the marquise de Sablé*, and the king's own cousin, the duchesse de Longueville, protected it. Mme de Lafayette* and Mme de Sévigné* also counted among its friends.

Jansenism's greatest contribution to women's learning was probably not the education* offered boarders at Port-Royal, which was much less innovative than the instruction given boys in the little schools. Rather, Jansenism promoted the inclusion of women in the audience for serious intellectual debate. Arnauld's *La Fréquente Communion* and Pascal's *Provinciales* gave women access to theological discussions that previously had been conducted in Latin among men. Likewise, at a time when the Church limited women's access to Scripture, Jansenist translations made the Bible* available to them.

After the renewed papal condemnation in 1713 by the bull *Unigenitus*, Jansenism became primarily a focus for protest against royal and papal authoritarianism. While women played little role in the agitation against *Unigenitus* among judges and the clergy, they were prominent in two other areas. They probably formed a majority of the convulsionaries whose trances and miraculous cures brought discredit to Jansenism in the eyes of the general public. After the closing of the Saint-Médard cemetery in 1732 forced these practices underground, women participated as equals with men in the conventicles where the convulsionary movement survived. On the other hand, the reputation of the Jansenists as heroic martyrs for truth owes much to Marguerite de Joncoux (1668–1715) and Marie de Théméricourt (1671–1745), who continued the historiographic work of Angélique de Saint-Jean by collecting and preserving the monastery's archives.

Thomas M. Carr, Jr.

BIBLIOGRAPHY

Primary Text

Arnauld d'Andilly, Angélique de Saint-Jean. *Relations de captivité*. Ed. Louis Cognet. Paris: Gallimard, 1954.

Secondary Texts

Adam, Antoine. *Du Mysticisme à la révolte. Les Jansénistes du XVIIe siècle*. Paris: Fayard, 1968.
Bugnion-Secretan, Perle. *La Mère Angélique Arnauld*. Paris: Cerf, 1991.
Chédozeau, Bernard. "Port-Royal et le jansénisme: La Revendication d'une autre forme du tridentinisme?" *XVIIe Siècle* (1991): 119–125.
Gazier, Cécile. *Les Belles Amies de Port-Royal*. Paris: Perrin, 1930.
Kreiser, B. Robert. *Miracles, Convulsions and Ecclesiastical Politics in Early Eighteenth-Century Paris*. Princeton: Princeton University Press, 1978.
Marie, Catherine-Laurence. *Les Convulsionnaires de Saint-Médard: Miracles, convulsions et prophéties à Paris au XVIIIe siècle*. Paris: Gallimard, 1985.
Mesnard, Jean. "Jansénisme et littérature." In *Le Statut de la littérature, mélanges offerts à Paul Bénichou*. Ed. Marc Fumaroli. Geneva: Droz, 1982. 117–135.
Sedgwick, Alexander. *Jansenism in Seventeenth-Century France: Voices from the Wilderness*. Charlottesville: University of Virginia Press, 1977.
Timmermans, Linda. *L'Accès des femmes à la culture (1598–1715)*. Paris: Champion, 1993.
———. "Une hérésie féministe? Jansénisme et préciosité." In *Ordre et contestation au temps des classiques*. Seattle: Biblio 17, 1992. 159–172.
Van Kley, Dale. *The Jansenists and the Expulsion of the Jesuits from France, 1757–1765*. New Haven: Yale University Press, 1975.

Weaver, F. Ellen. "Erudition, Spirituality, and Women: The Jansenist Contribution." In
   Women in Reformation and Counter-Reformation Europe. Ed. Sherrin Marshall.
   Bloomington: Indiana University Press, 1989. 189–205.
———. "Port-Royal." *Dictionnaire de spiritualité.* Paris: Beauchêne, 1985.

Jeanne d'Albret. *See* Albret, Jeanne d'.

Jodin, Marie-Madeleine (1741–1790). The daughter of Protestant immigrants,
Jodin had a tumultuous childhood and eventually joined Josse Rousselois's
troupe at the Polish court in Warsaw. Between 1765 and 1769, Diderot wrote
Jodin nineteen letters offering advice on acting, warning against the dangers of
theatrical life, and encouraging her to become an "honest" woman. In the years
preceding the Revolution*, she read extensively, acquiring the culture evident
in her brochure, *Vues législatives pour les femmes, adressées à l'Assemblée
nationale.* Following the epigraph, "Et nous aussi nous sommes citoyennes!"
(We, too, are citizens!), Jodin laments that women—despite being half the population—are denied influence in government. She proposes new laws to enhance
women's rights, seeks to eliminate prostitution*, gambling, and obscenity, and
advocates the creation of new legal courts—"conciliation" chambers to deal
with domestic matters, and "civil" chambers to handle public scandals. These
court buildings would also shelter poor and homeless women. Jodin envisages
a legislative assembly, composed exclusively of women, to formulate a "feminine code" of ethics. She concludes her brochure with strong support for divorce*. In *The Twilight of the Goddesses*, Madelyn Gutwirth cites Jodin's text
as a woman's response to "republican heroism."

Marie-Pascale Pieretti

BIBLIOGRAPHY

Primary Text

*Vues législatives pour les femmes, adressées à l'Assemblée nationale par Mademoiselle
   Jodin, fille d'un citoyen de Genève.* Angers: Mame, 1790.

Secondary Texts

Diderot, Denis. "Lettres à Mademoiselle Jodin." In *Oeuvres complètes. Correspondance.*
   Paris: Garnier, 1876. Vol. 2.
Proctor, Candice E. *Women, Equality, and the French Revolution.* Westport, CT: Green-
   wood Press, 1990.
Vernière, Paul. "Marie Madeleine Jodin, amie de Diderot et témoin des Lumières."
   Studies on Voltaire and the Eighteenth Century 58 (1967): 1765–1775.

Judaism. In medieval and early modern France, Jewish law and tradition regulated most aspects of life for the ghettoized Jewish communities, most of whose
members had few opportunities for contact with the outside world. Within such
traditional communities, Jewish women were in many ways religiously marginalized. No special ceremonies marked the birth of a girl or a girl's religious

majority. Women did not count toward a *minyan* (the quorum of ten men required for public religious prayer), were not called to read from the Torah, and were dispensed from studying the sacred texts that constitute the heart of Judaism, a dispensation which in practice became a virtual prohibition. They were also exempt from the fulfillment of all religious commandments required to be performed at specific times, on the grounds that such duties would interfere with the performance of their domestic roles.

Despite this alienation from the spiritual center of Judaism, women were nonetheless integral to the maintenance of a Jewish home, where much of Jewish ritual takes place. To them fell the main responsibility for keeping a kosher home and for preparing for the Sabbath and festivals, and in an age and a culture in which a clear separation between the spiritual and the mundane did not exist, women's domestic tasks could take on a religious meaning. Their contributions to the economic welfare of the family were important too; although theoretically women could own no property, in fact they took an often significant part in business activities. The medieval period also saw some improvements in the legal status of women, most notably with the abolition of polygamy and the prohibition of divorce* without the consent of the wife (although still only the husband could grant the wife a religious divorce).

The French Revolution* and the nineteenth century brought many changes for the Jews of France, who, as a result of political, social, and economic emancipation, slowly became integrated into the national community. As they faced the question of how to maintain a specifically Jewish identity in the modern secular world, many Jewish communal leaders paid a great deal of attention to women's position as mothers, arguing that as educators of the next generation, women were—or at least should be—the main conveyors of cultural identity. As the realization spread that mothers could not raise committed Jewish children if they themselves were ignorant of their religion, voices called for a more serious religious education* for girls; subsequently, some improvements were made in women's religious instruction and more attention was paid to women's religious roles in general. A religious initiation ceremony for both boys and girls became increasingly common, and a naming ceremony for newborn girls was instituted. Furthermore, while men retained firm control of communal administration, Jewish women did begin to take on increased responsibilities within the community, especially in the burgeoning field of Jewish philanthropy. They also took advantage of opportunities offered by the wider society, such as strengthened secular education and more extensive job prospects.

In twentieth-century France, the development of Liberal Judaism, which includes equality of the sexes as one of its central tenets, has opened up new possibilities for Jewish women. Liberal Judaism, however, represents only a small group within the Jewish community, and the official orthodox outlook on women remains largely traditional. But the birth of the organization Cooperation féminine in the 1960s, together with the fact that entire issues of the journals *Nouveaux Cahiers*, *Hamore*, and *Combat pour la Diaspora* have been devoted to Jewish women in general and Jewish girls' education in particular, indicates that the wider society's attention to women's issues has struck a chord within the Jewish community as well.

In recent decades, large numbers of Sephardic immigrants from North Africa arrived in France. The experiences of immigrant women of the Moroccan, Tunisian, and Algerian Jewish communities, as well as the impact of the demographic changes on attitudes toward Jewish women in general, provide new areas for research.

Jennifer I. Sartori

BIBLIOGRAPHY

Bebe, Pauline. *Le Judaïsme libéral*. Paris: Ed. Grancher, 1993.

Blumenkranz, Bernhard, ed. *Histoire des Juifs en France*. Toulouse: Edouard Privat, 1972.

"Femmes juives, voix d'elles." *Nouveaux Cahiers* 46 (Fall 1976).

Hyman, Paula E. *Gender and Assimilation in Modern Jewish History: The Roles and Representations of Women*. Seattle: University of Washington Press, 1995.

Lévy, Simon. *Discours sur la condition et les devoirs de la femme israélite, prononcés pendant l'hiver 1869*. Bordeaux: Impr. de E. Crugy, 1869.

Picard, Marianne. "Les Filles dans l'éducation juive." *Nouveaux Cahiers* 78 (1984): 40–43.

K

Kéralio-Robert, Louise Félicité Guynement de (1758–1822). Historian, editor, journalist, pamphleteer, novelist, translator, pedagogue, publisher, and printer, Kéralio-Robert fashioned a prodigious literary career that repeatedly challenged and expanded both the gender and genre boundaries that typically circumscribed the activities of "women of letters" during the revolutionary era. Born in 1758 into an old noble Breton family, she was recognized as a linguistic virtuoso, having mastered Ancient Greek, Latin, Italian, and English. At age eighteen Kéralio embarked upon her two most important works: a twelve-volume *Collection* of great French women writers (1786–1788), and a five-volume *Histoire d'Elisabeth, reine d'Angleterre* (1786–1788). The *Collection* and the *Histoire* elaborated what remain to this day the two main approaches to feminist historiography—one separatist, one integrationist. The *Collection* offers a series of exemplary portraits of exceptional literary women as models to women of her own age. The history of Elizabeth, by contrast, departs radically from the conventions of *femme forte* histories and is instead a critical constitutional history of Elizabeth's reign in the Whig tradition, but with a feminist twist: it includes a searing critique of the paradoxical nature of a female sovereign in a political culture that coded public virtue as inherently masculine. This work earned Kéralio immediate renown as the "first professional woman historian," and in 1787 she was the third woman ever to be elected to the Academy of Arras.

In the 1780s Kéralio secretly launched a publishing* house in Paris. In 1789 she threw herself into radical revolutionary politics, opening a printing shop and launching a career as journalist and pamphleteer. Her most important work during this period was an anonymously published indictment of Marie-Antoinette* entitled *Les Crimes des reines de la France* (1791). In 1790 she married a young Jacobin and future Jacobin deputy, François Robert. In 1808 she returned to publishing with several novels* and translations*. Her late novels are explicitly feminist, blending historical and fictional narrative forms, ceaselessly calling into question the normative oppositions between public and private; male and female; history and fiction; or past and present. Kéralio-Robert died in Brussels in 1822 at age sixty-four.

Carla Hesse

BIBLIOGRAPHY

Primary Texts

Adélaïde. Neuchâtel: Imprimerie de la Société typographique, 1782.

Collection des meilleurs ouvrages français composés par les femmes. Paris: [Lagrange, Kéralio], 1786–1788.

Histoire d'Elisabeth, reine d'Angleterre. Paris: [Lagrange, Kéralio], 1786–1788.

Journal de l'état et du citoyen. (1789). N.p. [Paris], 1790.

Observations sur quelques articles du projet de constitution de M. Mounier. Paris: Imprimerie de N. H. Nyon, n.d. [1789].

Addresse aux femmes de Montauban. N.p. [Paris], 1790.

Les Crimes des reines de la France depuis le commencement de la monarchie jusqu'à Marie-Antoinette. Paris: Prudhomme, 1791.

Amélia et Caroline. Paris: L. Collin, 1808.

Alphonse et Mathilde, ou la famille espagnole. Paris, 1809.

Rose et Albert. Paris, 1810.

Secondary Texts

Antheunis, L. *Le Conventionnel belge François Robert (1763–1826) et sa femme Louise de Kéralio (1758–1822)*. Wetteren: Editions Bracke, 1955.

Hesse, Carla. "Revolutionary Histories: The Literary Politics of Louise de Kéralio (1758–1822)." In *Culture and Identity in Early Modern Europe (1550–1800): Essays in Honor of Natalie Zemon Davis*. Ed. Barbara Diefendorf and Carla Hesse. Ann Arbor: University of Michigan Press, 1993.

Kofman, Sarah (1934–1994). Writer and professor of philosophy. Kofman's autobiographical *Rue Ordener, rue Labat* (1994) recounts her experience as a Jewish child in Paris during the German Occupation. Kofman wrote numerous works on philosophers and psychoanalysts such as Derrida, Kant, Nietzsche, Freud, and Comte. She viewed her philosophical writing as a form of feminist activity—part of the struggle to free women from the theoretical constructs in which men have imprisoned them. Kofman is best known for *L'Enigme de la femme* (1980), a work in which she presents a Derridean reading of Freud's essay on narcissism and critiques Irigaray's* interpretation of Freud (*Speculum de l'autre femme*). Kofman sees Freud's analysis of the narcissistic woman as potentially more productive than that of his rival René Girard in that Freud recognizes women's self-sufficiency and indifference to men's desire. She speculates that, fearing the implications of this independence, Freud failed to build on his insights, adopting instead a less threatening approach for men's narcissism.

In an earlier study, Kofman traces Comte's progression from his early conception of woman as a subordinate being to his later glorification of woman, which stems from his acceptance of femininity* in himself and others. Other works by Kofman include a text on Auschwitz, *Paroles suffoquées* (1987), an analysis of Freud's use of fiction (*Quatre romans analytiques*, 1974), and a study of aesthetic pleasure and the psychoanalytic interpretation of art (*L'Enfance de l'art*, 1985). In all of her work, Kofman supports a redefining of the categories of "masculine" and "feminine" writing.

                                          Susan Ireland and Patrice J. Proulx

BIBLIOGRAPHY

   Primary Texts

Quatre romans analytiques. Paris: Galilée, 1974.
Aberrations: Le Devenir-femme d'Auguste Comte. Paris: Flammarion, 1978.
L'Enigme de la femme: La Femme dans les textes de Freud. Paris: Galilée, 1980.
Le Respect des femmes: Kant et Rousseau. Paris: Galilée, 1982.
Lectures de Derrida. Paris: Galilée, 1984.
L'Enfance de l'art: Une Interprétation de l'esthéthique freudienne. Paris: Galilée, 1985.
Nietzsche et la scène philosophique. Paris: Galilée, 1986.
Paroles suffoquées. Paris: Galilée, 1987.
Le Mépris des juifs: Nietzsche, les juifs, l'anti-sémitisme. Paris: Galilée, 1994.
Rue Ordener, rue Labat. Paris: Galilée, 1994.

   Secondary Text

Jardine, Alice A., and Anne M. Menke, eds. *Shifting Scenes: Interviews on Women, Writing, and Politics in Post-68 France.* New York: Columbia University Press, 1991.

Kristeva, Julia (1941–). Writer, psychoanalyst, and professor of linguistics. Though she was born and raised in Bulgaria, Julia Kristeva's intellectual identity is so firmly rooted in her adopted country of exile that she has come to occupy a privileged, though not unproblematic, position in the development of French critical theory. Kristeva's earlier works, concurrent with her participation in the influential Tel Quel group, focus on the subversive potential of linguistic innovation as a symbolic response to political and economic oppression as evidenced for Kristeva in literary modernism's revolt against early capitalism. In *La Révolution du langage poétique* (1974), Kristeva refutes the structuralist vision of language as a monolithic system of interrelated signs and proposes in its place a symbolic order constituted through a destabilized, heterogenous movement between bodily drives (the semiotic) and symbolic representation (the symbolic). Rejecting the notion of a transcendent, unified speaking subject, Kristeva argues that the rhythmic dialectic of the symbolic is materially prefigured in the semiotic body whose consistently unsettling desire then fuels the construction of an illusively static discursive order. In other words, the signifying body is necessary to the symbolic function and is encoded as such from the moment of conception. This reintroduction of the speaking body into the field of representation takes on political—and even revolutionary—implications as the semiotic bodily moment of discourse, located in what Kristeva terms the prediscursive maternal chora, disrupts symbolic stability and ultimately prohibits definitive representation.

Though the focus of Kristeva's later works shifts more toward the psychoanalytic, her concern with liminal spaces and paradigms of representation remains thematically central. In her next three major texts, *Pouvoirs de l'horreur* (1980), *Histoires d'amour* (1983), and *Soleil noir: Depression et mélancolie* (1987), she theorizes the role of the pre-Oedipal maternal function in psychic development. Whereas Freud and Lacan read symbolic activity as a direct result of the paternal function via the Oedipal break, Kristeva argues that rejection of the maternal body and primary identification, already operative prior to language acquisition, maternally prefigure the psychic dialectic of the symbolic. As an analyst interpreting the symbolic representations of a theoretical analysand, Kristeva maintains that the subject's ambiguous relation to the maternal body reveals itself discursively through the semiotic drives without which both language and identity would become static and lifeless. Psychoanalysis, in this sense, demystifies individual subjectivity, blurs the borders of identity, and subverts the distinction between self and other. For Kristeva, psychoanalysis's exploration and acceptance of the other within the self opens the possibility for a new ethical system based on a comparable reception of the other in society.

The maternal body as embodiment of subjective alterity and the inherent inseparability of self and other metaphorically figures Kristeva's ethical project and opens her work to accusations of essentialism*. The pregnant woman— neither one nor two—represents the undecidability of the Kristevan split subject. For Kristeva, maternity* (insistently distinguished from womanhood) functions in a liminal space belonging to neither culture nor nature; the mother as ethical model also pushes at the margins of the social and expands the bounds of inclusivity. In *Etrangers à nous-mêmes* (1989), Kristeva's depiction of the immigrant experience in a xenophobic and racist France extends her analysis of the individual split subject to the social sphere. For Kristeva, just as the individual can learn to embrace the other within, so too can society as a whole begin to accept its own constitutive multiplicity.

While her ethical emphasis on difference and liminality has been read as politically progressive from a feminist point of view, Kristeva's explicit disavowal of feminism*, in addition to other more theoretical concerns (biologism, essentialism*), has created a certain wariness on the part of feminists with regard to her work. In her best-known commentary on feminism, "Le Temps des femmes" (1979), she labels first wave feminists as existentialists concerned with equality and power, and second wave feminists as essentialists concerned with patriarchal hierarchy reversal. Despite Kristeva's curious unopenness toward feminism, her work is most certainly useful to feminists concerned with questions of identity politics. For, though neither "French" nor "feminist," as her American labeling might indicate, her continued explorations of sociopsychic boundaries and her questioning of the symbolic confines imposed by traditional feminine archetypes (the Virgin mother, the hysteric) cannot but enhance a feminist understanding of these pressing issues.

Lisa Walsh

BIBLIOGRAPHY

Primary Texts

Seméiotikè: Recherches pour une sémanalyse. Paris: Seuil, 1969.
"Le Temps des femmes." *Cahiers de Recherches de Sciences des Textes et Documents* 33–44 (1979): 5–19.
La Révolution du langage poétique. Paris: Seuil, 1974.
Pouvoirs de l'horreur. Paris: Seuil, 1980.
Histoires d'amour. Paris: Denoël, 1983.
Soleil noir: Depression et mélancolie. Paris: Gallimard, 1987.
Etrangers à nous-mêmes. Paris: Fayard, 1989.
Les Nouvelles Maladies de l'âme. Paris: Fayard, 1993.
Sens et non-sens de la révolte: Pouvoirs et limites de la psychanalyse I. Paris: Fayard, 1996.

Secondary Texts

Fletcher, John, and Andrew Benjamin, eds. *Abjection, Melancholia and Love: The Work of Julia Kristeva.* New York: Routledge, 1990.
Moi, Toril, ed. *The Kristeva Reader.* New York: Columbia University Press, 1986.
Oliver, Kelly. *Reading Kristeva: Unraveling the Double-Bind.* Bloomington: Indiana University Press, 1993.

Krüdener, Barbara Juliane de (1764–1824). Born in Riga, Latvia, Barbara Juliane von Vietinghof married a diplomat twenty years her senior, baron von Krüdener, in 1782. Soon after the birth of a son, the baron became ambassador to Venice. A young secretary accompanied them to Italy and fell in love with Juliane. This is the historic basis of her pre-Romantic best-selling novel*, *Valérie* (1804). She left her husband to live in France, where she wrote this and other prose works. After her husband's death, Juliane had a religious conversion, and was instrumental in persuading Alexander of Russia to create the Holy Alliance (1815) with Austria and Prussia. The main theme of Madame de Krüdener's works is the search for love which gives meaning to her life. From an earthly concept of love, she moves to spiritual love for a human in *Valérie* and, after her conversion, to the all-embracing love of God.

Valérie is an epistolary novel including the letters of a Swede, Gustave de Linar, narrating his impossible love for the wife of his benefactor, the count of B. A victim of his passion, Gustave dies in a monastery after being forgiven by the count and Valérie. The themes of love and death alternate with that of climate which influences behavior. Gustave, the cool Northerner, is undone by warm, sensuous Italy as much as by the beautiful Valérie. Seen almost uniquely through the eyes of Gustave, the heroine becomes an idealized object rather than a real person.

Lucy M. Schwartz

BIBLIOGRAPHY

Primary Texts

Valérie ou lettres de Gustave de Linar à Ernest de G . . . . Paris: Henrichs, 1804.
Le Camp de vertus. Paris: Le Normant, 1815.
Lettre au baron de Berkheim. Karlsruhe: N.p., 1817.
Albert et Clara. Les Malheurs de l'Helvétie. Stuttgart: N.p., 1824.
Ecrits intimes et prophétiques de Madame de Krüdener: 1785–1807. Paris: CNRS, 1975.

Secondary Texts

Decreus van Liefland, Juliette. "La Baronne de Krüdener." In *Sainte-Beuve et la critique des auteurs féminins.* Paris: Boivin, 1949. 122–138.
Eynard, Charles. *Vie de Mme de Krüdener.* Paris: Cherbuliez, 1849.
Ford, Clarence. *The Life and Letters of Mme de Krüdener.* London: Adam and Charles Black, 1893.
Knapton, E. J. *The Lady of the Holy Alliance.* New York: Columbia University Press, 1939.
Kohler, Pierre. "*Valérie* ou maîtres et imitateurs de Mme de Krüdener." *Bulletin de l'institut national genevois* 45 (1922–1923): 193–222.
Le Breton, André. "*Claire d'Albe-Valérie.*" In *Le Roman français au XIXe siècle avant Balzac.* Paris: Boivin, 1901. 90–113.
Ley, Francis. *Bernardin de Saint-Pierre, Madame de Staël, Chateaubriand, Benjamin Constant et Madame de Krüdener.* Paris: Aubier-Montaigne, 1967.
———. *Mme de Krüdener et son temps.* Paris: Plon, 1961.
Mercier, Michel. "*Valérie": Origine et destinée d'un roman.* Dissertation, University of Paris IV, 1972.
Merlant, Joachim. "Mme de Krüdener—*Valérie.*" In *Le Roman personnel de Rousseau à Fromentin.* Paris: Hachette, 1905. 167–191.
Sainte-Beuve, Charles-Augustin. "Madame de Krüdner [*sic*]" and "Madame de Krüdner [*sic*] et ce qu'en aurait dit Saint-Evremond." In *Oeuvres.* Paris: Gallimard, 1956. 2: 764–784, 1327–1352.

Krysinska, Marie (1857–1908). This French symbolist writer of Polish origin played a significant role in the innovation of *vers libre.* Krysinska came to Paris at age sixteen. Once she abandoned her study of piano, she reveled with other bohemians, passing from the Hydropathes to the Je m'enfoutistes. Experimenting in turn with poetic writing, Krysinska published free verse before her male counterpart Gustave Kahn, who nonetheless claimed the precedence of his *vers libre.* By defending *his* innovation against *hers,* Kahn unwittingly supports the place that Krysinska occupies in French poetic history. Moreover, her poetry* and prose at the turn of the century announce a modern female subject coming to terms with the force of her own desire.

Adrianna M. Paliyenko

BIBLIOGRAPHY

Primary Texts

Le Chat noir. N.p., 1882, 1883, 1889, 1890, 1891, 1893.
Rythmes pittoresques. Paris: Lemerre, 1890.

L'Amour chemine. Paris: Lemerre, 1892.

Joies errantes. Paris: Lemerre, 1894.

Folle de son corps. Paris: Havard, 1896.

"Les Femmes des lettres anglaises." *Revue universelle* (November 16, 1901): 1085–1088.

Intermèdes. Paris: Messein, 1904.

La Force du désir. Paris: Société du Mercure de France, 1905.

Secondary Texts

Hauser, Fernand. "Madame Maria Krysinska." *Simple Revue* (May 16, 1894): 49–52.

Rachilde. "La Force du désir." *Mercure de France* 56 (July 1, 1905): 102–103.

Zanetto. "Profils de poètes: Mme Maria Krysinska." *Simple Revue* (November 1893): 332.

L

La Briche, Adélaïde-Edmée Prévost de (1755–1844). The only child of a doting mother, La Briche was well educated, became an accomplished musician, learned Italian, and studied mathematics. In marrying the younger brother of M. d'Epinay and Mme d'Houdetot, she entered the world of financiers. From an uncle she inherited a great fortune and the château du Marais near Paris. Widowed young, she never remarried, devoting her life to her daughter, extended family, and friends. During half a century, and regardless of the politics of the day, her salon* attracted men and women of letters, artists, members of government, financiers, and aristocrats, such as Saint-Lambert, Morellet, Marmontel, La Harpe, Fontanes, Chateaubriand, Pauline de Beaumont, Sophie Cottin*, Mme de Genlis*, Guizot, the Duke of Wellington, Talleyrand, and Walter Scott. She wrote—but did not publish—memoirs* and journals of her travels to Italy, Switzerland, England, and Scotland. Although she lived in turbulent times, she was never in danger, and continued to welcome relatives and friends in both her summer and winter houses and to give help and shelter to the needy. Loved and admired, she was universally known for her kindness.

Catherine Lafarge

BIBLIOGRAPHY
  Secondary Texts
Zurich, Pierre de. *Une Femme heureuse, Madame de la Briche*. Paris: E. de Boccard, 1934.
———. *Les Voyages en Suisse de Madame de la Briche*. Neuchâtel and Paris: Victor Attinger, 1934.

La Fite, Marie Elisabeth Bouée de (1750?–1794). The wife of a Protestant preacher living in La Haye, as a mother La Fite found that there were few books suitable for young children. In her *Entretiens, drames et contes moraux* (1778), dedicated to Queen Charlotte Sophia, wife of King George III of England, she expresses in the dedication and preface the desire to show goodness and morality in an entertaining manner, using children as characters in situations such as those that real children might encounter in everyday life. Through a series of dialogues between the young Julie, her mother Mme de Valcour, and her cousin Annette, and an intermingling of stories, plays, and letters, La Fite expects to influence her young, probably female, audience. Although some of her stories are translations* and adaptations from the German children's serial *Der Kinder Freund* (1775–1781) by Christian Felix Weisse, the majority of the work is original and was reprinted in at least four editions. La Fite published a second educational volume, *Eugénie et ses élèves* (1787), as well as *Lettres sur divers sujets* (1775). Published translations from German include works by Johann Lavater, Sophie de la Roche, and Johann Cramer. Additionally, she aided her husband with the periodical *Bibliothèque des sciences et des beaux arts.*

Sarah Harrell DeSmet

BIBLIOGRAPHY

Primary Texts

Lettres sur divers sujets. The Hague: P.-F. Gosse, 1775.
Entretiens, drames et contes moraux. The Hague: Detune, 1778.
Eugénie et ses élèves. Paris: Onfron et Née de La Rochelle, 1787.

Secondary Text

Buck, Claire, ed. *The Bloomsbury Guide to Women's Literature.* New York: Prentice-Hall, 1992.

La Force, Charlotte-Rose Caumont de (1654–1724). La Force was born to a high-ranking noble family known for defending the Protestant cause during the Wars of Religion, although she herself converted to Catholicism in 1686. She had numerous connections at court: she held the position of lady-in-waiting to the Dauphine, was intimately acquainted with Madame Palatine, dedicated several of her novels* to the Princesses of Conty, and even received a pension from Louis XIV. La Force also seems to have had connections to the Duc de Vendôme's libertine gatherings in the Temple section of Paris. Like several other late seventeenth-century women writers (notably, d'Aulnoy* and Murat*), she was associated with several public scandals: she was known to have had love affairs; her marriage*, which had been contracted without parental consent, was annulled by her husband's father; and she was exiled for a time to a convent* for composing impious Noëls. During her exile, she wrote a volume of fairy tales* (*Les Contes des contes*, 1697) and several historical novels (*Gustave Vasa*, 1697–1698; *Anecdote galante*, 1703). Three other novels had appeared before her exile: *Histoire secrète de Bourgogne* (1694), *Histoire secrète de Henry IV* (1695), and *Histoire de Marguerite de Valois, reine de Navarre, soeur de François Ier* (1696). Her fairy tales, republished several times in the eighteenth century, include ''Persinette,'' the first published version of the tale popularized by the Grimms as "Rapunzel." In many of her fairy tales, La Force includes thinly disguised erotic descriptions that defy the period's conventional representation of love. La Force's novels are almost exclusively of the "secret history" variety and are among the best known of this subgenre. The one exception is a novel published only in the nineteenth century, *Les Jeux d'esprit, ou la Promenade de la princesse de Conty à Eu*, which depicts the parlor games of a salon* and suggests the close links between these games and numerous literary forms. A well-known writer in her time, La Force was a member of the Accademia dei Ricovrati of Padua, a close friend of Deshoulières*, and in all likelihood acquainted with d'Aulnoy and Murat.

Lewis C. Seifert

BIBLIOGRAPHY

Primary Text

"Plus Belle que Fée," "Persinette," and "Tourbillon." In *Le Cabinet des fées*. Arles: Picquier Poche, 1994. 2: 9–57.

La Guesnerie, Charlotte-Marie-Anne Charbonnier de (1710?–1785). Very little is known about her except that she was born and remained in Angers and published four novels* anonymously. In a letter to the man who acted as her intermediary with publishers, La Guesnerie expresses her fear of the notoriety attached to the title of a woman author and refers to her work as "little nothings." At the same time, she discounts criticism of her work, standing firmly behind her aesthetic vision. This double discourse is characteristic of her work, in which she criticizes society's unjust treatment of women but stops short of condemning the institutions themselves. A stronger criticism is revealed, however, through her plots, which depict a harsh world where the wrong choice of a marriage* partner is critical in a legal system biased against women. Commentary on wider social issues is imbedded in the stories and serves as a counterpoint. The theme of women's friendship* as a compensatory and dependable alternative to male betrayal is common to all her work. La Guesnerie explores the condition of women in a hostile society, ranging from an examination of an education* suitable to sustain a woman once her youth has gone, to what love means to the mature woman.

Antoinette Marie Sol

BIBLIOGRAPHY

Primary Texts

Mémoires de Miladi B . . . par Madame R . . . . 4 vols. Amsterdam and Paris: Cuissart, 1760.
Iphis et Aglaé, par M***. 2 vols. London and Paris: Merlin, 1768.
Mémoires de Milady de Varmonti, comtesse de Barnshau, traduits ou imités de l'anglais par M. le Cte de M . . . , major du régiment de M . . . . London: N.p., 1778.
Les Ressources de la vertu par l'auteur des "Mémoires de Milady B." Amsterdam and Paris: J.-G. Mérigot le jeune, 1782.

Secondary Text

Soland, A. de. "Mlle de La Guesnerie." *Bulletin historique et monumental de l'Anjou*
    8 (1863–1866): 105–109.

La Guette, Catherine Meurdrac, dame de (1613–after 1676). Mme de La
Guette probably wrote her *Mémoires* soon after 1676, the date of the latest
episode recorded. She may still have been living at the time they were published
in 1681 in Holland.

She was born Catherine Meurdrac in 1613 to a village notable in Brie, but
neither she nor the soldier she married clandestinely held any traceable social
rank. She was a hardy young woman whose father was proud of her ability to
fence and use a pistol. During the Fronde* this intrepid woman protected her
people and property from the bloodthirsty brigands of invading armies. She
undertook a trip to Bordeaux at the request of the queen to negotiate with some
Frondeurs, including her husband. Otherwise she spent her life in Brie, where
she gave birth to ten children; she remained attached to her husband, whose
death in 1665 caused her great affliction. With no family left in France, she
moved to Holland to be with her son, whose death in 1676 left her destitute.
Claiming to be one of the rare women to do so, she wrote her *Mémoires*, recounting in a forthright manner and with little commentary the major events of
her life: her marriage* and eventual reconciliation with her father; her trip to
Bordeaux, duping an enemy army to help the royal cause; the massacres and
pillaging on her lands by foreign troops; and her move to Holland.

The *Mémoires* was perhaps intended to make Mme de La Guette's name and
story better known in the elite society of The Hague in which she was making
a new life. Her writing is engaging, visually lively, and gives a good sense of
this unusual woman.

Carmeta Abbott

BIBLIOGRAPHY

Primary Text

Mémoires. New ed. Micheline Cuénin. Paris: Mercure de France, 1982.

Secondary Text

Lougee, Carolyn Chappell. " 'Reason for the Public to Admire Her': Why Madame de
    La Guette Published Her Memoirs." In *Going Public: Women and Publishing in
    Early Modern France*. Ed. Elizabeth C. Goldsmith and Dena Goodman. Ithaca:
    Cornell University Press, 1995.

La Roche-Guilhen, Anne de (1644–1707). This prolific novelist, born in
Rouen, was descended from the lower ranks of the Huguenot nobility and was
distantly related to the poet Saint-Amant and the memorialist Tallemant des
Réaux. She spent the second half of her life in London, where she first arrived
in 1675; her refusal to abjure her Protestant faith despite the revocation of the

Edict of Nantes precluded a return to France in her later years. In 1677 she received the extraordinary honor of a royal commission: King Charles II had her compose a comedy-ballet (in French) to be performed as part of his birthday celebration. Arguably her most original work, *Rare-en-tout* is a skillful blend of comedy, singing, and dance, with one of the earliest depictions of the fatuous lady's man. She published some twenty volumes of fiction, starting in 1674; by her own admission she wrote fiction primarily to make money. Indeed, she is among the earliest French women to succeed in supporting themselves in this way. Her books must have sold very well, for some were reedited or translated into English in her lifetime, and there were even novels* falsely attributed to her. Her concern for marketability caused her to try a wide variety of novelistic possibilities, ranging from shortened and simplified adaptations of the Scudéry* model, to adventure stories set in exotic places, to novellas where she made a more conscientious effort to respect historical facts and customs.

Perry Gethner

BIBLIOGRAPHY

Primary Text

La Roche-Guilhen, Anne de. *Rare-en-tout*. In *Femmes dramaturges en France (1650–1750). Pièces choisies*. Ed. Perry Gethner. Seattle: Biblio 17, 1993.

Secondary Text

Calame, Alexandre. *Anne de La Roche-Guilhen, romancière huguenote 1644–1707*. Geneva: Droz, 1972.

La Sablière, Marguerite Hessein de Rambouillet de (1640–1693). Born to a family of Huguenot bankers, Marguerite Hessein was taught Latin and Greek and introduced to philosophy and mathematics, an extraordinary education* for a woman at the time. After thirteen years of marriage* she was forced into a legal separation by her husband, the poet and financier Antoine de Rambouillet; she was dispossessed of her children and much of her fortune. She then opened a famous salon* where leading literary and scientific figures debated, among other matters, the theories of Gassendi and Descartes. She offered hospitality and protection to La Fontaine, who praised her in a number of fables and in two "Discours à Madame de la Sablière." When her liaison with the poet La Fare ended in 1680, she devoted herself increasingly to charitable works and converted to Catholicism. She comforted the terminally ill at the Hôpital des Incurables until her death from breast cancer at the age of fifty-three. Her generosity, intelligence, and interest in philosophy and science (she even observed dissections) were praised by all (except Boileau) and made her one of the most influential *salonnières* of her day. Her extant works include *Maximes Chrétiennes*, published in 1705 with La Rochefoucauld's *Réflexions*, and fifty-four letters to her spiritual advisor, the Abbé de Rancé.

Gabrielle Verdier

BIBLIOGRAPHY

Primary Text

Menjot d'Elbenne, Samuel. *Madame de la Sablière, Pensées chrétiennes et ses Lettres à l'abbé de Rancé*. Paris: Plon-Nourrit, 1923.

La Suze, Henriette de Coligny, comtesse de (1618–1673). Daughter of Gaspard III de Coligny and Anne de Polignac, Henriette was raised in the Protestant enclave of Châtillon-sur-Loing, where she met and married Thomas Hamilton, third earl of Haddington (d. 1645). Coerced into a second marriage* to Gaspard de Champagne, comte de La Suze, she gained notoriety for winning its annulment (1661) after eight years' separation, and for conversion to Catholicism sponsored by Queen Anne (1653). Introduced to society at the Hôtels de Rambouillet and de Condé, she wrote verse early. Her poetry* gained prominence only in 1653 with eighteen poems in the collection published by the printer Sercy. The collection published under her name (and Pellisson's) in 1664 by the printer Quinet kept her associated with new lyric poetry through its reissues until 1748. She was one of the first women poets to have an independent collective edition of her poems published (1666): twenty-one odes, elegies, madrigals, airs, and epigrams. It was for her elegies, praised by Boileau and Saint-Amant among others, that she became truly famous. Confessional in tone, simplified in diction and rhythms, these dramatic monologues of triumphant passion opened up a new perspective for lyric poets; instancing a mimetic realism in stark contrast to *précieux* overrefinement, they were both popular and critical successes. They had a wide influence on other women poets, notably Mlle de Scudéry* (who celebrated them in Book VIII [1658] of *Clélie*) and Mme de Villedieu*. Independent of mind and taste, free in her affections as in their poetic expression, living in high and mixed society as she pleased, La Suze was also a more generally powerful role model of the emancipated woman. She was a center of many social circles rather than the hostess of an established large salon*. Revealing of both her mind and manner is the character Eulalie in *La Prétieuse* (1656), modeled on her by the abbé Michel de Pure. Attributions of poems to her and published texts after 1673 should be subject to caution.

Charles G. S. Williams

BIBLIOGRAPHY

Secondary Texts

Magne, Emile. *Madame de La Suze et la société précieuse*. Paris: Société du Mercure de France, 1909.
Niderst, Alain. *Madeleine de Scudéry, Paul Pellisson et leur monde*. Paris: Presses Universitaires de France, 1976.
Pelous, Jean-Michel. *Amour précieux, amour galant, 1654–1675*. Paris: Klincksieck, 1980.

La Vigne, Anne de (1634–1684). This daughter of a doctor cultivated both poetry* and science. She was born in Paris (or, some say, Vernon in Normandy).

Her verses are graceful and facile, in the manner of ladies of her time. It is in her more labored philosophical and feminist harangues that she is most interesting. An ode, "Monseigneur le Dauphin au Roi," was very successful and earned her a typical *précieux* present, a coconut box containing an enameled gold lyre and some lively verses. Another ode, "Les Dames à Mlle de Scudéry," congratulated the famous writer on winning a prize for eloquence at the French Academy. This ode was published by Pellisson with a reply from Mlle de Scudéry*, in his *Histoire de l'Académie française* (1672 edition). Her other poetry, particularly the sonnet "La Paysanne vaincue," appears in the *Vers choisis* of Dominique Bouhours without her name, but it is attributed to her by Lefort de la Morinière in his *Bibliothèque poétique*. Some poems by her are also collected in the *Parnasse des Dames* by Sauvigny. She was fond of the philosophy of Descartes and wrote an ambitious reply to his niece's poem, "L'Ombre de Descartes." She never married, but was known for her virtue, talents, and beauty. She died of kidney stones said to be caused by overwork at her literary pursuits. She belonged to the Accademia dei Ricovrati in Padua.

Dorothy Backer

BIBLIOGRAPHY

Secondary Texts

Biographie universelle ancienne et moderne. Ed. Eugène Ernest Desplaces and J. Fr. Michaud. Paris: Madame Desplaces, etc., 1854–1865.
Moréri, Louis. *Le Grand Dictionnaire historique.* Paris: Les Libraires Associés, 1759.

Labé, Louise (c. 1520–1566). From the 1530s to the 1550s the city of Lyons enjoyed a remarkable intellectual and cultural development as a cosmopolitan center, with a large Italian population of bankers and lawyers. Away from the Sorbonne's repressive scholastic authority, new intellectual ideas circulated freely. Several hundred printers had set up shops and thrived on best-sellers which included Greek philosophers, Latin poets, the *Roman de la Rose*, and Italian writers, especially Petrarch. The city was generously hospitable not only to sculptors, painters, and engravers but to scientists, mathematicians, and French writers including Clément Marot and François Rabelais.

In this favorable climate Louise Labé, the daughter and wife of industrious rope-makers, was able to rise to literary fame in spite of her relatively low social status. Raised, after her mother's death, by nuns who gave her a full-fledged classical education*, she was welcomed into the humanist circles of Lyons. In such an open intellectual climate, she familiarized herself with the contemporary writers, like Erasmus, and poets in the Petrarchan tradition. Her nickname, "La Belle Cordière" (the beautiful rope-maker), refers not only to her family's trade, but also to her skillful use of musical "cordes" (the lute strings) to accompany her poetry.

The posthumous publication of Pernette du Guillet's* *Rymes* (Lyons, 1545), a collection of love poems, may have prompted Labé to start writing her own poetry*. As she began composing her poems, Labé met Olivier de Magny, a translator and poet in his own right, who traveled through Lyons on his way to Rome, where he worked as secretary to the French ambassador. Nothing is clear about the relationship between Labé and Magny except their common passion for love poetry.

On March 13, 1555, Louise Labé formally asked the king for permission to publish her works. They were printed by Jean de Tournes, a respectable Lyons printer specializing in humanist writings. They included a liminary epistle dedicated to a female friend, Clémence de Bourges; the *Débat de Folie et d'Amour*, a mythological dialogue in prose; three elegies or fictional love letters in verse; and twenty-four love sonnets. Labé's own works were followed by another twenty-four poems written anonymously by Labé's friends and all dedicated to her greater glory.

The liminary epistle, which serves as a preface to the works, is an important document for the history of humanism and feminism*. Labé rejects the traditional attributes of the woman as object, her adornment with spectacular jewelry and sumptuous attire. What is important to her is her active participation in a new (or renewed) culture in which she can forge her own true identity. Her desire constitutes a kind of nascent refusal to be defined by others and a joy of recapturing an "être à soi," or fundamental being, which is independent of the objectifying desires of men.

At the same time Labé reformulates a typical problematic of the Renaissance: the acute awareness of the inevitable ravages of time and an urgent desire to escape time through fame. She knows that a lone woman, isolated in a cultural milieu which is at best disdainful, cannot hope to change an oppressive mentality. She invites her female audience to help each other along ("s'encourager mutuellement") in order to publicize their plight and mission. "Do not wile away your youth," she says to her friend Clémence, "don't waste your given talents; set yourself this minute to the study of Arts and Letters, for time is fleeting!"

The *Débat de Folie et d'Amour* is a mythological story in prose dialogue which illustrates, in allegorical fashion and with copious literary references, the conflictual aspects of passion and desire. The mythological setting provides the basis for an amusing parody. The gods suffer noticeably and do not escape ridicule. Jupiter himself evidences the irony of the Olympian gods, who appear as no better than mortals. Cupid depicts the tragic consequences of his blindness in burlesque fashion. As for Folly, she cannot resist peppering her opinions with scabrous double-entendres. Obscene jokes, however, so much a part of comical literature of the period, are absent from the *Débat*. Rather, the work can be described as a *facetia*, a literary genre long debated by Renaissance theorists and which relies heavily on surprise and cunning reversal. Labé sets men and women as the target for facetiousness, hinting at satire while delighting in total freedom. No one is spared.

Labé's three love elegies show her familiarity with Ovid's *Heroides*, which had appeared in several editions between 1507 and 1552. The dominant theme is the destructive passion that leads to folly. Evident here are several Propertian aspects of love's fury, or *furor amoris*: the slow poison which is distilled in the blood and leads to insomnia, anorexia, and finally, death. To express her poetic consciousness, as a woman, Labé turns to Sappho, the most illustrious woman poet of the Western tradition, to serve as her model. The evocation of the loves of Lesbos at the opening of the elegies is significant for a poet who was soon to be called the "Sapho lyonnaise" by her contemporaries.

The twenty-four sonnets (the first of them written in Italian) move from close imitation of the Neoplatonic mode (cosmic harmony) and Petrarchan style (idealized portrait of the lover) to an ironic commentary on the male-coded language of love. Since Petrarch's *Rime sparse*, the notion of a young man's "mistakes" ("giovanile errore") had been a commonplace predicament of European love poetry. Labé develops various connotations of "erreur" in contrast to the "irrevocable order" of the Neoplatonic cosmos. Her daring "revisionism" asserts her intellectual freedom within the tradition of the Renaissance amorous discourse. This is not the least of the enticements of Labé's oeuvre, which speaks to us today with the compelling intensity and fragility of a woman's voice.

François Rigolot

BIBLIOGRAPHY

Primary Texts

Evvres de Lovize Labé Lionnoize. A Lion par Jan de Tournes, MDLV. Avec Privilège du Roy (in-8). Lyons: Jean de Tournes, 1555 and 1556, with an erratum.
Oeuvres de Louise Labé. 2 vols. Ed. Charles Boy. Paris: A. Lemerre, 1887. Reprint. Geneva: Slatkine, 1968.
Oeuvres complètes. Ed. Enzo Giudici. Geneva: Droz, 1981.
Oeuvres complètes de Louise Labé. Ed. François Rigolot. Paris: Flammarion, 1986.

Secondary Texts

Baker, Dorothy Lesko. *The Subject of Desire: Petrarchan Poetics and the Female Voice in Louise Labé*. Lafayette, IN: Purdue University Press, 1996.
Jones, A. R. *The Currency of Eros: Women's Love Lyric in Europe, 1540–1620*. Bloomington: Indiana University Press, 1990. 155–200.
O'Connor, D. *Louise Labé: Sa Vie et son oeuvre*. Paris: Les Presses Françaises, 1926.
Rigolot, François. *Louise Labé Lyonnaise, ou la Renaissance au féminin*. Paris: Champion, 1997.

Lacanian literary theory. The neo-Freudian Jacques Lacan (1901–1981) turns from biology to structural linguistics and anthropology to illuminate analysis and identity formation. At six months, preverbal children enter the mirror stage, an exhilarating but false sense of unification, upon recognizing their reflections in the mirror. Self-cohesion thus begins visually, but subsequently the child

interacts with the Other through language. Language fills the empty space between the self and the symbolic Other, and through language the child negotiates
his needs, demands, and desires. Need (physical), demand (for a specific request
and relationship with the person fulfilling it), and desire (unsatisfiable) are situated in three Lacanian realms which suggest Freud's id-ego-superego: the preverbal Imaginary; the Symbolic, in language; and the Real, which, because it is
present, not absent, cannot be articulated within the Symbolic.

According to Lacan, the unconscious is structured like a language and is a
web of interrelated meanings within a larger system of signs. In this system, the
phallus as master signifier determines the speaking subject's position. Access to
language locates the speaking subject within a hierarchy of power relations depending on one's relationship to the phallus. Consequently, men can claim privilege and power, but women are portrayed as Lack. Nonetheless, Lacan deems
language acquisition an inevitable, salutary compromise of socialization.

Lacanian awareness of language has literary applications. Just as the unconscious becomes conscious through analytic dialogue, so, too, texts present themselves only through language. Lacan's seminar on Poe's *Purloined Letter* traces
the network of power relationships among the characters. The letter, a shifting
phallic signifier, constantly changes meaning and place, as do the characters'
relationships to it and to each other.

Lacan considered his own reading of Freud the most accurate, yet he draws
criticism from feminist writers, notably Hélène Cixous*, Luce Irigaray*, and
Julia Kristeva*, for creating a paradigm that devalues girls and women.

Susan Grayson

BIBLIOGRAPHY

Secondary Texts

Bowie, Malcolm. *Freud, Proust and Lacan: Theory as Fiction*. New York: Cambridge
    University Press, 1987.
Forrester, John. *The Seductions of Psychoanalysis: Freud, Lacan and Derrida*. New
    York: Cambridge University Press, 1990.
Grosz, Elizabeth. *Jacques Lacan: A Feminist Introduction*. London: Routledge, 1990.
Irigaray, Luce. *Spéculum de l'autre femme*. Paris: Minuit, 1974.
Kristeva, Julia. *Desire in Language*. Ed. Léons. Roudiez. Trans. Thomas Gora, Alice
    Jardine, and Léon S. Roudiez. New York: Columbia University Press, 1980.
Lacan, Jacques. *Ecrits I*. Paris: Seuil, 1966.
————. *Ecrits II*. Paris: Seuil, 1971.
————. *Le Séminaire de Jacques Lacan. Livre XI: Les Quatre Concepts fondamentaux
    de la psychanalyse*. Paris: Seuil, 1973.
Lee, Jonathan Scott. *Jacques Lacan*. Amherst: University of Massachusetts Press, 1990.
Mitchell, Juliet, and Jacqueline Rose. *Feminine Sexuality, Jacques Lacan and the école
    freudienne*. London: Macmillan Press, 1982.
Muller, John P., and William Richardson, eds. *The Purloined Poe: Lacan, Derrida and
    Psychoanalytic Reading*. Baltimore: Johns Hopkins University Press, 1988.
Roudinesco, Elizabeth. *Jacques Lacan and Co.: A History of Psychoanalysis in France,
    1925–1985*. Trans. Jeffrey Mehlman. Chicago: University of Chicago Press, 1990.

Lachmet, Djanet (1948–   ). Born in Algeria, and married and divorced at sixteen, Lachmet lived in Canada from 1968 to 1972 and currently resides in Paris, where she works in theater*. In *Le Cow-Boy* (1983), she examines the intersections of gender, race, and class through her portrayal of the childhood and adolescence of a young woman growing up in a wealthy Algerian family. The novel* focuses in particular on the protagonist's rebellion against her mother and her social milieu; her individual struggle to construct her identity is reflected in her country's collective fight for independence during the Algerian War. Rejected by her mother, who wanted a son, the protagonist seeks mother substitutes and friends among poor Algerian women whose social status offends her mother's image of womanhood. The novel also emphasizes the influence of the oral tradition of storytelling on the protagonist's identity.

Susan Ireland

BIBLIOGRAPHY

Primary Text

Le Cow-Boy. Paris: Belfond, 1983.

Secondary Texts

Ammar-Khodja, Soumya. "Djanet Lachmet: *Le Cow-Boy.*" In *Diwan d'inquiétude et d'espoir: La Littérature féminine algérienne de langue française.* Ed. Christiane Achour. Algiers: ENAG/Editions, 1991. 390–411.
Still, Judith. "Body and Culture: The Representation of Sexual, Racial and Class Differences in Lachmet's *Le Cow-Boy.*" In *Contemporary French Fiction by Women: Feminist Perspectives.* Ed. Margaret Atack and Phil Powrie. Manchester: Manchester University Press, 1990. 71–83.
———. "Djanet Lachmet's *Le Cow-Boy*: Constructing Self—Arab and Female." *Paragraph* 8 (October 1986): 55–61.

Lacombe, Claire (or Rose) (1765–?). Nothing is known of the childhood of this actress, women's rights advocate, and president of the short-lived Society of Revolutionary Republican Women, except that she began acting in the provinces before playing Paris. Although there is no early evidence of revolutionary sentiments, Lacombe addressed the French Legislative Assembly in 1792, denouncing constitutional monarchists, and offering herself as a warrior for the French nation. Pictured pike in hand, like her compeer Pauline Léon*, Lacombe turned more radical as the radicalism of the Revolution* increased.

Engaged in the 1792 demonstrations that toppled the monarchy, Lacombe was awarded a tricolor sash for her patriotic ardor. In spring 1793 she assisted in the expulsion of the Girondins from government, and by fall she was firmly preaching militant, democratic citizenship rights for women, and their rights to police domestic affairs. Allied ultimately with the Enragés, an egalitarian socialist group that rivaled the Jacobins, she inveighed against hoarders, demanded price controls, and pressured for outward markings of republican patriotism. This last demand created the environment for her political demise.

In September 1793 confrontations broke out between more conservative market women and the Revolutionary Republican Women over the revolutionary cockade and liberty bonnet. Taking their confrontation before the French National Convention, market women played into the growing misogyny of Jacobin-controlled politics. On October 30, the Revolutionary Republican Women were disbanded, and Lacombe was placed under arrest. In the words of government officials, militant women had stepped beyond the bounds of their sex. Their errant behaviors made them counterrevolutionaries according to the Rousseauist model of gender relations which the Jacobins espoused. Little more is known of Lacombe except that she became politically invisible while continuing an uninspired acting career.

Susan P. Conner

BIBLIOGRAPHY

Secondary Texts

Cerati, Marie. *Le Club des citoyennes républicaines révolutionnaires.* Paris: Editions sociales, 1966.

Lacour, Léopold. *Les Origines du féminisme contemporain: Trois Femmes de la Révolution, Olympe de Gouges, Théroigne de Méricourt, Rose Lacombe.* Paris: Plon-Nourrit, 1900.

Levy, Darline Gay, et al. *Women in Revolutionary Paris, 1789–1795.* Urbana: University of Illinois Press, 1979.

Melzer, Sara, and Leslie Rabine. *Rebel Daughters: Women and the French Revolution.* Oxford: Oxford University Press, 1992.

Rose, R. B. *The Enragés: Socialists of the French Revolution?* London: Cambridge University Press, 1965.

Lafayette, Marie-Madeleine Pioche de la Vergne, comtesse de (1634–1693). Mme de Lafayette is the mother of the French novel*. Her output was remarkably small: three novels (*La Princesse de Montpensier*, 1662; *Zayde*, 1669; and her great work, *La Princesse de Clèves*, 1678); a biography (*Histoire de Mme Henriette d'Angleterre*, 1720); a novella (*La Comtesse de Tende*, 1724); and *Mémoires de la Cour de France pour les années 1688 et 1689* (1731). Her reputation and impact rest on her psychological themes, stylistic finesse, and the complex but coherent organization of plot and structure.

Both of her parents were nobles of the robe. The firstborn of three daughters, she was a wealthy heiress highly placed in the firmly established social hierarchy that characterized life under Louis XIV, the Sun King. She grew up among the cultural elite of the Parisian aristocracy in a circle of well-to-do urban sophisticates that was closed but far from sheltered. Regardless of the historical or geographical settings she would choose for her heroines, her works reflect this fairly homogeneous, self-contained world.

Lafayette married well at the age of twenty-one; yet she and her husband lived virtually separate existences: he on a provincial estate, she raising the two sons of the couple in the townhouse her father had built in Paris. When her husband died in 1683, she chose to remain a widow "on her own."

Starting with her first work, *La Princesse de Montpensier*, the narrator voices the idea that a heroine's fragile happiness depends on self-possession defined in her own somewhat secular terms. The author forgoes the usual assortment of duels, disguises, and kidnappings that characterized fiction of her day in order to depict a contemporary, interior scene and power struggles. Two lovers are separated by the heroine's marriage* and complex political intrigues that finally destroy everyone. What is striking about *La Comtesse de Tende* is the crucial role of pregnancy and premature childbirth, hardly ever mentioned in literary depictions of women even by women.

The publication of *La Princesse de Clèves* marks the first time in history that a periodical *(Le Mercure galant)* conducted a public opinion survey on current literature. Most readers discredited the novel, both because its heroine disclosed to her husband her erotic attraction to another man and because she refused to marry the man she loved once her husband died. For Lafayette, sexual fulfillment offers no platonic image of perfection, shared by generous, free, and rational beings. Rather, love is a selfish, blinded, and blinding impulse, molded by social institutions made by and for the benefit of men. Subtly, she analyzes how social structures give shape and substance to psychological interactions. Thus, she writes of male sexual prerogatives in a calm, lucid way which shows their connection with social and political prerogatives. Her novels even show the appealing side of these prerogatives and the reasons why the emotional and legal bonds would be gladly accepted by both the sexes. On the other hand, some of her heroines die the way an anorexic would or exile themselves and die of natural causes. Nonetheless, her final word is not victimization. Rather, Lafayette exploits the intricacies of French grammar to create rich interior monologues that detail a stoic will to abide only by the lucid judgment of a jury of her peers. Her heroines dare raise questions about the place and voice of women in a society of extroverts.

Knowledgeable of the debates of her day, Mme de Lafayette skirts the issue of private and public domains or proper spheres; nor does she portray the nuclear family and monogamy as happiness. Yet the communication patterns she depicted still prevail today as the epitome of elegance when men court women. In depicting them so lucidly, she gave the French novel its mission for over three centuries.

Michael Danahy

BIBLIOGRAPHY

Primary Texts

Romanciers du XVIIe siècle. Ed. Antoine Adam. Paris: Gallimard, 1958.
Romans et nouvelles. Ed. Emile Magne. Paris: Garnier, 1961.
Vie de la princesse d'Angleterre. Ed. Marie-Thérèse Hipp. Geneva: Droz, 1967.
La Princesse de Clèves. Paris: Garnier-Flammarion, 1966.
La Princesse de Clèves et autres romans. Paris: Folio #778, n.d.

Secondary Texts

Beasley, Faith. *Revising Memory: Women's Fiction and Memoirs in Seventeenth-Century France*. New Brunswick, NJ: Rutgers University Press, 1991.

DeJean, Joan. *Libertine Strategies: Freedom and the Novel in Seventeenth-Century France*. Columbus: Ohio State University Press, 1981.

Henry, Patrick, ed. *An Inimitable Example: The Case for the Princesse de Clèves*. Washington, DC: Catholic University of America Press, 1992.

Lage de Volude, Béatrix-Stéphanie. *See* Volude, Béatrix-Stéphanie de Fuchsamberg d'Amblinont de Lage de.

Laguiller, Arlette (1940–). Writer and political figure. Laguiller is the spokesperson for the French far-left movement. While working as an entry-level bank employee, she ran for president in every national election between 1974 and 1995. For Laguiller, the term "communism" applies not to Stalinist ideology, but to the view that the workers' movement must be the driving force behind political change. In her autobiography*, *C'est toute ma vie*, she describes her first encounters with social injustice, the origins of her involvement in the Algerian War, and her activism in unions, political parties, and the feminist movement. Involved in the political arena as a worker and a woman, she has participated in many campaigns and strikes, including the fight to legalize contraception and abortion*, and has become a national symbol of the struggle for social justice and equal rights between the sexes.

Sylvaine Egron-Sparrow

BIBLIOGRAPHY

Primary Texts

Moi, une militante. Paris: Stock, 1974.
Une Travailleuse révolutionnaire dans la campagne présidentielle. Paris: Lutte Ouvrière, 1974.
Il faut changer le monde. Paris: Stock, 1988.
C'est toute ma vie. Paris: Plon, 1996.

Laïk, Madeleine (1944–). Playwright for stage and radio. Born in Oran, Laïk moved to France during the Algerian War. As a practicing psychologist, she wrote the theoretical text *Fille ou garçon* which examines the question of sexual identity in children. Turning to theater*, she joined with other women to form the writing workshop collective Les Téléphériques. Laïk's feminist plays explore the complex relationships between men and women. In *Transat* (1983), for example, the female protagonist is a childless writer who rents a child. Laïk views theater as a powerful way of depicting women's experiences, and in her work she skillfully weaves together the interior and exterior worlds of her characters.

Jan Berkowitz Gross

BIBLIOGRAPHY

Primary Texts

Fille ou garçon. Paris: Denoël, 1976.
La Peur qu'on a. Paris: Robert Laffont, 1979.
Transat. Paris: Théâtre Ouvert/Enjeux, 1983.
Double Commande et Les Voyageurs. Paris: Théâtre Ouvert Tapuscrit, 1985.
La Passerelle, Les Voyageurs, Didi Bonhomme. Paris: EDILIG, Théâtrales, 1989.

Secondary Texts

"Paroles de femmes au théâtre." Discussion. *Les Cahiers des Lundis.* Paris: Association
    THEATRALES, 1993–94. 21–30.
Surel-Turpin, Monique. "Ecrire autour de la peur et du manque: Madeleine Laïk, Dom-
    inique Chryssoulis." *Etudes Théâtrales* 8 (1995): 38.

Laisse, madame de (?–?). Very little is known about this writer, who married
a cavalry captain of an Artois regiment. She published collections of anecdotes,
tales, and proverbs with songs, which she believed to be innovative: *Recueil
d'anecdotes* (1773), *Nouveaux Contes moraux* (1774), *Ouvrage sans titre*
(1775), and *Proverbes dramatiques* (1777). Her dramatized proverbs follow the
fashionable trend set by Carmontelle, and include portraits, riddles, and maxims
designed as party games for elite society, or to be performed in private theaters.
Mme de Laisse's second collection, however, was more serious, and advocated
the education* of girls. In her playlets, she occasionally expressed philosophical
thoughts, and praised members of her sex. The light literary tone of her work,
combined with masquerades and touches of realism, is reminiscent of Marivaux's theater*.

S. Pascale Dewey

BIBLIOGRAPHY

Primary Texts

Recueil d'anecdotes. Amsterdam, 1773. [BN Z 23329]
"Lettre de Mme de Laisse, en réponse à la critique de Mme la baronne de Prinsen, dans
    Le Journal des Dames." *Mercure* (August 1774): 180–186.
Nouveaux Contes moraux. Paris: Valade, 1774.
Ouvrages sans titre. Paris: Saugrin, 1775.
Proverbes dramatiques mêlés d'ariettes connues. Amsterdam and Paris: Duchesne, 1777.
Nouveau genre de proverbes dramatiques mêlés de chants. Amsterdam and Paris: Pri-
    vately printed, 1778.
*Nouveau genre de proverbes dramatiques mêlés de chants pour servir de suite au premier
    volume.* Amsterdam and Paris: Privately printed, 1778.

Secondary Texts

Beach, Cecilia. *French Women Playwrights before the Twentieth Century: A Checklist.*
    Westport, CT: Greenwood Press, 1994.
Brenner, Carol. *A Bibliographical List of Plays in the French Language (1700–1789).*
    Berkeley: University of California Press, 1947.

Gethner, Perry, ed. *Femmes dramaturges en France: 1650–1750*. Paris: Biblio 17, 1993.
Rougemont, Martine de. *La Vie théâtrale en France au XVIIIe siècle*. Geneva: Slatkine, 1988.

Lambert, Anne Thérèse de (1647–1733). Born Anne Thérèse de Marguenat de Courcelles in Paris, she married Henri de Lambert, marquis de Saint-Bris, in 1666. His death left her a widow at thirty-nine with two children and her fortune in disarray. In an era when old age came early for women, the marquise opened her famous salon* at the age of sixty-three and became a protector of the arts and letters and one of the most powerful women in Paris. In 1726, nearly eighty years old, she became an author in spite of herself, when her *Avis d'une mère à son fils* was published without her knowledge. *Avis d'une mère à sa fille* followed two years later, and her *Traité de l'amitié* and *Traité de la vieillesse* appeared posthumously. In 1727 appeared her most substantial and most decidedly feminist work, *Réflexions nouvelles sur les femmes*, in which she asserts women's equality with men. According to Lambert, men usurped authority over women by force rather than by natural right. Her essays testify to studious meditation about woman's education*, her social and moral role, old age, and relations with men, and her insights are often conveyed in maxims such as "Beauty makes lovers, whereas the gifts of the mind make friends." She urged women to count on themselves rather than rely on men, and to cultivate their intellectual and moral faculties. But even with her independent mind, she also preached compliance with social expectations and respect for conventions.

Joan Hinde Stewart

BIBLIOGRAPHY

Primary Text

Oeuvres. Ed. Robert Granderoute. Paris: Honoré Champion, 1990.

Secondary Texts

Fassiotto, Marie-José. *Madame de Lambert (1647–1733) ou le féminisme moral*. New York: Peter Lang, 1984.
Granderoute, Robert. "*De l'éducation des filles* aux *Avis d'une mère à sa fille*: Fénelon et Madame de Lambert." *Revue d'histoire littéraire de la France* 1 (1987): 15–30.
Hine, Ellen McNiven. "Madame de Lambert, Her Sources and Her Circle: On the threshold of a New Age." *Studies on Voltaire and the Eighteenth Century* 102 (1973): 173–190.
Marchal, Roger. *Madame de Lambert et son milieu*. Oxford: Voltaire Foundation, 1991.
Timmermans, Linda. *L'Accès des femmes à la culture (1598–1715): un débat d'idées de Saint François de Sales à la Marquise de Lambert*. Paris: Honoré Champion, 1993.

Lambrichs, Louise (?–). Essayist and novelist. In *Journal d'Hannah*, Lambrichs recounts the trauma of a young Jewish woman struggling to deal with

memories of loss and personal guilt after her decision to have an abortion*
during the Occupation. Over a twenty-year period, Hannah watches the unborn
"Louise" come to life and mature in her secret diary. Plagued by insomnia and
depression, and little helped by the medical establishment, Hannah eventually
finds strength in conversations with a family physician and friend and through
the mediation of her living daughter. At the same time, Hannah comes to grips
with the loss of her family killed in the death camps. Lambrichs has also published books on dyslexia and the psychology of illness.

Jan Berkowitz Gross

BIBLIOGRAPHY

Primary Texts

Le Cercle des sorcières. Paris: Editions de la Différence, 1988.
La Dyslexie en question. Paris: Robert Laffont, 1989.
Journal d'Hannah. Paris: Editions de la Différence, 1993.
*La Vérité médicale: Claude Bernard, Louis Pasteur, Sigmund Freud: Légendes et réalités
    de notre médecine.* Paris: Robert Laffont, 1994.
Le Jeu du roman. Paris: Editions de la Différence, 1995.

Landre, Jeanne (1874–1936). Landre enjoyed a varied literary career as a journalist (with articles in *La Fronde* and *Minerva*), a critic (including studies on
Gavarni and Jehan Rictus), and a popular novelist. Fiction such as *Cri-cri, Bob
et Bobette,* and the *Echalote* series won her public recognition; she was noted
for the use of Montmartre as a bohemian setting, her colorful characters from
the theatrical milieu, and for a number of sexually uninhibited heroines who
enter into conflict with the overriding patriarchal codes of the time. World War
I* was her subject in a range of wartime publications, with a focus on the
sometimes controversial relationship between French soldiers and their *marraines de guerre.* As the founder of Aide aux femmes de professions libérales,
Landre was a champion of women's rights, and her vice presidency of the
Société des gens de lettres led to her being decorated with the Légion d'honneur.

Catherine O'Brien

BIBLIOGRAPHY

Primary Texts

Cri-cri. Paris: Offenstadt frères, 1900.
La Gargouille. Paris: L. Michaud, 1908.
Echalote et ses amants. Paris: L. Michaud, 1909.
Contes de Montmartre. Paris: Librairie universelle, 1910.
Gavarni. Paris: L. Michaud, 1912.
Puis il mourut. Paris: Renaissance du livre, 1916.
L'Ecole des marraines. Paris: A. Michel, 1917.
Loin des balles. Paris: A. Michel, 1918.
Bob et Bobette, enfants perdus. Paris: A. Michel, 1919.
Echalote, douairière. Paris: A. Michel, 1925.

"Les Soliloques du pauvre" de Jehan Rictus. Paris: Société française d'éditions littéraires
  et techniques, 1930.
Nouvelles Aventures d'Echalote. Paris: A. Michel, 1932.

Langfus, Anna (1920–1966). Born a Jew in Poland, Langfus was jailed for
being a member of the Polish Resistance. She immigrated to France in 1946. In
Le Sel et le soufre and *Les Bagages de sable*, Langfus revisits her past through
the fictional character of Maria. Her third novel* marks the beginning of a
distancing process from her own life, with a shift to a male narrator. It is,
however, when her vision of tragedy is mediated by a female consciousness,
and when she evokes the saving grace of bonding between women, that her
vision is the most powerful. Langfus's work is indirectly an indictment of history
through the depiction of its victims' psychological destruction and their unsuccessful attempts at overcoming the memory of evil and pain while negotiating
a new existence. Narrated in understated prose, her novels are remarkable for
their rejection of pathos and Manichaeism.

Madeleine Cottenet-Hage

BIBLIOGRAPHY
  Primary Texts
Le Sel et le soufre. Paris: Gallimard, 1960.
Les Bagages de sable. Paris: Gallimard, 1962.
Saute, Barbara. Paris: Gallimard, 1965.
  Secondary Text
Cottenet-Hage, Madeleine. "Anna Langfus et les risques de la mémoire." *Les Lettres
  Romanes* (1995): 25–39.

Lê, Linda (1963–). Novelist and short-story writer. Born in Vietnam, Lê currently lives and works in Paris. Her first novel*, *Un Si Tendre Vampire* (1987),
was one of the first novels of the Vietnamese diaspora to be published in France.
Lê's texts, which are characterized by their black humor, biting irony, and social
satire, depict the dark underside of society and the family*. Peopled largely by
losers, misfits, and pariahs of various ages, her stories convey strong emotions—
mostly negative—and focus on types of nonconformity, from madness, alcoholism, and suicide to incest (*Calomnies*) and cannibalism (*Les Evangiles du
crime*). Within Lê's dysfunctional familes, mothers often receive particularly
harsh criticism: the narrator of *Fuir*, rejected by his parents, recounts his problematic relationships with women, while *Un Si Tendre Vampire* depicts the
jealousy and desire for vengeance that characterize a mother-daughter relationship in which both protagonists are seduced by the same man. Finally, in *Les
Dits d'un idiot*, the handicapped narrator, who is confined to his wheelchair,
recounts how he is persecuted by his mother, and his angry, unpunctuated
monologue raises the questions of origins, filiation, and sacrifice that recur
throughout Lê's work.

Susan Ireland

BIBLIOGRAPHY

Primary Texts

Un Si Tendre Vampire. Paris: Table Ronde, 1987.
Fuir. Paris: Table Ronde, 1988.
Solo. Paris: Table Ronde, 1989.
Les Evangiles du crime. Paris: Julliard, 1992.
Calomnies. Paris: Christian Bourgois, 1993.
Les Dits d'un idiot. Paris: Christian Bourgois, 1995.
Les Trois Parques. Paris: Christian Bourgois, 1997.

Le Dantec, Denise (1939–   ). Poet, fiction writer, and specialist in horticulture and French garden history. Le Dantec, who has received the Grand Prix de Poésie de Bretagne, writes texts that blur the boundaries between poetry* and fiction. Her work, a philosophical meditation on life, is characterized by the intersections of the fleeting and the eternal, and the recurrent theme of nature. The land- and seascapes that run throughout texts such as the autobiographical *Suite pour une enfance* serve as metaphors for states of mind and raise existential questions, and Le Dantec uses precise technical terms to draw parallels between family members' lives and the cyclical rhythms of nature. A strong feminine presence is felt in many of Le Dantec's works, from *Le Jour* (1975), which underscores the themes of women's madness and oppression, to *Les Fileuses d'étoupe* (1985), with its emphasis on the traditional domestic arts of spinning and weaving.

Martine Motard-Noar

BIBLIOGRAPHY

Primary Texts

Métropole. Paris: P. J. Oswald, 1970.
Le Jour. Paris: Des femmes, 1975.
Les Joueurs de Go. Paris: Stock, 1977.
Les Fileuses d'étoupe. Bédée: Folle Avoine, 1985.
Le Roman des jardins de France. Paris: Plon, 1987.
Le Journal des roses. Paris: Bourin, 1991.
Opuscule d'Ouessant. Paris: Babel, 1992.
Suite pour une enfance. Paris: Des femmes, 1992.
Emily Bronte: Le Roman d'une vie. Paris: L'Archipel, 1995.
Le Livre du chagrin. Paris: C. de Bartillat, 1996.

Secondary Texts

Bishop, Michael. "De Denise Le Dantec à Marie Etienne: Passion, sérénité, profondeur."
    Dalhousie French Studies 29 (Winter 1994): 31–54.
———. "Denise Le Dantec." In *Contemporary French Women Poets*. Vol. 1. Amster-
    dam: Rodopi, 1995. 52–67.

Le Doeuff, Michèle (1948–). Philosopher, researcher at the Centre Nationale de la Recherche Scientifique, and translator of Bacon and Shakespeare. Le

Doeuff has been active in the women's cause on a practical as well as a theoretical level—participating in the events of May 1968, for example—and continues to act as a spokesperson for the women's movement in France. She is best known for her feminist critique of the Western philosophical tradition. Defining herself as both a feminist and a professional philosopher, Le Doeuff seeks to demonstrate that these two activities are not mutually exclusive. Her critique of philosophy both challenges its creation and perpetuation of negative discourses on women and reveals the masculinist assumptions that have led to philosophy's reputation as a superior discipline which has traditionally excluded women. In *L'Etude et le rouet* (1989), her analysis of the patriarchal foundations of philosophy, Le Doeuff discusses the few women philosophers of the past— Hipparchia of Thrace and Héloïse*, for example—and identifies the mid-eighteenth century as a turning point that marks the beginning of a misogynistic trend in the relations between philosophy and women, as seen in the work of Rousseau, Hegel, and Comte. Le Doeuff's first work, *L'Imaginaire philosophique* (1980), questions the masculine-feminine divisions established by earlier educational systems, divisions which characterize women as the intellectual inferiors of men, unable to think abstractly or in universal terms. In addition, Le Doeuff challenges the master-disciple, male-female model of philosophical learning that positions women in the subordinate role. She examines such philosophical "couples" as Abelard and Héloïse, Mill and Wollstonecraft, and Sartre and de Beauvoir*, to demonstrate how women's access to philosophy has traditionally been mediated by a male philosopher. Finally, Le Doeuff denounces the different forms of discrimination she believes women face when taking competitive exams and seeking teaching positions in philosophy. Le Doeuff has also worked in theater*, in particular on the play *La Soeur de Shakespeare*, and has written important essays on the seventeenth-century philosopher Bacon.

Susan Ireland and Patrice J. Proulx

BIBLIOGRAPHY

Primary Texts

L'Imaginaire philosophique. Paris: Payot, 1980.
La Nouvelle Atlantide: Voyage dans la pensée baroque. Paris: Payot, 1983.
L'Etude et le rouet. Paris: Seuil, 1989.
Vénus et Adonis. Shakespeare: Genèse d'une catastrophe. Paris: Alidades, 1989.

Secondary Texts

Grosz, Elizabeth. *Sexual Subversion: Three French Feminists.* Sydney: Allen and Unwin, 1989.
Moi, Toril, ed. *French Feminist Thought: A Reader.* Oxford: Blackwell, 1987.

Le Garrec, Evelyne (?–). Writer and journalist. Much of Le Garrec's work focuses on the traditional heterosexual couple. Her earliest text, *Les Messagères* (1976), emphasizes the need for an equal division of labor within the couple, while her best-known work, *Un Lit à soi* (1979), recalls and responds to Virginia Woolf's *A Room of One's Own*. Le Garrec argues that, despite the progress made in women's rights since Woolf's time—suffrage and the right to a legal abortion*, for example—women nonetheless remain "bound" to the conjugal bed, the symbol of the institutionalized couple. Through a series of interviews conducted with women of diverse ages and socioeconomic classes, she discusses the importance of pursuing independence through a negotiation of one's own space, either within or separate from the couple. A later study, also based on interviews with women (*Des Femmes qui s'aiment*, 1984), examines lesbian relationships.

In addition to her sociological studies, Le Garrec also wrote an autobiographical text (*La Rive allemande de ma mémoire*, 1980) that discusses her French and German origins, and a fictionalized account of the life of the journalist Séverine*, *Séverine, une rebelle (1855–1929)*.

Susan Ireland and Patrice J. Proulx

BIBLIOGRAPHY

Primary Texts

Les Messagères. Paris: Editions des femmes, 1976.
Un Lit à soi. Paris: Seuil, 1979.
La Rive allemande de ma mémoire. Paris: Seuil, 1980.
Séverine, une rebelle (1855–1929). Paris: Seuil, 1982.
Des Femmes qui s'aiment. Paris: Seuil, 1984.
Mosaïque de la douleur. Paris: Seuil, 1991.

Le Gendre, Marie (Dame de Rivery) (fl. sixteenth century). Writer of moral *discours*. Little is known of Marie Le Gendre's life, except that she may have hailed from Picardy and that she may possibly have been acquainted with aristocratic circles, for example the circle of the Princesse de Conty, to whom she dedicated one of her works, and François Le Poulchre, a *noble d'épée* from western France to whom she addressed a couple of sonnets and dedicated a dialogue. Two slender volumes are attributed to Marie Le Gendre: the *Cabinet des saines affections*, which appeared five times between 1584 and 1600 (the first three editions appeared anonymously from Abel L'Angelier, a respectable Parisian printer specializing in humanist writings) and was translated into both German and Italian in 1623, and the *Exercice de l'ame vertueuse*, published in 1596/1597. In addition to thirty moral *discours* thematically related to Montaigne's *Essais*, Marie Le Gendre wrote a lengthy dialogue in the Neoplatonic tradition, dealing with love, marriage*, and the mother-daughter bond, as well as a variety of short poems of uneven quality in which she aims at reconciling Christianity* with the morality of the ancient Stoic philosophy. She also composed a few stances and sonnets in which she laments the death of her husband and the sorrows of widowhood. It would hardly be surprising if Marie Le Gendre did not attend or at least hear about the humanist gatherings of the Palace Academy (founded in the 1570s by Henri III), which brought together the most prominent figures of her day: Ronsard, Desportes, Baif, Belleau, Du Perron, Jamyn, Pibrac, and Le Poulchre. The twelve *discours*, first included in the 1595 edition of the *Cabinet* and later published separately in the *Exercice*, constitute a group apart. They present obvious affinities of content and style with the humanist debates of the Palace Academy.

Marie Le Gendre's works are highly indicative of the direction in which women's writing is moving at the turn of the sixteenth century. She chose to write the bulk of her works in prose, applying her talents to two favorite humanist genres, the *discours* and the *dialogue*. Drawing from the same classical sources (Plato, Cicero, Seneca, and Plutarch) as the most eminent moralists of her age, she wrote on death, friendship*, virtue, honor, ambition, and envy, echoing Amyot, Body, Du Plessis-Mornay, Goulart, Montaigne, and Le Caron. Like them, she places the authority of reason foremost in her search for virtue. Her *discours* are important documents in the history of humanism and the revival of stoicism in the latter part of the sixteenth century.

Colette H. Winn

BIBLIOGRAPHY

Primary Texts

L'Exercice de l'ame vertueuse, dedié à très-haute, tres-illustre, et tres-vertueuse Princesse, Madame de Conty, par Marie Le Gendre, Dame de Rivery: Reveu, corrigé, & augmenté par elle-mesme d'un Dialogue des chastes Amours d'Eros, & Kalisti. Paris: Jean Le Blanc, 1596. (Bibliothèque Mazarine 27909A) (Arsenal 80 B.L. 20992 & 20993).

Cabinet des saines affections. Derniere Edition, augmentee de XII. Discours & quelques Stances sur le mesme sujet. Paris: Antoine Du Brueil, 1595. (Bibliothèque Mazarine 27934)

Oeuvres. Ed. Colette H. Winn. Paris: Champion, 1998.

Secondary Texts

Berriot-Salvadore, Evelyne. *Les Femmes dans la société française de la Renaissance.* Paris: Champion, 1990.

———. "Les Héritières de Louise Labé." In *Louise Labé: Les Voix du lyrisme.* Ed. Guy Démerson. Saint-Etienne: Publications de l'Université de Saint-Etienne, Editions du CNRS, 1990. 93–106.

———. "Marie Le Gendre et Marie de Gournay à la manière de . . . ." In *Le Lecteur, l'auteur et l'écrivain: Montaigne 1492–1592–1992.* Actes du Colloque International de Haïfa, April–May 1992. Ed. Ilana Zinguer. Paris: Champion, n.d.

Loviot, Louis. "*Cabinet des saines affections* (1595)." In *Revue des Livres Anciens.* Vol. 2. Paris: Fontemoing & Cie., 1917. 274–282.

Winn, Colette H. "Les *Discours* de Marie Le Gendre et l'Académie du Palais." In *La Femme lettrée à la Renaissance.* Ed. Michel Bastiaensen. Brussels: Université Libre de Bruxelles, Institut Interuniversitaire Renaissance et Humanisme, 1997. 165–175.

Yates, Frances A. *The French Academies of the Sixteenth Century.* London: Warburg Institute, 1947.

Zanta, Léontine. *La Renaissance du stoïcisme au XVIe siècle.* Paris: H. Champion, 1914.

Le Givre de Richebourg, madame (published c. 1735). Nothing is known with certainty about her life; even her name is unsure, as it appeared on title pages only as Mme. L.G.D.R. Three other interpretations, La Grange de Richebourg, Le Gendre de Richebourg, and La Garde de Richebourg, have been proposed. She adapted and expanded several Spanish works, including Cervantes's Byzantine romance, *Persile et Sigismonde, histoire septentrionale* (1738). Her own works, such as *Les Avantures de Zelim et de Damasine, histoire afriquaine* (1735), reflect the same genre, which offered her, as it did Isabelle de Montolieu*, both exotic adventures and a view of love as shared friendship*, focusing equally on the strengths of the male and female protagonists. But while Cervantes, like Richebourg's contemporaries Félicité de Genlis* and Mme Leprince de Beaumont*, portrayed intrepid religious heroines in the context of spiritual rebirth, Richebourg stressed women's capacities in the secular world for the new sciences and for decision making. Her female characters show initiative and resolve as well, in claiming their amorous choices, as the Counter-Reformation yielded to Deism and pre-Romantic destiny.

Marina Mazal Tov Compson and Clark Colahan

BIBLIOGRAPHY

Primary Texts

Avantures de Clamadès et de Clarmonde, tirées de l'espagnol. Paris, 1733.
Avantures de Dom Ramire de Roxas et de dona Leonor de Mendoce, tirées de l'espagnol. Paris, 1737 (bound with *Le Talisman*).
Avantures de Flores et de Blanche-Fleur, tirées de l'espagnol. Paris, 1735.
Les Avantures de Zelim et de Damasine, histoire afriquaine. The Hague, 1735.
Persile et Sigismonde, histoire septentrionale tirée de l'espagnol de Miguel de Cervantes. Paris, 1738.
La Veuve en puissance de mary, nouvelle tragicomique, avec deux divertissemens, dont l'un a pour titre Les caprices de l'amour, et l'autre La duppe de soi-même. Paris, 1732 (bound with *La Dupe de soi-mesme* and *Les Caprices de l'amour*).

Secondary Texts

Beach, Cecilia. *French Women Playwrights before the Twentieth Century.* Westport, CT: Greenwood Press, 1995.
Jones, S. Paul. *A List of French Prose Fiction from 1700 to 1750, with a Brief Introduction.* New York: Wilson, 1939.

Leclerc, Annie (1940–). Novelist, essayist, and professor of philosophy. Leclerc taught full-time from 1963 to 1975 before devoting herself to her writing; her teaching then took on more diverse forms, such as conducting writing workshops in prisons.

Leclerc is best known for her lyrical-philosophical text, *Parole de femme*, in which she challenges patriarchal language and proposes a new form of women's writing (*parole de femme*). In this provocative and controversial text, criticized by feminists such as Christine Delphy* for its essentialism*, Leclerc emphasizes the importance of the female body by urging women to listen to its corporeal rhythms and to rejoice in its life-affirming manifestations (menstrual cycles, pregnancy, and giving birth). A similar focus on women's relation to their bodies appears in her next book, *Epousailles*.

Leclerc's innovative style manifests itself again through a dialogue among Leclerc, Madeleine Gagnon, and Hélène Cixous* in *La Venue à l'écriture*, a text which affirms the desire of women to avoid imposing an authoritative (male) voice on others. Her interest in collaborative texts also leads to *Autrement dit*, in which she engages in a conversation with Marie Cardinal* on such topics as the effects of patriarchal structures on women. Her most recent work, *Exercices de mémoire*, is a personal meditation on the Holocaust* and the question of evil, inspired by Lanzmann's *Shoah*.

According to Leclerc, men's power to define the world and sexuality comes not only from their silencing of women, but from women's complicity in perpetuating male-constructed norms. Throughout her work, Leclerc explores gender-based differences between men and women and draws parallels between giving birth and giving life to a new language.

E. Nicole Meyer

BIBLIOGRAPHY

Primary Texts

Le Pont du nord. Paris: Gallimard, 1967.
Parole de femme. Paris: Grasset, 1974.
Epousailles. Paris: Grasset, 1976.
Au feu du jour. Paris: Grasset, 1979.
Hommes et femmes. Paris: Grasset, 1985.
Le Mal de mère. Paris: Grasset, 1986.
Origines. Paris: Grasset, 1988.
Clé. Paris: Grasset, 1989.
Exercices de mémoire. Paris: Grasset, 1992.
Leclerc, Annie, Hélène Cixous, and Madeleine Gagnon. *La Venue à l'écriture*. Paris: 10/ 18, 1977.

Secondary Texts

Brewer, Maria. "A Loosening of Tongues: From Narrative Economy to Women Writing." *Modern Language Notes* 99, no. 5 (December 1984): 1141–1161.
Powrie, Phil. "A Womb of One's Own: The Metaphor of the Womb-Room as a Reading-Effect in Texts by Contemporary French Women Writers." *Paragraph: A Journal of Modern Critical Theory* 12, no. 3 (November 1989): 197–213.

Lecouvreur, Adrienne (1692–1730). At age fifteen this actress and epistolary writer captivated audiences with her passionate performance as Pauline in *Polyeucte*. Throughout her career she championed a natural, emotional declamatory style. With guidance from Mlle Fonpré, director of the Lille theater*, Lecouvreur acquired a reputation that led her to the Comédie Française in 1717. Over thirteen years, she performed more than one hundred roles, including twenty-two premières, mostly in tragedies. She triumphed in 1724 as Constance in Houdard de la Motte's *Inès de Castro*.

Although unpublished until 1775, her prolific correspondence was renowned for its unique style. In her obituary (March 1730), the *Mercure* praised Lecouvreur's adherence to classical norms of moderation and clarity. The numerous letters she wrote to her lover, Maurice de Saxe, express her longing to reunite with him, and provide an interesting chronicle of the Regency, with its decadent mores and *libertinage**.

Voltaire was one of several poets to denounce the Church's refusal to bury Lecouvreur. His poem eloquently describes the ambiguous position of actresses in Old Regime France—adored yet ostracized. Rumors surrounding the circumstances of Lecouvreur's death inspired a play by Eugène Scribe and Ernest Legouvé (1848) which was later adapted for Cilea's opera *Adriana Lecouvreur*.

Marie-Pascale Pieretti

BIBLIOGRAPHY

Primary Text

Lettres d'Adrienne Lecouvreur. Ed. George Monval. Paris: Plon, 1892.

Secondary Texts

Germain, Pierre. *Adrienne Lecouvreur, tragédienne*. Paris: Fernand Lanore, 1983.
Richtman, Jack. *Adrienne Lecouvreur: The Actress and the Age*. Englewood Cliffs, NJ: Prentice-Hall, 1971.

Leduc, Violette (1907–1972). Novelist and journalist in a publishing* house. Childhood experiences and the context of her birth shape much of Leduc's writing. Unwanted by her mother, a servant for a wealthy family whose son fathered Leduc, the author experienced a guilt-ridden and isolated childhood; this unhappy situation was compounded by her grandmother's death and her mother's second marriage. Her work remained relatively unknown until the publication of the autobiographical *La Bâtarde* (1964). Leduc's novels*, often lyrical in style, depict a grotesque world of mental disorder and self-deprecation. The major themes include mother-daughter conflict, the dangers of pregnancy, rape*, and abortion*, as well as the stigma of illegitimacy, physical ugliness, poverty, and bisexuality. Her originality lies in her exploration of taboo subjects deemed particularly inappropriate for women—explicit passages on lesbian eroticism in *La Bâtarde*, references to homosexuality in *Ravages*. Although a protégée of Simone de Beauvoir*, who wrote the preface to *La Bâtarde*, Leduc remained a marginal writer during her lifetime; today, however, her focus on women's issues and female authorship has led critics to view her as a pioneer of women's writing.

Julia Lauer-Chéenne

BIBLIOGRAPHY

Primary Texts

L'Asphyxie. Paris: Gallimard, 1946.
L'Affamée. Paris: Gallimard, 1948.
Ravages. Paris: Gallimard, 1955.
La Bâtarde. Paris: Gallimard, 1964.
Thérèse et Isabelle. Paris: Gallimard, 1966.
La Folie en tête. Paris: Gallimard, 1970.
La Chasse à l'amour. Paris: Gallimard, 1973.

Secondary Texts

Ceccatty, René de. *Violette Leduc: Eloge de la Bâtarde*. Paris: Stock, 1994.
Courtivron, Isabelle de. *Violette Leduc*. Boston: Twayne, 1985.
Evans, Martha Noel. "Violette Leduc: The Bastard." In *Masks of Tradition: Women and the Politics of Writing in Twentieth Century France*. Ed. Martha Noel Evans. Ithaca: Cornell University Press, 1987. 102–122.
Rule, Jane. "Violette Leduc." *Lesbian Images*. Garden City, NY: Doubleday, 1975. 140–146.

Lefèvre, Kim (?–). Writer and actress. Born in Vietnam to a French father and a Vietnamese mother, Lefèvre moved to Paris in 1960. She has taught in several Parisian *lycées* and now works in theater*. She returned to Vietnam for the first time in 1990. The first of two autobiographical texts, *Métisse blanche*, describes the childhood of a Eurasian girl and focuses on her experience of marginalization in Vietnam because of her mixed blood and illegitimate birth. While *Métisse blanche* ends with the narrator's decision to leave for France, *Retour à la saison des pluies* recounts her return to Vietnam and her reunion with her family. Her rediscovery of the places associated with her past enables her to come to terms with the Vietnamese part of her identity, and her narrative is woven from stories told by the women with whom she is reunited—her mother, her three sisters, and old school friends. Throughout both texts, the narrator's personal story intersects with the collective history of Vietnam, especially its past as a colony of France. Similar themes recur in Lefèvre's historical novel* *Moi, Marina la Malinche* (1994). Here, she explores the notion of *métissage* by giving voice to Marina, an Indian woman from a noble Mexican family who is sold into slavery and becomes the interpreter for Cortés during his conquest of Mexico. Malina, the mother of his illegitimate child, is torn between the world in which she grew up and that of the Spanish conquerors.

Susan Ireland

BIBLIOGRAPHY

Primary Texts

Métisse blanche. Paris: Barrault, 1989.
Retour à la saison des pluies. Paris: Barrault, 1990.
Moi, Marina la Malinche. Paris: Stock, 1994.

Secondary Texts

Yeager, Jack. "Blurring the Lines in Vietnamese Fiction in French: Kim Lefèvre's *Métisse blanche.*" In *Postcolonial Subjects: Francophone Women Writers.* Ed. Mary Jean Green et al. Minneapolis: University of Minnesota Press, 1996. 210–226.

———. "Kim Lefèvre's *Retour à la saison des pluies*: Rediscovering the Landscapes of Childhood." *L'Esprit Créateur* 33, no. 2 (Summer 1993): 47–57.

Lemoine-Luccioni, Eugénie (1912–   ). Lemoine-Luccioni is a Lacanian psychoanalyst and a member of the Ecole Freudienne who has published books and articles on psychoanalysis, both individually and in collaboration with her husband, Paul Lemoine. She is also a translator and author of short stories* who sometimes writes under the name Gennie Lemoine. In *Psychanalyse pour la vie quotidienne* (1987), in which she discusses the future of psychoanalysis, she presents herself as a writer-analyst and as a woman who has a role to play in transmitting psychoanalysis to future generations. In *Partage des femmes* (1976), Lemoine-Luccioni's analysis of the duality of the female self is based on the concepts of mirroring and splitting. Positing that the gender division is reflected in an internal split (a second *partage*) in women's psyches, she argues that when a mother gives birth, her sense of loss—caused by another form of splitting—is translated into extreme narcissism or increased dependency on a man. Lemoine-Luccioni is best known for her disagreement with Luce Irigaray* over the relationship between pyschoanalysis, politics, and feminism*. In her review of Irigaray's *Spéculum de l'autre femme*, published in *Esprit* (March 1975), Lemoine-Luccioni uses a classical Lacanian argument to challenge Irigaray's views on the phallus and sexual difference. Irigaray, on the other hand, accuses Lemoine-Luccioni of being unable to break away from an orthodox patriarchal psychoanalytic approach that makes her deaf to the voice of women's unconscious desires.

Susan Ireland and Patrice J. Proulx

BIBLIOGRAPHY

Primary Texts

"*Speculum de l'autre femme.*" *Esprit* 444 (March 1975): 466–469.
Partage des femmes. Paris: Seuil, 1976.
Marches. Paris: Des femmes, 1977.
La Robe: Essai psychanalytique sur le vêtement. Paris: Seuil, 1983.
Psychanalyse pour la vie quotidienne. Paris: Navarin, 1987.
L'Histoire à l'envers: Pour une politique de la psychanalyse. Paris: Des femmes, 1992.

Secondary Texts

Gallop, Jane. *The Daughter's Seduction: Feminism and Psychoanalysis.* Ithaca: Cornell University Press, 1982.
Irigaray, Luce. "La Misère de la psychanalyse." *Critique* 365 (October 1977).
Jardine, Alice A., and Anne M. Menke, eds. *Shifting Scenes: Interviews on Women, Writing, and Politics in Post-68 France.* New York: Columbia University Press. 1991.

Lenclos, Anne (Ninon) de (1623?–1705). Although she wrote little, her convention-defying life made her a legend in her own time. With no family or fortune, Ninon of little virtue transformed herself into the respectable Mademoiselle de Lenclos, one of the most famous figures of seventeenth- and eighteenth-century culture, who was glorified by Voltaire and others as the patroness of the *philosophes*. Daughter of a libertine swashbuckler of doubtful nobility who taught her to play the lute before abandoning his family, she had to rely at an early age on her intelligence, musical talent, and other charms to support herself and her mother. A courtesan by necessity, she became a liberated woman; she had a succession of famous lovers whom she labeled "payers," "martyrs," and "favorites," whom, according to legend, she rarely kept longer than three months but retained as friends after her desire waned. A freethinker and nonbeliever who conversed with Scarron, Molière, and Saint-Evremond, and even charmed women who had been her rivals (Sévigné*, Maintenon*), she challenged the narrow gender roles of her times: rejecting chastity as the defining feminine virtue, she enjoyed the male prerogative of sexual freedom and practiced the higher "masculine" virtues of the *honnête homme*—probity, friendship*, generosity. Yet, as a consummately intelligent and cultured woman, she transformed sexuality into a refined art of love which she taught to generations of young men, all the while providing for her illegitimate son with discreet motherly devotion. Her few extant works include thirty letters and notes, many of them on Epicurean themes to Saint-Evremond, and *La Coquette vengée* (1659), a witty retort to Felix de Juvenel's misogynistic *Portrait de la Coquette*. The publication in 1750 of the apocryphal *Lettres de Ninon de Lenclos au Marquis de Sévigné*, composed by Damours, and in 1751 of biographies by Bret and Douxménil, all reprinted numerous times, elevated the legend of the long-lived seductress who philosophized "like a man" to the status of a myth that continues to intrigue historians and critics. These works inspired other apocryphal letters (by Ségur*, 1789) and dozens of plays about her (the most notable by Voltaire and Olympe de Gouges*) that attempt to reconcile the "danger" posed by her artful sexuality with her admirable probity and "virile" independence of thought.

Gabrielle Verdier

BIBLIOGRAPHY

Primary Text

Correspondance authentique de Ninon de Lenclos. Ed. Emile Colombey. Paris: Dentu, 1868.

Secondary Texts

Duchêne, Roger. *Ninon de Lenclos*. Paris: Fayard, 1984.
Magne, Emile. *Ninon de Lanclos* [sic]. Paris: Emile-Paul frères, 1948.
Verdier, Gabrielle. "Libertine, Philanthropist, Revolutionary: Ninon's Metamorphoses in the Age of the Enlightenment." *Continuum* 4, no. 2 (1992): 101–147.

Léo, André (1824–1900). Pseudonym of Léodile Béra formed by the names of her twin sons. Novelist, journalist, and socialist feminist activist. After the 1851 coup d'état Béra's family moved to Switzerland, where Léodile married the political refugee Grégoire Champceix. After Napoleon III's political amnesty in 1860, the couple moved to Paris and Léo's first novel* appeared: *Un Divorce*, serialized in the daily newspaper *Le Siècle*, and published at Léo's expense. Outspoken in her denunciation of male despotism and social inequality, Léo published many political articles in socialist periodicals and newspapers such as the Belgian *Coopérative* and the Swiss *Egalité*. She advocated workers' associations for both sexes, decried wage disparities both between city and country workers and between the sexes, and deplored the economic misery of the peasantry. Increasingly active in feminist circles, Léo participated in debates about girls' education* and founded the Society for the Demand of Women's Rights in 1866. Léo's essay "La Femme et les moeurs. Liberté ou monarchie" (1869) refuted the antifeminism of Proudhonism.

Léo's most active period of militancy and political journalism occurred after the Second Empire and during the Commune* (1871) when she helped found two newspapers, *La République des travailleurs* and *La Sociale*. Arguably the most prominent feminist socialist journalist of the Commune, in June 1871 Léo took refuge with her future second husband, Benoit Malon, in Switzerland, where she continued writing and speaking out for liberty, equality, and women's rights.

Cheryl A. Morgan

BIBLIOGRAPHY

Primary Texts

Un Divorce. Paris: Le Siècle, 1862.
Un Mariage scandaleux. Paris: Hachette, 1862.
Aline-Ali. Paris: A. Lacroix, Verboeckhoven et Cie., 1867.
La Justice des choses. Poitiers: P. Planchier, 1891.
Coupons le cable! Paris: Fischbacher, 1899.
La Femme et les moeurs. Liberté ou monarchie. Introduction and notes by Monique Biarnais. Tusson: Du Lerot, 1990.

Secondary Texts

Biarnais, Monique et al., ed. "André Léo, une journaliste de la Commune." *Le Lérot rêveur* 44 (March 1987).
Bellet, Roger. "André Léo, écrivain-idéologie." *Romantisme* 77 no. 3 (1992): 61–66.
Lejeune, P. "Une Grande Journaliste communarde: Léodile Champceix, dite André Léo." *Femmes en mouvements* 2 (February 1978): 58–59.

Léon, Anne Pauline (1758–?). In 1789 she was an unmarried chocolate maker living in Paris. An early and enthusiastic participant in Revolutionary political clubs and popular societies, Léon was among the petitioners at the Champs de Mars who were violently attacked by Lafayette's cavalry in 1791. In March

1792 she presented a petition to the Legislative Assembly demanding that women be authorized to "procure pikes, pistols, and sabres" in order to practice public maneuvers. Although Léon implied that such weapons would serve an exclusively defensive purpose in the hands of women, the petition was not honored. In May 1793, with Claire Lacombe*, Léon registered the first women's club in Paris, the short-lived Society of Revolutionary Republican Women—whose purpose was "to rush to the defense of the Fatherland"—and served as its president. In addition to patrolling grain markets, members played an aggressive role in ousting the Girondins from power. Their most notorious act was the administration of a public whipping to pro-Girondin Théroigne de Méricourt*. A Robespierrist backlash against the Society's growing influence resulted in the October 1793 suppression of all women's clubs. One month later, Léon married Théophile Leclerc, an *Enragé* from Lyons. Léon and Leclerc were arrested and imprisoned as suspected enemies of the state from April to August 1794. While in prison, Léon gave a statement in which she proudly reviewed her revolutionary activities, while maintaining that since her marriage* she had devoted herself to her wifely duties.

Mary McAlpin

BIBLIOGRAPHY

Secondary Texts

Levy, Darline Gay, Harriet Branson Applewhite, and Mary Durham Johnson, eds. and trans. *Women in Revolutionary Paris, 1789–1795*. Urbana: University of Illinois Press, 1979.

Rose, R. B. *The Making of the Sans-culottes*. Manchester: Manchester University Press, 1983.

Leprince de Beaumont, Jeanne-Marie (1711–1780). Although mostly known as the author of fairy tales*, such as *La Belle et la Bête* (adapted from Mme de Villeneuve's* original), and as Mérimée's great-grandmother, she published seventy volumes during her lifetime, including treatises on education*, grammar, and morals. As one of a large artistic family, she was compelled to support herself by teaching in the convent* of Ernemont, later giving music lessons and teaching girls at the court of Stanislas. After a brief marriage* to a man who squandered her money, she began a new life with her daughter in England, where she taught daughters of the aristocracy. Struck by the low level of education and status of English women, she became an advocate of women's education. The fairy tales she wrote to illustrate her lessons were published in *Le Magasin des enfants* (1757), *Le Magasin des adolescentes* (1760), and *Le Magasin des jeunes dames* (1764). She was thus the first to write entertaining educational material for children, especially girls. Her faith in the female mind and character and in the intellectual and social potential of women led her to propagate feminist ideas. She was the first woman to write and edit a magazine,

Le Nouveau Magasin français, in which she vindicated the rights of women and stressed the importance of education for women. During the fourteen years she spent in England she also published novels* (*Le Triomphe de la vérité*, 1748, and *Clivan*, 1754), and history and geography texts. She left England in 1762 for health reasons and, in 1768 bought a property near Annecy, where she refused offers of teaching positions in order to concentrate on her writing. She remained there until her death in 1780. Following in Fénelon's footsteps, she combined moral and intellectual education, and gave practical lessons as well as religious training in which pleasure was associated with useful tasks. Before Rousseau, she stressed the importance of adapting the education to the child: she wished to develop virtuous hearts and critical minds by adopting the question-and-answer system which would be used by many of her successors.

Rosena Davison

BIBLIOGRAPHY

Primary Texts

Le Triomphe de la vérité. Nancy: Thomas, 1749.
Le Magasin des enfants ou dialogues d'une sage gouvernante avec ses élèves de la première distinction. Lyons: Reguilliat, 1758.
Le Magasin des adolescentes. Lyons: Reguilliat, 1760.
Education complète ou abrégé de l'histoire universelle mêlé de géographie et de chronologie. Lyons: Duplain, 1762.
Le Magasin des jeunes dames. London: Nourse, 1764.
La Nouvelle Clarice. Lyons: Bruyset-Ponthus, 1767.
Contes moraux. Lyons: Bruyset-Ponthus, 1774.
Nouveaux Contes moraux. Lyons: Bruyset-Ponthus, 1776.
La Dévotion éclairée ou magasin des dévots. Lyons: Bruyset-Ponthus, 1779.
Contes moraux pour l'instruction de la jeunesse. Paris: Barba, 1806.
Récréations morales et amusantes de la jeunesse ou recueil de contes moraux et instructifs. Paris: Thiériot et Belin, 1824.
Contes de fées. Paris: Lebaüy, 1843.

Secondary Texts

Clancy, Patricia A. "A French Writer and Education in England: Mme Le Prince de Beaumont." *Studies on Voltaire and the Eighteenth Century* 201 (1982): 195–208.
Deguise, Alix. "Madame Leprince de Beaumont: Conteuse ou moraliste?" In *Femmes savantes et femmes d'esprit: Women Intellectuals of the French Eighteenth Century*. Eds. Roland Bonnel and Catherine Rubinger. New York: Peter Lang, 1994. 155–182.
Granderoute, Robert. "La Fable et La Fontaine dans la pédagogie de Fénelon à Rousseau." *Dix-huitième siècle* 13 (1981): 335–348.
Stewart, Joan Hinde. "Allegories of Difference: An Eighteenth-Century Polemic." *Romanic Review* 75 (1984): 283–293.
Woodward, Servanne. "Definitions of Humanity for Young Ladies by Madame Le Prince de Beaumont." *Romance Languages Annual* (1992): 184–188.

Leroyer de Chantepie, Marie-Sophie (1800–1888). Since her father had divorced and remarried, Marie-Sophie was considered a bastard born of an illicit relationship according to the revolutionary laws of the time. Her correspondence with Flaubert, Sand*, and others reveals the shame she felt because of the social stigma of such a beginning. These letters share personal details of her life as well as of her readings. Personal sympathy guides those readings (e.g., Flaubert's *Madame Bovary* and Sand's *Lélia*) and political sentiments. Indeed, Leroyer de Chantepie personally identified closely with Emma Bovary (despite Flaubert's objections of lack of similarity) and with George Sand.

She contributed to a local newspaper, *Le Phare de la Loire*. Some of her reviews of poetry* by Pierre-Jean de Béranger and Victor Hugo and of novels* by Madame de Staël* and George Sand were posthumously collected and published in her *Souvenirs et impressions littéraires*. This work explains some of her romantic leanings. In her *Chroniques et légendes* she recalled memories of her early childhood and wrote of her birthplace, Château-Gontier. In these and in her other writings, her romantic sympathies cause the fictional and the autobiographical to intermingle (see *Les Mémoires d'une provinciale*). The three women protagonists of this last work appear to express the author's views of women, love, and society. Leroyer de Chantepie's work shares Sand's concerns with women's sufferings and limitations in a contemporary male-dominated society.

E. Nicole Meyer

BIBLIOGRAPHY

Primary Texts

Angèle, ou le dévouement filial. Tours: A. Mame, 1860.
Chroniques et légendes. Château-Gontier: J.-B. Bezier, 1870.
Mémoires d'une provinciale. 2 vols. Paris: Dentu, 1880.
Nouvelles littéraires. Paris: Perrin, 1889.
Souvenirs et impressions littéraires. Paris: Perrin, 1892.
Luttes du coeur. Paris: Perrin, 1893.
Figures historiques et légendaires. Paris: Perrin, n.d.
Groupes de martyres: Les Duranti, Angèle de Chavigny, Zinetta la Bohémienne. Paris: Perrin, n.d.

Secondary Texts

Allen, James Smith. "A Republic of Romantic Letters: Marie-Sophie Leroyer de Chantepie and Her Literary Community." Ed. Graham Falconer. In *Autour d'un cabinet de lecture.* Toronto: Centre d'etudes romantiques Jean Sablé, forthcoming.
Brizemur, Daniel. "Une Correspondante de Flaubert: Mlle Leroyer de Chantepie." *Revue hébdomadaire,* October 18, 1919. Reprinted in *Les Amis de Flaubert* 16 (1960): 3–12, and 17 (1960): 3–10.
Flaubert, Gustave. *Correspondance.* Ed. Jean Bruneau. 3 vols. Paris: Gallimard, 1973–1991.
Sand, George. *Correspondance.* Ed. Georges Lubin. Paris: Garnier, 1964–1994.

Lesbianism. Though lesbianism, in France, was not severely repressed by law (as was the case with male homosexuality), lesbians were always regarded as disruptive elements. Till the nineteenth century, the discourse on lesbianism was essentially a male discourse focusing on the sexual aspect of women's love for women. Their sexual practices were imagined along the lines of male sexuality, and lesbians were seen as ridiculous or at best ineffective *hommes contrefaits*. But whereas in times of relative social harmony they were tolerated with amused disdain by men, in times of social unrest they posed a threat to the patriarchal order by questioning the institution of marriage* and traditional gender roles. In short, they represented, and still do to a certain extent, the grotesque but also dangerous figure of women's autonomy and individuality.

The word *tribade*, from the Greek to "rub" or "rub one another," was adopted in the sixteenth century to denote "lesbian," thus stressing the physical aspect. In that period, the interest in Sappho's poetry shaped an emerging discourse about love between women. Sappho's writings and persona became a mythical model around which both men and women projected their phantasms. Gifted poet, lascivious seducer of young women, *homme manqué*, tragic lover of Phaon, *femme damnée* or empowering figure of the woman artist, each age and group, subsequently, appropriated Sappho for its own purposes.

In the seventeenth century, the concept of love as mutual admiration spurred the advent of *les tendres amitiés*, which allowed women to carry on passionate friendships* in the public eye without being stigmatized. Indeed, women's expression of love for one another was quite acceptable until the nineteenth century in France. Whether those friendships had sexual, even genital, components is hard to ascertain. It seems, however, that the eighteenth century, under the liberating influence of the Enlightenment*, saw no reason to condemn women's expression of sexual feelings for their own sex.

This freedom was short-lived. As soon as the Revolution* started, there was an unleashing of hatred against lesbians. Women were sent back to their homes to serve as virtuous republican wives and mothers. The nineteenth century was a complex time that witnessed both the reaffirmation of an oppressive patriarchal code and the first outbursts of feminist revolts. This complexity is reflected in the highly ambivalent ways in which lesbians were represented. On the one hand, a female discourse on lesbianism emerged, as in Georges Sand's* *Lélia*, placing women's desire for women in the wider context of love. Significantly, the word "tribade" disappeared, to be replaced by "lesbian." The large number of lesbian artists of the period—such as Rosa Bonheur and Nathalie Micas, and later, the group of women around Natalie Barney*—emphasized the friendship aspect of their love because for centuries the spiritual and social dimension of lesbianism had been concealed. On the other hand, in reaction to their audacity, lesbians were reimprisoned in negative images. The image of *les femmes damnées* was a titillating mixture of sin and sex which cast lesbians as exotic creatures and also as a sort of alter ego of the decadent artists. And psychiatrists, Havelock Ellis for example, treated lesbians as inverts. Lesbianism became homosexuality, a perversion and an illness. Freud's theories completed the picture by turning lesbians into immature beings whose sexuality was arrested at the clitoral stage.

These negative images informed the perception and often the self-perceptions of lesbians till the 1960s. Women were caught between a shameful public image of lesbianism and their own personal experience. Colette* created lesbian images in direct opposition to Baudelaire's *femmes damnées* as well as to Proust's vision of Gomorrah. She insisted upon the healing effect of lesbian love, with its maternal overtone, which functions as an antidote to men's harsh treatment of women.

Although after the war, when women obtained the vote (1945), the lives of French women were to be forever changed, this transformation was not felt before 1968. As a consequence of the war, patriarchal structures and mentalities were reinforced and lesbians went back into the closet. While Simone de Beauvoir's* *Le Deuxième Sexe* presented an ambiguous picture of lesbians, Violette Leduc* in *La Bâtarde* and *Thérèse et Isabelle* wrote openly about sexual love between women. By liberating women's discourse on their own sexuality, she anticipated Cixous's* notion of *écriture féminine*.

May 1968, however, marked the liberation of the repressed. Lesbian feminists became the most radical voice, forcing women and men to reexamine accepted heterosexual norms. For many women, *becoming* lesbians was a political choice. In the 1970s, lesbian groups, such as les Gouines Rouges, and lesbian publications sprouted up everywhere. Essays by Hélène Cixous, Luce Irigaray*, and others turned women's polymorphic sexuality into a revolutionary weapon to dismantle the patriarchal order. Monique Wittig's* *Les Guérillères* and *Le Corps lesbien* were good representations of a radical lesbian feminist vision of a female utopia that put women's bodies at the center of the text.

As early as 1977, however, the French feminist movement split into fractional groups, some along hetero/homosexual lines, some within the lesbian groups themselves. If recent years have seen a growing tolerance toward homosexuality in general—a series of measures, from 1950 to 1990, removed all discrimination from the law—lesbians, however, now keep a low profile, especially compared to their American counterparts. It would certainly require another revolution to have lesbians not just tolerated but completely integrated into French society.

Colette T. Hall

BIBLIOGRAPHY

Secondary Texts

Beauvoir, Simone de. *Le Deuxième Sexe*. 2 vols. Paris: Gallimard, 1949. See Part 6 of Vol. 1.

Benstock, Shari. *Women of the Left Bank: Paris, 1900–1940*. Austin: University of Texas Press, 1986.

Bonnet, Marie-Jo. *Les Relations amoureuses entre les femmes du XVIe siècle au XXe siècle*. Paris: Ed. Odile Jacob, 1995.

Faderman, Lillian. *Surpassing the Love of Men: Romantic Friendship and Love between Women from the Renaissance to the Present*. New York: William Morrow, 1981.

Lago, Maria, and France Paramelle. *La Femme homosexuelle*. Paris: Casterman, 1976.

Lesselier, Claudine. "Le Regroupement de lesbiennes dans le mouvement féministe parisien (1970–1982)." In *Crises de la société, féminisme et changement*. Paris: Ed. Tierce, 1990.

Marks, Elaine. "Lesbian Intertextuality." In *Homosexualities in French Literature*. Ed. George Stambolian and Elaine Marks. Ithaca: Cornell University Press, 1979.

Martel, Frédéric. *Le Rose et le noir. Les Homosexuels en France depuis 1968*. Paris: Ed. du Seuil, 1996.

Mossuz-Lavau, Janine. *Les Lois de l'amour. Les Politiques de la sexualité en France (1950–1990)*. Paris: Casterman, 1995.

Lespinasse, Julie-Jeanne-Eléonore de (1732–1776). Born in Lyons under circumstances long kept secret, she was the illegitimate daughter of Julie d'Albon and presumably Gaspard de Vichy, Mme du Deffand's* brother. Vichy married Julie's older sister, thus becoming her brother-in-law. In 1754 Julie became du Deffand's companion and a member of her salon*. In 1764 she formed her own salon on rue Saint-Dominique in the house she shared with the mathematician and encyclopedist d'Alembert. Lespinasse was known as the "Muse of the Encyclopedia," and her famous salon was frequented by d'Alembert, Diderot, Condorcet, Turgot, the Chevalier de Chastellux, Malesherbes, and the Abbé Galiani. Her progressive views encouraged the free discussion of ideas, contributing to the intellectual activity associated with the Enlightenment*.

In 1767 Lespinasse fell in love with Gonsalve de Mora, son of the Spanish ambassador to France, but was unable to marry the gravely ill marquis, who subsequently died. In 1772 she met Count Jacques Hippolyte de Guibert, subsequently became his mistress, and began a correspondence that has earned her a distinguished place among epistolary writers. In the approximately 200 letters she wrote to him between 1773 and 1776, Lespinasse, torn between her love for Mora and Guibert, sought to differentiate herself from women writers she considered insincere, shallow, and hypocritical. Frustrated by Guibert's perceived coldness, and betrayed when he married another woman, Lespinasse, gravely ill and dying of tuberculosis, viewed herself as a superior but tragic heroine. Critical efforts have focused on her transformation into a literary figure, bridging the gap between truth and fiction and acting out a feminine destiny of love, abandonment, suffering, and death. However, in her writing, Lespinasse refused the role of victim. Writing, for her, constituted a source of strength and self-realization within masculine power structures. The letters explore the parameters of a woman's search for truth, focusing on Lespinasse's ability to express herself and interpret feelings. In addition to her correspondence with Guibert, Condorcet, d'Alembert, and numerous heads of state, two chapters in the style of Laurence Sterne's *A Sentimental Journey Through France and Italy* (1768), her partially completed memoirs*, and various short works are also attributed to Lespinasse.

Felicia B. Sturzer

BIBLIOGRAPHY

Primary Texts

Lettres de mademoiselle de Lespinasse, écrites depuis l'année 1773 jusqu'à l'année 1776 suivies de deux chapitres dans le genre de Voyage sentimental de Sterne, par le même auteur. Paris: L. Collin, 1809.

Lettres de Mlle de Lespinasse, suivies de ses autres oeuvres et de lettres de Madame du Deffand, de Turgot, de Bernardin de Saint-Pierre. Ed. Eugène Asse. Paris: Charpentier et Cie., 1876.

Lettres inédites à Condorcet, à D'Alembert, à Guibert, au comte de Crillon, publiées avec des lettres de ses amis, des documents nouveaux et une étude par M. Charles Henry. Paris: E. Dentu, 1887.

Correspondance entre Mlle de Lespinasse et le comte de Guibert, publiée pour la première fois d'après le texte original par le comte de Villeneuve-Guibert. Paris: Calmann-Lévy, 1906.

Lettres à Condorcet, suivies du portrait de Condorcet rédigé par Julie de Lespinasse en 1774. Ed. Jean-Noël Pascal. Paris: Editions Desjonquères, 1990.

Secondary Texts

Beaunier, André. *La Vie amoureuse de Julie de Lespinasse.* Paris: Ernest Flammarion, 1925.

Bouissounouse, Janine. *Julie de Lespinasse. Ses amitiés, sa passion.* Paris: Librairie Hachette, 1958.

Carrell, Susan L. *Le Soliloque de la passion féminine ou le dialogue illusoire.* Paris: Place-Narr, 1982.

Lacouture, Jean, and Marie-Christine d'Aragon. *Julie de Lespinasse. Mourir d'amour.* Paris: Editions Ramsay, 1980.

Pascal, Jean-Noël. ''Julie romancière.'' Préface. *Lettres de Mlle de Lespinasse, précédées de ''Mlle de Lespinasse'' par Sainte-Beuve, réimpression de l'édition Garnier de 1893 avec une préface inédite par J.-N. Pascal.* Plan-de-la-Tour: Editions d'aujourd'hui, 1978.

Ségur, Pierre Marie Maurice Henri, Marquis de. *Julie de Lespinasse.* Paris: Calmann-Lévy, 1906.

Letessier, Dorothée (1953–). Raised in a proletarian environment, Letessier was employed as a secretary in a Parisian office and as a worker in various factories in Brittany before beginning to write about the lives of working-class women. Her first and best-known novel*, *Le Voyage à Paimpol* (1980), tells the story of a woman who discovers the joy of independence when she leaves behind her child, her husband, and her job on an assembly line for a few bittersweet days of ''fresh air.'' In a direct, humorous, and down-to-earth style, Letessier gives a voice to poorly educated working-class women, and her work addresses both the class and gender issues that affect their lives.

Frédérique Chevillot

BIBLIOGRAPHY

Primary Texts

Le Voyage à Paimpol. Paris: Seuil, 1980.
Loïca. Paris: Seuil, 1983.

La Belle Atlantique. Paris: Seuil, 1986.
Jean-Baptiste ou l'éducation vagabonde. Paris: Gallimard, 1988.
La Reine des abeilles. Paris: Seuil, 1989.
L'Autocar. Paris: Flammarion, 1994.

Letter-writing. From the Middle Ages to the present day, French women writers have discovered in the letter an inexhaustible literary form. Unlike other literary genres (such as poetry* and theater*), in which established artistic rules constrained the writer's expression, the epistolary form allowed the writer greater imaginative freedom. Throughout literary history, genuine correspondences afforded women writers total privacy, and thus a sense of true artistic autonomy. And while a public literary career did not always ensure artistic freedom, epistolary writing provided women writers with a forum in which to express their personal views on marriage*, education*, friendship*, passion, and politics.

Much of the epistolary writing in France throughout history seems to bear traces of the Abélard-Héloïse correspondence of 1128–1134. Héloïse's* anguished letters from the convent* set the stage for the well-known ''seduced and abandoned'' theme, and many *épistolières* wrote either within or against the Héloïse tradition.

The medieval period is marked by the contributions of Marie de France* and Christine de Pizan*. Marie de France cannot technically be called an epistolary writer; nevertheless, the manner in which she addresses her *Lais* (1160–1170) to her royal patron Henry II captures something of the epistolary dynamic between sender and receiver. Christine de Pizan's 1399 text *Epître au dieu d'amour*, as well as the letters she sent to Jean de Montreuil and Jean and Pierre Col, identify her as France's first true *épistolière*. In these letters she vehemently objects to the misogynistic portrayals of women in *Le Roman de la rose* (1220, 1275) and in so doing launches the long-lived debate on the equality of women, known as the *Querelle des femmes** (Quarrel of Women). The French Renaissance produced a writer known primarily for her epistolary writing: Hélisenne de Crenne*. Hélisenne's *Les Epîtres familières et invectives* (1539) involved her in the *Querelle des femmes*. The text is comprised of thirteen personal letters and five ''invective'' letters. In them, the author protests the societal constraints on women—marriage, poor education, and geographical isolation—and defends a woman's right to achieve social and intellectual independence. One of the best-known poets of the French Renaissance, Louise Labé*, began her *Evvres de Lovize Labé Lionnoize* (1555) with an epistle to Clémence de Bourges which expresses a strident call for women's equality in society and therefore contributes significantly to the history of epistolary writing by women.

During the seventeenth century, the center of literary activity gradually moved from the court to the Parisian salon*, signaling an increase in artistic voice for women. In the literary salons of Mlle de Scudéry*, Mme de Lafayette*, and others, epistles real and imaginary were circulated and read aloud to theatrical effect. During this century, the letter form continued to provide women with an unrestricted literary outlet, and the so-called Great Century produced one of its greatest practitioners, Mme de Sévigné*.

Sévigné's correspondence of approximately 1,371 letters spans forty-eight years, ending with the year of her death in 1696. Present-day readers take particular interest in the great number of letters sent by Sévigné to her daughter in Provence; they reveal a degree of unfailing maternal devotion that counterbalances present-day theories of maternal ambivalence in early modern France. Another seventeenth-century writer, Marie-Catherine Desjardins de Villedieu*, is remembered for her poetry, theater, novels*, stories, and love letters. Her *Lettres et billets galants* (1668) was published (against her will) by her estranged husband.

Epistolary writing enjoyed an uncontested artistic vogue during the eighteenth century for several reasons, among them the reading public's taste for "exotic" perspectives and the favorable influence of Samuel Richardson's novels abroad. It is important to note that in contrast to earlier writers who wrote within a protected system of aristocratic patronage, the eighteenth-century woman wrote out of economic necessity. The financial pressures women writers faced coincided with the independence they enjoyed.

The eighteenth century saw a profusion of very original epistolary writers: Françoise de Graffigny*, the Marquise du Deffand*, Marie-Jeanne Riccoboni*, Jeanne Marie Leprince de Beaumont*, Julie de Lespinasse*, Claudine-Alexandrine Guérin de Tencin*, Isabelle de Charrière*, the comtesse de Genlis*, and Juliane von Krüdener*. Many of the published epistolary fictions of this period—most notably those of Graffigny and Charrière—were immensely popular with the reading public. In the fictions, the institutions within which women lived and died—marriage, family*, the convent—become the object of vigorous feminist scrutiny. The private correspondences (notably those of Lespinasse and du Deffand) are revealing in their tireless explorations of interior states of thinking and feeling.

Following this apex of epistolary writing in France, the form gradually fell out of favor with the reading public. Nineteenth-century realism* eclipsed the more exotic fictional settings that letter-writing had previously engendered, and lyric expression found new vigor in Romantic and Symbolist* poetry. George Sand* published several epistolary novels, among them *Jacques* (1834) and *Mademoiselle La Quintinie* (1863); in addition, her private correspondence has recently attracted well-deserved scholarly attention.

In this century, the very notion of genre has proven too limiting for the literary talents of women writers such as Cixous* and Duras*. However, the Senegalese writer Mariama Bâ achieved much notoriety for her 1979 epistolary novel entitled *Une Si Longue Lettre*. This fictitious correspondence between two female friends recasts the age-old epistolary paradox: that of intimacy achieved in the absence of presence.

Julia K. DePree

BIBLIOGRAPHY

Primary Texts

Charrière, Isabelle de. *Oeuvres complètes*. 10 vols. Ed. Jean-Daniel Candaux et al. Amsterdam: Van Oorschot, 1979–1984.

Graffigny, Françoise de. *Lettres d'une Péruvienne*. New York: Modern Language Association Texts and Translations, 1993.

Lespinasse, Julie de. *Lettres de Mademoiselle de Lespinasse, précédées d'une notice de Sainte Beuve*. Reprint of the 1893 Garnier edition. Plan-de-la-Tour: Editions d'Aujourd'hui, 1978.

Mustacchi, Marianna M., and Paul J. Archambault, eds. and trans. *A Renaissance Woman: Hélisenne's Personal and Invective Letters*. Syracuse: Syracuse University Press, 1986.

Riccoboni, Marie-Jeanne. *Oeuvres complètes*. 6 vols. Paris: Foucault, 1818.

Sand, George. *Mademoiselle la Quintinie*. Paris: Ressources, 1979.

Sévigné, Madame de. *Lettres*. 3 vols. Ed. Emile Gérard-Gailly. Paris: Bibliothèque de la Pléiade, Editions Gallimard, 1972–1978.

Tencin, Mme de. *Letters of Madame de Tencin and the Cardinal de Tencin to the Duc de Richelieu*. Paris: Editions Mazarine, 1967.

Willard, Charity C., ed. *The Selected Writings of Christine de Pizan*. New York: Persea Books, 1991.

Secondary Texts

Giraud, Yves. *Bibliographie du roman épistolaire en France: des origines à 1842*. Fribourg: Editions Universitaires, 1977.

Miller, Nancy K. ''Tender Economies: Mme de Villedieu and the Costs of Indifference.'' *L'Esprit Créateur* 23 (1983): 80–93.

Lévesque, Louise Cavelier (1703–1743? 1745?). Lévesque, one of the most prolific and distinguished writers of her time, wrote religious and comic poetry* and plays as well as short stories* and novels*. Her writings, though barely noted by literary historians, and absent from most collections, are nonetheless remarkable for their portrayals of strong, dynamic women characters. In *Le Prince des aigues marines* (1722) and *L'Auteur* (1740), written at a time when arranged marriages* were the norm, women freely choose their spouses. In the fantastical *Célénie* (1732) and *Le Prince invisible* (1722), constancy is rewarded and men's villainous *amour propre* exposed. In *Le Siècle* (1736) and *Le Prince des aigues marines*, and especially in *Le Soufflet* (1742), *L'Auteur*, and *Lilia* (1736), women are depicted as paragons of scientific knowledge and wisdom. And in *Lettres et Chansons* (1731), a blend of letters, songs, and poetry in which two women friends debate the merits of men and marriage, one of the young women chooses a life of solitude and independence the better to ensure the free exercise of the mind. Lévesque also wrote epistles and portraits, and her contemporaries praised her as a new Deshoulières*, a muse, a ''docte pucelle.''

Jennifer McGonagle

BIBLIOGRAPHY

Primary Texts

Le Prince des aigues marines. Paris: L. D. Vatel, 1722.
Le Prince invisible. Paris: L. D. Vatel, 1722.
Lettres et chansons de Céphise et d'Uranie. Paris: J.B.C. Ballard, 1731.
Célénie, histoire allégorique. Paris: P. Prault, 1732.
Lilia ou histoire de Carthage. Amsterdam: N.p., 1736.
Le Siècle ou les mémoires du Comte de S***. Paris: J. Clousier, 1736.
La Vie de Job en vers. Soissons: A. Sellier, 1736.
Augustin pénitent. London: P. Hebink, 1738.
L'Auteur/l'amour fortune. Paris: N.p., 1740.
Le Soufflet. Conte chinois. The Hague: H. Van Bulderen, 1742.

Secondary Texts

Dwyer, H., and B. Dwyer, eds. *Index biographique français.* London: Bowker-Saur, 1993.
Grente, Georges. *Dictionnaire des lettres françaises: Le Dix-Huitième Siècle.* Paris: Librairie Arthème Fayard, 1960.

Lézardière, Marie Charlotte Pauline Robert de (1754–1835). Born and raised in Vendée, she received an excellent education*, and decided, at an early age, to write about the political origins of France. Although her father tried to dissuade her, she persevered. A first version of her writings was shown to the politician Malesherbes, who encouraged her to continue her research, introduced her to other historians, and gave her access to the collections of the Bibliothèque du Roi and the Benedictine library in Poitiers. The first two parts of her major work, *Théorie des lois politiques de la monarchie française*, were published in 1792—the year the monarchy was abolished. Only a few copies of the book were saved from destruction. Lézardière then suffered the fate of many French aristocrats; she went into exile, and having survived the ruin of her family— her ancestral home with its rich library was burnt and three of her brothers killed—she returned to France in 1801 to live with an older brother. Deprived of her papers and books, and no longer able to pursue her studies, she led a quiet life until her death in 1835. In 1844 renewed interest in her writings encouraged her younger brother to publish an augmented edition of her work. Lézardière's major claim to fame is her lucid analysis of the progress of French civilization and its concomitant loss of freedom, and her determination, against all odds, to be a serious political writer.

Catherine Lafarge

BIBLIOGRAPHY

Primary Texts

Théorie des lois politiques de la monarchie française. Paris: Nyon l'aîné et fils, 1792.
Théorie des lois politiques de la monarchie française. Paris: Comptoir des imprimeurs-unis, 1844.
Ecrits inédits de Mlle de Lézardière. Introd. E. Carcassonne. Paris: Presses Universitaires de France, 1927.

Secondary Texts

Grente, Georges. *Dictionnaire des lettres françaises*. Edition revue et mise à jour par
    François Moureau. Paris: Fayard, 1995.
Nouvelle Bibliographie générale. Paris: Firmin-Didot, 1862.

Lezay-Marnésia, Charlotte Antoinette de Bressey, marquise de (?–1785).

Little is known about her. Daughter of one of Duke Leopold's chamberlains,
she married François-Gabriel, second marquis de Lezay-Marnésia, a descendant
of an ancient military aristocratic family from Franche-Comté. She entertained
a literary circle at her home in Nancy where prominent guests included, among
others, the chevalier de Boufflers and the Jesuit Cerrutti. Her only known work,
Lettres de Julie à Ovide, (1753), was published anonymously and attributed to
Marmontel until Lezay-Marnésia's son revealed that it was his mother's work.
This short epistolary poem, reedited several times, relates the passionate and
unfortunate love story between Julie and the famous Latin poet Ovid. Julie is
forced by the Emperor to marry his son, and Ovid is exiled; however, Julie finds
solace in the beauty and purity of nature. Idealized to suit the taste of salon*
society, and transformed into a vast inspiring garden, nature is depicted as a
perfect setting for the lovers' discourse. Ten years later, Rousseau developed
similar themes in *La Nouvelle Héloïse*.

S. Pascale Dewey

BIBLIOGRAPHY

Primary Text

Lettres de Julie à Ovide. Rome and Paris: Gattey, 1789.

Secondary Texts

Blanchard, J. M. "Style pastoral, style des lumières." *Studies on Voltaire and the Eigh-
    teenth Century* 114 (1973): 331–346.
Bonnel, Roland Guy. *Ethique et esthétique du retour à la campagne au XVIIIe siècle.
    L'oeuvre littéraire et utopique de Lezay-Marnésia, 1735–1800*. New York: Peter
    Lang, 1995.
Bourget-Besnier, Elisabeth. *Une Famille française sous la Révolution et l'Empire. La
    Famille de Lezay-Marnésia*. Paris: N.p., 1985.
Brelot, Claude. "La Noblesse en Franche-Comté de 1789 à 1808." *Annales littéraires
    de l'Université de Besançon* 134. Paris: Les Belles Lettres, 1972.
Kafker, Franz, and Serena Kafker. "The Encyclopedists as Individuals: A Biographical
    Dictionary of the Authors of the Encyclopédie." *Studies on Voltaire and the
    Eighteenth Century* 257 (1988): 1–430.
Maugras, Gaston. *La Cour de Lunéville au XVIIIe siècle*. Paris: Plon, 1904.
Mesmay, Jean Tiburce de. *Dictionnaire historique, biographique et généalogique des
    anciennes familles de Franche-Comté*. Paris: N.p., 1958.
Roposte, Roger. *La Maison de retraite Lezay-Marnésia de Saint-Julien-sur-Suran et son
    histoire*. Strasbourg: Amarel, 1986.
Veyre, Marius. *La Maison Lezay-Marnésia, 1240–1884*. Strasbourg: Beant, 1958.

Lhéritier de Villandon, Marie-Jeanne (1664?–1734). The daughter of a royal historiographer and the niece of Charles Perrault, Lhéritier received an exceptional education* for a woman of her day. Although little is known of her early life, she became a prominent participant in literary circles of the 1690s and 1700s, contributed frequently to the *Mercure galant*, won prizes sponsored by the Académie Française, was given honorary membership in the Académie des Laternistes de Toulouse and the Accademia dei Ricovrati of Padua, and is said to have inherited Madeleine de Scudéry's* salon* upon that writer's death. Throughout her lifetime, she published several collections of her works—poetry*, letters, novellas, and fairy tales*—including *Oeuvres meslées* (1695), *L'Erudition enjouée* (1702), *La Tour ténébreuse* (1705), and *Les Caprices du destin* (1718). She also edited the memoirs* of her protectress, the Duchesse de Nemours* (1709), and translated Ovid's *Heroides* into French (1723). Of all the late seventeenth-century French women writers, Lhéritier is arguably the most overtly feminist. Besides celebrating the accomplishments of prominent women writers (e.g., "Le Triomphe de Madame Deshoulières" [1694] and "L'Apothéose de Mademoiselle de Scudéry" [1702]), she wrote several responses to Boileau's misogynistic *Satire X* and, in her fiction, repeatedly defended women's education. This latter defense can be found in her fairy tale, "Les Enchantements de l'éloquence" (based on the same tale-type as Perrault's "Les Fées"), in which she explicitly defends women's reading and outlines a classically inspired "feminine" rhetoric. Lhéritier also repeatedly used the figure of the female cross-dresser to denounce inequalities between the sexes (e.g., "Eloge de Mlle de la Charce" and "Marmoisan"). However, the boldness of Lhéritier's feminism would seem to be tempered by her recurrent prescriptions for virtuous feminine conduct (e.g., the moralizing fairy tale, "L'Adroite Princesse," which was republished many times in the nineteenth and twentieth centuries).

Lewis C. Seifert

BIBLIOGRAPHY

Primary Texts

"Les Enchantements de l'éloquence." In *Contes de Perrault*. Ed. Gilbert Rouger. Paris: Garnier, 1967. 239–265.
La Tour ténébreuse et les jours lumineux. Nouveaux Cabinet des fées. Vol. 7. Geneva: Slatkine Reprints, 1978.
"Marmoisan ou l'innocente tromperie." In *La Fille en garçon*. Ed. Catherine Velay-Vallantin. Toulouse: Garae/Hesiode, 1992.

Liancourt, Jeanne de Schomberg, duchesse de. *See* Schomberg, Jeanne de.

Libertinage. *Libertinage* derives from a Latin word meaning "emancipated," and from the time it came into use in the early seventeenth century it connoted freedom associated with both unorthodox opinions and moral independence. The early *libertins* were stigmatized mostly for their impious or satirical writings, but they often indulged in a willful display of amorous (and other) license which, by the eighteenth century, came predominantly to define the word's meaning.

But it must be said that the *libertins* prominent in eighteenth-century novels* constitute more a literary type than the certifiable representation of a historical subclass. Seduction and abandonment are the *libertin* hero's standard behavioral mechanism, rationalized by an aesthetics of pleasure that demands constant change. He takes, however, a variety of forms, at times simply flighty, at others cynical, methodical, even philosophical—Meilcour in the former category and Versac in the latter (both in *Les Egarements du coeur et de l'esprit*, by Claude Crébillon, 1736–1738). Any number of novelists represent libertinage as simply a youthful phase in worldly life, one that may before long wind down as the maturing protagonist tires of constant infidelity (e.g., *Les Confessions du comte de**** by Charles Duclos, 1741). Another pertinent fact is that not a single libertine novel in France in the eighteenth century is known to have been written by a woman.

Woman's role with respect to the libertine male is similarly variable. When women are simply strewn in the *libertin*'s wake, they appear as the pathetic (but sometimes unlamented) consequence of an almost unconstrained male arrogance and prerogative, the waste product of a flagrant double standard. But libertinage is also a game that is played with two players on more or less equal footing; the young male is often, for example, initiated into its ways by an experienced, sometimes wily woman (Madame de Ferval in *Le Paysan parvenu*, by Marivaux, 1736; or Crébillon's Madame de Lursay), who may be just as intent on sexual adventurousness and the prestige of numerous ''conquests'' as he. Woman's own claim to erotic pleasure and freedom is highly explicit in novels like *Thérèse philosophe* (anonymous, 1748) and *Margot la ravaudeuse* (by Fougeret de Montbron, 1749/1750), whose female protagonists refuse to be victims and insist on sharing the prerogatives of their male counterparts. Thus there are *libertines* as well as *libertins*, and together they often seem to characterize an entire society, or a significant subset of it, given over to heady hedonism at a time of rapidly changing religious, intellectual, and moral norms.

Nonetheless, the woman is obliged to look to her reputation: the premise of the libertine code is not that immoral actions are wholly secret, only that they are in fact tolerated; and it is always assumed that while a man may be positively valued for his rakish reputation, a woman can be easily dishonored. Madame de Merteuil, in *Les Liaisons dangereuses* by Choderlos de Laclos (1782), is in every way Valmont's equal as partner and conspirator, but she must be much more clever and devious so as to keep her offenses quiet. Sometimes such heroines, like the men, end in repentance, ruin, or disrepute. Other possible consequences, in particular venereal disease and pregnancy, are only rarely acknowledged explicitly in a literature that is, after all, highly stylized.

Libertinage depends for its definition on the social constraints it defies: it is the fantasy that responds to strict official mores, and in its classical sense, with the abolition of aristocratic privilege and censorship, it comes to an end with the Revolution*.

Philip Stewart

BIBLIOGRAPHY

Secondary Texts

Cazenobe, Colette. "Le Système du libertinage de Crébillon à Laclos." *Studies on Voltaire and the Eighteenth Century* 282. Oxford: Voltaire Foundation, 1991.

Cryle, Peter. *Geometry in the Boudoir: Configurations of French Erotic Narrative*. Ithaca: Cornell University Press, 1994.

Laroch, Philippe. *Petits-maîtres et roués: Evolution de la notion de libertinage dans le roman français du XVIIIe siècle*. Quebec: Presses de l'Université Laval, 1979.

Moureau, François, and Alain-Marc Rieu, eds. *Eros philosophe: Discours libertins des Lumières*. Geneva: Honoré Champion, 1984.

Rustin, Jacques. *Le Vice à la mode: Etude sur le roman français de la 1re partie du XVIIIe siècle*. Paris: Ophrys, 1979.

Liébaut, Nicole Estienne, madame. *See* Estienne, Nicole.

Louise de Savoie. *See* Savoie, Louise de.

Lubert, Marguerite or Marie-Madeleine de (c. 1710–1779). Adult fairy tale* writer whose diverse work included verse (*Epître sur la Paresse*, 1746), an adaptation of *Amadis de Gaule*, and novellas such as *La Veillée galante* (1747), *Mourat et Turquia* (1752), and *Léonille* (1755); she also reedited fairy tales by Mme d'Auneuil and Mme de Murat*. Her wit charmed writers such as Fontenelle, Voltaire, and Mme de Graffigny*. Her fourteen fairy tales (published between 1743 and 1756), some of which are quite long, differ from the conventional model. The theoretical preface to *Sec et noir* (1743) emphasizes the self-conscious, playful nature of her work. Fantasy is combined with obsessional themes of monstrosity and metamorphoses. Licentious and scatological details abound, while images from marine life produce a surreal atmosphere. Sadomasochistic and homosexual tendencies, fears, and inhibitions, both conscious and unconscious, add an eccentric twist to her narratives. Exaggeration is pushed to its limits, creating thus an ironic dimension, associated with parody. Lubert's female characters are strong individuals inspiring fear in men, who are visualized as repellent, monstrous creatures. Only three stories have been reedited in the twentieth century: *La Princesse Coque d'oeuf et le Prince Bonbon* (1745), *La Princesse Camion* (1743), and *Le Prince Glacé et la Princesse Etincelante* (1743).

Olga B. Cragg

BIBLIOGRAPHY

Primary Texts

"Le Prince Glacé et la Princesse Etincelante." In *Le Cabinet des fées*. Arles: Philippe Picquier, 1988. 2: 127–173.

"La Princesse Camion." In *Le Cabinet des fées.* Arles: Philippe Picquier, 1988. 2: 81–125.
"La Princesse Coque d'oeuf et le Prince Bonbon." In *Il était une fois les fées. Contes du XVIIe et du XVIIIe siècles.* Ed. Raymonde Robert. Nancy: Presses Universitaires de Nancy, 1984. 49–190.

Secondary Texts

Barchilon, Jacques. *Le Conte merveilleux français de 1690 à 1790. Cent Ans de féerie et de poésie ignorées de l'histoire littéraire.* Paris: Honoré Champion, 1975.
Robert, Raymonde. *Le Conte de fées littéraire en France de la fin du XVIIe à la fin du XVIIIe siècle.* Nancy: Presses Universitaires de Nancy, 1982.
Von Franz, Marie-Louise. *An Introduction to the Interpretation of Fairy Tales.* New York: Spring Publications, 1970.
Warner, Marina. *From the Beast to the Blonde: On Fairy Tales and Their Tellers.* London: Chatto and Windus, 1994.
Zipes, Jack. *Fairy Tales and the Art of Subversion.* New York: Wildman Press, 1983.

Lussan, Marguerite de (1682–1758). Lussan's origins are shrouded in mystery. Possibly the illegitimate daughter of Prince Thomas de Savoie, who assured her care and education* throughout childhood, Lussan also maintained close ties to a fortune-teller named La Fleury (her mother or governess?). Thanks to her powerful protector, Lussan met and frequented the luminaries of Parisian society; she wrote her first novel* on the encouragement of Bishop Huet and dedicated works to the Prince de Condé and Mme de Pompadour*, who assigned her a pension. Loosely based on medieval history, her novels abound in crusades, tournaments, court intrigues, and tempestuous passions. Lussan's psychological analyses are particularly fascinating and often treat the conflict of love and duty. Indeed, the plot of the *Histoire de la comtesse de Gondez* resembles *La Princesse de Clèves* in many respects, except for a marriage* at the end. Lussan's most acclaimed work, *Anecdotes de la cour de Philippe-Auguste*, popularized the legend of Gabrielle de Vergy and Raoul de Coucy, and helped inspire the "troubadour" genre of the nineteenth century. Her fairy tales—*Les Veillées de Thessalie*—contributed to the vogue of the marvelous with a pedagogical bent: each concludes with a moral lesson.

Julia Douthwaite

BIBLIOGRAPHY

Primary Texts

Histoire de la comtesse de Gondez écrite par elle-même. Paris: M. Pepie, 1725.
Les Veillées de Thessalie. Paris: J. F. Fosse, 1731–1732.
Anecdotes de la cour de Childéric, roi de France. Paris: Prault père, 1736.
Anecdotes de la cour de François Ier. London: J. Nours, 1748. Paris: Lebègue, 1821.
Annales galantes de la cour de Henri second. Amsterdam: J. Desbordes, 1749.
Marie d'Angleterre, reine-duchesse. Amsterdam: J. Desbordes, 1749 [possibly written with Claude-Joseph Chéron de Boismorand].
Histoire du règne de Louis XI. Paris: Veuve Pissot, 1755 [also attributed to Nicolas Baudot de Juilly].

Vie de Louis Balbe-Berton de Crillon surnommé le Brave; et Mémoires des règnes de
   Henri II, François II, Charles IX, Henri III, et Henri IV, pour servir à l'histoire
   de son temps. Paris: Pissot, 1757, 1758.

Secondary Texts

Luff, Doris A. "Introduction à une étude sur Marguerite de Lussan et le roman historique
   au commencement du XVIIIe siècle." *Revue d'histoire littéraire de la France* 43
   (1936): 1–19.
Nikigorc, Anna. "Une Romancière oubliée: Mademoiselle de Lussan." *Acta Universi-
   tatis Wratislaviensis* 156 (1972): 3–18.

M

Maintenon, Françoise d'Aubigné, marquise de (1635–1719). Although she was the granddaughter of the famous Huguenot poet Agrippa d'Aubigné, she was born, and baptized Catholic, in a jail, the child of a disgraced father and an unaffectionate mother who would focus her care on her two sons. Following her family's journey to the Antilles in a failed attempt to seek fortune, and then her father's death, young Françoise was left to the care of a beloved aunt who raised her in the Protestant faith. As a new wave of religious intolerance was rising from the court, she was coerced into an Ursuline convent* where she eventually embraced Catholicism. By the age of sixteen, she was in Paris, penniless and without social protection. Rather than joining a convent, as expected in her situation, Françoise consented to marry the poet Scarron, crippled and much older but a celebrity in the Parisian salons*. Amid this refined *précieuse* society, she acquired much of the social education necessary to her future advancement. In the years of poverty following Scarron's death in 1660, she endeavored to maintain a certain level of respectability, which was finally acknowledged when she became governess of Mme de Montespan's bastards with Louis XIV. The year 1669 marked the rise of her phenomenal public career, which culminated in 1683 with her legitimate, though secret, marriage* to the king of France. Although for the next forty years she would be associated with the miseries of his reign, she cannot be personally blamed for the king's political mistakes, such as religious persecution, especially the revocation of the Edict of Nantes in 1685, and international politics in general. She was pious and respectful of the Church's dogma. Consequently, she incurred the wrath of the courtiers with her customary devotion that censured their libertine inclinations. In fact, her extraordinary elevation made her an easy scapegoat for the monarchy's failures. Despite accusations of religious hypocrisy and monstrous ambition, she was probably a woman of strong principles with a sense of destiny at the side of the aging king. She used her privileged position to promote reforms within the Catholic Church. But her correspondence and pedagogical *Instructions*, never meant for publication, showed the signs of an authentic spiritual life checked by an unfaltering respect for logic and reason. Her establishment in 1686 and lifelong governance of the school at Saint-Cyr* designed to educate poor daughters of noble ancestry are her crowning achievements and the best testimonial to her true character.

Marcelle Maistre Welch

BIBLIOGRAPHY

Primary Text

Maintenon, Françoise de. *Recueil des Instructions que Mme de Maintenon a données aux Demoiselles de Saint-Cyr*. Paris: J. Dumoulin, 1908.

Secondary Texts

Beaudrillard, Alfred. "Le Caractère et les idées de Madame de Maintenon d'après sa correspondance." *Le Contemporain* (March 1882): 441–470, (April 1882): 594–625.
Truc, Gonzague. *La Vie de Madame de Maintenon*. Paris: Librairie Gallimard, 1929.

Mallet-Joris, Françoise (1930–). *Nom de plume* of Françoise Lilar. Belgian-born Mallet-Joris spent a year at Bryn Mawr College in the United States before moving to France. She published a collection of poetry* entitled *Poèmes du dimanche* at the age of seventeen. This was followed by *Le Rempart des béguines* (1951), a critically acclaimed novel* that recounts the experiences of a young woman coming to grips with adulthood and female homosexuality. She continued this story in *La Chambre rouge* (1955), a bildungsroman in which the heroine's successes of the first novel are overturned. She published two historical novels, *Trois Ages de la nuit* (1968), which deals with the persecution of witches, and *Les Personnages* (1961), based on the life of Louise de Lafayette, a mistress of Louis XIII who remained loyal to the queen and later entered a convent*. She later wrote two biographies of women previously ignored by historians: Marie de Mancini*, niece of Cardinal Mazarin, and seventeenth-century mystic Jeanne Guyon*. In her autobiographical *La Maison de papier* (1973), Mallet-Joris reflects on issues important to her as a woman writer, in particular the problematic relationship between motherhood and writing. Taken as a whole, her introspective writing focuses on the misogynistic treatment of women throughout the centuries.

Ana M. de Medeiros

BIBLIOGRAPHY

Primary Texts

Poèmes du dimanche. Brussels: Editions des Artistes, 1947.
Le Rempart des béguines. Paris: Julliard, 1951.
La Chambre rouge. Paris: Julliard, 1955.
Les Personnages. Paris: Julliard, 1961.

Lettre à moi-même. Paris: Julliard, 1963.
Marie Mancini, le premier amour de Louis XIV. Paris: Hachette, 1964.
Trois Ages de la nuit. Paris: Grasset, 1968.
La Maison de papier. Paris: Grasset, 1970.
Jeanne Guyon. Paris: Flammarion, 1978.
Le Rire de Laura. Paris: Gallimard, 1988.
Divine. Paris: Flammarion, 1991.

Secondary Text

Becker, Lucille. *Françoise Mallet-Joris.* Boston: Twayne, 1985.

Malraux, Clara (1897–1982). Born in Paris, the only daughter of German-Jewish naturalized French citizens, Clara married André Malraux in 1921. They separated in 1939, and Clara lived out the German occupation with her daughter Florence in France. Her personal experiences—as the wife of a very important man, as a Jew, and as a member of the French Resistance—inform much of her writing. Her texts, both fictional and nonfictional, reflect her concern for disenfranchised groups: she spoke out against colonization and intolerance in Indochina, Cambodia, and the Orient, and in favor of Republican Spain, Zionism, and feminism*. She was the editor of the journal *Eléments*, which was dedicated to peace in the Middle East.

Roland A. Champagne

BIBLIOGRAPHY

Primary Texts

La Maison ne fait pas crédit. Paris: La Bibliothèque française, 1947.
Le Bruit de nos pas. 6 vols. Paris: Grasset, 1963–1979.
Rahel ma grande soeur. Paris: Ramsay, 1980.

Secondary Texts

Bartillat, Christian de. *Clara Malraux, Biographie—témoignage.* Paris: Perrin, 1985.
Courtivron, Isabelle de. *Clara Malraux, une femme dans le siècle.* Paris: L'Olivier, 1992.
Suleiman, Susan Rubin. "Malraux's Women: A Re-vision." In *Gender and Reading: Essays on Readers, Texts, and Contexts.* Ed. Elizabeth A. Flynn and Patrocinio P. Schweikart. Baltimore: Johns Hopkins University Press, 1986. 124–146.

Mancini, Hortense (1646–1699). Second youngest, most beautiful, and most favored of Mazarin's seven nieces, she was brought to France at age eight and married at fourteen to twenty-nine-year-old Charles de la Porte de la Meilleraye, to whom the cardinal bequeathed his fortune and his name. Her husband's possessive jealousy, fanatical prudishness, and ruinous obsession with lawsuits caused even-tempered Hortense to seek a legal separation in 1668. When the Parliament refused, she fled, dressed as a man, and sought refuge in Rome with her sister, Marie Mancini*. After a dangerous and peripatetic existence between Rome and Paris in the pursuit of her legal battle, she spent three peaceful years at the court of a former suitor, Charles-Emmanuel II, Duke of Savoie, in Chambéry, where she wrote her memoirs*, perhaps with the aid of Saint-Réal. At the duke's death in 1675, she fled to the court of another admirer, King Charles II of England, who established her at Saint James Palace. For the next quarter century she hosted a brilliant salon* that was the meeting place for the English elite and illustrious French expatriates, such as her friend Saint-Evremond. By publishing her *Mémoires D.M.L.D.M. à M**** at age twenty-nine (in Cologne), Hortense set a precedent in the history of memoir-writing by women. Recent criticism recognizes that, rather than the brazen confessions of an "adventuress," they should be read as the legal deposition of an independent woman who dared to make her marital grievances public.

Gabrielle Verdier

BIBLIOGRAPHY

Primary Text

Mémoires d'Hortense et de Marie Mancini. Ed. Gérard Doscot. Paris: Mercure de France, 1965.

Mancini, Marie (1639–1706?/1715?). Willful, dark-complexioned, cursed by an inauspicious prediction at birth, she was Mazarin's least-favored niece, but by her intelligence and culture she aroused the passion of the young Louis XIV. To ensure the King's marriage to the Spanish Infanta, Mazarin and Anne of Austria squashed the romance by sending away the troublesome Marie to marry a Roman prince, Laurent-Onuphre, Connétable de Colonna, in 1661. Multiple pregnancies, the birth of a third son that almost cost her life, and Colonna's infidelities prompted her to refuse conjugal relations after seven years of marriage. When her husband's tyranny increased, she followed the example of her sister, Hortense Mancini*, and fled Rome in 1672, appealing to Louis XIV for protection. Disappointed by the King's hostility, and deceived by Colonna's agents, she moved from convent* to convent in search of safety and independence, through France, Switzerland, Germany, Flanders, and finally Spain. After the publication of a slanderous apocryphal memoir* of her life (*Mémoires de M.L.P.M.M.*, 1676) that capitalized on the success of Hortense's memoirs, Marie published a refutation, *La Vérité dans son jour ou les véritables mémoires de Marie Mancini, Connétable de Colonne* (1676 or 1677). Addressing her testimony to the public, she sets the record straight with regard to her motives and lifelong struggle for self-affirmation, while acknowledging some mistakes in judgment. The text ends as she awaits the outcome of her appeal to the King of Spain and does not describe subsequent events, twelve more years of greater persecution after she refused to reconcile with her husband and resisted taking religious vows. When Colonna died in 1689, Marie, at fifty, was able to leave Spain, reunite with her children, and live the last part of her life in contentment. Defying feminine decorum and the conventions of the memoir genre, the Mancini sisters were the first to affirm that an account of a private life was as worthy of publication as historical testimony. Because the original Madrid edition of

La Vérité is not available today, modern editions reproduce a revision by the novelist Sébastien Brémond that first appeared in Leyden in 1678.

Gabrielle Verdier

BIBLIOGRAPHY

Primary Text

Mémoires d'Hortense et de Marie Mancini. Ed. Gérard Doscot. Paris: Mercure de France, 1965.

Mansour, Joyce (1928–1986). Born to anglophone parents in England, Joyce Mansour spent her early years in Egypt, where she mingled with both anglophone and francophone communities. In the late 1940s, she moved to Paris, where she began to write poetry* in French. Her first collection of poems, *Cris* (1953), attracted the attention of André Breton because of her fierce, provocative, and sensual images of pleasure mixed with pain in love. Breton welcomed her into the surrealist group. She remained intimately attached to surrealism* and continued to publish both poetry and prose until her death in 1986. She hosted several surrealist events, notably the ceremonial performance-burial of the Marquis de Sade in 1959 (commemorated by Breton in *Le Surréalisme et la peinture* [1965]). Her dark portrayal of love from the point of view of a traditional object of desire within surrealism redefines the image of Woman in surrealism.

Katharine Conley

BIBLIOGRAPHY

Primary Text

Prose & Poésie: Oeuvre Complète. Arles: Actes Sud, 1991.

Secondary Texts

Colvile, Georgiana. "Joyce Mansour et *Les Gisants satisfaits*, trente ans après." In *Femmes Frauen Women.* Ed. Françoise van Rossum-Guyon. Amsterdam: Rodopi, 1990. 107–119.
Conley, Katharine. "Joyce Mansour's Ambivalent Poetic Body." *French Forum* 20, no. 2 (1995): 221–238.
——— (Gingrass). "The Voice in the Bottle: The Love Poetry of Joyce Mansour and Robert Desnos." *Paroles Gelées* 8 (1990): 11–19.
Cottenet-Hage, Madeleine. "The Body Subversive: Corporeal Imagery in Carrington, Prassinos and Mansour." *Dada/Surrealism* 18 (1990): 76–95.
De Julio, Maryann. "Joyce Mansour and Egyptian Mythology." *Dada/Surrealism* 18 (1990): 114–122.
Dumas, Marie-Claire. "*Iles Flottantes*: Où ils et elle parlent. Un récit de Joyce Mansour." *Littérature* 97 (1995): 60–72.
Matthews, J. H. *Joyce Mansour.* Amsterdam: Rodopi, 1985.
Preckshot, Judith. "Identity Crises: Joyce Mansour's Narratives." *Dada/Surrealism* 18 (1990): 96–113.

Maraise, Marie-Catherine-Renée Darcel de (1737–1823). Born in Rouen into a family of merchants, Maraise was well educated and well read, gifted in mathematics, and versed in English; she excelled in accounting, bookkeeping, finance, and management. Her correspondence gives us a glimpse into the lives of the many forgotten women entrepreneurs—often widows—who headed large manufacturing and commercial enterprises and actively contributed to the economic growth of the eighteenth century.

At age thirty, she married Sarrasin de Maraise, business partner of the industrialist Oberkampf, in whose textile factory she was employed as a commercial agent, and with whom she maintained a regular correspondence. In addition to her responsibilities as wife and mother, she assumed full charge of the daily operations at the factory in Jouy-en-Josas from the date of her marriage* until the dissolution of the business partnership with Oberkamp twenty-two years later. Under her masterful leadership, company capital increased more than twentyfold, thus placing her *chef d'oeuvre* second only to the Manufacture royale des glaces de Saint-Gobain among French enterprises.

Although many of the documents pertaining to this remarkable capitalist have been lost, her letters to Oberkampf have been preserved with the industrialist's papers in the Archives Nationales. They offer a fascinating glimpse into the life of this forerunner of the modern businesswoman.

Samia I. Spencer

BIBLIOGRAPHY

Primary Text

Maraise, Madame de. *Une Femme d'affaires au XVIIIe siècle. La correspondance de Madame de Maraise, collaboratrice d'Oberkampf.* Ed. Serge Chassagne. Paris: Privat, 1981.

Secondary Text

Chassagne, Serge. *Oberkampf, un entrepreneur capitaliste au siècle des Lumières.* Paris: Aubier, 1980.

Marguerite d'Angoulême. *See* Navarre, Marguerite de.

Marguerite d'Autriche. *See* Autriche, Marguerite d'.

Marguerite de Valois. *See* Valois, Marguerite de.

Marguerite Durand Library. The first official French library of feminist documentation. Durand*, a feminist journalist, donated her extensive collection to the city of Paris in 1931. The collection now includes over 25,000 books and pamphlets in French and other languages dating from as far back as the seventeenth century; women's journals and feminist periodicals from France and abroad, mainly from 1850 to the present; dossiers on famous women; literary works and memoirs* written by women; theses by and about women; conference proceedings; autographed letters; visual materials such as postcards, photographs, posters, paintings, engravings, and artwork; information on the history of Paris (prisons, convents*, etc.); and reference manuals. The documents cover such issues as women's rights and feminism*, legislation, marriage* and sexuality, philosophy, religion, history, politics, pedagogy*, and social work.

Claire Marrone

BIBLIOGRAPHY

Secondary Text

Didier-Metz, Annie. *La Bibliothèque Marguerite Durand: Histoire d'une femme, mémoire des femmes*. Paris: Agence Culturelle de Paris, 1992.

Marie de France (twelfth century). Marie de France is the name given by the sixteenth-century literary historian Fauchet to the author of the late twelfth-century Anglo-Norman *Fables*, whose epilogue contains the signature "Me numerai pur remembrance: Marie ai nun, si sui de France," suggesting that she was a native of Ile de France transplanted to the English court. Marie is, therefore, the first woman author we know who wrote in French dialect in the Middle Ages. Two other Anglo-Norman texts, also signed by an author named Marie, are commonly attributed to Marie de France: the *Lais* (c. 1170) and *L'Espurgatoire Saint Patrice* (after 1189). It is impossible to know if the same Marie is responsible for all three texts, although the similar authorial stance— that of translator who perpetuates and disseminates texts otherwise inaccessible to her Francophone audience—would tend to support such a hypothesis.

Some scholars have even questioned whether the most widely studied of the three texts, the *Lais*, is the work of a woman author, but the presence of manuscript miniatures depicting a woman writing the *Lais* leads most scholars to feel comfortable in attributing the work to a woman. We know nothing more about Marie (or the Maries) than her name, and identification of her with various historical personnages—for example, Mary, Abbess of Shaftesbury, half-sister of Henry II (who is the presumed dedicatee of the *Lais*), or Mary of Meulan or Beaumont—is no more than speculation. Marie's popularity as the author of the *Lais* is confirmed by a churchman (c. 1170), who, in noting that she is "loved" by both male and female members of the aristocracy, gives evidence that her status as female author does not prevent her from being either known or appreciated.

Lais. In twelfth-century society, which knew only male authors of Latin texts, Marie was at a double disadvantage because she was a woman writing in the vernacular. In her Prologue to the *Lais*, Marie asserts her own authority as a writer by associating herself with a long tradition of learned writers dating back to antiquity, who, as some critics have argued, she believed to have written hermetically so as to engage later writer-commentators and readers in the glossing of their meaning. The substratum on which she intended to work her art constituted a third disadvantage, since it was not Patristic commentary or even

Latin literature, but rather ancient popular Celtic *lais*, whose perpetuation she proposed to assure by translating them into rhymed French texts. Her interest in exposing the origins and the *raison d'être* of this ancient folk art is associated in the Prologue with metaphors of fertility, thus, for some scholars, coupling textuality with female sexuality. This parallel between the production of stories and the generation of progeny (or lack thereof) is made explicit in many of the *lais*, for example, *Fresne, Deus Amanz, Yonec, Laustic, Milun, Chaitivel*, of which the final four follow each other in the Harley Manuscript. And for the other six *lais*, Marie's interest in uncovering the stages by which the narrative was built up usually shows itself in the *lai*'s prologue, which often discusses the etymological origin of its title, and/or in an epilogue treating its development. Many of the *lais* depict, in addition to the birth of a story, the creation of artifacts by female and male creative artists, and thus the individual *lais* represent *mises en abyme* of the textual creation which Marie hides behind the translating role of her authorial persona. Some scholars point to Marie's emphasis on the sharing of creative roles between the sexes (e.g., in *Chevrefeuille, Chaitivel, Laustic, Milun, Fresne*) as indicative of the androgynous persona which she, as a woman author, develops to assure her authority as a writing subject. If love is the unifying theme of the collection, Marie does not espouse ideological positions associated with either Occitan *fin'amors* or, conversely, the Church. Thus, if a woman's adultery* is presented unfavorably in *Equitan* and *Bisclavret*, Marie's "situational ethics" finds it quite acceptable in *Guigemar, Yonec, Milun*, and *Laustic*, where the husbands' failure to love and nurture their wives justifies the latters' entering into an extramarital bond.

Fables. As in the Prologue to the *Lais*, Marie enhances her *auctoritas* (authority) by associating herself with the long classical tradition of fabulists going back through Romulus to Aesop and by emphasizing the moral value of exemplary literature. Her allusions to Aesop and to King Alfred, whom she credits with the English version which she claims to have put into French, also enhance her authority, but scholars are certain that the first 40 of Marie's 103 fables are based on a fourth-century prose collection, the *Romulus Nilantii*. The fact that the 63 remaining fables are not known before Marie's text suggests the possibility that, as in the *Lais*, Marie had undertaken to collect vernacular fables and preserve them from oblivion. Recent revisionist readings of the *Fables* reverse an earlier scholarly trend that deprecated them as mere translations and stress their narrative consistency and effectiveness.

The animals and peasants Marie draws as characters often exemplify the worst in human conduct, allowing her in the concluding moral to criticize abuses of the poor by rich and powerful lords (e.g., "The Wolf and the Crane") and to examine the problems of kingship, whether those of proliferating administrators who may seize the throne ("The Eagle, the Hawk, and the Doves") or those unthinking subjects who do not recognize a good king when they have one ("The Frogs Who Asked for a King"). Several of her non-animal fables concern relationships between peasant husband and wife; unlike the misogynist male authors of the later fabliaux*, she sees one unfaithful wife who tricks her silly husband exemplifying a good sense more useful than riches or kin, although in another fable's moral, men see such a woman's "engin" (cleverness) as devilish. Also interesting are several fables with favorable portraits of female animals giving birth, rearing children, and protecting themselves from rape*.

L'Espurgatoire Saint Patrice. The Prologue, much longer than those of the *Lais* or the *Fables*, resembles them in the acknowledged desire to improve its lay audience morally and in the first-person allusions to the writer's craft. It also particularly resembles the Prologue of the *Fables* in claiming that, were it not for a male patron's insistence, Marie would not have undertaken her task. While earlier scholars considered this text inferior to the other two, recent work has focused on the paradigm of chivalric adventure—here, exclusively male, unlike the *Lais*—which Marie as redactor extracts from the Latin original.

Grace M. Armstrong

BIBLIOGRAPHY

Primary Texts

Ewert, A., and R. C. Johnson, eds. *Marie de France: Fables*. Oxford: Blackwell, 1942.
Jenkins, T. A., ed. *L'Espurgatoire Saint Patrice*. Philadelphia: Press of A. J. Ferris, 1894.
Rychner, J., ed. *Les Lais de Marie de France*. Paris: Champion, CFMA, 1969.

Secondary Texts

Burgess, Glyn. *The Lais of Marie de France: Text and Context*. Athens: University of Georgia Press, 1987.
———. *Marie de France: An Analytical Bibliography*. London: Grant and Cutler, 1977.
Foulet, A., and K. D. Uitti. "The Prologue of the Lais of Marie de France: A Reconsideration." *Romance Philology* 35 (1981–1982): 242–249.
Freeman, Michelle A. "Dual Nature and Subverted Glosses: Marie de France's *Bisclavret*." *Romance Notes* 25 (1985): 288–301.
———. "Marie de France's Poetics of Silence: The Implications of a Feminine 'Translatio.' " *PMLA* 99 (1984): 860–883.
Huchet, J. C. "Nom de femme et écriture féminine au Moyen Age: Les Lais de Marie de France." *Poétique* 12 (1980): 407–430.
Marechal, C., ed. *In Quest of Marie de France, a Twelfth-Century Poet*. Lewiston, NY: Mellen Press, 1992.
Mickel, E. J. *Marie de France*. New York: Twayne, 1974.
Pickens, R. "Marie de France and the Body Poetic." In *Gender and Text in the Later Middle Ages*. Ed. J. Chance. Gainesville: University of Florida Press, 1994.
Sienaert, E. *Les Lais de Marie de France: Du conte merveilleux à la nouvelle psychologique*. Paris: Champion, 1978.
Spitzer, L. "The Prologue to the Lais of Marie de France." *Modern Philology* 41 (1943–1944): 96–102.
Sturges, R. "Texts and Readers in Marie de France's *Lais*." *Romanic Review* 71 (1980): 244–264.
Vitz, E. B. *Medieval Narrative and Modern Narratology: Subjects and Objects of Desire*. New York: New York University Press, 1989.

Marie de l'Incarnation (née Marie Guyard) (1599–1672). Although she claimed aristocratic connections, Marie Guyard was born to a merchant family of Tours in 1599. At seventeen she married a master silk worker, Claude-Joseph Martin, who died two years later, leaving her with a bankrupt business and an infant son, her future editor, the Benedictine Claude Martin. The young widow immediately experienced divine visitations which she depicted in her *Relation* (1654); seeing herself immersed in blood, she was convinced that it was the blood of the son of God. Her spiritual life flourished despite her hard work as manager of her brother-in-law's haulage business on the Loire. Then suddenly, on January 25, 1631, the feast of the conversion of St. Paul, she quit work and family to enter the Ursuline convent* where she professed her vows two years later.

A dream vision of snowy Canada convinced her that God was calling her to join the mission to New France, and her letters to the ecclesiastical authorities, including the Jesuit Paul Le Jeune, finally prevailed. Her letters also persuaded a wealthy widow of Alençon, Madeleine de La Peltrie, to endow the Quebec convent and to go there as its foundress and benefactress. Queen Anne of Austria interviewed the two women before they embarked from Dieppe with four other nuns and their companions; they would anchor in the St. Lawrence at Tadoussac in August 1639. The Ursulines planned to instruct and convert the Amerindian women of Quebec, where their convent, the first school for girls in Canada, still thrives.

During the next thirty-two years, Marie bloomed as a writer who sent over 8,000 letters back to France to proclaim her progress and solicit support for the convent's work. In Quebec she rewrote her original *Relation* and created numerous other texts now lost, including dictionaries and grammars of the native languages. The ensemble of the letters recounts the triumphs and tribulations of the Ursulines and of the whole colony. Marie's self-reflexive and assured voice controls the plot, where she functions as both narrator and heroine.

On the night of December 30, 1650, a bakery fire burned the convent to the ground, devouring her *Relation* of 1633 as well as other documents. Undefeated by the destruction of her life's work, Marie rebuilt and enlarged her convent. She wrote a biography of her companion, Mother Joseph, who died in 1652, and recreated her own spiritual autobiography* in 1654. The letters to France soon resumed, and she composed a journal of her daily rounds among the Amerindians and French immigrants and her gradual assumption of power as spokesperson for the women of Quebec and, as Bossuet would say, the "Saint Theresa of our day and of the New World."

Mary Rowan

BIBLIOGRAPHY

Primary Texts

Marie de L'Incarnation, Ursuline de Tours, fondatrice des Ursulines de la Nouvelle-France. Ed. Albert Jamet. Paris-Quebec, 1935–1939.

La Correspondance. Ed. Guy-Marie Oury. Solesmes: Abbaye Saint-Pierre de Solesmes, 1971.

Marie-Antoinette (1755–1793). Daughter of Empress Maria-Theresa of Austria, Marie-Antoinette was married to the dauphin of France in 1770 and became queen upon his accession to the throne in 1774. She reigned with Louis XVI until the fall of the French monarchy in August 1792 and was executed on October 16, 1793. Although early in her reign the queen was admired for her beauty and regal bearing, her reputation suffered before the Revolution* from her active participation in court politics and the expensive and exclusive pastimes in which she indulged with close friends. After 1789 her image worsened as she threw in her lot with the staunchest opponents of the Revolution at court, and she was frequently represented as a harpy or a pig in popular engravings. In the course of her trial before the Revolutionary Criminal Tribunal in 1793, the accusations levied at her, such as the charge that she had sexually molested her young son, were exceptionally vicious, even by the standards of the time and place. Recent feminist scholarship has been less interested in the real woman Marie-Antoinette than in the meaning of the hostility directed at her both before and during the Revolution. Scurrilous pamphlet literature attacking the queen appeared as early as the late 1770s, some of it originating from the court itself. Both prerevolutionary underground pamphlets such as *Les Amours de Charlot et de Toinette* (1779) and revolutionary best-sellers like the *Essais historiques sur la vie de Marie-Antoinette* (1789; many reprints) claimed to reveal, with the help of graphic illustrations, the "French Messalina's" insatiable cravings for sex and power. Current scholarship sees this hostility as symptomatic of a widespread condemnation, most cogently articulated by Jean-Jacques Rousseau, of the Old Regime public culture in which prominent women such as salon* hostesses, royal mistresses, and female libertines played a conspicuous role. The increasing tension of the early revolutionary years intensified this trend and may have added a psychosexual dimension to it, casting Marie-Antoinette as the "bad mother" who had to be disposed of in order for revolutionary fraternity to flourish.

Sarah Maza

BIBLIOGRAPHY

Secondary Texts

Gutwirth, Madelyn. *The Twilight of the Goddesses: Women and Representation in the French Revolutionary Era.* New Brunswick, NJ: Rutgers University Press, 1992.

Hunt, Lynn. *The Family Romance of the French Revolution.* Berkeley: University of California Press, 1992.

Maza, Sarah. "The Diamond Necklace Affair Revisited (1785–1786): The Case of the Missing Queen." In *Eroticism and the Body Politic.* Ed. Lynn Hunt. Baltimore: Johns Hopkins University Press, 1991. 63–89.

Revel, Jacques. "Marie-Antoinette in Her Fictions: The Staging of Hatred." In *Fictions of the French Revolution.* Ed. Bernadette Fort. Evanston, IL: Northwestern University Press, 1991. 111–130.

Thomas, Chantal. *La Reine scélérate: Marie-Antoinette dans les pamphlets.* Paris: Le Seuil, 1989.

Marni, Jeanne (1854–1910). Pseudonym of Jeanne Marnière. She started her career as a theater* actress. After her husband's untimely death, she turned to her true vocation: writing. She published her first novel*, *La Femme de Silva*, in 1887. There followed a series of well-received novels, famous for their witty dialogue and realistic descriptions of women's lives: *Comment elles se donnent* (1895), *Comment elles nous lâchent* (1896), *Les Enfants qu'elles ont* (1897), *Celles qu'on ignore* (1899). Overall, she wrote fifteen novels and several plays, which brought her enduring success and literary fame.

Juliette Parnell-Smith

BIBLIOGRAPHY

Primary Texts

La Femme de Silva. Paris: Ollendorf, 1887.
Comment elles se donnent. Paris: Ollendorf, 1895.
Comment elles nous lâchent. Paris: Ollendorf, 1896.
Les Enfants qu'elles ont. Paris: Ollendorf, 1897.
Fiacres. Paris: Ollendorf, 1898.
Celles qu'on ignore. Paris: Ollendorf, 1899.
Pierre Tisserand. Paris: Ollendorf, 1907.
L'Une et l'autre. Paris: Pierre Laffite, 1908.
Souffrir. Paris: F. Juven, 1909.

Marquets, Anne de (c. 1533–1588). Poet. Richly endowed with privileges and revenues, possessing a magnificent library, and admitting primarily noble women, the Dominican Priory of Saint Louis at Poissy was founded in 1304 by Philippe IV le Bel. Anne de Marquets was sent to the priory, in all likelihood, as a young girl of nine or ten; she subsequently made her religious profession and remained there for the rest of her life. Exercising a large degree of self-government, the community also maintained close links with the court and an involvement in contemporary political and intellectual life. In her *Dit de Poissy* (c. 1400), Christine de Pizan* describes a visit she made to her daughter, a nun at Saint Louis. Christine, who herself probably retired to Poissy in her later years, celebrates the beauty of the conventual buildings and gardens, the material well-being of the sisters, the refinement of their life, and above all the independence of this exclusively female community. The profile of Poissy has also been discerned behind Christine's utopian *Cité des Dames* (1404–1405). If the observance of the monastic rule at times became quite relaxed (the order imposed extensive reforms in the first decade of the sixteenth century), the practice of letters flourished in the priory's cultured and learned environment. The religious life imposes its own particular constraints; nevertheless, given the severe controls to which lay women's lives were also subject at this time, it is clear that a community like Saint Louis could offer distinct social advantages.

Educated in the priory school where she herself would later teach, Marquets learned Latin and probably some Greek. She wrote her first collection of poetry*, *Sonets, prières et devises en forme de pasquins* (1562), published with liminary verse in her honor by Dorat and Ronsard, in response to the recent Colloquy of Poissy. Among the distinguished company that this ill-fated attempt to reconcile Protestants and Catholics brought to the priory were Marguerite de Valois*, the king's sister, and the noted theologian Claude d'Espence. Marquets always professed an extreme reluctance to appear in print, and the encouragement of d'Espence and Marguerite was instrumental in both the writing and the publication of her next works, the principal of which, *Les Divines Poesies de Marc Antoine Flaminius* (1568), is a translation of Flaminio's *De rebus divinis carmina*.

Marquets's most important and original collection of verse is her last, *Sonets spirituels* (1605), published posthumously by Marie de Fortia, a fellow religious and former pupil of the poet. The 480 sonnets guide the reader through the liturgical year; at once devotional and didactic, they reveal most clearly the influence of the texts of the divine office and the Mass, the Bible*, and the *Golden Legend*. Conservative in inspiration, the poems nevertheless engage with many issues of the day, including the ongoing *Querelle des femmes*. While on occasion Marquets's sonnets deliver a spirited attack on men's calumny of women, more frequently they celebrate sacred history's female exemplars. An emphasis on the notion of female community results in the evocation of a large sisterhood, embracing all the holy women who have served God throughout the ages. The *Sonets spirituels* also draws on and valorizes feminine experiences, such as childbirth and the nursing and care of infants. Elements of the nascent style of devotional sweetness are equally discernible: the human qualities of Christ are stressed, particularly those of humility, patience, and obedience, traditionally gendered as feminine; likewise, God appears as merciful, tender, and compassionate.

A comparison between Marquets and her contemporary Gabrielle de Coignard* reveals differences in both the material circumstances of their lives and the inflections of their poetic voices. Nevertheless, reflecting a particular feminine experience and forging a more feminine devotional discourse, the work of both poets heralds future developments. When the *Sonets spirituels* was published in the early years of the seventeenth century, devotional writing was evolving in response to the unprecedented degree of women's involvement in the Church's spiritual life during the post-Tridentine revival, and increasingly the readership for works of devotion was female.

Gary Ferguson

BIBLIOGRAPHY

Primary Texts

Les Divines Poésies de Marc Antoine Flaminius. Paris: Nicolas Chesneau, 1568.

Sonets, prières et devises en forme de pasquins, pour l'assemblée de Messieurs les Prélats et Docteurs, tenue à Poissy, M.D.LXI. Paris: Guillaume Morel, 1562.

Sonets spirituels . . . sur les dimanches et principales solennitez de l'année. Paris: Claude Morel, 1605. Ed. Gary Ferguson. Geneva: Droz, 1997.

Secondary Texts

Ferguson, Gary. "Biblical Exegesis and Social and Theological Commentary in the *Sonets spirituels* of Anne de Marquets." In *L'Exégèse biblique au XVIe siècle*. Ed. Colette H. Winn. *Oeuvres et Critiques* 20, no. 2 (1995): 111–121.

Fournier, Hannah S. "La Voix textuelle des *Sonets spirituels* d'Anne de Marquets." *Etudes littéraires* 20 (1987): 77–92.

Read, Kirk D. "French Renaissance Women Writers in Search of Community: Literary Constructions of Female Companionship in City, Family and Convent." Dissertation, Princeton University, 1991.

————. "Women of the French Renaissance in Search of Literary Community: A Prolegomenon to Early Modern Women's Participation in Letters." *Romance Languages Annual* (1993): 95–102.

Seiler, Mary Hilarine. *Anne de Marquets, poétesse religieuse du XVIe siècle*. Washington, DC: Catholic University Press of America, 1931. New York: AMS Press, 1969.

Marriage. Traditionally, marriage was an institution controlled almost exclusively by the Catholic Church and, thus, prohibited during periods of penance. As an indissoluble sacrament, it could not be broken, only annulled after long and costly trials in ecclesiastic courts. For both partners, the moral and economic benefits of marriage were considerable; however, the responsibilities it placed on women were taxing. Celibacy was rare: only 5 percent in rural areas, nearly double in cities. Widowers were numerous, due to the high rate of childbirth mortality, but they wasted no time before remarrying. Traditions prescribed parity of age, class, and social background between spouses; fiancés rarely lived more than five miles apart.

By the end of the Ancien Régime, the institution of matrimony was in a crisis, generally attributable to the aristocracy, for whom marriages of convenience were the rule. These concluded alliances between families and fortunes, without consideration for personal inclination. Spouses married early and felt uncommitted to their moral obligations to each other, and infidelity became widespread and largely accepted, even among broad segments of the urban bourgeoisie.

In matters of private life, bourgeois leaders of the Revolution* wanted to end the depravity of the previous era. The unmarried—female and male, laymen and clerics—were vigorously pursued as a threat to public morality. The campaign against celibacy was paralleled by an increased rate of marriage and a rising demand for divorce*. Henceforth, it was deemed that couples should be bonded by affection—the marital equivalent of fraternity—rather than by mercantile and indissoluble links. The fall of Robespierre triggered a reaction against the liberal trend, which escalated during the Directoire and culminated, legally, with the adoption of the Civil Code in 1804. That document greatly restricted divorce, and imparted to husbands unprecedented power and authority. During the Restoration, divorce was prohibited and the Napoleonic Code* remained almost intact. For a very long time, marriage was thus founded on a few simple rules, which were more or less rigorously followed.

Generally, parents were responsible for selecting their children's mates. Love was not a factor in these decisions; on the contrary, it was considered a cause of turmoil, leading inevitably to disaster. For members of the nobility, date of title was crucial; however, great wealth could, exceptionally, compensate for less glorious ancestry. Likewise, the bourgeois feared misalliances. If they could not aspire to marry into the nobility, they sought advancement within their own class. Among merchants of the petty bourgeoisie, an alliance between two fortunes could result in the establishment of a new business or the expansion of an existing one. Peasants had similar aspirations, appraising both the qualities of a neighbor's daughter and the worth of her land.

The only exception to this rule was among the new urban "slaves"—unskilled factory workers. Exiled in cities, far from parental guidance, they could not lay claim to even the smallest dowry, but only hope for a modest trousseau. Unable to afford the cost of a legal procedure and a wedding ceremony, they often neglected to legitimize their unions. However, if they ascended to the status of artisan or inherited a meager fortune, they aspired to the customs of the petty bourgeoisie.

The economic and social significance of marriage was displayed everywhere: in wedding announcements to relatives stating the amount of dowry; in etiquette books; and on the stage, in play after play. Exceptionally, personal qualities or education* could be taken into consideration. In all cases, however, great gaps between spouses were discouraged. For example, a very wealthy wife could be arrogant or contemptuous of a much less fortunate husband. Wisdom dictated that social advancement be achieved gradually, generation after generation.

Behind its strict moral and legal traditions, the nineteenth century witnessed a few signs of change. Ideologically, a few groups attempted to challenge existing family* structure. Their arguments focused on the efforts of feminists who sought to improve the status of women, on the romantic notion of upholding passionate love over social conventions, and on the vision of future harmony promoted by utopian socialists. Sociologically, the most significant shifts resulted from the spectacular growth of the bourgeoisie and the working class.

The dreadfully codified and restrictive lifestyle imposed upon bourgeoises afforded them, however, small windows of opportunity, with undeniable consequences. Although carefully circumscribed by social conventions, culture became more accessible to females, so that wives could become pleasant interlocutors for their husbands and their associates. Furthermore, the moral role of a wife extended beyond the household proper. Resting upon her were the education of children, especially daughters, and the imparting of values ensuring bourgeois dominance. Exemplary women were expected to care for the needy and devote ample time to charitable organizations. Thus, bourgeoises fulfilled a social and quasi-political role much greater than that of lower-class women. These responsibilities were probably a main reason for the involvement of some upper-class women in the struggle for freedom.

Resources of the working class were meager, but their use was much less motivated by selfish considerations. Generally, male workers kept a small amount of their pay for pocket money and gave the rest to their wives, who managed the budget. Since age difference between spouses were insignificant, relationships appear to have been amiable and friendly; authority emanated from external sources, employer, landlord, and so forth. The modern notion of the loving couple seems to have originated among the nineteenth-century working class.

The reestablishment of divorce in 1884 was an early sign of the renewed interest in marital harmony, and the increasing influence of the feminist movement was another cause for change. Legal progress, however, was slow, as an all-male body of judges and legislators continued to resist limitation of the husband's authority, which they considered fundamental for family cohesiveness. Gainfully employed wives struggled for seventeen years (1890–1907) before obtaining the right to control their own salaries. During World War I*, women assumed crucial responsibilities and, shortly thereafter, following the financial crisis, bourgeoises had to seek employment outside the home; yet, these women remained legal minors, submitted to the authority of their husbands.

In 1925 a parliamentary commission was appointed to remedy the situation; its recommendations were not enacted until 1938, when women reached legal adulthood and obedience to husbands was struck from the Civil Code. However, husbands continued to possess the right to prevent their wives from working and were solely responsible for selecting the family residence. In 1965 a new law abolished the system of dowry and focused on assets acquired during the marriage. Two years later, the Neuwirth Law legalized contraception,* and in 1970 parental authority became a shared responsibility. In 1975, at the height of the feminist movement, several laws were passed: the choice of family residence also became a shared responsibility; divorce by mutual consent was reestablished; and abortion* was legalized. With considerable delay, the legal system had finally caught up with social practice, and the Napoleonic Code was invalidated. A new concept of ''couple,'' defined as the free association of two equal individuals, replaced the traditional notion of ''nuclear family'' made up of master and subordinates. At about the same time a new phenomenon occurred: youthful cohabitation. Not only does this trend negate marriage, it may very well be the simplest and most basic concept of ''couple.''

Francis Ronsin and Samia I. Spencer

BIBLIOGRAPHY

Secondary Texts

Aimer en France. Actes du colloque international de Clermont-Ferrand. Clermond-Ferrand: Faculté des Lettres et Sciences humaines, 1980.

Duby, Georges, and Michelle Perrot, eds. *Histoire de la vie privée.* Paris: Editions du Seuil, 1987.

Dupâquier, Jacques, ed. *Histoire de la population française.* Paris: Presses Universitaires de France, 1988.

Flandrin, Jean-Louis. *Les Amours paysannes: Amour et sexualité dans les campagnes de l'ancienne France (XVIe–XIXe siècles)*. Paris: Gallimard-Julliard, 1975.

———. *Familles. Parenté, maison, sexualité dans l'ancienne société*. Paris: Hachette, 1976.

Fuchs, Rachel G. *Poor and Pregnant in Paris*. New Brunswick, NJ: Rutgers University Press, 1992.

Segalen, Martine. *Mari et femme dans la société paysanne*. Paris: Flammarion, 1980.

Shorter, Edward. *The Making of the Modern Family*. New York: Basic Books, 1975.

Zeldin, Theodore. *History of French Passions, 1848–1945*. Oxford: Clarendon Press, 1993.

Marron, Marie Anne Carrelet de (1725–1778). Marron was a gifted painter and sculptor whose *Conception* was hung in the cathedral of her hometown, Dijon. She did not begin her writing career until age forty-two, and within ten years she wrote nine *tragédies de société* and one *comédie*. Her early ''corrected versions'' of well-known classical works later gave way to plays firmly rooted in the emerging dramatic tradition of pathetic moralism. *La Comtesse de Fayel*, her only published play, is a typical but unusually forceful eighteenth-century plea for the rights of sons and daughters to determine their own destinies against the tyranny of fathers. Marron's startling portrait of an arranged marriage* and the fate of a woman at the hands of a violently jealous husband—the play concludes with the heroine's death on stage after her husband has tricked her into eating the heart of his rival—challenged prevailing notions of theatrical decorum. Voltaire wrote in 1775 that he had never seen a more extraordinary woman, and Lalande composed an elegy about her, published two years after her death in Bourg-en-Bresse.

Cecilia Beach and Charlotte Daniels

BIBLIOGRAPHY

Primary Text

La Comtesse de Fayel. Tragédie de société. Lyons: Les Frères Périsse, 1770.

Secondary Texts

Beach, Cecilia. *French Women Playwrights before the Twentieth Century: A Checklist*. Westport, CT: Greenwood Press, 1994.

Briquet, Marguerite-Ursule-Fortunée, Dame. *Dictionnaire historique, littéraire et bibliographique des Françaises et des étrangères naturalisées en France, connues par leurs écrits*. Paris: Gillé, 1804.

''La Comtesse de Fayel.'' *Journal des Savants* (February 1771): 100.

Depéry, Jean-Irénée. *Biographie des hommes célèbres du département de l'Ain, qui se sont distingués par leurs sciences, leurs talents ou leurs vices*. Geneva: Slatkine Reprints, 1971.

Hoefer, Dr., ed. *Nouvelle Biographie générale*. Paris: Firmin-Didot, 1968.

Lalande, Jérôme de. ''Eloge de Madame Marron.'' In *Nécrologe des hommes célèbres de France par une société de gens de lettres*. Paris: Moreau, 1780–1781. 15: 85–97.

Michaud, L. G., ed. *Biographie universelle*. Paris: Desplaces, 1834–1857.

Prudhomme, Louis Marie. *Biographie universelle et historique des femmes célèbres, mortes ou vivantes*. Paris: Lebigre, 1830. 40–41.

Marxist literary theory. While developing dialectical and historical material-ism* as a science to study economic and political change, Marxists have not ignored the dynamics of cultural production. Marx identified the aesthetic as one of the forms of consciousness through which we interpret the world; Lenin valued sensuous images as a means of concretely refuting abstract ruling-class ideologies; and Gramsci described the development of working-class intellec-tuals in the course of struggle against capitalist institutions. Marxist literary theory rests on the key concepts of reflection (all ideas arise from and depict material reality), alienation (workers are denied the fruits of their labor), and praxis (art is not an autonomous moment but is rooted in a community's social existence). Marxists bring historical context and class consciousness to literary studies. Marxist feminists have shown how sexual oppression intersects with racism and class exploitation, and they contribute to materialist feminist theory by critiquing the dichotomies of public/private, production/reproduction, crea-tion/procreation. Postcolonial critics such as Gayatri Spivak use Marxist analyses of imperialism and political economy to critique Western ideologies and prac-tices, while Trinh T. Minh-ha writes of the triple bind experienced by Third World women writers. Emergent literatures compel readers to reference the his-tory of colonial exploitation and indigenous resistance.

April A. Knutson

BIBLIOGRAPHY

Secondary Texts

Aguilar, Delia D. "The Limits of Postmodern Feminism." *Nature, Society, and Thought* 8, no. 3 (1995): 255–274.

Eagleton, Terry. *Criticism and Ideology: A Study in Marxist Theory*. London: Verso, 1978.

Gramsci, Antonio. *The Modern Prince and Other Writings*. London: Lawrence and Wis-hart, 1957.

Jameson, Frederic. "Criticism in History." In *Weapons of Criticism*. Ed. Norman Rudich. Palo Alto: Ramparts Press, 1976.

Le Sueur, Meridel. *Worker Writers*. Minneapolis: West End Press, 1982.

Lenin, V. I. *Materialism and Empirico-Criticism*. Moscow: Progress, 1970.

Lionnet, Françoise. " 'Logiques métisses': Cultural Appropriation and Postcolonial Rep-resentations." In *Postcolonial Subjects: Francophone Women Writers*. Ed. Mary Jean Green et al. Minneapolis: University of Minnesota Press, 1996.

Marx, Karl. "A Contribution to a Critique of Political Economy." In *Collected Works of Marx and Engels*. Vol. 16. New York: International Publishers, 1980.

Minh-ha, Trinh T. *Woman, Native, Other: Writing Postcoloniality and Feminism*. Bloom-ington: Indiana University Press, 1989.

San Juan, E. *From the Masses to the Masses: Third World Literature and Revolution*. Minneapolis: MEP Publications, 1994.

Spivak, Gayatri Chakravorty. *The Post-Colonial Critic.* New York: Routledge, 1990.
Williams, Raymond. *Marxism and Literature.* New York: Oxford University Press, 1977.

Materialism. The term denotes theories positing the primacy of matter as an explanatory category. In classical philosophy, materialism and natural law were opposed to idealism and metaphysics. In Marxist thought, materialism refutes essentialist notions of human nature by recognizing a relationship of causality between the material conditions of human life (economic organization) and human psychology, belief systems, and social institutions. Marxist feminists have provided valuable critiques of the universalizing tendencies in feminism* caused by ignoring the material condition of women's lives in their historical and cultural specificity or by treating gender in isolation from other categories. Recently, a new materialist feminism which combines Marxist, poststructuralist, and psychoanalytic notions of the materiality of language and subjectivity has posited subjectivity as a material effect of discourse. Conceiving of subjectivity as a discursive construction allows for the possibility of personal and social transformation through changes in systems of representation.

Katherine Stephenson

BIBLIOGRAPHY

Secondary Texts

Barrett, Michèle. *Women's Oppression Today: The Marxist Feminist Encounter.* London: Verso, 1988.
Butler, Judith. *Bodies that Matter: On the Discursive Limits of "Sex."* New York: Routledge, 1993.
Coward, Rosalind, and John Ellis. *Language and Materialism: Developments in Semiology and the Theory of the Subject.* London: Routledge, 1977.
Diprose, Rosalyn. *The Bodies of Women: Ethics, Embodiment and Sexual Difference.* London: Routledge, 1994.
Gatens, Moira. *Imaginary Bodies: Ethics, Power and Corporeality.* New York: Routledge, 1996.
Grosz, Elizabeth. *Volatile Bodies: Toward a Corporeal Feminism.* Bloomington: Indiana University Press, 1994.
Hamilton, Roberta, and Michèle Barrett, eds. *The Politics of Diversity: Feminism, Marxism and Nationalism.* London: Verso, 1986.
Hartmann, Heidi. "The Unhappy Marriage of Marxism and Feminism: Towards a More Progressive Union." In *Women and Revolution: A Discussion of the Unhappy Marriage of Marxism and Feminism.* Ed. Lydia Sargent. Boston: South End Press, 1981. 1–41.
Hennessy, Rosemary. *Materialist Feminism and the Politics of Discourse.* New York: Routledge, 1993.
Hypatia: A Journal of Feminist Philosophy 6, no. 3 (Fall 1991). "Feminism and the Body." Ed. Elizabeth Grosz.
Kuhn, Annette, and Ann-Marie Wolpe, eds. *Feminism and Materialism: Women and Modes of Production.* London: Routledge, 1971.

Landry, Donna, and Gerald MacLean. *Materialist Feminisms*. Cambridge, MA: Black-
     well, 1993.

Maternity. The mother in French literature has evolved over the centuries from
a mere accessory to the creation of the hero to a vital motivating force in the
hero or heroine's life and, finally, to a heroine in her own right. The image of
the mother in French fiction has reflected the many changes, and the few enduring values, in Western society and culture, from the dominance of Christianity* to the birth of psychoanalysis and beyond. Her triumph, the discovery of
her own voice, and the writing of her own experience represent the latest stage
in a long evolutionary process that begins with Rabelais.

   In the sixteenth century, the mother was a relatively marginal figure in French
literature. In accordance with the conception of childhood as an insignificant
stage during which the child is seen as a miniature adult, motherhood was just
one of women's many social functions, important but essentially uninteresting.
However, Rabelais presents readers with a disturbing account of childbirth in
Gargantua (1652). During Gargamelle's graphically described, if physiologi-
cally skewed, labor, she expresses a wish for her husband's castration to save
herself the pain of future childbirth. Her momentary renunciation of sexuality,
particularly of its pleasurable aspect, conforms to cultural expectations of maternal asexuality, illustrated in the Christian tradition by the dichotomy between
the maternal purity of the Virgin Mary and the overt sexuality of Mary Magdalene. Gargamelle then produces a large turd, while Pantagruel escapes through
her ear. This biological alteration of the birth process both denies and degrades
the maternal function, equating it with intestinal evacuation while emptying it
of its essential femaleness. Gargamelle, having fulfilled her function as accessory
to the hero, then conveniently disappears, both from the life of Gargantua and
from the text.

   In the seventeenth century, Madame de Chartres in *La Princesse de Clèves*
(1678) stands out as a fictional maternal figure whose motherhood is essential
to the story. Widowed and chaste, Madame de Chartres dedicates her life to the
education* of her only daughter. Mother and daughter coexist, far from the
outside world, in an imitation of the symbiotic unity of early infanthood. Mme
de Chartres derives her power from her maternity; sacrificing her chance for
selfhood, she attempts to appropriate her daughter's experiences. In her pursuit
of vicarious pleasures, she echoes the sentiments of a close friend of the author,
the Marquise de Sévigné*, whose passionate missives to her daughter have become a major landmark in the sociological and psychological evolution of maternity in France. By the act of writing letters, Mme de Sévigné constantly asks
for her daughter's approval, thereby risking a rejection that plunges her back
into the agonies of mother-daughter separation. Her intense maternal passion for
her daughter illustrates the fragile borderline between the maternal and the erotic
which will become a preoccupation of Romanticism*.

   With the family values of Jean-Jacques Rousseau in the eighteenth century comes a major shift in society's perceptions of the maternal role. Although he was not the first to glorify motherhood, Rousseau's emphasis on the emotional bonds between mother and child found an echo in the hearts of many female readers, including Germaine de Staël*. Traumatized by the death of his own mother, Rousseau imposes on his readers his own idealized image of a mother he never knew with his creation of Julie in *La Nouvelle Héloïse* (1761). After her return to reason and her entry into a loveless marriage, a young and passionate Julie is transformed into the model maternal figure whose influence can still be felt today. Rousseau reasons that, since women give birth, they should be solely responsible for childcare and domestic life, leaving the public sphere to men, who cannot produce children. His ideal mother, as represented by Julie, ceases to be a woman in the sensual sense; her sons, born not of love but of a sense of filial and conjugal duty, become the center of her universe, the focus of all her energies and ambitions. In giving her life to save that of her son, Julie reinforces Rousseau's ideal of maternal altruism, which continues to play an important role in maternal mythology more than two hundred years later.

Julie's ultimate sacrifice led to the creation in the nineteenth century of maternal figures who play the roles of both mother and mistress, devoted to the support of a succession of young heroes. While some of these women are allowed to be both sexual and maternal, nurturing their young lovers and initiating them in the ways of the world, most continue to follow the Christian tradition of alternating between the two roles. In Constant's *Adolphe* (1816), Ellénore, the hero's nurturer and companion, shows her devotion to her lover by abandoning her own children and is subsequently censored by society as "an unnatural mother." Balzac's *Le Lys dans la vallée* (1845) tells a tale of unconsummated passion between the young Félix and the virtuous Mme de Mortsauf, whose maternal obligations prevent her from acting on her desire. Stendhal creates a more ambiguous picture in *Le Rouge et le noir* (1830): Mme de Rênal both nurtures and actively desires Julien, the young peasant whose social and sexual education begins in her bedroom. In this coexistence of the maternal and the sexual lies a breakthrough for maternal autonomy that will be explored by women writers a century later.

Twentieth-century French literature opens the door to women who write, first of their ambiguous relationships with their own mothers, and finally of their own experiences of mothering. Colette*, Simone de Beauvoir*, and Violette Leduc* all created written accounts of their own mothers' lives, analyzed by loving but resentful daughters in the light of postmodern thought that includes psychoanalysis, existentialism*, and the dawning of a new feminist consciousness. In Beauvoir's works, an insightful analysis of the process of mothering coexists with a refusal of maternity, seen as a traditional excuse for the subjugation of women by a patriarchal society. Marguerite Duras's* writings also resound with the presence of the mother, her passions, her injustices, and her children's efforts to understand her. Not until the latter part of the century, however, have women dared to write *as* mothers, speaking not as accessories to the process of procreation but rather as human beings who have experienced the quickening of life within themselves and have nevertheless retained a sense of their own identities and desires. With such declarations of maternal independence as Hélène Cixous's *La Venue à l'écriture* (1977), women began to realize their own potential as women-who-mother and to create new literary maternal voices representing not the perceptions of the son or daughter but the inner workings of the maternal self. Chantal Chawaf*, in *Maternité* (1979) and other works, affirms the significance of the physical and emotional experience of motherhood as the authentic source of feminine literary creation. Her emphasis on the centrality of the mother and on the importance of finding a maternal voice marks the latest and perhaps most liberating development in the evolution of maternity in French literature.

Lisa G. Algazi

BIBLIOGRAPHY

Secondary Texts

Badinter, Elizabeth. *Mother Love: Myth and Reality. Motherhood in Modern History*. New York: Macmillan, 1980.
Beauvoir, Simone de. *Une Mort très douce*. Paris: Gallimard, 1964.
Chawaf, Chantal. *Maternité*. Paris: Stock, 1979.
Cixous, Hélène (in collaboration with Annie Leclerc and Madeleine Gagnon). *La Venue à l'écriture*. Paris: Union Générale d'Editions, 1977.
Garner, Shirley Nelson, et al. *The (M)other Tongue: Essays in Feminist Psychoanalytic Interpretation*. Ithaca: Cornell University Press, 1985.
Hirsch, Marianne. *The Mother/Daughter Plot: Narrative, Psychoanalysis, Feminism*. Bloomington: Indiana University Press, 1989.
Kristeva, Julia. *La Révolution du langage poétique: L'Avant-garde à la fin du XIXe siècle*. Paris: Seuil, 1974.
Lukacher, Maryline. *Maternal Fictions: Stendhal, Sand, Rachilde and Bataille*. Durham: Duke University Press, 1994.
Mann, Maria A. *La Mère dans la littérature française: 1678–1831*. New York: Peter Lang, 1989.
Rousseau, Jean-Jacques. *Julie, ou la Nouvelle Héloïse*. Paris: Flammarion, 1967.
Sévigné, Marie de Rabutin-Chantal, Marquise de. *Lettres*. Ed. and intro. by Emile Gérard-Gailly. Paris: Bibliothèque de la Pléiade, 1953–1957.
Stendhal. *Romans*. Paris: Seuil, 1969.

Maurel, Micheline (?–). Arrested as a political prisoner in Nazi-occupied France, Maurel became number 22,410 on the August 1943 convoy bound for Ravensbrück, and was later sent to the neighboring concentration camp of Neubrandeburg. Her texts describe in a matter-of-fact way the daily physical and emotional abuse suffered by the women of the camp—hunger, cold, illness, and beatings. *Un Camp très ordinaire*, for example, recounts the two years Maurel spent in Neubrandeburg and focuses in particular on the women prisoners' struggle to retain their dignity when faced with brutal conditions and violent female prison guards. Through the narratives and poems Maurel wrote on behalf of the incarcerated community, she gives voice to the seemingly unspeakable suffering of women.

Frédérique Chevillot

BIBLIOGRAPHY

Primary Texts

Un Camp très ordinaire. Paris: Minuit, 1957.
Him-Li-Co. Paris: Hatier, 1958.
La Vie normale. Paris: Minuit, 1958.
La Passion selon Ravensbrück. Paris: Minuit, 1965.
Contes d'agate. Paris: Hatier, 1961.
Dix-neuf Poèmes de déportées. Choisy-le-Roy: Amicale de Ravensbrück, Association des déportées et internées de la Résistance, 1971.

Medici, Catherine de (1519–1589). Queen, regent, poet, patron. Married to Henri II in 1533, Catherine de Médici remained a moving force in French politics through much of the sixteenth century. She acted as regent on several occasions: while Henri II campaigned abroad, while Charles IX was in his minority, and while Henri III traveled from Poland to France. She wrote some poetry* in Italian, but influenced the art and literature of the court through her patronage, particularly of the Pléiade poets. Most of her writing exists in the form of letters both personal and diplomatic. She spent a good portion of her energy writing a letter campaign and traveling through France in order to calm religious tensions. It was the marriage* of her daughter, Marguerite de Valois*, to Henri de Navarre that sparked the St. Bartholomew's Day Massacre in 1572. While many historians have linked her to both the assassination attempt on the Protestant leader, Gaspard de Coligny, and to the order to execute all of the Huguenot leaders in Paris, much of the villainy assigned to her stems from the biases of contemporary historiographers. Pierre de Ronsard saw her as the one person who was capable of preserving national unity, praising her in his *Discours des misères de ce temps.* Close examination of the evidence reveals that she relaxed Protestant repression with the Edict of January of 1562, which formally confirmed Protestantism as a legitimate and independent church, and the Peace of Saint-Germain in 1570.

Velvet Pearson

BIBLIOGRAPHY

Primary Text

Lettres de Catherine de Médicis. 10 vols. Ed. Hector de la Ferrière and Gustave Baguenault de Puchesse. Paris: Imprimerie nationale, 1880–1909.

Secondary Texts

Cloulas, Ivan. *Catherine de Médicis.* Paris: Fayard, 1981.
Folliott, Sheila. "Catherine de' Medici as Artemisia: Figuring the Powerful Widow." In

Rewriting the Renaissance: The Discourse of Sexual Difference in Early Modern Europe. Ed. Margaret W. Ferguson, Maureen Quilligan, and Nancy J. Vickers. Chicago: University of Chicago Press, 1986. 227–241.
Williamson, Hugh R. *Catherine de' Medici.* London: Joseph, 1973.

Medici, Marie de (1573–1642). Regent. Marie de Medici was a pivotal figure in the development of French women's political role. She assumed a preponderant role in the redefinition of authoritative identity. In the first years of her marriage to King Henri IV, she dedicated much time to the royal upbringing of her four children, sponsoring cultural events, and intriguing with her favorites. She indulged in fashion, jewels, and royal treasure, and made the royal palace the "fashionable" place to be. The assassination of Henri IV on May 4, 1610, brought a radical change. Nominated *Régente*, Marie de Medici took her responsibilities seriously. In her first political speech, she expressed her profound grief and adopted the reversed motto *possem, sed nolo*, indicating her willingness to comply with the rules and initiating an important political strategy. She now applied herself to political affairs with great dignity, and dedicated her time to counsel and government. But the firing of the economist Sully increased her unpopularity, and civil war started again. The Queen received bad advice and took up arms. She lost political control, especially in the eyes of her son, Louis XIII. After three years of exile in Blois, she returned and intrigued in favor of Richelieu. In a famous episode called "la journée des dupes" she was evicted by her son in favor of the Cardinal. She never regained any political power. Prisoner of the d'Estrées, she fled to Brussels and attempted to remove Richelieu and to convince her son of her loyalty. Her arrival in 1638 in London stirred up fears of a "popish plot." Unfounded rumors of the King conspiring with England's enemies were spread, but did not convince Louis XIII. Marie de Medici took refuge in Cologne in October, 1641. While the popish plot scare contributed eventually to Cromwell's revolution and Charles's death, it ruined the hopes of her return to the French court as a political leader. Marie de Medici died alone in 1642.

Marie de Medici's unpopularity is legendary. Numerous pamphlets written during her exile condemn her repeated efforts to regain power. Her accusations and defenses in response to her critics demonstrate her eagerness to intervene in parliament. Her denunciation of the merit-based power of Richelieu (as opposed to a power based on a theory of state and birthright) stayed strong until her death. During her reign, Marie de Medici commissioned many building projects, for example the aqueduct of Arcueil, Le Cours de la Reine on the Champs-Elysées, and an equestrian statue for Henri IV's death. Her most important architectural enterprise was the construction of the Luxembourg Palace, completed by Pierre le Muet. Statues and sculptures were added by Guillaume Berthelot, with paintings by Jacob and Ambroise Dubois. The memorable events of her life have been captured by Rubens in twenty-one portraits exhibited today at the Louvre.

Martine Sauret

BIBLIOGRAPHY

Secondary Texts

Kermina, Françoise. *Marie de Médicis, reine, régente et rebelle*. Paris: Librairie Académique Perrin, 1979.
Lord, Arthur Power. *The Regency of Marie de Médicis*. New York: Henry Holt, 1903.
Pillorget, René and Suzanne Pillorget. *France baroque et France classique*. Paris: Robert Laffont, 1995.
St. Germain. *Diverses Pièces pour défendre la Reine Mère*. 5 vols. Anvers, 1637.
Walecka, Anna. "Mère, déesse, reine: Marie de Médicis en Cybèle." *Atlantis* 19, no. 1 (1994): 134–145.

Melancholia. Contemporary feminist criticism examines the role of melancholia as a construct of patriarchal discourse in the constitution of the gendered subject and in its relation to artistic creativity. Derived from the Greek for "black bile," since the time of Aristotle melancholia has been associated, in Western culture, with male eminence in the arts, politics, and philosophy. During the Renaissance, Florentine humanist Marsilio Ficino revitalized this tradition, linking Platonic divine frenzy to the melancholic temperament as the source of intellectual accomplishment and creativity of gifted men, a tradition that culminated in the nineteenth-century Romantic hero. Although melancholia was often personified as a woman, as exemplified by Albrecht Dürer's engraving *Melencolia I*, women were generally not included among the great melancholics.

Today, the possibility and nature of female melancholia remain controversial. Current debate often concerns theories elaborated by Sigmund Freud in "Mourning and Melancholia" (1917) and "The Ego and the Id" (1921). For Freud, melancholia is associated with the superego, which is itself linked, in the terms of Jacques Lacan, with the Law of the Father. In melancholia, the superego or ego ideal acts as a harsh critic of the ego which has unconsciously identified itself with a lost object-choice (in Oedipal theory, the mother) that is both loved and hated. Freud employs the metaphor of an open wound to describe the process by which melancholia empties the ego of its cathartic energies. In her brilliant critique of Freudianism in *Le Speculum de l'autre femme*, Luce Irigaray* denies the possibility of female melancholia, arguing that woman functions as the open wound, hole, or lack in male imaginary and symbolic processes. An outsider to the signifying system, woman is unable to represent her loss and, indeed, herself. Julia Kristeva*, in *Soleil noir: Dépression et mélancolie*, also examines melancholia as discourse, although she has been criticized by some feminists for appearing to acknowledge the necessity of the matricidal drive in the constitution of the subject.

Mary Anne Garnett

BIBLIOGRAPHY

Primary Texts

Aristotle. "Problems, Book XXX." In *The Complete Works of Aristotle: The Revised Oxford Translation*. 2 vols. Ed. Jonathan Barnes. Princeton: Princeton University Press, 1984. 2: 1498–1506.

Freud, Sigmund. "The Ego and the Id." In *The Standard Edition of the Complete Psychological Works*. 24 vols. Trans. James Strachey. London: Hogarth, 1953–1974. 19: 12–66.

———. "Mourning and Melancholia." In *The Standard Edition of the Complete Psychological Works*. 24 vols. Trans. James Strachey. London: Hogarth, 1953–1974. 14: 243–258.

Irigaray, Luce. *Speculum of the Other Woman*. Trans. Gillian C. Gill. Ithaca: Cornell University Press, 1985.

Jackson, Stanley W. *Melancholia and Depression: From Hippocratic Times to Modern Times*. New Haven: Yale University Press, 1986.

Klibansky, Raymond, Erwin Panofsky, and Fritz Saxl. *Saturn and Melancholy: Studies in the History of Natural Philosophy, Religion, and Art*. New York: Basic Books, 1964.

Kristeva, Julia. *Black Sun: Depression and Melancholia*. Trans. Léon S. Roudiez. New York: Columbia University Press, 1989.

Schiesari, Juliana. *The Gendering of Melancholia*. Ithaca: Cornell University Press, 1992.

Secondary Texts

Abraham, Nicolas, and Maria Torok. "Introjection-Incorporation: *Mourning* or *Melancholia*." In *Psychoanalysis in France*. Ed. Serge Lebovici and Daniel Widlöcher. New York: International Universities Press, 1980.

Butler, Judith. "Freud and the Melancholia of Gender." In *Gender Trouble: Feminism and the Subversion of Identity*. New York: Routledge, 1990. 57–65.

Lechte, John. "Art, Love, and Melancholy in the Work of Julia Kristeva." In *Abjection, Melancholia and Love: The Work of Julia Kristeva*. Ed. John Fletcher and Andrew E. Benjamin. New York: Routledge, 1990. 24–41.

Melodrama. A drama in prose, usually in three acts, in which the literary text combines with music, dance, mime, and spectacular stage effects to create the total art form of "grand spectacle." Codified by Pixérécourt at the beginning of the nineteenth century (*Coelina*, 1800) the early French melodrama is based on a dramaturgy that respects the traditional rules of unities developed by classical theater* but follows its own rules and conventions with regard to language, themes, and characters. Often disparaged for its grandiloquent rhetoric and lack of realism, melodrama centers on a grand plot, the struggle between the forces of good and evil. Melodrama's rather stereotypical characters are clearly positions on each side of this Manichean world: the "good" ones include the innocent victim—usually a woman, sometimes orphaned children; the noble but powerless father; and the simpleton (*le niais*), who provides comic relief. Embodying evil all by himself, the villain (*traître*), usually a male, is the central and most powerful character. Between his arrival in a peaceful community and his banishment, which restores peace and order at the end of the play, the dramatic peripetia center on the innocent victim's persecution. The increasingly violent pathetic effects produced by her predicaments are a source of suspense and moral sublime, the heroine's function being to move the audience to recognize and admire in all its glory the virtue she embodies. The theme of persecution is sustained until the last scenes when it is abruptly replaced by the theme of recognition: a mother's ring or a written confession reveals the villain's accusations to be false. Invariably in the end, Providence prevails over fatality, good wins over evil, the innocent victim is vindicated and reunited with a long-lost relative or her community. In melodrama virtue is an essentially feminine quality, defined by the heroine's innocence, kindness, generosity, obedience, self-sacrifice, and devotion to duty; by her extreme capacity to endure sufferings; and by her unshakable faith in Providence. Based on a matriarchal ethics that proclaims women's moral superiority, melodrama nonetheless presents women as martyrs of humanity because of their sexual difference. From a feminist perspective, therefore, melodrama can be said to faithfully reflect the conservative imperial society, to echo the patriarchal laws of the Napoleonic Code* granting men—fathers and husbands—sole control over the family*. In that regard, women's contribution to the patriarchal genre of melodrama might appear paradoxical. Writing melodramas necessarily entailed, on the one hand, drawing on the emerging myths about women's difference and thereby adopting the dominant discourse of women's exclusion from the public sphere, and on the other hand, focusing on women's universal plight and thereby laying the ground work for the development of a feminist consciousness. For women playwrights such as Barthélémy-Hadot*, de Bawr, Leriche, Friedelle, or Hordé, writing melodramas was a way not only to assert their place as writers in a society that condemned most women to silence, but also to alter the image and role of women characters in the genre. Barthélémy-Hadot, for instance, tends to reward her women characters' high moral standards and their natural propensity to do good by emphasizing the theme of love more readily than her male counterparts. In her drama, the civilizing mission the genre traditionally ascribes to women is no longer presented as doomed, but as a real possibility.

Marie-Pierre Le Hir

BIBLIOGRAPHY

Secondary Texts

Le Hir, Marie-Pierre. *Le Romantisme aux enchères: Ducange, Pixérécourt, Hugo*. Philadelphia: John Benjamins, 1992.
Przybos, Julia. *L'Entreprise mélodramatique*. Paris: Corti, 1987.
Thomasseau, Jean-Marie. *Le Mélodrame sur les scènes parisiennes de Coelina à l'Auberge des Adrets*. Lille: Service de Reproduction des Thèses, 1976.

Memoirs. Memoirs are the narrative of past events of public interest as recorded by a participant in those events, or by an eyewitness, written from the perspective of the present. Temporal distance distinguishes them from diaries and journals, which purport to record events immediately upon their occurrence. Memoirs also remain distinct from autobiography* and biography by setting the author's experiences in the context of broader sociopolitical concerns so that they may be of wide public interest. Memoirs differ, too, from histories and chronicles by their inclusion of a substantial proportion of personal experiences, observations, and judgments which make the author as much an object of study as the events themselves. Although the hybrid nature of memoirs prompts scholars to question their authenticity and objectivity, it has not prevented historians of politics and literature from relying heavily on memoirs as important source material.

Relatively few examples are known to date from the French medieval period. Joinville's 1309 *Vie de Saint Louis* and Froissart's *Chroniques* (recording events from 1325 to 1400) incorporate characteristic elements, although they are not memoirs per se. With Philippe de Commynes's *Mémoires sur Louis XI*, the form begins to take tighter shape, since the narrative remains close to Commynes's own participation in political events between 1464 and 1498. Among the early female authors who contributed to France's historical record, Renaissance women underscore the need to formulate more explicitly women's place in history; Louise Labé* emphasizes that she and all women must cultivate a personal voice that establishes woman as a historical subject. Inasmuch as this position may be established through memoirs, women of the seventeenth century excelled in composing that historical subject. Detailed formulations of categories of memoirs indicate that the Classical Age respected the distinction between *mémoires d'état* and *mémoires particuliers*, the latter usually associated with women as keepers of the secret domain of private life and personal intrigue. Female memorialists were criticized for weaving egocentric confessions of only marginal interest, instead of carefully shaping useful firsthand accounts of major social and political events. Although often discredited, the works of female memorialists were plundered by historians for the verification of historical facts.

The memoirs of Cardinal de Retz (1717) and the Duc de Saint-Simon (1743) are traditionally considered of greatest significance. However, works of their female counterparts have gained renewed recognition. Of the many female participants who also documented the war of the Fronde*, Hortense Mancini* and the Duchesse de Montpensier* composed memoirs of particular literary and historical interest. Voltaire recognized the merits of the Marquise de Caylus's* memoirs, which he edited in 1770. Mme d'Aulnoy's* travels led to her lively court memoirs: *Mémoires de la cour d'Espagne* (1690) and *Mémoires sur la cour d'Angleterre* (1695). Memoirs implicitly raise the question of the limits between reality and fiction, an ambiguity that produced the seventeenth- and eighteenth-century memoir-novel (Prévost's *Manon Lescaut* is perhaps the most widely known example). A rich source of both gender and genre play, the travesties of this pseudo-memoir tease the reader into a gray area that breaks down rigid perspectives on what constitutes history and gender. Mme de Tencin* could freely borrow the male voice in *Mémoires du Comte de Comminges* just as numerous male authors attempt to authenticate the voice of a female narrator.

The degree to which women's memoirs reflect an active involvement in public life diminished during the eighteenth century until the revolutionary era, which produced Mme Roland's* *Mémoires particuliers* and *Portraits et anecdotes*, composed from her prison cell in 1793. These pages replaced her lengthy narrative that had been taken and burned, supposedly supplying sensitive details of her own involvement and that of many others in the revolutionary cause. No nineteenth-century female memorialist rivaled the political involvement for which Mme Roland was guillotined. The memoirs of the Comtesse d'Agoult* (pseudonym Daniel Stern), much as the celebrated *Mémoires d'outre-tombe* by Chateaubriand, constitute a highly personal narrative that attests more to Romantic melancholy and disillusionment than to the political and social upheavals associated with several generations of Romanticism*.

In the twentieth century, memoirs, pseudo-memoirs, and the memoir-novel enjoy a somewhat revived celebrity, despite the negative criticism disparaging the "intrusive" presence of a personal voice within the "objective" documents that constitute modern history. Marguerite Yourcenar*, the first woman to be elected to the Académie Française, authored autobiographical volumes including *Souvenirs pieux*. Ironically, it is her pseudo-memoir entitled *Mémoires d'Hadrien* that has captivated Yourcenar's reading public, particularly because of the depth and authenticity characterizing its male narrator's voice.

Personal accounts composed by Simone de Beauvoir* and Marguerite Duras* blend private narrative with a subtext of political engagement. Beauvoir's feminism* emerges from the pages of her four volumes of autobiographical narratives that begin with *Mémoires d'une jeune fille rangée*. Duras's early writing entitled *Douleur*, aptly translated into English as *The War: A Memoir*, also witnesses the return of women's active political involvement, recounting feelings and events experienced by a member of the French Resistance during 1944 as she awaits the release of her husband from a Nazi concentration camp. Duras's emotional narrative, on the border of fictional and factual representation (the narrative voice changes from first to third person, for example), also takes to the limit timely issues such as the female subject's solidarity with other females and her link to the larger context of twentieth-century life itself.

Virginia Marino

BIBLIOGRAPHY

Primary Texts

Aulnoy, Marie-Catherine, Comtesse d'. *Mémoires de la cour d'Espagne*. La Haye: Adrian Moetjens, 1691.
Beauvoir, Simone de. *La Force de l'âge*. Paris: Gallimard, 1960.
———. *La Force des choses*. Paris: Gallimard, 1963.
———. *Mémoires d'une jeune fille rangée*. Paris: Gallimard, 1958.
———. *Tout compte fait*. Paris: Gallimard, 1972.

Duras, Marguerite. *Douleur*. Paris: P.O.L., Editeur, 1985.

Montpensier, Anne-Marie-Louise-Henriette d'Orléans, duchesse de. *Mémoires*. 1718. Vols. 40–43, Collection des mémoires relatifs à l'histoire de France. Ed. M. Petitot. Paris: Foucault, 1825.

Roland, Marie-Jeanne Philipon, Mme. *Mémoires de Mme Roland*. Ed. Paul de Roux. Paris: Mercure de France, 1966.

Valois, Marguerite de. *Mémoires*. 1628. Paris: Mercure de France, 1971.

Yourcenar, Marguerite. *Essais et mémoires*. Paris: Gallimard, 1991.

    Secondary Texts

Beasley, Faith E. *Revising Memory: Women's Fiction and Memoirs in Seventeenth-Century France*. New Brunswick, NJ: Rutgers University Press, 1990.

Hipp, Marie-Thérèse. *Mythes et réalités: Enquête sur le roman et les mémoires 1660–1700*. Paris: Klincksieck, 1976.

Menopause. Before the twentieth century, explicit mention of menopause was rare because of rules governing taste and *bienséance*, and also because few women protagonists lived beyond fifty. In our time, literary menopause in France assumes the apocalyptic aspect of a crisis or definitive turning point in a woman's social, physical, and erotic life, regardless of whether the outcome is basically euphoric or dysphoric.

In *Le Deuxième Sexe*, Simone de Beauvoir* reminds us that menopause can represent for women a liberation from "the servitude of femininity" (2: 49) imposed at puberty. But Beauvoir emphasizes that the passage more often impoverishes the woman, who is traditionally unprepared by her lack of education* and experience to begin a new life (2: 285). This dilemma is illustrated by her character Monique in *La Femme rompue*. The desire to compensate for all one has missed in the past also usually ends in disappointment, as it does for Beauvoir's pre-menopausal character Anne in *Les Mandarins*, who goes to America, where she discovers real passion but is later abandoned. Beauvoir concedes that it is difficult for women to forge a new social identity when they are no longer considered desirable (1: 288). In *La Force de l'âge* she describes with loathing her middle-aged face in the mirror (656). A paroxysm of regret brings the essay to an end: "The moment has come to say: 'never again!' . . . never again a man . . . what breaks my heart, much more than these deprivations, is to find within myself no new desires . . . if this silence is to last, how long my brief future will seem!" (657). Women in France had lived with the unspoken assumption that their eroticism and hence their life ended when their traditional stories of love and courtship came to a close, and Beauvoir, like Anne, must invent her future. There is hope for both because they have consciously decided to accept their aging, and will no longer count on sexual desirability as a means of relating to others.

Colette's* menopausal character Marco in "Le Képi" is destroyed by the realization that her young lover perceives her as middle-aged and therefore less desirable. Léa in *Chéri* looks in the mirror at age forty-nine and sees that she is old. She wisely accepts this, and renounces all sexuality. But Léa's body is repeatedly described in *The End of Chéri* as grotesque, betraying the narrator's fundamental ambivalence at this point toward the aging woman. Colette's characters Julie de Carneilhan and "Colette" in *La Naissance du jour* are more positive examples of a resolution of the crisis of menopause. In one of the first literary references by a woman, Julie notes that she appears to be entering menopause, and this influences her decision to renounce her unrequited pursuit of her ex-husband. But "Colette" is the only Colettian protagonist to provide an idea of what her new life after the crisis will be like. Modeling her new values and behavior on her mother's late life, she too gladly renounces the love of men, following a long tradition of abstention but emphasizing a new cult of the self. "Colette" will write a new universe and create for herself a new kind of late life femininity* by redirecting her erotic drives into the production of her art.

Two pieces of fiction by women writers published in 1996 give us the beginning of a new, positive perspective on accepting the changes of menopause. In her story "Ménopause," Marianne Servouze Karmel describes a fifty-year-old banker who suffers from physical and emotional symptoms of menopause. For her, the crisis most directly concerns her childlessness, for now she will "never" have a child, and her other family members are dead. A night of insomnia ends with her determination to be the child she never had and to offer maternal care to herself. She will find a lover and ways to relate to young people that will satisfy her emotional and physical needs. In *La Dame en bleu*, Noëlle Châtelet's attractive, chic, fifty-two-year-old character Solange follows an elderly woman in the street and adopts her slower rhythm and style of life. She learns to empty her mind and merge peacefully with her surroundings. She finds a male companion who does not expect her to be seductive. She is happy, and when in the end she reenters the world of her age cohorts, we know that menopause and aging will no longer have the power to frighten her.

Bethany Ladimer

BIBLIOGRAPHY

Primary Texts

Beauvoir, Simone de. *La Femme rompue*. Paris: Gallimard, 1967.
———. *La Force de l'âge*. Paris: Gallimard, 1960.
———. *Les Mandarins*. 2 vols. Paris: Gallimard, 1954.
———. *La Vieillesse*. Paris: Gallimard, 1970.
Châtelet, Noëlle. *La Dame en bleu*. Paris: Stock, 1996.
Colette. *Chéri*. Paris: Fayard, 1920.
———. *Julie de Carneilhan*. Paris: Gallimard, 1941.
———. *La Naissance du jour*. Paris: Flammarion, 1928.
Karmel, Marianne Servouze. *Ménopause et autres récits*. Paris: Attique, 1996.

Secondary Text

Beauvoir, Simone de. *Le Deuxième Sexe*. 2 vols. Paris: Gallimard, 1949.

Menstruation. Since the time of ancient Greece menstruation has marked women as the biological "other." Medieval myths transmitted from Pliny about menstrual blood claimed that it could turn wine, kill crops, dull metal, and drive dogs mad. The menses, thought to be the product of "uncooked" blood, were expelled by the body to purify itself. While "good" menstrual blood nourished the embryo and produced mother's milk, diseases such as measles, smallpox, and even leprosy could be contracted in utero from its residues. Aside from medical and religious treatises, menstruation was a taboo subject.

Through the Enlightenment* women were treated as imperfect men, menstruation and the related pathology, hysteria*, being the visible symptoms of this dysfunction. The topic is rare in literature, although in his *Supplément au voyage de Bougainville* (1779), Diderot's chaplain learns that Tahitians wear gray veils during the "monthly sickness," and that sex during the menses is discouraged. Even the Marquis de Sade avoided breaking the menstrual taboo.

In the nineteenth century menstruation was an illness. The symptoms—physical frailty and mental instability—provided cause to confine and monitor women. Science proposed that menstruous women were prone to criminal tendencies for which they could not be held accountable. In literature, the courtesan in Alexandre Dumas's *La Dame aux Camélias* (1848) has the curious habit of carrying white camellias for twenty-five days of the month, red for the remaining five. The narrator coyly remarks that no one ever knew the reason. It was Emile Zola, however, who broke the boundaries of literary *bienséance*. He was influenced by Jules Michelet, who in *L'Amour* (1858) and *La Femme* (1859) describes menstruation as a "wound" which incapacitates women for fifteen to twenty days a month. In Zola's *Germinal* (1885), Catherine doesn't menstruate until she witnesses the slaughter of striking miners. Her mother's description of the menses as a "wound" which could only produce more downtrodden offspring underscores the miners' hopeless situation. The violence precipitating this scene reinforces the association of menstruation with wounding, labeling women as eternal victims. In *La Joie de vivre* (1884) women are victims of both biology and society. Pauline initially believes her menses to be a lethal hemorrhage, but medical textbooks convince her to view it as a celebration of her fertility. By the novel's end, however, Pauline's fortune has been drained, her love rejected, and her monthly cycles transformed into the dismal reminder of her failure to reproduce.

Simone de Beauvoir's* *Le Deuxième Sexe* (1949) demonstrates the strength of negative cultural views of menstruation. Beauvoir describes "the monthly annoyance" as a time of "semi-lunacy," inspiring disgust. Some writers and psychoanalytic theorists, on the other hand, embrace menstruation as symbolic of the irrepressible feminine psyche. Hélène Cixous* develops her theory of *écriture féminine*￼ in "Le Rire de la Méduse" (1975), and Luce Irigaray* celebrates fluid, unrestricted femininity in *Ce Sexe qui n'en est pas un* (1977). A novel depicting intersections of the body and feminine discourse is Marie Cardinal's* *Les Mots pour le dire* (1975). The narrator experiences torrential menstrual flows until she begins psychoanalysis. She discovers her voice, articulates repressed feelings, and begins to write. Of interest to literary criticism is Mary Jane Lupton's work on psychoanalytic theory*, which suggests that menstruation is repressed in the theory's fundamental concepts.

Katrina Perry

BIBLIOGRAPHY

Secondary Texts

Laqueur, Thomas. *Making Sex. Body and Gender from the Greeks to Freud.* Cambridge, MA: Harvard University Press, 1990.
Lupton, Mary Jane. *Menstruation and Psychoanalysis.* Urbana: University of Illinois Press, 1993.
Shapiro, Ann Louise. "Disordered Bodies/Disorderly Acts: Medical Discourse and the Female Criminal in Nineteenth-Century Paris." In *Gendered Domains: Rethinking Public and Private in Women's History.* Ed. Dorothy O. Helly and Susan M. Reverby. Ithaca, NY: Cornell University Press, 1992. 123–134.

Mérard de Saint-Just, Anne-Jeanne-Félicité d'Ormoy (1765–1830). Daughter of novelist, dramatist, and member of Rome Academy Charlotte Chaumet d'Ormoy*, she published her first work at age seventeen before marrying Mérard de Saint-Just, an amateur writer who edited her early work. "A little bit of everything" was Mérard de Saint-Just's motto. She wrote novels*, poetry*, pastorals, short works, and an almanac including a fierce defense of women writers. Her novels treat the internal and external forces shaping women's lives. In *Mon Journal d'un an* (1787) a young woman goes mad when forced to marry an old man she abhors. In *La Démence de Mme Panor* (1796), the same heroine returns to sanity. *Histoire de la baronne d'Alvigny* (1788) deals with a compulsive gambler who loses everything. *Six Mois d'exil ou les orphelines par la Révolution* (1805) follows a group of young women who help each other survive the Terror. Numerous episodes reflect the author's own experience.

Aurora Wolfgang

BIBLIOGRAPHY

Primary Texts

Bergeries et opuscules de Mlle d'O. l'aînée. Paris: Lamy, 1782.
Mon Journal d'un an, ou les mémoires de Mlle de Rozadelle-Saint-Ophelle, par *M.A.J.F.D.M.S.J.N.D.O., suivis de poésies fugitives, d'une anecdote cachémirienne et d'un conte pastoral.* Paris: N.p., 1787.
Histoire de la baronne d'Alvigny, par Mad. D.M.S.J.N.A.F. d'O. London: N.p., 1788.
Démence de Mme Panor, en son nom Rozadelle Saint-Ophèle, suivie d'un conte de fées, d'un fragment d'Antiquès, d'une anecdote villageoise et de quelques couplets. Paris: N.p., 1796.
Six Mois d'exil ou les orphelines par la Révolution par M. St.-J. Paris: Calixte Volland, an XIII [1805].

Secondary Texts

Dunkley, John. "Gambling: A Social and Moral Problem in France, 1685–1792." *Studies on Voltaire and the Eighteenth Century* 235. Oxford: Voltaire Foundation, 1985.

Stewart, Joan Hinde. *Gynographs: French Novels by Women of the Late Eighteenth Century.* Lincoln: University of Nebraska Press, 1993.

Mercoeur, Elisa (1809–1835) was a child prodigy and poet known as "la Muse armoricaine," for her Breton origins. In her quest for literary fame, Mercoeur was aided by Education Minister Guizot and Madame Récamier. Her greatest enemy, Baron Taylor, refused to accept her tragedy *Boabdil* for production at the Comédie Française. This rejection led to Mercoeur's physical and mental deterioration, ending with impoverishment and premature death. Her complete works were published posthumously by her mother in 1843.

Wendy Greenberg

BIBLIOGRAPHY

Primary Text

Oeuvres complètes. Paris: Pommeret, 1843.

Secondary Texts

Clarétie, Jules. *Elisa Mercoeur.* Paris: Collection du Bibliophile, 1864.

Greenberg, Wendy. "Elisa Mercoeur: The Poetics of Genius and the Sublime." *Nineteenth-Century French Studies* 24 (Fall-Winter 1996): 84–96.

Séché, Léon. "Elisa Mercoeur: A propos du Centenaire de sa naissance," *Les Annales Romantiques* (1909): 188–193.

Méricourt, Anne Josephe Théroigne de (1762–1817). A popular organizer and women's rights advocate during the Revolution*, Méricourt is best known as the "amazon*" who led the Women's March to Versailles in October 1789, armed, and astride a cannon.

An Ardennes peasant by birth, Méricourt spent her early years first in poverty, then as a domestic servant, and later as a companion, mistress, and music student. Abandoning her studies in 1789, she moved to Paris, where she became an ardent admirer of constitutional monarchy and popular sovereignty. As such, Méricourt participated in the fall of the Bastille, the return of the royal family to Paris, political organizing and oratory in the Amis de la loi and the Société fraternelle, and demonstrations against royalists. Her causes included the creation of women's clubs and an armed women's military battalion, along with citizenship instruction for working-class people.

During the turbulence of political rivalries in 1793, Méricourt allied with the Girondins against the victorious Jacobins. She was assaulted, flogged, and stripped by Jacobin women; and, according to accounts of the event, Méricourt experienced irreparable mental damage. She subsequently became permanently insane and died in La Salpêtrière, a women's prison-hospital in Paris, in 1817.

Just as royalist detractors had tried to equate her revolutionary ardor with behavior unnatural to her sex, Méricourt's revolutionary activities have often been treated as anomalies and minimized. Simon Schama's recent revisionist history of the French Revolution, for example, focuses primarily on Méricourt's madness as a metaphor for the revolution itself.

Susan P. Conner

BIBLIOGRAPHY

Secondary Texts

Lacour, Léopold. *Les Origines du féminisme contemporain. Trois femmes de la Révolution, Olympe de Gouges, Théroigne de Méricourt, Rose Lacombe.* Paris: Plon-Nourrit, 1900.
Ravelsberg, Ferdinand Strobel von. *Les Confessions de Théroigne de Méricourt, la fameuse amazone révolutionnaire.* Paris: L. Westhausser, 1892.
Roudinesco, Elisabeth. *Théroigne de Méricourt: A Melancholic Woman during the French Revolution.* New York: Verso, 1991.
Schama, Simon. *Citizens: A Chronicle of the French Revolution.* New York: Knopf, 1989.
Sokolnikova, Galina Osipovna. *Nine Women Drawn from the Epoch of the French Revolution.* Freeport, NY: Books for Libraries Press, 1931.

Michel, Louise (1830–1905). Anarchist, feminist, and writer. A schoolteacher by profession, she was quite involved with feminist and republican groups. In 1871 she played a major role during the Paris Commune*. Her bold attitude before the Versailles military tribunal was celebrated by Victor Hugo in his poem ''Viro Major.'' In 1873 she was deported to New Caledonia until 1880.

After her return to France, she devoted her life to anarchism*. She was jailed again from 1883 to 1886. During this period, she wrote propaganda for the anarchist movement. From 1886 to 1890, she published her memoirs* and the trilogy *Les Microbes humains* (1886), *Le Monde nouveau* (1888), and *Le Claque-dents* (1890). While these novels* tend to follow roman-feuilleton techniques, they nonetheless present innovative features such as the use of science fiction, political rhetoric, and unique narrative techniques. Louise Michel's primary goal was to educate and convert her readership to anarchy. She also created strong and bold women characters in her fictional works, echoing her feminist ideas. Several of her plays were produced in Paris, including *Le Coq rouge* (1888) and *La Grève* (1890). Michel also obtained some success with her poetry*.

In 1890 she moved to London for political reasons. While there, she published her most successful work, *La Commune* (1898). Shortly before her death, she wrote a second autobiography*, *Souvenirs et aventures de ma vie* (1905), in which she focused mainly on her political agenda and public actions, speaking little of her private life.

Louise Michel is better known for her political activism than for her literary works; her writings are worthy of being rediscovered. Keenly aware of the restrictions imposed on her gender, Louise Michel spoke up through her writings. She declared at the end of her life, "I do not speak much; however I do write."

Juliette Parnell-Smith

BIBLIOGRAPHY

Primary Texts

Légendes et chants de gestes canaques. Paris: Kéva, 1885.
Les Microbes humains. Paris: Dentu, 1886.
Le Monde nouveau. Paris: Dentu, 1888.
Le Claque-dents. Paris: Dentu, 1890.
La Commune. Paris: P. V. Stock, 1898.
A travers la vie et la mort. Intro. Daniel Armogathe and Marion Piper. Paris: Maspéro, 1982.
Souvenirs et aventures de ma vie. Intro. Daniel Armogathe. Paris: Maspéro 1983.

Secondary Texts

Stivale, Charles J. "Louise Michel's Poetry of Existence and Revolt." *Tulsa Studies in Women's Literature* 5, no. 1 (1986): 41–61.
Thomas, Edith. *Louise Michel ou la Velleda de l'anarchie.* Paris: Gallimard, 1971.

Ministry of Women's Rights. Created in 1974 by President Valéry Giscard d'Estaing, the Secretariat of State for Women's Condition aimed to promote equality and progress for women. Its first leader, Françoise Giroud*, established a blueprint for a modern society based on fairness and equality. Under her leadership, important legislation was passed to legalize abortion* and relax divorce* laws. She distanced herself from the feminist movement, however, in order to maintain credibility and effectiveness in the cabinet, and to avoid entanglement in the ideological disputes of radical feminists.

The history of the ministry reflects the state's reluctance to regulate women's issues—few ministries have had a more precarious existence or have undergone more frequent changes in structure, name, orientation. and mission. In less than twenty years, it was headed by nine different women before being reduced to a department within a ministry in 1993. The most feminist minister of women's rights was Yvette Roudy* who held offfice from 1981 to 1986 and who was the only leader to have had a full cabinet appointment.

Samia I. Spencer

BIBLIOGRAPHY

Secondary Texts

Adler, Laure. *Femmes politiques.* Paris: Editions du Seuil, 1993.
Cent mesures pour les femmes. Intro. Françoise Giroud. Paris: La Documentation Française, 1976.
Sur les chemins de l'égalité. Repères pour une histoire des droits des femmes. Preface by Simone Weil. Paris: Service des Droits des Femmes, n.d.
Giroud, Françoise. *La Comédie du pouvoir.* Paris: Fayard, 1977.

Jenson, Jane, and Mariette Sineau. "Une Création présidentielle: Le Ministère des droits de la Femme." In *Mitterrand et les Françaises. Un Rendez-vous manqué.* Paris: Presses de la Fondation Nationale des Sciences Politiques, 1995. 183–207, 360–366.

McBride Stetson, Dorothy. *Women's Rights in France.* Westport, CT: Greenwood Press, 1987.

Reynolds, Sian. "The Ministry of Women's Rights, 1981–1986." In *France and Modernisation.* Ed. John Gaffney. Aldershort, England: Avebury, 1988. 149–168.

Roudy, Yvette. *A cause d'elles.* Preface by Simone de Beauvoir. Paris: Albin Michel, 1985.

———. *La Femme en marge.* Preface by François Mitterrand. Paris: Flammarion, 1982.

———. *Mais de quoi ont-ils peur?* Paris: Albin Michel, 1995.

Spencer, Samia I. "Secretariat, Ministry, or Service? Searching for a Government Structure to Serve French Women." *Contemporary French Civilization* 21, no. 1 (Winter-Spring 1977): 61–85.

Miremont, Anne d'Aubourg de la Bove, comtesse de (1735–1811). Little is known about her life; however, her *Mémoires de la marquise de Crémy, écrits par elle-même* (Lyons, 1766; Paris, 1808) are said to be autobiographical. She is known primarily for her lengthy *Traité de l'éducation des femmes* (1779–1789), a detailed educational treatise aimed at girls ages seven to eighteen. They were expected to study not only traditional subjects such as religion, dance, and music, but also languages and literature, history and geography, and spelling. She placed the greatest emphasis on the six-year teacher-training curriculum, which included a wide-ranging reading program of modern philosophers, and writers of both sexes. Her ideas were remarkably modern: personal hygiene, a good diet, exercise, and plenty of fresh air were paramount for good health. She stressed the importance of acquiring both practical and theoretical information, and while imparting this knowledge, she attempted to appeal to the hearts of her students in order to capture their minds. Like many of her female contemporaries who wrote on this subject, she tried to demonstrate the importance of educating girls, attributing the general moral degeneracy of her age to the neglect of girls' education*. Since she considered women to be responsible for transmitting moral values to their children, the strength and grandeur of the nation's next generation depended on women's virtue and education. She claimed that a comparison between classical antiquity and the eighteenth century would confirm this: during her own century, women had become merely the playthings of men's passions, whereas in the classical age women were the preservers of virtue. A woman's duty was not only to her family*; even more important was her duty to society. Miremont's ideas were far removed from those of Rousseau. While she favored close contact between mothers and their children, she nevertheless felt that a woman's role far exceeded that of wife and mother.

Rosena Davison

BIBLIOGRAPHY

Primary Texts

Mémoires de la marquise de Crémy, écrits par elle-même. Lyons: Duplain, 1766.
Traité de l'éducation des femmes et cours complet d'instruction. Paris: P.-D. Pierres, 1779–1789.

Secondary Texts

Sonnet, Martine. "Une Fille à éduquer." In *Histoire des femmes.* 4 vols. Ed. Georges Duby and Michelle Perrot. Paris: Plon, 1991. 3: 111–139.
Spencer, Samia I. "Women and Education." In *French Women and the Age of Enlightenment.* Bloomington: Indiana University Press, 1984. 83–96.
Steinbrugge, Lieselotte. *The Moral Sex.* New York: Oxford University Press, 1995.

Mnouchkine, Ariane (1939–). The foremost woman theater* director in France, Mnouchkine helped launch the renowned Théâtre du Soleil in 1964. Dedicated to colorfully stylized, energetically choreographed productions that come to grips—sometimes metaphorically—with the thorniest political questions of our times, Mnouchkine's work has ranged from collective creations about the French Revolution* (*1789 ou la Révolution doit s'arrêter à la perfection du bonheur*) to her own adaptation of Klaus Mann's *Méphisto*, a novel* about artistic and ethical choice. In addition, her work includes reinterpretations, with a feminist focus, of Euripides's and Aeschylus's House of Atreus tragedies, *Les Atrides* (1990). Her marriage of Shakespearian texts (*Richard II, Henry IV*, and *Twelfth Night*) with traditional Asian theatrical techniques helped establish her as one of the most daring and original stage practitioners of today. With playwright Hélène Cixous*, Mnouchkine has also examined the horrors of civil war in decolonized regions of the world (*L'Histoire terrible et inachevée de Norodom Sihanouk, Roi du Cambodge* [1985] and *L'Indiade ou l'Inde de leurs rêves* [1988]), and has courageously exposed the responsibility of the French medical establishment in HIV-contaminated blood transfusions in *La Ville parjure ou le réveil des Erinyes* (1994).

Judith G. Miller

BIBLIOGRAPHY

Primary Text

Méphisto, le roman d'une carrière. Paris: Editions Théâtre du Soleil, 1979.

Secondary Texts

Bablet, Denis, and Marie-Louise Bablet. *Le Théâtre du Soleil, diapolivre.* Paris: Editions du C.N.R.S., 1979.
Feral, Josette. *Dresser un monument à l'éphémère: Rencontres avec Ariane Mnouchkine.* Paris: Editions Théâtrales, 1995.
Kiernander, Adrian. *Ariane Mnouchkine and the Théâtre du Soleil.* Cambridge: Cambridge University Press, 1993.
Kourilsky, Françoise, ed. *Mephisto. Theatre and Politics: An International Anthology.* New York: Ubu Repertory Theatre, 1990.

Lallias, Jean-Claude, Jean-Jacques Arnault, and Evelyne Ertel, eds. *Théâtre aujourd'hui: La Tragédie grecque, Les Atrides au Théâtre du Soleil.* Paris: Ministère de l'Education et de la Culture, 1992.

Mignon, Paul Louis. *Le Metteur en scène au pouvoir ou de Jacques Copeau à Ariane Mnouchkine.* Paris: Palais de l'Institut, 1994.

Richardson, Helen. "The Théâtre du Soleil and the Quest for Popular Theatre in the Twentieth Century." Dissertation, University of California at Berkeley, 1990.

Singelton, Brian. "The Interpretation of Shakespeare by Ariane Mnouchkine and the Théâtre du Soleil." Dissertation, University of Birmingham, England, 1988.

Théâtre du Soleil. *1789 ou la Révolution doit s'arrêter à la perfection du bonheur.* Ed. Helmut Schwartz and Helga Wandel. Frankfurt am Main: Verlag Moritz Diesterweg, 1989.

Films

Mnouchkine, Ariane, dir. and author. *Molière.* 1978. Videocassette. TF1 Entreprises, 1995.

Mnouchkine, Ariane, dir. *1789.* 1974. Videocassette. Ariane Video, 1990.

Mogador, Céleste Venard, later comtesse de Chabrillan (1824–1909). Mogador suffered poverty and an abusive family early in life. As a teenager, she became a *fille inscrite*, a prostitute registered with the Paris police. Brothel life led to contacts in the entertainment world. While a dancer, she was crowned "La Mogador," after the Moroccan city assaulted by French troops. She endured a stormy liaison with the Count of Chabrillan, whom she eventually married. Her early years, her affair with Chabrillan, and their flight to Australia are recounted in the *Mémoires de Céleste Mogador* (1854). The sequel, *Un Deuil au bout du monde: Suite des Mémoires de Céleste Mogador* (1857), treats the couple's life in Australia and Mogador's early writing career. She published numerous novels*, her first, *Les Voleurs d'or* (1857), set in Australia, plays, operetta librettos, poems, and songs. Some speculate that she inspired Bizet's *Carmen*.

Claire Marrone

BIBLIOGRAPHY

Secondary Texts

Curtis, Mina. *Bizet and His World.* New York: Knopf, 1958.

Marrone, Claire. "Male and Female *Bildung*: The *Mémoires de Céleste Mogador.*" *Nineteenth-Century French Studies* 25, no. 3/4 (Spring/Summer 1997): 335–347.

McClary, Susan. *Georges Bizet's "Carmen."* Cambridge: Cambridge University Press, 1992.

Mokeddem, Malika (1949–). Doctor and writer. Born in southern Algeria, Mokeddem now lives and works in Montpellier. Her four novels* all focus on the situation of Algerian women in a society traditionally dominated by men. In *Les Hommes qui marchent* (1990), a grandmother's lyrical evocations of the desert express her nostalgia for the nomadic life that came to an end when the tribe dispersed in the early 1940s, while her granddaughter seeks to break out of the traditional mold of womanhood by studying medicine. *Le Siècle des sauterelles* (1992) recounts the marginalization of a daughter whose father, a poet and nomad, teaches her to write. Mokeddem's two most recent texts, *L'Interdite* (1993) and *Des Rêves et des assassins* (1995), contain an impassioned denunciation of the reign of fear and violence created by the political crisis in contemporary Algeria, especially as it affects women. While *Des Rêves et des assassins* addresses the betrayal of women after independence, *L'Interdite* focuses on women's opposition to the rise of Islamic fundamentalism.

Susan Ireland

BIBLIOGRAPHY

Primary Texts

Les Hommes qui marchent. Paris: Ramsey, 1990.
Le Siècle des sauterelles. Paris: Ramsey, 1992.
L'Interdite. Paris: Grasset, 1993.
Des Rêves et des assassins. Paris: Grasset, 1995.

Secondary Texts

Albet, Maguy. "De la lecture à l'écriture, des livres au livre, résistance ou survie: Malika Mokeddem." In *Multi-culture, multi-écriture: La Voix migrante au féminin en France et au Canada*. Ed. Lucie Lequin and Mair Verthuy. Paris: L'Harmattan, 1996. 51–57.
Chaulet-Achour, Christiane. "Place d'une littérature migrante en France: Matériaux pour une recherche." In *Littérature des immigrations*. Vol. 2. Paris: L'Harmattan, 1995. 2: 115–124.

Monbart, Marie Joséphine (de Lescun) de (afterwards Mme Sydow) (c. 1750–?). Product of a long convent* education*, Monbart expresses frustration and bitterness about her youth in *Les Loisirs d'une jeune dame* (1776). Married life proved more eventful; in *Les Loisirs* she also recounts the dangers and excitement of traveling with her husband to Berlin, where she apparently spent the rest of her life. Inspired by Rousseau's *Emile*, Monbart penned a treatise on education, *Sophie ou de l'éducation des filles* (1777), which places woman in a network of social and moral roles and argues that her happiness depends upon fulfilling those functions. Her last work, however, reveals an effort to create a female community in the world of letters. Subtitled *Suite aux Lettres péruviennes* (1786) (an allusion to Graffigny's* *Lettres péruviennes*, Monbart's *Lettres taï-tiennes* tells of an exotic woman's encounter with European culture, her struggles with language, and her eventual mastery of writing. The novel's portrayal of Europeans in Tahiti also constitutes a timely commentary on colonialism*. While the press sensationalized the Tahitian woman as the object of male desire, Monbart showed the actual results of such myths*, portraying Europeans raping the island women and corrupting the indigenous culture.

Julia Douthwaite

BIBLIOGRAPHY

Primary Texts

Les Loisirs d'une jeune dame. Berlin: G. J. Decker, 1776; Breslau: W. G. Korn, 1784.
Sophie ou de l'éducation des filles. Berlin: Rottman, 1777.
Mélanges de littérature. Breslau: W. G. Korn, 1779.
De l'éducation d'une princesse. Berlin: C. F. Himburg, 1781.
Lettres taïtiennes, suite aux Lettres péruviennes. Breslau: W. G. Korn, 1784; Paris: Les Marchands de Nouveautés, 1786.

Secondary Text

Douthwaite, Julia V. *Exotic Women: Literary Heroines and Cultural Strategies in Ancien Régime France*. Philadelphia: University of Pennsylvania Press, 1992.

Monnet, Marie Moreau (1752–1798). Born in La Rochelle to a wigmaker, Monnet received a good education*, thanks to a noble female benefactor. At age sixteen this precocious poet, novelist, and playwright wrote *Stances sur le bonheur de la sagesse*, which she retouched at nineteen before sending it to Voltaire. The philosopher responded with a flattering letter in which he compared her to Sappho. In Paris she was welcomed by Diderot and Thomas—author of an essay on women—who became a fervent admirer. Her wit, sensitivity, and pleasant personality earned her great praise and many friends among the *philosophes*. In her late twenties she married the chemist Antoine Monnet. Her most popular novel*, *Contes orientaux ou les récits du sage Caleb, voyageur persan*, appeared in several editions before being translated into Russian, and earned her the nickname Caleb. In 1784 a sequel, *Histoire d'Abdal Mazour*, was published, followed in 1787 by a third novel, *Lettres de Jenny Bleinmore*. She is also the author of two comedies in prose, *Zadig ou l'épreuve nécessaire* and *Les Montagnards*, set during the Revolution* and published in 1795, three years before her death in Paris.

Catherine Lafarge

BIBLIOGRAPHY

Primary Texts

Histoire d'Abdal Mazour, suite des contes orientaux. Paris: P.-F. Gueffier, 1784.
Lettres de Jenny Bleinmore and *Zadig ou l'épreuve nécessaire*. Paris: Regnault, 1787.
Essais en vers. Paris: Demonville, 1788.
Les Montagnards. Paris: Mme Toubon, an III (1795).
Contes orientaux ou les récits du sage Caleb, voyageur persan. Paris: Mérigot, 1779.

Secondary Texts

Le Cabinet des fées ou Collection choisie des contes de fées. Geneva and Paris: Chez Barde, Manget, 1785.
Grente, Cardinal Georges. *Dictionnaire des lettres françaises*. Edition revue et mise à jour par François Moureau. Paris: Fayard, 1995.
Nouvelle Bibliographie générale. Paris: Firmin-Didot, 1862.

Montanclos, Marie Emilie Maryon, baronne de Princen, later Mme de (1736–1812). She was the third female editor of the *Journal des Dames* (1774–1775), and dedicated her paper to the adolescent dauphine Marie-Antoinette*. The widow of a German nobleman, she remarried and soon withdrew from court circles, turning in her paper to serious discussions of the responsibilities of motherhood inspired by Rousseau, but stressing also the importance of intellectual achievements for women. For example, she praised Laura Bassi, a determined bourgeoise who had earned a doctorate in physics and a teaching post at the University of Bologna, and hoped that someday soon such female accomplishments would be the rule rather than the exception. She showed by her own example that women could manage a very public career. It is noteworthy that she separated from her second husband almost immediately and had him draw up papers granting permission for her to function independently in her journalistic business. She raised her daughters, to whom she would remain very close, alone. She was a prolific poet and dramatist in her own right, but suffered many indignities at the hands of the Comédie Française. "O, la cruelle chose d'être auteur femelle!" she lamented in the midst of a struggle to get one of her plays performed. Her protest against the royally privileged theater* may have been the root of her friendship with Louis Sébastien Mercier, who helped behind the scenes at the *Journal des Dames*, whose work she increasingly admired and featured in her paper, and to whom she eventually sold it.

Nina Rattner Gelbart

BIBLIOGRAPHY

Primary Text

Journal des Dames.

Secondary Texts

Gelbart, Nina Rattner. "Female Journalists." In *A History of Women in the West.* Ed. Georges Duby and Michelle Perrot. Vol. 3. *Renaissance and Enlightenment Paradoxes.* Ed. Natalie Zemon Davis and Arlette Farge. Cambridge, MA: Harvard University Press, 1993. 420–435.

———. *Feminine and Opposition Journalism in Old Regime France: Le Journal des Dames, 1759–1778.* Berkeley: University of California Press, 1987.

———. "The *Journal des Dames* and Its Female Editors: Politics, Censorship and Feminism in the Old Regime Press." In *Press and Politics in Pre-Revolutionary France.* Ed. Jack Censer and Jeremy Popkin. Berkeley: University of California Press, 1987. 24–74.

Van Dijk, Suzanna. *Traces des femmes. Présences féminines dans le journalisme français du XVIIIe siècle.* Amsterdam: APA-Holland University Press, 1988.

Montenay, Georgette de (1540?–1607). Poet. Her family, of solid and ancient nobility, was from Normandy, but after her marriage* she moved to Languedoc. Her parents and six of their servants died when she was quite young, but whether this tragedy resulted from the devastating epidemics of the time or from a catastrophic accident that spared the five Montenay children is not known.

In 1562 she married an older Catholic gentleman of lesser nobility. Guyon du Goust had long enjoyed a superb reputation as an officer, was much appreciated at court, and was most likely a protégé of the Duc de Vendôme. It was after the Peace of Amboise that he took his young wife to Languedoc. Georgette's family had common ancestors with both Jeanne d'Albret* and her husband Antoine de Bourbon-Vendôme, which explains why she was a frequent guest at the court of Pau and of Nérac.

Whether she had been drawn to the Reformation* while still in Normandy or converted at the Navarre court, it is undeniable that Georgette de Montenay, a zealous Protestant, ardently admired and revered the Queen of Navarre, with whom she must have shared her project to write Christian emblems in French.

The *Privilège* of the *Emblèmes ou devises chrestiennes*, Georgette de Montenay's only known work, was granted in Paris on October 18, 1566, undoubtedly with the help of Jeanne d'Albret, but the 100 emblems, the prefatory epistle, and various poems to the reader were not published until 1571. The 100 emblems of the volume are all of Christian inspiration. Each engraving (*pictura*) illustrates the message of an eight-line decasyllabic poem (*subscriptio*) and contains a Latin inscription (*inscriptio*) generally culled from Scripture. Most emblems invite the readers to worship, to examine their faith, and to live according to the lesson of the Bible*, yet to remain constantly aware of the danger that awaits them. The pope, the Roman Church, and more particularly its clergy are not spared. Peace and harmony are advocated without much hope for success. The proselytizing aim of this eloquent work is undeniable, but the reader cannot fail to be impressed by the fervor and the sincerity of the author's message. Furthermore, the beauty of the engravings, the elegance of the print, and the refinement of the page-setting prove how painstakingly Georgette de Montenay had conceived the work in its most minute details.

The author stresses that hers was the first book of Christian emblems printed in French. What she did not say is that it was the first (and only) book of emblems written in any language by a woman. She availed herself of the fact that, while translating Scripture into French was forbidden and punishable by death, emblems were a fashionable literary genre at the time. She also sensed that emblems printed in French would reach a far greater audience than those written in Latin, and could be an effective means by which to be heard by her fellow Protestants and to convince those who still wavered in their beliefs. Her *Emblèmes ou devises chrestiennes* was immensely popular from the moment it was published. It was translated in a polyglot edition and used in numerous Protestant communities all over Europe after her death. A childless widow in 1573, she settled permanently in her castle of Saint-Germier, devoting herself to the Protestant cause and helping the poor.

Régine Reynolds-Cornell

BIBLIOGRAPHY

Primary Text

Reynolds-Cornell, Régine. *Witnessing an Era: Georgette de Montenay and the Emblèmes ou Devises Chrestiennes.* Birmingham: Summa Publications, 1987.

Secondary Texts

Labrousse, Elisabeth, and Jean-Philippe Labrousse. "Georgette de Montenay et Guyon du Gout son époux." *Bulletin de la Société archéologique, historique, littéraire et scientifique du Gers.* Auch, 1990.
Zezula, J., and R. J. Clements. "La Troisième Lyonnaise: Georgette de Montenay." *L'Esprit Créateur* 5 (1965): 90–101.

Montesson, Charlotte Jeanne Béraud de la Haye de Riou, marquise de (1737–1806). Born in Paris, married at nineteen to the elderly marquis of Montesson, and widowed at age thirty-two, she was secretly married to Louis-Philippe, duc d'Orléans, grandson of the regent, in 1773, and widowed again in 1785. She then led a quiet life, generously providing food and other amenities to the unfortunate. She was briefly imprisoned during the Terror and, through her close friendship* with Joséphine de Beauharnais, later received the protection of Napoleon. She was the author of sixteen comedies and tragedies as well as stories and poetry*. She is best known as an excellent actress in her private theater*, which she organized for the amusement of the duc d'Orléans and where her plays, however faulty, were nevertheless well received. Montesson played a role in the largely female world of the salons* and in the proliferation of private theater that animated eighteenth-century Paris. Her themes of love, marriage*, and family* life place her work within the tradition of the *drame bourgeois* and *comédie larmoyante.*

Mary Cisar

BIBLIOGRAPHY

Primary Text

Oeuvres anonymes, théâtre et mélanges par Mme de la Haie de Riou, marquise de Montesson. Paris: Imprimerie de Didot l'aîné, 1782–1785.

Secondary Texts

Briquet, Marguerite Ursule Fortunée. *Dictionnaire historique, littéraire et bibliographique des Françaises, et des étrangères naturalisées en France.* Paris: Gillé, 1804.
Chaponnière, Paul. *Madame de Montesson et ses oeuvres anonymes. Etude publiée dans la Revue des Livres Anciens.* Paris: N.p., 1914.
Olah, Lillian. *Une Grande Dame auteur dramatique et poète au XVIIIe siècle, Madame de Montesson.* Paris: Champion, 1928.
Saint-Laudernt, Vincent. "Montesson (Charlotte-Jeanne Béraud de la Haie de Riou, marquise de)." In *Biographie universelle ancienne et moderne.* Ed. L. G. Michaud. Paris: Desplaces, 1834.
Turquan, Joseph. *Madame de Montesson, douairière d'Orléans, 1738–1806. Etude de femmes et de moeurs au XVIIIe siècle.* Paris: J. Tallandier, 1904.

Montolieu, Isabelle de (1751–1832). Born into a noble family of Lausanne, she married Benjamin de Crousaz in 1769, bore one son, and was widowed at twenty-four. In 1786 she married Baron Louis de Montolieu and was widowed again in 1800. She had a wide circle of acquaintances among the Swiss gentility, was admired by Gibbon, and was a correspondent of Félicité de Genlis*. Author of an intense literary production extending over a quarter century, Isabelle de Montolieu had difficulty, as a woman living far from Paris, in getting paid for her published stories. These are mostly translations*, adaptations, or imitations, for example, *Le Nécromancien* (1811), after Schiller, *Le Robinson suisse* (1816), after Wyss, and *Raison et sensibilité* (1815), after Jane Austen. Her best work, however, was her first: *Caroline de Lichtfield* (1786), a substantial novel* inspired by a short German tale. A youthful Caroline is cajoled by her father into marrying a physically unattractive man; horrified, she separates from him after the wedding ceremony. But his appearance belies his generosity and courage. Moreover, with proper nutrition, an artificial eye, and the passage of time, he becomes a good-looking chap, and Caroline learns—after three years and numerous peripeteia—to love him. With its humor and happy ending, the novel was an immediate and enduring best-seller.

Joan Hinde Stewart

BIBLIOGRAPHY

Primary Texts

Caroline de Lichtfield. Paris: Buisson, 1786.
Recueil de contes. Geneva: J. J. Paschoud, an XI (1803).
Emmerich. Paris: H. Nicolle, 1810.
Le Nécromancien. Paris: P. Blanchard, 1811.
Raison et sensibilité ou les deux manières d'aimer. Paris: N.p., 1815.
Les Châteaux suisses, anciennes anecdotes et chroniques. Paris: A. Bertrand, 1816.
Le Robinson suisse. Paris: A. Bertrand, 1816.
La Jeune Aveugle. Paris: P. Bertrand, 1819.
La Famille Elliot. Paris: A. Bertrand, 1821.

Secondary Texts

Berthoud, Dorette. *Le Général et la romancière, 1792–1798: Episodes de l'émigration française en Suisse, d'après les lettres du général de Montesquiou à Mme de Montolieu*. Neuchâtel: La Baconnière, 1959.
Sévery, Monsieur et Madame William de. *La Vie de société dans le pays de Vaud à la fin du dix-huitième siècle*. Lausanne: Bridel; Paris: Fischbacher, 1911.
Stewart, Joan Hinde. *Gynographs: French Novels by Women of the Late Eighteenth Century*. Lincoln: University of Nebraska Press, 1993.
———. "Sensibility with Irony: Madame de Montolieu at the End of an Era." *Kentucky Romance Quarterly* 25, no. 4 (1978): 481–489.

Montpensier, Anne-Marie-Louise-Henriette d'Orléans, duchesse de (called "La Grande Mademoiselle") (1627–1693). Her direct ancestors included Marguerite de Navarre* and Henri IV; she also inherited the immense Montpensier fortune from her mother, who died giving birth to her. Raised at the court of her aunt and uncle, Anne d'Autriche and Louis XIII, the richest heiress in France struggled to protect her fortune from her greedy father, Gaston d'Orléans, and grew up expecting a royal marriage*, as befitting her rank. Among the possible matches were Louis XIV and Charles II of England, her first cousins. During the Fronde* rebellion, she played a glorious military role in the opposition to Mazarin: she led her father's troops to secure Orléans, his fiefdom; to save Condé and the Frondeurs, she ordered the Bastille cannons to be fired against the royal army besieging Paris in 1652. The "amazon's"* deeds, denigrated by her male counterparts, ruined all hope of her becoming queen of France and earned her several years of exile in one of her properties, Saint-Fargeau, where she began writing her memoirs*. Intimately involved with events at court and literary matters after her pardon, Mademoiselle, who had refused all marriages beneath her rank, fell passionately in love with a scheming courtier, the Count de Lauzun, in 1670. After Louis XIV forbade their marriage and imprisoned Lauzun, she spent ten years and much of her fortune securing his release, only to be disappointed by his ingratitude. She devoted her last years to her memoirs and the building of a chateau at Choisy, to surpass Versailles in comfort and elegance. Her stormy life and headstrong character have inspired numerous, often condescending, biographies. Only recently has her importance as historian and literary figure been recognized. The literary activities of her court at Saint-Fargeau inspired *Les Nouvelles françaises* (1656), written by her secretary, Segrais; she fashioned the literary portrait genre by publishing the first collection, *Divers portraits* (1659), and wrote utopian and satirical fiction. Her four volumes of memoirs (first published in 1718 in a "corrected" version) rewrite public and private history from a feminocentric perspective, just as she modified official architecture to create feminine spaces in her various residences. By valorizing her own experience and the particularizing detail neglected by male historians, she upsets political and social hierarchies and creates an alternative female order.

Gabrielle Verdier

BIBLIOGRAPHY

Primary Text

Mémoires de Mlle de Montpensier. 4 vols. Ed. A. Cheruel. Paris: Charpentier, 1857–1859.

Secondary Texts

Beasley, Faith E. *Revising Memory: Women's Fiction and Memoirs in Seventeenth-Century France.* New Brunswick, NJ: Rutgers University Press, 1990.
Garapon, Jean. *La Grande Mademoiselle mémorialiste.* Geneva: Droz, 1989.

Montrelay, Michèle (?–). Montrelay is best known for *L'Ombre et le nom* (1977), her study of the concept of femininity* in which she examines female desire and psychoanalytic theories* of the feminine. Her analysis focuses on the opposing views of Sigmund Freud and Ernest Jones on the nature of female sexuality (phallocentric versus concentric). Montrelay posits the existence of two stages in the development of a girl's femininity. The first, a primary female identity linked to the child's discovery of the vagina, is associated with the image of "l'ombre" (the shadow), while the second, which corresponds to her entry into the Symbolic, is related to the "nom," the Name/No of the Father. Montrelay's examination of mother-daughter relations and of women's relationship to the body explores the notions of pleasure and *jouissance*, and draws parallels between female *jouissance* and writing. Her discussion of women's writing makes frequent references to the work of writers such as Marguerite Duras*, Chantal Chawaf*, and Jeanne Hyvrard*.

Susan Ireland and Patrice J. Proulx

BIBLIOGRAPHY

Primary Text

L'Ombre et le nom: Sur la féminité. Paris: Minuit, 1977.

Secondary Texts

Jardine, Alice A., and Anne Menke, eds. *Shifting Scenes: Interviews on Women, Writing, and Politics in Post-68 France*. New York: Columbia University Press, 1991.
Moi, Toril. *French Feminist Thought: A Reader*. Oxford: Blackwell, 1987.

Moreton de Chabrilland, Elisabeth Céleste Venard de. *See* Mogadar, Céleste Venard.

Motteville, Françoise Bertaut, dame de (1621–1689), was the daughter of a courtier of Louis XIII and a lady-in-waiting of Queen Anne d'Autriche. Like the queen, her mother was of Spanish origin. In 1628 Françoise was also named a lady-in-waiting of the queen because of her ability to speak Spanish. In 1639 Françoise married Nicolas Langlois, seigneur de Motteville, a man already in his eighties. Widowed in 1641, Motteville returned to court in 1643 when Louis XIII died and Anne d'Autriche became regent for her son, Louis XIV. She remained a lady-in-waiting for Anne d'Autriche until Anne's death in 1666, after which she left the court to lead a pious life and to write.

Motteville was friends with some of the leading female figures of the day, including Henriette-Marie de France, the princesse de Montpensier*, the marquise de Sévigné*, and Mme de Lafayette*. Motteville is best known for her *Mémoires pour servir à l'histoire d'Anne d'Autriche*, which she composed after the queen's death from notes she had taken since 1643. In her preface she distinguishes her history from all others, stating that her privileged relationship allows her to include details no one else knows. The *Mémoires* was first published in 1723, but most likely circulated in manuscript form before then.

Motteville also composed a portrait of Anne d'Autriche for Montpensier's *Galerie des portraits*. She had a lengthy and fascinating correspondence with Montpensier around 1660 in which they discussed women's roles in society, concluding that marriage* has given men power over women, so it is best to reject it. They wrote of creating a utopian place in the world where women could be their own mistresses. At the end of her life Motteville composed a number of religious treatises.

Faith E. Beasley

BIBLIOGRAPHY

Secondary Texts

Beasley, Faith E. *Revising Memory: Women's Fiction and Memoirs in Seventeenth-Century France.* New Brunswick, NJ: Rutgers University Press, 1990.
Hipp, Marie-Thérèse. *Mythes et réalités.* Paris: C. Klincksieck, 1976.

Mouvement de Libération des Femmes. The French media coined the term Mouvement de Libération des Femmes (MLF) in 1970. Feminists quickly adopted the acronym, despite the deliberate lack of formal organization that characterized the movement. The first public demonstration by MLF activists was the 1970 attempt to commemorate the unknown soldier's equally unknown wife at the Arc de Triomphe. Throughout the 1970s, some within the MLF successfully pursued issues such as the legalization of abortion*, an issue brought to public attention by the "Manifesto of 343" (signed by Simone de Beauvoir*, Christiane Rochefort*, and others who admitted to having had illegal abortions), and by Gisèle Halimi's* well-publicized defense in the 1972 Bobigny trial. Other groups, like Antoinette Fouque's* Psychanalyse et Politique*, focused on the liberation of women's desires and creativity through psychoanalysis. In 1980 Fouque's group obtained exclusive legal rights to the acronym MLF. This controversial move highlighted the growing discord among feminist factions and, for many marked the end of the movement's productive life.

Miléna Santoro

BIBLIOGRAPHY

Secondary Texts

Albistur, Maïté, and Daniel Armogathe. *Histoire du féminisme français de l'empire napoléonien à nos jours.* Vol. 2. Paris: Des femmes, 1977.
Burke, Carolyn Greenstein. "Report from Paris: Women's Writing and the Women's Movement." *Signs* 3, no. 4 (1978): 843–855.
Delphy, Christine. "Libération des femmes an dix." *Nouvelles Questions Féministes* 7 (February 1980): 3–13.
———. "Les Origines du Mouvement de Libération des Femmes en France." *Nouvelles Questions Féministes* 16–18 (1991): 137–148.
Duchen, Claire. *Feminism in France: From May '68 to Mitterrand.* London: Routledge, 1986.
Fouque, Antoinette. "Entrevue avec Antoinette Fouque." *Gravida* 1 (Fall 1983): 22–42.
———. "Entrevue avec Antoinette Fouque, suite et fin." *Gravida* 2 (Winter 1984): 55–74.
Kaufman-McCall, Dorothy. "Politics of Difference: The Women's Movement in France from May 1968 to Mitterrand." *Signs* 9, no. 2 (1983): 282–293.

"Libération des femmes, année zéro." Special Issue. *Partisans* 54–55 (July-October 1970).

Makward, Christiane P. "Les Editions des femmes: Historique, politique et impact." *Contemporary French Civilization* 5 (Spring 1981): 347–355.

Marks, Elaine, and Isabelle de Courtivron, eds. *New French Feminisms.* New York: Schocken, 1981.

Tristan, Anne, and Annie de Pisan. *Histoires du MLF.* Paris: Calmann-Lévy, 1977.

Murat, Henriette-Julie de Castelnau, comtesse de (1668?–1716). Little is known of Murat's early life, except that she was born to a family with an illustrious military past and that she was married in 1691 to Nicolas de Murat. Several accounts speak of her reputation in court circles as a person of great wit and eloquence. However, she was also involved in at least two high-profile public scandals. The first involved accusations of sexual impropriety, to which Murat responded with her *Mémoires de Madame la Comtesse de*** avant sa retraite, ou la Défense des dames* (1695). Using her case as an example of many women's plight, the narrator recounts her forced marriage* to an older, jealous husband, her flight to a convent*, her request for a separation from her husband, and her attempts to restore her tarnished reputation after her husband's death. The novel* is significant as a depiction of the considerable legal and social obstacles faced by seventeenth-century women who found themselves in unhappy or abusive marriages. In the second scandal, Murat was denounced for lesbianism* and banished by Louis XIV to Loches. During her exile, Murat kept an unpublished "journal" (including letters, poems, and short stories*) that provides valuable insight into the literary activities of a late seventeenth-century salon* woman. Between the first and second scandals, Murat published two collections of fairy tales*, *Nouveaux contes de fées* (1698) and *Histoires sublimes et allégoriques* (1699), and a novel, *Voyage de campagne* (1699). In her fairy tales, Murat displays an unusual predilection for unhappy endings, declaring at the end of "Heureuse peine," for instance, that "a wedding is almost always a sad occasion." Not unlike other seventeenth-century women novelists, Murat points to the transience of love and desire, especially for her heroines. Her *Histoires sublimes et allégoriques* also includes an important dedicatory letter in which Murat valorizes the fairy tales of her fellow women writers, which she clearly distinguishes from the oral storytelling of lower-class women. Murat's novel *Voyage de campagne* portrays a salon-like gathering of young aristocrats in which women, especially, display their wit and intelligence through conversation and experimentation with literary genres (comedy proverbs, ghost stories, and a fairy tale). Murat had numerous contacts with other women writers of her time; she was acquainted with La Force* and Lhéritier*, and was elected to honorary membership in the Accademia dei Ricovrati of Padua.

Lewis C. Seifert

BIBLIOGRAPHY

Primary Text

"Le Prince des feuilles." In *Le Cabinet des fées*. Arles: Picquier Poche, 1994. 2: 61–82.

Mystères. Medieval dramatic compositions that, during the late Middle Ages, could become exceedingly long and complex, including hundreds of roles and requiring many days for public presentation. The taxonomic designation *mystère* is, however, imprecise, often being used along with *miracle* to identify any religious play. Of the texts referring to themselves as *mystères*, most follow biblical sources but embellish them considerably, particularly in the creation of dialogue. Unsurprisingly, the common female figures featured in the plays are Eve, the Virgin, and Mary Magdalene. The last offered ample possibilities for drama, with the emphasis on her conversion balanced by a colorful depiction (in the *Mystère de la Passion d'Arras*, for example) of her earlier sinful life.

Beyond the predictable veneration of Mary and condemnation of Eve, generalizations about the presentation of women are no easier in regard to the *mystères* than in other medieval genres. One of the most remarkable treatments of a female character is offered by the *Mystère d'Adam* (also called the *Jeu d'Adam*). Dating from the third quarter of the twelfth century, this text presents the conversations between the serpent (Diabolus) and Eve, emphasizing the ease with which he deceives her by playing on her curiosity, her gullibility, and her susceptibility to flattery. On the other hand, a play such as the *Sacrifice d'Abraham* is capable of developing an exceedingly moving portrait of Sarah as a complex and admirably forceful woman.

Norris J. Lacy

BIBLIOGRAPHY

Secondary Texts

Craig, Barbara M. *The Evolution of a Mystery Play*. Birmingham, AL: Summa Publications, 1983.
Frank, Grace. *The Medieval French Drama*. Oxford: Clarendon Press, 1954.

Myth. Myth is a fundamental component of the work of many French feminist writers today. Most contemporary writers subscribe to Barthes's view of myths as arbitrary constructs of archetypal belief systems. Writers and theorists such as Julia Kristeva* and Elisabeth Badinter* use myths primarily in a metaphorical sense, treating them as continuously changing paradigms of social and political behavior associated with a particular historical moment. Badinter, for example, looks at myths of motherhood from the eighteenth to the twentieth centuries in *L'Amour en plus* (1980).

Luce Irigaray's* philosophical essays, along with Hélène Cixous's* poetical and philosophical works, emphasize the need to reconnect with certain mythical figures which have been neglected in the predominantly male-oriented conceptualization of myths. Along with authors such as Chantal Chawaf* and Jeanne Hyvrard*, Cixous and Irigaray posit that the creative "feminine" energy they find in such figures as Demeter, Hecate, Medusa, and Promethea is essential to the rediscovery of prerational, preverbal connections which will lead to new perspectives in relationships, art, and society.

In their texts, contemporary French feminist writers use myths as complex, powerful symbolic tools to create new versions of figures representing various types of social behavior: mother-daughter relationships (Demeter-Persephone) and woman to woman encounters (Amazons*), but also father-daughter (Creon-Antigone) and woman-man (Eurydice-Orpheus) mythical paradigms. Michèle Sarde's* *Histoire d'Eurydice pendant la remontée*, for example, uses the well-known literary myth of Orpheus and replaces the central male figure with a predominant female voice. In theory as in fiction, women writers use "feminine" mythical models in order to emphasize the role of literature in transforming inequitable social conditions.

Metka Zupančič

BIBLIOGRAPHY

Primary Texts

Badinter, Elisabeth. *L'Amour en plus*. Paris: Flammarion, 1980.

Chawaf, Chantal. *Le Corps et le verbe*. Paris: Presses de la Renaissance, 1992.

Cixous, Hélène. *Entre l'écriture*. Paris: Editions des Femmes, 1986.

Hyvrard, Jeanne. *La Pensée corps*. Paris: Editions des Femmes, 1989.

Sarde, Michèle. *Histoire d'Eurydice pendant la remontée*. Paris: Seuil, 1991.

Secondary Texts

Barthes, Roland. *Mythologies*. Paris: Seuil, 1970.

Garcia, Irma. *Promenade familière, I, II*. Paris: Editions des Femmes, 1981.

Irigaray, Luce. *Je, tu, nous*. Paris: Grasset, 1990.

Kristeva, Julia. "Hérétique de l'armour." *Tel Quel* 74 (Winter 1977): 30–49.

Larrington, Carolyne, ed. *The Feminist Companion to Mythology*. London: Pandora Press, 1992.

Makaryk, Irene, ed. *Encyclopedia of Contemporary Literary Theory*. Toronto: University of Toronto Press, 1993.

Walker, Barbara. *Women's Encyclopedia of Myths and Secrets*. New York: Harper-Collins, 1983.

N

Names and pseudonyms. The altering of a given proper name, whether by an external entity or circumstance, or by the author herself, carries with it significant ideological ramifications. On the one hand, societal events such as marriage* and adoption often provoke the changing of a name, which in these instances is no more than an onomastic shift preserving patriarchal continuity. Moreover, literary history sometimes participates in this gesture, as a number of women writers are primarily known by their married titles (Madame de Sévigné*, Madame de Lafayette*, Madame de Staël*, the Comtesse de Ségur*, etc.). On the other hand, women authors have frequently changed their names when signing a literary text, a gesture that ideologically outlines the onomastic appropriation of an origin and subsequent reinvention of a public self in the pseudonym. Beyond the simple invention of a pen name whose form is determined according to its difference to the existing name, other kinds of women writers' pseudonyms exist. Some women, often for practical purposes, have sought to cloak their gender in a male pseudonym (George Sand*, Marc de Montifaut, etc.). Another strategy women have employed has been to invent a single name by which they are known (Rachilde*, Gyp*, etc.), a designation whose willful ambiguity conflates first and surnames and effectively subverts the referentiality of the proper noun in sociolinguistic hierarchies. Within a literary text, changed names can have significant import. In Colette's* *Chéri*, the courtesan Léonie Vallon has rendered herself aristocratic by renaming herself Léa de Lonval, and her lover Alfred Peloux infantile by his nickname. The mutilated name of the main character of Marguerite Duras's* *Le Ravissement de Lol V. Stein* (1964) reflects a consciousness ostensibly mutilated by the world. The invented or altered name, then, often signifies a paratextual or textual disruption of the social and ideological constitution of language.

Leonard R. Koos

BIBLIOGRAPHY

Secondary Texts

Laugaa, Maurice. *La Pensée du pseudonyme*. Paris: Presses Universitaires de France, 1986.

Taylor, Archer, and Frederic J. Mosher. *The Bibliographical History of Anonyma and Pseudonyma*. Chicago: Chicago University Press, 1951.

Napoleonic Code. The Code civil des Français, with its 2,281 articles grouped in thirty-six laws, was promulgated on March 21, 1804. Although internationally acclaimed as a model of the modern legal system which abolished the feudal hierarchical order, the Code became the grantor of equality for men only. In direct opposition to the experiences of the French Revolution*, women, no longer recognized as *citoyennes*, were explicitly expelled from the public sphere and confined to domesticity. A team of jurists—entrusted with the stabilization of the Napoleonic state—legitimized this exclusion through a syllogistic interpretation of "nature" differently defined for each sex. Women, believed to be weaker and unruly, as opposed to physically stronger men, seemed to be in need of surveillance.

The shift from equality to difference is most visible in the provisions on marital regimes. Limited to her role of wife/childbearer who "owes obedience to her husband," a woman is obliged to live with her husband and to "follow him wherever he judges it appropriate to live" (213, 214). Reduced to the status of a legal minor, she is forbidden to buy, sell, sign contracts, have identity papers or a bank account, or exercise any independent occupation, without the authorization of the husband whose *puissance maritale* can further control her acquaintances and correspondence (215–219). She loses property rights recognized by the French Revolution as a fundamental value in promoting social and financial emancipation. She is not allowed to acquire an estate or inherit without the written consent of the husband, who as chief administrator of the community (1421) can alienate the funds without her consent (1428). To protect the matrimonial contract for men, the Code makes divorce* more difficult and suppresses divorces for incompatibility granted to many women under the law of 1792 (278). Striking double standards are maintained in the case of infidelity. While the adulterous wife may be sent to prison or a house of correction for a period of three months to two years (298), the husband's extramarital affairs can be subject to a nominal monetary fine only if he entertains a mistress in his matrimonial home (230).

The Napoleonic law finds mothers unfit to supervise their own children and grants the father alone parental authority during the marriage* (373, 389). Furthermore, to secure the peace of the patriarchal family*, the Code frees men from responsibility for out-of-wedlock children, and fixes all burden upon the mother, who is legally forbidden to determine the paternity of the child (340).

The provisions concerning women's sexuality and reproduction further curtail women's choices by making them criminally responsible for infanticide and abortion* (300, 302, 317).

Still in force, the Code incapacitated women for more than a century and a half. Some of the most oppressive features of the family law were abrogated in the 1960s and 1970s.

Karyna Szmurlo

BIBLIOGRAPHY

Arnaud, André-Jean. *Essai d'analyse structurale du Code civil français: La Règle du jeu dans la paix bourgeoise*. Paris: Librairie générale de droit et de jurisprudence, 1973.

Arnau-Duc, Nicole. "Women Entrapped: From Public Non-existence to Private Protection." In *Women's Rights and the Rights of Man*. Ed. A. J. Arnaud and E. Kingdom. Aberdeen: Aberdeen University Press, 1990. 9–24.

Fuchs, Rachel G. "Public Power and Women's Bodies: Abortion, Infanticide, and the Penal Code in the Nineteenth Century." *Proceedings of the Annual Meeting of the Western Society for French History* 18 (1991): 567–577.

Furet, François, and Mona Ozouf, eds. *A Critical Dictionary of the French Revolution*. Trans. Arthur Goldhammer. Cambridge, MA: Belknap Press of Harvard University Press, 1989. 440–448.

Pope Corrado, Barbara. "Revolution and Retreat: Upper-Class French Women after 1789." In *Women, War and Revolution*. Ed. Carol R. Berkin and Clara M. Lovett. New York: Holmes and Meier, 1980. 215–236.

Rogers, Adrienne. "Women and the Law." In *French Women and the Age of Enlightenment*. Ed. Samia I. Spencer. Bloomington: Indiana University Press, 1984. 33–48.

Sagnac, P. *La Legislation civile de la Révolution française (1798–1804)*. Paris: Hachette, 1898.

Vogel, Ursula. "Whose Property? The Double Standard of Adultery in Nineteenth-Century Law." In *Regulating Womanhood*. Ed. Carol Smart. New York: Routledge, 1992. 147–219.

Naturalism (1860–1893). The movement was partly inspired by Gustave Flaubert, Claude Bernard, and the Goncourt brothers' influential novel* *Germinie Lacerteux*. Emile Zola and his followers, known as the Médan group, believed novels should reflect reality and follow a scientific methodology. Zola's monumental opus, *Les Rougon-Macquart, Histoire naturelle et sociale d'une famille sous le Second Empire*, is thus the study of heredity and its effect on a family*.

Naturalist writings about the female body abound, in large measure due to the degree of dependence by Zola on medical sources. To study the woman in Naturalism in a feminist context requires that particular attention be paid to woman's generative organs, in particular her uterus, and the issue of blood, long associated with sexual taboos. For instance, images of bleeding uteruses abound in Naturalist writings, from Zola's "Voreux" in *Germinal* to Rachilde's* slaughterhouse in *La Marquise de Sade*. References to menstruation* can appear as detailed metaphors (where the inessential detail covers up a repressed image of menstrual blood), as displaced synecdoches (bodily fragments or vestitular fragments that point to menstruation), as metamorphosed feminine images of the "monstrous" (such as the vampire woman with blood on her lips, or the anemic who drinks animal blood), and as associated with the pathological and fetishistic objects of male desire for the taboo linked with feminine sexuality.

Sylvie L. F. Richards

BIBLIOGRAPHY

Primary Texts

Aurevilly, Barbey d'. *Oeuvres romanesques complètes*. 2 vols. Paris: Editions de la Pléiade, 1966.
Huysmans, J. K. *Oeuvres complètes*. Geneva: Slatkine, 1972.
Maupassant, Guy de. *Contes et nouvelles*. Paris: Editions de la Pléiade, 1974.
Rachilde. *Le Grand Saigneur*. Paris: Flammarion, 1922.
———. *La Marquise de Sade*. Paris: Mercure de France, 1887.
Zola, Emile. *Les Rougon-Macquart*. Paris: Edition de la Pléiade, 1960–1967.

Secondary Texts

Bernheimer, Charles. "Huysmans: Writing against (Female) Nature." *Poetics Today* 6 (1985): 311–324.
Colatrella, Carol. "Representing Liberty: Revolution, Sexuality and Science in Michelet's Histories and Zola's Fictions." *Nineteenth-Century French Studies* 20 (1991–1992): 27–43.
Gilman, Sander. "Black Bodies, White Bodies: Toward an Iconography of Female Sexuality in Late Nineteenth-Century Art, Medicine and Literature." *Critical Inquiry* 12 (1985): 204–242.
Lukacher, Maryline. *Maternal Fictions: Stendhal, Sand, Rachilde and Bataille*. Durham: Duke University Press, 1994.
Schor, Naomi. *Reading in Detail: Aesthetics and the Feminine*. New York: Methuen, 1987.
Suleiman, Susan Rubin. "Rewriting the Body: The Politics and Poetics of Female Eroticism." *Poetics Today* 6 (1985): 43–65.

Navarre, Marguerite de (1492–1549). Queen of Navarre, poet, playwright, author of novellas. Living at the court of her brother, King François I, Marguerite spent much of her life in the public eye. At the same time, she lived an intensely private spiritual life that found expression in her writings, most of which were published posthumously. Religion was at the center of both her public and private life. Although she remained outwardly obedient to the Church of Rome, she was responsive to Luther's call for reform and supported attempts to simplify and revitalize the Gallican Church.

She wrote a great deal of poetry*, most of which expresses the travail of the Christian wayfarer who, seeking to follow Christ, moves from anguished entanglement in the material and carnal world to rapturous pleasure in contemplation of the spiritual world attainable by faith and faith alone (the *sola fides* of early Reformers), a world in which the humble believer will be folded back into the Godhead.

Marguerite's early works remained in manuscript until they were rediscovered by scholars in the late nineteenth century and twentieth century. During her lifetime, three volumes were published: *Le Miroir de l'âme pécheresse* (1531), reprinted in a slightly expanded version in 1533; *Marguerites de la Marguerite des princesses* (1547); and *Suyte des marguerites* (1547). The 1533 edition of the *Miroir* contained an early poem, *Dialogue en forme de vision nocturne*, in which Marguerite raised controversial religious matters such as grace and free will. The Sorbonne, the center of religious orthodoxy, condemned the work. The condemnation was retracted, however, at the insistence of François I. Several of her major poems were not published until recent times: *La Navire*, a long allegorical text of astonishing metrical complexity, is both a tribute to François and a meditation on the meaning of a Christian life; and *Les Prisons*, which, in imitation of Dante's *Divine Comedy*, is divided into three books, traces the journey of the narrator through various "prisons" in which he was held captive because of his love for the things of this world. Eventually he learns that he must turn his back on the world if he hopes to follow Christ.

Marguerite also wrote plays. Several of them deal with biblical subjects such as the birth of Christ, the visit of the three wise men, the flight into Egypt, and the massacre of the Innocents. Others are close to the medieval tradition of the morality play and dramatize confrontations between figures that incarnate principles of evangelical Christianity* and those that incarnate bigotry, ignorance, and idolatry. At least some of the plays were probably performed by the ladies at the court.

Until recently, Marguerite was best known for her collection of novellas inspired by Boccaccio's *Decameron*. Left unfinished at the time of her death, the work was partially published in 1558 under the title *Histoires des amans fortunez*. A corrected version of seventy-two novellas was published in 1559 under the title *Heptaméron*. Ten aristocratic travelers, five men and five women, are stranded for ten days in a monastery. While waiting for a bridge to be built, they tell each other stories. After each story has been told, they discuss it, often in considerable detail. An intricately designed work, the *Heptaméron* presents a remarkable picture of courtly life in which aristocratic ideals and mores are constantly at odds with the ideals of evangelical Christianity. The text can be read on many different levels, one being that of a case book illuminating the infinite number of ways in which men and women relate to each other. Though the *Heptaméron* is not a feminist tract, Marguerite's sympathetic treatment of women has attracted the attention of readers in search of early modern works that present women as equals of men in intelligence and education* and that, further, examine the ways in which women are molded and shaped by powerful societal forces and patriarchal values.

Robert D. Cottrell

BIBLIOGRAPHY

Primary Texts

Marguerites de la Marguerite des princesses, très illustre Royne de Navarre and *Suyte des marguerites*. 2 vols. Lyons: J. de Tournes, 1547. Facsimile reprint, Intro. Ruth Thomas. New York: S. R. Publishers; Johnson Reprint, Mouton, 1970.
Suyte des Marguerites de la marguerite des princesses. Lyons, 1547. Intro. Ruth Thomas. The Hague: S. R. Publishers, 1970.
La Navire, ou Consolation du Roi François I à sa soeur Marguerite. Ed. Robert Marichal. Paris: Champion, 1956.
Petit Oeuvre dévot et contemplatif. Ed. Hans Sckommodau. Frankfurt am Main: V. Klostermann, 1960.
L'Heptaméron. Ed. Michel François. Paris: Garnier, 1963.
Chansons spirituelles. Ed. B. Dottin. Geneva: Droz, 1971.
La Coche. Ed. Robert Marichal. Geneva: Droz, 1971.
Les Prisons. Ed. S. Glasson. Geneva: Droz, 1978.
Théâtre profane. Ed. Verdun L. Saulnier. Geneva: Droz, 1978.
Dialogue en forme de vision nocturne. Ed. Renja Salminen. Helsinki: Suomalainen Tiedeakatemia, 1985.

Secondary Texts

Cottrell, R. D. *The Grammar of Silence: A Reading of Marguerite de Navarre's Poetry*. Washington, DC: Catholic University of America Press, 1986.
Tetel, Marcel. *Marguerite de Navarre's "Heptameron": Themes, Language, and Structure*. Durham, NC: Duke University Press, 1973.

Ndiaye, Marie (1967–). Born in France to a French mother and a Senegalese father, Ndiaye is often associated with the new generation of Minuit writers of the 1980s and 1990s. Ndiaye's male and female characters are marginalized in their relationships with their families, their friends, and a bureaucratic society. The novel* *En Famille*, with its central theme of displacement and alienation, depicts a young girl's desperate search to find her place in a family* that has rejected her because of her racial difference. Ndiaye's use of the fantastic in many of her texts is reinforced by mythological allusions, particularly in relation to female characters—Leda in *En Famille* and the Devil in *La Femme changée en bûche*. In her latest novel, *La Sorcière*, Ndiaye resituates the traditional figure of the witch in a modern suburban setting.

Martine Motard-Noar

BIBLIOGRAPHY

Primary Texts

Quant au riche avenir. Paris: Minuit, 1985.
Comédie classique. Paris: P.O.L., 1987.
La Femme changée en bûche. Paris: Minuit, 1989.
En Famille. Paris: Minuit, 1990.

Un Temps de saison. Paris: Minuit, 1994.
La Sorcière. Paris: Minuit, 1996.

Necker, Suzanne Curchod (1739–1794). Born into a Swiss Protestant family, Suzanne Curchod received an excellent humanist education*. In her mid-twenties she went to Paris, where she met and married Swiss banker Jacques Necker, who eventually became finance minister under Louis XVI. The Neckers were known as one of the most devoted couples of their time.

Suzanne Necker established an influential salon*, frequented by such intellectuals as Diderot, Grimm, d'Alembert, and Buffon. While maintaining cordial friendships with the freethinking philosophes, she remained faithful to her Protestant beliefs; she was both ridiculed and admired for her rigid personality and integrity of character. She worked among the poor, and organized a hospital that became a model in its care for indigent patients.

Little of her writing was published during her lifetime. Her *Réflexions sur le divorce* appeared posthumously in 1794. This essay argued that the very possibility of divorce* (legalized in France in 1792) created a climate of moral instability that threatened all sense of family* commitment; she was adamantly opposed to it. After her death, Jacques Necker published five volumes of her personal reflections, entitled *Mélanges*.

Her view of woman's place is complex. She maintained that women's particular aptitude was that of living in and for others, rather than seeking fame for themselves. Yet she cultivated her own influence as a *salonnière* and labored constantly to make her own mind more retentive and more powerful. She deplored women's lack of mental discipline, which she attributed to nature, not to upbringing. If women have not excelled, she said, it is because they have exhausted their energy in overcoming obstacles. She worked devotedly to give her brilliant daughter Germaine, the future Madame de Staël*, the serious education that most women lacked.

Janet Whatley

BIBLIOGRAPHY

Primary Texts

Hospice de charité. Paris: Imprimerie Royale, 1780.
Des inhumations précipitées. Paris: Imprimerie Royale, 1790.
Réflexions sur le divorce. Lausanne: Durand-Ravanel, 1794.
Mélanges extraits des manuscrits de Mme Necker. Ed. Jacques Necker. Paris: Pougens, 1798.
Nouveaux Mélanges extraits des manuscrits de Mme Necker. Ed. Jacques Necker. Paris: Pougens, 1801.

Secondary Texts

Andlau, Béatrix, comtesse d'. *La Jeunesse de Mme de Staël*. Geneva: Droz, 1970.
Balayé, Simone. *Madame de Staël: Lumières et liberté*. Paris: Klincksieck, 1979.
Corbaz, André. *Mme Necker, humble Vaudoise et grande dame*. Lausanne: Payot, 1945.

Hannin, Valérie. ''Une Ambition de femme au siècle des Lumières: Le Cas de Madame Necker.'' *Cahiers staëliens* 36 (1985): 5–29.

Haussonville, Gabriel Paul Othenin de Cléron, comte d'. *Le Salon de Madame Necker d'après des documents tirés des archives de Coppet.* Geneva: Slatkine Reprints, 1970.

Necker de Saussure, Albertine. *Notice sur le caractère et les écrits de Madame de Staël. Oeuvres complètes de Madame la baronne de Staël.* Vol. 1. Paris: Treuttel et Würtz, 1820.

Soumoy-Thibert, Geneviève. ''Les Idées de Madame Necker.'' *Dix-huitième Siècle* 21 (1989): 357–368.

Nemours, Marie d'Orléans-Longueville, duchesse de (1625–1707). Cousin of the Bourbons and related to most of the European royal families, heiress to an immense fortune, she received an exceptional education* thanks to the governess her mother gave her, Catherine Arnauld. She learned not just the arts but Latin, jurisprudence, how to administer her fortune, and how to govern her subjects. She virtually founded independent journalism by commissioning the gazetteer Loret to bring her weekly news (in burlesque verse) omitted from Renaudot's official *Gazette*. During the Fronde* she maintained an independent stance, refusing to follow her imperious stepmother, the duchesse de Longueville. She was eager to marry James, Duke of York, and offer her fortune to her exiled Stuart cousins, but Mazarin thwarted the match and married her to Henri de Savoie, duc de Nemours (1657). Soon a childless widow, she refused to remarry and join the court at Versailles. Instead, opening her residences to artists and writers, she befriended unfortunate women of letters, among them the Comtesse de la Suze* and Mme de Villedieu*, who addressed the *Mémoires de la vie d'Henriette-Sylvie de Molière* to her extraordinary patroness. When the Condés, invoking the Salic law*, attempted to dispossess her and Louis XIV sought to impose his foreign policies on her sovereign principality of Neuchâtel, she won over public opinion by the brilliant letters she published in European newspapers. Around 1686–1687 she composed her memoirs* of the Fronde years, which were published posthumously in 1709 by her protégée, Mlle L'Héritier*. Unlike other memorialists, she deliberately avoids personal revelations and, following the historian Mézeray, writes an objective, lucid account of the events and personalities. Though considered eccentric, she was admired for her great intelligence, strength of character, nonconformism, and generosity.

Gabrielle Verdier

BIBLIOGRAPHY

Primary Text

Mémoires de Marie d'Orléans, Duchesse de Nemours. Ed. Micheline Cuénin. Paris: Mercure de France, 1990.

Neo-Malthusianism. Thomas Malthus (1766–1834), a British pastor and liberal economist, proposed to fight poverty by eliminating aid to the poor, and encouraging them to marry late and have fewer children. Soon, radical British and American scholars stretched his ideas and advocated the use of contraception, thus creating a new movement known as neo-Malthusianism.

Paul Robin (1837–1912), a militant revolutionary with ties to Bakounine and Marx, launched the neo-Malthusian movement in France. Two slogans clearly summarized Robin's revolutionary orientation. The first, "No more pleasure fodder, labor fodder, or canon fodder!," urged the proletariat to stop providing prostitutes, laborers, and soldiers to the bourgeoisie. The second, aimed at women, urged them to go on a "womb strike."

Until 1914 the movement grew steadily in France, thanks to the support of, among others, radical feminists such as Gabrielle Petit, Nelly Roussel*, and Madeleine Pelletier*. However, in 1920 the rising support for increased fecundity resulted in the passing of a law banning information on contraception and abortion*. Nevertheless, neo-Malthusians, gathered around Eugène Humbert (Paul Robin's disciple since 1902) and his wife, Jeanne, continued their struggle until World War II*.

After 1956 the French Movement for Family Planning adopted Margaret Sanger's approach, and promoted birth control* as a means to ensure family* happiness.

Francis Ronsin and Samia I. Spencer

BIBLIOGRAPHY

Girioud, Gabriel. *Paul Robin*. Paris: Editions Mignolet et Storz, 1937.
Guerrand, Roger Henri. *La Libre Maternité*. Paris: Casterman, 1971.
Himes, Norman. *Medical History of Contraception*. New York: Schocken Books, 1936.
Le Bras, Hervé. *Marianne et les lapins*. Paris: Olivier Orban, 1991.
McLaren, Angus. *Sexuality and Social Order: The Debate over the Fertility of Women and Workers in France, 1770–1920*. New York: Holmes and Meier, 1983.
Mossuz-Lavau, Janine. *Les Lois de l'amour*. Paris: Editions Payot, 1991.
Pelletier, Madeleine. *L'Emancipation sexuelle de la femme*. Paris: Giard et Brière, 1912.
Roling, Hugo, and Francis Ronsin. *Catalogue d'exposition: Le néo-malthusianisme en France et aux Pays-Bas*. Amsterdam: Internationaal Instituut voor Sociale Geshiedenis, 1995.
Ronsin, Francis. *La Grève des ventres. Propagande néo-malthusienne et baisse de la natalité en France, 19e–20e siècles*. Paris: Aubier, 1980.
Roussel, Nelly. *Quelques Lances rompues pour nos libertés*. Paris: Giard et Brière, 1912.

Niboyet, Eugénie (1796–1883). Feminist journalist, writer, and social reformer. Of Swiss Protestant origin, Eugénie Mouchon married Paul-Louis Niboyet, by whom she had a son, Paulin, in 1823. She eventually went to Paris and entered the Saint-Simonian hierarchy around 1830. She later separated from the movement and in 1833 launched her own Lyons-based weekly paper, the *Conseiller des femmes*. Inspired by Fanny Richomme's *Journal des femmes*, Niboyet sought to publish women's writing and to educate her readers, but she was also concerned with working-class women. She founded an "Athenée des femmes" (an educational center dedicated to reading and discussion) to foster solidarity among all women and to educate them in enlightened motherhood. The mother's civilizing influence was essential to Niboyet's vision of social regeneration. The *Conseiller* gave way to the more literary *Mosaïque lyonnaise*. When this failed, Niboyet returned to Paris, where she contributed to *Le Citateur féminin, La Gazette des femmes*, and *La Mère-institutrice*. Active in the Society for Christian Morality, Niboyet wrote on the abolition of the death penalty, education for the blind, and prison reform. In 1844 she launched *La Paix des deux mondes*, a weekly devoted to "universal fraternity" and "social interests." During the mid-1840s, Niboyet published some literary work but is best known as director of the first French feminist daily newspaper, *La Voix des femmes*, in 1848. This paper sparked controversy by nominating George Sand* for candidacy in the spring legislative elections following the February 1848 revolution. Jeanne Deroin*, Desirée Gay, and Niboyet formed the Société des Voix des Femmes and organized public meetings. Internal disagreement and government crackdown on the press led to the demise of the paper. Debt-ridden, Niboyet retreated to relative obscurity in the following years, writing articles under the pseudonym Saint-Aignan and seeking to regain the literary pension awarded her in 1839 and withdrawn in 1848. *Le Vrai Livre des femmes*, written in response to the Countess Dash's *Livre des femmes*, offers Niboyet's noticeably more conservative opinion on women's place in greed-ridden society. In the final, autobiographical chapter Niboyet describes 1848 as the most painful period of her life. Later, Niboyet directed yet another periodical, *Le Journal pour toutes*, for several years during the Second Empire. After this, she sent letters to Richer's *Le Droit des femmes* and to the government on behalf of families of deported Communards. Her name appears on a guest roster of the International Congress for the Rights of Woman in Paris in 1878.

Cheryl A. Morgan

BIBLIOGRAPHY

Primary Texts

Conseiller des femmes (Ed., 1833–1834).
La Mosaïque lyonnaise (Ed., 1834–1835).
La Paix des deux mondes (Ed., 1844–1845).
La Voix des femmes (Ed., March 20–June 20, 1848).
Le Vrai Livre des femmes. Paris: E. Dentu, 1863.
Le Journal pour toutes (Ed., 1864–1867).

Secondary Texts

Czyba, Lucette. "L'Oeuvre lyonnaise d'une ancienne Saint-Simonienne: *Le Conseiller des femmes* (1833–34) d'Eugénie Niboyet." In *Regards sur le Saint-Simonisme et les Saint-Simoniens*. Sous la direction de J. R. Derre. Lyons: Presses Universitaires de Lyon, 1986. 103–139.
Riot-Sarcey, Michèle. *La Démocratie à l'épreuve des femmes: Trois Figures critiques du pouvoir, 1830–1848*. Paris: Albin Michel, 1994.

————. "Histoire et autobiographie: *Le Vrai Livre des femmes* d'Eugénie Niboyet." *Romantisme* 17, no. 56 (1987): 59–68.

Rude, Fernand. "Eugénie Niboyet." In *Un Fabuleux Destin: Flora Tristan.* Dijon: Presse Universitaire de Dijon, 1985. 120–143.

Strumingher, Laura. "The Struggle for Unity among Parisian Women: The *Voix des femmes*, March–June 1848." *History of European Ideas* 11 (1989): 273–285.

Noailles, Anna de (1876–1933). Poet, novelist, and one of the most celebrated literary personalities of her day, she was born Princesse Anna-Elisabeth de Brancovan, of Romanian and Greek parents. Noailles grew up in the fashionable circles of Paris and on the family's country estate, where her love for nature inspired her first verses. After her marriage* to the Comte de Noailles, she published her first volume of poetry*, which instantly became a bestseller. Noailles was a prolific writer who produced ten volumes of poetry, four novels*, a biography, and several collections of short stories*. Her many official honors include a seat in the Belgian Academy, the first given to a woman. She was also the first woman named Commander of the Legion of Honor. Noailles's writing appealed to the general public as well as to the literary elite, who praised her intense sensual lyricism influenced by the Romantics. Her poetry reflects her hypersensitive nature in its exuberant celebration of love, life, nature, and especially the senses, but also reveals a darker side, as she contemplates her mortality. Critics of Noailles attributed her popularity to snob appeal and labeled her poetry characteristically "feminine" because it is undisciplined, narcissistic, and inspired. Indeed, she played into this negative stereotype by flouting conventional versification as too restrictive for her inspired lyricism. Although the feminine label trivializes Noailles's writing, her work is currently poised for revival as critics reassess her impact on the writers of her generation and the unconventional frankness with which she expresses her passionate nature.

Tama Lea Engelking

BIBLIOGRAPHY

Primary Texts

Le Coeur innombrable. Paris: Calmann-Lévy, 1901.
La Nouvelle Espérance. Paris: Calmann-Lévy, 1904.
Le Visage émerveillé. Paris: Calmann-Lévy, 1904.
Les Forces eternelles. Paris: A. Fayard, 1921.
Le Livre de ma vie. Paris: Mercure de France, 1976.
Choix de poésie. Intro. Jean Rostand. Paris: Bernard Grasset, 1979.

Secondary Texts

Engelking, Tama Lea. "Anna de Noailles." In *French Women Writers: A Bio-Bibliographical Source Book.* Ed. Eva Martin Sartori and Dorothy Wynne Zimmerman. Westport, CT: Greenwood Press, 191. 335–345.

Higonnet-Dugua, Elisabeth. *Anna de Noailles, coeur innombrable: Biographie-Correspondance.* Paris: Michel de Maule, 1989.

Mignot-Ogliastri, Claude. *Anna de Noailles.* Paris: Méridiens Klincksieck, 1986.

Waelti-Walters, Jennifer. *Feminist Novelists of the Belle Epoque: Love as a Lifestyle.* Bloomington: Indiana University Press, 1990.

Nouveau Roman. The *Nouveau Roman* or New Novel, which appeared in France in the 1950s, was the name given to the works written by a group of predominantly male writers including Michel Butor, Robert Pinget, Alain Robbe-Grillet, Jean Ricardou, Nathalie Sarraute*, and Claude Simon. The *Nouveaux Romanciers* rejected the conventions of the traditional realist novel (embodied by Balzac) as well as the politically committed *roman à thèse* (Sartrean *engagement*, for example). They replaced the linear plots, well-rounded characters, and psychological analysis of the traditional novel* with temporal discontinuity, fragmented characters, shifting points of view, and multiple, contradictory meanings. Their writing is further characterized by its intertextuality, reflexivity, and use of ludic textual structures. Many of these issues are discussed in such texts as Sarraute's *L'Ere du soupçon* (1953), Robbe-Grillet's *Pour un Nouveau Roman* (1963), and Ricardou's *Problèmes du Nouveau Roman* (1967).

Sarraute's texts, which abandon traditional narrative structures and their exploration of unspoken emotions, bear witness to her pioneering role in the *Nouveau Roman*. In addition to her theoretical essays in *L'Ere du soupçon*, she wrote several works in the *Nouveau Roman* style, including *Tropismes* (1939), *Le Planétarium* (1959), and *Entre la vie et la mort* (1968). Marguerite Duras*, who uses similar experimental structures and fragmented characters to express the unconscious, is often associated with the *Nouveau Roman*, although she distanced herself from it. Through their search for original forms of expression, the *Nouveaux Romanciers* opened up new possibilities for both male and female writers.

Susan Ireland and Patrice J. Proulx

BIBLIOGRAPHY

Primary Texts

Sarraute, Nathalie. *Entre la vie et la mort.* Paris: Gallimard, 1968.
———. *Le Planétarium.* Paris: Gallimard, 1959.
———. *Tropismes.* Paris: Denoël, 1939.

Secondary Texts

Briton, Celia. *The Nouveau Roman.* New York: St. Martin's Press, 1992.
Butor, Michel. *Essai sur "Les Essais."* Paris: Gallimard, 1968.
Janvier, Ludovic. *Une Parole exigeante: Le Nouveau Roman.* Paris: Minuit, 1964.
Oppenheim, Lois, ed. *Three Decades of the French New Novel.* Urbana-Champaign: University of Illinois Press, 1986.
Ricardou, Jean. *Pour une théorie du Nouveau Roman.* Paris: Seuil, 1971.
———. *Problèmes du Nouveau Roman.* Paris: Seuil, 1967.
Ricardou, Jean, and Françoise van Rossum-Guyon, eds. *Nouveau Roman: Hier, aujourd'hui.* Paris: Union Générale d'Editions, 1972.
Robbe-Grillet, Alain. *Pour un Nouveau Roman.* Paris: Minuit, 1963.
Sarraute, Nathalie. *L'Ere du soupçon.* Paris: Gallimard, 1953.

Novel. The novel has been a genre of special interest to women as readers; and as writers, women have made significant contributions to its development. There are several reasons for this relationship: the novel has had more flexible rules than other genres, allowing more experimentation than fixed forms such as epic poetry* or tragic drama. And certain genres such as the two just mentioned have been considered "noble" and therefore inaccessible to women. Female writers have felt more free to write novels, diaries, and letters than poetry or theater*. Nevertheless, many female novelists have published their work anonymously or under a male name; others have refrained from publishing* their work at all.

The novel as a genre has its origins in the Latin and Greek works of the first and second centuries. These works, called *romances*, have complex plots and stock characters. Following this tradition, the medieval French *roman* was born. Most of the medieval French works called *romans* are in verse like epic poems, and recount legendary adventures of heroes. In the twelfth century, the *lais* appeared, which are attributed to Marie de France*. She is believed to have been an abbess born in France but living in England. The *lais* are short forms in verse which tell a story. Compared to the medieval *romans*, they give more place to female characters, love plots, and psychological analysis. Many of the *lais* include Celtic material surrounding the Arthurian legends which were later used by Chrétien de Troyes in his famous *romans*.

In 1538 Hélisenne de Crenne* wrote *Les Angoysses douloureuses qui procedent d'amours*, called the first "sentimental novel" in France. It follows the Greco-Latin romance traditions but tells the story of a wife who is abused by her husband. Later in the sixteenth century, Marguerite de Navarre*, the sister of King François I, wrote *L'Heptaméron*, a collection of tales with prologues and discussions following the patterns of Boccaccio's *Decameron*. Marguerite introduces an expanded frame story and gives the genre new depth and significance by using the tales and portraits of the storytellers to explore her definition of platonic love and to expound her mystical evangelical views on life and the nature of truth. In 1594 Marie Le Jars de Gournay*, Michel de Montaigne's "adopted daughter," published *Le Proumenoir de M. de Montaigne*, including a new version of a tale by Taillemont which serves as a frame for Gournay's moral lessons to women about the faithlessness of men.

In the seventeenth century, French women had a significancet impact on the genre of the novel. At the beginning of the century, social gatherings devoted to literary and intellectual discussions at the homes of prominent women helped to encourage new ideas. These salons* included males as well as females and served to supplement the often deficient education* of females. The women, who were often called *précieuses*, have been satirized as pretentious and overly meticulous by male writers of the seventeenth century. However, their contributions to literature are beginning to be recognized. Madeleine de Scudéry*, who published novels under her brother Georges's name, wrote *Artamène ou le Grand Cyrus* (1648–1653) and *Clélie, histoire romaine* (1654–1660). These ten-volume novels were best-sellers and outstanding examples of the heroic novel.

Extremely complex, with many subplots, these works use ancient history as a backdrop for portraits of contemporaries and for the analysis of amorous feelings and conduct. They develop a code of spiritual love called *galanterie*. But tastes changed and moved away from these long novels. In the latter half of the century, shorter novels using psychological analysis and recent history as a frame became popular. Madame de Lafayette's* celebrated *La Princesse de Clèves*, which was published anonymously in 1678, is the model for this genre and is considered the first modern French novel. This historical novel was carefully researched and portrays many actual people; however, the heroine is a fictional character. The novel caused great controversy because of a scene in which the heroine confesses to her husband that she loves another man although she has not been unfaithful. This work, like those of Madeleine de Scudéry, teaches women that love will make them unhappy. This was also the moral of Marie-Catherine de Villedieu's* *Les Désordres de l'amour* (1675), which has some resemblances to Lafayette's work.

In the eighteenth century women became associated with fairy stories, memoirs*, and letters. Marie-Catherine d'Aulnoy* and Marie Leprince de Beaumont* are the most famous of the fairy tale* writers. They and others used magical elements (inherited from the *lais* of Marie de France) and unlikely plots to empower their heroines and to imagine a world where women would not be cloistered and denied an education. Many of the authors of fairy tales also wrote memoirs in a more realistic genre to show the everyday reality of women's lives. The most famous of these pseudo-memoirs is Louise d'Epinay's* *Histoire de Madame de Montbrillant* (1762). In this work she portrays, under fictitious names*, many of the most famous people of her time, giving an especially negative image of Jean-Jacques Rousseau.

The (real) letters of Marie de Sévigné* were published posthumously in 1725. After their success, epistolary novels became popular; a majority of them were written by women. Françoise de Graffigny* wrote *Lettres d'une Péruvienne*, published anonymously in 1747, which tells the story of a Peruvian princess who is separated from her fiancé and taken to France. This novel, which is both sentimental and philosophic, uses the princess as a naive observer to criticize French society. After she learns to speak French and to express her thoughts, she refuses to marry the Frenchman who had been kind to her. This outcome violates novelistic conventions but corresponds to her attainment of knowledge and a sense of her own value.

Isabelle de Charrière*, a Dutch woman living in Switzerland and writing in French, used epistolary novels such as *Lettres écrites de Lausanne* (1785–1787) to protest women's boring and tedious lives, which make marriage* the prime preoccupation for mothers as well as daughters. It was in this period that novels (and letters and memoirs) became known as ''feminine'' literature. Feminine ''sensibility'' was seen as the opposite of masculine rationality. Best-selling authors of this period include Sophie Cottin* and Marie-Jeanne Riccoboni*.

The principal theorist for the French Romantic movement, Germaine de

Staël*, wrote two novels. *Delphine* (1802) was the first great novel to use a sentimental plot as a pretext for the exposition of revolutionary ideas. *Corinne ou l'Italie* (1807) showed that artistic conquests outlast military ones. Both novels contain extraordinary women who are outcasts because of their genius*. Staël's work caused her to be exiled by Napoleon. Claire de Duras* further explored the outcast in her novels *Ourika* (1824) and *Edouard* (1825), which analyze the plight of individuals who, because of their race or class, are unable to marry the ones they love. *Edouard* inspired passages in Stendhal's *Le Rouge et le noir*, and Duras's unpublished *Olivier* inspired his novel *Armance*.

Undoubtedly the most influential female novelist of the French nineteenth century was George Sand*, the pen name of Aurore Dupin Dudevant. In her more than sixty novels she challenged traditional stereotypes of women, workers, peasants, and the poor, arguing for equality between men and women in marriage and in the world. This could only take place, she believed, through improved education for women and the working class. Using her works to preach social reform, Sand was the first to portray farmers, workers, and children in her novels. She invented the genre called *le roman pastoral*, which not only took the form of oral tales told around the fireplace, but also used transformed speech from the Berry region, recording social customs and traditions which were rapidly disappearing with the coming of the industrial revolution.

In the early twentieth century Sidonie Gabrielle Colette*, who wrote under the pen name Colette, began the reexamination of the notion of genre that has characterized the century. Blurring the line between autobiography* and fiction, she also analyzed a wide range of gender issues in her works which gravitate around the theme of love. Nathalie Sarraute*, a French citizen of Russian extraction, became the theorist of the *Nouveau Roman* when she published *L'Ere de soupçon* in 1956. She explored the notion of *tropismes*, which she invented in 1939 to explain the subconscious movements which she sees as essential to human interaction. Like Sarraute, Marguerite Duras* wrote novels without linear chronology, clearly identifiable characters, or conventional plots. However, in her novels beginning with *Moderato cantabile* (1958), she began to eliminate the barriers between novels, theater, and film. Duras was more intent than Sarraute on following one or more narrative voices, but her interest was especially in the silences which often communicate more than speech.

Lucy M. Schwartz

BIBLIOGRAPHY

Secondary Texts

Aubaud, Camille. *Lire les femmes de lettres*. Paris: Dunod, 1995.
Coulet, Henri. *Le Roman jusqu'à la Révolution*. Paris: Armand Colin, 1967.
François, Carlo. *Précieuses et autres indociles*. Birmingham, AL: Summa Publications, 1987.

King, Adele. *French Women Novelists: Defining a Female Style*. New York: Macmillan,
    Basington, 1989.
Lougee, Carolyn C. *Le Paradis des Femmes: Women, Salons and Social Stratification
    in Seventeenth Century France*. Princeton: Princeton University Press, 1976.
Mercier, Alain. *Le Roman féminin*. Paris: PUF, 1976.

O

Oldenbourg, Zoé (1916–). Historian, novelist, and playwright. Born in Russia, Oldenbourg emigrated to France with her parents in 1925. *Réveillés de la vie* (1956) and *Les Irréductibles* (1958), two of her early works which depict the Russian *émigré* community in Paris, also evoke her troubled relationship with a dominating father who attempted to control her life and her writing. Oldenbourg is best known for her historical novels* and plays, most of which are set in the Middle Ages. In her historical works, she presents both ordinary women and famous figures such as Aliénor of Aquitaine and Catherine the Great. The exiled Oldenbourg articulates her quest for origins in the autobiographical *Visages d'un autoportrait* (1977), a work that reveals her empathy for the socially marginalized, especially women. Oldenbourg, who has always considered herself a feminist, portrays women as stronger than their male counterparts throughout her work.

Susan Ireland and Patrice J. Proulx

BIBLIOGRAPHY

Primary Texts

Argile et cendres. Paris: Gallimard, 1946.
La Pierre angulaire. Paris: Gallimard, 1953.
Réveillés de la vie. Paris: Gallimard, 1956.
Les Irréductibles. Paris: Gallimard, 1958.
Le Bûcher de Monségur: 16 mars 1244. Paris: Gallimard, 1959.
Les Cités charnelles ou l'histoire de Roger de Montbrun. Paris: Gallimard, 1961.
Les Croisades. Paris: Gallimard, 1963.
Catherine de Russie. Paris: Gallimard, 1965.
Visages d'un autoportait. Paris: Gallimard, 1977.
Déguisements. Paris: Gallimard, 1989.
Aliénor. Paris: Gallimard, 1992.

Secondary Text

Becker, Lucille Frackman. "Toward a Female Subject: Elsa Triolet and Zoé Oldenbourg." In *Twentieth-Century French Women Novelists*. Boston: Twayne, 1989.
44–65.

Orientalism. Western European fascination with the Middle East and East Asia
intensified during the nineteenth century. Within a European frame of reference,
Orientalism created an East-West dichotomy, a dominated-dominator dynamic
where the East became the silent mirror image of the West. The 1847 French
victory in Algeria marked the culmination of African conquests begun by Napoleon's 1798–1801 Egyptian expedition. European imperialism was paralleled
by increased interest in Oriental philosophies, literature, and art, as exposed by
scholars such as Raymond Schwab and Edward Said.

Informed by colonialism*, European artistic fascination with the East also
represented novelty and escape from European societal strictures. Historian Ed-
gar Quinet captured this notion with the term "Oriental Renaissance" (1842),
expressing the popular hope that Europe and East Asia would come together,
forming an alliance for their common ground. In French literature, Orientalism
combined embellished description, rendered by European travel writers such as
Gérard de Nerval, Gustave Flaubert, and Théophile Gautier, and painters such
as Jean-Léon Gérôme and Eugène Delacroix, with exotic fantasies of the East.
Orientalism is both the voice of colonization and the expression of Western
fantasies about self-gratification and escape.

Symbolic of fantasies about the East was a growing obsession with Oriental
women and forbidden female space, such as the harem or the geisha house. As
the Orient became a popular artistic and literary motif, it was tied to the female
image: mysterious and silent, desirable in her veiled remoteness, an object to
be conquered. Running parallel to the military domination of the East, the Western quest to enter the harem and unveil its women was common in the visual
arts and literature of the period: European appropriation of its Eastern neighbors
was related to men's desire to dominate women. In addition to the need to see
unveiled the cloistered beauty of Oriental women, European interest was piqued
by the sexual charge of this space and by the sexual license of the women,
including lesbian activities depicted in paintings and written accounts of the
harem. Examples of Western curiosity about the Orient include Hugo's *Les
Orientales* (1829), Nerval's *Voyage en Orient*, and Flaubert's *Salammbo*.

Some writers, such as Judith Gautier*, although interested in the artistic appeal of the Orient, took exception to the tone of Orientalism. In her work she
transformed the passive image of the Orient, allowing characters to reappropriate
the power that was rightfully theirs. The focus shifted from the European travel
writer-narrator to Eastern voices, demystifying Asia and the Middle East: original Oriental intertexts, diction, and traditions inform works such as *Le Dragon
impérial* (1868–1869) and *Princesses d'amour (courtisanes japonaises)* (1900).

These representations of Eastern cultures form a bridge between the fantasies of the Romantic movement and the concrete description of Realism*.

Elizabeth Fisher Goldsmith

BIBLIOGRAPHY

Secondary Texts

Harper, Mary J. "Recovering the Other: Women and the Orient in Writings of Early Nineteenth-Century France." *Critical Matrix* 1, no. 3 (1985): 1–31.
Kabbani, Rana. *Europe's Myths of Orient: Devise and Rule*. London: Macmillan, 1986.
Lewis, Reina. *Gendering Orientalism: Race, Femininity and Representation*. London: Routledge, 1996.
Lowe, Lisa. *Critical Terrains: French and British Orientalists*. Ithaca: Cornell University Press, 1991.
Miller, Christopher. "Orientalism, Colonialism." In *A New History of French Literature*. Ed. Denis Hollier. Cambridge, MA: Harvard University Press, 1989, 689–704.
Nochlin, Linda. "The Imaginary Orient." *Art in America* 71 (May 1983): 119–31, 186–191.
Porter, Dennis. "Orientalism and Its Problems." In *The Politics of Theory*. Ed. Francis Barker, Peter Hulme, Margaret Iverson, and Diana Loxley. Colchester: University of Essex, 1983.
Said, Edward. *Orientalism*. New York: Vintage Books, 1978.
———. "Orientalism Reconsidered." In *Europe And Its Others*. Ed. Francis Barker, Peter Hulme, Margaret Iverson, and Diana Loxley. Colchester: University of Essex, 1983.
Schwab, Raymond. *La Renaissance orientale*. Paris: Payot, 1950.
Young, Robert. *White Mythologies: Writing History and the West*. London: Routledge, 1990.

Orléans, Charlotte Elisabeth, duchesse d'. *See* Palatine, Elisabeth-Charlotte von der Pfalz.

Ormoy, Charlotte Chaumet d' (1732–1791). In *Les Malheurs d'Emélie pour servir d'instruction aux âmes vertueuses et sensibles* (1777), the heroine's tale of innocence besieged and chastity rewarded is posited against that of her friend la soeur Saint-Ange, who does give in to temptation. *La Vertu chancelante ou la vie de Mlle d'Amincourt* (1778) is narrated by a heroine who escapes the corruption of the city and its offers of money for mistresshood by retiring to the countryside under the assumed name of Babet with only her maidservant Fanchon and a cow for company. D'Amincourt heroically defends her chastity against an onslaught of suitors before finally marrying and having a child with the man she loves. Even this most virtuous of heroines is not beyond the cruel blows of destiny. D'Amincourt learns of her husband's death on the battlefield just a few days after her son dies of smallpox, and narrates her tale of woe from the base of the golden box that contains her husband's heart. In addition to her novels*, Ormoy edited a literary journal, *Journal de Monsieur*, which she distributed from her home, and later devoted herself to composing plays.

Charlotte Daniels

BIBLIOGRAPHY

Primary Texts

Les Malheurs de la jeune Emélie pour servir d'instruction aux âmes vertueuses et sensibles. Paris: La Veuve Duchesne, 1777.

La Vertu chancelante ou la vie de Mlle d'Amincourt. Liège-Paris: Moureau, 1778. (Generally attributed to Ormoy, though Barbier, in his *Dictionnaire des ouvrages anonymes*, claims this novel was written by Pierre-François-Canien Baugin, Rossel, Mercier, and Mérard de Saint-Just.)

Journal de Monsieur. Ed. Charlotte Chaumet d'Ormoy. Paris, 1779–1780.

Zelmis ou la jeune sauvage. Opéra comique en un acte, mêlé d'ariettes. London and Paris, 1780.

La Belle dans le souterrain. London and Paris, 1781.

Le Lama amoureux. Conte oriental. London and Paris, 1781.

Les Dangers de la passion du jeu. N.p., n.d.

Secondary Texts

Briquet, Marguerite-Ursule-Fortunée, Dame. *Dictionnaire historique, littéraire et bibliographique des Françaises et des étrangères naturalisées en France, connues par leurs écrits*. Paris: Gillé, 1804.

Le Mercure 1 (January 1777): 124–129.

Le Petit Almanach de nos grandes femmes. London: S.n., 1789. 73.

Prudhomme, Louis Marie. *Biographie universelle et historique des femmes célèbres, mortes ou vivantes*. Paris: Lebigre, 1830.

P

Palatine, Elisabeth-Charlotte von der Pfalz, later duchesse d'Orléans (known as Madame) (1652–1722). Born in Heidelberg to the royal family of the Palatinate, she spent four of her happiest childhood years in Hanover with her dear Aunt Sophie (granddaughter of England's James I), to whom she would eventually write several thousand letters. The years at Hanover furnished Liselotte with treasured playmates, including William III, future king of England, and instilled in her a love of festivals, such as the Christkindl, and the hymns and Bible* of Luther. Her genuine faith and systematic daily reading of the German Bible throughout her life would bring her courage and tranquillity in spite of her marriage* to Philippe d'Orléans, Louis XIV's homosexual brother (called Monsieur), and her disappointment with the frivolities of the French court. Liselotte's father's ambition and Louis XIV's politics of expansion were the galvanizing factors behind her forced conversion to Catholicism and the marriage, described by biographer Dirk Van der Cruysse as a sacrifice on the altar of a Franco-Palatine alliance.

According to the conservative estimates of Van der Cruysse, Madame is the author of at least 60,000 letters, about half in French and half in German, with only one-tenth conserved, due to the custom of burning letters of the deceased. Her epistolary network extended to practically all the royal courts in Europe. These letters provide an exceptional mirror of a crucial period in early modern Europe. Because Madame intended her letters only for the eyes of her correspondents (although she knew that they were read by the *cabinet noir*, the postal censorship office), they possess an irresistible spontaneity and frankness, revealing her innermost self. Despite her comparison of herself to Molière's Monsieur Jourdain writing prose without knowing it, Liselotte scholars find an explicit literary self-awareness in the letters. They are filled with literary allusions and proverbs. The French letters sometimes contain German expressions, especially in passages relating to youthful memories, education*, religion, customs, medicine, even language acquisition.

Featuring firsthand accounts of European rulers, their families and courts, Madame's letters are vast in scope and varied in tone. She tackles thorny theological questions such as the immortality of the soul, rejoices at scientific discoveries, reveals her interest in history and antiquity in her discussions of coins and medals, and relates with Rabelaisian humor the stercoraceous habits at court. She devotes much attention to the theater*, a passion since her youth, and to anthropological and philosophcal considerations. Madame's correspondence leaves many questions unanswered; scholars do not agree about her linguistic gallantry or her feminism*.

Christine McCall Probes

BIBLIOGRAPHY

Primary Texts

Forster, Elborg, ed. *A Woman's Life in the Court of the Sun King: Letters of Liselotte von der Pfalz.* Baltimore: Johns Hopkins University Press, 1984.
———, ed. *Madame Palatine, lettres françaises.* Ed. Dirk van der Cruysse. Paris: Fayard, 1989.

Secondary Texts

Albert, Mechthild. " 'Une ermite au milieu de la cour': La Mélancolie de Madame Palatine." In *Diversité, c'est ma devise.* Ed. Frank-Rutger Hausmann, Christoph Miething, and Margarete Zimmermann. Seattle: Biblio 17, 1994.
Brooks, William S., and Peter Yarrow. *The Dramatic Criticism of Elizabeth Charlotte, Duchesse d'Orléans.* Lewiston, NY: Edwin Mellen Press, 1996.
Le Roy Ladurie, Emmanuel. "Auprès du roi, la cour." *Annales: Economies, sociétés, civilisations* 38 (1983): 21–41.
Probes, Christine McCall. " 'Moi je vous dirai *auff gut pfältzisch*': Les Expressions allemandes au service de Madame Palatine, épistolière française." In *Contacts culturels et échanges linguistiques au XVIIe siècle en France.* Ed. Yves Giraud. Paris, Seattle: Papers on Seventeenth Century Literature, 1997.
Sweetser, Marie-Odile. "Aspects autobiographiques dans la correspondance de Madame Palatine." *Cahiers Saint-Simon* 23 (1995): 49–54.
Van der Cruysse, Dirk. *Madame Palatine, princesse européenne.* Paris: Fayard, 1988.

Parmelin, Hélène (1915–). Parmelin has devoted her life to writing, art, and politics as expressed from a woman's point of view. She and her late husband, the artist Paul Pignon, were close friends of Picasso, who was the subject of several of Parmelin's studies, including *Picasso sur la place* (1963). Among her other essays are an album on war and art, and an exploration of "anartism," that is, "art anti-art." She has also written over twenty novels*. Like many members of her generation who lived through the German Occupation, she joined the Communist Party in 1944, serving from that time until 1953 as art critic and journalist for the Party's daily, *L'Humanité.* In *La Désinvolture* (1983) Parmelin writes of her love for the world she lives in, even though it is difficult, unjust, and tragic—even murderous. This world, she contends, exhibits a violence in love, anger, and creation that she as a woman could never have imagined. It has transformed her into a woman warrior in the different struggles she has undertaken.

Margaret Collins Weitz

BIBLIOGRAPHY

Primary Texts

La Montée au mur. Paris: Éditeurs Français Réunis, 1950.
Les Mystères de Moscou. Paris: R. Julliard, 1956.
Picasso dit. Paris: Denoël-Gonthier, 1966.
La Femme-crocodile. Paris: Julliard, 1968.
La Femme-écarlate. Paris: Stock, 1975.
Voyage en Picasso. Paris: Robert Laffont, 1980.
La Désinvolture: Auto-pamphlet. Paris: Christian Bourgois, 1983.

Secondary Text

Verthuy, Maïr. *Fenêtre sur cour: Voyage dans l'oeuvre romanesque d'Hélène Parmelin.* Laval: Trois, 1991.

Parnassian poets (c. 1850–1875). The Parnassian movement repudiated Romanticism's* sentimental excesses in favor of an objective poetic stance. Taking its name from the review *Le Parnasse contemporain*, this group of poets, albeit diverse, shared an anti-utilitarian aesthetic characterized by the quest for formal perfection. The movement's central figures (Gautier, Leconte de Lisle, Banville, Mendès, Heredia) offered a poetic model described in masculine terms: the poetic line was hard as granite, shaped not with fine hands into fluid fillets, but rather vigorously chiseled into enduring monuments. This muscular conception of the poetic act, coupled with the banishment of affect, would seem particularly uninviting to women poets, heretofore permitted a voice only under the sentimental and subjective romantic guise. Indeed, more so than surrounding poetic movements of the nineteenth century, Parnassianism relegated ''woman'' to the role of object, a passive and impassive incarnation of idealized beauty.

There were in fact eight women Parnassians who numbered among the almost one hundred poets represented in the three volumes of the *Parnasse contemporain*. Absent from the all-male first volume, the following integrated the final two: Louise Colet* (1810–1876), Louise Ackermann* (1813–1890), Léocadie Penquer (1817–1889), Malvina Blanchecotte* (1830–1897), Mélanie Bourotte (1832-?), Isabelle Guyon (1833–1911), Nina de Villard* [or Callias] (1843–1884), and Louisa Siefert* (1845–1877). Since, to this date, critics have largely ignored them or addressed their contributions with condescension and generalizations, a reevaluation of the *Parnassiennes* is long overdue.

This is an eclectic list, including the well-established Ackermann and Colet, both having made their first marks on literary history under Romanticism, alongside younger poets, such as Louisa Siefert and Nina de Villard. Blanchecotte, the *poète-ouvrière*, rubs elbows with the aristocratic Guyon. While their contributions are often dismissed as romantic and sentimental—decidedly un-Parnassian—it must be noted that most female contributors explored either the sonnet form, impersonal voice, or orientalist themes favored by the movement. The feminist content of their poems is sometimes explicit, as in the case of Penquer's "Paradis retrouvé," which offers an antidote to Milton by glorifying Eve's sexual awakening. At other times it is ironic, more often simply oppositional thanks to feminine perspectives and subject matter.

Gretchen Schultz

BIBLIOGRAPHY

Primary Text

Le Parnasse comtemporain. 3 vols. Ed. Alphonse Lemerre. 1866, 1869/71, 1876.

Secondary Texts

Badesco, Luc. *La Génération poétique de 1860, la jeunesse des deux rives.* 2 vols. Paris: Editions Nizet, 1971.

Johnson, Barbara. "Dream of Stone: 1866, the First Volume of *Le Parnasse contemporain* Appears." In *A New History of French Literature.* Ed. Denis Hollier. Cambridge, MA: Harvard University Press, 1989. 743–748.

Schaffer, Aaron. *The Genres of Parnassian Poetry.* Baltimore: Johns Hopkins University Press, 1944.

Somoff, J.-P., and A. Marfée. *Les Muses du Parnasse.* Paris: A. Rebours, 1979.

Parthenay, Catherine de (1554–1631). The only child of fervently Protestant parents, she received a thorough classical education*, and her earliest work was a translation from Greek into French of *Isocrates's Precepts to Dominique.* In 1568 she married Charles du Quélennec, baron du Pont, who was killed in the 1572 St. Bartholomew's Day Massacre. According to La Croix du Maine, she wrote touching elegies in memory of her husband and Admiral de Coligny, but these have been lost. In 1573 she took refuge in the Protestant stronghold of La Rochelle, where she wrote a tragedy, *Holopherne.* This text has also been lost.

In 1575 she married René de Rohan, with whom she had two sons, Henri (future duc de Rohan) and Benjamin de Soubise, and three daughters, Catherine, Henriette, and Anne. After Rohan's death in 1585, she devoted herself to her children's education and advancement, but her continued political involvement is evident in her correspondence with Duplessis-Mornay. She composed three ballets for her friend Catherine de Bourbon*: *Ballet representé devant Madame au Château de Pau le 23 aoust 1592, Au Balet de Madame,* and *Autre Balet,* the latter two performed at Tours in 1593. These ballets, more properly called political plays, call for an end to the religious wars, beseech Henri IV to remain Protestant, and urge him to consent to his sister's marriage*. Parthenay's most controversial work is the 1596 *Apologie pour le roi Henri IV envers ceux qui le blasment de ce qu'il gratifie plus ses ennemis que ses serviteurs.* This biting satire chastises the king for having abandoned the reformed religion, denounces his favoritism toward his former enemies to the detriment of his supporters, and berates him for his treatment of his sister.

Her defiant resistance during the 1627 siege of La Rochelle rallied her co-religionists and convinced them to accept an alliance with England. She sacrificed her horses to provide food for the citizens, more than half of whom had died of hunger. After La Rochelle's capitulation, Louis XIII granted amnesty to the rebels, except for Parthenay and her daughter, Anne, who were imprisoned at the château de Niort for four months. She retired to her chateau at Parc-Soubise in Poitou, where she died on October 26, 1631. She was praised by both Protestants and Catholics for her intelligence, outspoken honesty, and courage.

Christie St-John

BIBLIOGRAPHY

Primary Text

Baletz representez devant le roy à la venue de Madame à Tours 1593. Tours: Jamet Mettayer, n.d. (Bibliothèque nationale, Rés. Yf. 1822 in-40; Bibliothèque municipale de Tours, N.F. 2517).

Secondary Texts

Maine, François La Croix du et du Verdier. *Les Bibliothèques françoises de La Croix du Maine et de du Verdier, sieur de Vauprivas.* 4 vols. Ed. Rigoley de Juvigny. Paris: Saillaut & Nyou, 1772–1773.
Merland, M. C. *Catherine de Parthenay.* Nantes: Mellinet Imprimeur, 1875.
Paquot, Marcel. "Madame de Rohan, auteur de Comédies-Ballets?" *Revue Belge de Philologie et d'Histoire* 8 (1929): 801–829; and "Comédies-Ballets représentées en l'honneur de Madame, soeur du roi Henri IV." *Revue Belge de Philologie et d'Histoire* 10 (1931): 965–995.
Ritalongi, G. Puig de. *Catherine de Parthenay.* Parthenay: Cante Libraire-Editeur, n.d..
Ritter, Raymond. *Catherine de Parthenay, Dame de Rohan: Ballets allégoriques en vers 1592–1593.* Paris: Champion, 1927.

Parturier, Françoise (1919–1995). Essayist and novelist. Parturier championed women's rights in the columns she wrote for *Le Figaro* (1956–1975), and later for *Le Monde.* In 1970 she created a scandal when she became the first woman since 1893 to submit her candidacy to the Académie Française.

The transgressive character of Parturier's work is reflected in her *Lettre ouverte aux hommes* (1968), published several months before the revolution of May 1968. This text, written in the form of a male-female dialogue, critiques misogynistic ideologies which define woman as physically and mentally inferior to man. Parturier continues the debate in *Lettre ouverte aux femmes* (1974), challenging women to acknowledge their complicity in the perpetuation of patriarchal power structures and urging them to embrace the concept of female solidarity.

Patrice J. Proulx

BIBLIOGRAPHY

Primary Texts

La Prudence de la chair. Paris: Editions R. Julliard, 1963.
Lettre ouverte aux hommes. Paris: Albin Michel, 1968.

Antoine ou L'Amant de cinq jours. Paris: Plon, 1971.
Lettre ouverte aux femmes. Paris: Albin Michel, 1974.
Calamité, mon amour. Paris: Albin Michel, 1978.
Les Hauts de Ramatuelle. Paris: Albin Michel, 1983.
Le Sexe des anges. Paris: Editions de Fallois, 1991.
Nicole [Françoise Parturier], and Josette Raoul-Duval. *Les Lions sont lâchés*. Paris: Editions R. Julliard, 1955.

Pascal, Françoise (1632–?). The daughter of a well-connected customs commissioner in Lyons, Pascal was active as a poet by the age of fifteen. Between 1657 and 1664 she published six plays (three short farces and three full-length tragicomedies), along with some shorter poems. Around 1667 she moved to Paris, for reasons unknown, and managed to support herself by painting portraits, giving drawing and music lessons, and publishing religious poetry*, including collections of Christmas hymns designed to be sung to popular tunes of the day. There is no record of her death, although she is known to have been still alive in 1698. Pascal deserves mention as one of the first women writers known to have made a living by her artistic talents and yet remain socially respectable. She was the first Frenchwoman to compose her stageworks with professional acting companies in mind and was likewise the first to have her plays staged by them. Pascal had an unusually acute sense of what the public wanted. She based her tragicomedies on best-selling novels* of the period, on subjects as diverse as Christian martyrs, ancient history, and classical mythology. Her *Endymion* was the sole machine play of the century written by a woman. She chose to cultivate the one-act farce just as it was beginning to regain literary respectability, and managed to combine rapid physical action with themes taken from the salons*. She was also among the first French women to issue a collection of letters, *Le Commerce du Parnasse*. Pascal deserves credit for achieving financial independence, for insisting that her publications were exclusively her own work, and for arguing that women ought to be valued primarily for their minds.

Perry Gethner

BIBLIOGRAPHY

Primary Text

L'Amoureux extravagant. In *Femmes Dramaturges en France (1650–1750)*. Ed. Perry Gethner. Seattle: Biblio 17, 1993.

Secondary Text

Baldensperger, Fernand. "Françoise Pascal, fille lyonnaise." In *Etudes d'histoire littéraire*. Paris: Droz, 1939. 1–31.

Pascal, Gilberte, later Madame Périer (1620–1687). Her early education made Pascal competent in Latin, history, philosophy, and mathematics. In 1641 she married Florin Périer; she bore four children between 1642 and 1647. Won over to Jansenism* by her siblings Blaise and Jacqueline Pascal*, she became an important interlocutor for them in matters spiritual, as is seen in their correspondence and in written accounts of their conversations. Many of Blaise's *pensées* are in Gilberte's hand, apparently dictated to her by her brother. After his death, she turned to Port-Royal* for assistance in publishing his notes for an apology of the Christian religion, and subsequently fought to preserve the integrity of the work, resisting any embellishments or clarifications other editors wanted to impose on the text. Shortly after Blaise's death, Gilberte Pascal wrote her *Vie de Pascal*, a biographical account of her brother's life and work; she similarly composed a *Vie de Jacqueline* as a tribute to her younger sister. As biography was not an established genre in the seventeenth century, Pascal's texts are rather innovative. Recent criticism suggests that the passages devoted to Blaise's apology were written by a theologian and philosopher rather than by Gilberte Pascal, but it is generally believed that she is the author of most of the text. Pascal's *Vies* offer a frank, albeit idealized, account of Blaise's and Jacqueline's intellectual and spiritual passions, while acknowledging the weaknesses of each. The *Vie de Pascal* was not published with the first edition of the *Pensées*, though her son Etienne borrowed heavily from his mother's text when composing his own preface for that edition. A version of Gilberte Pascal's *Vie de Pascal* was first published in 1684, as a preface to an Amsterdam edition of the *Pensées*.

Suzanne C. Toczyski

BIBLIOGRAPHY

Primary Texts

[Périer, Gilberte, Jacqueline Pascal, and Marguerite Périer.] *Lettres, opuscules et mémoires de Madame Périer et de Jacqueline Périer, soeurs de Blaise Pascal, et de Marguerite Périer, sa nièce*. Ed. Prosper Faugère. Paris: Auguste Vattier, 1845.
Ernst, Pol. "Le Témoignage de 'Gilberte Pascal' sur l'Apologie." *Dix-septième siècle* 75 (1967): 23–47.
Pommier, Jean. *La Vie de Pascal, par Gilberte Périer*. Archives des lettres modernes 57. Paris: Lettres modernes, 1964.

Secondary Text

Sainte-Beuve, Charles Augustin. *Port-Royal*. Paris: Hachette, 1922.

Pascal, Jacqueline, Soeur Sainte-Euphémie (1625–1661). Sister of Blaise and Gilberte* Pascal; subprioress of Port-Royal* des Champs at the time of her death. An early introduction to verse led Pascal to compose a brief, five-act comedy at age eleven; she studied theater* with Mondory, and played Cassandre in Georges de Scudéry's *L'Amour tyrannique* in 1639. Her verses found favor with the queen and Richelieu, and Pierre Corneille encouraged her to compete in a poetry* contest in Rouen; she won the Tour d'Argent for her stances on the Immaculate Conception in 1640. Converted to Jansenism* with the rest of her family in 1646, Pascal desired to join the community at Port-Royal de Paris.

When her father refused his permission, Pascal continued to pursue her religious education* through letters exchanged with members of the Port-Royal community. At the request of her priest, Pascal translated *Jesu, nostra redemptio* into French verse in 1648, but renounced any further translations on the advice of Mère Agnès, abbess of Port-Royal, who feared that such work would inspire vanity in the young woman. In 1651 Pascal composed an *Ecrit sur le mystère de Jésus*. After her father's death, Pascal's pursuit of her religious vocation dismayed her siblings, but she took her final vows in June 1653. Her spiritual devotion contributed greatly to her brother's conversion in 1654. In April 1657 Pascal wrote the *Règlement pour les enfants de Port-Royal*, a codification of the role of the teacher's language in the disciplining and conversion of young children. Pascal regretted her brother's participation in the writing of the Mandement of 1661, which urged the religious of Port-Royal to sign the Formulary condemning the teachings of Cornelius Jansen. Though Pascal did eventually sign, the conflict between her conscience and her oath of obedience to her superiors seems to have contributed to her death shortly thereafter.

Suzanne C. Toczyski

BIBLIOGRAPHY

Primary Text

All of Pascal's extant writings have been published in *Oeuvres de Pascal*. Ed. Léon Brunschvicg and Pierre Boutroux. Paris: Hachette, Grands Ecrivains, 1904–1914.

Secondary Texts

Cousin, Victor. *Jacqueline Pascal. Premières Etudes sur les femmes illustres et la société du XVIIe siècle*. Paris: Didier, 1862.
Lagarde, François. "Instruction et conversion: Le 'Règlement pour les enfants de Port-Royal.' " *Travaux de littérature* 2 (1988): 125–135.
Sainte-Beuve, Charles Augustin. *Port-Royal*. Paris: Hachette, 1922.

Pedagogy. Man's fear of woman as temptress and as source of disorder began with his first teacher: Eve handed Adam fruit from the Tree of Knowledge, and Catholic France has always remembered to punish her and her kind for wanting to learn and to teach. Keeping women out of schools and out of the teaching profession has for centuries preoccupied French clergy and politicians alike. When bishops and kings were not fighting with each other about who would control education* in France, they agreed to exclude women from it, except as the latter might train themselves and each other to run their household and to raise mannerly Christian children.

This plan succeeded for university teaching until the early twentieth century: in 1906 Marie Curie was the first woman ever named to a French university post. Besides her unquestionable brilliance, the deciding factors were that she had been married to the just-dead Pierre Curie and that together they (with Becquerel) had won a Nobel Prize. Clearly, few women could fulfill those particular requirements. In fact, few women have ever fulfilled any requirements at all: as late as 1988, only 9 percent of university professors were female (along with 35 percent of assistants and 31 percent of *maîtres de conférences*) (Lelièvre, 185–186). Meanwhile, the lower ranks have undergone a "feminization," a phenomenon deplored by those who use it to devalue the profession of teaching: in 1990 women made up 95 percent of pre-elementary, 74 percent of elementary, and 55 percent of secondary school teachers (*International Encyclopedia of Education*, 2383).

In order to teach, she had to learn; but like Eve, the learned woman was considered dangerous; and the French language wields negative epithets that date from the Renaissance (*pédante*) and the seventeenth (*précieuse, femme savante*) and eighteenth (*bas bleu**) centuries. The culture deprecated learned female teachers in other ways—"faded at age twenty-five, most seem frankly ugly" (*La Revue bleue* 1913, quoted in Mayeur, 174)—and until the end of World War I* forbade them to marry. For centuries only small numbers of women taught, and only at the lowest levels. Years of educational discrimination kept them disadvantaged when they tried to earn their living by teaching. The circularity of this phenomenon is well known to historians of women's access to culture and of their entry into the workplace: systematic disadvantaging yields perceived inferiority, which is then used to justify continued disadvantaging. Here, as in other areas, nature (itself a construct) dictates social behavior, making it natural that women teach young children, which work is then devalued even as women are held responsible for instilling morality and citizenship.

Other double binds include the overdetermining of female teachers for younger students: history and gender combine with the state's urgent need for teachers when education becomes free (in 1881 for primary grades) and compulsory (in 1882 for ages six to twelve), and at the same time female leadership is condemned as unnatural, and the drive for success as unfeminine. This paradox touches the whole question of professional status for teaching, along with nursing and social work, all predominantly female and therefore treated by men as not "real" but instead "semi" professions, that is, as not meeting standards of elite knowledge and autonomy. This exclusion of lower-level teachers from professional status causes particularly hypocritical reasonings since, unlike nursing and social work, teaching is divided between female, in the lower ranks, and male, in the upper, elite stratum. University professors, at least 90 percent of whom are male, are thus particularly subject to panic over the "woman peril," over the profession's becoming feminized. A feminist analysis of this reaction might say that the concept of professionalism is a "historical and social construct shaped by the male-defined conception of elite knowledge as quantifiable, objective, and abstract" (*International Encyclopedia of Education*, 6722).

History. The Revolution* and the later official separation of church and state did little to improve women's place in teaching; emphasis fell on the idea of education as a national, secular concern and as the key to political freedom and to a strong national identity. Since women did not vote in France until after World War II*, their claims to political freedom were minimal; and they entered the profession in greater numbers mostly because during the nineteenth and early twentieth centuries schooling gradually became compulsory and universal. There were more children to teach and more women, educated and without jobs, to be swept up in teaching them.

In this centuries-long alternation between resistance and expediency, there are a few thinkers, male and female, who stand out for their vision and for experimentation with woman's place in education: Christine de Pizan* (*La Cité des dames*, 1405; *Le Livre des trois vertus*, 1405); Louise Labé* (*Préface* to *Poèmes*, 1555; *Débat de Folie et d'Amour*, 1555); Marie de Gournay* (*Egalité des hommes et des femmes*, 1622); Fénelon (*Traité de l'éducation des filles*, 1687) and Mme de Maintenon*, founder of Saint-Cyr*, convent* school for daughters of impecunious aristocrats, one of many schools closed by the Revolution; Poulain de la Barre (*De l'égalité des deux sexes*, 1673; *De l'éducation des dames pour la conduite de l'esprit dans les sciences et dans les moeurs*, 1674). The *salonnières* of the seventeenth and eighteenth centuries must be considered unofficial teachers: by inviting groups of artists and writers to their homes, they created the kinds of affinity groups that encouraged all their members to write and think, including women who could both learn and teach during the informal exchange of ideas. The eighteenth century struggled with ideas of gender specificity and so of unequal education and with those of gender equality and its correlate, equal education. Rousseau and Condorcet represent, respectively, opposing thoughts on women's capacities: the first isolates their abilities and responsibilities—nurturance, feeling, morals (*Emile*, 1762); and the second, like Poulain a century earlier, believes reason to be genderless. Condorcet concludes from this that women should not be excluded from the teaching profession and that the same subjects should be taught to both sexes. Félicité de Genlis*, lady-in-waiting, then governess in a royal house, exemplifies aspects of both. A remarkably innovative pedagogue, she used invention and fantasy in her methods of home schooling, papering hallways and stairwells with maps of foreign countries, for example, expanding the kinds of concrete demonstrations seen in *Emile*. She and her employer, the duc de Chartres, departed from Rousseau, however, in educating male and female children together and in having all subjects taught by a woman. Among her writings are didactic plays (*Théâtre d'éducation*, 1779) written for her young pupils. Napoleon named her inspector of primary schools.

In the nineteenth century, teacher-training was established by the state (*cours normaux, écoles normales*) and remained the object of controversy. The schoolmistress makes virtually no appearance in nineteenth-century novels*, but in the twentieth century female teachers appear in the writings of women especially and in a favorable light: *agrégées* who taught for a time, Simone de Beauvoir*, and, more recently, Annie Ernaux* exemplify authors who discuss and depict the lives of female intellectuals who belong to the pedagogical profession. There and throughout their history, female pedagogues have suffered patriarchy's ambivalence: because they wield certain powers, they augment patriarchal anxieties, and so they encounter resistance and blame.

Carol Sherman

BIBLIOGRAPHY

Secondary Texts

Beauvoir, Simone de. *Mémoires d'une jeune fille rangée*. Paris: Gallimard, 1958.
Ernaux, Annie. *Une Femme*. Paris: Gallimard, 1987.
International Encyclopedia of Education. Tarrytown, NY: Pergamon, 1996.
Lelièvre, Françoise, and Claude Lelièvre. *Histoire de la scolarisation des filles*. Paris:
     Nathan, 1991.
Mayeur, Françoise. *L'Education des filles en France au XIXe siècle*. Paris: Hachette,
     1979.

Pelletier, Madeleine (1874–1939). Self-educated from the age of twelve, Pelletier attended medical school and practiced medicine. She achieved fame as a feminist, socialist, Freemason, journalist, and novelist. Her cross-dressing* and radical theories distanced her from mainstream feminism*. In the autobiographical novel *La Femme vierge* (1933), the celibate heroine denounces marriage* and motherhood for enslaving women. In the utopian work *Une Vie nouvelle* (1932), Pelletier depicts an egalitarian society where families* and gender inequalities have disappeared. Pelletier also supported neo-Malthusianism* and abortion* rights. Charges of having assisted in abortions led to her commitment to a mental asylum, where she died.

Juliette Parnell-Smith

BIBLIOGRAPHY

Primary Texts

La Femme en lutte pour ses droits. Paris: Giard et Brière, 1908.
L'Education féministe des filles. Paris: Giard et Brière, 1914.
La Femme émancipée. Paris: Montaigne, 1927.
Une Vie nouvelle. Paris: Figuière, 1932.
La Femme vierge. Paris: Valentin Bresle, 1933.
La Rationalisation sexuelle. Paris: Editions du Sphinx, 1935.

Secondary Texts

Bard, Christine, ed. *Madeleine Pelletier (1874–1939): Logiques et infortunes d'un com-
     bat pour l'égalité*. Paris: Côté-femmes, 1992.
Gordon, Felicia. *The Integral Feminist: Madeleine Pelletier, 1874–1939*. Cambridge:
     Polity Press, 1990.
Maignien, Claude, and Charles Sowerwine. *Madeleine Pelletier. 1874–1939. Une Fé-
     ministe dans l'arène politique*. Paris: Editions ouvrières, 1992.
Mitchell, Claudine. "Madeleine Pelletier (1874–1939): The Politics of Sexual Oppres-
     sion." *Feminist Review* 33 (Autumn 1989): 79–92.
Scott, Joan Wallach. *Only Paradoxes to Offer: French Feminists and the Rights of Man*.
     Cambridge, MA: Harvard University Press, 1996.
Sowerwine, Charles. "Madeleine Pelletier 1874–1939: Femme, médecin, militante."
     L'Information psychiatrique 9 (November 1988): 1183–1193.
———— "Militantisme et identité sexuelle: La Carrière politique et l'oeuvre théorique de

Madeleine Pelletier (1874–1939).'' *Le Mouvement social* 10–12, no. 157 (1991): 9–32.

Penrose, Valentine Boué (1898–1978). French-born Valentine Penrose and her husband, English artist Roland Penrose, were affiliated with surrealism* during its heyday in the late 1920s and early 1930s, at a time when no women were acknowledged members of the movement—despite the centrality of the feminine muse to the surrealist aesthetic. Penrose's work was considered marginal until recent critical attention, galvanized by the special issue of *Obliques* (1977) on surrealist women, gave due recognition to the particular originality of women surrealists. An emerging feminist voice is heard in Penrose's revisionist text (*Le Nouveau Candide*, 1936), in the exploration of feminine perversion in her fictional biography of the sixteenth-century Hungarian female counterpart to Gilles de Rais (*Erzsébet Bathory, la comtesse sanglante*, 1962), and in her poetry* and collages (*Dons des féminines*, 1951), whose images counter the male erotic prevalent in surrealist writing by associating women with sensuality, grace and creative forces in nature.

Judith E. Preckshot

BIBLIOGRAPHY

Primary Texts

Herbe à la lune. Preface by Paul Eluard. Paris: G.L.M., 1935.
Le Nouveau Candide. Illus. Wolfgang Paalen. Paris: G.L.M., 1936.
Martha's Opera. Paris: Fontaine, 1946.
Dons des féminines. Paris: Les Pas Perdus, 1951.
Erzsébet Bathory, la comtesse sanglante. Paris: Mercure de France, 1962.
Les Magies. Lith. Joan Miro. Paris: Les Mains Libres, 1972.

Secondary Texts

Chadwick, Whitney. *Women Artists and the Surrealist Movement*. Boston: Little, Brown, 1985.
La Femme Surréaliste. Obliques 14–15 (1977).
Gauthier, Xavière. *Surréalisme et sexualité*. Paris: Gallimard, 1971.
Hubert, Renée Riese. ''Lesbianism and Matriarchy: Valentine and Roland Penrose.'' In *Magnifying Mirrors: Women, Surrealism, and Partnership*. Lincoln: University of Nebraska Press, 1994. 87–111.
Suleiman, Susan Rubin. ''A Double Margin: Women Writers and the Avant-Garde in France.'' In *Subversive Intent: Gender, Politics, and the Avant-Garde*. Cambridge, MA: Harvard University Press, 1990. 11–32.

Périer, Françoise Gilberte Pascal. *See* Pascal, Gilbert.

Perrein, Michèle (1930–). Novelist, playwright, and essayist. Born in La Réole, Perrein studied law in Bordeaux before beginning her career as a journalist in Paris. In her first novel*, *La Sensitive* (1956), written in epistolary form, she creates a female character fighting for her place and rights in a male-dominated world. This figure reappears in her later novels, in which Perrein reflects on the female condition and on the relationship between the sexes. In such fictional works as *La Chineuse* (1970) and *Comme une fourmi cavalière* (1980), her female characters are often marginalized figures, best symbolized by the recurring metaphor of the parenthesis. These characters engage in a quest for their identity and their own means of communication, rejecting the roles society defines for women. In the semi-autobiographical texts *Le Mâle aimant* (1975) and *Entre chienne et louve* (1978), she addresses political questions of language and identity from a feminist perspective. Perrein continues to explore what it means to be a writer and a woman, and her most recent novels celebrate woman-centered language.

Ana M. de Medeiros

BIBLIOGRAPHY

Primary Texts

La Sensitive. Paris: Julliard, 1956.
Le Cercle. Paris: Julliard, 1962.
La Chineuse. Paris: Julliard, 1970.
Le Buveur de Garonne. Paris: Grasset, 1973.
Le Mâle aimant. Paris: Julliard, 1975.
Entre chienne et louve. Paris: Grasset, 1978.
Comme une fourmi cavalière. Paris: Grasset, 1980.
Les Cotonniers de Bassalane. Paris: Grasset, 1984.
La Sensitive ou l'innocence coupable. Paris: Grasset, 1986.
La Margagne. Paris: Grasset, 1989.

Secondary Texts

O'Nan, Martha. "Naming Would-Be Overthrowers of Men in the Novels of Michèle Perrein." *Literary Onomastics Studies* 9 (1982): 53–63.
Parker, Gabrielle. "Celle par qui le scandale arrive: Michèle Perrein and the Notion of Scandal." *Modern and Contemporary France* 33 (April 1988): 24–32.
———. "Michèle Perrein: The Parenthesis as Metaphor of the Female Condition." In *Contemporary French Fiction by Women: Feminist Perspectives*. Ed. Margaret Atack and Phil Powrie. Manchester, UK: Manchester University Press, 1990. 116–127.

Pétigny de Saint-Romain, Marie-Louise-Rose Lévesque de (1768–?). Pétigny's *Idylles ou contes champêtres* (1786) was published when she was just sixteen and earned the author praise for her sensitivity and wisdom. The *Idylles* begins with a warning about love but ends by extolling its virtues. Twenty years later, the females in her epistolary novel* *Aurélie ou l'intéressante orpheline* (1806) are the wise and outspoken ones from whom males seek advice. Pétigny advocated education* for women, which she believed should be expanded beyond the traditional female arts of song and dance to the study of arduous subjects such as history and geography.

Jennifer McGonagle

BIBLIOGRAPHY

Primary Texts

Idylles, ou Contes champêtres. Paris; Bailly, 1786.
Aurélie, ou l'intéressante orpheline. Nevers: N.p., 1806.

Secondary Text

Dwyer Helen, and Barry Dwyer. *Index biographique français.* 4 vols. London: K. G. Saur, 1993.

Pisier, Marie-France (1944–). Pisier, who was born in Indochina and later spent six years in New Caledonia, earned both law and political science degrees in France. Best known for her acting, for which she has received two Cesars for supporting actress, she has written three novels*, acted in numerous films and television series, and directed the film version of her first and most well known novel, *Le Bal du gouverneur* (1984). In this work, set in the colonies at the end of the Fourth Republic, Pisier depicts adolescent female sexuality and its attendant emotional extremes.

E. Nicole Meyer

BIBLIOGRAPHY

Primary Texts

La Belle Imposture. Paris: Grasset, 1982.
Le Bal du gouverneur. Paris: Grasset, 1984.
Je n'ai aimé que vous. Paris: Grasset, 1986.
Le Deuil du printemps. Paris: Grasset, 1997.

Pizan, Christine de. *See* Christine de Pizan.

Plantier, Thérèse (1911–). An independent, militant feminist poet, Plantier is prone to controversial statements, such as her comment that the publishing* house Des femmes is controlled by a group of extremist lesbians. Initially she endorsed surrealism* as the only viable form of revolutionary expression able to subvert art as a vehicle for bourgeois thinking. She is skeptical of language inasmuch as it reflects the values of patriarchy, but is nevertheless convinced that self-expression as a subject is the key to women's autonomy. Since 1980 she has published essays on diverse aspects of male discourse as well as literary criticism, including an essay on Sade and a scathing attack on George Sand*.

Karen Bouwer

BIBLIOGRAPHY

Primary Texts

Chemins d'eau. Paris: Guy Chambelland, 1963.
Mémoires inférieurs. Paris: La Corde, 1966.
C'est moi Diégo. Paris: Saint-Germain-des-Prés, 1971.
Jusqu'à ce que l'Enfer gèle. Paris: Oswald, 1974.
La Loi du silence. Paris: Saint-Germain-des-Prés, 1975.

Le Sonneur. Paris: Atelier des Grammes, 1977.
La Portentule. Paris: Saint-Germain-des-Prés, 1978.
Le Discours du mâle. Paris: Anthropos, 1980.
Provence ma haine. Saint-Cyr-sur-Loire: Christian Pirot, 1983.
George Sand ou Ces Dames voyagent. Lyons: Atelier de création libertaire, 1986.
Je ne regrette pas le Père Ubu. Paris: Cerisiers, 1988.
Qouiza. Saint-Martial-de-Nabirat (Dordogne): Laporte H., 1988.

Plisson, Marie Prudence (1727–1788). Midwife and author, Plisson wrote a wide variety of poems, novellas, and essays. Her widely read "Promenade de Province" (*Mercure*, April 1755) presents a lively assortment of humorously drawn eighteenth-century types: the wed, the unwed, the re-wed, alchemists, actresses, and a broad array of would-be writers. Her *Réflexions critiques sur les écrits qu'a produits la légitimité des naissances tardives* (1765), published "to be of use to her sex," was written in response to a published debate among male doctor-philosophers concerning the normal length of pregnancy. The essay points to the gender bias in scientific arguments of the day and considers the concrete results of such biases in the lives of women. Plisson's highly personal preface provides a remarkable portrait of this self-assured woman of letters.

Charlotte Daniels

BIBLIOGRAPHY

Primary Texts

"La Promenade de province, nouvelle." *Le Mercure* (August 1755): 48–65.
"Les Charmes du caractère, histoire vraisemblable, suite de la Promenade de Province." *Le Mercure* (November 1755): 9–40.
Projet pour soulager la misère des pauvres dans les campagnes. Chartres: N.p., 1758.
Réflexions critiques sur les écrits qu'a produits la légitimité des naissances tardives, suivies d'une dissertation sur les hommes marins. Paris: La Veuve Duchesne, 1765.
Maximes morales d'un philosophe chrétien. Rome: Lamy, 1783.

Secondary Texts

Briquet, Marguerite-Ursule-Fortunée, Dame. *Dictionnaire historique, littéraire et bibliographique des Françaises et étrangères naturalisées en France, connues par leurs écrits*. Paris: Gillé, 1804.
Prudhomme, Louis Marie. *Biographie universelle et historique des femmes célèbres, mortes ou vivantes*. Paris: Lebigre, 1930.

Poetry. Women have participated in the creation and history of French poetry throughout the centuries, not only as writers, but as patrons, publishers, and catalysts of the poetry of others. Although women poets have been in general excluded from most literary schools, their compositions show the imprint, nonetheless, of all of the notable stylistic movements, such as romanticism* and surrealism*. Moreover, women's poetry exists at all points where history and literature intersect: from the songs of the medieval *trobairitz** to poems of resistance during World War II*. It is difficult to categorize women's poetry in French, for the themes vary with the personal concerns and social condition of the writer, as well as with the important historical issues of the particular time period. However, there do seem to be certain themes that are unique to women's poetry: maternal love, childbearing, physical closeness to the child, and conjugal bliss. More important, though, women poets share the experience of writing from the position of the marginalized other. This excluded status derives historically from the phallocratic belief that the intricate demands of combining elevated thoughts and elaborate language according to a prescribed rhythm require a level of cerebral activity not innate in women. This centuries-old debate on the ability of women to engage in poetic activity and on the value of their writing often manifests itself in the works of women poets as they weave an attitude of dissent into their poetic creations.

Perhaps the most striking and, in France, the earliest, manifestation of this opposition to the patriarchal bias that women were not capable of being poets lies in the example of Marie de France* (twelfth century). Her short narrative poems, or *lais*, attest to her literary vocation in which the poet's toil and labor produce the poetic value of the work and also represent an innovation in poetic expression. She states in several of her *lais* that she has transformed traditional folk material, presumably songs of feminine origin, such as weaving songs (*chansons de toile**), into high literary art destined for an audience at court. Her contribution is thus threefold: she is France's first known woman of the pen; she popularized a new poetic form; and she translated feminine folk art into a poetic form that won acceptance at court and in the canon. In the late Middle Ages, another woman poet, Christine de Pizan*, (1364–1431) initiated a debate that would become known as the *Querelle des femmes** when she attacked the misogyny of her time and its literary conventions. She committed herself and her writing to the defense of women and the recognition of their accomplishments.

The *Querelle des femmes* occupies an equally prominent place in the poetry of women in later centuries. Sixteenth-century poets reiterated Christine's defense of women and also asserted through their poems their right to define relationships with men not according to the chivalric tradition of courtly love*, but in their own way. For Louise Labé*, love is an expression of intense personal desire, while for Pernette du Guillet*, it is a mystic communion between two souls. Madeleine des Roches's* poems of marriage* and widowhood unite her personal experience with that of her readers. Marie Romieu's* poems challenge her era's misogyny by asserting women's good faith and sincerity, and Nicole Estienne's* "Misères de la femme mariée" is one of the more famous examples of the numerous contemporary apologia of women. The works of these poets made women more visible in the world of literature and, further, raised issues that were of particular interest to women.

Religious themes are generally prevalent in women's poetry, and often the poet relates her religious experience as a sensual one. This is the case in Gabrielle Coignard's* poetry from the late sixteenth century. This blending of the religious with the sensual continues into the seventeenth century with Jeanne-Marie Guyon*, whose works unite the erotic and mystic and provoked an important religious debate. The treatment of religious themes in the passionate realism* of Elisabeth Chéron* influenced Nicolas Gilbert. Sensuality and eroticism are also important elements in the suggestive fables* of Louise-Geneviève de Saintonge, who appropriated in her bacchic songs a voice normally reserved for males.

The literary salons* that arose in the seventeenth century were both established and controlled by aristocratic women who were seeking to revive elements of the gallant literary tradition of the past. The salons and the women who frequented them exercised a great deal of influence over many aspects of intellectual life, including literary conventions. Several writers enjoyed widespread fame during their lifetimes: Antoinette Deshoulières*, famous for her contribution to the pastoral poetry so popular in the seventeenth century, was the first woman accepted into a literary academy; Catherine Bernard's* poetry won many prizes from the Académie Française; and Henriette de Coligny de La Suze* was renowned for her passionate elegies, her *préciosité**, and her salon. The increased acceptance of women as writers at this time marked their prominence as practitioners of literature in addition to the significant cultural role they played as *salonnières.*

In the eighteenth century literary salons continued to provide an important vehicle for the participation of women writers. Anne Marie du Bocage* enjoyed international fame for her salon and her poetry that idealized pastoral life. This century also witnessed the fame of several writers recognized for the quality of their comedies and tragedies in verse: Marie-Anne Barbier*, Charlotte Bourrette*, Madeleine-Angélique Poisson, dame Gomez*, and Charlotte Jeanne Béraud de la Haye de Riou Montesson*. Both Adélaïde Dufrénoy* and Marguerite Babois* were known for their elegies, the former for her passionate evocation of heroism, the latter for her themes that heralded the onset of romanticism.

Romanticism, the first major poetic movement to value originality over imitation, coincides with the French Revolution* and the nineteenth century. It was also a period during which people began to reevaluate the role of women in society. The contemporaries of Marceline Desbordes-Valmore* (1786–1859), an early romantic, regarded her as a genius*. Her many volumes of poetry reveal the emotional pressures of everyday life; her emphasis on melody and the exploration of different rhythms influenced Verlaine and the later symbolists*. Other romantic poets include Clémence Robert, Amable Tastu*, and Louisa Siefert*. Delphine Gay de Girardin* was celebrated for her public spirit and poems of national interest. The powerful and dignified poetry of Louise Ackermann* reflected the active role that philosophy and science enjoyed in the nineteenth century. Augustine Blanchecotte's* poetry bore witness to her poverty and the working conditions of women. Increasingly, women's poetry echoed the reality of the social milieu in which the writers operated, and the themes indicate their concerns with issues of wide significance, such as industrialization*.

The poetry of women is present in the various attempts to revitalize poetic expression in the name of modernism. This effort to enlarge the domain of poetry in form, content, and readership began in the latter part of the nineteenth century and in many ways continues to this day. The movement toward inclusion in form was matched by an increasingly receptive public for women poets; accordingly, as poetry questioned its identity, women poets asserted their own individuality. Bridging the turn of this century are several very different poets whose celebrity gained for them a substantial audience. Marie Krysinska*, heralded as the inventor of the *vers libre*, explored musicality and form in her poems. Anna de Noailles* in particular enjoyed worldwide fame for a personal lyricism that exalted the heroic and the passionate. Renée Vivien*, known as the French Sappho, and who translated many poems of that Greek writer, celebrated women's bodies in her own poetry through striking images of a multifaceted sensuality. Louise de Vilmorin was drawn to the spirit of experimentation in form, and her poetry shows her skill at drawing word pictures without rejecting musicality. The more traditional verse of Gérard d'Houville* bespoke the gravity of the human condition through careful attention to harmony and the beauty of words. Lucie Delarue-Mardrus* evoked her native Normandy and examined the condition of women and other marginalized members of society. The desire to investigate previously unknown poetic language and themes characterizes the works of several innovative poets. The works of surrealists Valentine Penrose* and Joyce Mansour* have been praised for their ability to create fantastic worlds and for the versatility of their language. Violence and savagery are important elements in the works of Mansour, recognized as a major figure in twentieth-century poetry. Thérèse Plantier's* poetry approaches surrealism, but its unique qualities and individualism resist classification. Rhythmic sensuality highlights the powerful celebration of nature in Annie Salager's* verse.

Circumstances in regions outside of France and the accompanying interrelationship of language and identity in the lives of women mark the poetry of several writers. The Caribbean experience influences Jeanne Hyvrard's* works, as does that of Québec in the poems of Anne Hébert*, and the Middle East in the writings of Andrée Chedid*. The poetry of both Hébert and Chedid is appreciated by a worldwide audience and universally heralded for its blend of transcendence and presence and its powerful and evocative imagery.

Monica L. Wright and Nancy Sloan Goldberg

BIBLIOGRAPHY

Primary Texts

Bishop, Michael. *Contemporary French Women Poets*. 2 vols. Atlanta: Rodopi, 1995.

Deforges, Régine. *Poèmes de femmes, des origines à nos jours*. Paris: Cherche-Midi, 1993.

Moulin, Jeanne. *Huit Siècles de poésie féminine 1170–1975*. Paris: Seghers, 1981.

Secondary Texts

Metzidakis, Stamos. *Understanding French Poetry: Essays for a New Millennium*. New York: Garland, 1994.

Nichols, Stephen J. "Working Late: Marie de France and the Value of Poetry." In *Women in French Literature*. Ed. Michel Guggenheim. Saratoga, CA: Anma Libri, 1988.

Sabatier, Robert. *Histoire de la poésie française*. 9 vols. Paris: Albin Michel, 1975–1988.

[Useful as an index only, due to sexist commentary and unfounded judgments.]

Stanton, Domna, ed. *The Defiant Muse: French Feminist Poems from the Middle Ages to the Present*. New York: Feminist Press, 1986.

Poitiers, Diane de (1499–1566). More than a mistress to Henri II (king of France, 1547–1559), she wielded greater political influence and often received more official recognition as Henri's consort than his queen, Catherine de Medici*. Born into a noble family and well educated, Diane began her court career at a young age and, after a marriage* that left her widowed at thirty, became mistress to the young dauphin, sixteen years her junior. Upon his accession to the throne and throughout his reign, he kept her by his side in every aspect of royal affairs: she received ambassadors and was often present at counsel; she signed royal documents and had access to treasury accounts; she used her vast influence to manipulate court politics and—as she was known for her familiarity with the latest medical practice, notably in midwifery and pediatrics—was even given the charge of overseeing the health and education* of the king's children. The couple's device, an "H" with intertwining "D's," appeared everywhere; he wore her colors publicly. Her power being entirely dependent on that of the king, she left the court after his death in a jousting accident in 1559 gave Catherine the power of regent.

Besides a hundred or so letters—none of her private missives to Henri survives—Diane left only two short poems. Perhaps her most striking legacy was to have encouraged the development of a new aesthetic around the myth* of Diana the Huntress, a personal mythology reflecting her will—keeping Henri in the role of a willing Acteon—and perpetuated through allegorical designs in the galleries at Fontainebleau and Chenonceaux and throughout her own château, Anet, designed by the master architect Philippe Delorme. Royal allegorical *entrées* (Lyons 1548, Paris 1549, Rouen 1550) represented her patron goddess in central roles and in various incarnations as *la dame aux cerfs* mastering beasts (signifying Henri's adversaries, or Henri himself) or Apollo/Henri's chaste sister fighting by his side in battle. A century later Diane appears in Mme de Lafayette's* *La Princesse de Clèves* as the troubling, semi-mythic figure who—unlike the protagonist—is able successfully to join Eros with power and public acceptance. Patroness of the arts (Du Bellay, Ronsard, Olivier de Magny and others wrote works for her), she had a great influence on the literary and artistic imagination of her era.

Francis T. Bright

BIBLIOGRAPHY

Primary Text

Guiffrey, Georges. *Lettres inédites de Dianne de Poytiers*. Paris: Veuve J. Renouard, 1866.

Secondary Texts

Bardon, Françoise. *Diane de Poitiers et le mythe de Diane*. Paris: PUF, 1963.
Erlanger, Philippe. *Diane de Poitiers*. Paris: Gallimard, 1955.
Roussel, Pierre Désiré. *Histoire et description du château d'Anet*. Paris: D. Jouaust, 1875.

Pompadour, Jeanne-Antoinette Poisson, marquise de (1721–1764). The first official mistress of a French king to come from the bourgeoisie, Pompadour married in 1741, but abandoned her husband four years later to become the mistress of Louis XV. Rechristened marquise de Pompadour, she took up residence at Versailles and soon established herself as a powerful figure at court. Although her relationship with Louis XV was platonic from around 1750, she remained his confidante until her death.

Pompadour's reputation has varied greatly over time according to the beneficial or nefarious consequences attached to her influence over the king. Her role in shaping the artistic taste of her era has attracted the least criticism, given the indifference of Louis XV. Pompadour significantly increased her power in this domain by appointing a relative as General Director of Buildings, in charge of spending on the arts. While the extent of her direct involvement with this agency is disputed (see Posner), it is certain that she was the guiding force behind such projects as the Royal Porcelain Factory at Sèvres, and that she filled her many residences with government-purchased artistic treasures, thus subsidizing her favorite artists. Pompadour was herself an accomplished actress and singer, and established a much-admired private theater* at Versailles. She had ties to various literary figures of the time, including Voltaire, whom she met as a young woman, and who remained a lifelong friend.

Pompadour was much vilified during her lifetime for her extravagance, as well as for the perception that she used her position to intervene in political as well as artistic affairs of state. While her influence in the aesthetic domain has since been extolled as civilizing and feminine, her behind-the-scenes political maneuvering has been almost universally condemned. Even Pompadour's detractors have admired the intellectual and psychological force she manifested in rising from relatively humble origins to a position of great power. It is all the more remarkable that she occupied her tenuous post for some twenty years, dying in her apartments at Versailles.

Mary McAlpin

BIBLIOGRAPHY

Secondary Texts

Gallet, Danielle. *Madame de Pompadour ou le pouvoir féminin*. Paris: Fayard, 1985.
Goncourt, Edmond and Jules de. *Madame de Pompadour*. Paris: Firmin-Didot et Cie., 1888.
Posner, Donald. "Mme de Pompadour as a Patron of the Visual Arts." *Art Bulletin* 72, no. 1 (March 1990): 74–105.

Popular literature. The phrase "popular literature" and the related term "best-seller" did not come into use in France until the nineteenth century. As a result of the ease of production and the consequent lower prices that characterized the book industry during the nineteenth century, books aimed specifically at women readers came to dominate the market. Oftentimes, as they are today, these books were written simply, thus making them easy for less-educated women to read, and had romance as their principal topic. This was true throughout the twentieth century and is still an accurate description of much popular literature today. "Popular literature" can be difficult to define; however, most critics agree that it is constituted by texts read by a large number of individuals during a given period. Nonetheless, it is often very difficult to determine the precise readership of a given nineteenth-century book.

The dominant genre of popular literature during the nineteenth and twentieth centuries is the novel*, although other genres such as comic strips are also considered popular literature. During the nineteenth century and the first half of the twentieth century, popular novels generally spoke of the contemporary society of the readers and writers, generally bourgeois or aristocratic. They had plots in which good and bad were easily distinguished, and they are the predecessors of Harlequin romance novels that are still popular in France today. Early in the nineteenth century Sophie Cottin* was an extremely popular writer for just these reasons. As Resa Dudovitz notes, her books are generally about persecuted but intelligent women who ultimately triumph over disreputable lovers. Cottin's novels were reprinted often during the first half of the nineteenth century, and her two most popular, *Elizabeth* (1808) and *Claire d'Albe* (1799), sold over 30,000 copies between 1816 and 1840. Laure de Saint-Ouen was another widely read writer of the same period. Although her *Histoire de France* (1835?) was not a novel, over 90,000 copies of this text were printed between 1835 and 1850. Like Madame Bovary in the novel by Gustave Flaubert, the nineteenth-century women readers preferred "amours, amants, amantes," and historical subjects.

From 1885 to 1933 one of the most popular women writers was Gyp* (the comtesse de Martel de Janville), who wrote over 100 best-sellers. Many of her books feature hideous Jewish characters, and *Israel* (1898) in particular mirrors the anti-Semitic mood of France during the Dreyfus Affair (1898–1905). Although some people have claimed that Gyp was a feminist due to her athletic heroines who married for love and were modeled on the writer herself, her biographer notes that she always aggressively rejected this characterization. The period just after World War I* manifests another boom in popular novels written by women. Romance novels by the Dellys (the brother/sister team of Marie and Frédéric Petitjean de la Rosière) were perhaps the most popular books of this period, thanks to the escapist tone of the romances described, so desperately needed after the horrors of the war.

The phenomenal popularity of Françoise Sagan's* *Bonjour Tristesse* (1954) can be ascribed to its depiction of disillusioned youth. After the harsh post–

World War II years, young French women recognized the ease with which society can be destroyed and then rebuilt. The best-sellers of the 1960s and 1970s assumed a more political tone, as exemplified by the work of Christiane Rochefort*, whose popular novel *Les Petits Enfants du siècle* (1961) tells the story of a working-class girl who tries to escape from the suburban wasteland of French low-income housing, only to end up pregnant and married, fated to continue in the footsteps of her mother and the women around her. The more politically and class-conscious women of the 1960s wanted to see themselves mirrored in the novels they read. With the rise of feminism*, many of the books written during the 1970s were based on a search for self-identity, as in *Le Jeu du souterrain* (1973) by Françoise Mallet-Joris*. However, in the 1980s the popular literature once again becomes quite escapist in nature. One of the most read writers of this period was Régine Deforges*, whose trilogy of romantic, historical novels, *La Bicyclette bleue* (1983), *101 Avenue Henri-Martin* (1983; 1986), and *Le Diable en rit encore* (1984), were extremely popular; the first volume alone sold over 3 million copies. Perhaps the popularity of these historical novels can be explained by the reading public's need for perspective; life may be difficult today, but it is much easier than it was fifty years ago. An important element that all of these novels have in common is the style in which they are written; each one is formally conventional and easy to read. One extremely popular book, which is radically different both in style and theme from novels such as Deforges's, is *L'Amant* (1984). Marguerite Duras's* tale of forbidden love sold over 750,000 copies the first year of its publication. Although it touches on complex issues such as colonialism* and racism and is truly erotic in tone, *L'Amant*'s remarkable popularity can be attributed in part to the theme of love and the easily read quality of the prose, but also to the prestigious Prix Goncourt it won in 1984.

Gayle A. Levy

BIBLIOGRAPHY

Secondary Texts

Dudovitz, Resa L. *The Myth of Superwoman: Women's Bestsellers in France and the United States*. London: Routledge, 1990.

Martin, Henri, and Roger Chartier, eds. *Histoire de l'édition française: Le Temps des éditeurs*. Vol. 3. Paris: Promodis, 1985.

Olivier-Martin, Yves. *Histoire du roman populaire en France de 1840 à 1980*. Paris: Albin Michel, 1980.

Silverman, Willa Z. *The Notorious Life of Gyp: Right-Wing Anarchist in Fin-de-Siècle France*. New York: Oxford University Press, 1995.

Weiner, Susan E. *Heroes of Everyday Life: Women Writers in 1950s France*. Ann Arbor: UMI, 1993.

Port-Royal (1204–1709). Founded in the Chevreuse valley in 1204, the abbey of Port-Royal housed a Cistercian community of women religious. In the seventeenth century the abbey also accepted male laity who sought refuge and solitude there, and most historical accounts of Port-Royal focus on the contributions of these *Solitaires* (Antoine Arnauld, Pierre Nicole, Blaise Pascal, and others). Recent research, however, has revealed the prominent role of the women of Port-Royal. Notable among them was Angélique Arnauld* who, at age eleven, was named abbess in 1602. In 1608, desiring to amend the relatively lax observation of monastic vows at the abbey, Mère Angélique introduced severe reforms, including the cloistering of all religious, strict observation of the vow of poverty, increased solitude, silence and prayer, and spiritual and physical mortification designed to help the religious live the Passion of Christ through perpetual sacrifice. Advocating uniformity among the sisters, Mère Angélique believed the communal life of the cloister to be an affirmation of liberty from the material world. Under her direction, life at Port-Royal consisted of prayer and good works (feeding and clothing the poor and providing limited medical assistance when possible). While Mère Angélique discouraged the religious from learning to write, believing that activity to be in contradiction with the simplicity of monastic life, she herself carried on an abundant correspondence, particularly with other women. In 1626 malaria forced the community to leave Chevreuse; the religious relocated to Port-Royal de Paris, where they would stay until 1648, when Port-Royal had been made safe for habitation. In 1630 the newly elected abbess Geneviève Le Tardif reformed the process of educating novices at Port-Royal. Most significantly, Mère Geneviève insisted that women religious learn to write as a means of developing their reason. This second wave of religious, which included intelligent and well-educated women such as Jacqueline Pascal*, helped to found the schools of Port-Royal, which were closed in 1661 during the persecution of the abbey by the Jesuits and Louis XIV. Objecting to Port-Royal's espousal of Jansenism*, the Parisian Assembly of the Clergy demanded that all priests and religious sign an oath condemning the movement's teachings. While the *Solitaires* eventually signed the Formulary, the women religious of Port-Royal proved to be more obstinate in their resistance, proclaiming their willingness to die for their beliefs. The persecution of Port-Royal continued until the Church granted a Pax Ecclesiae in 1668; in 1679, however, pressure to eradicate Jansenism from France grew. In 1709, under orders of the pope, the remaining religious were expelled from Port-Royal. All structures save one were razed, and the abbey's cemetery was desecrated.

Suzanne C. Toczyski

BIBLIOGRAPHY

Chroniques de Port-Royal. Bulletin de la Société des Amis de Port-Royal. Paris: Bibliothèque Mazarine, 1992.
Courcelles, Dominique de. *Le Sang des autres*. Paris: L'Herne, 1994.
Mémoires pour servir à l'Histoire de Port-Royal et à la Vie de la Révérende Mère Marie Angélique Arnauld Réformatrice de ce Monastère. 3 vols. Utrecht: N.p., 1742.
Sainte-Beuve, Charles Augustin. *Port-Royal*. Paris: Hachette, 1922.

Postcolonialism. The term ''postcolonial'' appeared for the first time in reference to British Commonwealth literatures and cultures in the mid-1980s. In its most literal meaning, postcolonialism designates that which follows modern European colonization, and for this reason has been accused of ignoring neocolonialism. While the term has many meanings, its most popular usage refers to counterdiscursive practices which seek to revise and decenter Western master narratives about formerly colonized peoples. It is used, for example, to designate the work of writers from former colonies and of minority groups such as the *Beurs* in France.

The relationship of postcolonialism to feminism* in general, and to French feminism in particular, stems from feminists' adoption of a terminology describing the condition of women throughout history as one of exploitation and colonization by men. Writers such as Hélène Cixous* and Claudine Herrmann* adapt the language of colonization to feminist purposes, and show how language and knowledge have been instrumental in the cultural colonization of women. A further parallel can be drawn between feminist strategies for rereading patriarchal texts and postcolonial strategies for revising texts written from a Western hegemonic position.

The appropriation of the language of postcolonialism to serve First World universalizing ends has provoked tensions between First and Third World women. Although the identification of gender-specific issues is a common concern of both First World and Third World feminisms, critics have denounced Western feminists' ethnocentrism. Over a decade ago, Gayatri Spivak strongly criticized French feminists for their theoretical positions that remained blind to cultural and class differences. In response to their double silencing as women and as colonized subjects, postcolonial writers such as Assia Djebar* have given voice to women in narratives that counter the patriarchal and colonialist discourses that claim to define them.

S. Pascale Bécel

BIBLIOGRAPHY

Secondary Texts

Cixous, Hélène, and Catherine Clément. *La Jeune Née*. Paris: Union Générale d'Editions, 1975.

Djebar, Assia. *L'Amour, la fantasia*. Paris: Lattès, 1985.

Green, Mary Jean, Karen Gould, Micheline Rice-Maximin, Keith L. Walker, and Jack A. Yeager, eds. *Postcolonial Subjects: Francophone Women Writers*. Minneapolis: University of Minnesota Press, 1996.

Herrmann, Claudine. *Les Voleuses de langue*. Paris: Des femmes, 1976.

Kristeva, Julia. *Des Chinoises*. Paris: Des femmes, 1974.

Lionnet, Françoise. *Postcolonial Representations: Women, Literature, Identity*. Ithaca: Cornell University Press, 1995.

Lionnet, Françoise and Ronnie Scharfman, eds. ''Post/Colonial Conditions: Exiles, Migrations, and Nomadisms.'' *Yale French Studies* 82–83 (1993).

Minh-ha, Trinh T. *Woman, Native, Other: Writing Postcoloniality and Feminism.* Bloomington: Indiana University Press, 1989.

Mohanty, Chandra. "Under Western Eyes: Feminist Scholarship and Colonial Discourses." *Feminist Review* 30 (Autumn 1988): 61–87.

Mudimbe-Boyi, Elisabeth, ed. "Post-colonial Women's Writing." *L'Esprit créateur* 33, no. 2 (Summer 1993).

Schor, Naomi. "French Feminism Is a Universalism." *Differences: A Journal of Feminist Cultural Studies* 7, no. 1 (1995): 15–47.

Spivak, Gayatri Chakravorty. "French Feminism in an International Frame." *Yale French Studies* 62 (1981): 154–184.

Postmodernism. A term originally used in the field of aesthetics, postmodernism has become one of the most ubiquitous, yet difficult to define, critical terms of today. It is most accurately described as a critical stance that opposes Enlightenment* ideals of modernity. Postmodernity, a particular historical and cultural moment, and postmodern projects of various kinds have many traits in common, such as fragmentation, instability, pluralism, micropolitics, and suspicion of theory. Postmodernism shares much with poststructuralist critiques of the foundations of Western thought and its investigations into the play of signification and the materiality of language, although postmodernism is much broader and more interdisciplinary in scope, more political and radical in its contestation of the certainties of the past. Indeed, the beginning of postmodern criticism is often associated with Jean-François Lyotard's description of the breakdown of modernity's totalizing explanatory narratives of philosophy, science, and social theory, and of their legitimating metanarratives that served as the foundations of truth and knowledge in the West. Postmodern feminists deconstruct numerous long-standing Enlightenment assumptions. In particular, they expose the privileging of male perspectives and interests in what are presented as absolute, universal truths, thus revealing the so-called universal subject to be male and all knowledge to be partial and necessarily situated. Postmodern feminists also reject the notion of the transparency of language, choosing instead to explore its role in constructing rather than merely reflecting the truths and realities it conveys. Thus, in place of a universalized subject conceptualized as a cohesive, stable identity, they describe an already sexed—that is, embodied—subjectivity that is socially and discursively constructed within politically motivated relations of power. Because of its situatedness within language, culture, biology, and history, this means of conceptualizing subjectivity responds to the desire to account for differences among women and to the need to situate both political action and ways of knowing in female subjects.

Katherine Stephenson

BIBLIOGRAPHY

Secondary Texts

Best, Steven, and Douglas Kellner. *Postmodern Theory: Critical Interrogations.* New York: Guilford Press, 1991.

Butler, Judith. *Bodies that Matter: On the Discursive Limits of "Sex."* New York: Routledge, 1993.

Butler, Judith, and Joan W. Scott, eds. *Feminists Theorize the Political.* New York: Routledge, 1992.

Docherty, Thomas, ed. *Postmodernism: A Reader.* New York: Columbia University Press, 1993.

Flax, Jane. *Thinking Fragments: Psychoanalysis, Feminism, and Postmodernism in the Contemporary West.* Berkeley: University of California Press, 1990.

Grosz, Elizabeth. "Bodies and Knowledges: Feminism and the Crisis of Reason." In *Space, Time, and Perversion.* New York: Routledge, 1995. 25–43.

Hekman, Susan. *Gender and Knowledge: Elements of a Postmodern Feminism.* Cambridge: Polity, 1990.

Hutcheon, Linda. *The Politics of Postmodernism.* London: Routledge, 1989.

Jaggar, Alison, and Susan Bordo, eds. *Gender/Body/Knowledge: Feminist Reconstructions of Being and Knowledge.* New Brunswick, NJ: Rutgers University Press, 1989.

Lyotard, Jean-François. *The Postmodern Condition: A Report on Knowledge.* Trans. Goeff Bennington and Brian Massumi. Minneapolis: University of Minnesota Press, 1984.

Nicholson, Linda J., ed. *Feminism/Postmodernism.* New York: Routledge, 1990.

Waugh, Patricia, ed. *Postmodernism: A Reader.* London: Edward Arnold, 1992.

Poststructuralism. This term comprises a broad range of theoretical positions that have emerged from structuralism's focus on the structural relations of the linguistic sign and the application of a linguistic model of signification to other fields. The theorists most commonly identified as poststructuralist are Roland Barthes, Jacques Lacan, Jacques Derrida, Michel Foucault, and, in the rare accounts including feminist theorists, Hélène Cixous*, Luce Irigaray*, and Julia Kristeva*, who have in common their critique of structuralist accounts of how meaning is produced and their rejection of traditional categories of Western thought. With this "linguistic turn" in Western thought, truth and traditional modes of legitimating knowledge were revealed to be discursive effects of the workings of power, and unquestioned faith in the stability of sign systems, representation, meaning, and the subject gave way to a growing awareness and investigation of their inherent instability. Consequently, the focus moved from the analysis of objects to that of materialist processes: from meaning to how meaning is produced, from truth to representation, from text as product to text as process, from author as source and legitimator of a text to the indeterminacy of the text and to readers as its co-producers, from a unified subject to a decentered, discursively constituted subject.

Poststructuralist critiques have provided the foundation for identifying and analyzing how knowledge is politically motivated and discursively constructed, thus helping feminists to deconstruct patriarchal knowledge and truth claims, to explain why women accept confinement in roles and institutions defined by the patriarchy, and to understand the importance of providing alternative, more socially equitable, definitions and representations of women.

Katherine Stephenson

BIBLIOGRAPHY

Secondary Texts

Barrett, Michèle, and Anne Phillips, eds. *Destabilizing Theory: Contemporary Feminist Debates*. Stanford: Stanford University Press, 1992.

Butler, Judith, and Joan Scott, eds. *Feminists Theorize the Political*. New York: Routledge, 1992.

Culler, Jonathan. *On Deconstruction: Theory and Criticism after Structuralism*. Ithaca: Cornell University Press, 1982.

Diamond, Irene, and Lee Quinby, eds. *Feminism and Foucault: Reflections on Resistance*. Boston: Northeastern University Press, 1988.

Diprose, Rosalyn, and Robyn Ferrell, eds. *Cartographies: Poststructuralism and the Mapping of Bodies and Spaces*. Sydney: Allen and Unwin, 1991.

Grosz, Elizabeth. *Jacques Lacan: A Feminist Introduction*. London: Routledge, 1990.

———. *Sexual Subversions: Three French Feminists: J. Kristeva, L. Irigaray, M. Le Doeuff*. Sydney: Allen and Unwin, 1989.

Gunew, Sneja, ed. *Feminist Knowledge: Critique and Construct*. New York: Routledge, 1990.

Moore, Pamela, and Devoney Looser. "Theoretical Feminisms: Subjectivity, Struggle, and the 'Conspiracy' of Poststructuralisms." *Style* 27, no. 4 (Winter 1993): 530–558.

Sarup, Madan. *Introductory Guide to Post-Structuralism and Postmodernism*. Athens: University of Georgia Press, 1993.

Silverman, Kaja. *The Subject of Semiotics*. New York: Oxford University Press, 1983.

Young, Robert, ed. *Untying the Text: A Post-Structuralist Reader*. New York: Routledge, 1987.

Pougy, Liane de (1869–1950). Liane de Pougy, née Anne-Marie Chassaigne, has been remembered as one of the most beautiful, decadent, and literary courtesans of the turn-of-the-century era in France. However, both the beginning and the ending of her life were quite different from the erotic and hedonistic images that have traditionally been preserved for posterity.

She was born to the bourgeois family Chassaigne. Her father was an officer in the French army. Her mother's strict religious values required that Anne-Marie be educated in a convent*. She was married at age sixteen to Armand Pourpe, a naval lieutenant, gave birth to one son, then fled to Paris, where she became immersed in the opulent lifestyle of the "demi-mondaines" and took up the name Liane de Pougy (Pougy was one of her first male conquests in Paris).

After several years of success as an actress, mime, and dancer, and numerous affairs with artists, noblemen, politicians, and wealthy bankers from all over Europe, Liane decided to write a novel* about her experiences. In 1898 the *roman à clé L'Insaisissable* appeared and sold extremely well, going through nineteen editions in the first year alone. In 1899 her second novel, on a similar subject, *Myrrhille*, also met with a popular success. During that same year, she met Natalie Barney*, the American expatriate and writer, and it was while they pursued their passionate twelve-month love affair that Liane began writing one of her most famous works, *Idylle sapphique*, which appeared in 1901. Although her contemporaries described her writing as "the style of an artificial blonde," they also noted that her prose contained an originality in its phrasing and spiritual quality. *Idylle sapphique* was also shocking: it openly chronicles and celebrates Pougy's lesbian love affair with Barney, at the same time that it mocks and trivializes bourgeois mentality and heterosexual love.

After nearly twenty years as a courtesan in Paris, Liane de Pougy met Prince Georges Ghika in 1908 and married him in 1910, subsequently growing distant from the intimate women's community, her literary career, and the tumultuous lifestyle that she had developed and led for two decades. Thus, at age forty, she gave up her nom de plume, became Princess Anne-Marie Ghika, and tried to enter the "respectable" society of the *grand monde* in Paris. Her efforts, however, were unsuccessful, given her past life of disorder and easy virtue. Her old friends and new artists continued to come to her home for friendship*, advice, and literary and artistic exchange.

Liane de Pougy began her last work, *Mes Cahiers bleus*, in 1920 and continued to write this combination memoir/diary for over twenty years. She chronicled events happening to her during those years, but also reviewed previous moments in her chaotic life as a courtesan.

During the 1930s, she became involved in charitable work for the St. Agnes Asylum for mentally disturbed children. After fifteen years of physical and mental decay, her husband Georges died in 1943. With the help of the director of the St. Agnes Asylum, Liane de Pougy abandoned her title of Princess Ghika to become a lay nun in the order of St. Dominic. She remained Sister Anne-Marie until she died in Lausanne at the end of 1950.

Juliette M. Rogers

BIBLIOGRAPHY

Primary Texts

L'Insaisissable. Paris: Librairie Nilsson, 1898.
Myrrhille. Paris: Librairie Nilsson, 1899.
Idylle sapphique. Paris: Librairie de la Plume, 1901. (Réedition chez Jean-Claude Lattès, 1979.)
Ecce homo. Paris: Société parisienne d'édition, 1903.
Les Sensations de Mademoiselle de La Bringue. Paris: Albin Michel, 1904.
Yvée Lester. Paris: Ambert, 1906.
Yvée Jourdan. Paris: Ambert 1908.
Mes Cahiers bleus. Paris: Plon, 1977.

Secondary Texts

Chalon, Jean. *Liane de Pougy: Courtisane, princesse, et sainte*. Paris: Flammarion, 1994.
Jacob, Max, and Salomon Reinach. *Lettres à Liane de Pougy*. Paris: Plon, 1980.

Poulain, mademoiselle (eighteenth century). Very little is known about her life, except that she came from Nogent-sur-Seine, a small town southwest of Paris, and wrote during the latter years of the eighteenth century. Still, her works show a talented author who wrote both fiction and nonfiction, poetry,* and prose. Her *Histoire de Port-Royal* (1786) and *Tableau de la parole ou une nouvelle manière d'apprendre à lire aux enfants en jouant* (1783) show a broad range of interests in social and historical subjects. The idea that children could learn to read while having fun clearly indicates that Mademoiselle Poulain favored new and inventive methods over rote memorization. In addition to her works of nonfiction, she published *Poésies diverses* (1787), and a novel*, *Lettres de Madame la comtesse de Rivière à Madame la baronne de Neufpont, son amie* (1777). While this novel appears similar in style to many of the epistolary novels popular at the time, Mademoiselle Poulain's originality lies in the technique she uses to convince her readers of the work's authenticity. While she claims that these letters are written by a family member—an often-used technique—she skillfully weaves her own name, Poulain de Nogent, and birthplace into the introduction, thereby increasing the belief that these letters must be authentic.

Jeanne Hageman

BIBLIOGRAPHY

Primary Texts

Lettres de Madame la comtesse de Rivière à Madame la baronne de Neufpont, son amie. Paris: Froulle, 1777.
Tableau de la parole ou une nouvelle manière d'apprendre à lire aux enfants en jouant. Paris: Nyon l'aîné, 1783.
Anecdotes intéressantes de l'amour conjugal, revues et exposées avec précision. Paris: Hardouin et Gattey, 1786.
Nouvelle histoire abrégée de Port Royal. Paris: Varin, 1786.
Poésies diverses. Paris: Varin, 1787.

Pozzi, Catherine (1882–1934). Born of an affluent family, Pozzi manifested her independence of spirit and desire to break away from traditional female roles at an early age. She temporarily distanced herself from her family* to study at Oxford, and later divorced her husband, playwright Edouard Bourdet. Her work exhibits a continuing effort to define her own identity and affirm her freedom. Her complex and sophisticated poetry* expresses her attempts to create a new path which would make use of and surpass the poetic endeavors of her male predecessors. She is best known for her *Journal*, a large part of which is devoted to her stormy relationship with the poet Paul Valéry and to her struggle to protect her own ideas and inspiration—in particular those expressed in her philosophical essay, *Peau d'Ame*. Pozzi feared both that Valéry would appropriate them and that critics and the public would not recognize them as hers.

Hélène Julien

BIBLIOGRAPHY

Primary Texts

Peau d'Ame. Preface by Gérard d'Houville. Paris: Corréa, 1935.
Journal 1913–1934. Preface by Lawrence Joseph. Ed. Claire Paulhan. Paris: Ramsay, 1987.
Agnès. Preface by Lawrence Joseph. Paris: Editions de la Différence, 1988.
Oeuvres poétiques. Ed. Lawrence Joseph. Paris: Editions de la Différence, 1988.

Secondary Texts

Aury, Dominique. "Un Eclair de génie." *Nouvelle Revue Française* 243 (April 1988): 59–60.
Joseph, Lawrence. *Catherine Pozzi: Une Robe couleur du temps*. Paris: Editions de la Différence, 1988.

Prassinos, Gisèle (1920–). Born in Istanbul, Prassinos emigrated to France in 1922. Her early "automatic" texts, written in her mid-teens, were hailed by Breton and the surrealists for their nonsensical, subversive, and cruel humor (*La Sauterelle arthritique*, 1935). A fifteen-year silence ended with *Le Temps n'est rien* (1958), her poetic autobiography*. For six years, Prassinos experimented with the genre of the novel*, abandoning it after writing *Le Grand Repas* (1966), with its haunting blend of realism*, poetry*, and the fantastic. Since then, she has published several collections of short stories* and poems, including some for children. Though Prassinos makes no feminist claim, her work challenges conventional representations of reality, in particular gender boundaries, through her use of androgynous characters.

Madeleine Cottenet-Hage

BIBLIOGRAPHY

Primary Texts

Le Cavalier. Paris: Plon, 1961.
Le Visage effleuré de peine. Paris: Grasset, 1964.
Les Mots endormis. Paris: Flammarion, 1967.
La Vie la voix. Paris: Flammarion, 1971.
Brelin le Frou ou Le Portrait de famille. Paris: Belfond, 1976.
Trouver sans chercher. Paris: Flammarion, 1976.
Le Ciel et la terre se marient. Paris: Les Editions Ouvrières, 1979.
Mon Coeur les écoute. Paris: Liasse à l'Imprimerie Quotidienne, 1982.
La Confidente. Paris: Grasset, 1992.
La Table de famille. Paris: Flammarion, 1993.

Secondary Texts

Caws, Mary Ann, Rudolf E. Kuenzli, and Gwen Raaberg, eds. *Surrealism and Women*. Cambridge, MA: MIT Press, 1991.
Cottenet-Hage, Madeleine. *Gisèle Prassinos ou Le Désir du lieu intime*. Paris: Jean-Michel Place, 1988.

Préciosité. Although the term may be traced to the Middle Ages, *préciosité* has long been described as a literary and social phenomenon which flourished in France between 1650 and 1661. The literary inspiration of seventeenth-century *préciosité* consisted primarily of the correspondence of Balzac and Voiture, Voiture's poetry*, Pierre Corneille's plays, and, to a lesser extent, Honore d'Urfé's *L'Astrée*. These works contributed greatly to the social phenomenon of *préciosité*, which has come to be associated with the salons* of Catherine de Rambouillet* and Madeleine de Scudéry* and the circles of Mlle de Montpensier* and Mme de Lafayette*. In its social manifestation, *préciosité* is said to represent a desire for refinement and elegance, a taste for rarefied language purified of vulgarity, and a search for distinction within an exclusive world that celebrated brilliant conversation, platonic love, *galanterie, générosité*, and heroism. The literature produced in this intellectual yet playful social milieu valorized love and an idealized conception of woman as perfect yet inaccessible. It relied upon paradox and surprise, hyperbole, antithesis, strong imagery and metaphors, and paraphrase to create an effect. *Préciosité* purified and enriched the French language; its themes inspired intricate novels* featuring psychological analysis and idealism (cf. Scudéry, Lafayette, Montpensier). The ostensible proponents of *préciosité* were featured in Michel de Pure's *La Prétieuse* (1656–1658), while Baudeau de Somaize's *Grand Dictionnaire des Prétieuses* (1661) purported to explain allusions and expressions associated with the *précieux*. Yet, from the time of its first appearance in 1654, virtually all references to the word *précieuse* are found in satires or parodies such as Molière's *Les Précieuses ridicules* (1659), and the term was associated primarily with prudes and/or coquettes who were hostile to marriage* and promoted the right of women to autonomy and intellectual distinction; *préciosité* came to be synonymous with a tendency toward affectation and excess. The limited body of textual references to *précieuses* has led contemporary critics to question the historical validity of the term. Women who came to be known as *précieuses* neither applied that term to themselves nor considered it an ideal to emulate. *Précieuse* now seems, at best, an unstable substantive which eludes precise definition; at worst, a fictional invention of historians who sought to reconstruct the nonexistent "true" *précieuses* as a group to be admired. Some recent critical approaches include psychoanalytical models. Domna Stanton has maintained that the term *précieuse* names a caricature born of men's fear of women's power over language, whereas Philippe Sellier suggests that *précieuses* can be better understood using modern descriptions of hysteria*, frigidity, homosexuality, and phobia. Clearly, the phenomena associated with the term are diverse and complex; *préciosité* has perhaps best been described by Lathuillère as a convergence of literary and social tendencies resisting synthesis or formal definition. Yet historically, the phenomena associated with *préciosité* contributed greatly to the movement of women from the private sphere to the public space of writing, and as such must be included in any account of the beginnings of French feminism* in seventeenth-century France.

Suzanne C. Toczyski

BIBLIOGRAPHY

Secondary Texts

Backer, Dorothy. *Precious Women*. New York: Basic Books, 1974.

Bray, René. *La Préciosité et les précieux, de Thibaut de Champagne à Jean Giraudoux*. Paris: A. Michel, [1948].

Lathuillère, Roger. *La Préciosité: Etude historique et linguistique*. Geneva: Droz, 1966.

Pelous, Jean-Michel. *Amour précieux, amour galant (1654–1675)*. Paris: Klincksieck, 1980.

Stanton, Domna C. "The Fiction of *Préciosité* and the Fear of Women." *Yale French Studies* 62 (1981): 107–134.

Press, feminist. Following the French Revolution* of 1789 and the Napoleonic Code's* exclusion of women from the polis, French women used the press to denounce their subordinate civil, cultural, and political status, or to claim a superior feminine difference. An instrument of enlightenment, protest, or coalition building, the press became a primary means for women to constitute themselves publicly as subjects. The first such publications appeared during the July Monarchy, exploded in the Third Republic, and continued to proliferate during the twentieth century. Yet, for all its vitality and capacity for regeneration, the French feminist press has regularly suffered from financial pressures, both personal and ideological, as well as from national crises.

If the general political press during much of the nineteenth century struggled against government control and repression, the earliest publications for and by women were deemed inherently apolitical. Nonetheless, from 1822 to 1881 women were legally prohibited from managing newspapers and journals. While some women managed to circumvent this law, others succeeded in using the so-called feminine press to feminist ends.

During the early decades of the nineteenth century, women were the audience for fashion and instructive journals. Journals such as Sophie de Senneterre's *Athenée des femmes* (1808) were also an outlet for women writers' political and literary pieces. In the early July Monarchy, Fanny Richomme's *Journal des femmes* (1832–1836) was a strong advocate for women's right to professional authorship. Eugénie Niboyet's* Lyons-based *Conseiller des femmes* (1833–1834) and *Le Citateur féminin* (1833–1835) both stressed the importance of women's writing, while *La Gazette des femmes* (1836–1838) was the first publication to campaign for women's right to petition the government.

In contrast to these periodicals, the proletarian Saint-Simonian women's autonomous *La Femme libre* (1832–1834) articulated a class-conscious, radical feminism* and offered a critique of the dominant sexual morality. In 1848 several women from this paper rallied around the first French feminist daily, Niboyet's *La Voix des femmes*. For a brief moment, feminists from both the middle and the working classes used this paper to publicize their aggressive campaign for the right to vote*.

Léon Richer and Maria Deraisme's* *Droit des femmes* (1868) became an important feminist publication in the early Third Republic. Anticlerical and republican, the paper focused on women's civil, professional, and educational formation and rights. Its silence on women's suffrage prompted socialist Hubertine Auclert* to launch *La Citoyenne* (1881–1891) with suffrage as its objective. Maria Martin maintained the paper's pro-suffrage stance when she transformed *La Citoyenne* into the nonpartisan *Journal des femmes* (1891–1904).

At the end of the century the numerous feminist publications reflected the fractured nature of the movement, which split along Republican, socialist, Catholic, and independent lines. Of these, Marguerite Durand's* *La Fronde* (1897–1905; 1914; 1926–1928) was the first feminist daily to be owned, managed, written, and printed by women. It launched campaigns supporting Dreyfus, voluntary motherhood, pacifism, and women's economic emancipation.

During the early years of the twentieth century, feminists were divided about the extent of suffrage. Madeleine Pelletier's* *La Suffragiste* (1908–1914; 1919–1920) favored integral suffragism, while Jane Misme's *La Française* (1906–1940), the mouthpiece of the National Council of French Women and later of the French Union for Women's Suffrage, advocated limited suffrage. Division among socialist feminists also led to separate publications. Louise Saumonneau's *La Femme socialiste* (1901–1902) repudiated bourgeois feminism in favor of class struggle, while Gabrielle Petit's neo-Malthusian and syndicalist *La Femme affranchie* (1904–1909) remained open to organized feminism.

After World War I*, paper shortages, financial losses, and pressing concerns such as depopulation, national recovery, and employment weakened feminist journalism. Many radical socialist feminists defected, even if temporarily, to the new Communist Party's section for women and its periodical, *L'Ouvrière* (1921–1927). The most important radical feminist publication of this period was Colette Reynaud's *La Voix des femmes* (1917–1939), which attracted seasoned feminist journalists such as Hélène Brion*, Nelly Roussel*, Séverine*, and Madeleine Pelletier.

After World War II*, American-inspired women's magazines such as *Marie-Claire* and *Elle* offered upbeat consumer messages, while the communist-linked Union of French Women launched the weekly *Femmes françaises* and the monthly *Heures claires* in 1944. The only avowedly feminist publication, *Droit des femmes*, quietly but doggedly pressured for reform of marriage* law. The association newsletter *Maternité heureuse* addressed women's health issues, laying important groundwork for the campaigns of the 1960s against the 1920 law that banned the distribution of information about contraception and abortion*. In 1961, non-communist women's rights activists published the magazine *La Femme au XIXe siècle*, written mostly by Yvette Roudy* and Colette Audry.

The explosion of women's voices in periodicals, newsletters, and broadsheets after May 1968 signaled "new" provocative and revolutionary French feminists. Different teams of women produced the issues of the radical feminist *Le Torchon*

Brûle (1971–1973), which dispensed with formal layout, rubrics, by-lines, and even typeface in its refusal of polished journalism. In the 1970s the MLF (Mouvement de Libération des Femmes*) split along different lines of approach to issues of gender, class, and difference. Simone de Beauvoir* co-founded *Questions féministes* (1977–1980), which theorized the oppression of women as a social class, while the Psychanalyse et Politique* (Psych et Po) group focused on psychoanalytical theories* of the feminine. Psych et Po had the funds to found a publishing* house and bookstore, des femmes, and to publish a weekly magazine, *des femmes en mouvements* (1978–1982). Xavière Gauthier's* *Sorcières* (1976–1979) explored women's relationship to writing, while *Pénélope* (1979–1985) published reports of feminist research on women in history. *Les Pétroleuses* (1974–1976) and *Femmes travailleuses en lutte* (1974–1978) were feminist publications focused on class struggle.

Signs of a feminist press abound throughout France today, although, as ever, the plural nature of French feminism, shifts in French government support, and the perennial lack of capital make for fragile if exuberant publications. Two success stories of the 1990s are Catherine Gonnard's longest-running lesbian and feminist *Lesbia Magazine* and the university review *Clio*, which produces the latest scholarship in gender and history. Recent developments in technology present new opportunities for broadly distributed feminist journalism. Indeed, by the twenty-first century, it is likely that Web sites such as the *Annuaire au feminin* (http://www.iway.fr/femmes/docs) will make the French feminist press available online.

Cheryl A. Morgan

BIBLIOGRAPHY

Secondary Texts

Adler, Laure. *A l'Aube du féminisme: les premières journalistes (1830–1850)*. Paris: Payot, 1979.

Morgan, Cheryl A. "Unfashionable Feminism: Designing Women Writers in the *Journal des Femmes*." In *Making the News: Modernity and the Mass Press in Nineteenth-Century France*. Ed. Dean de la Motte and Jeannene M. Przyblyski. Amherst: University of Massachusetts Press, 1999.

"La Presse et les femmes." *Pénélope* 1 (June 1979).

Roberts, Mary-Louise. "The Frondeuses, Gender Identity and Journalism in Fin-de-Siècle France." In *Making the News: Modernity and the Mass Press in Nineteenth-Century France*. Ed. Dean de la Motte and Jeannene M. Przyblyski. Amherst: University of Massachusetts Press, 1999.

Sullerot, Evelyne. *Histoire de la presse féminine en France des origines à 1848*. Paris: Armand Colin, 1966.

Pringy, madame de (fl. 1694–1709). Little is known of her life, except that she was the daughter of M de Marenville, the guardian of the treasury of the Chamber of Accounts in Paris, that she was first married to the comte de Pringy, and later to M d'Aura, seigneur d'Entragues, and that she was a prolific writer.

Her published works include *Les Différents Caractères des femmes du siècle* (1694; the 1699 edition is dedicated to the duchesse de Nemours*, Pringy's protector); two novels*, *Junie, ou les sentimens romains* (1695; also attributed to Lesconvel), and *L'Amour à la mode, satyre historique* (1695); *A la gloire de Mgr. le Dauphin—Discours académique sur son retour d'Allemagne* (1698, published in *La Nouvelle Pandore*); *La Critique de la prévention* (1702); *La Vie du Père Bourdaloue* (1705); and a *Traité des vrais malheurs de l'homme* (1707).

Mme de Pringy is mainly remembered today for *Les Différents Caractères des femmes du siècle*, a work inspired both by La Bruyère's *Caractères* and by François Poulain de la Barre's educational theories. Of particular interest are her arguments on women's education* and her apology for science.

Colette H. Winn

BIBLIOGRAPHY

Primary Texts

Les Différents Caractères des femmes du siècle, avec la description de l'amour propre, contenant six caractères et six perfections. Paris: Médard-Michel Brunet, 1699.
Les Différents Caractères. Ch. VI, "La Science." In *Protestations et revendications féminines—Textes inédits et oubliés sur l'éducation féminine (XVIe–XVIIe siècle)*. Ed. Colette H. Winn. Paris: Champion, forthcoming.

Secondary Text

Timmermans, Linda. *L'Accès des femmes à la culture (1598–1715)*. Paris: Champion, 1993.

Prison writing. The term "prison writing" refers to memoirs*, letters, diaries, prison narratives, poems, and fictionalized accounts written by women during or after incarceration. The first examples of prison writing appeared in the eighteenth century, after the imprisonment of several women (Madame de Staal-Delaunay* and the Comtesse de la Motte) involved in political plots. Staal-Delaunay's *Mémoires* (1755) recount the conspiracies of the period of the Regency. The Duchesse de Duras's *Mémoires*, published during the revolutionary period, relate the pain of separation from her family*, and her incomprehension of other prisoners' frivolity in the face of death. Madame Roland's* *Mémoires* are a frank account of her childhood and private life, and also a political testimony of the first years of the Revolution*.

The post-revolutionary era saw the establishment of a more psychologically repressive penal system, which stifled almost all prison writing. Notorious exceptions to this silencing include Madame de Campestre, and particularly Marie Cappelle Lafarge, whose *Mémoires* were published despite the tremendous pressure exerted on her publishers.

The genre blossomed in the twentieth century, with the publication of the autobiographical works of Marguerite Steinheil, Anne Huré, Albertine Sarrazin*, Nicole Gérard, and Béatrice Saubin. Sarrazin, the best known of these writers, created a literary sensation in the 1960s with the publication of the first prison novels*, *L'Astragale* and *La Cavale*, in which she moves away from self-justification to a fictional exploration of a woman prisoner's experience of incarceration and social marginalization.

Prison texts written by women have many themes in common—the recounting of the author's childhood and the circumstances that led to her arrest, the description of prison conditions, and the denunciation of the repressive treatment of women prisoners. In every case, the writers of these texts were found guilty of transgressing traditional feminine roles and were condemned for their writing, which was considered scandalous at the time of their publication.

Anna Norris

BIBLIOGRAPHY

Primary Texts

Cappelle, Marie. *Mémoires de Marie Cappelle (veuve Lafarge) écrits par elle-même*. 4 vols. Paris: René, 1841.
Huré, Anne. *En prison*. Paris: Julliard, 1963.
La Motte, Comtesse de la (Jeanne de Valois). *Recueil de mémoires et autres pièces concernant l'affaire de M. le grand aumonier*. Paris: N.p., 1786.
Lafarge, Madame (née Marie Cappelle). *Heures de prison*. 3 vols. Paris: Librairie Nouvelle, 1854.
Roland, Madame. *Mémoires de Madame Roland*. Paris: Mercure de France, 1966.
Sarrazin, Albertine. *L'Astragale*. Paris: Pauvert, 1964.
———. *La Cavale*. Paris: Pauvert, 1967.
Staal-Delaunay, Madame de. ''Mémoires de Madame de Staal, écrits par elle-même.'' In *Oeuvres*. Paris: Renouard, 1821.
Steinheil, Marguerite. *Mes Mémoires*. Paris: Ramlot, 1911–1912.

Secondary Texts

Gelfand, Elissa. *Imagination in Confinement: Women's Writings from French Prisons*. Ithaca: Cornell University Press, 1983.
Lambert, Benjamin. *La Cavale, Mémoires d'Albertine*. Paris: Nizet, 1994.

Prostitution. Despite the sociopolitical marginality of the world of prostitution, prostitutes have been a frequent figure in French literature from the medieval fabliaux* to the most recent novels*. Their presence in literature, moreover, often betrays an ideological preoccupation only tangentially related to realist representational exigencies. The plethora of words and expressions, in various degrees of euphemism or pejorativeness, used to designate the prostitute (*courtisane, femme galante, fille, fille publique, fille des rues, fille perdue, poule, hétaïre, peripatéticienne, raccrocheuse, belle de nuit, trimardeuse, tapineuse, ribaude, fenestrière, pouiffiasse, roulure, putain, pute*, etc.) as well as related terms (*femme vénale, femme de mauvaise vie, cocotte, lorette, maitresse, maison close, faire le trottoir*, etc.) not only provide a taxonomy of the varieties of prostitution, but also frequently convey the position occupied by a literary text employing one term or another on a continuum from high to popular culture. While marginal genres (erotica and pornography) freely represented the transgressive figure of the prostitute, pre–nineteenth-century canonical texts nearly always semantically and discursively euphemized her, as with the courtesan who was a welcome denizen of upper-class circles despite her scandalous profession. In the eighteenth and early nineteenth centuries, in tracts like Restif de La Bretonne's *Le Pornographe* (1769) and Parent-Duchâtelet's *De la prostitution dans la ville de Paris* (1836), prostitution became a social problem comparable to hygiene and urban sanitation. Nineteenth-century French literature experienced a veritable explosion in representations of prostitutes of all types, as the works of Balzac, Sue, the Goncourt brothers, Maupassant, Zola, and Huysmans attest. Moreover, prostitutes were the main characters in many texts from this period, for example, Barbey d'Aurevilly's "La Vengeance d'une femme" from *Les Diaboliques* (1874), Huysmans's *Marthe, histoire d'une fille* (1876), Edmond de Goncourt's *La Fille Elisa* (1877), Zola's *Nana* (1880), Maupassant's *La Maison Tellier* (1881), Lorrain's *La Maison Philbert* (1904), and Margueritte's *Prostituée* (1907). These literary prostitutes performed a variety of ideological functions, often embodying a projection of male fantasy of fear in the form of misogynistically motivated versions of a *femme fatale*. In the twentieth century, the figure of the prostitute has been appropriated for still other purposes, as in Sartre's *La Putain respectueuse* (1946), wherein the American racial question is explored, and Genet's *Le Balcon* (1956), in which Madame Irma's prostitutes freely participate in or subvert the political order. Throughout the history of French literature, the prostitute has been a protean figure that writers have appropriated in order to express a wide range of political agendas.

Leonard R. Koos

BIBLIOGRAPHY

Secondary Texts

Adler, Laure. *La Vie quotidienne dans les maisons closes: 1830–1930*. Paris: Hachette, 1990.

Bernabou, Erica-Marie. *La Prostitution et la police des moeurs au XVIIIe siècle*. Paris: Perrin, 1987.

Bernheimer, Charles. *Figures of Ill Repute: Representing Prostitution in Nineteenth-Century France*. Cambridge, MA: Harvard University Press, 1989.

Corbin, Alain. *Les Filles de noce: Misère sexuelle et prostitution*. Paris: Aubier Montaigne, 1978.

Geremek, Bronislaw. *The Margins of Society in Late Medieval Paris*. Trans. Jean Birrell. Cambridge: Cambridge University Press, 1987.

Harsin, Jill. *Policing Prostitution in Nineteenth-Century Paris*. Princeton: Princeton University Press, 1985.

Matlock, Jann. *Scenes of Seduction: Prostitution, Hysteria, and Reading Difference in Nineteenth-Century France*. New York: Columbia University Press, 1994.

Prou, Suzanne (1920–1995). Novelist and short story* writer, Prou spent her early childhood years in Algeria and Indochina. During World War II* she wrote for *L'Espoir*, an underground journal denouncing anti-semitism, and in the 1950s and 1960s she spoke out against human rights abuses that occurred during the Algerian War. Prou was also active in l'Union des Femmes Françaises (UFF), a women's rights group.

Many of Prou's literary works, set in her native Provence, focus on female characters attempting to achieve self-realization from within a traditional bourgeois milieu which privileges the married woman with children. In *La Terrasse des Bernardini* (Prix Renaudot, 1973), her best-known work, two former rivals join forces against the man who has been exploiting them. Prou thus refutes the traditional marriage* plot, emphasizing female solidarity and presenting a possible lesbian subtext.

Patrice J. Proulx

BIBLIOGRAPHY

Primary Texts

Méchamment les Oiseaux. Paris: Albin Michel, 1971.
La Terrasse des Bernardini. Paris: Calmann-Lévy, 1973.
Les Demoiselles sous les ébéniers. Paris: Calmann-Lévy, 1976.
La Notairesse. Paris: Albin Michel, 1978.
Mauriac et la jeune fille. Paris: Editions Ramsay, 1982.
Le Dit de Marguerite. Paris: Calmann-Lévy, 1985.
La Petite Tonkinoise. Paris: Calmann-Lévy, 1987.
Le Temps des innocents. Paris: Albin Michel, 1988.
La Maison des champs. Paris: Editions Grasset, 1993.
L'Album de famille. Paris: Editions Grasset, 1995.

Psychanalyse et Politique. In 1968 Antoinette Fouque* founded the controversial women's group Psychanalyse et Politique, which associated itself with the class struggle and was to become the intellectual center of the Mouvement de Libération des Femmes* (MLF). Although this avant-garde organization never publicly stated its ideological position, group members refused to become engaged in any overt political action, seeking to align themselves with psychoanalysis rather than politics in an effort to repudiate phallocentric power systems. They explored the potential of both psychoanalysis and historical materialism, undertaking a theoretical analysis of women's unconscious and a reevaluation of history. Well-known feminist theorists such as Cixous*, Kristeva*, and Irigaray* were all associated with Psych et Po. Considered counterrevolutionary by some women's groups, Psych et Po has been criticized for its legal fight to obtain exclusive rights to the MLF logo for the trademark of its publishing* house, Editions des femmes.

Susan Ireland and Patrice J. Proulx

BIBLIOGRAPHY

Duchen, Claire, ed. *French Connections: Voices from the Women's Movement in France.* Amherst: University of Massachusetts Press, 1987.

Jouve, Nicole Ward. " 'Bliss was it in that dawn . . . ': Contemporary Women's Writing in France and the Editions des femmes.'' In *Contemporary French Fiction by Women: Feminist Perspectives.* Ed. Margaret Atack and Phil Powrie. Manchester: Manchester University Press, 1990. 128–140.

Psychoanalytic theory. Divisible into Freudian and object relations schools. Object relations analysts examine attachment, loss, separation, and individuation in the pre-Oedipal child. Melanie Klein studies the infant's relationship to the maternal breast and the paranoid and depressive reactions to loss of the mother; Kohut concentrates on primary narcissism, and Chodorow on the problem of diffuse boundaries and the girl's complicated differentiation from the mother. The writing styles and works of Cixous* and Irigaray*, in contrast, celebrate the relationship with the mother and her body as a source of creativity. Without endorsing essentialism*, they question the patriarchal bias of Western rational thought, philosophy, and language as unsuited to explaining women's inner and interpersonal lives.

Psychoanalytic theory applies broadly to the study of language, themes, and structure in literary texts. Fruitful readings of poetry*, stream-of-consciousness language, and primary process or prerational thought can incorporate the free-association technique on which analysis relies to undo repression. Similarly, symbols and hidden themes in the text may be clarified using the methods of dream interpretation. Metaphor and metonymy, for example, are poetic versions of condensation and displacement. Traumas and unrecognized, displaced conflicts within or between characters can play themselves out in patterns most skillfully interpreted by the trained reader or analyst. Additionally, literary characters and voices may evince primitive defense mechanisms like splitting, in which the contradictory love object is alternately good and bad, giving and withholding, mirroring or fragmenting. Finally, readers may view texts as case history, dreams, or transference (Skura).

Susan Grayson

BIBLIOGRAPHY

Bion, Wilfred. *Seven Servants: Four Works by Wilfred R. Bion.* New York: Jason Aronson, 1977.

Chodorow, Nancy. *Feminism and Psychoanalytic Theory.* New Haven: Yale University Press, 1989.

Guntrip, Harry. *Psychoanalytic Theory, Therapy, and the Self.* New York: Basic Books, 1973.

———. *Schizoid Phenomena, Object Relations and the Self.* New York: International Universities Press, 1978.

Klein, Melanie. *Narrative of a Child Analysis.* N.p.: Delacorte Press, 1975.

Kohut, Heinz. *The Analysis of the Self*. New York: International Universities Press, 1971.
———. *The Restoration of the Self*. New York: International Universities Press, 1977.
Mahler, Margaret, Fred Pine, and Anni Bergman. *The Psychological Birth of the Human Infant, Symbiosis and Individuation*. New York: Basic Books, 1975.
Skura, Meredith. *The Literary Use of Psychoanalysis*. New Haven: Yale University Press, 1981.
Winnicott, D. W. *The Maturational Process and the Facilitating Environment*. New York: International Universities Press, 1965.

Publishing. The term ''publisher'' has changed meanings since the advent of the age of print. The modern definition of a publisher, an individual responsible for the bringing to print and sale of a book, dates only from the nineteenth century. From the sixteenth through the eighteenth centuries the roles of printer, publisher, and bookseller were combined in a designation initially indicated simply by the term *libraire*, and later *libraire-éditeur*. This evolution in the concept and function of publishing has had a particular relevance for women. Inventories of booksellers indicate that women were active in the business from the beginning, first mostly as widows of booksellers who assumed control of the family business (the title page of a book published by a bookseller's widow would indicate that it was printed ''chez la veuve Barbin,'' for example), then also by women who had learned the trade from their fathers or who had otherwise been able to establish themselves as independent *libraires-éditeurs*. In Paris in the 1550s there were around thirty women bookseller-printers, some of them major distributors: Charlotte Guillard, Yvonne Bonhomme, and Madeleine Boursette, for example, all managed large businesses on the rue Saint-Jacques.

Seventeenth-century salon* women acted as publishers of the works of writers who wished to have their works known but did not want to commit them to print. Vincent Voiture, for example, a greatly admired poet, never had his works printed. The public order of court society placed little value on the printed work. Women writers, as well as many male writers from the nobility, were reluctant to assume the identity of professional author. Getting a piece of writing published and recognized often meant simply putting it into limited circulation and orchestrating publicity to influence its reception, via private correspondence, conversations, or printed gazettes. Salon women like Madame de Rambouillet*, Mademoiselle de Scudéry*, and Madame de Lafayette* all acted as publishers, in this sense, of others' works as well as their own. Eighteenth-century *salonnières* prolonged this tradition to some extent, but the new Republic of Letters engaged a broad community of readers which could best be reached through the printed work. As the publishing industry flourished, more women participated as bookseller-publishers as well as published authors. Delalain's lists of *libraires-éditeurs* in Paris at the time of the Revolution* reveal that more than one in ten were women. But in the early decades of the nineteenth century major technological changes in the printing process (the invention of linotype, for example), together with a rapid increase in the reading population, transformed the industry. The number of books printed and sold rose, but among the bookseller-publishers there were waves of bankruptcy in the 1830s and 1840s. Between 1850 and World War I*, the production and marketing of books came to be dominated by large publishing houses, many of whose names are still familiar today—Hachette, Garnier, Plon, Larousse. None of these was managed or owned by women.

While throughout the nineteenth century salon women continued to act as culture-brokers with considerable influence over literary reputations, a new and larger sphere of activity in the world of book publishing came to be controlled by a new figure, that of the publisher-industrialist. This new type of *éditeur* depended for professional survival on the support of investors and on access to credit on a scale that was not easily available to women. Even publishing houses specializing in books written by women, or in those aimed at a female reader-ship, did not have women in the position of publisher. Research on this topic is scant, but studies suggest that only in the years immediately following World War I did French women again begin to play an important role as professional booksellers also involved in publishing. Adrienne Monnier is a frequently men-tioned bookseller-publisher of this type; she played a major role in facilitating the publication and sale of works by writers including Paul Valéry, Jules Ro-mains, and André Gide. Over the last fifty years women writers and intellectuals have launched ventures challenging the hold of mainstream publishers over the industry—the most famous examples include Simone de Beauvoir's* role in the founding of Les Temps Modernes and the collaboration of Hélène Cixous* and Antoinette Fouque* in establishing the feminist publishing house des femmes.

A few women in the 1930s and 1940s occupied important positions in the large publishing houses. Denise Tual was an important figure in the publishing firm of Gaston Gallimard. In the early 1930s she launched the Synops agency, which produced screenplays from Gallimard publications. For the most part, though, executive positions in major French publishing houses were not occu-pied by women until very recently, when the post of *attaché de presse* began to assume greater importance in the marketing strategies of publishing compa-nies. Women have been the majority occupants of these positions for some time, and since the 1970s they have increasingly been promoted to the position of publisher through this career path.

Elizabeth C. Goldsmith

BIBLIOGRAPHY

Secondary Texts

Armbruster, Carol, ed. *Publishing and Readership in Revolutionary France and America.* Westport, CT: Greenwood Press, 1993.
Assouline, Pierre. *Gaston Gallimard.* Paris: Editions Balland, 1984.
Chartier, Roger and Henri-Jean Martin, eds. *Histoire de l'édition française.* 4 vols. Paris: Promodis, 1982–1986.

Delalain, Paul. *L'Imprimerie et la librairie à Paris de 1789 à 1813*. Paris: Delalain, 1869.

Goldsmith, Elizabeth C., and Dena Goodman, eds. *Going Public: Women and Publishing in Early Modern France*. Ithaca: Cornell University Press, 1995.

Schuwer, Philippe. *Editeurs aujourd'hui*. Paris: Retz, 1987.

Viala, Alain. *Naissance de l'écrivain*. Paris: Minuit, 1992.

Puisieux, Madeleine d'Arsant de (1720–1798). A Parisian by birth and education*, she wrote poetry*, tales, novels*, a comedy, a history of the reign of Charles VII, and moral and pedagogical works. Her friendship with Diderot led to collaboration on several of his tales, causing her *Conseils à une amie* (1749) and *Les Caractères* (1750) to be falsely attributed to him when they first appeared. To seek redress, she attacked the tendency of critics to minimize women's writings or attribute them to men ("Preliminary Discourse" to the second edition of *Les Caractères*). Her five novels deal with social and philosophical issues, and denounce religious intolerance, forced religious vows, and the injustice of the judicial system. In addition, her *Histoire de Mademoiselle de Terville* (1768) and the *Mémoires d'un homme de bien* (1768) contain critical analyses of women's plight in the eighteenth century. Puisieux deplored women's inadequate education in her moral and pedagogical writings, but her proposals for change may not properly be called feminist. In *Conseils à une amie*, the narrator insists that women are naturally equal to men and should pursue knowledge, but she advises her young female friend to hide her education, respect appearances, and submit to society's unjust gender hierarchy. Most striking is Puisieux's avowed distrust of women, the majority of whom she deemed too frivolous to heed the advice expressed in her works. She received a pension from the Convention in 1795, possibly for *Prospectus sur un ouvrage important* (1772), in which she sets out her ideas for educating better male and female citizens.

Michèle Bissière

BIBLIOGRAPHY

Primary Texts

Les Caractères. London: N.p., 1750.

L'Education du Marquis de *** ou mémoires de la Comtesse de Zurlac. Berlin and Paris: Bauche, 1753.

Zamor et Almanzine ou l'inutilité de l'esprit et du bon sens. Amsterdam and Paris: Hochereau l'aîné, 1755.

Alzarac ou la nécessité d'être inconstant. Cologne and Paris: Charpentier, 1762.

Histoire de Mademoiselle de Terville. Amsterdam and Paris: Veuve Duchesne, 1768.

Les Mémoires d'un homme de bien. Paris: Delalain, 1768.

Prospectus sur un ouvrage important. Minerve: Valleyre, 1772.

Conseils à une amie. Paris: Librairie des bibliophiles, 1882.

Secondary Texts

Laborde, Alice M. *Diderot et Madame de Puisieux*. Stanford French and Italian Studies 36. Saratoga, CA: Anma Libri, 1984.

Silver, Marie-France. ''Madame de Puisieux ou l'ambition d'être femme de lettres.'' In *Femmes savantes et femmes d'esprit: Women Intellectuals of the French Eighteenth Century*. Ed. Roland Bonnel and Catherine Rubinger. New York: Peter Lang, 1994. 183–201.

Q

Querelle des anciens et des modernes. The frequently renewed debate over the relative merits of ancient wisdom and modern genius* was revived in the late 1680s and prolonged (in what is called the Quarrel's second phase) by the polemic surrounding a new translation of *The Iliad* (1711). The translator, Madame Dacier*, wished to bring the beauties of the Greek text to a broader French public and thereby add support to the Ancients' side of the debate. Exceptionally well educated, Dacier had learned Greek and Latin from her father and had several translations to her credit by the time of her marriage to André Dacier, classicist and secretary of the French Academy. Houdar de La Motte, a leader of the Modernist opposition, held that Homer was an imperfect writer and published his own "improved" translation. He was supported by the prominent *salonnière* Madame de Lambert*. Discussion of the issue continued over the next decade and produced, among others, Fénelon's famous letter to the French Academy. Control of that body was a prize coveted by both sides. Lambert's efforts were crucial both in electing pro-Moderns to the Academy and in bringing about a reconciliation of the two sides. Many issues raised by the Quarrel were significant for eighteenth-century women. If few men of the period could read classical Greek, even fewer women were allowed that privilege. It is arguable that educated women would naturally choose the Moderns' role, given their historic exclusion from classical education. Furthermore, as the Moderns argued from Cartesian principles of clarity and reason against the weight of authority, they found allies among women whose emerging rights were often at odds with traditional authority. The relationship between progress in the arts, letters, and science, on the one hand, and the status of women, on the other, was clearly a logical one. The debate further illustrates the role of the salon* itself as an important site of cultural discourse.

Caryl L. Lloyd

BIBLIOGRAPHY

Secondary Texts

Becq, Annie. "La Querelle des Anciens et des Modernes et l'émergence de l'esthétique française moderne." In *Lumières et modernité: de Malebranche à Baudelaire*. Orléans: Paradigme, 1994.

DeJean, Joan. *Ancients Against Moderns: Culture Wars and the Making of a Fin de Siècle*. Chicago: University of Chicago Press, 1997.

Fénelon, François de. *Lettre à l'Académie*. Geneva: Librairie Droz, 1970.

Marchal, Roger. *Madame de Lambert et son milieu*. Oxford: Voltaire Foundation, 1991.

Rigault, Hippolyte. *Histoire de la Querelle des Anciens et des Modernes*. Paris: Hachette, 1856.

Warwick, Barbara. Introduction and Commentary. In *Fénelon's Letter to the French Academy*. Lanham, MD: University Press of America, 1984.

Querelle des femmes. A literary debate, dating back to the late twelfth century and reaching its peak during the mid-1500s, which had for its central focus the social status and the rights of women. While there were countless influences and inspirations behind the dispute, it was Jean de Meung's slanderous invectives against the feminine sex in the second half of the *Roman de la Rose* (1265), coupled with the anti-matrimonial *Lamentations de Mathéolus* (c. 1280) that sparked what was to grow into a vast movement of attacks and counterattacks circling the question of women's inferiority, equality, and superiority in their relation to men. Christine de Pizan*, whose *Epistre au dieu d'amours* (1399) and *La Cité des dames* (1404) served as rebuttals to masculine disparagements of feminine character, played a crucial role in the development of the debate and was among the earliest champions of her sex.

During the Middle Ages the scope of the *Querelle* was for the most part limited to discussions of love and marriage*, its participants usually drawing on age-old theories preaching the innate maliciousness of women. Pizan's claims of women's rights to an education* fell by the wayside and lay in waiting for more progressive times. Authors of the fifteenth century, influenced by the rise in bourgeois mentalities, dominated the scene with their ruthless satires of the woes of husbands and lovers, in works like *Les Quinze Joyes du mariage*. Idolization of the feminine, so prevalent in the courtly literature of authors like Chrétien de Troyes and Guillaume de Lorris, had given way to masculine hostility and disdain. Literary representations of women such as Alain Chartier's *La Belle Dame sans mercy* (1424) promoted these negative attitudes. Amid the many vindictive voices, however, declamations in defense of women were on the rise. Martin le Franc opposed antagonists with his praises of the excellence of women and feminine virtues in his *Champion des dames* (1430–1440).

Poets, moralists, jurists, doctors, and philosophers engaged in this relentless rhetorical war, which progressed from medieval rehashings of ideas about the evils of feminine nature to Renaissance examinations of the repercussions of social law in the lives of women. It was not until the sixteenth century, with humanist and reformist involvements, that the *Querelle* advanced to a discussion of issues relating more to the *reality* of the feminine condition. Although André Tiraqueau and Jean Nevizan had taken the matrimonial vein of the debate to its antifeminist extreme in their diatribes, *De legibus connubialibus* (1513) and *Sylvae Nuptialis* (1521), respectively, there were increasing efforts during this period, fostered by works like Vivès's *Institution de la femme chrétienne* (1523) and Erasmus's *Institution du mariage chrétien* (1526), to rehabilitate the institution of marriage. These publications also brought about an important shift to considerations of women's intellectual capacities and the consequences of limitations on feminine education. Such deliberations provided ground for feminist queries into women's unjustified exclusion from political, social, and religious positions of authority.

Polemic writings of the sixteenth century were crucial to the propagation of the debate. Apologists' laudings abounded, beginning early in the century with Symphorien Champier's *La Nef des dames vertueuses* (1503), and gaining momentum with Henri Cornélius Agrippa's highly successful *De la noblesse et preéxcellence du sexe féminin* (1530). In the detractors' camp was the infamous Gratien du Pont, seigneur de Drusac, who contributed one of the most misogynistic additions to the debate with his *Controverses des sexes masculin et feminin* (1534). It was the works, however, of Guillaume Postel and François Billon, both passionate defenders of the female sex, that prevailed during the latter half of the century. Postel glorified women in *Les Très Merveilleuses Victoires des femmes du nouveau monde* (1553), as supreme spiritual guides and leaders of worldly progress. Billon's *Le Fort inexpugnable de l'honneur du sexe féminin* (1555) was an attempt to prove the equality of the sexes, as well as an authoritative history of the *Querelle*.

The controversy was continued throughout the Renaissance, extending to, and paralleling, Neoplatonist trends and the *Querelle des amyes*, capturing as well the interest of authors like Rabelais, Marguerite de Navarre*, and Montaigne. Nevertheless, the import of the *Querelle des femmes* was not so significant as to change much as far as the reality of women was concerned. In effect, it remained, on the whole, a verbal game of theoretical exchange. The debate did, nonetheless, draw critical attention to the plight of women and put their subordination into question. The *Querelle des femmes* reflected the development of consciousness during the sixteenth century that encouraged at least preliminary challenges, more actively pursued in the centuries to follow, to the culturally prescribed constraints under which women lived.

Melanie E. Gregg

BIBLIOGRAPHY

Primary Texts

Agrippa, Henri Cornélius. *De la noblesse et preéxcellence du sexe féminin*. Paris: Denys Janot, 1530.

Billon, François de. *Le Fort inexpugnable de l'honneur du sexe fémenin*. Paris: I. d'Allyer, 1555.

Champier, Symphorien. *La Nef des dames vertueuses*. Paris: I. de la Garde, 1515.

Du Pont, Gratien. *Les Controverses des sexes masculin et femenin*. Toulouse: J. Colomies, 1534.

Le Franc, Martin. *Le Champion des dames*. Ed. A. Piaget. Lausanne: Payot, 1968.

Mathéolus. *Les Lamentations de Mathéolus et le livre de leesce de Jehan le Fèvre, de Resson*. 2 vols. Paris: E. Bouillon, 1892–1905.

Meung, Jean de. *Roman de la Rose*. Ed. E. Langlois. 5 vols. Paris: Firmin-Didot & Cie., 1914–1924.

Pizan, Christine de. *Le Livre de la cité des dames*. Ed. E. Hicks and T. Moreau. Paris: Stock, 1986.

Postel, Guillaume. *Les Très Merveilleuses Victoires des femmes du nouveau monde*. Paris: Jehan Rueille, 1553.

Secondary Texts

Angenot, Marc. *Champion des femmes: Examen du discours sur la supériorité des femmes, 1400–1800*. Montreal: Presses de l'Université de Québec, 1977.

Albistur, Maïté, and Daniel Argomathe. *Histoire du féminisme français du moyen âge à nos jours*. Paris: Editions des femmes, 1977.

Maclean, Ian. *Woman Triumphant: Feminism in French Literature, 1610–1652*. Oxford: Clarendon Press, 1977.

R

Rachilde (pseudonym of Marguerite Eymery Vallette) (1860–1953). Any attempt to discuss feminism* in relation to the life and work of Rachilde must recognize the obstacle posed by her claim to reject feminism in the 1928 tract *Pourquoi je ne suis pas féministe*. Taken at face value, this short book is an explicit rejection of feminism, but closer reading reveals that it is less a reasoned political argument against feminism than an autobiographical, highly idiosyncratic collection of remarks grouped under general topics such as religion and education*. Rachilde did oppose votes for women, but it would be a mistake to assume that suffrage was synonymous with feminism for many French women of her era. Moreover, given Rachilde's cynicism regarding politics, her belief that women would be better off not participating in this realm makes the meaning of her opposition more ambiguous. Rachilde also made various statements about the intellectual inferiority of women, but given her desire, evident elsewhere, to be provocative, as well as her general misanthropy, such statements call for careful and measured interpretation.

Certainly Rachilde's life, as opposed to her writing, offers ample evidence of a belief that women are entitled to independence, economic equality, careers, sexual expression, freedom from unwanted pregnancy, and most of the other demands associated with contemporary feminism. She asserted her independence early in her life, becoming a writer while still a teenager, and later never shied from controversy. She wrote throughout her life and continued to support herself through writing after the death of her husband, Alfred Vallette, a founding editor of *Mercure de France*, in 1935.

She always favored the underdog and defended those attacked for nonconformity, and this attitude extended to a lifelong sympathy with homosexuals. This sympathy began at an early age, continued in her early years in Paris, when she befriended, among others, Jean Lorrain and the sexually ambiguous Alfred Jarry, and is also evident in her defense of Oscar Wilde and Alfred Douglas. In the 1920s she collaborated on a number of books with André David, most notably the controversial *Le Prisonnier* (1928), which presented the perspective of an older gay man attracted to his young ward. In the 1920s and 1930s she formed part of the "French clan" of the lesbian salon* hostess Natalie Clifford Barney*. However, while Rachilde seems to have identified with gay men, the close bond of sympathy seems lacking in her relationship with lesbians, as with women in general.

Although her personal life was not as scandalous as she allowed the public to imagine (her marriage*, which she claimed was monogamous and faithful, lasted from 1889 to 1935), Rachilde depicted nonnormative forms of sexuality in her works on a regular basis. These depictions verge on exploitation, since they often occur in narratives apparently intended to shock, but it can be argued that by depicting such characters and bringing such forbidden topics into discourse, Rachilde was indirectly forcing society to admit and accept their existence. Her most celebrated creation is Raoule de Vénérande, transvestite heroine of the much-debated *Monsieur Vénus* (1884), but other notable creations, many of them women, include the sadistic Mary Barbe of *La Marquise de Sade* (1887); the bisexual Marcel(le) Deshambres of *Madame Adonis* (1888); the incestuous and homosexual de Fertzen brothers of *Les Hors Nature* (1897); the necrophiliac, hair-fetishist lighthouse keeper of *La Tour d'Amour* (1899); and the perverse heroine of *La Jongleuse* (1900), Eliante Donalger, whose great love is a Greek vase.

There is debate about Rachilde's feminism, but there is no doubt that recent feminist criticism has found much that is worthy of note in Rachilde's depictions of unorthodox gender roles and her explorations of "deviant" sexualities. Whether it is through a revisionist view of the hysteric as heroine, the way turn-of-the-century women writers have responded to cultural gendering of writing as male, or the implicit questioning of gender roles, Rachilde's work is proving a fertile source of feminist reevaluation.

Melanie Hawthorne

BIBLIOGRAPHY

Primary Texts

Monsieur Vénus. Brussels: Brancart, 1884.
La Marquise de Sade. Paris: Monnier, 1887.
Madame Adonis. Paris: Monnier, 1888.
Les Hors Nature. Paris: Mercure de France, 1897.
La Tour d'Amour. Paris: Mercure de France, 1899.
La Jongleuse. Paris: Mercure de France, 1900.
Pourquoi je ne suis pas féministe. Paris: Editions de France, 1928.
[with André David] *Le Prisonnier*. Paris: Editions de France, 1928.

Secondary Texts

Felski, Rita. *The Gender of Modernity*. Cambridge, MA: Harvard University Press, 1995.
Gordon, Rae Beth. *Ornament, Fantasy, and Desire in Nineteenth-Century French Literature*. Princeton: Princeton University Press, 1992.

Hawthorne, Melanie. "Rachilde." In *French Women Writers: A Bio-Bibliographical Source Book*. Ed. Eva Martin Sartori and Dorothy Wynne Zimmerman. Westport, CT: Greenwood Press, 1991. 346–356.

Kelly, Dorothy. *Fictional Genders: Role and Representation in Nineteenth-Century French Narrative*. Lincoln: University of Nebraska Press, 1989.

Kingcaid, Renee A. *Neurosis and Narrative: The Decadent Short Fiction of Proust, Lorrain, and Rachilde*. Carbondale: Southern Illinois University Press, 1992.

Lukacher, Maryline. *Maternal Fictions: Stendhal, Sand, Rachilde, and Bataille*. Durham: Duke University Press, 1994.

Rambouillet, Catherine de Vivonne de Savelli, later marquise de (1588–1665). Italian by birth, she came to Paris in 1600 after her marriage* to Charles d'Angennes, future marquis de Rambouillet. Around 1613 she retired semi-permanently to her home, which was built according to her innovative design, after the physical ailments resulting from childbearing made it difficult to participate in courtly life at the Louvre. By 1620 and over the next twenty years, the Hôtel de Rambouillet became the center of early seventeenth-century literary culture. The gatherings over which Mme de Rambouillet presided were so influential that Richelieu, always on the watch for threats against the monarchy, requested that the marquise keep him apprised of the activities there; she declined.

Invited by the incomparable "Arthénice" (Malherbe's anagram for the marquise's first name), writers of all genres and of all levels of experience came together to share their literary creations and to debate minutiae of the French language. The elite guest list at the Hôtel de Rambouillet included Malherbe, Chapelain, Balzac, Conrart, Voiture, and countless others. While the Hôtel de Rambouillet did indeed play an important role in the aesthetics of French seventeenth-century literature, the primary purpose of the salon* was, in effect, to pursue a type of pleasure and amusement in high society that only wit and delicacy could provide. Although poetry*, which was particularly effective in this respect, appears to be a privileged genre there, the salon also gave rise to a new vogue for the *lettre galante*. Committed to courtly love* and the playful language games that would eventually become defining elements of *préciosité*, the Hôtel de Rambouillet is often credited with restoring a much-needed *politesse* to the aristocracy following the bloody religious wars. Although Arthénice's receptions were less frequent in the 1650s, she continued her influential role of hostess until her death in 1665.

Holly Tucker

BIBLIOGRAPHY

Secondary Texts

Krajewska, Barbara. *Mythes et découvertes: Le Salon littéraire de Madame de Rambouillet dans les lettres des contemporains*. Paris: Biblio 17, 1990.

Picard, Roger. *Les Salons littéraires et la société française, 1610–1789*. New York: Brentano's, 1943.

Rape. In the Middle Ages, there was no word to correspond to the modern French term "viol"—instead, the term most commonly used was "fame esforcer" (to force a woman). This was defined as having carnal knowledge of a woman against her will and despite her resistance and came under the jurisdiction of separate ecclesiastical and civil courts. Of the two, the more lenient Church court did not make rape a capital offense, and, in general, rape was seen as a crime against the family*. In northern France, rape, punishable by death, was considered the equivalent of crimes like murder. However, in the very few cases that reached the courts, penalties depended on the status of both victims and perpetrators. Assaults on girls, particularly if they had been deflowered in the process, were treated as more serious crimes than attacks on adult women.

When laws were eventually centralized under the Penal Code of 1791, rape was defined as either simple or aggravated. The two were distinguished by the nature of the punishment; the sentence could be doubled for the latter, and charges of "aggravated rape" were justified by the victim's age, the number of attackers, and the level of violence used. The reformed 1810 penal code did not make a distinction between rape and violent assaults on a woman's chastity, although attacks on those under the age of fifteen continued to be subject to more severe punishments. When the code was revised subsequently in 1832 and 1865, rape remained a specifically male crime defined as the violent penile penetration of a vagina; all other types of sexual assault were considered "attentats à la pudeur" (violations of decency), and the level of violence used was seriously considered by courts generally skeptical of women's testimony. Moreover, rape within the context of marriage* was not held to exist.

Rape moved from the realm of courts to become the object of intense public debate during World War I* when publication of government reports on the violation of civilians by German soldiers reached the public in January 1915. This sparked a debate carried out in press accounts as well as literary and visual texts over the consequences of rape—the children of the barbarous enemy that might result, and whether abortion* should be allowed—rather than violence against women. Although the discussion of rape was widespread, the question faded after the war, and would not reemerge in the same manner during World War II*. In the postwar era, rape became an important issue in the women's movement of the 1960s and 1970s. Rape and abortion again became intertwined issues as the fight for legalized abortion focused attention on the plight of women who had abortions after having been raped and impregnated. The appearance in 1976 of both a translation of Susan Brownmiller's *Against Our Will* and Marie-Odile Fargier's *Le Viol* gave new visibility to rape and prompted feminist organizing against the way rape and its victims had been publicly regarded and treated by the legal system. Adopting such slogans as "La chasse aux femmes est ouverte toute l'année" (the hunt for women is open year round), the women's liberation movement began to campaign for the reform of existing laws. In 1980, Article 332 of the penal code was finally rewritten to define "all acts of sexual penetration" violently committed by one person against another as rape. Rape was now punishable by five to ten years in prison, and up to twenty years in cases that involved particularly vulnerable persons (minors or pregnant women) or particular circumstances (the use of arms or gang rapes).

Susan R. Grayzel

BIBLIOGRAPHY

Secondary Texts

Arnaud-Duc, Nicole. "The Law's Contradictions." Trans. Arthur Goldhammer. In *A History of Women in the West IV: Emerging Feminism from Revolution to World War*. Ed. Geneviève Fraisse and Michelle Perrot. 1991. Cambridge, MA: Harvard University Press, 1993.

Audoin-Rouzeau, Stéphane. *L'Enfant de l'ennemi 1914–1918*. Paris: Aubier, 1995.

Brownmiller, Susan. *Against Our Will: Men, Women and Rape*. New York: Simon and Schuster, 1975.

Dossier Viol. Bibliothèque Marguerite Durand, Paris.

Fargier, Marie-Odile. *Le Viol*. Paris: Bernard Grasset, 1976.

Gravdal, Kathryn. *Ravishing Maidens: Writing Rape in Medieval French Literature and Law*. Philadelphia: University of Pennsylvania Press, 1991.

Harris, Ruth. "The 'Child of the Barbarian': Rape, Race and Nationalism in France during the First World War." *Past and Present* 141 (October 1993).

Laubier, Claire, ed. *The Condition of Women in France, 1945 to the Present: A Documentary Anthology*. London: Routledge, 1990.

Mossuz-Lavau, Janine. *Les Lois de l'amour: Les Politiques de la sexualité en France (1950–1990)*. Paris: Payot, 1991.

Tomaselli, Sylvana, and Roy Porter, eds. *Rape: An Historical and Social Enquiry*. Oxford: Basil Blackwell, 1986.

Wishnia, Judith. "Natalisme et nationalisme pendant la Première Guerre Mondiale." *Vingtième Siècle* 45 (1995).

Realism (c. 1850–1870). The term "Realism" refers both to a certain mode of representing reality "sincerely" or "directly" (when used to describe authors as historically diverse as Villon and Duras*), and to a specific literary historical doctrine of the 1850s and 1860s to which few authors actually adhered. Mid-nineteenth-century Realism in France set itself forth as a break from the sentimentality of Romanticism* by claiming to represent all aspects of contemporary life, with a focus on the sociological, the economic, and, later, with its outgrowth Naturalism*, on the scientific. Hence the preference of Realists for the novel*.

As a literary historical category, it is quite problematic. Stendhal and Balzac were so labeled only retroactively; Flaubert repeatedly rejected the term. Self-proclaimed Realists include the brothers Goncourt, Feydeau, Duranty, and Champfleury, author of the 1857 manifesto *Le Réalisme*.

From the point of view of modern feminist scholarship, it becomes clear that the great majority of Realist works, self-proclaimed or not, depend upon representations of women, focusing on prostitution*, hysteria*, and adultery* as the foundation of their Realistic enterprise and its claim to sociological accuracy.

On the one hand, these focuses make evident the often more hidden misogynist anxieties about femininity* that dominate traditional literary representations of women. On the other hand, by breaking with Romantic sentimentality, they helped open the field of literature to later discussion of the oppressed condition of women at all socioeconomic levels from a more properly feminist perspective.

Christopher G. Fox

BIBLIOGRAPHY

Primary Texts

Champfleury [Jules Husson]. *Le Réalisme*. Paris: Lévy Frères, 1857.
Duranty, Louis Emile Edmond. *Le Malheur d'Henriette Gérard*. Paris: Poulet Malassis et de Broise, 1860.
Feydeau, Ernest. *Fanny*. Paris: Amyot, 1858.
Flaubert, Gustave. *Madame Bovary*. Paris: M. Lévy Frères, 1857.
Goncourt, Edmond, and Jules Goncourt. *Germinie Lacerteux*. Paris: Charpentier, 1864.

Secondary Text

Bernheimer, Charles. *Figures of Ill Repute: Representing Prostitution in Nineteenth-Century France*. Cambridge, MA: Harvard University Press, 1989.

Redonnet, Marie (1948–). Novelist, playwright, and poet. Regardless of genre, Marie Redonnet's writings share the simplicity of conceit and the transparency of style that have come to be her hallmarks. The principle of expressive economy guides all of her works; her novels*, her plays, and her poems are marked by a wry laconism, a deceptively naive manner, and a rigorous minimalist aesthetic. Her first book, *Le Mort et Cie*, exemplifies that aesthetic in a series of 484 three-line poems of varying syllabic length. Redonnet is best known for her novelistic triptych, composed of *Splendid Hôtel* (1986), *Forever Valley* (1987), and *Rose Mélie Rose* (1987). Though the stories they tell are different, the three novels are united by a common thematic concern: in each of them, a young female protagonist struggles to come to terms with a world dominated by devolution, decay, and death. Redonnet's theater*, in texts such as *Tir & Lir, Mobie-Diq* (1989), and *Seaside*, tells much the same sort of human story, played out on a stark, painfully bare stage. It is her distinctive world view that characterizes Redonnet's writing most profoundly. Renouncing conventional literary flourish, Redonnet wagers instead on a studiously impoverished, literalist style to convey the deprivation of her characters' condition.

Warren Motte

BIBLIOGRAPHY

Primary Texts

Le Mort et Cie. Paris: POL, 1985.
Doublures. Paris: POL, 1986.
Splendid Hôtel. Paris: Minuit, 1986.
Forever Valley. Paris: Minuit, 1987.
Rose Mélie Rose. Paris: Minuit, 1987.

Tir & Lir. Paris: Minuit, 1988.
Mobie-Diq. Paris: Minuit, 1989.
Silsie. Paris: Gallimard, 1990.
Candy Story. Paris: POL, 1992.
Seaside. Paris: Minuit, 1992.
Le Cirque Pandor, suivi de Fort Gambo. Paris: POL, 1994.
Nevermore. Paris: POL, 1994.

Reformation (1520s–1620s). Both Huguenot and Catholic writers in the sixteenth century emphasized the importance of women in the establishment and spread of the Protestant Reformation in France. Nancy Roelker has documented the involvement of about fifty noblewomen in the pre-Reformation evangelical movement, in the period of the Religious Wars, and in the later sixteenth and early seventeenth centuries. Natalie Zemon Davis has drawn attention to the activities of city women who read their New Testaments and disputed with priests, as well as to the potential for and the limits to freedom of expression for both Catholic and Protestant women.

Many of the women who were active in the Reform movement were already independent, strong-minded, and literate. Marguerite de Navarre* is the best known. Concerns that appear in her correspondence with the evangelical theologian Guillaume Briçonnet are central to her writing, and she was equally important as a protector of evangelical reformers. Several generations of articulate noblewomen can be traced, beginning with Anne de Beaujeu and including Louise de Savoie*, Renée de France, Marguerite de Navarre, her daughter Jeanne d'Albret*, their entourages, and their daughters and granddaughters. A number, like Charlotte de Laval, wife of the Huguenot leader Gaspard de Coligny, were converts before their husbands and/or influenced them and their sons to adopt or to continue in the reformed faith. Several corresponded with Calvin. While their impact on his thinking about the role of women is debatable, and influential Protestant leaders adopted St. Paul's insistence on women's silence, these women clearly found in Protestantism an encouragement for an extension of their household and family* responsibilities into the public realm.

A number of Huguenot women produced written texts, including letters (Eléonore de Roye, Charlotte de Bourbon*, Louise de Coligny, Charlotte-Brabantine de Nassau, Elizabeth de Nassau), memoirs* (Charlotte Dupléssis Mornay, Jeanne d'Albret), poetry* (Catherine de Bourbon*), pamphlets (Marie Dentière*), and an emblem book (Georgette de Montenay*). Many of these were not published at the time. They were nonetheless public documents, circulated in manuscript, and had an impact on events. In her *Mémoires*, Jeanne d'Albret defended her conversion and her actions during the second War of Religion. Dentière's and Montenay's works were published during their lifetimes. Dentière's "Epistre . . . à la Reine de Navarre" includes a lively defense of the duty of women to speak the truth which has been revealed to them. Sara Matthews Grieco has analyzed Montenay's more subtle defense of women in her choice of images of educated and spiritually superior women for her emblems. These texts by early modern women are now attracting critical attention as literary and not simply as historical documents.

The letters and memoirs of many of these women have been edited in full or reproduced in part in their biographies. For publication information, consult the studies listed in the bibliography.

Jane Couchman

BIBLIOGRAPHY

Secondary Texts

Bainton, Roland H. *Women of the Reformation in France and England.* Boston: Beacon Press, 1973.

Berriot-Salvadore, Evelyne. "L'Epouse compagne: Quelques Grandes Dames de la Réforme." In *Les Femmes dans la société française de la Renaissance.* Geneva: Droz, 1990. 119–156.

Blaisedell, Charmaine Jenkins. "Renée de France between Reform and Counter-Reform." *Archiv für Reformationsgeschichte* 63 (1972): 196–225.

Couchman, Jane. "What Is 'Personal' about Sixteenth-Century French Women's Personal Writings?" *Atlantis* 19 (Fall-Winter 1993): 16–22.

Davis, Natalie Zemon. "City Women and Religious Change." In *Society and Culture in Early Modern France.* Stanford: Stanford University Press, 1975. 65–95.

Grieco, Sara Matthews. "Georgette de Montenay: A Different Voice in Sixteenth-Century Emblematics." *Renaissance Quarterly* 47, no. 4 (Winter 1994): 793–871.

Head, Thomas. "Marie Dentière: A Propagandist for the Reform." In *Women Writers of the Renaissance and Reformation.* Ed. Katharina M. Wilson. Athens: University of Georgia Press, 1987. 260–283.

Roelker, Nancy L. "The Appeal of Calvinism to French Noblewomen in the Sixteenth Century." *Journal of Interdisciplinary History* 2 (Spring 1972): 391–418.

———. *Queen of Navarre: Jeanne d'Albret.* Cambridge, MA: Belknap Press, 1968.

———. "The Role of Noblewomen in the French Reformation." *Archiv für Reformationsgeschichte* 63 (1972): 168–195.

Thompson, John Lee. *John Calvin and the Daughters of Sarah: Women in Regular and Exceptional Roles in the Exegesis of Calvin, His Predecessors, and His Contemporaries.* Geneva: Droz, 1992.

Régnier, Marie de. *See* Houville, Gérard d'.

Rémusat, Claire Elisabeth Jeanne Gravier de Vergennes, comtesse de (1780–1821). Claire de Rémusat was the daughter of a counselor to the Parliament of Bourgogne who was a victim of the guillotine* in 1794. While taking refuge with her mother in Saint-Gratien, she became acquainted with Josephine de Beauharnais, the future wife of Napoleon. When Napoleon became First Consul, Josephine invited Mme de Rémusat to become her lady-in-waiting while her husband, Augustin de Rémusat became a court chamberlain. Her most famous works, published posthumously, are her memoirs* of this life at court.

They reflect her growing disillusion with Napoleon as his megalomania increased, at the same time presenting a sympathetic portrait of Josephine. Her vividly recreated scenes of life in the Palace of the Tuileries, at Saint-Cloud, and at Fontainebleau make fascinating reading. Her letters to her husband, written when he traveled abroad with the Emperor, were also published posthumously. They are less candid than the *Mémoires* because she feared they would be opened. They provide a picture of her life in Paris and at court, and reveal a deep devotion to her husband and two sons. Her older son became the journalist and politician Charles de Rémusat; his son became the editor of her works, providing her first biography in his preface to the *Mémoires*. She also wrote an *Essai sur l'éducation des femmes*, where she advocates that women not write for publication, but remain modestly in their household realm. Thus, though endowed with abundant gifts and an inclination for authorship, she accepted the strictures of her era against women writers and confined her writing to a circle of friends and family.

Dorothy Wynne Zimmerman

BIBLIOGRAPHY

Primary Texts

Essai sur l'éducation des femmes. Paris: Ladvocat, 1824.
Mémoires de Madame de Rémusat, 1802–1808. Ed. Paul de Rémusat. 3 vols. Paris: Calmann-Lévy, 1880.
Lettres de Madame de Rémusat, 1804–1808. Ed. Paul de Rémusat. 2 vols. Paris: Calmann-Lévy, 1881.

Secondary Text

Ozouf, Mona. *Les Mots des femmes: Essai sur la singularité française*. Paris: Fayard, 1995.

Reval, Gabrielle (1870–1938). Nom de plume of Gabrielle Fleuret. Following her graduation from the Ecole Normale de Sèvres and several years as a high school teacher, Reval wrote a trilogy about the privileges and problems of attending Sèvres and the trials that awaited young women schoolteachers in provincial France: *Sèvriennes* (1900), *Un Lycée de jeunes filles* (1901), and *Lycéennes* (1902). Reval published other novels* with independent female protagonists, as well as works of nonfiction such as *L'Avenir de nos jeunes filles* (1904), which provides advice on career options for young women. In 1924 she published *La Chaîne des dames*, a collection of essays on sixteen contemporary women writers including Colette*, Anna de Noailles*, Rachilde*, Séverine*, and Marcelle Tinayre*.

Juliette M. Rogers

BIBLIOGRAPHY

Primary Texts

Sèvriennes. Paris: Ollendorff, 1900.
Un Lycée de jeunes filles. Paris: Ollendorff, 1901.

Lycéennes. Paris: Ollendorff, 1902.
L'Avenir de nos jeunes filles. Paris: A. Hatier, 1904.
Le Ruban de Vénus. Paris: Calmann-Lévy, 1906.
La Bachelière. Paris: Ed. de Mirasol, 1910.
La Bachelière en Pologne. Paris: Ed. de Mirasol, 1911.
La Chaîne des dames. Paris: Ed. G. Crès, 1924.

Revolution, French (1789–1799). If, as Charles Fourier wrote in 1808, "the extension of women's privileges is the general principle for all social progress," then the French Revolution must first be described as ambivalent, then progressive, and finally repressive. The revolutionary era was beset by experiments in constitutionalism, political factionalism, and radically differing interpretations of sovereignty. Framed initially in Enlightenment* language, subjects became citizens, absolute monarchy became constitutional monarchy and then republicanism, and women's roles underwent significant redefinition.

The women's rights debate during the French Revolution found its immediate antecedents in the eighteenth century. The literary debate known as the *Querelle des femmes** was actively renewed, *taxation populaire* became more frequent (popular demonstrations in which goods were seized and sold at a "just price"), and a number of *cahiers de doléances* dealt explicitly with women's issues. Among items included in these lists of grievances were demands for legal equality in marriage*, educational and vocational opportunities for girls, public instruction and licensing of midwives, employment opportunities for women including protected employment in the embroidery and dressmaking trades, the right to divorce*, widows' control of property, and widowed mothers' control over their minor children. Other demands included the suppression of prostitution*, vocational training for former prostitutes, and the right to wear trousers.

Although the *cahiers* were not consulted during the early phase of the Revolution, many of the issues raised therein were widely debated. In framing definitions of citizenship for the Constitution of 1791, for example, women were designated as passive citizens, that is, having the guarantees of civil society, but without the right to vote*. Condorcet, an outspoken advocate for women, had asked for an even broader commitment: legal equality along with suffrage for women of property. His *Essai sur l'admission des femmes au droit de la cité*, however, was a minority opinion in legislative circles.

In the environment that spawned *cahiers* and pamphlets, women themselves had become politicized. While many of the pre-revolutionary activities of working-class women might be considered pre-political in nature, by the time of the Women's March to Versailles in October 1789, economic demands had merged with the vocabulary of politics. While women of the streets demonstrated for bread, lower tariffs, employment, and guaranteed subsistence, they also wrote petitions, met in groups, frequented the galleries of the legislative bodies, and courted Parisian and national leaders. There was nothing idle about their presenting Lafayette with a bouquet or their confirmation that political activities actually made them better wives and mothers as they reared future citizens of France. Such had been the arguments of actress-pamphleteer Olympe de Gouges* when she issued her famous *Declaration of the Rights of Woman* in 1791. Her pamphlet demanded the expansion of the guarantees of the 1789 *Declaration of the Rights of Man* to women. Gouges's widely quoted pamphlet called for ''the right [of women] to mount to the tribune,'' and included a template for a prenuptial agreement which would protect women's property rights.

In the period from 1791 through 1793, significant legislative change had taken place for women: marriage and divorce had been confirmed as contractual relationships, illegitimate children were given inheritance rights, women became the legal guardians of their minor daughters, and limited employment opportunities were provided in locally and nationally funded spinning workshops. Women remained visible and vocal in the galleries of the National Convention and assisted the Jacobins in ousting their rival Girondins from the Convention in 1793. By then, a well-articulated women's agenda was present, further promoted by the first significant women's political club, the Society of Revolutionary Republican Women. Founded by chocolatière Pauline Léon* and led by actress Claire Lacombe*, the club initially espoused Jacobin politics, but eventually allied itself with the more radical Enragés. Its women's agenda, which included full equality and expanded educational and vocational opportunities, also included stringent measures against hoarders, radical economic policies, and expanded women's militancy.

In October 1793, after the execution of Marie-Antoinette*, Manon Roland*, and Olympe de Gouges, the Revolutionary Republican Women were disbanded. Women who ''sought to be men'' were excoriated as counterrevolutionaries; politics had become the domain of civic virtue where only men trod. Classical and Rousseauist definitions of separate spheres dominated the discourse of the Revolution. By 1795 women were banned from government galleries, and assemblies of over five citizens were outlawed, thereby punitively sanctioning any further popular organizing. The final rescission of women's rights occurred in Napoleon's Civil Code, which placed women explicitly under their husband's control—their persons, their property, and their offspring.

The revolutionary women's rights movement was not forgotten, however. It found voice in the writings of Saint-Simonian women, Flora Tristan*, women of the Commune*, and nineteenth-century feminists.

Susan P. Conner

BIBLIOGRAPHY

Secondary Texts

Hufton, Olwen. *Women and the Limits of Citizenship in the French Revolution.* Toronto: University of Toronto Press, 1992.
Landes, Joan. *Women and the Public Sphere in the Age of the French Revolution.* Ithaca: Cornell University Press, 1988.

Levy, Darline Gay, Harriet Branson Applewhite, and Mary Durham Johnson. *Women in Revolutionary Paris, 1789–1795.* Urbana: University of Illinois Press, 1979.

Proctor, Candice. *Women, Equality and the French Revolution.* Westport, CT: Greenwood Press, 1990.

Yalom, Marilyn. *Blood Sisters: The French Revolution in Women's Memory.* New York: Basic Books, 1993.

Revolution of 1848 (1848–1851). The Second French Republic was declared in February 1848. It brought immediate social reforms and high hopes that women as well as men might benefit from social democracy in France. In this turbulent period, women were quick to demonstrate, to establish political clubs, and to join men in the fight for a representative government in France, even on the barricades. Many hoped to make suffrage truly universal by extending the right to vote* to the sex relegated to the private sphere. Women were a driving force in the movement to reform education* and establish social programs. The most radical claimed the right to work and the right to run for office for women themselves.

Women were also quick to seize the pen in support of the nascent Republic in the new, censorship-free climate. The women's press, dormant in the repressive late 1830s and 1840s, flourished once again. The most important women's newspaper was *La Voix des femmes,* under the direction of Eugénie Niboyet* in collaboration with Désirée Gay, Jeanne Deroin*, Suzanne Voilquin*, and Elisa Lemonnier. The newspaper's editors established a club of the same name. Despite the first surge of feminist spirit and solidarity, however, activist women, like the nation as a whole, soon split along class lines. Clubs and newspapers collapsed under pressures from within and without.

Women's participation in the public sphere left an indelible mark on the collective imagination. Popular caricatures like Daumier's *Les Divorceuses* or images of the *Vésuviennes,* a group of women who supposedly had crossed gender lines to assume masculine roles, derided revolutionary women. An orderly group of working-class women did indeed march as the *Vésuviennes* and presented demands to share domestic and civic responsibilities, thus rendering the image a more positive one. Later in the century, Flaubert relied heavily on images of the women of 1848 in *L'Education sentimentale* (1869), his masterpiece about the failure of an entire generation.

The revolutionary experience informs much of women's literary production thereafter. Recent analyses have shown the extent to which George Sand's* disillusionment shaped works like *La Petite Fadette* (1848). Marie d'Agoult* achieved her greatest success with her *Histoire de la Révolution de 1848* (1862). Other women drew on their experience to write memoirs*, fiction, poetry*, and political works.

Mary Rice-DeFosse

BIBLIOGRAPHY

Primary Texts

Agoult, Marie d' (Daniel Stern). *Histoire de la Révolution de 1848.* 2 vols. Paris: Charpentier, 1862.
Flaubert, Gustave. *L'Education sentimentale.* Paris: Lévy, 1869.
Sand, George. *Souvenirs de 1848.* Plan de la Tour: Aujourd'hui, 1976.

Secondary Texts

Bidelman, Patrick K. *Pariahs Stand Up! The Founding of the Liberal Feminist Movement in France, 1858–1889.* Westport, CT: Greenwood Press, 1982.
Moon, S. Joan. "Woman as Agent of Social Change: Woman's Rights during the Second French Republic." In *Views of Women's Lives in the Western Tradition.* Ed. Frances R. Keller. New York: Mellen, 1990.
Moses, Claire Goldberg. *French Feminism in the Nineteenth Century.* Albany: State University of New York Press, 1984.
———. "Feminist Activism during the Revolutionary Upheavals of 1848–1851." Chapter 6 of *French Feminism in the Nineteenth-Century.* Albany: State University of New York Press, 1984. 126–49.
Riot-Sarcy, Michèle. "La Conscience féministe des femmes de 1848: Jeanne Deroin et Désirée Gay," In *Un Fabuleux Destin: Actes du Premier Colloque International Flora Tristan.* Ed. Stéphane Michaud. Dijon: Editions Universitaires de Dijon, 1985.
———. *La Démocratie à l'épreuve des femmes: Trois Figures critiques du pouvoir 1830–1848.* Paris: Albin Michel, 1994.
———. "A Public Life Denied by History—Jeanne Deroin or the Forgetfulness of Self." *History of European Ideas* 11 (1989): 253–261.
Strumingher, Laura S. "The Struggle for Unity among Parisian Women: The *Voix des femmes,* March–June 1848." *History of European Ideas* 11 (1989): 273–285.
———. "The Vésuviennes: Images of Women Warriors in 1848 and Their Significance for French History." *History of European Ideas* 8 (1987): 451–488.
Walton, Whitney. "Writing the 1848 Revolution: Politics, Gender, and Feminism in the Works of French Women of Letters." *French Historical Studies* 18 (Fall 1994): 1001–1024.

Rey, Françoise (1951–   ). Little biographical information is available on this writer of erotic*—some would say pornographic—novels*. Written from a woman's perspective, Rey's texts reshape the traditional masculine orientation of the genre by placing male and female characters on the same level of erotic performance. Full of salacious and quick-witted humor, her female characters often engage in the written exploration of their sexual fantasies before putting them into practice. For these reasons, Rey's texts can be called feminist erotic novels.

Frédérique Chevillot

BIBLIOGRAPHY

Primary Texts

La Femme de papier. Paris: Ramsay/Jean-Jacques Pauvert, 1989.
Des Camions de tendresse. Paris: Ramsay, 1991.
La Rencontre. Paris: Spengler, 1993.
Nuits d'encre. Paris: Spengler, 1994.
"Le Patin à roulettes." In *Troubles de femmes: Nouvelles*. Ed. Marc Dolisi. Paris: Spengler, 1994.
Marcel facteur. Paris: Spengler, 1995.
Le Gourgandin. Paris: Edition Blanche, 1996.
Rey, Françoise, and Remo Forlani. *En Toutes Lettres*. Paris: Ramsay, 1992.

Reyes, Alina (1956–). Novelist. Alina Reyes established herself in the literary world with her first novel*, *Le Boucher* (1988), which elicited both critical acclaim and commercial success. A sexual fable* told from the point of view of a young woman, *Le Boucher* questions the boundaries of eroticism and pornography and enacts a feminist appropriation of those traditionally male genres. In *Derrière la porte*, that critical dimension becomes even more explicit, as Reyes offers a compendium of the commonplaces of erotic writing, subverting them one after the other with parody and ironic play. Although they were not conceived as such, it is tempting to regard Reyes's novels as a cycle, for they resemble each other formally in their fragmentary, terse style, and their female protagonists share meditations on gender, love, and sexuality. Reyes stages the writing subject dramatically; in each of her novels, the writing of desire translates the love of writing.

Warren Motte

BIBLIOGRAPHY

Primary Texts

Le Boucher. Paris: Seuil, 1988.
Lucie au long cours. Paris: Seuil, 1990.
Au Corset qui tue. Paris: Gallimard, 1992.
Quand tu aimes, il faut partir. Paris: Gallimard, 1993.
Derrière la Porte. Paris: Laffont, 1994.
La Nuit. Paris: Joëlle Losfeld, 1994.
Le Chien qui voulait me manger. Paris: Gallimard, 1996.

Secondary Text

Motte, Warren. "Temptations of the Flesh." *L'Esprit Créateur* 31, no. 4 (1991): 51–58.

Riccoboni, Marie-Jeanne (1713–1792). Her early years seem the stuff of fiction: a father whose bigamy, discovered, would deprive the child of his love and fortune; an uncaring mother, and a convent* education* which she would remember only with bitterness. Marriage* to Antoine-François Riccoboni, an actor at the Comédie Italienne, seemed an escape, but it did not bring happiness.

Her husband was a spendthrift, hot-headed and ill-tempered. Her liaison with the comte de Maillebois, who served (most agree) as the model for the unfaithful Albert of Riccoboni's first novel, did not bring happiness either. Friendship*— with both men and women—provided some compensation for life's deceptions. Separated from her husband in 1755 (although continuing to pay his debts and being with him when he died), Riccoboni shared an apartment with Thérèse Biancolelli, an actress like herself, with whom she lived and worked until her death.

Riccoboni acted at the Comédie Italienne for twenty-six years. She wrote essays and short fiction, corresponded with the likes of Diderot and Garrick, translated English plays and Fielding's *Amelia*, and engaged in a celebrated exchange with Laclos about Mme de Merteuil. For her contemporaries, however, she was a best-selling novelist, widely read, and acclaimed by critics for her sensibility, her pure and elegant style. She began her literary career on a dare, imitating Marivaux (to whom she is sometimes compared) and writing a conclusion for *La Vie de Marianne*. In seventeen years, she produced eight novels, retiring from her acting career when she could support herself through the sale of her books. Her best-known works are her earliest: *Lettres de Mistriss Fanni Butlerd* (1757), *Histoire du Marquis de Cressy* (1758), and *Lettres de Milady Juliette Catesby à Milady Henriette Campley, son amie* (1759), although *Histoire de Miss Jenny* (1764) and others have also received recent critical attention. All of her shorter novels have been published in modern editions.

Although they are frequently set in a conventional, aristocratic England and an epistolary mold, Riccoboni's novels are not of a piece. Fanni Butlerd's monophonic letters are classically simple; Jenny's story is long and romanesque. The philosophical polyphonic *Lettres de Mylord Rivers à Sir Charles Cardigan* (1777) has been compared to Montesquieu's letters. Yet the common thread is female experience, viewed through the explicitly female perspective of a narrator or correspondent. Her heroines comment on their relationship with men and the dichotomy between the sexes. Sensitive, intelligent, superior women who follow their hearts and consciences, they find themselves involved with vain and faithless, sensual and selfish men who do not appreciate them and seek only the satisfaction of desire. Aware of the sexual inequalities and the society that sanctions them, they strongly protest the double standard, but they do not change the social order. They accept as inevitable the consequences of male privilege, and, more traditional than the novelist herself, seek their identity in love and marriage. Happiness frequently eludes them.

Ruth P. Thomas

BIBLIOGRAPHY

Primary Texts

Histoire de Miss Jenny, écrite et envoyée par elle à Milady, comtesse de Rosemonde, ambassadrice d'Angleterre à la cour de Dannemark. Paris: Volland, 1786.
Histoire du marquis de Cressy. Ed. Olga B. Cragg. *Studies on Voltaire and the Eighteenth Century* 266. Oxford: Voltaire Foundation, 1989.

Les Lettres de Mylord Rivers. Ed. Olga B. Cragg. Geneva: Droz, 1993.

Lettres de Milady Juliette Catesby à Milady Henriette Campley, son amie. Preface by Sylvain Menant. Paris: Desjonquères, 1983.

Lettres de Mistriss Fanni Butlerd. Ed. Joan Hinde Stewart. Geneva: Droz, 1979.

Secondary Texts

André, Arlette. "Le Féminisme chez Mme Riccoboni." *Studies on Voltaire and the Eighteenth Century* 193 (1980): 1988–1995.

Cazenobe, Colette. "Le Féminisme paradoxal de Madame Riccoboni." *Revue d'histoire littéraire de la France* 88 (1988): 23–45.

Demay, Andrée. *Marie-Jeanne Riccoboni: ou De la pensée féministe chez une romancière du XVIIIe siècle.* Paris: La Pensée universelle, 1977.

Piau, Colette. "L'Ecriture féminine? A propos de Marie-Jeanne Riccoboni." *Dix-Huitième Siècle* 16 (1984): 369–385.

Stewart, Joan Hinde. *Gynographs: French Novels by Women of the Late Eighteenth Century.* Lincoln: University of Nebraska Press, 1993.

———. *The Novels of Mme Riccoboni.* Chapel Hill: North Carolina Studies in the Romance Languages and Literatures, 1976.

Richebourg, Madame Le Givre de. *See* Le Givre de Richebourg, madame.

Right to vote. Since the early days of the French Revolution*, women have sought equal access to citizenship, including the right to participate in the political process. Unfortunately, their hopes were crushed when the Constitution of 1793 awarded the right to vote to men only; two years later, women were formally excluded from participation in political activities, although they could still be legally prosecuted and sent to the guillotine*.

In the middle of the nineteenth century, voting rights were extended to all citizens, except minors, criminals, the mentally ill, and women. Despite the heroic efforts of such ardent militants as Hubertine Auclert*, Jeanne Deroin*, Marguerite Durand*, and Pauline Roland*, and the powerful voice of Eugénie Niboyet's* *La Voix des femmes*, the suffragist movement remained marginal, and the constitutions of the Second and Third Republics continued to bar women from the political process. However, in the years following World War I*, suffragists gained wide support as groups from the entire political spectrum, ranging from communists to Catholics (including the pope in 1919), backed their cause. Under increasing public pressure, legislators were urged to debate the political rights of women. Various laws advanced by enlightened and influential men such as Joseph Barthélémy, Jean Bon, Aristide Briand, and René Viviani were introduced and passed by the lower chamber. The Senate, however, adamantly opposed to women's suffrage, prevented the enactment of these laws. The breakthrough occurred during World War II* when Charles de Gaulle promised to give women the right to vote—ironically at a time when the suffragist movement was inactive. De Gaulle kept his word. As of 1945 women have been able to participate in the political process as voters and as legislators.

Since 1945 the number of female voters has steadily increased, although the number of female legislators has not. While women constitute 53 percent of the electorate and vote in nearly the same percentage as men, there was only a minimal increase or a decline in the percentage of female deputies and senators between 1945 and 1993. However, at lower levels of government, the percentage of female officials improved. Since 1981, in order to offset the paucity of female legislators, governments have increased the presence of women in the executive and judiciary branches, giving them more judgeships and cabinet posts.

The pattern of the women's vote indicates a noticeable shift in their political orientation. In the early years, women tended to support candidates from the right. Since the early 1980s, however, they have leaned to the left, except in 1993, when they outnumbered men in voting against the Socialists. In the mid-1990s, women from the entire political spectrum joined forces to demand "political parity," that is, a revision of the present political system, perhaps through a constitutional amendment, which would allow women fair access to political office and the legislative arena.

Samia I. Spencer

BIBLIOGRAPHY

Secondary Texts

Albistur, Maïté, and Daniel Armogathe. *Histoire du féminisme français du moyen âge à nos jours*. Paris: Editions des femmes, 1972.

Aubin, Claire, and Hélène Gisserot, eds. *Les Femmes en France: 1985–1995. Rapport établi par la France en vue de la quatrième conférence mondiale sur les femmes*. Paris: La Documentation française, 1994.

Badinter, Elisabeth. *Les Femmes. Contours et caractères*. Paris: Insée, 1995.

———. *Paroles d'hommes (1790–1793)*. Paris: P.O.L., 1989.

Gaffrey, John. *France and Modernization*. Brookfield, VT: Avebury, 1988.

Gaspard, Françoise, Claude Servan-Schreiber, and Ann Le Gall. *Au pouvoir citoyennes!; liberté, égalité, parité*. Paris: Editions du Seuil, 1992.

Halimi, Gisèle. *Choisir la cause des femmes, moitié de la terre, moitié du pouvoir. Plaidoyer pour une démocratie paritaire*. Paris: Gallimard, 1994.

Huard, Raymond. *Le Suffrage universel en France (1848–1946)*. Paris: Aubier, 1991.

Jenson, Jane, and Mariette Sineau. "The Same or Different? An Unending Dilemma." In *Women and Politics Worldwide*. Ed. Barbara Nelson and Najma Chowdhury. New Haven, CT: Yale University Press, 1944. 243–260.

Roudy, Yvette. *Mais de quoi ont-ils peur? Un vent de misogynie souffle sur la politique*. Paris: Albin Michel, 1995.

Stetson, Dorothy McBride. *Women's Rights in France*. Westport, CT: Greenwood Press, 1987.

Rivoyre, Christine de (1921–). Novelist and journalist. Rivoyre worked for *Le Monde* before becoming the literary editor of *Marie-Claire*. In her fictional works, she analyzes the relations between the sexes. *Reine-Mère* (1985), for example, depicts a strong female character who opposes the violence of the modern world with her love for all living creatures. Two of her novels* use the context of war as a backdrop—the occupation of France in *Le Petit Matin* (1968) and the Spanish Civil War in *Boy* (1973). In *Racontez-moi les Flamboyants* (1995), the earthy sensuality of the characters and their love of life and of all creatures are reminiscent of the themes of other well-known women writers such as Colette*.

Ana M. de Medeiros

BIBLIOGRAPHY

Primary Texts

L'Alouette au miroir. Paris: Plon, 1955.
La Mandarine. Paris: Plon, 1957.
La Tête en fleurs. Paris: Plon, 1960.
Les Sultans. Paris: Grasset, 1964.
Le Petit Matin. Paris: Grasset, 1968.
Le Seigneur des chevaux. Paris: Julliard, 1969.
Fleur d'agonie. Paris: Grasset, 1970.
Boy. Paris: Grasset, 1973.
Le Voyage à l'envers. Paris: Grasset, 1977.
Belle Alliance. Paris: Grasset, 1982.
Reine-Mère. Paris: Grasset, 1985.
Racontez-moi les Flamboyants. Paris: Grasset, 1995.

Robert, Marie-Anne Roumier (1705–1771). Robert was born into a bourgeois family. Her father was a businessman, her mother a lawyer's daughter. Well educated, she was influenced by her father's friend, the philosopher Fontenelle. Upon her parents' death and the family's financial losses in the John Law scandal, she was sent to a convent*, then married an esteemed lawyer, M. Robert. She published three novels*, one imaginary voyage, and a novel-length *conte*. The number of editions of these works belies their decidedly mixed critical reception. Portraying women, often of foreign, lower-class, or unknown origin, Robert explores Enlightenment* values in a gendered context to reveal hidden inconsistencies. *Les Ondins* and *Voyages de Milord Céton* represent the advantages and dangers of different forms of government, only to conclude with the ideally and equally shared rule of king and queen, husband and wife. The other more realistic novels reveal a less optimistic vision in their examination of female autonomy, class, race, and gender. Robert's work, using the conventions of the philosophic tradition, continues in the steps of women novelists (Scudéry*, Lafayette*, Graffigny*, etc.), situating cultural, social, and political critiques in a gendered context.

Antoinette Marie Sol

BIBLIOGRAPHY

Primary Texts

La Paysanne philosophe ou mémoires de Mme la Comtesse *** par Mad. de R.R. Amsterdam: Les Libraires Associés, 1761–1762.

La Voix de la nature ou les aventures de Mme la marquise de *** par Mad. de R.R., auteur de la Paysanne philosophe. Amsterdam: N.p., 1763.

Voyages de Milord Céton dans les sept planètes, ou, le nouveau mentor, traduits par Mme de R.R. M.-A. The Hague and Paris: Despilly, 1765–1766.

Nicole de Beauvais ou l'amour vaincu par la reconnaissance, par Mme Robert. The Hague and Paris: Desaint, 1767.

Les Ondins. Conte moral, par Mme Robert. London and Paris: Delalain, 1768.

Secondary Text

Harth, Erica. *Cartesian Women: Versions and Subversions of Rational Discourse in the Old Regime.* Ithaca, NY: Cornell University Press, 1992.

Rochefort, Christiane (1917–1998). Novelist and essayist. Rochefort began her career as a cinema* reporter. She earned instant success with her first novel*, *Le Repos du guerrier* (1958), which attacks middle-class values and portrays a woman in an exploitative relationship. Rochefort, who was active in the French women's movement of the 1970s, criticizes patriarchal institutions such as the educational system, the church, the judicial system and the police—institutions she sees as encouraging rampant consumerism. She critiques Western society and raises political consciousness in an ironic, derisory style, using neologisms and puns with the goal of subverting the language of the oppressors. Her best known social critique, *Les Petits Enfants du siècle* (1961), which recounts how a young girl living in a Parisian housing project finds herself unable to break out of the cycle of poverty, questions the relationship between capitalism and social policies. *Les Stances à Sophie* (1963), narrated by a woman character, depicts her disillusionment with bourgeois marriage* and reflects her concern with patriarchal power structures. In this satirical work, Rochefort explores a variety of sexual relationships, including a lesbian relationship between the protagonist and her best friend. In addition to women, Rochefort deals with children, another segment of society she considers oppressed. She turns to her favorite genre, the utopian novel, in *Encore heureux qu'on va vers l'été*, which focuses on a group of children who reject school in favor of real-world experiences. As in her other utopian works, this text starts with an escape, after which the protagonists build a new world free of gender-based hierarchies and rooted in sexual freedom without guilt, an important theme of Rochefort's work. In her well-known feminist utopian text, *Archaos ou le jardin étincelant*, Rochefort parodies the Oedipus myth*, proposes a decentralized anarchist community, and stresses the notion of androgyny* as a way of breaking down rigid definitions of male and female. In her work, Rochefort subverts feminine and masculine clichés through her use of irony, subversive vocabulary, and her emphasis on the transformation and interchangeability of the sexes.

Isabelle Constant

BIBLIOGRAPHY

Primary Texts

Le Repos du guerrier. Paris: Grasset, 1958.
Les Petits Enfants du siècle. Paris: Grasset, 1961.

Les Stances à Sophie. Paris: Grasset, 1963.
Une Rose pour Morrisson. Paris: Grasset, 1966.
Printemps au Parking. Paris: Grasset, 1969.
Archaos ou le jardin étincelant. Paris: Grasset, 1972.
Encore heureux qu'on va vers l'été. Paris: Grasset, 1975.
Les Enfants d'abord. Paris: Grasset, 1976.
Ma Vie revue et corrigée par l'auteur. Paris: Stock, 1978.
Le Monde est comme deux chevaux. Paris: Grasset, 1984.
La Porte du fond. Paris: Grasset, 1988.

Secondary Text

Holmes, Diane. "Realism, Fantasy and Feminist Meaning: The Fiction of Christiane Rochefort." In *Contemporary French Fiction by Women: Feminist Perspectives.* Ed. Margaret Atack and Phil Powrie. Manchester, UK: Manchester University Press, 1990. 26–40.

Roches, Dames des (Madeleine Neveu, 1520–1587; Catherine Fradonnet, 1542–1587). The Dames des Roches, mother and daughter, lived their entire lives in and around Poitiers. Madeleine likely frequented humanist circles during Poitiers's first period of literary fame (1545–1555) that included the poets J. Pelletier, J. Tahureau, and J.-A. de Baïf. Twice married to lawyers whose library holdings would have been available to her, Madeleine devoted herself to the education* of Catherine, her sole surviving child. She encouraged the pursuit of learning for its own sake, in contrast to a more traditional, utilitarian female education that taught household management and obedience to one's husband. Catherine never married due to her desire to pursue a life of learning and writing with her mother. Two of her suitors, C.-J. de Guersens and C. Pellejay, dedicated certain of their works to her to sway her toward marriage*; but Catherine, instead, expressed pride in women who resist social constraints to become known for themselves.

The Dames des Roches's publications first appeared in the 1570s when they established a salon*. In 1577 the court's three-month residence in Poitiers prompted them to write several poems lauding members of the royal family. These poems were included in their first volume of works, published in Paris in 1578 by the well-known bookseller Abel L'Angelier, who also brought out an expanded second edition the following year. That the first edition sold out so quickly attests to their growing fame, which attracted to their salon Parisian lawyers present at the 1579 assizes or "grands jours" of Poitiers. Among them was E. Pasquier who, upon sighting a flea on Catherine's bosom, suggested a contest of versified wit. This led to the beginning of *La Puce de Madame des Roches*, a ninety-three folio collection of *blasons* by the habitués of the salon. Before their deaths in 1587, the Dames des Roches published two more volumes of works, including *Les Missives*, the first collection of private letters by women in France. These publications include a wide variety of poetic genres, prose dialogues, letters, a tragicomedy, and first translations of Latin works. Madeleine's contribution, entirely in verse except for her letters, covers largely personal subjects such as her health, a thirteen-year lawsuit, her love for her daughter, the misfortunes of Poitiers during the religious wars, marital love, and the role of women. In her preface to the first volume, she urges the *Dames*, her contemporaries, to realize that if "silence, the ornament of women," does not put them to shame, neither does it bring them any honor; therefore, they should read her work. Catherine's contribution is more extensive and is marked with a more developed feminist consciousness. Two of her major dialogues, "Dialogue de Placide et Severe" and "Dialogue d'Iris et Pasithée," likely emerged from salon discussions concerning women in society and the goals of female education. They bring together three distinct views, the traditionalism of the misogynist (Severe), the paternalism of the humanist (Placide), and the independence of the feminist (Pasithée). These dialogues daringly defend the single woman who pursues an independent existence. Also integral to Catherine's feminist economy is her praise of the distaff in her often-anthologized "A ma Quenouille" (1579). Catherine is the first to challenge humanist norms that consider female learning as necessarily subservient to household management, and that treat learned women as exceptions to their sex, unfit for traditional feminine occupations.

The Dames des Roches's singular commitment to each other was recognized, and to a limited extent criticized, during their lifetime. They wrote of and for each other, repeatedly dedicating their works to each other. The valorization of the mother-daughter bond is one of the most striking features of their works. The daughter's appeal to maternal discourse is embodied in her independent-minded heroines Agnodice, Pasithée, Charite, the Amazons*, Proserpina, Pallas Athena, the "Femme forte" of Proverbs, and Phyllis, who constitute so many legitimizing "foremothers" in her quest for poetic origins.

The des Roches were highly appreciated by a community of humanists, scholars, and poets. Their conciliatory feminism* parallelled their conservative political and religious beliefs. They aimed at strengthening the national consciousness and the glory of the weak monarchy and defended the superiority of French culture. Denouncing the Reform movement, they were Catholics and pacifists. Both mother and daughter died on the same day in 1587 of the plague.

Anne R. Larsen

BIBLIOGRAPHY

Primary Texts

Les Oeuvres de Les Dames des Roches de Poitiers, mere et fille. Paris: Abel L'Angelier, 1578.

Les Oeuvres [. . .] seconde edition. 4 vols. Paris: Abel L'Angelier, 1579.

La Puce de Madame des Roches [. . .]. 4 vols. Paris: Abel L'Angelier, 1582, 1583.

Les Secondes Oeuvres de Mes-dames des Roches de Poitiers, Mere et Fille. Poitiers: Nicolas Courtoys, 1583.

Les Missives de Mes-dames des Roches de Poictiers, mere et fille, avec le Ravissement de Proserpine prins du Latin de Clodian. Et autres imitations et meslanges poë-tiques. 4 vols. Paris: Abel L'Angelier, 1586.

Les Oeuvres. Ed. Anne R. Larsen. Geneva: Droz, 1993.

Secondary Texts

Berriot-Salvadore, Evelyne. *Les Femmes dans la société française de la Renaissance.* Geneva: Droz, 1990.

———. ''Les Femmes dans les cercles intellectuels de la Renaissance: De la fille prodige à la précieuse.'' In *Mélanges Pitti-Ferrandi. Etudes corses, études littéraires.* Paris: Le Cerf, 1989. 210–237.

Diller, George. *Les Dames des Roches. Etude sur la vie littéraire à Poitiers dans la deuxième moitié du XVIe siècle.* Paris: Droz, 1936.

Jones, Ann Rosalind. *The Currency of Eros: Women's Love Lyric in Europe, 1540–1620.* Bloomington: Indiana University Press, 1990.

Larsen, Anne R. ''The French Humanist Scholars: Les Dames des Roches.'' In *Women Writers of the Renaissance and Reformation.* Ed. Katharina M. Wilson. Athens: University of Georgia Press, 1987. 232–259.

Sankovitch, Tilde. ''Catherine des Roches's *Le Ravissement de Proserpine*: A Humanist/Feminist Translation.'' In *Renaissance Women Writers: French Texts/American Contexts.* Ed. Anne Larsen and Colette H. Winn. Detroit: Wayne State University Press, 1994. 55–66.

Winn, Colette H. ''Mère/fille/femme/muse: Maternité et créativité dans les oeuvres des Dames des Roches.'' *Travaux de Littérature* 4 (1991): 53–68.

Yandell, Cathy. ''Of Lice and Women: Rhetoric and Gender in *La Puce de Madame des Roches.*'' *Journal of Medieval and Renaissance Studies* 20 (1990): 123–135.

Rohan, Anne de (1584–1646). Youngest daughter of Catherine de Parthenay* and René II, viscount of Rohan. Her correspondence, in which she shares the gossip of the court with friends, is witty and lighthearted, yet her piety and sensitivity are evident in her poetry*. Agrippa d'Aubigné praised her for her intelligence (she knew Latin and Hebrew) and her virtue. A constant companion to her mother, she shared with her the hardships during the siege of La Rochelle and their imprisonment afterwards. Her writings include a long remonstrance entitled ''Les Larmes et regrets de Mademoiselle Anne de Rohan sur la desroute de Monsieur de Soubize son frère, et sur sa rebellion contre le roy'' (1612), and twenty-five poems that have been found to date. Seven of the poems treat serious or religious themes, but eighteen express her sorrow on the deaths of friends and family, the earliest being an octet in 1595. Three relate to the death of her sister, Catherine, and appeared in the 1606 *Tombeau de la Duchesse de Deux-Ponts.* She wrote three elegies on the death of her friend Catherine de Lorraine, duchess of Nevers, in 1618. Four poems lamenting the death of Catherine de Parthenay appear in the 1636 edition *Plaintes de très-illustre princesse Mlle Anne de Rohan, sur le trépas de Mme de Rohan, sa mère.* Her 1610 ''Stances sur la mort du Roi Henri IV'' was widely published, and D'Aubigné included several lines from it at the end of his *Histoire universelle.* She repaid his homage to her with a ''Sonnet à la ville de Genève sur la mort de M. d'Aubigné''

(1630). Her longest poem, "La Patience" (550 lines in alexandrine), was dedicated to Louise de Coligny after the death of her son, Frédéric-Henri de Nassau, to whom Rohan had been engaged. She never married, and little is known of her later life. She died in Paris on September 20, 1646.

Christie St-John

BIBLIOGRAPHY

Primary Texts

Plaintes de très-illustre princesse Mlle Anne de Rohan, sur le trépas de Mme de Rohan, sa mère. Geneva, 1636.
Poésies d'Anne de Rohan-Soubise et Lettres d'Eléonore de Rohan-Montbaron. Ed. A. Aubry. Paris: A. Aubry, 1862.
Bonnet, Jules. "Un Poème inédit, 'La Patience' par Anne de Rohan, publiée d'après le manuscrit de la Bibliothèque Royale de la Haye." *Mélanges littéraires* (February 1886): 1–18.
Lettres de Catherine de Parthenay . . . et de ses deux filles Henriette et Anne à Charlotte-Brabantine de Nassau. Ed. Hugues Imbert. Niort: Société des Antiquaires de l'Ouest, n.d.

Secondary Texts

Marchegay, Paul. "Un Poème inédit de Mademoiselle Anne de Rohan-Soubise." *Mélanges littéraires* (June 1884): 1–16.
————. ed. *Recherches sur les poésies de Mlle de Rohan-Soubise.* Les Roches: Baritaud, 1874.

Rohan, Marie-Eléonore de (1628–1681). Daughter of the highest nobility, Marie-Eléonore de Rohan was born in 1628 to the notorious Mme de Montbazon, second wife of Hercule de Rohan-Guéménée, a courtier of Henri IV. When the child was seven, her family dispatched her to the Benedictine Abbey of Montargis to be educated under her aunt's protection. She would return there as a postulant in 1644, professing final vows in 1646. Almost immediately, Louis XIV appointed her abbess of La Trinité, known as the Abbaye des Dames, in Caen, Normandy. The abbess wielded exceptional power in this royal foundation, which received only girls of the upper classes. There, Pierre-Daniel Huet, future bishop of Avranches, encouraged Marie-Eléonore's initial literary project: a translation and paraphrase of the Books of Proverbs, Ecclesiastes, and Wisdom, later augmented with the Penitential Psalms. Marie-Eléonore used the originals as a pretext for her personal meditations on the snares of life at court, which she expressed in precious style. Published anonymously in 1665, *La Morale du Sage* reappeared in 1667 and in 1681, and posthumously in 1691 with the author's engraved portrait. The work was aimed at the ladies of the salon* rather than cloistered nuns.

As she carried out her duties as abbess at Caen, then at Malnoue in Brie, and finally at Notre Dame de la Consolation in Paris, where she transferred in 1669, Marie-Eléonore frequented the most distinguished salons of the capital. She contributed several portraits to the *Divers Portraits* issued by Mlle de Montpensier* (Anne-Marie-Louise d'Orléans) in 1659. In her self-portrait, she presents both her best features (such as gratitude, facility in understanding most sorts of things, and facility in speaking and writing), without sparing her defects (such as willfulness and vindictiveness).

Madeleine de Scudéry* disguised Marie-Eléonore as "La Grande Vestale" in Book VIII of her novel *Clélie*. Known also as "Octavie" and "Mélagire," she frequented the salon of Mme de Sablé* and knew the Jesuit critics Fathers Bouhours and Rapin. She corresponded with Pellisson and La Rochefoucauld, among many important figures of the era.

Mary Rowan

BIBLIOGRAPHY

Secondary Text

Nouvelle Biographie générale. Ed. M. Hoefer. Paris: Firmin Didot Frères, 1852–1877.

Roland, Marie-Desirée Pauline (1805–1852). Writer, journalist, socialist feminist, and educator. Raised in Normandy by her mother, Pauline was drawn to Saint-Simonianism*. In 1832 she became an instructor and contributed to *La Tribune des femmes* as Marie-Pauline. Consciously breaking her vow of celibacy, Roland became pregnant in 1834 with her first child by Adolphe Guéroult. She then took another lover, Saint-Simonian Jean Aicard, by whom she would have three more children. Acting as head of the family*, Roland supported her children through writing and freelance journalism. Throughout the July Monarchy, she contributed to Pierre Leroux's periodicals such as *L'Encyclopédie nouvelle, La Revue indépendante*, and *La Revue sociale*. After breaking with Aicard, Roland struggled in Paris before assuming teaching responsibilities at Boussac, Leroux's community, from 1847 until December 1848. Her articles of this period advocate worker associations and equal education for men and women of all classes. Abjuring the "slavery of the senses," Roland now argued that education*, love, and fidelity could indeed transform marriage*. Still a "sacred duty," maternity* was not, however, woman's only mission. Roland also reported on Parisian workers' associations in *La République*, and in 1850 joined Deroin* to found the Union of Workers' Associations and Teachers' Association, for which both women received a six-month prison sentence. Writing from prison, Roland published articles in the *Liberté de penser* and refuted Emile de Girardin's reactionary article on women. Released in 1851, she tried to resurrect the Teachers' Association but was arrested again in February 1852 for her alleged role in the Parisian insurrection following the December coup d'état. Deported in June 1852 to Algeria, Roland remained there until freed in November 1852 despite her refusals to request a government pardon. En route to Paris, she became ill and died in Lyons.

Cheryl A. Morgan

BIBLIOGRAPHY

Primary Texts

Lefrançais, G., Pauline Roland, and Perot. *Aux Instituteurs: L'Association des institu-
teurs, institutrices et professeurs socialistes.* Paris: Impr. Schneider, 1849.
———. *Association fraternelle des instituteurs, institutrices et professeurs socialistes:
Programme d'éducation.* Paris: Chez le citoyen Perot, 1849.
———. "La Femme a-t-elle droit à la liberté?" *La Feuille du peuple,* April 25, 1851.
Roland, Pauline, Arthur Ranc, and Gaspard Rouffet. *Bagnes d'Afrique. Trois Transportés
en Algérie après le coup d'état du 2 décembre 1851.* Textes établis, annotés et
présentés par Fernand Rude. Paris: François Maspéro, 1981.

Secondary Texts

Gordon, Felicia, and Mire Cross. *Early French Feminisms, 1830–1940: A Passion for
Liberty.* Cheltenham, UK: Edward Elgar, 1996.
Groult, Benoîte. *Pauline Roland, ou, comment la liberté vint aux femmes.* Paris: Robert
Laffont, 1991.
Lejeune-Resnick, Evelyne. *Femmes et associations (1830–1880).* Paris: Publisud, 1991.
Michaud, Stéphane. "Deux Approches du changement social: Flora Tristan et Pauline
Roland au miroir de leur correspondance." In *Flora Tristan, George Sand, Pau-
line Roland: Les Femmes et l'invention d'une nouvelle morale 1830–1848.* Etudes
réunies par Stéphane Michaud. Paris: Créaphis, 1994.
Moses, Claire Goldberg. *French Feminism in the Nineteenth Century.* Albany: State
University of New York Press, 1984.
Moses, Claire Goldberg, and Leslie Wahl Rabine. *Feminism, Socialism, and French
Romanticism.* Bloomington: Indiana University Press, 1993.
Riot-Sarcey, Michèle. *La Démocratie à l'épreuve des femmes: trois figures critiques du
pouvoir 1830–1848.* Paris: Albin Michel, 1994.
Thomas, Edith. *Pauline Roland: Socialisme et féminisme au XIXe siècle.* Paris: Marcel
Rivière, 1956.

Roland de la Platière, Marie Jeanne (Manon) Phlipon (1754–1794). The only
child of a middle-class couple, she showed a predisposition for serious study
and voracious reading: Plutarch, Montaigne, Montesquieu, Locke, and Voltaire
were among her favorite authors, and she became imbued with the ideals of the
Enlightenment*. But it was Rousseau who revealed to her her spiritual being.
Henceforth, she would remain his enthusiastic and faithful disciple in all matters
regarding politics, morality, and the "woman question."

In 1789, after a protracted courtship, she married Jean-Marie Roland de la
Platière, an inspector of manufactures twenty years her senior, a union that
produced a daughter, Eudora. Manon Roland soon became the close collaborator
of her husband. In 1789 she greeted the Revolution* with overwhelming enthusiasm and became the Egeria of the ill-fated Girondins. Roland's appointment
as Minister of the Interior in 1792 furthered her activities, but also put her at
the center of a political maelstrom that would eventually bring about her demise.

When the Jacobins came to power, the Rolands and their Girondin allies found themselves outmaneuvered. In the meantime, her private life had come to an impasse, she having fallen in love with François Buzot, a Girondin deputy. But like Rousseau's virtuous Julie, she would remain faithful to her husband.

Arrested on May 31, 1793, Manon Roland was executed on November 8, 1793. According to eyewitnesses, she showed exemplary courage during her imprisonment and trial, and her last words, uttered at the foot of the guillotine*—"O Liberty! What crimes are committed in your name!"—have been immortalized. Paradoxically, even though as a loyal disciple of Rousseau, Manon Roland felt that women should find their fulfillment as wives and mothers, she seemed unable to curb her writing urge or to resist her overwhelming need to play a part in the Revolution. As a result, she authored a not inconsiderable body of letters and personal essays as well as political documents signed by her husband and, most notably, her poignant and eloquent memoirs*, patterned after Rousseau's *Confessions* and penned during her incarceration.

Gita May

BIBLIOGRAPHY

Primary Texts

Oeuvres de Jeanne-Marie Phlipon Roland. Ed. Luc-Antoine Champagneux. Paris: Baidaut, 1899.
Mémoires. Ed. Claude Perroud. Paris: Imprimerie Nationale, 1900–1902.
Lettres. Ed. Claude Perroud. Paris: Imprimerie Nationale, 1900–1902.
Lettres. Nouvelle série. Ed. Claude Perroud. Paris: Imprimerie Nationale, 1913–1915.
Roland et Marie Phlipon. Lettres d'amour (1777–1780). Ed. Claude Perroud. Paris: Picard, 1909.

Secondary Texts

Chaussinand-Nogaret, Guy. *Madame Roland: Une Femme en révolution.* Paris: Seuil, 1985.
May, Gita. *Madame Roland and the Age of Revolution.* New York: Columbia University Press, 1970.
Michelet, Jules. "Madame Roland." *Les Femmes de la Révolution française.* Ed. F. Giroud. Paris: Carrère, 1989.
Ozouf, Mona. "Madame Roland." *Les Mots des femmes. essai sur la singularité française.* Paris: Fayard, 1995.
Trouille, Mary. "The Circle of the Republic: Mme Roland, Rousseau, and Revolutionary Politics." *Literate Women and the French Revolution of 1789.* Ed. Catherine R. Montfort. Birmingham, AL: Summa Publications, 1994.
Winegarten, Renee. "Marie-Jeanne Roland." In *French Women Writers.* Ed. Eva Martin Sartori and Dorothy Wynne Zimmerman. Westport, CT: Greenwood Press, 1991. 380–389.

Rolin, Dominique (1913–   ). Novelist and playwright. Belgian by birth, Rolin moved to Paris in 1946 and succeeded Marguerite Yourcenar* in the Belgian

Royal Academy in 1989. In her first novel*, *Les Marais* (1942), Rolin depicts the claustrophobic atmosphere of family* life which suppresses selfhood. Autobiographical elements often underlie her characters' struggles to deal with difficult moments in their lives: *Maintenant*, for example, was written after the death of Rolin's mother, leading her to reflect on her own double role as daughter and mother of a daughter. In *Le Jardin d'agrément*, Rolin recalls her own evolution as a writer through the creation of two women writers of different ages—both named Domi—whose initial animosity finally dissolves into a shared identity. Rolin often depicts conflicts between mothers and daughters, as in the story "Repas de famille" (1936) and in the strained restaurant conversation between daughter and mother in *Deux Femmes un soir* (1992), in which the two alternating points of view emphasize the distance separating the two women.

Jan Berkowitz Gross

BIBLIOGRAPHY

Primary Texts

Les Marais. Paris: Denoël, 1942.
Les Deux Soeurs. Paris: Denoël, 1946.
Souffle. Paris: Seuil, 1952.
La Maison, la forêt. Paris Denoël, 1965.
Deux. Paris: Denoël, 1975.
L'Infini chez soi. Paris: Denoël, 1980.
Trente Ans d'amour fou. Paris: Gallimard, 1988.
Deux Femmes un soir. Paris: Gallimard, 1992.
Les Géraniums: Nouvelles de jeunesse, et quelques autres. Paris: Editions de la Diffé-
    rence, 1993.
Le Jardin d'agrément. Paris: Gallimard, 1994.
L'Accoudoir. Paris: Gallimard, 1996.

Secondary Texts

De Haes, Frans. *Le Bonheur en projet: Hommage à Dominique Rolin*. Brussels: Editions
    Labor, 1993.
Dossier: Dominique Rolin. Ed. Paul Renard. *Nord* 27 (June 1996).
Nys-Mazure, Colette. "De mères en filles." *Nord* 27 (1996): 27–42.

Roman champêtre. A genre created and practiced by George Sand*, and associated almost exclusively with her. Sand initially hoped to document peasant life and speech in her native Berry before they disappeared. The trilogy composed of *La Mare au diable* (1846), *La Petite Fadette* (1849), and *François le champi* (1850) is among the best examples of this genre, but all of her pastoral novels* are included, as are similar works, such as the novels of Marguerite Audoux*. Recent criticism has shown the complexities of a genre once considered charming but simplistic.

Mary Rice-DeFosse

BIBLIOGRAPHY

Primary Texts

Audoux, Marguerite. *Marie-Claire*. Paris: Fasquelle, 1910.
Sand, George. *François le Champi*. Intro. Pierre Salomon and Jean Mallion. Paris: Garnier, 1981.
———. *La Mare au diable*. Intro. Pierre Salomon and Jean Mallion. Paris: Garnier, 1981.
———. *La Petite Fadette*. Intro. Pierre Salomon and Jean Mallion. Paris: Garnier, 1981.

Secondary Texts

Naginski, Isabelle Hoog. *George Sand: Writing for Her Life*. New Brunswick, NJ: Rutgers University Press, 1991.
Powell, David, ed. *George Sand Today*. Proceedings of the Eighth International George Sand Conference, Tours, 1989. New York: University Press of America, 1992.
Schor, Naomi. *George Sand and Idealism*. New York: Columbia University Press, 1993.

Romanticism. A literary and artistic movement, Romanticism represented a turn away from the rationalism that had dominated previous centuries. Instead of reason and logic, the Romantics privileged sensibility. Romanticism ostensibly placed women, long associated with feeling rather than rational thought, in the position of individual subjects, equally capable of strong passions and spiritual exaltation as well as deep alienation and melancholia*.

With its emphasis on extraordinary feelings and capabilities, Romanticism represented a move from the universal to the particular. The Romantic hero or heroine was often personified as a unique being or genius* in exile in a mediocre world. The Romantic impulse included a turn away from society's conventions. The Romantic soul instead found communion—and transcendence—in nature and in the company of other, singular individuals. In an attempt to escape the ennui of the present, Romantics looked to the distant past, to the Christian heritage, or to the faraway and exotic as alternatives to contemporary reality, but reimagined all of these alternatives according to the Romantic code, with little regard for historical or cultural context. The other thus became a projection and an extension of the Romantic ego.

Romanticism had its roots in Rousseau's thought, but reached its zenith in the early nineteenth century, in the works of writers like Mme de Staël*, Chateaubriand, Lamartine, Vigny, and Hugo. The movement developed in France later than in England or Germany. Mme de Staël was one of the movement's most important representatives, not only because she emphasized the importance of differences in cultural context, but, from a feminist standpoint, because of the strong heroines she created in works like *Delphine* and *Corinne*. Hugo's play *Hernani*, first performed in 1830, is often said to mark the triumph of Romanticism, a movement that rejected restrictive literary conventions in favor of freer modes of expression, and seemed to signal a period of greater artistic, political, and social freedom. Romanticism's emphasis on the solitary genius nonetheless reinforced notions of an elite, thereby undercutting egalitarian ideals.

A similar tension is seen in questions of gender. While Romanticism opened up new possibilities, valorizing traits in the speaking subject once considered "feminine" and therefore portraying them as inferior no more, Romantic literature often reduced women themselves to absent objects of masculine desire. Likewise, although women were often associated with nature rather than with culture, this did not place them in the superior position of the individual masculine subject. Instead, the masculine and feminine were often subsumed into a single (male) subject whose androgyny* may be seen as a repressive reaction against true difference.

Romanticism in fact often reinforced stereotypical feminine roles, like those of the virgin, the mother, or the muse, idealized, but essentially passive. Women who took up the pen were frequently denigrated as "blue-stockings" (*bas-bleus**) who had lost their feminine identity by crossing gender lines. George Sand*, whose own androgynous persona and literary voice made her notorious, represents the double bind in which the Romantic woman was caught, as do novels* like *Lélia*. Some women, like Sand and Marceline Desbordes-Valmore*, were able to create a distinctly feminine Romantic voice, but others, like Louise Colet* or Elisa Mercoeur*, were measured against masculine standards and found lacking. If they succeeded, they were denatured women. If they failed, it was because they were seen as too conventional to embody the singularity of Romantic genius.

Romanticism, as a movement, was at least partially eclipsed by Realism* and Parnassianism. Flaubert's *Madame Bovary* is an ironic portrait of the Romantic woman whose illusions lead her nowhere. Yet the Romantic movement, with its reinvention of the social code and of identity itself, has had a lasting impact on French literature and culture.

Mary Rice-DeFosse

BIBLIOGRAPHY

Secondary Texts

Bowman, Frank Paul. *French Romanticism: Intertextual and Interdisciplinary Readings.* Baltimore: Johns Hopkins University Press, 1990.

Fraisse, Geneviève. *Muse de la raison: La Démocratie exclusive et la différence des sexes.* Aix-en-Provence: Alinéa, 1989.

Kelly, Dorothy. *Fictional Genders: Role and Representation in Nineteenth-Century French Narrative.* Lincoln: University of Nebraska Press, 1989.

Mellor, Anne K., ed. *Romanticism and Feminism.* Bloomington: Indiana University Press, 1988.

Moses, Claire Goldberg, and Leslie Wahl Rabine. *Feminism, Socialism, and French Romanticism.* Bloomington: Indiana University Press, 1993.

Naginski, Isabelle. *George Sand: Writing for Her Life.* New Brunswick, NJ: Rutgers University Press, 1991.

Peyre, Henri. *What Is Romanticism?* Trans. Roda Roberts. University: University of
    Alabama Press, 1977.

Romieu, Marie de (1545?–1590). Poet chiefly remembered for her work *Brief
Discours de l'excellence des femmes.* Her brother Jacques, also a poet, was both
her publisher and mentor. The brother and sister were of noble extraction and
followed the entourage of their beneficiary, Jean de Chastellier, a finance minister of the kings Charles IX and Henri III. Consequently, many of Romieu's
sonnets, epigrams, epitaphs, hymns, and eclogues laud the merits of Chastellier
and other benefactors. She was married and had at least one son.

We have scant biographical information about the author of the *Premières
Oeuvres poétiques* (1581). For many years it was assumed that this collection
was composed by Jacques. Well educated in the liberal arts, Romieu, like many
fellow poets of the day, devoted much of her literary effort to the translation of
Italian and neo-Latin works. Stylistically, she was most influenced by Ronsard.
Her poetry* reveals a preference for his lyrical vocabulary and themes.

Largely derivative of the Italian Renaissance and French Pléiade traditions,
Romieu's writing is not considered today to have significant literary merit but
does reveal an enthusiasm for the cultural and humanist concerns of the day.
Her choice of translations and adaptations reveals a keen interest in the role of
women. She is believed by many critics, but not all, to be the translator of
Alessandro Piccolomini's *Dialogo dove si ragiona della bella creanza delle
donne,* entitled *Instruction pour les jeunes dames* (1573). Most notably, Romieu
was sensitive to the role of educated women and to contemporary female poets.
Her *Brief Discours* praises female writers such as Catherine de Clermont, Marguerite de Navarre*, Hélisenne de Crenne*, and Madeleine and Catherine des
Roches*. Written in response to her brother Jacques's invective against women,
this 356-line poem composed in alexandrine couplets traces the excellence of
women and culminates in a proclamation of their superiority over men. Romieu's discourse does not follow Christine de Pizan's* outline of Christian
ethics as a basis for the dignity of women seen in *La Cité des dames* but, rather,
closely imitates a passage from Charles Estienne's *Paradoxes* (1553), in turn
adapted and translated from Ortensio Landi's defense of women, *Paradossi*
(1543). The arguments in Romieu's version ultimately appear to be as much
parries in a literary game as sincere praises of women.

A generation younger than the early feminists of Lyons, Pernette du Guillet*
and Louise Labé*, Romieu, while weighing in on the *Querelle des femmes** in
defense of women, rarely attempts to establish her own narrative voice on issues
of love, marriage*, or life in general, as do her female predecessors. Instead,
she prefers to imitate what she considers the best poetry, whether by men or
women. Unlike Louise Labé, Romieu's love poetry serves, first, as a means to
describe her patron's love for others, and second, as a translation exercise. Romieu's original compositions are always erudite and often indicate an austere
sensibility. Few of Romieu's own preferences or emotions are revealed other

than the great value she places on education* and learning. In a sonnet addressed to her son she reminds him that knowledge is the only virtue that does not disappear. It appears that Romieu preferred to be a full-time poet and scholar. In the preface to her collection of poems she tells her brother that her *discours* has been written with much dedication but in great haste because her household duties leave her no free time.

There has been no substantial research on Romieu since Winandy's 1972 edition of *Premières Oeuvres poétiques*. Several of her poems continue to be anthologized as examples of the Pléiade poetic tradition.

Margaret Harp

BIBLIOGRAPHY

Primary Texts

Les Premières Oeuvres poétiques. Ed. P. Blanchemain. Paris: N.p., 1878.
Les Premières Oeuvres poétiques. Ed. André Winandy. Geneva: Droz, 1972.

Secondary Texts

Le Sourd, Auguste. *Recherches sur Jacques et Marie de Romieu*. Paris: Villefranche, 1934.
Raymond, Marcel. *L'Influence de Ronsard*. Vol. 2. Paris: N.p., 1927.

Romilly, Jacqueline de (1913–). Author of over forty works on classical subjects, classical scholar Romilly had a long and distinguished teaching career, from 1939, when she taught in a girl's *lycée* in Bordeaux, to 1973, when she joined the prestigious Collège de France. In 1975, when named to the Académie d'Inscriptions et de Belles-Lettres, she became the first woman member of the Institut de France, which encompasses five academies, including the Académie Française, to which de Romilly was named in 1990, making her the second woman so honored. These and subsequent honors can be attributed to the breadth and impact of her scholarship, which covers Greek history, culture, and literature. In recent years she has devoted several studies to the problem of education* in France.

Margaret Collins Weitz

BIBLIOGRAPHY

Primary Texts

Nous Autres Professeurs. Paris: Fayard, 1969.
L'Enseignement en détresse. Paris: Presses Pocket, 1985.
Lettre aux parents sur les choix scolaires. Paris: Editions de Fallois, 1994.

Roudy, Yvette (1929–). Born into a working-class family in Pessac, Roudy started to work in a factory at age sixteen. Gradually, this self-made woman became a staunch feminist and an ardent socialist, fully committed to the ideals of justice, equality, and respect for human rights. Her long and distinguished career in politics includes membership in the European Parliament (1979–1981) and the French National Assembly (1986–1993), the mayorship of Lisieux (1989–present), and an appointment as Minister for Women's Rights (1981–1986)—an office that allowed her to pursue an ambitious program aimed at eliminating prejudice against women in family* law and in the workplace. Throughout her life, Roudy's work as a political leader and a talented writer and translator has focused unequivocally on improving the status of women.

Samia I. Spencer

BIBLIOGRAPHY

Primary Texts

Les Métiers et les conjoints. N.p.: Editions du CAL, 1965.
La Réussite de la femme. N.p.: Editions du CAL, 1969.
La Femme en marge. Preface by François Mitterrand. Paris: Flammarion, 1975.
A cause d'elles. Preface by Simone de Beauvoir. Paris: Albin Michel, 1985.
Mais de quoi ont-ils peur? Paris: Albin Michel, 1995.

Roussel, Nelly (1878–1922). Roussel's major contributions to feminist literature are her political speeches and essays: between 1899 and 1922, she wrote nearly 200 articles and gave 236 speeches throughout Europe. Her speeches focused on topics such as women's suffrage, women's citizenship, and contraception. As a member of the neo-Malthusian movement, she was particularly interested in the question of population control. Her most famous published speech, "L'Eternelle sacrifiée," which covers all these topics as well as presenting her views on women's position in French society, provides an excellent example of Roussel's feminist stance.

Juliette M. Rogers

BIBLIOGRAPHY

Primary Texts

Par la Révolte. Intro. Sébastien Faure. Paris: Privately printed, 1903.
Quelques Discours. Paris: Privately printed, 1907.
Pourquoi vont-elles à l'Eglise? Paris: Privately printed, 1910.
Quelques Lances rompues pour nos libertés. Paris: Giard et Brière, 1910.
Paroles de combat et d'espoir. Preface by Madeleine Vernet. Paris: Editions l'Avenir Social, 1919.
Ma Forêt. Paris: Editions l'Avenir Social, 1921.
Trois Conférences. Preface by Mme O. Laguerre. Paris: Giard, 1930.
Derniers Combats. Preface by Han Ryner. Paris: Imprimerie Emancipatrice, 1932.
L'Eternelle sacrifiée. 1906. Ed. Daniel Armogathe and Maïté Albistur. Paris: Syros, 1979.

S

Sablé, Madeleine de Souvré, marquise de (1599–1678). Sablé is best known for the Jansenist salon* over which she presided after her self-sequestration in a home immediately adjacent to Port-Royal* in the late 1650s. More notable salon participants included Nicole, Arnauld, Domat, Pascal, La Rochefoucauld, and on occasion Madame de Lafayette*. From their collaborative inquiries on the human condition, the salon developed and nurtured the austere and evocative genre of the maxim. Sablé is herself the author of eighty-one maxims, which were first published posthumously in 1678. She also left in manuscript a collection of maxims entitled *De l'amitié*. Given the striking similarities between her maxims and those of La Rochefoucauld, there has been much speculation about the extent of Sablé's influence on the celebrated moralist. Literary historians have suggested that the salon may have likewise played an important role in the composition of Pascal's *Pensées*. La Rochefoucauld's letters confirm that Sablé also wrote a treatise, *L'Instruction des enfants*, when there was some possibility of the Duke's becoming guardian to the Dauphin; it is not extant. Sablé was an active participant at Mme de Rambouillet's* *chambre bleue*, where she engaged in an affectionate correspondence with the poet Voiture, among others; Chapelain praised her *esprit* and *finesse* in letters to Balzac. Sablé's conflict-ridden personal life provided rich fodder for the famed novelist Madeleine de Scudéry*, who painted a detailed verbal portrait of Sablé as ''Parthénie'' in *Le Grand Cyrus*. After unsuccessfully protesting her arranged marriage* at the age of fifteen to Philippe-Emmanuel de Laval, marquis de Sablé, she succeeded in separating from him only after his scandalous behavior threatened to ruin both of them. The Marquise's own love affairs, love of good food, and lifelong propensity for hypochondria were often the subject of gossip in the intimate social circles of the salons.

Holly Tucker

BIBLIOGRAPHY

Primary Text

La Rochefoucauld, François, duc de. *Réflexions ou sentences et maximes morales, suivi de Réflexions diverses et des Maximes de Mme de Sablé.* Ed. Jean Lafond. Paris: Gallimard, 1976.

Secondary Texts

Cousin, Victor M. *Madame de Sablé: Nouvelles Etudes sur la société et les femmes illustres du XVIIe siècle.* Paris: Didier, 1859.
Ivanoff, N. *La Marquise de Sablé et son salon.* Paris: PUF, 1927.
Lafond, Jean. "Madame de Sablé et son salon." In *Images de la Rochefoucauld: Actes du tricentenaire.* Ed. Jean Lafond and Jean Mesnard. Paris: PUF, 1984. 201–216.

Sagan, Françoise (1935–). The rebellious daughter of a wealthy Parisian family, Sagan shocked the publishing world in 1954 with the phenomenal success of her racy first-person narrative *Bonjour Tristesse* (1954), in which a teenage girl orchestrates the disastrous breakup of her playboy father's relationship with an admirably responsible and elegant fashion executive. Since this first bestseller, Sagan has written seventeen other novels* which charmingly and often satirically treat the triangular romances and bourgeois social codes prevalent in a certain segment of French society. *Aimez-vous Brahms* (1959), for example, traces an aging beauty's dependency on an eternally adolescent man, while *La Chamade* (1966) shows how an otherwise feisty girl cannot afford emotionally to stray too far from her middle-aged protector. Sagan has also produced nine light comedies for the stage, among them *Château en Suède* (1960). Known for their witty, fast-paced dialogue and socially deviant characters, Sagan's plays create a fantasy space free of social conventions and constraints. Independent, outspoken, and daring, Sagan has made of herself an intellectual counterpart to Brigitte Bardot's sexually liberated woman. Her heroines, on the contrary, are often victims of romantic thralldom—their subjugation subtly conveying the limits of women's possibilities within patriarchy. Yet in her short stories*, *Des Yeux de soie* (1976) and *Musiques de scènes* (1981), and in her most innovative recent novel, *Un Orage immobile* (1983), Sagan also creates contemporary Amazons*, Sphinxes, and Medusas who playfully wreak havoc with patriarchal norms, subverting the sex-gender system and deconstructing the family* romance. Likewise, in her memoirs*, *Avec mon Meilleur Souvenir* (1984), Sagan reveals her kinship to a community of literary and political mentors, such as Jean-Paul Sartre and Billie Holiday, whose irreverence and courage reflect her own commitment to impassioned, progressive causes and a highly crafted personal style.

Judith G. Miller

BIBLIOGRAPHY

Primary Texts

Bonjour Tristesse. Paris: Julliard, 1954.
Aimez-vous Brahms. . . . Paris: Julliard, 1959.
La Chamade. Paris: Julliard, 1965.
Des Bleus à l'âme. Paris: Flammarion, 1972.
Des Yeux de soie. Paris: Flammarion, 1976.
Réponses 1954–1974. Paris: J.-J. Pauvert, 1974.
Musiques de scènes. Paris: Flammarion, 1981.
Un Orage immobile. Paris: J.-J. Pauvert, 1983.
Avec mon Meilleur Souvenir. Paris: Gallimard, 1984.

Secondary Texts

Miller, Judith Graves. *Françoise Sagan*. Boston: G. K. Hall, 1988.
Poirot-Delpech, Bertrand. *Bonjour Sagan*. Paris: Herscher, 1985.
St. Onge, Marian. ''Narrative Strategies and the Quest for Identity in the French Female
    Novel of Adolescence: Studies in Duras, Mallet-Joris, Sagan, and Rochefort.''
    Dissertation, Boston College, 1984.

Sainctonge (or Saintonge), Louise-Geneviève Gillot, dame de (1650–1718).
Little is known of her life, except that her mother was also a woman of letters
and that she married a lawyer. She was the first woman in France to write opera
libretti. Both of her *tragédies lyriques, Didon* (1693) and *Circé* (1694), with
music by Henri Desmarets, were staged at the Opéra; these are competent texts
in the manner of Quinault. A third libretto, *Les Charmes des saisons*, helped
inaugurate the tradition of opera-ballet, though a cabal prevented its performance. Some of her short entertainments (mostly freestanding opera prologues)
were performed for the royalty of Spain and Bavaria. In addition, she wrote two
spoken comedies, *L'Intrigue des concerts* (apparently performed in Dijon), an
amusing comedy of manners in the tradition of Dancourt, with as heroine a
professional singer who refuses to sacrifice her virtue, and *Griselde, ou la Princesse de Saluces*, which retells the Griselda story from a woman's point of view.
The bulk of her corpus consists of short, light-hearted poems, in the Epicurean
tradition, with particular emphasis on the pleasures of friendship*, as opposed
to love, and on the joys of conviviality. She also published *Histoire secrète de
dom Antoine roi de Portugal*, for which she used the files of her maternal
grandfather (who knew that prince), an adaptation of Montemayor's *Diana*, and
some short fiction.

Perry Gethner

BIBLIOGRAPHY

Secondary Text

Nouvelle Biographie universelle. Paris: Fermin Didot, 1852–1866.

Saint-Balmon, Alberte-Barbe d'Ernecourt, madame de (1607–1660). Called a "Christian Amazon" by her contemporary biographer, this pious French woman of Lorraine protected the statue of the Virgin at the pilgrimage shrine of Benoîtevaux by fighting off brigands and vandals. During the Thirty Years War she commanded a small cavalry and an infantry in the service of France; her patriotic military career came to the attention of Louis XIII, who sought to put her in charge of royal regiments. A large equestrian portrait of her attired in men's clothing hangs in the Musée Historique Lorrain. Although three plays are attributed to her, only one has survived: *Les Jumeaux martyrs*, published in 1650. This tragedy exalts the faith of two young Romans, Marc and Marcelin, twin brothers who have converted to Christianity.* When their faith is most vulnerable, St. Sebastian appears to strengthen their convictions. To one character, the mother, Saint-Balmon gives the speech that persuades a judge to help the family.* Saint-Balmon's style is vigorous and direct; she handles rhymed couplets with assurance. Her writing suggests that she knew contemporary theater in Paris, probably including Corneille's *Polyeucte*. She aims to inspire in spectators constancy in faith; the play may have been the centerpiece of a pious entertainment for a people in wartime. She is said to have written religious verse, none of which has been positively identified. A copy of her version of the events at Benoîtevaux is included in her biography, as are a few letters. Although writing was an important activity, she did not think of herself as a literary figure, nor even as an unusual person, but simply as a woman of action in the service of God.

Carmeta Abbott

BIBLIOGRAPHY

Primary Text

Saint-Balmon, Barbe d'Ernecourt, Madame de. *Les Jumeaux Martyrs*. Critical ed. by Carmeta Abbott and Hannah Fournier. Geneva: Droz (TLF), 1995.

Secondary Texts

Cuénin, Micheline. *La Dernière des Amazones: Madame de Saint Baslemont*. Nancy: Presses Universitaires de Nancy, 1992.

Vernon, Jean-Marie Du Cernot de. *L'Amazone chrestienne ou les avantures de Mme de S.-Balmon, qui a joint une admirable dévotion et la pratique de toutes les vertus avec l'exercice des armes et de la guerre*. Paris: Gaspar Meturas, 1678.

Saint-Chamond, Claire-Marie de la Vieuville, marquise de (1731–?). Born in Paris, Claire-Marie Mazarelli had already published a "Portrait" (1751) and an *Eloge historique de Maximilien de Béthune, duc de Sully* (1764) before her marriage,* in 1765, to Charles-Louis de la Vieuville, marquis de Saint-Chamond. A novel*, *Camédris*, and an *Eloge de René Descartes* followed in 1765. Saint-Chamond often used her writing to criticize a society governed by outdated laws and traditions, one in which women had few rights. In a three-act comedy, *Les Amants sans le sçavoir* (1771), Saint-Chamond shows that a woman need not hide her education* to find a husband, and condemns the practice of marriage for economic gain. In her final work, *Jean-Jacques à M. S . . . sur des réflexions contre ses derniers écrits* (1784), she clearly demonstrates the need for social change. Seeking to defend Rousseau, Madame de Saint-Chamond shows a profound knowledge of his works by citing passages that point to errors of his critics. However, she refutes his vision of the subservient woman and decries the double standards by which women are judged, particularly the absurdity of giving all powers to men while ascribing their weaknesses to women. Although little is known about Saint-Chamond's education*, her eloquent eulogies, wit, and rational ability to denounce injustice show a woman of great intelligence and character.

Jeanne Hageman

BIBLIOGRAPHY

Primary Texts

Camédris. Paris: Duchesne, 1765.
Eloge de René Descartes. Paris: Duchesne, 1765.
Les Amants sans le sçavoir. Paris: Monory, 1771.
Lettre à Jean-Jacques Rousseau. Paris: N.p., 1771.
Lettres de Madame la comtesse de Mal . . . à Madame la marquise d'A . . . . Paris: N.P., 1776.
Jean-Jacques à M. S . . . sur des réflexions contre ses derniers écrits. Paris: Belin, 1784.
Eloge historique de Maximilien de Béthune, duc de Sully. Lyons: B. Duplain, 1963.

Secondary Texts

Condamin, James. *Histoire de Saint-Chamond et de la Seigneurie de Jarez*. Paris: Alphonse Picard, 1890.
Streckeisen-Moultou, M. G. *J. J. Rousseau, ses amis et ennemis*. Paris: Michel-Lévy Frères, 18○○.
Toussaint Le Moyne, Nicolas. *Les Siècles littéraires de la France*. Geneva: Slatkine, 1971.

Saint-Cyr, school of (1686–1793). With the financial support of Louis XIV, Mme de Maintenon* founded this institution in the village of Saint-Cyr, near Versailles. Mansart directed the school's construction in a record fifteen months. Originally known as the Institut des Dames de Saint-Louis, it was conceived as a secular school for impoverished girls from old nobility, where they would acquire a strong Christian foundation infused with the necessary social graces of their station. However, under the direction of the fashionable Mme de Brinon, worldly concerns quickly overshadowed their moral education*. Thus, the successful productions of Racine's *Esther* (1689) and *Athalie* (1691), both commissioned for the school, convinced Mme de Maintenon that public adulation, as well as exposure to works of fiction, would corrupt her pupils' minds. The reform of 1692 transformed the school into an Augustinian convent*. Thereafter, and until the Convention government ordered its suppression in 1793, the Maison Royale de Saint-Cyr, as it would continue to be known, functioned according to Mme de Maintenon's vision.

Specifically, the religious community comprised eighty-six nuns, half of whom were recruited from the school monastery's alumnae. Their mission remained pedagogical as Mme de Maintenon was named officially the first *institutrice* of Saint-Cyr. She was a born organizer and a born teacher. The school took complete charge of 250 girls until they were ready to enter a religious order or matrimony; they received 3,000 French pounds upon their departure. Students were divided into four classes identified by the specific color of their uniform belt: the Reds, ages seven to ten; the Greens, eleven to thirteen; the Yellows, fourteen to sixteen; and the Blues, seventeen to twenty. The girls were subsequently divided into "families" of eight to ten members, according to their level of instruction, with the older classmates playing a leadership role for the youngsters. Catholic education, inspired by François de Sales, and manual tasks, intended to develop housewives' skills, dominated their days.

Mme de Maintenon profoundly distrusted women's intellectual empowerment. As she believed in the natural inequality of the sexes, her detailed *Instructions* to her school's teachers emphasized domestic moral values prevalent in the Old Regime patriarchal society. Her personal experience might also have contributed to the school's pessimistic slant on marriage*, leading to the large number of religious vocations among her students. She cherished her daily visits to Saint-Cyr, far from the court's intrigues, as she felt most at ease among the children. She retired there after 1715, remaining until her death in 1719.

Marcelle Maistre Welch

BIBLIOGRAPHY

Secondary Texts

Daniélou, Madeleine. *Madame de Maintenon éducatrice.* Paris: Editions Bloud & Gay, 1946.
Lavallée, Théophile. *Histoire de la Maison Royale de Saint-Cyr (1686–1793).* Paris: Furne et Cie., 1853.
Timmermans, Linda. *L'Accès des femmes à la culture (1598–1715). Un Débat d'idées de Saint-François de Sales à la Marquise de Lambert.* Paris: Nizet, 1993.

Saint-Phalier Dalibard, Françoise-Thérèse Aumerle de (?–1757). Little is known about the life of this novelist, poet, and playwright. Her first novel*, *Le Portefeuille rendu ou les lettres historiques* (1749), consists of a series of intercalated stories about the dangers of love, seduction, and marriage* for women. Her second, *Les Caprices du sort ou l'histoire d'Emilie*, was published in 1750, followed by *Recueil de poésie* in 1751. She signed these works with only the initials to her maiden name, Mlle S*** or Mlle de St. Ph***. In 1752 her three-act comedy, *La Rivale confidente*, was performed at the Italian Theater in Paris without much success. It was published the same year, along with *Mourat et*

Turquia (1752), a work falsely attributed to Mlle de Lussan*, who seems to have lent her name to it and to Marguerite de Lubret.

Aurora Wolfgang

BIBLIOGRAPHY

Primary Texts

Le Portefeuille rendu ou les lettres historiques, par Mlle S***. London: N.p., 1749.
Les Caprices du sort, ou l'histoire d'Emilie, par Mlle de St. Ph***. N.p., 1750.
Recueil de poésie, par Mlle de St. Ph***. Amsterdam: N.p., 1751.
Mourat et Turquia, histoire africaine. Paris: N.p., 1752.

Secondary Texts

Stewart, Joan Hinde. *Gynographs: French Novels by Women Writers of the Late Eighteenth Century*. Lincoln: University of Nebraska Press, 1993.
Versini, Laurent. *Laclos et la tradition*. Paris: Klincksieck, 1968.

Saint-Simonianism. Reacting against the excesses of laissez-faire liberalism, the Saint-Simonians preached love, the emancipation of women and the proletariat, and the bettering of the human condition through science. Their ideas on urban planning and on mobilizing credit to support transportation networks made a lasting impression on the financial world. Although critical of bourgeois values—in particular the institutions of marriage*, inheritance, and property—Saint-Simonianism largely appealed to rising middle-class professionals, especially to bankers, entrepreneurs, and engineers. The Saint-Simonian Society was formed after the death of Henri, Comte de Saint-Simon in May 1825, and developed Saint-Simon's scientific approach to re-structuring social relations. Like Saint-Simon, the Saint-Simonians saw industry and association (as opposed to the free market spirit of competition) as the fulcrum for the new social order. Although the movement was of short duration, peaking in popularity from late 1829 to summer 1832, it was extensively documented. Its influence lasted well into the Second Empire and spread throughout Europe, Egypt, Russia, and the Americas. The Saint-Simonians' newspapers (*Le Producteur* [1825–1826], *L'Organisateur* [1829–1831], and *Le Globe* [IX-XII, 1830–1832]) were widely distributed, and their sermons, or predications, were well attended. The society adopted a family structure: two of the founders, Prosper Enfantin and Saint-Amand Bazard, were Supreme Fathers, influential women were mothers, and members were sons or daughters. Handsome and charismatic, Enfantin became the group's leader after he and Bazard parted ways over the woman question in 1831. Unlike Bazard, Enfantin affirmed women's equality and right to establish paternity. Enfantin appealed to women to articulate the new moral law, placing an empty chair next to him on the speaker's platform as a symbol of the call to the Supreme Mother (Enfantin's female equivalent). Due to its doctrine embracing free love and women's equality, the movement came under close scrutiny.

Saint-Simonianism waned in popularity in late 1832, after several leaders were charged and incarcerated for outrage to public morals. In 1833—the Year of the Mother—Enfantin and some followers left for Egypt to search for the Mother (and to help construct the Suez Canal).

Saint-Simonianism both offers a critique of women's condition under the Civil Code and posits the entry to subjectivity through sexuality. Yet there are many paradoxes to this early feminism*. Enfantin felt that the doctrine was incomplete without women's experience, yet he determined himself that feminine essence should be the opposite of the male. Although women participated in the inner workings of the family, they never had an equal share of the power. Of special interest to feminists is the work of the Saint-Simoniennes—the newspaper *Tribune des femmes* and the writings of women such as Pauline Roland*, Claire Démar*, and Suzanne Voilquin*—on moral law and feminine sexuality.

Annie Smart

BIBLIOGRAPHY

Secondary Texts

Allemagne, Henry-René, d'. *Les Saint-Simoniens, 1827–1837*. Paris: Librairie Grund, 1930.
Bulciolu, Maria Teresa. *L' Ecole saint-simonienne et la femme: notes et documents pour une histoire du rôle de la femme dans la société saint-simonienne*. Pisa: Goliardica, 1980.
Carlisle, Robert B. *The Proffered Crown: Saint-Simonianism and the Doctrine of Hope*. Baltimore: Johns Hopkins University Press, 1987.
Charlety, Sébastien. *L' Histoire du Saint-Simonisme*. Paris: Gonthier, 1931.
Derr, J. R., ed. *Regards sur le Saint-Simonisme et les Saint-Simoniens*. Lyons: Presses Universitaires de Lyon, 1986.
Goldstein, Leslie. ''Early Feminist Themes in French Utopian Socialism: The Saint-Simonians and Fourier.'' *Journal of the History of Ideas* 43 (1982): 91–108.
Manuel, Frank. *The Prophets of Paris*. Cambridge, MA: Harvard University Press, 1962.
Moses, Claire Goldberg. *French Feminism in the Nineteenth Century*. Albany: State University of New York Press, 1984.
Moses, Claire Goldberg, and Leslie Wahl Rabine. *Feminism, Socialism, and French Romanticism*. Bloomington: Indiana University Press, 1993.
Saint-Simon, Henri de, and Prosper-Barthélémy Enfantin. *Oeuvres de Saint-Simon et d'Enfantin*. 47 vols. Paris: E. Dentu, Ernest Leroux, 1865–1878.
Voilquin, Suzanne. *Souvenirs d'une fille du peuple, ou la Saint-Simonienne en Egypte*. Intro. Lydia Elhadad. Paris: François Maspéro, 1978.

Salager, Annie (?–   ). Poet and Spanish teacher. Since Salager was raised in a Quercy village, and has lived in Paris and Lyons, she always feels she is from ''elsewhere.'' Her poetry* denounces war and capitalism and hails a new era in which women, more fortunate than their ''gagged'' foremothers, will be free. Also central to her poetic enterprise are the poems presented under the aegis of Daphne, whose mother turned her into a laurel bush to save her from the amorous Apollo. The metamorphoses of ''The Shrub-Woman'' and ''The Desert-

Woman'' explore the relationship between language and reality and demonstrate Salager's belief in the power of poetry to transform women's lives.

Karen Bouwer

BIBLIOGRAPHY

Primary Texts

La Nuit introuvable. Lyons: A. Henneuse, 1961.
Présent de sable. Paris: G. Chambelland, 1964.
Histoire pour le jour. Paris: Seghers, 1968.
Dix Profils sur la toile, l'été. Paris: A. Henneuse, 1971.
La Femme-buisson. Paris: Saint-Germain-des-Prés, 1973.
Les Fous de Bassan. Paris: Saint-Germain-des-Prés, 1976.
Figures du temps sur une eau courante. Paris: P. Belfond, 1983.
Chants. Ill. Jean-Noël Baches. Paris: COMP'ACT, 1989.
Marie de Montpellier: Une Reine au temps de Philippe Auguste. Montpellier: Presses du Languedoc, 1991.

Secondary Texts

Brindeau, Serge, ed. ''De l'onirisme aux combats: Annie Salager.'' In *La Poésie contemporaine de langue française depuis 1945.* Paris: Saint-Germain-des-Prés, 1973. 110–111.
Chedid, Andrée. ''En route vers le mot'' (pour Annie Salager); ''Renaître et veiller'' (Entretien avec Annie Salager). In *Rencontrer l'inespéré.* Vénissieux: Paroles d'Aube, 1993. 9–14.
Hermey, Carl. ''Annie Salager: The Distilling Eye.'' In *Contemporary French Women Poets: A Bilingual Critical Anthology.* Van Nuys, CA: Perivale Press, 1977. 44–49.

Salic law (1400s–1500s). During the 1400s, the Salic law, allegedly a founding law of the French kingdom, was fabricated to exclude women from monarchic rule. Drawn from a Carolingian redaction of the Franco-Germanic Salic Law Code (802–803), that ordinance ''On allodial lands (De allodio),'' reads: ''Indeed, concerning Salic land no part of the inheritance may pass to a woman, but all the inheritance of land goes to the virile sex.'' Taken out of context, the ordinance is misleading, because it was mediated by other titles in the code, which permitted women to inherit allodial lands (essentially, family farms); sometimes favored transmission through female lines; and also allowed other lands, even if held in grant from rulers, to pass (in the absence of men) to women. Around 1000, when Salic and Roman laws were meshed through usage, the Salic Code disappeared for a time. In northern France, from the 1100s to the 1300s, where regional customary laws (*coutumiers*) developed, were compiled by kings (1454, 1494, 1509), and were redacted in the Custom of Paris (Coutume de Paris, 1510, 1580), women succeeded to lands, and some who did not inherit directly passed inheritance rights to successors, as practiced in the Paris region.

The first to speak of a ''Salic law'' by name, Richard Lescot, in *Genealogy of the Kings of France* (*Genealogia aliquorum regum Francie*, 1358), provided no text of the ordinance; and his insinuation that it secured male succession elicited no official interest. French ordinances were promulgated by kings to regulate succession, father to eldest son (1375, 1392, 1407); but they did not specifically block a daughter, or her son (if no sons survived), and did not cite a Salic law. As a result, the attempt to transform a Salic ordinance from a civil law of the Salian Franks (regulating inheritance of allodial lands in the 800s) into a public law of the French kingdom (regulating succession to the royal domain and monarchic rule in the 1400s) triggered a long political debate over the exclusion of women from rule.

The debate was provoked by Christine de Pizan* in *Le Livre de la cité des dames* (1405); she validated rule by women (actually and potentially), negated the defamation litany of moral precepts on female inferiority (body, hence mind), and exposed efforts to legitimize female exclusion by resort to defamation. Reinterpreting an important tenet of political thought (the body politic–body mystic analogy likening kings and bishops), which refused to queens the sacred anointment given to kings in the French coronation (like bishops in ordination), she carved out a female route to coronation; and she did not treat a Salic law because it had not yet been invented. In the *La Cité des dames*, written while Queen Isabelle of Bavaria was regent for the incapacitated King Charles VI, Pizan also recalled a recent epistolary quarrel waged over defamatory practices (1399–1404). There, she criticized Jean de Meun, who, in *Le Roman de la rose* (1275–1280), had defamed woman, the entire sex, and by association, Jean de Montreuil, who praised Meun and defamed Pizan, denying her intellectual capacity (as woman) and labeling her a courtesan for taking writings to the public. Between 1406 and 1409, as *La Cité des dames* circulated in political quarters, Montreuil decided to refute Pizan's case for rule by women.

In "To All the Knighthood" ("A toute la chevalerie," c. 1409–1413), Montreuil produced a text of the Salic ordinance, but that fragment was marred by an interpolation (in italics) which effected a forgery: "Indeed no part in the realm may pass to a woman." Next, in the *Traité contre les Anglais* (1413, 1416), he provided a fuller correct passage—"No part of the inheritance may pass to a woman, but all the inheritance of land goes to the virile sex . . ."—but attached to it his unsuported claim: that this Salic law absolutely "excludes women from succession to the crown of France" and also excludes "their sons." Attempting to negate Pizan's specific arguments, Montreuil resorted to the defamation litany, but it had just been publicly contested. So he fabricated a Salic law fixed in perpetuity (unlike French custom, subject to change over time). Around 1418 a royal official read a copy of the Salic ordinance and ignored it; and by 1420 French custom proponents made an alternative case.

Grounding French custom in nature, Jean de Terre Rouge, in *Contra rebelles suorum regum* (c. 1420), did not mention a Salic law. Admittedly beholden to Aristotelian biological concepts of propagation—the superior male capacity (female incapacity) to generate and transmit formative seed—Terre Rouge politicized that view. Moving from nature, male reproductive replication (father-son "filiation"), he shaped a political parallel, male monarchic replication (king-dauphin, "simple succession"), positing the metaphysical notion of a body politic incorporated in the king's one body regenerated over time. Although several royal officials and scholars read the Salic law, 1430s–1440s, and bypassed it, advocates held on.

Confirming Montreuil and Terre Rouge, disputing Pizan, Jean Juvénal des Ursins, in *Audite celi que loquor* (1435), and "Most Christian, Most Great, Most Powerful King" ("Tres crestien, tres hault, tres puissant roy," 1446), reproduced correctly the whole Salic ordinance, yet rationalized both forged and fabricated versions, insisting "Salic land" was the "royal domain" of France and Salic law a public law. Dispelling legal doubt with moral certainty, he also invoked the defamation litany, now girded with a biological precept holding virility a male trait. By the 1450s, writers troubled by an inadequate Salic law text, which required manipulation, offered a compromise.

Turning to French custom, Noël de Fribois, in the *Abrégé des chroniques de France* (1459), rooted a political model of male command in a structural homology of immortal corresponding spheres, nature and polity. Following nature, French custom grounded rulership in the regenerative capacity of a series of kings who embodied the polity, actually and potentially, in the king's one body. Dictated by nature, imprinted in the male body, impressed on French custom, and transformed into public law, the male right to rule was mirrored in all law—natural, Roman, canon, and French—including the Salic ordinance, which meant to identify the virile sex as male (comment in italics): "No part of the inheritance may pass to a woman but all the inheritance of land goes to the virile sex"—"which means man." Although salvaged by Fribois, Salic law was dislodged from a primary position (as a founding law of the kingdom) to an ancillary one (as an ordinance that reflected a more ancient French custom of male affiliation writ in nature). In the 1460s, Salic law advocates retaliated.

The *Grand Traité de la loy salique* (anonymous, c. 1464) produced a flagrantly forged text through an extended interpolation (in italics, my brackets): "No part of Salic land may pass as an inheritance to a woman, because [Salic land] is interpreted as the royal domain [of France] which is not dependent or subject to anyone in contrast to the precept that covers other allodial land which is divisible, but all the inheritance [of Salic land = royal domain] goes to the virile sex." Pronouncing Salic law a French public law, that gross forgery, aided by defamatory injunctions, was circulated into the 1480s, printed in 1488, and reprinted five times, 1522–1557, as the *Grand Traité*, retitled, Salic Law, First Law of the French (Loy salique, première loy des françois), made its mark.

From the 1460s through the 1500s, rule by women—queens in Spain, England, and Scotland, queen-regents in France—was witnessed in Europe (as predicted by Pizan), examples contradicting exclusion and defamation. And between the 1540s and 1550s, French jurists, who discovered uncorrupted copies of the Salic ordinance, discarded the fraudulent Salic law. Bereft of a juridical base for excluding women from rule, they formulated an early modern political theory of male right still grounded in the law of nature but soon juridically institutionalized in French public law and civil law, which underwrote a system of marital regime government upholding male rule in parallel entities, household and state, from the 1550s through the 1700s.

Sarah Hanley

BIBLIOGRAPHY

Primary Texts

Christine de Pizan. *The Book of the City of Ladies*. Trans. Earl Jeffrey Richards. New York: Persea Books, 1982.

Drew, Katherine. *The Laws of the Salian Franks*. Philadelphia: University of Pennsylvania Press, 1991.

Eckhardt, Karl August. *Monumenta germaniae historica, leges nationum germanicorum: Pactus legis salicae*. Vol. 4, pt. 1 (Merovingian redaction c. 507–511); and pt. 2, Lex salica (Carolingian, 802–803). Hanover: Historisches Institut des Werralandes, Göttingen, 1962, 1969 [article 6, title 34, Systematic version; title 62, Standard version].

Juvénal des Ursins, Jean. *Ecrits politiques de Jean Juvénal des Ursins*. Vols. 1 and 2. Ed. Peter S. Lewis. Paris: Klincksieck, 1978, 1985.

Lescot, Richard. *Chronique de Richard Lescot, religieux de Saint-Denis (1328–1344) suivi de la continuation de cette chronique (1344–1364)*. Ed. Jean Lemoine. Paris: Laurens, 1896.

Montreuil, Jean de. *Opera: L'Oeuvre historique et polémique*. Vol. 2. Ed. E. Ornato, N. Grévy, and G. Ouy. Turin: G. Giappichelli, 1975.

Terre Rouge, Jean de. *Contra rebelles suorum regum*. Ed. J. Bonaud de Sauset. Lyons: N.p., 1526.

Secondary Texts

Kathleen Daly, and Ralph E. Giesey. "Noel de Fribois et la loi salique" (Appendix). Bibliothèque de l'Ecole des Chartes, Vol. 151, 1993.

Giesey, Ralph E. "The Juristic Basis of Dynastic Right to the French Throne." *Transactions of the American Philosophical Society*. Philadelphia: American Philosophical Society, Vol. 51, 1961.

Hanley, Sarah, "Identity Politics and Rulership in France: Female Political Place and the Fraudulent Salic Law in Christine de Pizan and Jean de Montreuil." In *Changing Identities in Early Modern France*. Durham, NC: Duke University Press, 1997.

———. "La Loi salique." In *Encyclopédie politique et historique des femmes*. Ed. Christine Fauré. Paris: Presses Universitaires de France, 1997.

———. "Mapping Rulership in the French Body Politic: Political Identity, Public Law and the King's One Body." *Historical Reflections/Reflexions Historiques* 23, no. 2 (1997).

Saliez (or Saliès), Antoinette de Salvan, comtesse de (1638–1730). The "Muse of Albi," as she was called, spent her entire life in that city. Following the death of her husband in 1672, she chose not to remarry, devoting herself instead to literary pursuits. She published a historical novel*, *La Comtesse d'Isembourg*, a volume of Christian meditations, a set of verse paraphrases of the Psalms, plus miscellaneous letters, poems, and other short pieces that appeared in the *Mercure gallant* and various collections. Having for many years hosted a respected salon*, she decided in 1704 to establish a Société des Chevaliers et des Chevalières de la Bonne Foi; its statutes banned love, while exalting friendship*, the shared love of letters, and the intellectual equality of the sexes. She was held in high esteem for her wit, good taste, piety, and affability, and was elected to the Accademia dei Ricovrati in Padua. Her novel recounts with great sympathy the misadventures of a German noblewoman, trapped in an unhappy marriage*, who finally runs off to France and attempts to lead an independent, solitary life.

Perry Gethner

BIBLIOGRAPHY

Secondary Texts

Nouvelle Biographie générale. Ed. M. [Jean Chrétien Ferdinand] Hoefer. Paris: Firmin Didot, 1852–1877.
Laporte, Joseph de. *Histoire des femmes qui se sont rendues célèbres dans la littérature française*. Paris: J. P. Costard, 1771.

Sallenave, Danièle (1940–). Novelist, playwright, essayist, translator, and professor of theater*. In *Le Voyage d'Amsterdam*, an early novel* written in *Nouveau Roman** style, Sallenave constructs the gaze of an anonymous woman lost in a solitary present as she seeks to revive a richly erotic past. Sallenave adopts a more traditional narrative style in her later and best-known works, such as *Les Portes de Gubbio* (Prix Renaudot, 1980) and *La Vie fantôme* (1986), in which she contrasts male and female perspectives on a modern-day love triangle. In response to criticism of her return to traditional forms, Sallenave speaks out against what she sees as artistic self-indulgence, and in *Le Don des morts: Sur la littérature* she advocates an ''ethics of literature'' based on the reestablishment of the links between readers and writers that she accuses certain forms of literary experimentation of having broken. Through her diverse narrative styles, Sallenave depicts female characters whose experiences resonate among women of all ages. In *Conversations conjugales*, stark dialogue communicates the latent tensions between a husband and wife, while stories such as ''La Visite,'' ''Une Lettre,'' ''Louise,'' and ''Eternellement Joyeux'' (*Un Printemps froid*) provide poignant glimpses of women's solitude and old age.

Jan Berkowitz Gross

BIBLIOGRAPHY

Primary Texts

Le Voyage d'Amsterdam ou les règles de la conversation. Paris: Flammarion, 1977.
Les Portes de Gubbio. Paris: Hachette, 1980.

Un Printemps froid. Paris: P.O.L., 1983.
La Vie fantôme. Paris: P.O.L., 1986.
Adieu. Paris: P.O.L., 1987.
Conversations conjugales. Paris: P.O.L., 1987.
Les Epreuves de l'art. Arles: Actes Sud, 1988.
Le Don des morts: Sur la littérature. Paris: Gallimard, 1991.
Le Principe de ruine. Paris: Gallimard, 1994.
Les Trois Minutes du diable. Paris: Gallimard, 1994.
Lettres mortes. De l'enseignement des lettres en général et de la culture générale en particulier. Paris: Editions Michalon, 1995.

Secondary Text

Salgas, Jean-Pierre. "Entretien: Danièle Sallenave et l'éthique de la littérature." *La Quinzaine Littéraire* 478 (January 16–31, 1987): 11–12.

Salons. Salons exhibited a great variety with respect to their formal aspects and the contents of their discourses. In the most general definition they were mixed-sex gatherings hosted by women at regular intervals and in private settings. While the definitive work on the salon has yet to be written, its origin is generally situated in the Renaissance. Among the earliest *salonnières* Madeleine and Catherine des Roches*, a mother and daughter, shared their generation's love of learning and sociability. They attracted humanists and writers to their salon in Poitiers. Topics ranging from contemporary events to history, literature, and philosophy alternated with games and lighter conversation. Letters were read to the assembled habitués, establishing the chain that would link women writers, salons, and the epistolary genre. Louise Labé* gathered other women poets in Lyons, where they read their works aloud and discussed the new ideas circulating from Italy throughout France.

It is certain that one of the topics discussed from the earliest salons onward was the nature of women and their role in society. The seventeenth-century salon of the Marquise de Rambouillet*, like that of Madeleine de Scudéry*, who followed her, provided a venue for discussion of marriage* and women's education* as well as for the reading of recent works by the period's leading dramatists.

While much remains to be studied in this area of cultural history, it is generally agreed that the eighteenth-century version of these social occasions became increasingly devoted to public issues and less to private concerns. Recent studies of the seventeenth-century salon deemphasize the ludic and family-oriented aspects of salons, such as matchmaking and gossip, focusing instead on the mentoring of younger women and the flourishing epistolary genre associated with salon conversation. It could be argued, somewhat paradoxically, that where the seventeenth-century salon created an alternative feminine discourse, the eighteenth-century salon (to the extent that it joined debate of public issues) both increased in importance and lost its specificity.

Among the most prominent *salonnières*, Mesdames Condorcet*, du Deffand*,

Geoffrin*, Holbach, Helvétius, Lambert*, Lespinasse*, Necker*, and Tencin* spanned the century, providing venue and structure for dissemination of new ideas or defense of old ones. If the salons of Lambert separated the purely social from the intellectual, others merged participants in free-flowing talk and performance. Philosophers were regulars in the drawing rooms of Sophie Condorcet and Anne-Catherine Helvétius but were soon unwelcome in the home of du Deffand, whose letters convey scorn for their ideas and their manners. Lambert used her afternoons to promote the fortunes of would-be academicians; Geoffrin and Necker shared the challenge of anti-authoritarian discourse with the likes of Voltaire, Montesquieu, and Rousseau. During the Revolution*, meetings in the salon of Adélaïde Filleul (Flahaut) were part of the feverish political maneuvering regarding constitutional provisions and formation of ministries.

Contemporary perceptions of salon life, whether favorable or critical, were invariably related to gender. André Morellet, a regular participant at Geoffrin's gatherings and a firm believer in the civilizing role of female conversation, nonetheless praised Madame d'Holbach's deferential role when her husband's friends assembled. Rousseau considered leadership by women to be a reversal of natural law and part of the emasculating effect of social life. Defenders of men's gatherings often contrasted their wholesome virility to salon frivolity.

Current scholarship on the role of the Enlightenment* salon is linked to several critical issues. Joan Landes analyzes the participation and exclusion of women in the creation of a public sphere and, in so doing, offers a revisionist view of Habermas's class-based history of public spaces. Dena Goodman reconsiders the private-public dichotomy and defines a seriousness of intent among *salonnières* as they participated in the Republic of Letters. If sociability indeed became the dominant value not only of Enlightenment theory but of modern democracies, then salons must be seen as the emblematic social institution, one which was led by women and which created their most significant space.

Caryl L. Lloyd

BIBLIOGRAPHY

Secondary Texts

Goodman, Dena. *The Republic of Letters: A Cultural History of the French Enlightenment*. Ithaca: Cornell University Press, 1994.
Harth, Erica. "The Salon Woman Goes Public . . . or Does She?" In *Going Public: Women and Publishing in Early Modern France*. Ed. Elizabeth C. Goldsmith and Dena Goodman. Ithaca: Cornell University Press, 1995. 179–193.
Landes, Joan. *Women and the Public Sphere in the Age of the French Revolution*. Ithaca: Cornell University Press, 1988.

Sand, George (1804–1876). By birth Amantine-Aurore-Lucile Dupin, and by marriage* the Baroness Dudevant, George Sand chose a pen name that reflects her unconventional life. Born less than a month after the wedding of her aristocratic father and plebeian mother, she received most of her education* through tutoring at her paternal grandmother's country manor in the province of Berry. From age thirteen to fifteen she attended a Paris convent* school run by English nuns. The pseudonym contains the Berry peasant name, Georges, in its English spelling, and that of her first well-known lover, Jules Sandeau, who collaborated on her earliest texts. Sand's family provided much raw material for her works. Her mother, daughter of a Paris bird merchant, inspired the writer's lifelong defense of the less privileged and her portraits of the "fallen woman." Linked to French and Polish royalty through her paternal grandmother, the illegitimate daughter of Maurice de Saxe, Sand wrote of the unwed mother, the adulterer, the bastard, and the foundling, as well as charitable adoption. The rivalry between her grandmother and mother, especially bitter after the early death of Sand's father, fueled the theme of two women who love the same man. Sand's difficult marriage, without the possibility of divorce* (outlawed in France between 1816 and 1884), to a man totally uninterested in intellectual and cultural activities, who had control over her person and property under the Napoleonic Code*, led to her focus on the egalitarian couple. Throughout her life and her work, Sand sought ideal love, the ideal family*—as revealed by her many love affairs and fictional couples, people of different socioeconomic status, age, or education who must pass through a series of trials in order to be worthy of each other. Her life was a model for other women: she earned her living and supported her family (and others) through her writing; she circumvented the double standard and took lovers as openly as her male counterparts; she cross-dressed for practical reasons; she counted among her friends the artists, politicians, and other intellectuals of Europe.

Sand wrote over sixty novels*, twenty-six short stories*/novellas, numerous essays (travel pieces, prefaces, art and literary criticism, unsigned contributions to the *Bulletin de la République* for the provisional government in 1848), and saw twenty-five of her plays professionally staged. She also wrote a celebrated autobiography*, *Histoire de ma vie* (1854–1855). Her published *Correspondance (1812–1876)*, impeccably edited by Georges Lubin, totals twenty-six volumes. From her earliest independently written narrative, *Indiana* (1832), to her last major novel, *Nanon* (1872), Sand experimented with a wide variety of techniques—from epistolary, diary, or dialogue form to the Berry oral tale. Her constant goal remained social reform, not revolution, but gradual, small-scale transformation. For Sand, that reform began with the family. Most of her works, therefore, have as their nucleus the couple. Their very titles frequently reveal Sand's focus on women. Some give only a first name, suggesting that the woman will forge her own identity. Sand often took familiar motifs, such as Pygmalion and Galatea in *François le Champi* (1850), reassuring the reader, but then subverting that motif. Madeleine, an unhappy wife, adopts the seemingly retarded foundling, François, and brings him up to be an exceptional, androgynous man—the ideal husband, but for herself! Sand also wrote apparently simple stories of Berry peasants, where the women, more knowledgeable than those around them, educate others, by-passing official institutions. Sand gave high priority to female education, but also considered male re-education essential. She dared to explore women's sexuality in *Lélia* (1833, 1839). She examined gender by creating, in *Gabriel* (1840), a female child brought up, in isolation, as a male, and then released into the world, in female attire, with a male's education and expectations for freedom of action. In *Isidora* (1846), she treated the courtesan whose ambition could be satisfied only by subjugating men, a woman who later attains mature self-knowledge and is then ready to adopt a daughter, whom she will save from a similar fate. Sand's women are strong and energetic, not delicate, as custom willed. They may sing and compose, like the heroine of one of Sand's finest works, *Consuelo* (1843–1844). They may amass real estate, like Nanon, or run a factory, like Tonine of *La Ville noire* (1861).

These exceptional women, however, rarely have close relationships with other women. Most are motherless; if the mother is alive, she is generally separated from her daughter. When a couple forms, the woman distances herself from female friends, rivals for the man's affections. Sand herself preferred the company of men, disliking the traditional woman's lack of education and her frivolity. Sand's library held an extensive collection of works by women, but she rarely praised women writers. Though generous to women in private and author of an essay on women's difficult condition, *Lettres à Marcie* (1837), she harshly rejected the symbolic compliment of the journalists of *La Voix des femmes*, who wished to propose her candidacy in 1848. Scholars the world over, but especially in North America, have written on George Sand's enormous literary production. Two of the best recent studies, Isabelle Naginski's analysis of Sand's exceptional narrative experiments, and Naomi Schor's pinpointing of the demise of the once-popular vein of idealism as a cause of Sand's "decanonization," join the controversy over whether or not to term George Sand a feminist. Although the answer may well be no, in the twentieth-century sense, Sand did in many ways raise women's status, as she vowed to do. If one replaces her in the nineteenth-century context, then by all means George Sand was an early feminist, a writer whose life and work inspired other women writers and gave courage to women around the world.

Annabelle M. Rea

BIBLIOGRAPHY

Primary Texts

"Lettres à Marcie." In *Mélanges*. Paris: Perrotin, 1843. 157–219.
Histoire de ma vie. In *Oeuvres autobiographiques*. 2 vols. Ed. Georges Lubin. Paris: Gallimard, 1970–1971.
François le Champi. Ed. Pierre Salomon and Jean Mallion. Paris: Garnier, 1981.
Consuelo/La Comtesse de Rudolstadt. 3 vols. Ed. Simone Vierne and René Bourgeois. Meylan, France: Aurore, 1983.
Indiana. Ed. Pierre Salomon. Paris: Garnier, 1985.
Lélia. 2 vols. Ed. Béatrice Didier. Meylan, France: Aurore, 1987.
Nanon. Ed. Nicole Mozet. Meylan, France: Aurore, 1987.
Gabriel. Ed. Janis Glasgow. Paris: Des femmes, 1988.

La Ville noire. Ed. Jean Courrier. Meylan, France: Aurore, 1989.
Isidora. Ed. Eve Sourian. Paris: Des femmes, 1990.

Secondary Texts

Naginski, Isabelle. *George Sand: Writing for Her Life.* New Brunswick, NJ: Rutgers University Press, 1991.
Schor, Naomi. *George Sand and Idealism.* New York: Columbia University Press, 1993.

Sarde, Michèle (?–). Novelist, essayist, and professor of literature. Born during World War II* to a Jewish family, Sarde was marked by the persecution of the Jews and later by her involvement in leftist organizations supporting the Algerian War for Independence.

In her two novels*, *Le Désir fou* (1975) and *Histoire d'Eurydice pendant la remontée* (1991), Sarde emphasizes the importance of woman's desire and freedom of choice. The first novel deals with a forbidden love which reveals the masochistic tendencies of the female protagonist. In the second novel, a new Eurydice emerges from a series of conflicts involving issues of identity, politics, and love; the protagonist must reinvent herself after discovering her Jewish origins.

Sarde's works of nonfiction also illustrate her interest in women's writing, revisionist mythmaking, and the history of myths*. Her works on Colette* and Marguerite Yourcenar* give voice to two precursors of contemporary feminism*. Her main contribution to the history of French feminism is the vast study *Regard sur les françaises: Xe siècle–XXe siècle* (1983), which combines sociological and philosophical approaches to the writing and the sociohistorical context of French women throughout the centuries.

Metka Zupančič

BIBLIOGRAPHY

Primary Texts

Le Désir fou. Paris: Stock, 1975.
Colette: Libre et entravée. Paris: Stock, 1978.
Regard sur les françaises: Xe sièele–XXe siècle. Paris: Stock, 1983; abridged version, 1985.
Histoire d'Eurydice pendant la remontée. Paris: Seuil, 1991.
Vous, Marguerite Yourcenar: La Passion et ses masques. Paris: R. Laffont, 1995.

Secondary Texts

Plate, Liedeke. "Breaking the Silence: Michèle Sarde's *Histoire d'Eurydice pendant la remontée.*" *Women in French Studies* 3 (1995): 90–99.
———. "Orphée, le regard et la voix: Pour une analyse narratologique de la réécriture des mythes." *Religiologiques* 15 (Spring 1997).
Proulx, Patrice J. "Of Myth and Memory: Reading Michèle Sarde's *Histoire d'Eurydice pendant la remontée.*" *Religiologiques* 15 (Spring 1977): 179–187.

Sarraute, Nathalie (1900–). Novelist, essayist, playwright. Born into an educated middle-class Jewish family in Ivanovo, Russia, Sarraute moved definitively to Paris in 1909. Between 1918 and 1925, she studied English literature and law in Paris, art history in Oxford, and philosophy in Berlin. In 1936 she joined the fight for women's suffrage and participated in the first conference on English women writers sponsored by the Maria Verone Association. In 1942 the German occupation forced Sarraute and her daughters to flee Paris under false names; she returned in 1944 and devoted herself to writing.

Between 1932 and 1937, Sarraute wrote *Tropismes* (1939), a series of short narratives which was to become one of the seminal works associated with the *Nouveau Roman**. In Sarraute's work, a tropism (a word borrowed from biology) refers to instinctive inner movements concealed by our words and actions. This emphasis on unspoken emotion recurs in various forms throughout her work.

In the collection of essays *L'Ere du soupçon* (1953), Sarraute articulates her rejection of traditional narrative forms. Through her readings of Dostoyevsky, Proust, Joyce, and Woolf, she reflects on significant issues in her own writing, including the nonverbal, questions of authenticity, and the creation of meaning. Sarraute continues her exploration of inner consciousness in such early texts as *Le Planétarium* (1959), with its shifting points of view, and *Entre la vie et la mort* (1968), which abandons plot and characters. Sarraute's texts also exemplify her specific focus on art and writing—from the satirical reactions to the novel *En abyme* in *Les Fruits d'or* (1963) and the portrayal of a writer's consciousness in *Entre la vie et la mort*, to reflections on art and aesthetic values in *Vous les entendez* (1972). *Disent les imbéciles* (1976) and *L'Usage de la parole* (1980)— with their multiple, disembodied voices—focus on language, in particular on lack of communication and the effects of language on others.

Sarraute's theater*, with its anonymous characters and minimal gestures, also deals with the meanings hidden beneath dialogue. In *Le Silence* (1967), for example, one of the unnamed characters remains silent throughout the play, while the others seek the reason for his mutism. In the autobiographical *Enfance* (1983), she tries—through a dialogue with her double—to return to the emotions of her childhood, articulating the ambivalent feelings caused by the tragic realization of her separation from the mother figure.

Sarraute prefers the neutral term "writer" to that of "feminist" or "woman writer," and this stance has brought her outspoken disapproval from many feminists. However, her role as precursor in rejecting traditional narrative forms and her exploration of language, in particular the preverbal, have been seen as crucial in the textual expression of women's unconscious.

Véronique Flambard-Weisbart

BIBLIOGRAPHY

Primary Texts

Tropismes. Paris: Denoël, 1939.
L'Ere du soupçon. Paris: Gallimard, 1953.
Le Planétarium. Paris: Gallimard, 1959.

Les Fruits d'or. Paris: Gallimard, 1963.
Entre la vie et la mort. Paris: Gallimard, 1968.
Isma: ou ce qui s'appelle rien. Suivi de Le silence et Le mensonge. Paris: Gallimard, 1970.
Enfance. Paris: Gallimard, 1983.
Ici. Paris: Gallimard, 1995.

Secondary Texts

Becker, Lucille. *Twentieth-Century French Women Novelists.* Boston: Twayne, 1989.
Benmussa, Simone. *Nathalie Sarraute. Qui êtes-vous?* Lyons: La Manufacture, 1987.
Flambard-Weisbart, Véronique. ''Ecrire neutre versus écrire féminin: Nathalie Sarraute.'' *Francographies* (1997): 103–113.
Phillips, John. *Nathalie Sarraute: Metaphor, Fairy-Tale and the Feminine of the Text.* New York: Lang, 1994.

Sarrazin, Albertine (1937–1967). Novelist, diarist, and poet. Abandoned at the Welfare Office in Algiers at her birth, Albertine Sarrazin was adopted at age two by an elderly couple and was raised in Aix-en-Provence. Sent to reform school for truancy in her mid-teens, she escaped in 1953 and hitchhiked to Paris, where she turned to prostitution* and burglary. She died during a kidney operation on July 10, 1967, having spent most of her adult life in prison. The prison experience colors most of Sarrazin's writings. She is best known for her three largely autobiographical novels, *L'Astragale* (1965), *La Cavale* (1965), and *La Traversière*, which are animated by an eloquent discourse on personal and political liberation. There and in her other works, Sarrazin deals powerfully with the themes of constraint and freedom, love and sexuality, and the manner in which power is deployed in human relationships, both intimate and social.

Warren Motte

BIBLIOGRAPHY

Primary Texts

L'Astragale. Paris: Jean-Jacques Pauvert, 1965.
La Cavale. Paris: Jean-Jacques Pauvert, 1965.
La Traversière. Paris: Jean-Jacques Pauvert, 1966.
Romans, lettres et poèmes. Paris: Jean-Jacques Pauvert, 1967.
Poèmes. Paris: Jean-Jacques Pauvert, 1969.
Lettres à Julien, 1958–60. Ed. Josane Duranteau. Paris: Jean-Jacques Pauvert, 1971.
Lettres et poèmes. Paris: Livre de Poche, 1971.
Journal de prison, 1959. Pref. Josane Duranteau. Paris: Editions Sarrazin, 1972.
La Crèche. Paris: Editions Sarrazin, 1973.
Lettres de la vie littéraire. Ed. Josane Duranteau. Paris: Jean-Jacques Pauvert, 1974.
Le Passe-peine, 1949–1967. Ed. Josane Duranteau. Paris: Julliard, 1976.
Biftons de prison. Intro. Brigitte Duc. Paris: Jean-Jacques Pauvert, 1977.

Savoie, Louise de (1476–1531). Widowed at the age of nineteen, Louise de Savoie educated her children, Marguerite and François, by retaining the best available humanist scholars, although she herself instructed them in French and Spanish. Her personal library and those inherited from her father and husband numbered over 200 volumes. Her interest in education* and children—her motto was *litris et liberis*—was probably due in part to her experience in the court of Anne de Beaujeu, who wrote *L'Enseignement des filles* for her own daughter. After her son was crowned François I, Louise acted as regent during his captivity in Pavia and Madrid in 1525. At that time both she and her daughter acted on his behalf to gain his freedom. Representing French political interests, she negotiated the Treaty of Cambrais (1529) with the representative of Holy Roman Emperor Charles V. Often called the Ladies' Peace because Charles V's representative was his aunt, Marguerite de Savoie, the treaty ended the second war against Charles V. Her regency and diplomatic efforts illustrate how women could and did perform traditionally male functions even as early as the sixteenth century.

Her personal journals reflect an obsessive concern not only with her son's activities in general, but also with her ambition that he become king. In stark contrast to an entry in which she records that she told François that she would be lost if he died, there are relatively few remarks about her daughter.

Velvet Pearson

BIBLIOGRAPHY

Primary Texts

"Journal de Louise de Savoie." In *Nouvelle Collection des mémoires pour servir à l'histoire de France*. 5 vols. Ed. Joseph Michaud and Jean Poujoulat. Paris: Chez l'éditeur du Commentaire analytique du Code Civil, 1836–1839. 5: 83–93.
Journal depuis 1476 jusqu'à 1522, [par] Louise de Savoie, mère de François Ier. Paris: Didier, 1854.
Comptes de Louise de Savoie et de Marguerite d'Angouleme. Paris: Champion, 1905.

Secondary Texts

Bordeaux, Paule H. *Louise de Savoie*. Paris: Plon, 1954.
Mayer, Dorothy M. *The Great Regent: Louise of Savoy, 1476–1531*. New York: Funk and Wagnalls, 1966.

Schomberg, Jeanne de, duchesse de Liancourt (1600–1674). Born into an illustrious family from Germany, Jeanne de Schomberg was first married to François de Cossé, comte de Brissac, for whom she had a strong dislike. The marriage* was annulled, and she married the duc de Liancourt, remembered today for his association with Antoine Arnauld and the Jansenist party. This marriage was a happy one in spite of the duke's early debauchery and his extramarital affairs. Mme de Liancourt, who saw a call from God to fulfill the ideal of perfection that she had set for herself, employed her entire life to save her husband's soul and detach him from the court. To achieve her goal, she designed the plans of the magnificent château de Liancourt and spent a fortune on its realization. She became famous for her genuine kindness and her piety.

She devoted herself to the love of God, her husband, and her fellow men, trying to reduce her wants and live modestly. Her works include some mediocre poems published in Père Bouhours's *Recueil de vers choisis* (1693) and a courtesy book, *Réglement donné par une Dame de haute qualité à Mxxxx sa petite-fille*, written for her granddaughter, Jeanne-Charlotte de La Rocheguyon, the sole daughter of her only son, killed at an early age in the siege of Mardick. The *Réglement*, followed by another *Réglement que ceste Dame avoit dressé pour elle-mesme* (an intimate journal in which Schomberg describes her everyday activities and the principles that govern her life) was published in 1698 by Abbé Jean-Jacques Boileau, who had been acquainted with Schomberg during the last eleven years of her life. It enjoyed considerable popularity in the eighteenth and nineteenth centuries (seven editions altogether).

Jeanne de Schomberg was quite traditional in her thoughts about gender. She considered women's subordination to man within the family* as quite natural. Her *Réglement* contains the ideal of modesty, humility, patience, obedience, self-control, and thrift recommended by the most eminent educators from Vivès to Fénelon. A young woman must be chaste, modest in dress and behavior, courteous in all her actions, and temperate in eating and drinking. She should not engage in gossip or mockery. Her language should be modest and reserved. Schomberg emphasizes moral and religious instruction, warns against uncontrolled passion and extramarital affairs, and reminds her granddaughter that she will be rewarded or punished depending on how she lived. While her own education* was unusually broad for a woman of this time (her father introduced her to literature, art, and various sciences), Jeanne de Schomberg supported the view that education was to prepare the young girl for motherhood and efficient homemaking, the only career open to her.

The *Réglement*, heavily influenced by the long tradition of conduct books, parental advice books, and books of piety addressed to women of the nobility (such as François de Sales's *Introduction à la vie dévote*, from which Schomberg draws considerably), is of particular interest for the history of mentalities and mores, and is typical of early experiments with autobiographical forms.

Colette H. Winn

BIBLIOGRAPHY

Primary Texts

Boileau, Abbé. *Vie de Madame la Duchesse de Liancourt, Avec le Réglement qu'elle donna à sa Petite-Fille pour sa conduite et pour celle de sa Maison.* Paris: Chez Cretté, nos. 94 and 98, 1814.

Schomberg. *De l'éducation chrétienne des jeunes gens et des jeunes demoiselles; ouvrage utile et nécessaire aux enfans de l'un et de l'autre sexe, ainsi qu'aux Instituteurs et Institutrices, et aux parens qui veulent donner la dernière instruction à leur famille: Terminé par quelques Anecdotes chrétiennes et morales.* Paris: Cretté et Belin, 1811.

———. *Réglement donné par la Duchesse de Liancourt à la Princesse de Marsillac avec une notice sur la Duchesse de Liancourt par la Marquise de Forbin d'Oppede.* Paris: E. Plon et Cie., 1881.

―――. *Réglement donné par une Dame de haute qualité à Mxxx sa petite-fille pour sa Conduite, & pour celle de sa Maison. Avec un autre Réglement que cette Dame avoit dressé pour elle-mesme.* Ed. Colette H. Winn. Paris: Champion, 1997.

Secondary Texts

Constant, Paule. *Un Monde à l'usage des demoiselles.* Paris: Seuil, 1987. 322–324.

Lesaulnier, Jean. "Les Liancourt, leur hôtel et leurs hôtes (1631–1674)." In *Images de La Rochefoucauld, Tricentennaire.* Ed. Jean Lafond and Jean Mesnard. Paris: Presses Universitaires de France, 1984. 167–200.

Winn, Colette H. "La *Dignitas mulieris*: Les Enjeux idéologiques d'une appropriation— du XVe au XVIIe siècle." In *Ecrits de femmes à la Renaissance.* Ed. Anne R. Larsen and Colette H. Winn. *Etudes littéraires* 27, no. 2 (Autumn 1994): 11–24.

―――. "La Fille à l'image de la mère: Jeanne de Schomberg, *Réglement donné par une dame de haute qualité . . . à sa petite-fille . . .* (1698)." *Papers on French Seventeenth-Century Literature* 22, no. 43 (1995): 359–467.

Scudéry, Madeleine de (1607–1701). Scudéry, a pivotal figure in the era's upsurge of women's writing, was an orphan of obscure aristocratic lineage educated in Rouen by her uncle. At age thirty she set out for Paris, where her brother, the academician Georges de Scudéry, introduced her to the Hôtel de Rambouillet. "Sapho," as she was known, eventually presided over her own salon*, the Samedi, which attracted prominent literati and inspired her admirer Paul Pellisson's *La Chronique du Samedi* and *La Gazette de Tendre.* She published three multivolume heroic novels* (set in antiquity, but imbued with contemporary mores as glimpsed through elaborate subplots), a compendium of illustrious women, three *nouvelles* (short novels), and five collections of conversations. Although her works appeared under her brother's name or anonymously, she claimed authorship in her correspondence. She was honored by the French Academy for her *Discours sur la gloire* (1671), appointed to the Accademia dei Ricovrati of Padua (1684), and pensioned by the king (1683).

Scudéry's contemporaries Antoine de Somaize (*Le Dictionnaire des Précieuses*, 1661) and the Abbé de Pure (*La Prétieuse ou le mystère des ruelles*, 1656–1658) describe her as a cultivated *précieuse* adept in the arts of conversation and writing. Her long novels, translated into several languages, were best-sellers acclaimed by the likes of La Fontaine and La Bruyère. Marie-Jeanne Lhéritier's* homage, "L'Apothéose de Mademoiselle de Scudéry" (1702), eulogizes "Sapho" as a model for aspiring women writers. Nicolas Boileau, who criticizes her novels for undermining morals (*Satire X*, 1694) and injudiciously melding history and fiction (*Dialogue des héros de roman*, 1703), strikes a dissonant note in an otherwise laudatory chorus.

Scudéry departs from the conventional topoi of the sentimental novel to introduce conversations that expose the art of sociability while highlighting women's public role in the shaping of culture. The episode "Histoire de Sapho,'' in the second long novel, *Artamène ou le Grand Cyrus* (1649–1653), relates the musings of ladies who, like the habitués of the Samedi, examine questions of love, marriage*, and women's education* and social role. *Artamène* portrays contemporary personages disguised as historical figures and includes the Prince de Condé as well as Pellisson and Scudéry herself. Recalling the earlier Sapho character in *Les Femmes illustres* (1642), "Histoire de Sapho" boldly exhibits Scudéry's self-portrait as a writer skilled in analyzing affairs of the heart. The third long novel, *Clélie, histoire romaine* (1654–60), includes the "Carte de Tendre," an amorous geography that bypasses marriage in favor of an idealistic love based on genuine emotion. While certain critics stress the spiritual dimension of *amour tendre*, current scholarship gives greater weight to its emphasis on sincerity and individual choice; "tender love" foreshadows the eighteenth-century cult of *sensibilité*. In the later-published *Conversations*, Scudéry draws upon the discussions of the Samedi to display her talents as a feminist theoretician of *honnêteté* (sociability).

Patricia Hannon

BIBLIOGRAPHY

Primary Texts

Les Femmes illustres ou Les Harangues héroïques. 1642–1644. 2 vols. Paris: Côté-femmes, 1980.
Artamène ou Le Grand Cyrus. 10 vols. Paris: Courbé, 1649–1653. Reprint. Geneva: Slatkine, 1972.
Clélie, histoire romaine. 10 vols. Paris: Courbé, 1654–1660. Reprint. Geneva: Slatkine, 1973.
Choix de Conversations de Mlle de Scudéry. Ed. Phillip J. Wolfe. Ravenna: Longo Editore, 1977.

Secondary Texts

Aronson, Nicole. *Mademoiselle de Scudéry.* Boston: G. K. Hall, 1978.
DeJean, Joan. *Tender Geographies: Women and the Origins of the Novel in France.* Chicago: Chicago University Press, 1989.
Munro, James S. *Mademoiselle de Scudéry and the Carte de Tendre.* Durham: University of Durham, 1986.
Niderst, Alain. *Madeleine de Scudéry, Paul Pellisson et leur monde.* Paris: PUF, 1976.

Sebbar, Leïla (1941–). Novelist and short story* writer. Born and raised in Algeria by an Algerian father and a French mother, both of whom taught in a French-language elementary school in Algeria, Sebbar has lived in Paris since the age of seventeen. In the 1970s she was actively engaged in the feminist struggle in France, contributing to the feminist journals *Cahiers du GRIF* and *Sorcières*, the leftist *Les Temps modernes*, and *Sans frontière*, a journal about immigration. She calls herself *une croisée* (a person of mixed descent/a crusader/ at the crossroads), a French writer on the margins, caught between French and Algerian cultures. French is her mother tongue, but it was the separation from her father's language and country that prompted her to write. The act of writing allows her to transform her feelings of exile into a sense of belonging. The protagonists of her novels* and short stories are usually children of Maghrebian immigrants *(Beurs)* living in France. They are mostly teenagers, male or female, grappling with their hybridity and attempting to cope with their difficult position by running away and creating an alternative reality for themselves (*Shérazade* trilogy [1982, 1985, 1991]; *Le Chinois vert d'Afrique* [1984]). Sebbar's protagonists are always in motion, searching various places for traces of their history to help them construct a new identity. In all of her work, especially the *Shérazade* trilogy, Sebbar rewrites the male Orientalist tradition in painting and literature by juxtaposing historical and contemporary sources, both Arabic and Western. She foregrounds her characters' responses to these sources, as they either appropriate them for their own purposes or reject them. Sebbar repeatedly underscores the colonial confrontation which causes violence, war, and exile, but also suggests potentially more positive encounters among very diverse characters. She focuses on wars in several parts of the world, from Algeria and Vietnam to the struggles in the Middle East and, more recently, Bosnia.

Sebbar's work reflects a concern for the welfare of all exiled people. Her purpose is to give children of immigrants a legitimate place in French literature, hoping perhaps to symbolically facilitate their access to a legitimate position in French society, which continues to marginalize them.

Anne Donadey

BIBLIOGRAPHY

Primary Texts

Fatima ou les Algériennes au square. Paris: Stock, 1981.
Shérazade, 17 ans, brune, frisée, les yeux verts. Paris: Stock, 1982.
Le Chinois vert d'Afrique. Paris: Stock, 1984.
Parle mon fils parle à ta mère. Paris: Stock, 1984.
Les Carnets de Shérazade. Paris: Stock, 1985.
J. H. cherche âme soeur. Paris: Stock, 1987.
La Négresse à l'enfant. Paris: Syros Alternatives, 1990.
Le Fou de Shérazade. Paris: Stock, 1991.
Le Silence des rives. Paris: Stock, 1993.
La Jeune Fille au balcon. Paris: Seuil, 1996.
Sebbar, Leïla, and Nancy Huston. *Lettres parisiennes: Autopsie de l'exil.* Paris: Bernard Barrault, 1986.
———, eds. *Une Enfance d'ailleurs: Dix-sept écrivains racontent.* Paris: Belfond, 1993.

Ségur, Sophie Rostopchine, comtesse de (1799–1874). Born in St. Petersburg, Ségur moved to France as a recently converted Roman Catholic, a faith which would shape her life and her writing. She married Eugène de Ségur in 1819 and, while her family went back to Russia, she established herself in her adopted country, sharing her time between Paris and Les Nouettes, her own property in Normandy. She started to write in 1855, dedicating her first book to her granddaughters; she would not stop writing for children until 1871. Her books were best-sellers, attracting a wide readership among children of the imperial court as well as in orphanages. Starting with a stylistically traditional collection of fairy tales*, *Les Nouveaux Contes de fées* (1857), she innovated quickly after that, creating novels* of a semi-autobiographical nature which incorporated realistic details, dialogues, humor, and action. Ségur's works allow for a feminist reading seditiously embedded in a self-avowed moralistic conservatism. In her early novels *Les Malheurs de Sophie* (1850), which addresses preteen readers, Ségur manages to present the title heroine as an independent, creative, and energetic character growing up in a community of women, a portrait that is barely tempered by a few admonitions to obedience and humility. In later works, such as *Après la pluie le beau temps* (1871), which focus on older, less rambunctious characters appropriate for an older readership, Ségur presents more concrete ways of avoiding arranged marriages* and ways of retaining one's dowry. As a very popular author for children, Ségur's influence was prodigious: her life and her novels allowed many readers, such as Simone de Beauvoir*, to see through the social expectations of moral tales and to identify with lifelike female heroines who escaped the angel/devil dichotomy.

Christine Lac

BIBLIOGRAPHY

Primary Text

Oeuvres. 3 vols. Ed. Claudine Beaussant. Paris: Robert Laffont-Bouqins, 1990.

Secondary Texts

Beaussant, Claudine. *La Comtesse de Ségur ou l'enfance de l'art*. Paris: Robert Laffont, 1988.
Lac, Christine. "Sophie Rostopchine, Comtesse de Ségur." In *French Women Writers. A Bio-Bibliographical Source Book*. Ed. Eva Martin Sartori and Dorothy Wynne Zimmerman. Westport, CT: Greenwood Press, 1991.
Malarte-Feldman, Claire-Lise. "La Comtesse de Ségur, a Witness of Her Time." *Children's Literature Association Quarterly* 20, no. 3 (Fall 1995): 135–139.

Serreau, Geneviève (1915–1981). Novelist, playwright, and literary critic. Serreau is best known for her work in theater* and has written both plays and critical works. In *Histoire du nouveau théâtre* (1966)—her discussion of playwrights such as Adamov, Beckett, Genet, and Ionesco—she critiques the theories of Lukács, Barthes, and Robbe-Grillet. She co-founded the Théâtre de Babylone with director Jean-Marie Serreau; *En Attendant Godot* was first performed there in 1953. In the early 1960s, she adapted Marguerite Duras's* *Un Barrage contre le Pacifique* for the theater. In the collection of short stories* *Dix-huit Mètres cubes de silence* (1976), as in most of her fiction, Serreau deals with alienated female characters and challenges the notion of *écriture féminine**.

Serreau's marginalized characters are known for their transgression against the social order.

Ana M. de Medeiros

BIBLIOGRAPHY

Primary Texts

Bertolt Brecht: Dramaturge. Paris: L'Arche, 1955.
Le Soldat bourquin. Paris: Julliard, 1955.
Le Fondateur. Paris: Julliard, 1959.
Histoire du nouveau théâtre. Paris: Gallimard, 1966.
Ricercare. Paris: Denoël, 1973.
Dix-huit Mètres cubes de silence. Paris: Denoël, 1976.
La Lumière sur le mur. Paris: Gallimard, 1979.
Un Enfer très convenable. Paris: Gallimard, 1981.
Théâtre complet. Paris: L'Arche, 1988.

Secondary Text

Fairley, Ian. "Geneviève Serreau: Theatre of Fiction." In *Contemporary French Fiction by Women: Feminist Perspectives.* Ed. Margaret Atack and Phil Powrie. Manchester: Manchester University Press, 1990. 99–115.

Séverine (1855–1929). Pseudonym of Charlotte Rémy Guebhard, journalist, feminist, and polemical writer. Sometime between 1879 and 1880 she met Jules Vallès, who became her mentor. She assisted him in his writing and worked with him on his paper, *Le Cri du peuple.* At his death, she took over the paper as its manager. She remained close to Vallès's anarchist ideology. As manager of *Le Cri du peuple*, she tried to open it to the full range of the political left: socialists, Marxists, anarchists, and others, but she eventually resigned in 1888 because of perpetual infighting among the different leftist political groups. Already a journalist of renown, she was given columns in bourgeois papers such as *Le Gaulois* and *Gil Blas.* In her articles, she continually fought for the poor and oppressed. She reached unprecedented notoriety for a woman journalist and was especially known for her passionate and lively editorials. In 1897 she joined the ranks of *La Fronde*, the first daily newspaper entirely run, written, and published by women. She wrote the column "Notes d'une frondeuse." Séverine was one of the first to publicly defend Alfred Dreyfus and covered his trial on a daily basis. During World War I* she was heavily censored because of her antimilitarism. Politically, she was always sympathetic to the anarchist cause but joined the Communist Party in 1921 because of her admiration for the Bolshevik Revolution. Quickly disillusioned, she left the party in 1923.

Séverine wrote six thousand editorials and articles that were later published in books. She also published an autobiographical novel, *Line.* An original thinker, she refused political categorization. Nonetheless, she always fought for the rights of the oppressed.

Juliette Parnell-Smith

BIBLIOGRAPHY

Primary Texts

Pages rouges. Paris: Simonis Empis, 1893.
Notes d'une frondeuse. Paris: Simonis Empis, 1894.
En marche. Paris: Simonis Empis, 1895.
Pages mystiques. Paris: Simonis Empis, 1895.
Vers la lumière. Paris: P. V. Stock, 1900.
Sainte Hélène. Paris: Giard-Brière, 1904.
Sac à tout. Paris: Juven, 1905.
Line. Paris: G. Cres, 1921.
Choix de papiers. Ed. Evelyne Le Garrec. Paris: Editions Tierce, 1982.

Secondary Texts

Le Garrec, Evelyne. *Séverine, une rebelle (1855–1929).* Paris: Seuil, 1992.
Maricourt, Thierry. *Histoire de la littérature libertaire en France.* Paris: Albin Michel, 1992.

Sévigné, Marie de Rabutin-Chantal, marquise de (1626–1696). A woman of wit, appreciated in her social circles for her lively conversational skills, she thought that her main claim to fame was to be a Rabutin-Chantal married to a Sévigné, and would be surprised to be remembered today for the letters written to her cousin and to her daughter. In fact, when she died at Grignan, neither of the gazettes mentioned her letters in her obituary. However, since the first editions of her letters in the eighteenth century, Sévigné quickly arose as the letter writer par excellence, overshadowing even the masters of the epistolary genre, Balzac and Voiture. *Mondains*, philosophers, and scholars alike admired her "natural" style. Later in the century, in the wake of the ascendant bourgeoisie, the *"spirituelle"* marquise of Voltaire gradually appeared in a new light: serious, pious, edifying. She soon became the symbol of motherly love, order, and respectability. From the early years of the nineteenth century on, collections of her letters proliferated, playing a prominent part in the education* of the young in France, a trend that lasted well into the 1960s. Fourteen volumes of her letters inaugurated the prestigious series *Les Grands Écrivains de la France*, published by Hachette starting in 1862. Sévigné was easily accepted into the canon because she was no threat to the patriarchy: writing in the epistolary genre was viewed as an appropriate mode of expression for women. Even her passionate love for her daughter was misread as the ideal of motherly love, rather than as the stifling love that it was. Moreover, the editors of school versions had a social or moral agenda and presented Sévigné as an antisepticized lay saint who told lively stories about a glamorous time in French history. Today, though many people know of her existence, few people read her except scholars. Of interest to them are her biography, her relationships with intellectuals of her time, with friends, with family members, and with her daughter, her impact on later writers, and her use of language and style. However, some feminist scholars, searching for precursors, go too far in claiming that Sévigné aspired to the status of author, whereas all evidence suggests that she wrote without publication in mind. Roger Duchêne has shown that it is only through a series of miracles that her letters were ever published. Also, her letters did not generally circulate in seventeenth-century salons* (a legend originated by Monmerqué in the nineteenth century). One final point: we do not possess Sévigné's original letters. The letters that we have were "corrected" by Bussy, by his son, and finally by Perrin in the eighteenth century to be more palatable to the public.

There are several bases of continuing interest in Mme de Sévigné. First, readers continue to be interested in a woman who discovered herself as she wrote. Second, the letters offer a unique opportunity to study the texture of social interaction and the rules of communication in the seventeenth century. Finally, the open, nonstructured form of the letters and their diversity of content and style are akin to twentieth-century tastes. Her fate as a woman writer will remain unique, for she never planned to be an author and yet was easily canonized— a feat seldom achieved by women writers until the twentieth century.

Catherine Montfort

BIBLIOGRAPHY

Primary Texts

Madame de Sévigné: Correspondance. 3 vols. Paris: Gallimard (Bibliothèque de la Pléiade), 1972–1978.
Lettres. Choix. Preface by Roger Duchêne. Commentaires et notes de Jacqueline Duchêne. Paris: Librairie générale française, 1987.

Secondary Texts

Duchêne, Roger. *Naissances d'un écrivain: Mme de Sévigné*. Paris: Fayard, 1996.
Europe. "Mme de Sévigné, un féminin pluriel." Numéro spécial consacré à Mme de Sévigné. 76, nos. 801–802 (1996).
Longino, Michèle Farrell. *Performing Motherhood: The Sévigné Correspondence*. Hanover, NH: University Press of New England, 1991.
Montfort, Catherine R. "Grouvelle, lecteur de Mme de Sévigné: La 'Scandaleuse Edition' de 1806." *Papers on French Seventeenth Century Literature* 19, no. 37 (1992); 501–514.
———. "Mme de Sévigné: Seventeenth Century Feminist?" *French Studies* 50, no. 2 (1996): 144–156.
Revue d'histoire littéraire de la France. "Images de Mme de Sévigné." Numéro spécial consacré à Mme de Sévigné (1996).

Short story. Perceived as a minor literary form, the *nouvelle* is often dismissed as immature, simple, and inferior to the longer novel*. These prejudices place women *nouvellistes* in a classic double bind: their work is devalued because of gender and genre. Rare is the anthology of short stories in French that includes stories by women authors with the exception of a tale from Marguerite de Navarre's* *Heptaméron* (1558–1559), Mme de Lafayette's* *La Princesse de Mont-*

pensier (1662), and an occasional story by Colette*. However, the evolution of the short story—from its medieval origins in the oral tradition to its contemporary manifestation as "short fiction" *(fiction courte/brève)*—owes much to women writers. In the seventeenth century, the development of a brief, single narrative was advanced by stories such as Mme de Villedieu's* *Cléonice ou le roman galant, nouvelle* (1669) and Catherine Bernard's* *Les Malheurs de l'amour, première nouvelle, Eléonore d'Yvrée* (1687). Throughout the seventeenth and eighteenth centuries, women were successful in publishing* both *nouvelles galantes* and *nouvelles historiques*. A representative sample of authors and works would include Mme d'Aulnoy's* *Les Nouvelles d'Elisabeth, reyne d'Angleterre* (1674) and *Les Nouvelles espagnoles* (1692), Anne La Roche-Guilhen's* *Almanzaïde* (1674), Mme Gomez's* *Les Cent Nouvelles nouvelles* (1732–1739), Mlle de Lubert's* *Léonile, nouvelle* (1755), Mlle de Lussan's* *Les Annales galantes de la cour de Henri second* (1749), and Mme Riccoboni's* *Histoire du marquis de Cressy* (1758). Indeed, Bernard and La Roche-Guilhen were among the most popular *nouvellistes* of their time. The rise of the short story in the nineteenth century is attributed to the increase in the daily and periodical press. Louise Colet*, Marceline Desbordes-Valmore* *(Contes*, 1989), the Duchesse d'Abrantès, and George Sand* *(Nouvelles*, 1869) were among the early contributors of short stories to the popular press. However, as the genre met with increasing favor, the number of published stories by women decreased. Selections by women writers are absent from anthologies of nineteenth-century short stories, and critical studies of this culminating moment in the genre's history focus on the dominant male authors. Thus, there exists a lacuna for women's contribution at this key moment in the genre's history. Despite the decline in short story writing during the first half of the twentieth century, three collections deserve recognition: Colette's *La Femme cachée* (1924), Marguerite Yourcenar's* *Nouvelles orientales* (1938), and Elsa Triolet's* *Le Premier Accroc coûte deux cent francs* (1945), which was awarded the Prix Goncourt in 1945. Since the 1970s the short story has had a resurgence in France and appears to be a favorite among women writers in France and other francophone countries. The genre's predilection for marginal characters—those not in a position of power—may explain its appeal to women who find themselves at odds with the dominant culture. Furthermore, the open, flexible qualities of the short story offer women a means to introduce new subject matter, transform the status quo, and give voice to previously unspoken issues. The present diversity of short story writing by women echoes the multiplicity of women's lived experiences. A partial list of outstanding writers and collections would include S. Corinna Bille's *La Demoiselle sauvage* (1974), Andrée Chedid's* *Le Corps et le temps, suivi de L'Etroite peau* (1978), Annie Saumont's *Quelquefois dans les cérémonies* (1981), and Pierrette Fleutiaux's* *Les Métamorphoses de la reine* (1984)—all recipients of the Bourse Goncourt de la nouvelle. Among those known for their "feminist" short stories are Anne Bragance and Jeanne Hyvrard*. Despite the obvious contribution of women writers to the history of the short story, critical studies combining gender and the *nouvelle* as genre remain to be undertaken.

Jeanette Marie Hecker

BIBLIOGRAPHY

Secondary Texts

Borgomano, Madeleine. "Le Lieu de vertige." *Notre librairie* 111 (Fall 1992): 10–16.
Borgomano, Madeleine, and Elisabeth Ravoux Rallo. *La Littérature française du XXe siècle*. Vol. 1. Paris: Armand Colin Editeur, 1995.
Bryant, David. *Short Fiction and the Press in France, 1829–1841*. Studies in French Literature, Vol. 24. Lewiston, NY: Edwin Mellen Press, 1995.
Dubuis, Roger. *Les Cent Nouvelles nouvelles et la tradition de la nouvelle en France au Moyen Age*. Grenoble: Presses Universitaires de Grenoble, 1973.
Eagleton, Mary. "Gender and Genre." In *Re-reading the Short Story*. New York: St. Martin's Press, 1989.
Godenne, René. *Histoire de la nouvelle française aux XVIIe et XVIIIe siècles*. Geneva: Librairie Droz, 1970.
———. *La Nouvelle française*. Paris: Presses Universitaires de France, 1974.
Issacharoff, Michael. *L'Espace et la nouvelle*. Paris: Corti, 1976.
Raynal, Marie-Aline. *Le Talent de Madame de La Fayette: La Nouvelle française de Segrais à Madame de La Fayette*. Paris: Editions de Paris, 1926. Geneva: Slatkine Reprints, 1978.
Sozzi, Lionello. *La Nouvelle française de la Renaissance*. 2 vols. Turin: G. Giappichelli Editore, 1973.
Viegnes, Michel. *L'Esthétique de la nouvelle française au vingtième siècle*. New York: Peter Lang, 1989.

Siefert, Louisa Pène (1845–1877). A lifetime of mental anguish and physical suffering inspired this Romantic writer who ranks among the strongest women poets in nineteenth-century France. Consumption, among other ailments that would cut Siefert's life tragically short, often confined her to bed, and thus to her reverie. Apart from sojourns in Aix, Geneva, Paris, and Pau, and a brief marriage*, she remained in the family home near the village of Saint Cyr, close to Lyons, her birthplace. Betrayed in love at age eighteen, Siefert consoled herself with verse. She later married René d'Asté Pène in 1876, only to die shortly thereafter, at age thirty-two. Siefert's resplendent southern retreat nurtured her remarkable debut on the poetic stage in 1868. Yet the miles that separated her from Paris, the literary center of nineteenth-century France, may account for her waning success and, hence, eventual erasure from most anthologies of poetry*. *Rayons perdus* instantly established Siefert's literary reputation. Charles Asselineau, prefacing the second edition of this best-selling collection, remarks on her originality in a male-dominated tradition. Harmoniously joining content and form, she expresses with vibrant verse the dialogue of reality and fantasy. Emmanuel Des Essarts attributes Siefert's strong poetic voice to a highly developed inner life cultivated by reading and contemplation.

Her subsequent writings, too, received critical acclaim. *Les Stoïques*, in particular, offers a perfection of form that distinguishes Siefert from most of her female counterparts. This text, a philosophical meditation on patriotism, challenges the view prevalent among nineteenth-century critics that women who attempted to write verse were limited by personal themes and a lack of style. Both Siefert's poetry and prose develop the Romantic propensity to nostalgia while circulating to the public a girl's physical and emotional struggle with unrequited love. *Georgette* and *Méline*, a poetic "talking cure," which harks back to Duras's* *Ourika* (1823), present a female subject who feels the lack of love in her body as she recalls her desire. Rereading Siefert's self-analysis may enable us to reconstruct yet another chapter of female identity formation that Freudian psychoanalysis has covered over and French poetic history has obscured.

Adrianna M. Paliyenko

BIBLIOGRAPHY

Primary Texts

Rayons perdus. Paris: Lemerre, 1868.
L'Année républicaine. Paris: Lemerre, 1869.
Les Stoïques. Paris: Lemerre, 1870.
Les Saintes colères. Paris: Lemerre, 1871.
Comédies romanesques. Paris: Lemerre, 1872.
Méline. Paris: Lemerre, 1875.
Georgette (unpublished novella). *Lyon-Revue* 1 (1880): 80–99, 163–169, 312–318; 2 (1880): 78–89.
Souvenirs rassemblés par sa mère, Poésies inédites. Paris: Fischbacher, 1881.

Secondary Texts

Des Essarts, E. "Louisa Siefert." *Revue bleue* 2 (1881): 307–310.
Peyrouton, Abel. "Louisa Siefert et son oeuvre." *Lyon-Revue* 1 (1880): 32–43.
Spizio, Ludovic. "L'Ame féminine: Louisa Siefert." *Revue internationale* 15 (1887): 567–584.

Sommery, Mademoiselle Fontette de (?–1790). Little is known of her life, except that she was educated in a convent*, that she lived an independent existence thanks to an annuity provided at the death of her benefactor, the maréchale de Brissac, that her friendships* included distinguished literary figures, and that she died after an attack of apoplexy. All her writings—which included *Doutes sur différentes opinions reçues dans la société*, a philosophical work reminiscent of La Rochefoucauld and La Bruyère; two epistolary novels*; and one of the longest short stories* of the eighteenth century—were published anonymously. *Lettres de Mlle de Tourville à Mme la comtesse de Lénoncourt* juxtaposes two very different women, one conventional and one extraordinary. *Lettres de Mme la comtesse de L*** à M. le comte de R**** describes the convent milieu, the typical education* of women, and the expectations for women's lives. The work is interesting as a document of eighteenth-century *sensibilité*. Certain scenes, in their use of gesture and pathos, recall paintings by Greuze, the *drame bourgeois*, and the *comédie larmoyante* of the middle of the eighteenth century.

Mary Cisar

BIBLIOGRAPHY

Primary Texts

Doute sur différentes opinions reçues dans la société. Paris: Cailleau, 1782. Paris: Barrois l'aîné, 1784.
Lettre à Deslon, magnétiseur. Paris: N.p., 1784.
Lettres de Mme la comtesse de L*** à M. le comte de R***. Paris: Barrois l'aîné, 1785.
Lettres de Mlle de Tourville à Mme la comtesse de Lénoncourt. Paris: Barrois l'aîné, 1788.
L'Oreille, conte asiatique. Paris: Barrois l'aîné, 1789.
Le Rosier et le brouillard par l'auteur de ''l'Oreille.'' Paris: Cailleau, 1791.

Secondary Texts

''Fontette de Sommery, Mlle.'' In *Dictionnaire des lettres françaises: Le Dix-huitième Siècle*. Ed. Georges Grente. Paris: Fayard, 1960.
La France littéraire ou dictionnaire bibliographique des savants, historiens et gens de lettres de la France. Paris: Ed. J. M. Quérard, 1827–1864.
Laporte, Hippolyte de. ''Sommery, Mademoiselle de.'' In *Biographie universelle ancienne et moderne*. Ed. L. G. Michaud. Paris: A. T. Desplaces, 1825.
''Sommery, Mademoiselle Fontette de.'' In *Dictionnaire historique, littéraire et bibliographique des Françaises et des étrangères naturalisées en France*. Ed. Marguerite Ursule Fortunée Briquet. Paris: Gillé, 1804.
''Sommery, Mlle Fontette de.'' In *Les Siècles littéraires de la France ou nouveau dictionnaire historique, critique et bibliographique de tous les écrivains français, morts et vivants*. Ed. Nicolas Toussaint Le Moyne des Essarts. Paris: N.p., 1800–1801.

Staal-Delaunay, Marguerite-Jeanne Cordier, baronne de (1684–1750). Her *Mémoires* offers an eyewitness account of life and the political struggles at court and the Bastille at the end of the reign of Louis XIV and the beginning of the Regency. Her life was dominated by her superior intelligence, romantic passion, and service to the duchesse du Maine. Adopted by an abbess who brought her up like a lady and gave her an education* suited to her outstanding ability, she found herself destitute upon the death of the abbess, failed to obtain the job of governess for which she qualified, and was placed instead as a chambermaid in the household of the duchesse du Maine. She was drawn out of obscurity by a satirical letter she wrote to Fontenelle, and participated in the preparation of evening entertainments at the court of Sceaux. In 1718 she was sent to the Bastille for being the confidante of the duchesse and for being instrumental in efforts to establish contact with the king of Spain. In prison, she found freedom from servitude and the happiness of a seemingly lasting reciprocal love with the chevalier de Menil. After the captivity, in which she displayed heroic loyalty and courage, she was lifted in rank, but not out of bondage, by marriage to an officer of the Duc de Maine. Her *Mémoires* is characterized by lucid psychological analysis, wise maxims, exquisite clarity, precision, and wit. Written in unusual circumstances, her letters to the two men she loved, Menil and Silly, are masterpieces of the epistolary genre. She also wrote two delightful comedies of manners, *L'Engouement* and *La Mode*. Her writings were published posthumously in 1755 to great popular acclaim.

Pauline Kra

BIBLIOGRAPHY

Primary Texts

Oeuvres de Madame de Staal. London: N.p., 1755.
Lettres de Mlle Delaunay. Paris: L. Collin, 1806.
Mémoires de Madame de Staal. Ed. M. de Lescure. Paris: A. Lemerre, 1877.

Secondary Texts

Fréron, Elie-Catherine. *L'Année littéraire*. Amsterdam: Lambert, 1755. 6: 221–245.
Grimm, Frédéric Melchior. *Correspondance*. 16 vols. Ed. Maurice Tourneux. Paris: Garnier, 1877. 3: 73–77.
Herold, J. Christopher. *Love in Five Temperaments*. London: Hamish Hamilton, 1961. 101–162.

Staël-Holstein, Anne-Louise-Germaine Necker de (1766–1817), essayist, political theorist, critic, novelist, and historian whose liberal views unleashed Napoleon's hostility. The daughter of Louis XVI's finance minister, Jacques Necker, and of Suzanne Curchod, a well-known *salonnière*, Germaine was a phenomenon hard to reconcile with traditional notions about the modesty expected from her sex. From earliest youth, surrounded by Encyclopedists, diplomats, and writers—among them Denis Diderot, d'Alembert, Helvétius, Buffon, Grimm, Abbé Raynal, and the comte de Guibert—she charmed them all with her intellectual brilliance, vibrant energy, and genius* for conversation. At age nineteen she consented to marry Baron Eric Magnus de Staël-Holstein, the Swedish ambassador to the French court, chosen for her by the Neckers. Although the marriage* dissolved quickly and the couple's only child, Gustavine, died before she was two, the young ambassador's wife managed to gain economic independence and assure herself a distinguished place in society with a salon* of her own. Many lovers influenced Staël's life: the comte de Narbonne, a short-term minister of war in 1791, with whom she had two sons, Auguste and Albert; Count Adolphe Ribbing, the Swedish regicide in exile; and Benjamin Constant, the writer and politician who fathered Albertine. All the love affairs ended in abandonment. Only shortly before her death did Staël enjoy the boundless devotion of a young hussar, John Rocca, whom she secretly married in 1811.

While Staël's pursuit of happiness and defiance of public opinion brought parental criticism, the influence of her Parisian salon, frequented by the liberal aristocracy and later by opponents of the Empire—led her to the adventure of expatriation. Repeatedly forced into exile, first by the Jacobin terror in 1793 and then by Napoleon's increasingly cruel interdictions between 1802 and 1812, she retreated to the family estate at Coppet in Switzerland, which became a hospitable haven for Europe's intellectuals.

Born with the capacity to transform defeat into victory, Staël looked abroad for the inspiration and literary glory refused her in Paris. Already the well-known author of a work of literary criticism, *De la littérature* (1800), and of *Delphine* (1802), her first novel* on the role of intellectual women—both attacked by Napoleon's press—Staël traveled extensively in Italy and Germany, building a circle of friends among the greatest thinkers and writers of her time, including Goethe, Schiller, August Schlegel, Humboldt, Villers, and Sismondi. Her second novel, *Corinne ou l'Italie* (1807), in which she glorified the independence of the Woman/Nation instead of Napoleon's military conquests, was coldly received by the imperial press. *De l'Allemagne* (1813), with its open cosmopolitan sympathies, was destroyed, the plates broken at the printing press. Fearing imprisonment, Staël fled Coppet and traveled through Germany, Poland, Russia, Scandinavia, and England to incite the strongest European courts to battle tyranny. She became the political agent of Bernadotte, the republican general, in an attempt to establish him on the throne. After Napoleon's fall in 1814, she returned to Paris to work on the apologetic treatise devoted to her beloved father and his role during the Revolution*. She died, paralyzed, on Bastille Day, 1817.

Liberty is the pivotal concept in Staël's work. She proclaims freedom for individuals and nations, and, despite historical calamities, she believed in the universal progress of enlightenment and democracy. From *De la littérature* (1800) through the *Considérations sur la Révolution française* (1818), Staël demonstrated the dialectical interdependence between a nation's institutions and its culture, calling for the social responsibility of a writer. Her numerous works are proof of her passionate engagement. In the *Réflexions sur la paix adressées à M. Pitt*, the *Réflexions sur la paix intérieure*, and the *Circonstances actuelles*, she promoted peace and the republican order against fanaticism and violence. In *De l'influence des passions sur le bonheur des individus et des nations*, she sought remedies for post-Revolutionary sufferings. She took up the defense of Marie-Antoinette* awaiting the guillotine* in the *Réflexions sur le procès de la Reine* and built a monument for all nations that endured the scourge of Napoleonic imperialism in her *Dix Années d'exil*.

Staël ascribed a critical role to women as agents of historical advancement and insisted on their intellectual emancipation. Her fictional works dramatize women's attempts at freedom. The antinomy of self-affirmation and restriction on the existential level provides structure for the novellas of Staël's youth, the *Histoire de Pauline, Adélaide et Théodore, Mirza*, and *Zulma*, and the two proto-feminist novels, *Delphine* and *Corinne*, whose greatly talented heroines are annihilated by society. Unlike Staël's theoretical writings, her fiction emphasizes the danger of women's longing for recognition through the representation of suffering, fragmentation, and death. In her plays, performed at Coppet and written for her circle of close friends, she ridicules the threatening social order.

While Staël's studies on cultural relativism assured her a permanent place in literary anthologies as a founder of comparative literature and a precursor of Romanticism*, her novelistic production remained marginalized by the canon. Generations of critics, unable to perceive the prophetic aspect of Staël's fiction, systematically mocked the excesses of her female protagonists as autobiographical, self-aggrandizing fantasies of the writer who dared to step out of her socially assigned position. Increasingly, revisionist insights started to appear in the second half of the twentieth century as a result of the activities of the Société des Etudes Staëliennes led by Simone Balayé. Most recently, feminist criticism joined the movement, reexamining Staël's novels as crucial references for women's studies and extending the search for Staël's affiliations with other women writers as well as noting her importance as a philosopher of language. Ellen Moers's *Literary Women* and Madelyn Gutwirth's *Madame de Staël, Novelist: The Emergence of the Artist as Woman* in particular, and translations by Avriel Goldberger contributed heavily to the renaissance of Staël studies.

Karyna Szmurlo

BIBLIOGRAPHY

Primary Texts

Considérations sur la Révolution française. Ed. Jacques Godechot. Geneva: Droz, 1971.
Corinne ou l'Italie. Ed. Simone Balayé. Paris: Gallimard, 1985.
De la littérature. Ed. Paul Van Tieghem. Geneva: Droz; Paris: Minard, 1959.
De l'Allemagne. 5 vols. Ed. Jean de Pange. Intro. Simone Balayé. Paris: Hachette, 1958–1960.
Delphine. Ed. Simone Balayé and Lucia Omanici. Geneva: Droz, 1987.
Dix Années d'exil. Ed. Simone Balayé and Marielle Vianello. Paris: Fayard, 1996.

Secondary Texts

Balayé, Simone. *Madame de Staël: Lumière et liberté.* Paris: Klincksieck, 1979.
Gutwirth, Madelyn. *Madame de Staël, Novelist: The Emergence of the Artist as Woman.* Urbana: University of Illinois Press, 1978.
Moers, Ellen. "Performing Heroism: The Myth of Corinne." In *Literary Women: The Great Writers.* New York: Doubleday, 1976.
Szmurlo, Karyna, ed. *The Novel's Seductions: Staël's "Corinne" in Critical Inquiry.* Lewisburg, PA: Bucknell University Press, 1997.

Suchon, Gabrielle (1631–1703). Suchon was born in Semur to a respectable family. A Jacobinic nun for some years, she fled the convent* and went to Rome to obtain the pope's authorization to renounce her vows. Her request was granted, but her parents objected and the Parliament of Dijon ordered her to return to the convent. She did not comply and spent the rest of her life close to her mother, reading, writing, and teaching children.

Her works include the *Traité de la morale et de la politique* (1693), which she published at her own expense, and *Du Célibat volontaire ou la vie sans engagement* (1700). Obviously composed hastily, the *Traité* is divided into three parts: the first concerns morality, politics, and liberty; the second, science; and the third, the authority and power of those who govern, the submission and dependence of those who are obliged to obey, and the perfection of the female sex. Of particular interest are the chapters dealing with the condition of women. It is not their lack of competence, Suchon contends, that prevents women from participating in government and management, but the laws and customs that were introduced to the disadvantage of women. As its title indicates, *Du Célibat volontaire* is an apology for voluntary celibacy. Comparing it to monastic life, which she finds not suited to everyone, and to marriage*, which she describes as a state of total subjection, Suchon demonstrates that the only way for a woman to attain happiness and realize herself fully is to remain single.

Colette H. Winn

BIBLIOGRAPHY

Primary Texts

Traité de la morale et de la politique, divisé en trois parties, sçavoir la liberté, la science et l'autorité où l'on voit que les personnes du sexe pour en être privées, ne laissent pas d'avoir une capacité naturelle, qui les en peut rendre participantes. Avec un petit traité de la foiblesse, de la legereté, et de l'inconstance, qu'on leur attribuë mal à propos. Lyons: B. Vignien, 1693.

Du Célibat volontaire, ou la vie sans engagement par Damoiselle Gabrielle Suchon. Paris: Chez J. et M. Guignardin, 1700.

Traité de la morale et de la politique. Part III, Ch. XX, "Les Personnes du sexe sont capables des sciences." In *Protestations et revendications féminines—Textes inédits et oubliés sur l'éducation féminine (XVIe–XVIIe siècles).* Ed. Colette H. Winn. Paris: Champion, forthcoming.

Secondary Texts

Geffriaud-Rosso, J. "Gabrielle Suchon: Une Troisième Voie pour la femme." In *Ouverture et Dialogue. Mélanges offerts à Wolfgang Leiner à l'occasion de son soixantième anniversaire.* Tübingen: G. Narr, 1988. 669–678.

Timmermans, Linda. *L'Accès des femmes à la culture (1598–1715).* Paris: Champion, 1993.

Sullerot, Evelyne (1924–). A pioneer of the French feminist movement, Sullerot is an internationally known historian and sociologist. Her doctoral dissertation on the French feminine press was published in 1963. Since that time, she has published almost twenty books, largely devoted to women's issues. She has also written many reports for organizations such as the European Economic Community, the United Nations, the Bureau International du Travail, and various French government councils. From a staunchly patriotic Protestant family,

Sullerot was arrested at sixteen for Resistance activities and took her *baccalau-réat* exams in prison. In the mid-fifties, she co-founded the French Family Planning Movement. Sullerot's long-standing concerns include socioeconomic issues and the history of women. She taught one of the first courses on women's history at the University of Paris X. To deal with the problems of French women trying to enter the job market, Sullerot conceived of and founded the Retravailler Centers. The success of these training facilities was such that they were soon copied not only throughout France, but around the world. Sullerot also anticipated and called attention to many of today's prominent social issues, such as the problems of aging, child care, single parenthood, father's rights, and, particularly, the ongoing question of women and work. Retravailler and her expertise on women's issues have taken her to many Third World countries. For a number of years, she taught courses at the University of Tunisia. Her 1978 study of the condition of women brought together over twenty years of reflection on the problem. In recent years, she has also published several novels*—with autobiographical elements—dealing with the period of the Occupation.

Margaret Collins Weitz

BIBLIOGRAPHY

Primary Texts

La Presse féminine. Paris: Armand Colin, 1963.
Demain les femmes. Paris: Laffont, 1965.
Histoire de la presse féminine en France des origines à 1848. Paris: Armand Colin, 1966.
Histoire et sociologie du travail féminin. Paris: Denoël-Gonthier, 1968.
La Femme dans le monde moderne. Paris: Hachette, 1970.
Les Françaises au travail. Paris: Hachette, 1973.
Histoire et mythologie de l'amour: Huit Siècles d'écrits féminins. Paris: Hachette, 1974.
Le Fait féminin. Paris: Fayard, 1978.
Pour le meilleur et sans le pire. Paris: Fayard, 1984.
L'Enveloppe. Paris: Fayard, 1987.
Alias. Paris: Fayard, 1996.

Surrealism. Surrealism was codified in André Breton's *Manifeste du surréalisme* (1924) as a literary and artistic movement that sought to explore the creative potential of the unconscious via the practice of automatism. Eventually automatism became less practiced as a technique, but the idea of a completely uncensored automatic moment of inspiration remained essential to surrealist thinking. No women participated in the group as active members in the 1920s, but women were everywhere visible as muse figures for writing and art produced by the men. The concept of reciprocal love was exalted. Mentally unstable women were admired within surrealism, as the publication of Breton's *Nadja* (1928) attests, because of the clairvoyant poetic powers they were perceived to have.

Starting in the 1930s, women became increasingly active in the group, both as partners to the men and as independent artists. They began to add their names to surrealist tracts and to show their work in surrealist exhibitions. These women included Meret Oppenheim, Lee Miller, Leonora Carrington, Valentine Hugo, Gisèle Prassinos*, Dora Maar, Nusch Eluard, and Frida Kahlo. With their self-portraits in art and writing, these women redefined the image of Woman in surrealism as a powerful figure capable of producing art on her own. In the 1950s and 1960s, after World War II*, more women came to surrealism, including Joyce Mansour*, Unica Zürn, Bona de Mandiargues, and Mimi Parent. Surrealism as a movement ended officially in 1969 with an announcement in *Le Monde*, three years after Breton's death.

Katharine Conley

BIBLIOGRAPHY

Bonnet, Marguerite. *André Breton: Naissance de l'aventure surréaliste*. Paris: Corti, 1988.
Breton, André. *Oeuvres complètes*. 2 vols. Paris: Gallimard-Pléiade, 1988, 1992.
————. *Le Surréalisme et la peinture*. Paris: Gallimard, 1965.
Caws, Mary Ann, Rudolf Kuenzli, and Gwen Raaberg, eds. *Surrealism and Women*. Cambridge, MA: MIT Press, 1991.
Chadwick, Whitney. *Women Artists and the Surrealist Movement*. Boston: Little, Brown, 1985.
Chadwick, Whitney, and Isabelle de Courtivron. *Significant Others: Creativity and Intimate Partnership*. London: Thames and Hudson, 1993.
Chénieux-Gendron, Jacqueline. *Le Surréalisme*. Paris: PUF, 1984.
Conley, Katharine. *Automatic Woman: The Representation of Woman in Surrealism*. Lincoln: University of Nebraska Press, 1996.
Foster, Hal. *Compulsive Beauty*. Cambridge, MA: MIT Press, 1994.
Hubert, Renée Riese. *Magnifying Mirrors: Women, Surrealism, and Partnership*. Lincoln: University of Nebraska Press, 1994.
La Révolution surréaliste (periodical, 1920s).
Suleiman, Susan Rubin. *Subversive Intent: Gender, Politics and the Avant-Garde*. Cambridge, MA: Harvard University Press, 1990.

Surville, Laure (1800–1871). Born to a bourgeois family from Tours, she was Honoré de Balzac's younger sister. A stringent critic and admirer of her brother's work, she published several critical books on him after his death. She was also a writer in her own right, starting her career by publishing anonymously or under the pen name of Lélio in children's literary magazines. She later published under her married name. Her short stories—some of which served as a direct source of inspiration for her brother—often convey her ambiguous feelings toward the status of married female writers.

Valérie Lastinger

BIBLIOGRAPHY
  Primary Texts
Le Compagnon du foyer. Paris: Giraud, 1854.
Balzac, sa vie et ses oeuvres d'après sa correspondance. Paris: Librairie Nouvelle Jaccottet, Bourdilliat and Cie., 1858.

Les Rêves de Marianne. Paris: Calmann-Lévy, 1878.
Lettres à une amie de province (1831–1837). Paris: Plon, 1932.
Les Femmes de Balzac (anonymously). Paris: Janet, 1951.

Secondary Texts

Helm-Floyd, Juanita. *Les Femmes dans la vie de Balzac.* Paris: Plon, 1926.
Planté, Christine. *La Petite Soeur de Balzac.* Paris: Seuil, 1989.

Symbolist poetry (c. 1875–1914). Stylistically, Symbolism suggests the inten-
sification of figurative language, including the use of symbols to evoke objects,
experiences, and sensations obliquely. Its poetry* tended toward rhythmic fluidity and musicality, moving away from the strictness of the Parnassian poets*.
Many longstanding rules of French prosody and rhyme were overturned, leading
to the softening of the alexandrine, toward *vers libéré* and the advent of free
verse. Symbolist poets experimented with a new form, the prose poem, which
would become a major genre in the twentieth century. Along with new forms,
they explored new subjectivities, returning to lyrical perspectives forgotten since
Romanticism*, although often exchanging cynical irony for romantic sentimentality and candor. Such a freeing-up of poetry favored the creation of not only
female, but also homosexual lyric voices at the end of the century.

Strictly defined as a school or movement by conventional literary historians,
Symbolism involved a burgeoning of poetic activity between 1885 and 1895 to
which women are generally accorded only a footnote. This indicates less a paucity of women poets before the turn of the century than the problem of writing
literary histories in terms of manifestos and *cénacles*. Descriptions of literary-
social scenes favoring the formation of male-dominated movements invariably
obscure the production of women writers. And yet, defined in broader terms,
the symbolist era, characterized by countless splinter groups and offshoots, witnessed the participation of women from its earliest manifestations in the 1870s
to the years before World War I*, often referred to as post-symbolist.

Nina de Villard* (1843–1884) had an early and prominent role in the *Cercle
zutique*, keeping company with Cros, Verlaine, and Rimbaud, among others.
Marie Krysinska* (1857–1908) frequented the *Hydropathes* alongside the decadent poet Jules Laforgue. She was one of the first practitioners of free verse
in France and perhaps its inventor. Other women who published in symbolist
reviews included Judith Gautier* (1846–1917), Marie Daguet (1860–1942), Jane
Catulle Mendès (1867–1965), and Gérard d'Houville* (pseud. of Marie de Régnier, 1875–1963). While there have been contributions to the scholarship on
these poets in recent years, much remains to be explored.

Although not a poet, Rachilde* (1860–1953) must be remembered for her
role in the publication of a number of symbolist reviews, as well as for her
symbolist theater*, decadent prose, criticism, and memoirs*. Some nonliterary
women supported and were supported by the symbolists, including the *communarde* Louise Michel* and the actress Sarah Bernhardt.

At the turn of the century, a significant number of women poets were composing in a variety of veins. Although often grouped together as neo-romantics (by, among others, the poet and critic Charles Maurras, who founded the nationalist and neoclassical *Ecole romane* as a reaction to Symbolism), these women clearly wrote and must be read in the context of the themes, styles, and obsessions of the symbolist era. One such figure is Anna de Noailles* (1876–1933), whose literary fame began in 1901 with the publication of her first collection of poetry, *Le Coeur innombrable*. She is associated with the poetic tendency called *naturisme*, which began around 1895 as a response to Symbolism's anti-materialism, favoring rustic and quotidian themes.

Another poet crucial to the development of the symbolist period's female tradition is Renée Vivien* (1877–1909). Her lesbian poems and translations of Sappho were in keeping with the sexually liberatory thematics of much symbolist production, as her focus on death relates to decadent morbidity. Natalie Clifford Barney* (1877–1972) brought together Vivien, Noailles, and other women writers, including Lucie Delarue-Mardrus* (1875–1945), in her noteworthy salon*. The group, later named Sapho 1900 (Billy), was a center for female literati and became one of the few lesbian salons in French literary history.

Gretchen Schultz

BIBLIOGRAPHY

Secondary Texts

Barre, André. *Le Symbolisme: Essai historique sur le mouvement symboliste en France de 1885–1900*. 1911. New York: Burt Franklin, 1968.

Benstock, Shari. *Women of the Left Bank: Paris, 1900–1940*. Austin: University of Texas Press, 1986.

Billy, André. *L'époque 1900*. Paris: Tallandier, 1951. [See especially "Les Femmes de lettres," 214–233.]

Cornell, Kenneth. *The Symbolist Movement*. New Haven: Yale University Press, 1951.

Décaudin, Michel. *La Crise des valeurs symbolistes 1895–1914*. Geneva: Slatkine, 1981. [See especially "Le Lyrisme féminin," 155–165.]

Maurras, Charles. "Le Romantisme féminin." In *L'Avenir de l'intelligence*. 1903. Paris: Flammarion, 1927. 115–134.

T

Tastu, Amable (1798–1885). Widely published in numerous genres, Tastu wrote most of her works during the first half of her long life. Her poems, both elegiac and historic, enjoyed popular success during the 1820s and 1830s and then fell into critical oblivion, a fate shared by many other women romantics.

Winner of the Jeux Floraux prize on several occasions, she was highly praised by her contemporaries, including Mme Dufrénoy*, Lamartine, and Sainte-Beuve. She subsequently abandoned poetry* for more ''marketable'' writings, including educational treatises. She also edited volumes for youths, literary histories, travel chronicles, and translations from many languages (including translations of the English poet Felicia Hemans).

Gretchen Schultz

BIBLIOGRAPHY

Primary Texts

Poésies. Paris: A. Dupont, 1827.
Chroniques de France. Paris: Delangle frères, 1829.
Poésies nouvelles. Paris: Denain et Delamare, 1835.
Education maternelle. Paris: Renduel, 1836.
Cours d'histoire de France. Paris: Lavigne, 1836–1837.
Eloge de Mme de Sévigné. Paris: F. Didot frères, 1840.
Education morale. Paris: Didier, 1841.
Tableau de la littérature allemande. Tours: A. Mame, 1843.
Tableau de la littérature italienne. Tours: A. Mame, 1843.
Voyage en France. Tours: A. Mame, 1846.

Secondary Texts

Baale-Uittenbosch, Alexandrina Elisabeth Maria. *Les Poétesses dolantes du Romantisme*. Haarlem: De Erven F. Bohn, 1928.

Sainte-Beuve, Charles. ''Madame Tastu.'' In *Causeries du lundi: Portraits de femmes et portraits littéraires*. Paris: Garnier Frères, 1926. 1–21.

Wailly, Léon de. ''Madame A. Tastu.'' In *Les Poètes français*. Ed. Eugène Crépet. Paris: Maison Quantin, 1887. 203–214.

Teisson, Janine (?–). Teisson has published a poignant first novel*, *La Petite Cinglée* (1993), whose title plays on the two meanings of the word *cinglée*: the narrator, a young girl, is both whipped and called crazy. Told with humor and gentleness, the narrative is composed of a series of fragmented family memories structured around forty-four chapters, each centering on the definition of a word. The awakening of the girl's awareness of gender, motherhood, and womanhood is shaped by the domestic violence she endures and witnesses, by the fears it generates—especially that of being mad—and by her resistance to the dysfunctional behavior of her family*.

Joëlle Vitiello

BIBLIOGRAPHY

Primary Text

La Petite Cinglée. Castelnau-le-Nez: Les Editions Climat, 1993.

Tencin, Claudine-Alexandrine Guérin de (1682–1749). Born in Grenoble, into a family that had risen from obscurity through hard work, good marriages*, and the practice of sacrificing the younger children in favor of the oldest males in order to conserve and perpetuate the family's* fortune, Claudine-Alexandrine, as the youngest of five, was placed at the age of eight as a boarder in the Dominican convent* of Montfleury to prepare her for a life as a nun. That she was unhappy with this fate is made clear by her repeated and desperate attempts to resist her father's orders. But despite her entreaties, she was coerced into taking the veil at the age of sixteen, upon which she immediately initiated legal proceedings that eventually led to the annulment of her vows fourteen years later in 1712, when she was thirty.

Attractive-looking, intelligent, resourceful, bold, and sensuous, she became notorious for her numerous liaisons, some with the most powerful and famous men of her time, notably with the regent himself as well as with Lord Bolingbroke and Matthew Prior. The offspring of one of her illicit love affairs turned out to be Jean Le Rond d'Alembert, the mathematician and co-editor of the *Encyclopédie**. She relentlessly furthered the career of her brother Pierre and eventually succeeded in having him elevated to the rank of cardinal. The salon* she established in Paris was frequented by such well-established literary figures as Lamotte-Houdar, Fontenelle, Montesquieu, and Marivaux, as well as up-and-coming writers such as Marmontel, Duclos, and Helvétius. Ironically, this notorious adventuress inherited the habitués of the salon of the irreproachable marquise de Lambert* upon the latter's death in 1733. Madame de Tencin published anonymously (as was then the custom) a number of novels* that enjoyed

wide popularity throughout Europe in her lifetime, but were subsequently largely
forgotten until their recent inclusion in the literary canon as major works of
fiction deserving of serious critical consideration, notably the *Mémoires du
comte de Comminge* (1735), *Le Siège de Calais* (1739), *Les Malheurs de
l'amour* (1747), and *Anecdotes de la cour et et du règne d'Edouard II* (completed by Madame Elie de Beaumont* and published posthumously in 1767).

Gita May

BIBLIOGRAPHY

Primary Texts

Oeuvres complètes de Mesdames de La Fayette, de Tencin et de Fontaines. Paris: Moutardier, 1832.
Mémoires du comte de Comminge. Ed. Jean Decottignies. Lille: Giard, 1969.

Secondary Texts

Decottignies, Jean. "Roman et revendication feminine, d'après les *Mémoires du comte de Comminge* de Madame de Tencin." In *Roman et Lumières au XVIIe siècle.* Paris: Editions sociales, 1970. 311–320.
Masson, Pierre-Maurice. *Une Vie de femme au XVIIIe siècle: Madame de Tencin.* Geneva: Slatkine, 1970.
Parker, Alice. "Madame de Tencin and the 'Mascarade' of Female Impersonation." *Eighteenth-Century Life* 9, no. 2 (1985): 65–77.
Sartori, Eva Martin. "Claudine-Alexandrine Guérin de Tencin." In *French Women Writers: A Bio-bibliographical Source Book.* Ed. Eva Martin Sartori and Dorothy Wynne Zimmerman. Westport, CT: Greenwood Press, 1991. 473–483.
Stewart, Joan Hinde. "The Novelists and Their Fictions." In. Ed. Samia I. Spencer. *French Women and the Age of Enlightenment.* Bloomington: Indiana University Press, 1984. 197–211.

Theater. The history of French women's theater begins in the sixteenth century
with a few exceptionally well educated noble women. The first known woman
playwright in France, Marguerite de Navarre*, wrote a number of plays, both
religious and secular, to be performed at the court in about the 1530s. In the
second half of the sixteenth century, a period when the theater was condemned
by both church and state, three other women are known to have written plays:
Madeleine des Roches* and her daughter Catherine, whose plays were most
likely performed in the privacy of their literary salon* in Poitiers, and Catherine
de Rohan-Soubise, a Calvinist imprisoned after the siege of La Rochelle, during
which her tragedy *Holoferne* (1574) was performed. Later, having befriended
Henri IV's sister, she wrote three *comédies-ballets* which were performed at the
royal court in the 1590s.

As the French stage revived in the 1630s, a number of women played an
important role as actresses, administrators, patrons, and critics, but it was not
until the second half of the century that women began to be recognized as
playwrights. Madame de Villedieu*, best known as a poet and novelist, is probably the first woman in France whose plays were performed in a professional

the^ater. Though she did not depend on writing plays for her living like her English contemporary Aphra Behn, she did prove that it was possible to be recognized as a writer in the very male-dominated and highly competitive milieu of the French stage. She had three plays published, two of which were performed at the Hôtel de Bourgôgne and one at the court in Versailles. Before the end of the century, three other women playwrights would follow her example: Antoinette Deshoulières*, Madame de Longchamps, and Catherine Bernard*. The late seventeenth century also saw a breakthrough in lyric theater when, immediately after the death of Lulli in 1693 and the subsequent end of his monopoly over the performance of opera in France, Madame de Sainctonge* became the first woman librettist.

Compared to the women playwrights of the Renaissance, those writing during the seventeenth century were of more varied social, economic, and educational backgrounds, ranging from Deshoulières, who frequented the aristocratic salon of the Hôtel de Rambouillet to Longchamps, an actress at the Comédie Française. The democratization of play writing would become more pronounced during the following centuries, contributing to an increase in the number of women playwrights from 17 in the seventeenth century to 80 in the eighteenth and 350 in the nineteenth. This increase can be attributed to a number of important developments in the French theater during the eighteenth century: the diversification of genres and the redefinition of comedy, which would replace tragedy as the preferred genre of women playwrights; the development of salon theater or *théâtre de société* and the proliferation of small private theaters; and the increasing number of actresses and other professional women of the theater who wrote for the stage. The Théâtre Italien, where more women's plays were performed than in any other single theater in eighteenth-century France, was particularly favorable to works written by actresses such as Flaminia Riccoboni and Marie Justine Favart*.

Another important factor in the rise of women's theater is the development and femininization of children's theater. Rather than use adult plays, often in Latin, to educate young men, as had been the tradition since the sixteenth century in France, mid-eighteenth-century novelist and playwright Madame de Graffigny* was commissioned by Empress Maria-Theresa to write plays specifically for the education* of the archdukes of Austria. Several decades later, Madame de Genlis* would be made responsible for the education of the Orléans children, for whose education and entertainment she wrote numerous plays, published in a seven-volume collection in 1785.

A number of women took advantage of the fervent theatrical activity during the French Revolution*. Some remained safely within the less ideological genres of comedy, vaudeville, or melodrama*, while others, like Olympe de Gouges*, wrote plays with an explicit ideological or political message. Olympe's fate is representative of the paradox of women's role in the Revolution: if the Revolution allowed her to speak out more than ever in the political sphere, it also succeeded in radically silencing her voice: Olympe went to the guillotine* in

1793, having written over twenty overtly political plays, thus paving the way for the numerous politically and socially active women playwrights of the nineteenth and twentieth centuries.

While the eighteenth-century developments in the theater discussed above remained relevant, a number of new factors related to the history of women also contributed to the importance of women playwrights in the nineteenth century, notably substantial improvements in women's education. Women's voices in the theater became less marginal throughout the nineteenth century. Over thirty-five plays by authors such as Virginie Ancelot, Sophie Gay*, Delphine Gay de Girardin*, and George Sand* were performed at the Comédie Française alone. The coincident development of feminism* and a more socially conscious theater in the second half of the century also led to the birth of a feminist theater. Aside from isolated women like Marie-Anne Barbier*, who had framed her plays with feminist prefaces, or Olympe de Gouges, few women before this period had openly exposed their feminist ideologies in their dramatic works. At the end of the nineteenth century and into the twentieth, playwrights in France began bringing to the stage a variety of themes relating to the status of women in contemporary French society. Feminist activists like Maria Deraismes*, Nelly Roussel*, and Madeleine Pelletier* were also playwrights, as was Louise Michel*. The first feminist theater was founded by Marya Cheliga in 1897 in order to promote the works of women playwrights and the feminist cause.

The development of women's theater slowed down considerably during World War I*, only to rise dramatically during the interwar period, reaching a peak in the 1930s when over two hundred plays by women were performed in Paris alone. Critics spoke with enthusiasm of the great diversity of women's theater in the thirties, of the audacity and even genius* of playwrights like Marie Leneru and Marcelle Maurette, who were seen as taking possession of the Parisian stage. Unfortunately, this wave of women's theater was to be broken and virtually erased from theater history with the onset of World War II*.

It would take another forty years for women's theater to attain and surpass such a level of activity. While authors like Duras*, Sagan*, Chedid*, Dorin, and Sarraute* all began writing for the stage in the sixties, plays by women were still relatively rare. The seventies saw three interrelated developments: an increase in politically engaged theater by women inspired by the militant fervor of 1968 and the rebirth of the feminist movement; the creation of a number of women-centered collective theater troupes like La Carmagnole or Lo Teatre de la Carriera; and the central role of women in *café-théâtre* performances, notably the one-woman show. Nevertheless, the participation of women in the theater beyond the role of actress remained relatively marginal until the 1980s, which brought on a veritable explosion of theater by and about women, from experimental drama to the Boulevard, from adaptations of the history of women to explorations of the feminine psyche. Although we cannot speak of a tradition of French women's theater, since the playwrights of each new generation generally ignored the existence of their predecessors, we can speak of a history of women's theater, a history that is rich and diverse and largely unexplored.

Cecilia Beach

BIBLIOGRAPHY

Primary Texts

Gethner, Perry, ed. *Femmes dramaturges en France: 1650–1750.* Paris: Biblio 17, 1993.
Mawkward, Christiane, and Judith G. Miller, eds. *Plays by French and Francophone Women: A Critical Anthology.* Ann Arbor: University of Michigan Press, 1994.

Secondary Texts

Beach, Cecilia, comp. *French Women Playwrights before the Twentieth Century: A Checklist.* Westport, CT: Greenwood Press, 1994.
———. *French Women Playwrights of the Twentieth Century: A Checklist.* Westport, CT: Greenwood Press, 1996.
Goldwyn, Henriette. "Femmes Auteurs dramatiques au dix-septième siècle: La Condition humaine." In *Cahiers du dix-septième siecle: An Interdisciplinary Journal* 4, no. 1 (1990): 51–61.
Krakovitch, Odile. "Les Femmes Dramaturges et la création au théâtre." *Pénélope pour l'histoire des femmes* 3 (Fall 1980): 29–36.
Lamar, Celita. *Our Voices, Ourselves: Women Writing for the French Theater.* New York: Peter Lang, 1991.
Millstone, Amy Blithe. "Feminist Theatre in France: 1870–1914." Dissertation, University of Wisconsin-Madison, 1977.
Mittman, Barbara. "Women and Theater Arts." In *French Women and the Age of Enlightenment*, Ed. Samia I. Spencer. Bloomington: Indiana University Press, 1984. 155–169.
Showalter, English, Jr. "Writing Off the Stage: Women Authors and Eighteenth Century Theater." *Yale French Studies* 75 (1988): 95–111.
Surel-Tupin, Monique. "La Prise de parole des femmes au théâtre." In *Le Théâtre d'intervention depuis 1968.* Ed. Jonny Epstein and Phillipe Ivernel. Lausanne: L'Age d'homme, 1980. 56–78.

Thiroux d'Arconville, Marie-Geneviève-Charlotte Darlus (1720–1805). Author of seventy mostly anonymous volumes of fiction, poetry*, drama, essays on science, history, and translations from English, she married Louis Lazare, chief investigator at the court of Paris, had three sons, and lived in the Marais. Among her acquaintances were well-known writers and scientists: Voltaire, Gresset, Jussieu, Lavoisier, Turgot, Bougainville, Condorcet, and Macquer. After contracting smallpox at age twenty-two, she devoted her time to family obligations, charitable actions, and writing. Her translations from English best confirm Arconville's austerity and interest in moral works. The most distinctive characteristic of her activities was her research in physics, anatomy, natural history, agriculture, botany, and chemistry. Her *Essai pour servir à l'histoire de la putréfaction* and sixteen medical publications were widely recognized. In

1759 she translated Peter Shaw's *Leçons de chimie*, and Monro's *Traité d'ostéologie* with thirty-one plates drawn under her direction. Having access to the king's library, she started publishing historical essays at age fifty: *Vie du Cardinal d'Ossat, Marie de Médicis*, and *Histoire de François II*. At age eighty, she was still preparing an adaptation of Goldsmith's *Histoire d'Angleterre*. Although well informed about revolutionary events through her son, Thiroux de Crosne, a police lieutenant in Paris who stayed in direct contact with the king, Arconville did not comment on the Revolution*. She survived her son's decapitation in 1794, regained a large part of her property, and died in the Marais without having published for twenty years. Her copious memoirs*, given to a friend, have been lost.

Karyna Szmurlo

BIBLIOGRAPHY

Primary Texts

Pensées et réflexions morales sur divers sujets. Avignon: S.n., 1760.
Traité de l'amitié. Amsterdam and Paris: Desaint, 1761.
L'Amour éprouvé par la mort ou lettres modernes de deux amants de Vieille-Roche. Paris: Musier fils, 1763.
Traité des passions. Paris: s.n., 1764 (both *Traités* wrongly placed in Diderot's *Oeuvres*, Amsterdam, 1773).
Essai pour servir à l'histoire de la putréfaction. Paris: Chez P. F. Didot le jeune, 1766.
Mémoires de Mlle de Valcourt. Paris and Amsterdam: Lacombe, 1767.
Dona Gratia d'Ataïde, comtesse de Ménézès. Histoire portugaise. Paris: Lacombe, 1770.
Vie du Cardinal d'Ossat avec son discours sur la Ligue. Paris: Herissant, 1771.
Vie de Marie de Médicis, princesse toscane, reine de France et de Navarre. Paris: Prault, 1774.
Mélanges de littérature, de morale et de physique. Amsterdam: Aux dépends de la Compagnie, 1775–1776.
Histoire de François II roi de France. Paris: Belin, 1783.

Secondary Texts

Campbell Hurd-Mead, Kate. *A History of Women in Medicine*. Haddam, CT: Haddam Press, 1938.
Girou-Swiderski, Marie-Laure. "Vivre la Révolution. L'incidence de la Révolution sur la carrière et la vie de trois femmes de lettres." In *Les Femmes et la Révolution française*. Toulouse: Le Mirail, 1989. 2:239–249.

Thomas, Edith (1909–1970). Thomas, the daughter of nonpracticing Catholic parents, converted to Protestantism at sixteen, thus displaying an early example of the independence that characterized her life. As a journalist, she wrote reports on the Spanish Civil War. In 1942 she joined the Communist Party (which she later left) and helped found the Comité National des Ecrivains, which published *Les Lettres françaises*, the leading journal of French intellectual resistance. During the same period, she also wrote pamphlets for the Union des Femmes Françaises, the principal women's organization of the Resistance. Using a pseudonym, she published the *Contes d'Auxois*, a collection of short stories* based on Resistance activities. Trained as an archivist, Thomas wrote extensively: seven novels*, eight historical and critical studies, collections of short stories, memoirs*, poems, and journalistic accounts. Her writings reveal her feminist concerns. *Eve et les autres*, for example, is a feminist re-creation drawn from tales of women in the Bible*. She also wrote on Joan of Arc, Pauline Roland*, George Sand*, Louise Michel*, the women of 1848, and the *Pétroleuses*.

Margaret Collins Weitz

BIBLIOGRAPHY

Primary Texts

Le Refus. Paris: Editions Sociales Internationales, 1936.
Contes d'Auxois. Paris: Editions de Minuit, 1943.
Etudes de femmes. Paris: Editions Colbert, 1945.
Jeanne d'Arc. Paris: Editions Hier et Aujourd'hui, 1947.
Les Femmes de 1848. Paris: P.U.F., 1948.
Eve et les autres. Paris: Gizard, 1952.
Pauline Roland: Socialisme et féminisme au XIXe siècle. Paris: Librairie Marcel Rivière, 1956.
George Sand. Paris: Classiques du XIXe siècle, 1959.
Les "Pétroleuses." Paris: Gallimard, 1963.
Louise Michel ou la Velléda de l'anarchie. Paris: Gallimard, 1971.
Le Témoin compromis. Ed. Dorothy Kaufman. Paris: Vivian Hamy, 1995.

Secondary Text

Kaufmann, Dorothy. " 'Le Témoin compromis': Diaries of Resistance and Collaboration by Edith Thomas." *L'Esprit Créateur* 33, no.1 (Spring 1993): 17–28.

Tinayre, Marcelle (1877–1948). Marcelle Tinayre, née Marguerite-Suzanne-Marcelle Chasteau, was a prolific novelist and a journalist for several Parisian magazines, including *Le Temps* and *La Vie heureuse*. Her most famous protagonists, Hellé de Riveyrac from the novel* *Hellé* (1899) and Josyane Valentin from *La Rebelle* (1905), are both independent thinkers who believe that women have the right to pursue their own ideas of happiness, unfettered by patriarchal laws and customs. Even in more traditional marriages*, Tinayre's female characters rebel against the daily inequities and injustices that wives and mothers confront in conservative bourgeois and working-class families. Their revolts are depicted in subtle ways that may not be considered "feminist" or "activist" according to today's definitions of those terms, but their actions were considered daring and intelligent by feminists of the Belle Epoque, and Tinayre's works received much praise and discussion at the turn of the century.

Juliette M. Rogers

BIBLIOGRAPHY

Primary Texts

Avant l'amour. Paris: Mercure de France, 1897.
La Rançon. Paris: Mercure de France, 1898.

Hellé. Paris: Mercure de France, 1899.
L'Oiseau d'orage. Paris: Calmann-Lévy, 1900.
La Maison du péché. Paris: Calmann-Lévy, 1902.
La Rebelle. Paris: Calmann-Lévy, 1905.
L'Ombre de l'amour. Paris: Calmann-Lévy, 1910.
Madeleine au miroir. Journal d'une femme. Paris: Calmann-Lévy, 1912.

Translation (Renaissance). Never has the work of translation seemed as vital as in the Renaissance, and in this respect the French sixteenth century is no exception. In the religious area, the Reformation* encouraged translation of scriptural texts in order to invite a wider participation in the Protestant Reform; in the humanistic sphere of erudition and creativity, translation, which often merged with imitation and interpretation, was seen, on the one hand, as an indispensable connection with the illustrious cultures of Rome and Greece, as well as with contemporary humanist expressions in neo-Latin and in other vernaculars; and, on the other hand, as a means of enriching the French idiom by an increased stylistic and linguistic sensitivity to the semantics and the aesthetics of texts. Translation was thus recognized as an essential undertaking both in the religious and in the humanistic domains. The spiritual and intellectual life of women was seriously affected and altered by the ongoing project of translation, for it opened up for them horizons of knowing and of learning that had been unsuspected until this time. As patrons, as consumers, as practitioners, women had indeed an important stake in the enterprise of translation, as it allowed them to enter into new modes of thinking and imagining, and to discover new intellectual activities, new possibilities of participation in the world around them, and new ways of exploration (including self-exploration) and expression.

The new Calvinist liturgy stressed the use of the vernacular, and hence of translations, in order to integrate all potential adherents, including women, into the rites and ceremonies of religion. Following the Protestant example, the Roman Church also engaged in vernacular translation of scriptural works. Women were now enabled to read and study the Bible* as well as other previously forbidden religious texts, and so to construct wider dimensions to their spiritual experience. High-born women, such as Marguerite de Navarre*, and prestigious abbesses, such as Louise de Bourbon, abbess of Fontevrault, played significant roles as protectors and patrons of biblical, theological, and devotional translations. This opening up of the life of the soul allowed women not only to engage in piety, as they had always been encouraged to do, but also to reflect critically on the bases and modalities of their own intellectual and emotional engagement with their faith, and on their traditional religious practices and roles. Although the actual functions of women, both in the Reformed and in the Catholic churches, remained limited, women who desired to do so could lead an autonomous spiritual life grounded in their own capacity for study, reflection, and meditation.

In the humanistic sphere, the widening of possibilities was even more striking, since women, equally active as patrons and consumers of translation, functioned also as practitioners of the erudite craft that was among the prevalent activities of the male humanists. More women had gained access to advanced education*, and many of them were eager to engage in all aspects of the humanist enterprise, namely, study, writing, and translation. The latter activity was especially meaningful since it allowed women to practice their hard-won learning and to apply their erudition in a recognized and generally credited and respected fashion. For women, translation was a way of establishing for themselves a foothold in the world of authorship and thus of authority: as manifestly learned women they displayed the same familiarity with the great nourishing works of humanism, both past and present, as the male scholars and authors, and, like them, contributed significantly to the ongoing transmission of culture. Women's translation activity bridged not only the gap between historically and geographically distant cultures and their literary, philosophical, and scientific expressions; it also bridged the gap between women and the dominant culture in which they lived, namely, the culture of Renaissance humanism. It is, then, not surprising that many of the well-known, as well as lesser-known, women authors of the period engaged in the work of translation, whether they inserted translations of classical passages in their own writings, or whether they undertook complete translations of classical, neo-Latin, or Italian authors. Among sixteenth-century women authors who engaged in translation were Marie de Cotteblanche*, Hélisenne de Crenne*, Marie de Gournay*, Anne de Graville, Anne de Marquets, Madeleine and Catherine des Roches*, and Marie de Romieu*. Most of their translations do not exist in modern editions, a lack that, it is to be hoped, will be remedied by current researchers.

Tilde Sankovitch

BIBLIOGRAPHY

Primary Texts

Gournay, Marie le Jars de. *Le Proumenoir de Monsieur de Montaigne, par sa fille d'alliance*. Ed. Patricia F. Cholakian. Delmar, NY: Scholars' Facsimiles and Reprints, 1985.

Roches, Madeleine and Catherine des. *Les Oeuvres*. Ed. Anne R. Larsen. Geneva: Droz, 1993.

Romieu, Marie de. *Les Premières Oeuvres poétiques*. Ed. André Winandy. Geneva: Droz, 1972.

Secondary Texts

Berriot-Salvadore, Evelyne. *Les Femmes dans la société française de la Renaissance*. Geneva: Droz, 1990.

Chavy, Paul. *Traducteurs d'autrefois: Moyen Age et Renaissance. Dictionnaire des traducteurs de la littérature traduite en ancien et moyen français (842–1600)*. 2 vols. Paris and Geneva: Champion-Slatkine, 1988.

Davis, Natalie Zemon. "City Women and Religious Change." In *Society and Culture in Early Modern France*. Stanford: Stanford University Press, 1975.

Feugère, Léon. *Les Femmes poètes au XVIe siècle*. Paris, 1860. Geneva: Slatkine Reprints, 1969.

King, Margaret L. *Women of the Renaissance*. Chicago: University of Chicago Press, 1991.

McKinley, Mary. " 'Fleurs estrangeres': Gournay's translation of Montaigne's Quotations in the 1617 Essais." *Montaigne Studies* 7 (1995): 119–130.

Norton, Glen P. *The Ideology and Language of Translation in Renaissance France and Their Humanist Antecedents*. Geneva: Droz, 1984.

Sankovitch, Tilde. "Catherine des Roches's *Le Ravissement de Proserpine*. A Humanist/ Feminist Translation." In *Renaissance Women Writers. French Texts/American Contexts*. Ed. Anne R. Larsen and Colette H. Winn. Detroit: Wayne State University Press, 1994.

Wiesner, Merry E. *Women and Gender in Early Modern Europe*. Cambridge: Cambridge University Press, 1993.

Travel literature. Unlike their noteworthy contribution to such genres as epistolary writing, moral literature, and romance fiction, French women are not noted for their contribution to the genre of travel writing for several important reasons.

First, travel writing has generally been defined as the first-person account of a voyage of adventure, discovery, or exploration of a particular part of the globe. Its subject is often the attainment of a difficult and physically demanding goal, the account of scientific and technological advances in either the means of transportation itself or in the discovery of new territories, or the retelling of a process of colonization. Few Frenchwomen participated in enterprises of this kind, though they frequently wrote about their travels within the framework of their autobiography* or as a means of discussing social mores and etiquette abroad. The genre itself would therefore have to be somewhat redefined to include the types of travel narratives that were often written by women.

Second, and as an offshoot of the first reason for women's relative absence from the genre of travel, is the fact that travel has been linked since antiquity to the acquisition of knowledge. In early modern Europe this type of link between travel and knowledge has been formulated and codified by the notion of the Grand Tour in which a young man of noble standing spends several years traveling as a way of completing his formal education*. Since women were rarely provided with the kind of education which men customarily received and which was a prerequisite to the undertaking of travel (see, for example, Rousseau's stipulations in *Emile ou de l'éducation*) there are fewer accounts of European travels by women than by men.

Finally, travel was a most undomestic pursuit as well as an arduous undertaking before modern-day conveniences enabled people to travel with ease and comfort to distant parts of the world. Defined by and confined largely to the domestic sphere, few women ventured to undertake the kind of travel that is most often the subject of grand narratives of travel. For moral reasons, furthermore, they had difficulty traveling alone without being taken for "loose women'' if they did venture into the public sphere on their own (see Flora Tristan's* comments about her frequent tribulations during her travels as a result of social mores and perceptions of what is proper and improper conduct for women in her *Pérégrinations d'une paria*).

And yet there were French women who did travel and who wrote about their experiences. Their numbers increased dramatically during the nineteenth century—particularly around the 1850s—as travel itself was conducted more frequently and with greater ease, and as greater numbers of women from the middle class were able to participate in this activity. Travel also increased during this period due to the great upheavals of the Revolutionary wars, which forced many families into exile. Women who traveled for this reason were not aware of themselves specifically as travelers, but perceived travel as descriptive of a portion of their lives. As such, women who were exiled often wrote about their travel experiences in their autobiographical accounts. See for example Stéphanie-Félicité de Genlis's* *Mémoires inédits*, as well as Henriette-Lucie Dillon, the Marquise de La Tour du Pin's *Journal d'une femme de cinquante ans* in which she describes her flight from France to England and later to the United States. The most detailed and self-conscious account of travel as a result of exile can be found in Germaine de Staël's* *Dix Années d'exil*, which recounts her flight throughout Europe in the attempt to escape Napoleon's clutches.

Like these accounts of exiled noblewomen, earlier accounts of travel tend also to be written by women of the aristocracy. Madame d'Aulnoy* is noted not only for her fairy tales* but also for her *Mémoires de la cour d'Espagne* and *Relation du voyage d'Espagne*, which focus largely on court society, personal relations, and gossipy details of high society life in Spain. These texts were extremely popular in their day, going through several editions, though modern scholarship contends they are composed of bits and pieces lifted from other authors' accounts of Spanish courtly life. Madame du Bocage*, who wrote about her experiences in England, Holland, and Italy, as well as of her travels to the New World, is also among the better-known women travelers before the nineteenth century.

Among the numerous female travelers of the nineteenth century are Flora Tristan, Suzanne Voilquin*, George Sand*, and Isabelle Eberhardt. Unlike their predecessors, these female travelers often went to more remote parts of the world, traveled alone, and produced accounts in which they are self-conscious of themselves as travelers. They are no longer exclusively from the upper classes, and, as is the case with Tristan and Voilquin, their travels are part of a socialist, radical vision to improve the state of society and to emancipate women. Modern-day women travelers who have followed in their footsteps—writers like Simone de Beauvoir* and Julia Kristeva*—have also linked travel to personal liberation and to the search for utopian alternatives. Their writings reveal that travel has continued to represent a contestation of the educational, social, and moral limitations that delimit women's place in society.

Yaël Schlick

BIBLIOGRAPHY

Primary Texts

Aulnoy, Marie-Catherine. *Mémoires de la cour d'Espagne*. Paris: C. Barbin, 1690.
———. *Relation du voyage d'Espagne*. Paris: C. Barbin, 1690.
Beauvoir, Simone de. *L'Amérique au jour le jour*. Paris: Morihien, 1948; Paris: Gallimard, 1954.
Du Bocage, Marie-Anne. *La Colombiade, ou la foi portée au Nouveau Monde*. Paris: Desaint et Saillant, 1756.
Eberhardt, Isabelle. *Notes de route*. Paris: E. Fasquelle, 1908.
Genlis, Stéphanie-Félicité, comtesse de. *Mémoires inédits de Madame la Comtesse de Genlis sur le dix-huitième siècle et la révolution française, depuis 1756 jusqu'à nos jours*. Paris: Ladvocat, 1825.
Kristeva, Julia. *Des Chinoises*. Paris: Edition des femmes, 1974.
La Tour du Pin, Henriette-Lucie, marquise de. *Journal d'une femme de cinquante ans*. Paris: Berger-Levrault, 1924–1925.
Sand, George. *Un Hiver à Majorque*. Paris: Michel-Lévy frères, 1867.
———. *Journal d'un voyageur pendant la guerre*. Paris: Michel-Lévy, 1871.
———. *Lettres d'un voyageur*. Paris: Garnier-Flammarion, 1971.
Staël, Anne-Louise-Germaine Necker. *Dix Années d'exil*. Paris: Garnier frères, 1906.
Tristan, Flora. *Pérégrinations d'une paria*. Paris: Arthus-Bertrand, 1838.
———. *Promenades dans Londres*. Paris: H.-L. Delloye, 1840.
———. *Le Tour de France*. Paris: Maspéro, 1980.

Secondary Text

Monicat, Bénédicte. "Pour une bibliographie des récits de voyages au féminin (XIXe siècle)." *Romantisme* 77, no. 3 (1992): 95–100.

Triolet, Elsa (1896–1970). Triolet was a prolific novelist, literary critic, journalist, and translator, yet ironically she is often most remembered through her association with two men: her first husband, André Triolet, whose name she chose to retain to the end of her life, and, more significantly, her second husband, Louis Aragon, who immortalized his wife/muse Elsa in works such as *Les Yeux d'Elsa* (1942). Although it is only quite recently that Triolet's writing has begun to attract serious critical attention, she was in her own lifetime a well-known figure on the literary left. She was active in the Resistance, and, in 1945, became the first woman to be awarded the Prix Goncourt, for her collection of short stories* about the Resistance and the Occupation (*Le Premier Accroc coûte deux cents francs*). Her novel* *Le Cheval blanc* (1943) also received votes for the 1943 Goncourt. Triolet's first novels were written in her native Russian, but the majority of her work was composed in her adopted language, French. Alienation, solitude, exile, and homesickness are recurrent themes in her works and are frequently embodied in her female characters. These preoccupations reflect Triolet's own experience of insecurity as a foreigner, living in exile and writing in a foreign language, as a Jew, and as a woman whose status in France depended first on André Triolet and then on Aragon. Much recent research on

Triolet has a biographical focus, although studies are concentrating increasingly on the gendered nature of her work.

Angela Kimyongür

BIBLIOGRAPHY

Primary Text

Oeuvres romanesques croisées de Louis Aragon et Elsa Triolet. 42 vols. Paris: Robert Laffont, 1964–1974.

Secondary Texts

Adereth, Max. *Elsa Triolet and Louis Aragon: An Introduction to Their Interwoven Lives and Works*. Lewiston, NY: Edwin Mellen Press, 1994.

Breed, Nancy Jane. "Feminine Self-Consciousness and Masculine Referent: The Image of Woman in the Novels of Elsa Triolet." Dissertation, Princeton University, 1979.

Holmes, Diana. "Elsa Triolet (1896–1970): Stories of Exile and Resistance." In *French Women's Writing, 1848–1994*. Atlantic Highlands, NJ: Athlone, 1996.

Mackinnon, Lachlan. *The Lives of Elsa Triolet*. London: Chatto and Windus, 1992.

Madaule, Jacques. *Ce que dit Elsa*. Paris: Denoël, 1961.

Marcou, Lilly. *Elsa Triolet. Les Yeux et la mémoire*. Paris: Plon, 1994.

Tristan, Flora (1803–1844). Social reformer, writer, and union organizer. She was the child of a French bourgeoise and a Peruvian noble who were married in a religious ceremony in Spain, but who had never registered the marriage* with the civil authorities as required. After Don Mariano Tristan's premature death in 1807, the family found themselves in reduced circumstances, since his widow and her two children had no legal claim to his estate. As a result, the family moved from Paris to the countryside, where Tristan received only a sporadic education* and was largely self-taught. At the age of seventeen she found work in Paris as a lithographic colorist and married her employer, the engraver André Chazal, in 1821. The marriage was an unhappy one, and Flora left her abusive husband in 1825 when pregnant with their third child, Aline.

Society treated Tristan as a pariah, and doubly so, for she was not only an illegitimate child but also a wife who had abandoned her husband. Tristan worked and traveled as a lady's companion, but she was eventually forced to leave her only surviving son with Chazal and to board Aline. In a quest to reestablish her social status, Tristan embarked on a journey to Peru in 1833, hoping that her father's family would at last recognize her as his legitimate heir. While these efforts failed, Tristan's journal of the voyage served as the basis for her first major work, *Pérégrinations d'une paria* (1838). She also received a small allowance from her uncle, which gave her the financial means needed to devote herself to a career as a writer.

Tristan's early works reflect her personal experience, which informs her appeals for social reforms on a wider scale. *Nécessité de faire bon accueil aux* *femmes étrangères* (1835) is a pamphlet about unattached women travelers and their needs in a society whose mores restrict or exclude them. Her petition on divorce*, addressed to the French Chamber of Deputies, argued for the reinstitution of a legal means to dissolve marriages like her own. Yet it was her autobiographical narrative of her travels in South America that established her literary reputation. It was also the probable provocation for Chazal's dramatic attack on his estranged wife in a Paris street in broad daylight. He shot her at point-blank range, then was tried and convicted of the crime, but not before Tristan herself gained notoriety for her own conduct. She also regained custody of her children and promptly changed their surname to her own patronymic.

Tristan's only work of fiction, *Méphis* (1838), a novel* about a victimized wife who falls in love with a revolutionary worker-artist, was poorly received. The writer returned to her forte, the social documentary. *Promenades dans Londres* (1840) is a detailed analysis and acerbic critique of the social abuses she had observed on travels to England.

Tristan's attention soon turned once again to the country of her birth and the exploitation of the men and women of France's nascent proletariat. *L'Union ouvrière* (1843) is a manifesto for the international organization of the working classes, although the focus is clearly on France. In it, Tristan appeals to workers to help themselves, and to include their wives, sisters, mothers, and daughters. She proposes a concrete agenda for social reform through organization and mutual aid. Although Tristan was heavily influenced by utopian socialism, her own social theory is unique in that she fused socialism with feminism*, for she insisted that women be constituted as a separate class. She also presented practical solutions designed for immediate implementation.

The next step in the process was to take her message to the workers themselves, in a *tour de France* modeled on the traditional journeyman's circuit around the country, a tour made popular at the time by writers like Agricol Perdiguier and George Sand*. In 1844 Tristan visited workshops, union halls, and the homes of workers and bourgeois alike in her efforts to convince people of the need for the reforms she envisioned. The journal she kept was published posthumously as *Le Journal du tour de France* (1973). The author never lived to complete her *tour de France*. Tristan succumbed to typhoid fever in Bordeaux in September and died there in November 1844.

Flora Tristan's writings fell into obscurity for over a century. In the last twenty years, however, they have been recognized as significant contributions to socialist and feminist literature and theory.

Mary Rice-DeFosse

BIBLIOGRAPHY

Primary Texts

Méphis. Paris: Ladvocat, 1838.
Promenades dans Londres. Ed. François Bédarida. Paris: Maspéro, 1978.
Pérégrinations d'une paria. Paris: Maspéro, 1979.

Flora Tristan's London Journal. Trans. Dennis Palmer and Giselle Pincetl. Cambridge, MA: Charles River Books, 1980.

Lettres. Ed. Stéphane Michaud. Paris: Seuil, 1980.

Le Tour de France. Ed. J. L. Puech. 2 vols. Paris: Seuil, 1980.

L'Union ouvrière. Ed. Daniel Armogathe and Jacques Grandjonc. Paris: Des femmes, 1986.

Nécessité de faire bon accueil aux femmes étrangères. Ed. Denys Cuche. Paris: L'Harmattan, 1988.

Secondary Texts

Cross, Maíre, and Tim Gray. *The Feminism of Flora Tristan*. Providence, RI: Berg, 1992.

Michaud, Stéphane, ed. *Un Fabuleux Destin: Flora Tristan*. Proceedings of the First Flora Tristan Colloquium. Dijon: Editions Universitaires de Dijon, 1985.

Rice-DeFosse, Mary. "Flora Tristan." In *French Women Writers: A Bio-Bibliographical Source Book*. Ed. Eva Martin Sartori and Dorothy Wynne Zimmerman. Westport, CT: Greenwood Press, 1991. 484–494.

Struminger, Laura S. *The Odyssey of Flora Tristan*. New York: Peter Lang, 1988.

Trobairitz. As a naturalized word, "troubadour" connotes a widely recognized phenomenon, the first vernacular lyric poets who began singing in the south of France at the end of the eleventh century. Less well known but the subject of intense scrutiny in recent decades are the women troubadours, or *trobairitz*, some twenty named poets who can be dated from approximately 1170 to 1260. According to the evidence of the extant manuscripts, women troubadours start singing once the poetic system of the troubadours has reached its classical expression; their voices cease before the last generation of troubadours falls silent. In a kind of mirroring effect, the marginality of women in medieval society's structuring of values and power reappears in the marginality of the *trobairitz's* reception. Starting with the written anthologies of the *chansonniers* (song manuscripts) of the thirteenth and fourteenth centuries and continuing into the modern era, interest in the women troubadours has ebbed and flowed, rising with the moving tides of feminism*. Although their numbers and corpus are small in comparison with the 400 or so named troubadours who have left us over 2,500 songs, such a large group of women poets composing in Occitan inevitably raises tantalizing questions about who they were and what they said.

The lives of the women poets themselves, all noblewomen insofar as they have been identified, are clearly connected to the Occitanian courts in which troubadour lyric flourished in the give-and-take of live performance. *Vidas* (biographies) and *razos* (commentaries) included in some *chansonniers* mention thirteen *trobairitz* by name (including Gaudairenca, wife of the troubadour Raimon de Mirval, of whom no poems have survived; the other names appear in poems and rubrics). Mixing historical information and literary inventions inspired by the songs, the introductions (primarily written for a later Italian public) suggest that the women troubadours enjoyed multiple interactions with their male counterparts. Historical research outside the lyric texts confirms that women troubadours like Tibors, Almucs de Castelnau, Maria de Ventadorn, Garsenda de Forcalquier, and Clara d'Anduza were associated with courts that patronized troubadour lyric; the women poets were relatives, friends, and patronesses, as well as objects and subjects of troubadour song.

Difficult to delimit with any exactitude, their repertoire divides primarily between *cansos* (love songs) and *tensos* (debate poems), with a small sampling of other lyric genres: several political poems or *sirventes* (two anonymous, plus one by Gormonda de Montepellier, who offers a spirited defense of Rome in reply to Guilhem Figueira's famous polemic against the Roman church); a *planh* (lament poem), an *alba* (dawn song), and a *balada* (dance song), all anonymous but spoken in a woman's voice; and a *salut d'amor* (love letter). Five or six women composed *cansos*, the most prestigious and by far the dominant form in the troubadour repertoire. The majority of women troubadours participated in dialogue poems: exchanges of *coblas* (stanzas); *partimens* (a debate in which a particular question is argued from opposing sides); and *tensos*. Exchanges between male and female voices dominate these debates (twenty-three out of twenty-six poems in Rieger's edition). The problematic recognition of real women poets behind the unsubstantiated first names and anonymous *domnas* is complicated by our knowledge that some *tensos* were fictive. Editors and readers will differ in their final tabulations, but the existence of a historically verified group of women poets in Occitania argues for admitting the possibility that some—perhaps many—of these voices were indeed shaped by *trobairitz*. The active role women troubadours played in dialogue with male poets underscores an important aspect of troubadour song in general: the balance of power between the sexes and the relative hierarchy of lovers and ladies furnish topics for endless mediation and debate, whether interpreted by troubadours or *trobairitz*. The disagreements do not always coincide with the division of the sexes, but the tensions generated between male and female rivalries add their spice to the linguistic and erotic fireworks.

A social and literary game, highly polished through the rhetoric of love poetry*, troubadour lyric plays unceasingly across the borders of reality and fiction, the social and the personal: the ''I'' who sings is and is not the real poet, who dons a mask and invents a variety of personae to reveal secrets of the heart for a public of connoisseurs. When women poets compose in this style, the question of what they can and do say has frequently been a polemical one. *Fin'amor* (perfect love) and the *canso* are generally conceived from the point of view of the male lover who seeks to persuade his beautiful (but reluctant) lady that he loves loyally and suffers with a desire refined through the delays of poetry. He deserves mercy for his love service in song, but the lady—who owes him recompense, just as the lord rewards his faithful vassal—necessarily remains silent in the poet lover's own *canso*. The women troubadours who break out of that silence are by no means unanimous in the points of view they express; nor do they restrict themselves to simply putting on the image of the *domna* constructed by the male lover, especially since the underlying situation implied in their lyrics identifies them as lovers, already committed to an *amic* (beloved) who has failed to respond to their trust and loyalty. The Comtessa de Dia* and Castelloza* are particularly outstanding examples of different ways the *trobairitz* can manipulate and individualize the lyric system just as the troubadours do. They invent new combinations for the woman speaker by borrowing, adapting, and reinventing the humble stance of the lyric lover, the pride and worth of the superior lady, and the sensuous longing of the female subject who sings her own and her lover's charms in the tradition of woman's song.

   The *trobairitz* enlarge the troubadour tradition by interjecting women's points of view; their voices both confirm and contest the power plays of *fin'amor*. If earlier generations were sometimes unable to discern and appreciate the difference of the *trobairitz* (often because they expected there to be none), current readers, scholars, and critics have been drawn to and richly rewarded by this small group of women poets and their marginal repertoire. Their songs help nuance and deepen our understanding of medieval society and the places women occupied within it through the art of poetry and exploration of love.

Matilda Tomaryn Bruckner

BIBLIOGRAPHY

Primary Texts

Bruckner, Matilda Tomaryn, Laurie Shepard, and Sarah White, eds. *Songs of the Women Troubadours*. New York: Garland, 1995.

Secondary Texts

Bruckner, Matilda Tomaryn. "Debatable Fictions: The Tensos of the Trobairitz." In *Literary Aspects of Courtly Culture: Selected Papers from the Seventh Triennial Congress of the International Courtly Literature Society*. Ed. Donald Maddox and Sara Sturm-Maddox. Cambridge: D. S. Brewer, 1994. 19–28.

Gradval, Kathryn. "Metaphor, Metonymy, and the Medieval Women Trobairitz." *Romanic Review* 83 (1992): 411–426.

Kay, Sarah. *Subjectivity in Troubadour Poetry*. Cambridge: Cambridge University Press, 1990.

Paden, William D., ed. *The Voice of the Trobairitz*. Philadelphia: University of Pennsylvania Press, 1989.

Shapiro, Marianne. "The Provençal Trobairitz and the Limits of Courtly Love." *Signs* 3, no. 2 (Spring 1978): 560–571.

V

Valois, Marguerite de (popularly known as "La Reine Margot" (1553–]1615). Queen of Navarre and memorialist. Her *Mémoires*, composed in Usson prior to 1600, and perhaps as early as 1594, is the first full-length autobiographical text written by a woman in the French language. It was also the first to apply the Plutarchan model of life-writing to a woman's story. Written in response to Brantôme's biographical portrait of her in *Les Dames illustres*, her memoirs* were hailed at the time of publication in 1628 as the French equivalent of Caesar's *Gallic Commentaries*. Unfortunately, the original manuscript was lost, and the published text breaks off abruptly in the middle of 1582. Frequently republished in the seventeenth century, they inspired another famous woman memorialist, Mademoiselle de Montpensier*.

Valois was the daughter of Henri II and Catherine de Medici*, and the sister of the last Valois kings—François II, Charles IX, and Henri III. In August 1572 she was married to Henri de Navarre, the grandson of her great-aunt, Marguerite de Navarre* who wrote the *Heptaméron*. This alliance between an avowedly Catholic daughter of the royal family and a Protestant leader set off the Saint Bartholomew's Day Massacre. Although the couple were sometimes on amicable terms, they had no children. They separated for political and personal reasons around 1585. Following this, she was consigned to the fortress-castle of Usson, where she was forced to live as a virtual prisoner until she was permitted to return to Paris in 1605. In 1599, after her husband's accession to the throne as Henri IV, she agreed to a divorce* so that he could remarry and produce an heir. During her final years, she became a generous patron of the arts, inviting such renowned literary figures as Gournay*, Malherbe, Racan, Maynard, and Urfé to her grandiose receptions. Although novels*, like Dumas's *La Reine Margot* (1845), as well as a host of popular biographies, have sensationalized Valois's story, Eliane Viennot has reestablished the historical facts of her life and shown that many of the anecdotes attached to her name are fictitious.

In her *Mémoires*, Valois provides an eyewitness picture of court life at the end of the sixteenth century. She also explores the intellectual, political, and spiritual dimensions of her own existence, thus expanding the emerging genre of historical *mémoires* and departing from the conventions of men's *mémoires*, which concentrated on war and politics. She recounts her childhood, her marriage* and its bloody sequel, the court intrigues spawned by rivalry between Catholics and Protestants during the Wars of Religion, her diplomatic mission to Flanders, her sojourn with her husband in Gascony, and the events leading up to their estrangement. As she narrates her experiences, she seeks to interpret the forces that determined her unhappy destiny. In spite of her vulnerability and powerlessness as a royal daughter, she affirms a strong sense of self based on intellectual and spiritual strengths rather than public achievements. Calling attention to her sound judgment, steadfastness of character, and political acumen, she implicitly supports Brantôme's contention that she deserved to succeed her brothers. She maintains a sober style marked by objective analysis and good taste. Although she has been vilified by misogynist gossip as one of the most promiscuous women of all time, she refuses to discuss her love life. Throughout, she portrays herself as a tolerant and supportive wife whose loyalty to her husband never wavered in spite of *his* numerous extramarital affairs.

In addition to her *Mémoires*, Valois wrote the "Mémoire justificatif pour Henri de Bourbon," a treatise exonerating her husband from accusations of treason; a pro-feminist response to François Loryot's misogynist essay "Pourquoy le sexe feminin est fort honoré de l'homme" (*Secrets moraux*, 1614), and a number of letters. "La Ruelle mal assortie," a poetic satire of platonic love, is attributed to her, but Viennot argues persuasively that she is not the author.

Patricia Francis Cholakian

BIBLIOGRAPHY

Primary Texts

Les Mémoires de la roine Marguerite. Paris: Chappellain, 1628.
Mémoires et lettres de Marguerite de Valois. Ed. M. F. Guessard. Paris: Jules Renouard, 1842.
Mémoires et autres écrits de Marguerite de Valois, la reine Margot. Ed. Yves Cazaux. Paris: Mercure de France, 1971.

Secondary Texts

Bauschatz, Cathleen. " 'Plaisir et proffict' in the Reading and Writing of Marguerite de Valois." *Tulsa Studies in Women's Literature* 7, no. 1 (Spring 1988): 27–48.
Cholakian, Patricia Francis. "Marguerite de Valois and the Problematics of Female Self-Representation." In *Renaissance Women Writers: French Texts/American Contexts.* Ed. Anne R. Larsen and Colette H. Winn. Detroit: Wayne State University Press, 1994. 65–81.
Mariéjol, Jean H. *La Vie de Marguerite de Valois, reine de Navarre et de France (1553–1615).* Paris: Hachette, 1928. Geneva: Slatkine Reprints, 1970.
Schrenck, Gilbert. "Brantôme et Marguerite de Valois: D'un genre à l'autre ou les Mé-

moires incertains." In *La Cour au miroir des mémorialistes: 1530–1682.* Ed.
Noémi Hepp. Paris: Klincksieck, 1991. 183–92.
Viennot, Eliane. "Marguerite de Valois et *La Ruelle mal assortie*: Une Attribution er-
ronée." *Nouvelle Revue du seizième siècle* 10 (1992): 81–98.
———. *Marguerite de Valois: Histoire d'une femme, histoire d'un mythe.* Paris: Payot,
1993.

Viardot, Pauline (1821–1910). Pauline Garcia was born to the Spanish tenor
Manuel Garcia and was the sister of the famous contralto Maria Malibran. Her
mother, a singer, was her voice instructor, and Franz Liszt her piano teacher.
She married the journalist Louis Viardot but led an independent life and was
the intimate of writers and composers including George Sand*, Ivan Turgenev,
and Charles Gounod. The protagonist of Sand's *Consuelo* is drawn from her.
Viardot was renowned for her *double voix*; she could sing both soprano and
contralto voices. Her bisexual voice troubled some: the Goncourt brothers dis-
dainfully noted that an autopsy would reveal that she possessed male genitals.
    Viardot sang Desdemona in Gioacchino Rossini's *Otello* in 1839 and went
on to sing the title roles in Gounod's *Sapho* and Hector Berlioz's version of
Christoph Gluck's *Orphée et Eurydice*, as well as Rachel in Fromental Halévy's
La Juive. Giacomo Meyerbeer and Camille Saint-Saëns wrote roles specifically
for her. She performed widely throughout Europe. Admired for her dramatic
talent and intelligence, Viardot was also a teacher and composer; she collaborated with Sand on "La Mare au diable" and with Turgenev on several works,
notably "Le Dernier Sorcier." She wrote both the music and libretto of the
opéra-comique Cendrillon. In 1910 she received the *Légion d'honneur.*
    The Association des Amis d'Ivan Tourguéniev, Pauline Viardot, Maria Mal-
ibran publishes a *Cahiers*. The Department of Music of the Bibliothèque Nationale houses Viardot's musical compositions, transcriptions, and editions.

Marie Lathers

BIBLIOGRAPHY

Secondary Texts

Barry, Nicole. *Pauline Viardot.* Paris: Flammarion, 1990.
Dulong, Gustave. *Pauline Viardot, tragédienne lyrique.* Paris: Association des amis
    d'Ivan Tourguéniev, Pauline Viardot, Maria Malibran, 1987.
Fitzlyon, April. *Price of Genius: A Life of Pauline Viardot.* New York: Appleton-
    Century, 1964.
Marix-Spire, Thérèse, ed. *Lettres inédites de George Sand et de Pauline Viardot (1839–
    1849).* Paris: Nouvelles Editions Latines, 1959.

Vigée-Lebrun, Louise-Elisabeth (1755–1842). Famous and extraordinarily successful, she was patronized by monarchs and aristocrats across Europe. Daughter
of a minor painter, she showed a precocious talent for drawing and had established herself as a professional portrait painter by 1770. Excluded as a woman
from the studio system, she was primarily self-taught and learned her craft from

copying old and modern masters. She married the artist, dealer, and critic Jean-Baptiste Lebrun in 1776, was admitted to the Royal Academy of Painting and Sculpture in 1783, and exhibited regularly during the 1780s. Her literary and musical salon* was one of the most fashionable in pre-revolutionary Paris, famous for her staged Grecian dinner (1788). Vigée-Lebrun painted the leading figures of her day including the entire royal family. She is best remembered for her sensitive portraits, among them *Marie-Antoinette and Her Children* (1787, Versailles) and her *Self-Portrait* (1790, Uffizi).

Calumniated by the press and endangered by her royal connections, Vigée-Lebrun escaped the Revolution*, traveled widely in Italy, Austria, Germany, and Russia, and earned her living by painting portraits. Repatriated after twelve years in exile, she lived in London and settled in France in 1805. Her anecdotal *Souvenirs* (1835), which chronicle her artistic triumphs and brilliant social life, portray her as she wished to be remembered. One of the foremost portrait painters of her era and an international celebrity, Vigée-Lebrun was influential in propagating the Neoclassical style and a more simplified style of dress. Influenced by past art and the French tradition, she endowed her portraits with a refined sensibility and a relaxed sense of intimacy. In her memoirs*, she constructed a multifaceted image of herself as a devoted mother and a dedicated professional artist. Ironically, Vigée-Lebrun's exceptional success in the male-dominated art world and the royal favor she enjoyed have proved a liability. Earlier biographers focused on her social pedigree and seriously underrated her artistic accomplishments. Recent scholarship seeks to redress the equation by reconsidering her exemplary art and life in the context of gender and cultural politics in Revolutionary France.

Heather McPherson

BIBLIOGRAPHY

Primary Text

Souvenirs. Ed. Claudine Herrmann. Paris: Des femmes, 1986.

Secondary Texts

Baillio, Joseph. *Elisabeth Louise Vigée-Lebrun, 1755–1842*. Forth Worth: Kimball Art Museum, 1982.

Blum, André. *Madame Vigée-Lebrun: Peintre des grandes dames au XVIIIe siècle*. Paris: L'Edition d'art, 1919.

Hautecoeur, Louis. *Madame Vigée-Lebrun*. Paris: Librairie Renouard, 1926.

Schaefer, Jean Owens. "The Souvenirs of Elisabeth Vigée-Lebrun: The Self-Imaging of the Artist and the Woman." *International Journal for Women's Studies* 4 (1981): 35–49.

Sheriff, Mary D. *The Exceptional Woman: Elisabeth Vigée-Lebrun and the Cultural Politics of Art*. Chicago: University of Chicago Press, 1996.

———. "Woman? Hermaphrodite? History Painter? On the Self-Imaging of Elisabeth Vigée-Lebrun." *The Eighteenth Century: Theory and Interpretation* 35 (Spring 1994): 3–28.

Villard, Nina de (also known as Nina de Callias) (1843–1884). An influential and colorful bohemian figure, Villard is remembered above all for the salon* she held from 1863 to 1882, called "le plus vivant et le plus intellectual de Paris" (Raynaud). With her mother, Villard provided a flamboyant meeting place for artists, musicians, political figures, and writers. Manet left her image as "La Dame aux éventails" (1873). An acclaimed pianist, she also composed and was among the first to champion the new music of Wagner. She welcomed republicans during the final years of the Second Empire; Villard's relationship with them prompted her temporary exile following the Paris Commune*. Literary habitués of her salon included Coppée, Cros, France, Mallarmé, Mendès, Nouveau, Verlaine, and Villiers de L'Isle-Adam.

One of the few women included in the *Parnasse contemporain*, Villard also collaborated with poets ("la bande à Nina") who frequented her salon during the heyday of the Parnassian poets* and the dawning of Symbolism (*see* Symbolist poetry). Her only collection of poems, *Feuillets parisiens*, was published posthumously. Much of what is known about Villard must be gleaned from the memoirs*, fiction, poetry*, and biographies of the male figures who surrounded her. She is consequently figured, in most cases, as an eccentric *salonnière* rather than a writer in her own right. A new edition of *Feuillets parisiens* would be necessary for an appreciation of Villard as a writing subject.

How, then, to gauge her contributions to any sort of literary tradition, be it normative, feminist, or avant-garde? We might begin by giving her brilliant and eccentric personality its due and noting that her salon was rarely known to open its doors to other women artists, musicians, and writers. We must also recognize Villard's importance to both Parnassianism and the pre-Symbolist *zutistes*, as one of the few women to integrate, to influence, and, finally, to satirize these poetic circles in her poetry and collaborations.

Gretchen Schultz

BIBLIOGRAPHY

Primary Texts

"Deux Sonnets." *Le Parnasse contemporain* 2 (1869/1871).
Dixains réalistes, par plusieurs auteurs. Paris: Librairie de l'eau-forte, 1876.
La Duchesse Diane, saynette en vers. Paris: Michaud, 1882.
Feuillets parisiens, poésies. Paris: Messager, 1885.

Secondary Texts

Bersaucourt, Albert de. *Au temps des Parnassiens: Nina de Villard et ses amis*. Paris: La Renaissance du livre, 1922.
Dufay, Pierre. "Chez Nina de Villard." *Mercure de France*, June 1, 1927, 324–352.
Harismendy-Lony, Sandrine. "De Nina de Villard au Cercle Zutique: Violence et représentation." Dissertation, University of California, Santa Barbara, 1995.
Raynaud, Ernest. "La Jeunesse de Nina." *Cahiers de la quinzaine* 19, no. 15 (1930): 71–141. Issue entitled *La Bohème sous le second Empire: Charles Cros et Nina*.
Zayed, Georges. "Un salon parnassien d'avant-garde: Nina de Villard et ses hôtes."

Aquila 2 (1973): 177–229 (Chestnut Hill Studies in Modern Languages and Literatures).

Villedieu, Marie-Catherine Desjardins (later known as Madame de) (1640?– 1683). One of the first women in France to live by her pen, she was a prolific writer of prose fiction, poetry*, and plays. So well known in her own time that spurious works were published under her name to assure their good sales, and popular in England thanks to contemporary translations, Villedieu made significant contributions to the evolution of the French novel*. Villedieu's life situation was quite unusual and bears a strong relationship to her writing practice. Freed early from the normal family restrictions placed on young women, she lived on her own recognizance. On the death of her lover, Antoine de Boësset, sieur de Villedieu, who had betrayed his promise to marry her, Mademoiselle Desjardins took his name and from then on signed her works Madame de Villedieu. She spent much of her writing career among rich and powerful members of the high aristocracy who were her protectors, although she herself came from only the most minor nobility and an impoverished family. Paid by the page by the fashionable publisher Claude Barbin, Villedieu was socially and economically on her own in a time when women were, with rare exceptions, under male legal domination from birth to death. Her public literary career, which spanned the period from 1659 to 1675, ended with her marriage* to a minor noble, although other works appeared during her marriage and after her death. During the eighteenth and nineteenth centuries Villedieu, like a number of other women writers of the late seventeenth century, underwent a process that Joan DeJean has aptly named decanonization. The last collected edition of her work was published in 1741. No new editions appeared until the 1970s.

Living by her pen, Villedieu practiced many genres, and adapted to each. Her work is thus beset with contradictions, and it is deceptive to assume that a full picture of her views or techniques can be derived from any single work. Central themes include mask and disguise—often a necessity for female characters whose gender places them in jeopardy—and the rewriting of history, inflecting it away from the grand gestures of great men and toward human interactions. All of her texts touch on the issues raised by marginality and ask subtle questions about gender roles. Among Villedieu's most striking texts are the para-autobiographical *Mémoires de la vie de Henriette-Sylvie de Molière*; the novella *Le Portefeuille*, which anticipates eighteenth-century portrayals of society; and the three tales collected in *Les Désordres de l'amour*, reflecting the more pessimistic stance on love and life of many of Villedieu's later works.

Donna Kuizenga

BIBLIOGRAPHY

Primary Texts

Oeuvres complètes. 12 vols. Geneva: Slatkine, 1971. [Reprint of Paris edition of 1720. Contains most but not all of her works, and includes a number of spurious ones.]

Lettres et billets galants. Ed. Micheline Cuénin. N.p.: Société d'étude du XVIIe siècle, 1975.

Les Mémoires de la vie de Henriette-Sylvie de Molière. Ed. Micheline Cuénin. Tours: Editions de l'Université François Rabelais, 1977.

Secondary Texts

Beasley, Faith E. *Revising Memory: Women's Fiction and Memoirs in Seventeenth-Century France.* New Brunswick, NJ: Rutgers University Press, 1990.

Cuénin, Micheline. *Roman et société sous Louis XIV: Madame de Villedieu (Marie-Catherine Desjardins 1640–1683).* 2 vols. Paris: Honoré Champion, 1979.

Démoris, René. *Le Roman à la première personne.* Paris: A. Colin, 1975.

Flannigan, Arthur. *Madame de Villedieu's "Les Désordres de l'Amour": History, Literature and the Nouvelle Historique.* Washington, DC: University Press of America, 1982.

Hipp, Marie-Thérèse. *Mythes et réalités, enquête sur le roman et les mémoires, 1660–1700.* Paris: Klincksieck, 1976.

Jensen, Katharine Ann. *Writing Love: Letters, Women, and the Novel in France, 1605–1776.* Carbondale: Southern Illinois University Press, 1995.

Kuizenga, Donna. '' 'La Lecture d'une si ennuyeuse histoire' '': Topoï de la lecture et du livre dans les *Mémoires de la vie de Henriette-Sylvie de Molière.*'' In *L'Epreuve du lecteur. Livres et lectures dans le roman d'Ancien Régime.* Ed. Jan Herman and Paul Pelckmans. Louvain-Paris: Editions Peeters, 1995. 120–128.

Margitic, Milorad, and Byron R. Wells, eds. *Actes de Wake Forest.* Paris: Biblio 17, 1987.

Miller, Nancy K. ''Tender Economies: Mme de Villedieu and the Costs of Indifference.'' *Esprit Créateur* 23, no. 2 (1983): 80–93.

Schwartz, Debora B. ''Writing Her Own Life: Villedieu, Henriette-Sylvie de Molière and Feminine Empowerment.'' In *Women in French Literature.* Ed. Michel Guggenheim. Saratoga, CA: Anma Libri, 1988. 77–90.

Villeneuve, Gabrielle Suzanne Barbot de Gallon de (1695–1755). Her life continues to be eclipsed by her celebrated fairy tale*, *Belle et la bête*, which has taken on a life of its own, spawning literary revisions, staged and televised productions, picture books, novels*, and poetry*. Born into the aristocracy, Villeneuve was married to Monsieur de Gallon, seigneur de Villeneuve. Writing under the pseudonym Madame D. V., she penned at least two collections of short stories*, *Le Beau-Frère supposé* and *La Jeune Amériquaine et les contes marins*, within which *Belle et la bête* first appeared. Following the patterns of the genre set forth by the classical fable* *Cupid and Psyche*, the heroine of *Belle et la bête* is an archetypal character, representing inner goodness, manifested outwardly by her perfect beauty, love, sense of duty, and virtue. Yet, Villeneuve's female muse breaks with the binding ties of tradition. Unlike the classical Psyche, who suffers because men shun her, Beauty refuses repeated propositions by male suitors, even the Beast's, until the story's denouement. It is the Beast who lies pining away while Beauty resolves her inner conflicts over duty to her father and trueness to herself and her desires. Indeed, it is Beauty who saves the Beast. Finally, Psyche is unschooled, while Beauty is well read. Although Villeneuve's tale ends in typical marital bliss, she seems to have been very conscious of her young female readers, cleverly revealing that the subservient female condition is transcendable.

T. Denean Sharpley-Whiting

BIBLIOGRAPHY

Primary Texts

La Jeune Amériquaine et les contes marins. Paris: N.p., 1740.
Le Beau-Frère supposé. Paris: N.p., 1752.
Belle et la bête. Paris: Grasset, 1984.

Secondary Texts

Apuleius. *The Most Pleasant and Delectable Tale of the Marriage of Cupid and Psyche, Done in English by William Adlington.* London: David Nutt, 1887.
Le Prince de Beaumont, Madame. *Le Magasin des enfants ou dialogues entre une sage gouvernante et plusieurs de ses élèves de la première distinction.* London: J. Haberkorn, 1756.
Perrault, Charles, and Madame d'Aulnoy. *Cabinet des fées ou collection des fées et autres contes merveilleux ornés de figures.* Paris: Rue et Hôtel Serpente, 1786.
Quiller-Couch, Arthur Thomas. *Sleeping Beauty and Other Fairy Tales from Old French.* New York: Hodder and Stoughton, 1910.

Vivien, Renée (1877–1909). Pen name of the Anglo-American poet Pauline Mary Tarn, whose translations of Sappho and Sappho-inspired poetry* helped revive interest in the Greek poet. Vivien is considered one of the most talented of the generation of women poets who emerged in Paris at the turn of the century. Called ''Sappho 1900'' by one critic, her work is frequently discussed in relation to the sapphic tradition, and to ''Paris-Lesbos,'' the woman-centered community of writers and artists living in Paris during the early twentieth century. Drawing from the rich imagery of Symbolist poetry* and the Pre-Raphaelites, as well as more traditional love lyrics, Vivien's finely crafted poems typically rely on conventional forms and alexandrine meter. It is the lesbian content of her work, however, which initially shocked early twentieth-century readers, that has in recent years attracted the attention of the gay press and the feminist press* in both the United States and France, resulting in several reprints and English translations of Vivien's work.

The daughter of an American mother and a wealthy British merchant, Vivien was primarily educated in French boarding schools. She wrote poetry from the age of ten, adopting French as her literary language of choice, and by age fifteen she declared her vocation to be a poet. Her father's death left her under the control of her unsympathetic mother, who eventually attempted to take over her daughter's inheritance by having her declared insane. The courts intervened, and when Vivien reached her majority she became financially independent and returned to Paris, where she became part of the ''Paris-Lesbos'' circle centered around Natalie Clifford Barney*. Publishing her first two volumes under the names "R. Vivien" and "René Vivien," she first used her pen name to hide her gender and her sexual orientation. Eventually, however, she signed her work "Renée Vivien": re-née means reborn, and Vivien was the powerful enchantress who so fascinated the Pre-Raphaelites.

The direction Vivien's poetry would take was largely determined by her fateful meeting with the beautiful American heiress Natalie Clifford Barney in 1899. Barney not only became her first lover, but also introduced Vivien to the poetry of the ancient Greek poet Sappho, who would become Vivien's principal muse. Early in their relationship, the two women studied French prosody together under the direction of the classicist Charles-Brun, who quickly recognized Vivien's superior talent and became her lifelong friend, Greek instructor, and literary assistant. She learned ancient Greek so she could translate Sappho's poems into modern French, and, along with Barney, eventually visited the island of Lesbos, where they hoped to establish a woman-centered artistic community. Although their mutual dream was never realized, Barney transferred much of her early idealism to the salon* she hosted in Paris and to her lesbian lifestyle, while Vivien's sapphism seemed more rooted in her writing than in her life. Vivien's relationship with Barney inspired numerous poems and an autobiographical novel*, Une Femme m'apparut . . . (1904), where the unfaithful Barney appears as a femme fatale. Barney was replaced by the wealthy Baroness Hélène de Zuylen de Nyevelt, under whose influence Vivien was exceedingly productive.

During her short but prolific career, Renée Vivien produced more than a dozen volumes of poetry, several collections of short stories*, and prose poems, an autobiographical novel, and a biography of Anne Boleyn, as well as a volume of translations of Sappho and the other known Greek women poets. Vivien's translations of Sappho, published anonymously in 1903, include literal translations along with poetic interpretations built around sapphic fragments, a technique she also uses in many of her own original poems. In these works Vivien is intent on reclaiming Sappho as a lesbian by retelling the story of her loves and death with an emphasis on the Greek poet's love for women, a far cry from the heterosexual Sappho promoted by centuries of classical scholars. Her poems and short stories also feature feminist revisions of many myths* and legends about strong and rebellious women, such as Lilith and Cleopatra, whom she recasts as heroines.

The affirmative, "sapphic" phase of her career was not to last, however. Suspicious of her readers and sensitive to harsh critical judgments, Vivien gradually retreated from the public and withdrew most of her work from circulation, preferring instead to direct her efforts toward future generations of women readers. Her later poems, devoid of references to Sappho, became increasingly dark, and are characterized by a longing for death and feelings of rejection and paranoia. These themes are reflected in Colette's* portrait of the poet included in

Ces Plaisirs . . . (1932), which focuses on Vivien's decadent lifestyle and self-destructive behavior. Indeed, Vivien's early death, at age thirty-two, was hastened by alcoholism and anorexia.

Colette's disturbing portrait is among those that have contributed to the myths surrounding the mysterious Renée Vivien, some of them perpetuated by the poet herself, others by male admirers of her work who tried to cover up her sexual orientation and who played up her disputed deathbed conversion to Catholicism. One of these, Salomon Reinach, went so far as to collect her personal documents, and allegedly had them sealed in the Bibliothèque Nationale until the year 2000 in order to protect her reputation. While Renée Vivien remains mysterious, it seems clear that the increasing availability of her rich and complex poetry will continue to inspire a renaissance of interest among the "women of the future" for whom she wrote.

Tama Lea Engelking

BIBLIOGRAPHY

Primary Text

Oeuvre poétique complète de Renée Vivien (1877–1909). Ed. Jean-Paul Goujon. Paris: Régine Deforges, 1986. Contains *Etudes et préludes* (1901).

Secondary Texts

Benstock, Shari. *Women of the Left Bank: Paris, 1900–1930.* Austin: University of Texas Press, 1986.
Colette. *Ces Plaisirs.* Paris: Ferenczi et fils, 1932.
Engelking, Tama Lea. "Renée Vivien's Sapphic Legacy: Remembering the 'House of Muses.' " *Atlantis: A Women's Studies Journal* 18, nos. 1 & 2 (Fall-Summer, 1992–1993): 125–141.
Goujon, Jean-Paul. *Tes Blessures sont plus douces que leurs caresses: Vie de Renée Vivien.* Paris: Régine Deforges, 1986.
Jay, Karla. *The Amazon and the Page: Natalie Clifford Barney and Renée Vivien.* Bloomington: Indiana University Press, 1988.

Voilquin, Suzanne (1801–1877). Born in Paris to working-class parents, Suzanne Voilquin joined the Saint-Simonians in 1830. While Voilquin did not always agree with the Saint-Simonian doctrine, it did foster her interest in women's issues. She participated in the journal *La Femme libre* (finally to become the *Tribune des femmes*), which she later helped edit. *La Femme libre,* written for and by women, focused on social reform, particularly with regard to women's and working-class concerns. Voilquin led a difficult but remarkable life. She traveled—generally alone—through France and to Egypt (1834–1836); she worked in Russia (1839–1846) and lived in Louisiana (1848–1859). Throughout her life, Voilquin remained firm in her Saint-Simonian beliefs and devoted to the cause of women's emancipation.

In addition to many journal articles, Voilquin wrote two autobiographical works, *Souvenirs d'une fille du peuple, ou la Saint-Simonienne en Egypte* (1866) and *Mémoires d'une Saint-Simonienne en Russie* (published posthumously). Her writings are valuable historical documents, offering a frank account of a working-class woman's experience, a valuable (although often Orientalist) perspective on women of other cultures, and an insider's view of the Saint-Simonian family. Often unjustly dismissed as conventional, Voilquin's writing is of interest to the literary theorist in that it raises the question of woman both as autobiographical and historical subject. Her writings reflect the difficulty of representing a woman's experience in a "female" way of writing, and of writing from the margins. Although Voilquin's memoirs* may seem traditional in style, her attempts to create female solidarity and to rework the autobiographical pact are certainly unconventional.

Annie Smart

BIBLIOGRAPHY

Primary Texts

Mémoires d'une Saint-Simonienne en Russie. Paris: Editions des femmes, 1977.
Souvenirs d'une fille du peuple, ou la Saint-Simonienne en Egypte. Intro. Lydia Elhadad. Paris: Maspéro, 1978.

Secondary Texts

Bulciolu, Maria Teresa. *L'Ecole Saint-Simonienne et la femme.* Pisa: Goliardica, 1980.
Moses, Claire Goldberg. *French Feminism in the Nineteenth Century.* Albany: State University of New York Press, 1984.
Moses, Claire Goldberg, and Leslie Wahl Rabine. *Feminism, Socialism, and French Romanticism.* Bloomington: Indiana University Press, 1993.

Volude, Béatrix-Stéphanie de Fuchsamberg d'Amblimont de Lage de (1764–1842). Born into a noble naval family, she was chosen by the princesse de Lamballe as her companion in 1779 and adopted her ideas of virtue, piety, and charity. In 1782 she married Lage de Volude and had three daughters. On the surface, her life appeared to be devoted to the Ancien Régime's "douceur de vivre" among a group of young women attached to Marie-Antoinette* which included Mme Elisabeth (Louis XVI's sister) and the princesse de Lamballe. Simultaneously, she was developing her mind and judgment with books, such as Fénelon's *Education des filles* and Rousseau's *Emile*. Her deep attachment to the royal family and her hatred of enemies of the monarchy forced her to go into exile during the French Revolution*, although she continued, at great personal risk, to spend long periods of time in France. Once she was officially declared an *émigrée*, the account of her life (in her memoirs*) reads like an adventure novel*. The executions of the king, of Mme de Lamballe, then of the queen underlined the precariousness of her existence. Unable to accept Napoleon's popularity, and oppressed by personal tragedy, she spent much of her life in exile, traveling in Spain, England, Scotland, Switzerland, and Germany, until the restoration of the monarchy. Few women endured with such courage one of the most tumultuous and tragic periods of French history; her writing offers a unique glimpse into it.

Rosena Davison

BIBLIOGRAPHY

Primary Text

Souvenirs d'émigration de Madame la marquise de Lage de Volude 1792–1794. Lettres à Madame la Comtesse de Montijo, publiées par M. le baron de la Morinerie. Evreux: A. Herissey, 1869.

Secondary Texts

Chuquet, Arthur. "La Marquise de Lage." In *Episodes et portraits*. 3 vols. Paris: Plont-Nourrit, 1909. 1: 210–232.

Mézières, Alfred. "La Marquise de Lage de Volude." In *Pages d'automne*. Paris: Hachette, 1911.

W

Weil, Simone (1909–1943). Political and spiritual philosopher and writer of prewar and wartime France, Weil explored issues of science, language, and theology. One of the few recognized women scholars of her generation, she completed a thesis on perception in Descartes. In this rewriting of the *Méditations*, Weil produced one of the first documents on modern existentialism*. A teacher of philosophy, Weil also vigorously pursued a life of intense political and social commitment.

Weil published many prewar studies of German society and politics, as well as comparative commentaries on French and German history. During a year of labor and research as a production-line worker in the Renault and Alsthom factories, Weil wrote *La Condition ouvrière* (1951), one of the most important studies of women's working conditions in French factories. Her daily journal entries documented the inequities between women's and men's wages, and the accidents and physical suffering of women forced to labor in dangerously unprotected sweatshops. Active in the labor union movement, Weil helped industrial leaders and factory owners reform the factory environment.

In 1937 Weil served in Spain as an independent volunteer for the Republican struggle against Franco. When Hitler invaded France, the Weil family fled first to Marseilles, then to America. Weil returned to Europe and worked for De Gaulle's Free French organization in London; during this time, she completed a commissioned study on the reasons for France's fall in 1940—a provocative work that was published posthumously by Camus as *Enracinement* (1949). Having limited herself to the ration of food and drink allowed her French compatriots living under German occupation, Weil died in 1943 from pulmonary pneumonia. Through her activism and writings, Weil helped to enlighten society as to the inequities and cruelty imposed on workers—women in particular— and inspired in ensuing generations a more humane ethos and a renewal of spirituality, based on the reintegration of individual understanding and public action.

Betty L. McLane-Iles

BIBLIOGRAPHY

Primary Texts

Enracinement. Paris: Gallimard, 1949.
Attente de Dieu. Paris: La Colombe, 1950.
La Condition ouvrière. Paris: Gallimard, 1951.
Oppression et liberté. Paris: Gallimard, 1955.
Ecrits historiques et politiques. Paris: Gallimard, 1960.
Sur la science. Paris: Gallimard, 1966.

Secondary Texts

Cliff, Michelle. "Sister-Outsider—Some Thoughts on Simone Weil." In *Between Women*. Ed. Carol Ascher, Louise Salvo, and Sara Ruddick. Boston: Beacon Press, 1994.
Maroger, Nicole. "Simone Weil: Images de la condition féminine." *Cahiers Simone Weil* 13, no. 4 (December 1990): 355–373.
McLane-Iles, Betty L. *Uprooting and Integration in the Writings of Simone Weil*. New York: Peter Lang, 1987.
Panichas, George A., ed. *The Simone Weil Reader*. New York: David McKay, 1977.
Pétrement, Simone. *La Vie de Simone Weil I et II*. Paris: Fayard, 1973.
White, George Abbott, ed. *Simone Weil: Interpretations of a Life*. Amherst: University of Massachusetts Press, 1981.

Wittig, Monique (1935–). Little biographical information is available on Wittig, yet she remains one of the most recognized French women writers alive today, largely because of the international influence of her four novels*, her lesbian lexicon, and a handful of theoretical articles. Wittig's first book, *L'Opoponax* (1964), won her critical acclaim and the Médicis Prize. The narrative perspective is that of a schoolgirl who develops from an undifferentiated member of her peer group, referred to by the pronoun *on*, into an individual "I" empowered by love for another girl. Wittig pursues her interest in the impact of language on life in her most influential novel, *Les Guérillères* (1969). This experimental epic, punctuated by symbolic circles and women's names*, describes an Amazon* society, which is designated as *elles*; this universal *elles* deposes the patriarchy by dismantling its linguistic codes, its essentialist myths*, and its army. Wittig's utopian vision prefigures later feminist debates. *Le Corps lesbien* (1973), Wittig's most radical exploration of lesbian desire, introduces the pronoun *J/e*, which marks both the vexed place of lesbian subjects in language and the threat they represent for heterosexuality. Less formally experimental but still powerfully subversive is Wittig's parodic rewriting of Dante, *Virgile, non* (1985), in which Wittig the character searches for a language appropriate to a lesbian paradise free from the physical and psychological tortures inflicted on women in patriarchal society. A prominent activist within the Mouvement de Libération des Femmes* (MLF), Wittig demonstrated at the Arc de Triomphe in 1970, and founded the group Féministes révolutionnaires. In collaboration with Sande Zeig, she produced *Brouillon pour un dictionnaire des amantes* (1976) and the play *Le Voyage sans fin*. She has contributed theoretical essays to *Questions féministes*, under Simone de Beauvoir's* editorship, and to *Feminist Issues*. Wittig now lives and teaches in the United States.

Miléna Santoro

BIBLIOGRAPHY

Primary Texts

L'Opoponax. Paris: Minuit, 1964.
Les Guérillères. Paris: Minuit, 1969.
Le Corps lesbien. Paris: Minuit, 1973.
Virgile, non. Paris: Minuit, 1985.
Le Voyage sans fin. Paris: Vlasta, 1985.
The Straight Mind and Other Essays. Boston: Beacon Press, 1992.
Wittig, Monique, and Sande Zeig. *Brouillon pour un dictionnaire des amantes*. Paris: Grasset, 1976.

Secondary Texts

Crowder, Diane Griffin. "Amazons or Mothers? Monique Wittig, Hélène Cixous and Theories of Women's Writing." *Contemporary Literature* 24, no. 2 (1983): 117–144.
Fuss, Diana. "Monique Wittig's Anti-essentialist Materialism." In *Essentially Speaking: Feminism, Nature and Difference*. New York: Routledge, 1989. 39–53.
Lindsay, Cecile. "Body/Language: French Feminist Utopias." *French Review* 60, no. 1 (1986): 46–55.
Wenzel, Hélène Vivienne. "The Text as Body/Politics: An Appreciation of Monique Wittig's Writings in Context." *Feminist Studies* 7, no. 2 (1981): 264–287.

Women in French. WIF is an organization that promotes "research on women writing in French, on women in literature and culture of French expression, and other domains of feminist literary criticism" (bylaws). Founded in 1977 as a division of the Women's Caucus of the Modern Languages (WCML), WIF is now an independent allied organization of the Modern Language Association (MLA). The organization publishes a journal, *WIF Studies*, once a year as well as a biannual newsletter that includes bibliographies on Francophone women writers, conference news, and information on journals and recent publications. It also sponsors book projects and student prizes, organizes sessions for the MLA Convention (including regional conferences), and maintains a mentoring network for junior scholars. Further, WIF is committed to sharing information and concerns about the status of women in higher education in the United States. The *MLA Directory* gives information regarding current officers.

Claire Marrone

Women's organizations. Dozens of groups and associations provide assistance to women. The following list gives information on some of the best-known organizations:

Association européenne contre les violences faites aux femmes au travail (established 1985) provides legal and moral support to victims of discrimination and sexual harassment. It publishes a newsletter and a journal.

Association Parité-Infos, founded to achieve political parity between women and men, publishes a newsletter.

Choisir (established 1971), initially founded to promote sexual education, contraception, and abortion* rights, is also active in the "Parité" movement, and has published extensively on these issues.

Collectif féministe contre le viol offers a hotline for rape* victims (male and female), provides medical and legal advice, and organizes workshops to sensitize school and security personnel to the plight of victims.

Condition masculine-Soutien de l'enfance (established 1975) and its affiliates, Ligue du Droit des Pères and SOS Divorce, monitor new legislation to ensure fairness toward men, especially in matters of divorce and custody. These organizations publish newsletters and fight against reverse discrimination and sexist images of men in the media.

Fédération nationale solidarité femmes brings together dozens of associations providing shelter for victims of domestic violence.

Planning familial (established 1956) is the umbrella organization for associations and centers distributing information on birth control* and abortion. Recently, it has had to counter the growing influence of militant anti-abortion groups such as Laissez-les vivre, La Trève de Dieu, SOS Tout-Petits, Mère de miséricorde, and Avenir de la culture, and has faced increasing violence from "commandos anti-IVG" (Interruption volontaire de grossesse), whose tactics are inspired by the anti-abortion movement in the United States, and whose funding is supplied by the Front National and foreign sources.

Union féminine civique et sociale (established 1925) provides information on a multitude of issues, including consumer protection, education, discrimination, politics, prostitution*, bioethics, and the environment.

Information on these organizations and their publications may be obtained from the following sources:

Association européenne contre les violences faites aux femmes au travail. Founder and President Marie-Victoire Louis. 71, rue St Jacques, 75005 Paris. Tel. 43.29.86.52. Fax 45.83.43.93.

Association Parité-Infos. Founders and Presidents Françoise Gaspard and Claude-Servan-Schreiber. 14 bis, rue Jean Ferrandi, 75006 Paris. Tel. and fax 42.22.58.05.

Choisir. Founder and President Gisèle Halimi*. 102, rue St Dominique, 75007 Paris. Tel. 42.77.44.21. Fax 45.51.56.10.

Collectif féministe contre le viol (previously SOS Femmes Alternative). 96, boulevard Masséna, 75013 Paris. Tel. 45.82.73.00.

Condition masculine-Soutien de l'enfance. Founder and President Antoine Leenhardt. 221, Faubourg St Honoré, 75008 Paris. Tel. 45.63.93.88. Fax 42.56.00.73.

Fédération nationale Solidarité femmes. President Viviane Monnier. 102, quai de la Rapée. 75012 Paris. Tel. 40.02.03.23. Fax 40.02.02.88.

Planning familial. Founders Evelyne Sullerot and Marie-Andrée Lagroua-Weil Hallé; Director Colette Gallard. 4 square Ste Irénée, 75011 Paris. Tel. 48.07.29.10. Fax 47.00.79.77.

Union féminine civique et sociale. President Sylvie Ulrich. 6, rue Béranger, 75003. Tel. 44.54.50.54. Fax 44.54.50.66.

Additional resources and information may be obtained from:

Catherine Lesterpt. Service des Droits des femmes. 31, rue Le Peletier, 75009 Paris. Tel. 47.7.41.58. Fax 42.46.99.69.

Monique Dental. President, Réseau Femmes Ruptures. 38, rue Polonceau, 75018 Paris. Tel. 42.23.78.15. Fax 42.23.60.47.

Samia I. Spencer

World War I. Anthologies of French World War I literature have created an androcentric canon (revering Henri Barbusse, Roland Dorgelès, et al.) and have ensured that women writers appear noticeably silent in the face of the unprecedented carnage. Although questions of sexual politics are confronted in the barriers (both emotional and geographical) which existed between the sexes, women are regarded as the objects of male creativity rather than as the producers of textual meaning. With a few notable exceptions (e.g., Paul Géraldy's *La Guerre, Madame*), the focus is firmly fixed upon the soldier's experience, reducing female characters to a lowly status by virtue of their noncombatant role.

Jean Vic's comprehensive *La Littérature de guerre*, published in 1923, catalogues women's writings which subsequently disappeared from the indexes as the result of postwar value judgments. Women's wartime literary responses were varied in genre and ideology, from Marcelle Tinayre's* *La Veillée des armes*, a novel* that offers an ultimately nationalistic reaction amid the fervor of mobilization, to Marcelle Capy's *Une Voix de femme dans la mêlée*, a publication whose pacifist sentiments were stifled by censorship. Lucie Delarue-Mardrus's* *Un Roman civil en 1914* combines a story of wartime service in the Red Cross with issues of gender conflict; Jeanne Landre* ventures to the fighting front with tales of soldiers and their sexually liberated *marraines de guerre*; Camille Mayran allows her eponymous heroine to be executed in the *Histoire de Gotton Connixloo* (for which she was awarded the Prix du roman in 1918); and the patriotic tone of Colette's* journalistic anecdotes in *Les Heures longues 1914–*

1917 contrasts with Rachilde's* ironic outpourings in *Dans le puits ou la vie inférieure 1915–1917.*

Feminist historians continue to assess the importance of 1914–1918 as a watershed in the history of women's liberation, underlining the fact that women's war work crossed the traditional margins of gender division but did not lead to the envisaged goal of suffrage. Women's written responses reflect this time of upheaval, as pro-war propaganda promoted binary oppositions, while men's immobilization in the trenches contrasted with a degree of female autonomy on the home front. The predominant themes are acquiescence rather than emancipation, and an attempt to express sacrifice and loss within a patriarchal vocabulary, in a body of literature that belies the common assumption that French women had nothing to say about a war that destroyed a generation of men.

Catherine O'Brien

BIBLIOGRAPHY

Primary Texts

Capy, Marcelle. *Une Voix de femme dans la mêlée.* Paris: Ollendorf, 1916.
Colette. *Les Heures longues 1914–1917.* Paris: Arthème Fayard, 1917.
Delarue-Mardrus, Lucie. *Un Roman civil en 1914.* Paris: Bibliothèque-Charpentier, 1916.
Géraldy, Paul. *La Guerre, Madame.* Paris: G. Crès, 1916.
Landre, Jeanne. *. . . puis il mourut.* Paris: La Renaissance du livre, 1916.
Mayran, Camille. *Histoire de Gotton Connixloo suivie de L'Oubliée.* Paris: Librairie Plon, 1918.
Rachilde. *Dans le puits ou la vie inférieure 1915–1917.* Paris: Mercure de France, 1918.
Tinayre, Marcelle. *La Veillée des armes.* Paris: Calmann-Lévy, 1915.

Secondary Texts

Bard, Christine. *Les Filles de Marianne: Histoire des féminismes 1914–1940.* Paris: Fayard, 1995.
Cruickshank, John. *Variations on Catastrophe.* Oxford: Clarendon Press, 1982.
Thébaud, Françoise. *La Femme au temps de la guerre de 14.* Paris: Editions Stock, 1986.
Vic, Jean. *La Littérature de guerre.* 5 vols. Paris: Les Presses françaises, 1923.

World War II: Collaboration. Collaborators, like resisters, were a minority of the French population during the Occupation years of 1940–1944—but a dangerous minority. What constituted collaboration during this period is not easily defined. The 1939 French Penal Code addressed serious crimes of collaboration with the enemy—that is, treason—but did not envision the context of the Occupation and the range of offenses that took place in varying circumstances. The term "collaboration" was used to designate a choice or constraint, a means of social promotion, or an ideological commitment: in most cases, it was a state of mind. While Marshal Pétain invited the French to collaborate with the enemy, most of the population restricted their activities to support for his government. Black-market trading was pervasive in France, in most instances because of acute food shortages. The Vichy regime provided Hitler with administrators and civil servants to carry out his directives. In general, there were more collaborators among the upper bourgeoisie, the industrial right, and high-level administrators than among the rank and file. A recent study (Burrin) holds that women collaborators were few in number—they included wives, companions, and daughters of militants and of members of the notorious Militia (the French equivalent of the SS). Assessment of collaboration in wartime France is hindered by access to archives; some are still closed. Documentation on women collaborators appears in the transcripts of postwar trials. At the Liberation in 1944, head shaving became a widespread punishment for women thought to have collaborated. Virtually all women so treated were of modest background; few upper-class women—such as *couturière* Coco Chanel or well-known actresses— were persecuted. The intensity of the vengeance unleashed against these women is striking; major industrialists and businessmen got off lightly. Viewed as symbols of the nation, women were seen as having defiled France by having physical relations with the enemy. *See also* World War II: Resistance.

Margaret Collins Weitz

BIBLIOGRAPHY

Primary Text

Duras, Marguerite. *Hiroshima mon amour*. Paris: Gallimard, 1960.

Secondary Texts

Brossat, Alain. *Les Tondues: Un Carnaval moche*. Paris: Manya, 1992.
Burrin, Philippe. *La France à l'heure allemande*. Paris: Seuil, 1995.
Gordon, Bertram. *Collaborationism in France during the Second World War*. Ithaca: Cornell University Press, 1980.
Hirschfeld, Gerhardt, and Patrick Marsh, eds. *Collaboration in France: Politics and Culture during the Nazi Era, 1940–1944*. New York: St. Martin's, 1989.
Kedward, H. Roderick. *Occupied France: Collaboration and Resistance, 1940–1944*. London: Blackwell, 1985.
Novick, Peter. *The Resistance versus Vichy: The Purge of Collaborators in Liberated France*. New York: Columbia University Press, 1968.
Weitz, Margaret Collins. *Sisters in the Resistance: How Women Fought to Free France*. New York: Wiley, 1995.

Film

Hiroshima mon amour. Dir. Alain Resnais. Argos Films, 1960.

World War II: Resistance. Women were an important presence in virtually every aspect of France's war-within-a-war, the Resistance. However, their important contribution has been largely overlooked. Part of this absence from the historical accounts that detail France's efforts to combat the German occupiers and the collaborationist Vichy regime may be attributed to women's reticence. They did not seek official recognition after the war as did their male counterparts. They did not see themselves as "veterans"; they only did "what had to be done." Another factor in women resisters' marginalization has been the tendency of historians to focus on military campaigns and projects such as the *maquis*, even though these clandestine paramilitary fighting groups did not really develop until the last years of the war. Furthermore, the *maquis* could never have existed without the many women and girls who supplied them—at great risk. What women did in the French Resistance was largely an extension of their everyday activities, and was for this reason marginalized. Clandestine secretaries typed, edited, and distributed underground tracts and papers, and coded and decoded secret documents. Doing "errands," liaison agents and couriers—largely young women—delivered messages, material, and, in some cases, weapons. Women of all ages offered hospitality to "guests" pursued by the Nazis or their Vichy colleagues: political refugees, Allied airmen, Jews, and underground agents.

All these activities undertaken for the Resistance were fraught with peril for the women and their families. Many women were imprisoned; some were tortured, deported—even executed. The Resistance experience helped many of these women attain a fuller awareness of their own potential and gave them the opportunity to use unsuspected skills. After the war, some used the wartime experience as a platform for politics: not in the traditional political arena, but in organizations dealing with social issues. Nevertheless, most resumed their prewar roles in spite of the exceptional freedom the war years afforded. Clandestine wars require secrecy; thus the exact number of women resisters will never be known. At best, those involved in the Resistance represented only a very small part of the population. However, their contribution was arguably as important as that of their male counterparts. Indeed, de Gaulle claimed that French women had earned the right to vote* (first exercised in 1945) because of their participation in the Resistance—an affirmation that ignores the long history of women's efforts to become enfranchised. Women writers who served in the Resistance have drawn upon their experience in their memoirs* and fiction. Among the most prominent are Marguerite Duras*, Clara Malraux*, Edith Thomas*, Marie-Madeleine Fourcade, and Elsa Triolet*. The best known memoir is Lucie Aubrac's *Ils partiront dans l'Ivresse*, which is also the subject of two films. *See also* World War II: Occupation.

Margaret Collins Weitz

BIBLIOGRAPHY

Primary Texts

Albrecht, Mireille. *La Grande Figure féminine de la Résistance: Berty*. Paris: Laffont, 1986.

Aubrac, Lucie. *Ils partiront dans l'Ivresse*. Paris: Seuil, 1984.

Bohec, Jeanne. *La Plastiqueuse à la bicyclette*. Paris: Mercure de France, 1975.

Chevrillon, Claire. *Code Name Christiane Clouet: A Woman in the French Resistance*. College Station: Texas A & M University Press, 1995.

Fourcade, Marie-Madeleine. *L'Arche de Noë*. Paris: Fayard, 1968.

Frang, Brigitte. *Regarde-toi qui meurs*. Paris: Plon, 1970.

Malraux, Clara. *Le Bruit de nos pas*. Vols. 5 and 6. Paris: Grasset, 1976, 1979.

Secondary Texts

Atack, Margaret. *Literature and the French Resistance—Cultural Politics and Narrative Form, 1940–1950.* Manchester: University of Manchester Press, 1989.

Kedward, H. Roderick. *Resistance in Vichy France.* Oxford: Oxford University Press, 1978.

Laska, Vera, ed. *Women in the Resistance and in the Holocaust: The Voices of Eyewitnesses.* Westport, CT: Greenwood, 1983.

Rossiter, Margaret L. *Women in the Resistance.* New York: Praeger, 1986.

Weitz, Margaret Collins. *Sisters in the Resistance: How Women Fought to Free France, 1940–45.* New York: John Wiley and Sons, 1995.

Worms, Jeannine (1923–). Novelist, essayist, and playwright. Argentinian-born Worms uses absurdist language and situations in her comic theater* in order to depict compulsive greed and self-centeredness. In *Mougnou-Mougnou* (1989), for example, young mothers become so engrossed in discussing what they humorously term ''Oedipisation'' that they fail to notice their infant sons are devouring each other. With greater subtlety, Worms created *Archiflore* (1965) to show four generations of Flore women, each harboring the same illusions about love, being abandoned by a recurring archetypal male figure named Léopold. The female protagonists in *Avec ou sans arbres* (1985) and *Liens* (1989) face similar defeat in their quest for independence and self-definition. Feeling used and trapped by the men in their lives, these women discover that their ties (*liens*) are strangling them. Providing few easy solutions, Worms's theater presents penetrating moments of female experience.

Jan Berkowitz Gross

BIBLIOGRAPHY

Primary Texts

Avec ou sans arbres. Paris: Actes Sud-Papiers, 1985.
Archiflore. Paris: Actes Sud-Papiers, 1988.
Un Chat est un chat. Paris: Librairie Théâtrale, 1989.
Liens. Paris: Actes Sud-Papiers, 1989.
Pièces de femmes: Le Goûter, Mougnou-Mougnou, Le Palace. Paris: Librairie Théâtrale, 1989.
Entretiens avec Roger Caillois. Paris: Editions de la Différence, 1991.
Vies de la mort. Paris: Editions de la Différence, 1992.

Secondary Texts

Ferrua, Pietro. ''L'Itinéraire narratif et métaphysique de Jeannine Worms.'' *Cincinnati Romance Review* 3 (1984): 112–185.

Lamar, Celita. ''Couples.'' In *Our Voices, Ourselves.* New York: Peter Lang, 1991. 83–89.

Y

Yaguello, Marina (1947–). Born in Paris of Russian immigrant parents, Yaguello credits her bilingual childhood for her early interest in linguistics. She is a professor at the University of Paris VII, where her current research focuses on French and English syntax and on Wolof. With her essay *Les Mots et les femmes* (1978), Yaguello broke new ground in the study of women and language at a time when few linguists even considered the question noteworthy—only a few, such as Verena Aebischer, have ever followed her lead. Yaguello's observations on gender-based linguistic biases in language debunk the myth* of women's lack of linguistic creativity and their perceived dominance in verbal interaction, while at the same time questioning the presuppositions underlying scientific studies of language that reinforce popular stereotypes and reflect the asymmetries embedded in language itself. Yaguello's *Le Sexe des mots* (1989) further develops the analysis of the sexism inherent in the French language. In *Alice au pays du langage* (1981), *Les Fous du langage* (1984), and *En écoutant parler la langue* (1991), she introduces abstract linguistic notions to a general public often mystified by a jargon that is frequently patriarchal in nature.

Christine Lac

BIBLIOGRAPHY

Primary Texts

Les Mots et les femmes. Essai d'approche socio-linguistique de la condition féminine. Paris: Payot, 1978.
Alice au pays du langage. Paris: Seuil, 1981.
Les Fous du langage. Paris: Seuil, 1984.
Catalogue des idées reçues. Paris: Seuil, 1988
Le Sexe des mots. Paris: Belfond, 1989.
Histoires de lettres. Paris: Seuil, 1990.
En écoutant parler la langue. Paris: Seuil, 1991.

Secondary Text

Aebischer, Verena. *Les Femmes et le langage. Représentations sociales d'une différence.*
    Paris: PUF, 1985.

Yourcenar, Marguerite (1903–1987). Nom de plume of Marguerite de Cray-
encour. Born in Brussels to a wealthy family, Yourcenar was raised by her father
and classically educated at home. During World War II*, she moved to Maine,
where she established a home with her companion, Grace Frick. Between 1929
and 1939, Yourcenar published twelve books that introduce the major themes
of her opus: Greek ideals and Oriental values, the many forms of love and
pleasure, the search for God and the sacred, dream and reality, and political
virtue and oppression. Her international fame began with *Mémoires d'Hadrien*
(1951) and continued with two other historical novels, *L'Oeuvre au noir* (1968)
and *Comme l'eau qui coule* (1982). Their respective protagonists, Hadrian the
emperor, Zeno the alchemist, and Nathanael the common man, form a triptych
that illustrates strength of mind, soul, and heart. The women characters—even
those Yourcenar admired greatly—remain in the background. They are often
seen as traditional Mary or Eve figures, selfless or self-serving, Mother or temptress. When they appear in mythological contexts or comparisons, as in *Feux*
(1936) and in much of her poetry* and theater*, women are often cast in the
role of goddess or heroine.

In the 1950s, Yourcenar began to simplify both her lifestyle and her literary
approach, to revise her early work, to take a public stand on political issues,
and to explain her fiction through her nonfiction. She wrote essays and prefaces
dealing with issues such as world history, her travels, spirituality, and the art of
writing itself. Her interest in preservation led her to translate hitherto inaccessible texts from English, Japanese, Hindi, and Greek. These translations include
works by well-known women such as Sappho, Virginia Woolf, and Murasaki
Shikibu, and lesser-known authors like Hortense Flexner.

Her autobiographical *Labyrinthe du monde* (1974–1988), like many of her
works, defies traditional genre definitions. Yourcenar herself rarely appears in
the text, and she presents her family as only one of many examples of human-
kind. A rich cross-section of women characters—from prototypical mothers to
the hated Noémi—illustrate domestic life through the ages, while war, over-
population, fear, and art also play a prominent role.

Yourcenar spoke from a universal perspective, and her concerns led her from
a historical to a ''geological'' approach. While she believed women were the
equals of men, and she supported ''simple justice''—equal pay and choice in
reproductive rights—she rejected any consideration of differences based on nationality, religion, or gender. She mostly expressed her ideas through male bi-
sexuals, her best-known protagonists. Although Yourcenar's representation of
women accurately reflects women's role in history, her fictional heroines sometimes appear idealized in their capacity for love and sacrifice, and her female
villains are portrayed as particularly negative.

Yourcenar's manuscripts, journals, and correspondence are housed in Harvard's Houghton Library, and there are extensive archives in Tours and Brussels. Her work has always received critical recognition, and she was the first woman to be elected to the prestigious Académie Française (1980). Feminist critics are sharply divided over Yourcenar's treatment of women's issues. Some dismiss Yourcenar as a "phallic" woman, while others see feminist elements in her life and writing, especially in her autobiography*. Never following trends or being unduly swayed by her critics, Marguerite Yourcenar garnered impressive international honors and set a standard for women's literary accomplishments in the twentieth century.

C. Frederick Farrell, Jr., and Edith R. Farrell

BIBLIOGRAPHY

Primary Texts

Le Jardin des chimères. Paris: Perrin, 1921.
Les Charités d'Alcippe et autres poèmes. 1956. Paris: Gallimard, 1984.
Fleuve profond, sombre rivière: Les Negro Spirituals. Trans. and ed. Paris: Gallimard, 1964.
Théâtre. 2 vols. Paris: Gallimard, 1971.
La Couronne et la lyre: Poèmes traduits du grec. Trans. and ed. Paris: Gallimard, 1979.
Les Yeux ouverts: Entretiens avec Matthieu Galey. Paris: Editions du Centurion, 1980.
Discours de réception de Mme Marguerite Yourcenar à l'Académie Française et réponse de M. Jean D'Ormesson. Paris: Gallimard, 1981.
Oeuvres romanesques. Paris: Gallimard, 1982.
Essais et mémoires. Paris: Gallimard, 1991.
Lettres à ses amis et quelques autres. Ed. M. Sarde and J. Brami. Paris: Gallimard, 1995.

Secondary Texts

Bonali-Fiquet, Françoise. *Reception de l'oeuvre de Marguerite Yourcenar. Essai de bibliographie chronologique (1922–1994)*. Tours: Société d'Etudes Yourcenariennes, 1994.
Sarde, Michèle. *Vous, Marguerite Yourcenar*. Paris: Robert Laffont, 1995.

Yver, Colette (1874–1953). Nom de plume of Antoinette de Bergevin. In 1903 Yver began writing novels* about women professionals and their struggle to balance a career with domestic duties. She won the Prix Femina for her 1907 novel *Princesses de sciences*, which portrays a variety of women scientists. Even though most of her novels present independent, intelligent women, critics labeled her texts reactionary, because they usually conclude with the female protagonist's decision to abandon her career to please her husband. Although Yver wrote more conventional romance and society novels and hagiographies after World War I*, her depictions of professional women during the Belle Epoque earn her an important place in feminist literary history.

Juliette M. Rogers

BIBLIOGRAPHY

  Primary Texts

Les Cervelines. Paris: Juven, 1903.
La Bergerie. Paris: Juven, 1904.
Comment s'en vont les Reines. Paris: Calmann-Lévy, 1905.
Princesses de sciences. Paris: Calmann-Lévy, 1907.
Dames du palais. Paris: Calmann-Lévy, 1909.
Le Métier du roi. Paris: Calmann-Lévy, 1911.
Un Coin de voile. Paris: Calmann-Lévy, 1912.
Les Sables mouvants. Paris: Calmann-Lévy, 1913.
Dans le Jardin du féminisme. Paris: Calmann-Lévy, 1920.

Appendix A: General Bibliography

Abensour, Léon. *La Femme et le féminisme avant la Révolution*. Paris: Ernest Leroux, 1923.

Aebischer, Verena. *Les Femmes et le langage. Représentations sociales d'une différence*. Paris: PUF, 1985.

Albistur, Maïté, and Daniel Armogathe. *Histoire du féminisme français du moyen âge à nos jours*. 2 vols. Paris: Des femmes, 1977.

Atack, Margaret, and Phil Powrie. *Contemporary French Fiction by Women: Feminist Perspectives*. New York: Manchester University Press, 1990.

Backer, Dorothy. *Precious Women*. New York: Basic Books, 1974.

Bastiaensen, Michel, ed. *La Femme lettrée à la Renaissance*. Brussels: Université Libre de Bruxelles, Institut Interuniversitaire Renaissance et Humanisme, 1997.

Beach, Cecilia. *French Women Playwrights before the Twentieth Century: A Checklist*. Westport, CT: Greenwood Press, 1994.

———. *French Women Playwrights of the Twentieth Century*. Westport, CT: Greenwood Press, 1996.

Beasley, Faith. *Revising Memory: Women's Fiction and Memoirs in Seventeenth-Century France*. New Brunswick, NJ: Rutgers University Press, 1990.

Beauvoir, Simone de. *Le Deuxième Sexe*. 2 vols. Paris: Gallimard, 1949.

Becker, Lucille. *Twentieth Century French Women Novelists*. Boston: Twayne, 1989.

Beizer, Janet. *Ventriloquized Bodies: Narratives of Hysteria in Nineteenth-Century France*. Ithaca: Cornell University Press, 1994.

Benstock, Shari. *Women of the Left Bank: Paris, 1900–1940*. Austin: University of Texas Press, 1986.

Berriot-Salvadore, Evelyne. *La Femme dans la société française de la Renaissance*. Geneva: Droz, 1990.

Bishop, Michael. *Contemporary French Women Poets*. 2 vols. Amsterdam: Rodopi, 1995.

Boetcher, Ruth Ellen, and Elizabeth Mittman, eds. *Women's Essays: Genre Crossings*. Bloomington: Indiana University Press, 1993.

Bonnel, Roland, and Catherine Rubinger, eds. *Femmes savantes et femmes d'esprit: Women Intellectuals of the French Eighteenth Century*. New York: Peter Lang, 1994.

Bruckner, Matilda Tomaryn. "Fictions of the Female Voice: The Women Troubadours." *Speculum* 76 (1992): 865–891.

Bruneau, Marie-Florine. *Women Mystics Confront the Modern World: Marie de L'Incarnation and Madame Guyon*. Albany: State University of New York Press, 1998.

Buck, Claire, ed. *The Bloomsbury Guide to Women's Literature*. New York: Bloomsbury, 1992.

Bullough, Vern L., and Bonnie Bullough. *Cross-Dressing, Sex, and Gender*. Philadelphia: University of Pennsylvania Press, 1993.

Cohen, Margaret, and Christopher Prendergast, eds. *Spectacles of Realism: Body, Gender, Genre*. Minneapolis: University of Minnesota Press, 1995.

Conley, Katharine. *The Representation of Woman in Surrealism*. Lincoln: University of Nebraska Press, 1996.

Davis, Natalie Zemon. *Society and Culture in Early Modern France*. Stanford: Stanford University Press, 1965.

DeJean Joan, *Libertine Strategies: Freedom and the Novel in Seventeenth-Century France*. Columbus: Ohio State University Press, 1981.

DeJean, Joan, and Nancy K. Miller, eds. *Displacements: Women, Tradition, Literatures in French*. Baltimore: Johns Hopkins University Press, 1991.

———. *Tender Geographies: Women and the Origins of the Novel in France*. New York: Columbia University Press, 1991.

Déjeux, Jean. *La Littérature féminine de langue française au Maghreb*. Paris: Karthala, 1994.

Dijkstra, Bram. *Idols of Perversity: Fantasies of Female Evil in Fin-de-Siècle Culture*. New York: Oxford University Press, 1986.

Douthwaite, Julia V. *Exotic Women: Literary Heroines and Cultural Strategies in Ancien Régime France*. Philadelphia: University of Pennsylvania Press, 1992.

Duby, Georges. *Love and Marriage in the Middle Ages*. Trans. Jane Dunnett. Chicago: University of Chicago Press, 1991.

Duby, Georges, and Christine Klapisch-Zuber. *A History of Women in the West*. Vol. 2: *Silences of the Middle Ages*. Cambridge, MA: Harvard University Press, 1993.

Duchen, Claire. *Feminism in France: From May '68 to Mitterrand*. Boston: Routledge and Kegan Paul, 1986.

Evans, Martha Noel. "Colette: The Vagabond." In *Masks of Tradition: Women and the Politics of Writing in Twentieth-Century France*. Ithaca: Cornell University Press, 1987.

Felski, Rita. *The Gender of Modernity*. Cambridge, MA: Harvard University Press, 1995.

Gaunt, Simon. *Gender and Genre in Medieval French Literature*. Cambridge: Cambridge University Press, 1993.

Gelfand, Elissa. *Imagination in Confinement: Women's Writings from French Prisons*. Ithaca: Cornell University Press, 1983.

Gethner, Perry, ed. *Femmes Dramaturges en France: 1650–1750*. Paris: Biblio 17, 1993.

Gold, Penny Schine. *The Lady and the Virgin: Image, Attitude and Experience in Twelfth-Century France*. Chicago: University of Chicago Press, 1985.

Goldsmith, Elizabeth C., ed. *Writing the Female Voice: Essays on Epistolary Literature.* Boston: Northeastern University Press, 1989.

Goldwyn, Henriette. "Femmes Auteurs dramatiques au dix-septième siècle: La Condition humaine." In *Cahiers du dix-septième siècle: An Interdisciplinary Journal* 4, no. 1 (1990): 51–61.

Goodman, Dena. *The Republic of Letters: A Cultural History of the French Enlightenment.* Ithaca: Cornell University Press, 1994.

Gordon, Felicia, and Marie Cross. *Early French Feminisms, 1830–1940: A Passion for Liberty.* Brookfield, VT: Edward Elgar, 1996.

Green, Mary Jean, Karen Gould, Micheline Rice-Maximin, Keith L. Walker, and Jack A. Yeager, eds. *Postcolonial Subjects: Francophone Women Writers.* Minneapolis: University of Minnesota Press, 1996.

Gutwirth, Madelyn. *The Twilight of the Goddesses: Women and Representation in the French Revolutionary Era.* New Brunswick, NJ: Rutgers University Press, 1992.

Hargreaves, Alec G. *Voices from the North African Immigrant Community in France: Immigration and Identity in Beur Fiction.* Providence, RI: Berg, 1991.

Harth, Erica. *Cartesian Women: Versions and Subversions of Rational Discourse in the Old Regime.* Ithaca: Cornell University Press, 1992.

Hoffmann, Paul. *La Femme dans la pensée des Lumières.* Paris: Ophrys, 1977.

Holmes, Diana. *French Women's Writing 1848–1994.* Atlantic Highlands, NJ: Athlone Press, 1996.

Jardine, Alice A., and Anne Menke, eds. *Shifting Scenes: Interviews on Women, Writing, and Politics in Post-68 France.* New York: Columbia University Press, 1991.

Jensen, Katharine Ann. *Writing Love: Letters, Women, and the Novel in France* (1605–1776). Carbondale: Southern Illinois University Press, 1995.

Jones, Ann Rosalind. "Assimilation with a Difference: Renaissance Women and Literary Influence." *Yale French Studies* 62 (1981): 135–153.

———. *The Currency of Eros: Women's Love Lyric in Europe, 1540–1620.* Bloomington: Indiana University Press, 1990.

———. "Inscribing Femininity: French Theories of the Feminine." In *Making a Difference: Feminist Literary Criticism.* Ed. Gayle Greene and Coppelia Kahn. New York: Routledge, 1985.

Kelly, Dorothy. *Fictional Genders: Role and Representation in Nineteenth-Century French Narrative.* Lincoln: University of Nebraska Press, 1989.

King, Adele. *French Women Novelists: Defining a Female Style.* New York: St. Martin's Press, 1989.

Lamar, Celita. *Our Voices, Ourselves: Women Writing for the French Theatre.* New York: Peter Lang, 1991.

Larsen, Anne R., and Colette H. Winn, eds. *Renaissance Women Writers: French Texts/ American Contexts.* Detroit: Wayne State University Press, 1994.

Lionnet, Françoise. *Postcolonial Representations: Women, Literature, Identity.* Ithaca: Cornell University Press, 1995.

Lomperis, Linda, and Sarah Stanbury, eds. *Feminist Approaches to the Body in Medieval Literature.* Philadelphia: University of Pennsylvania Press, 1993.

Maclean, Ian. *Woman Triumphant: Feminism in French Literature, 1610–1652.* Oxford: Clarendon Press, 1977.

Makward, Christiane P., and Madeleine Cottenet-Hage, eds. *Dictionnaire littéraire des femmes de langue française: De Marie de France à Marie Ndiaye.* Paris: Karthala, 1996.

Marks, Elaine, and Isabelle de Courtivron, eds. *New French Feminisms: An Anthology.* New York: Schocken Books, 1981.

Miller, Nancy. "Women's Autobiography in France." In *Subject to Change: Reading Feminist Writing.* New York: Columbia University Press, 1988.

Milligan, Jennifer E. *The Forgotten Generation: French Women Writers of the Inter-war Period.* New York: Berg, 1996.

Moers, Ellen. *Literary Women: The Great Writers.* New York: Doubleday, 1976.

Moi, Toril. *French Feminist Thought: A Reader.* Oxford: Blackwell, 1987.

Monicat, Bénédicte. *Itinéraires de l'écriture au féminin: Voyageuses du 19e siècle.* Atlanta: Rodopi, 1996.

Moses, Claire Goldberg. *French Feminism in the Nineteenth Century.* Albany: State University of New York Press, 1984.

Moses, Claire Goldberg, and Leslie Wahl Rabine. *Feminism, Socialism, and French Romanticism.* Bloomington: Indiana University Press, 1993.

Moulin, Jeanne. *Huit Siècles de poésie féminine 1170–1975.* Paris: Seghers, 1981.

Roelker, Nancy L. "The Appeal of Calvinism to French Noble Women in the Sixteenth Century." *Journal of Interdisciplinary History* 2, no. 4 (Spring 1972): 391–418.

Sankovitch, Tilde A. *French Women Writers and the Book: Myths of Access and Desire.* Syracuse, NY: Syracuse University Press, 1988.

Sartori, Eva M., and Dorothy W. Zimmerman, eds. *French Women Writers: A Bio-Bibliographical Source Book.* Westport, CT: Greenwood Press, 1991.

Schor, Naomi. *Breaking the Chain: Women, Theory, and French Realist Fiction.* New York: Columbia University Press, 1985.

———. *Reading in Detail: Aesthetics and the Feminine.* New York: Methuen, 1987.

Seifert, Lewis C. *Fairy Tales, Sexuality and Gender in France, 1690–1715: Nostalgic Utopias.* Cambridge: Cambridge University Press, 1996.

Smith, Bonnie. *Ladies of the Leisure Class: The Bourgeoises of Northern France in the Nineteenth Century.* Princeton: Princeton University Press, 1981.

Spencer, Samia I., ed. *French Women and the Age of Enlightenment.* Bloomington: Indiana University Press, 1984.

Spivak, Gayatri Chakravorty. "French Feminism in an International Frame." *Yale French Studies* 62 (1981): 154–184.

Stanton, Domna, ed. *The Defiant Muse: French Feminist Poems from the Middle Ages to the Present.* New York: Feminist Press, 1986.

Stewart, Joan Hinde. *Gynographs: French Novels by Women of the Late Eighteenth Century.* Lincoln: University of Nebraska Press, 1993.

Suleiman, Susan Rubin. "Rewriting the Body: The Politics and Poetics of Female Eroticism." *Poetics Today* 6 (1985): 43–65.

Thomas, Edith. *Les Femmes de 1848.* Paris: PUF, 1948.

———. *Les "Pétroleuses."* Paris: Gallimard, 1963.

Timmermans, Linda. *L'Accès des femmes à la culture (1598–1715).* Paris: Nizet, 1993.

Van Dijk, Suzanna. *Traces des femmes. Présences féminines dans le journalisme français du XVIIIe siècle.* Amsterdam: AOA-Holland University Press, 1988.

Waelti-Walters, Jennifer, and Stephen C. Hause, eds. *Feminisms of the Belle Epoque: A Historical and Literary Anthology.* Lincoln: University of Nebraska Press, 1994.

Wilson, Katharina M., ed. *An Encyclopedia of Continental Women Writers*. 2 vols. New York: Garland, 1991.

Winn, Colette H., and Donna Kuizenga, eds. *Women Writers in Pre-Revolutionary France: Strategies of Emancipation*. New York: Garland Press, 1997.

Appendix B: Chronology of French Women Writers

The chronology is organized by date of birth. Writers with unknown birth dates appear at the beginning of each century. An asterisk marks the name under which the author is entered in *The Feminist Encyclopedia of French Literature*.

MIDDLE AGES

*Castelozza (12th century?, 13th century?)

Comtessa de *Dia (end of 12th century?)

*Marie de France (12th century)

*Héloïse (c. 1100–1163)

*Christine de Pizan (c. 1364–c. 1431)

SIXTEENTH CENTURY

Marie *Le Gendre (?–?)

Marie de *Cotteblanche (?–?)

Katherine d'*Amboise (?–1550)

Marie *Dentière (?–1561)

Anne de *Bretagne (1476–1514)

Louise de *Savoie (1476–1531)

Marguerite d'*Autriche (1480–1530)

Marguerite de *Navarre (1492–1549)

Diane de *Poitiers (1499–1566)

Hélisenne de *Crenne (1510?–1560?)

Catherine de *Médici (1519–1589)

Madeleine des *Roches (1520–1587)

Pernette du *Guillet (1520?–1545)

Louise *Labé (c. 1520–1566)

Jeanne d'*Albret (1528–1572)

Anne de *Marquets (c. 1533–1588)

Jeanne *Flore (1537–15??)

Georgette de *Montenay (1540?–c. 1581)

Catherine des *Roches (1542–1587)

Marie de *Romieu (1545?–1590)

Nicole *Estienne (1545–1584/1596)

Madeleine de l'*Aubespine (1546–1596)

Charlotte de *Bourbon (1546/1547–1582)

Gabielle de *Coignard (c. 1550–c. 1586)

Marguerite de *Valois (1553–1615)

Catherine de *Parthenay (1554–1631)

Catherine de *Bourbon (1558–1604)

Louise (Boursier) *Bourgeois (1563–1636)

Marie Le Jars de *Gournay (1565–1645)

Jeanne-Françoise Frémyot *Chantal (1572–1641)

Marie de *Médici (1573–1642)

Anne de *Rohan (1584–1646)

Catherine Vivonne de Savelli de *Rambouillet (1588–1665)

Marie Guyard, later *Marie de l'Incarnation (1599–1672)

Madeleine de *Sablé (1599–1678)

SEVENTEENTH CENTURY

Marguerite Buffet (?–?)

Mlle *Poulain (?–?)

Marie-Françoise *Certain (?–?)

Catherine *Durand, dame Bédacier (?–1736)

Mme de *Pringy (fl. 1694–1709)

Jeanne de *Schomberg (1600–1674)

Alberte-Barbe d'Ernecourt de *Saint-Balmon (1607–1660)

Madeleine de *Scudéry (1607–1701)

Catherine Meudrac, dame de *La Guette (1613–after 1676)

Marthe *Cosnard (1614–after 1659)

Jacqueline Bouette de *Blémur (1618–1698)

Henriette Coligny de *La Suze (1618–1673)

Charlotte Saumaise de Chazan, comtesse de *Brégy (Brégis) (1619–1693)

Gilberte *Pascal (Périer) (1620–1687)

Françoise Bertaut, dame de *Motteville (1621–1689)

Anne (Ninon) de *Lenclos (1623?–1705)

Jacqueline *Pascal (1625–1661)

Marie d'Orléans-Longueville, duchesse de *Nemours (1625–1707)

Marie de Rabutin-Chantal de *Sévigné (1626–1696)

Anne-Marie-Louise Henriette d'Orléans, duchesse de *Montpensier (1627–1693)

Marie-Eléonore de *Rohan (1628–1681)

Marie Pech (Puech) de *Calages (1630–1661)

Gabrielle *Suchon (1631–1703)

Françoise *Pascal (1632–?)

Anne de *La Vigne (1634–1684)

Marie-Madeleine Pioche de la Vergne de *Lafayette (1634–1693)

Françoise d'Aubigné de *Maintenon (1635–1719)

Antoinette du Ligier de la Garde, Madame *Deshoulières (1637–1694)

Antoinette, dame Salvan de *Saliez (Saliès) (1638–1730)

Marie *Mancini (1639–1706/1715)

Marie Catherine Desjardins de *Villedieu (1640?–1683)

Marguerite Hessein de Rambouillet de *La Sablière (1640–1693)

Anne de *La Roche-Guilhen (1644–1707)

Hortense *Mancini (1646–1699)

Elisabeth-Sophie *Chéron (1647–1711)

Anne Thérèse de *Lambert (1647–1733)

Jeanne-Marie Bouvier de la Mothe, dame *Guyon (1648–1717)

Marie-Catherine Le Jumel de Barneville, baronne d' *Aulnoy (1650/1651–1705)

Louise-Geneviève Gillot de *Sainctonge (Saintonge) (1650–1718)

Elisabeth-Charlotte von de Pfalz, Madame *Palatine (1652–1722)

Charlotte-Rose Caumont der *La Force (1654–1724)

Anne Le Fèvre *Dacier (1654–1721)

Anne de Bellinzani *Ferrand (1657–1740)

Catherine *Bernard (1663–1712?)

Anne-Marguerite Petit, dame *du Noyer (1663–1719)

Marie-Jeanne *Lhéritier de Villandon (1664?–1734)

Henriette-Julie de Castelnau, comtesse de *Murat (1668?–1716)

Marie-Anne *Barbier (1670–1745)

Marthe-Marguerite de *Caylus (1673–1729)

Marguerite de *Lussan (1682–1758)

Claudine-Alexandrine Guérin de *Tencin (1682–1749)

Madeleine-Angélique Poisson, dame de *Gomez (1684–1770)

Marguerite-Jeanne Cordier de Launay de *Staal (1689–1750)

Adrienne *Lecouvreur (1692–1730)

Charlotte Elisabeth *Aïssé (c. 1694–1733)

Gabrielle Suzanne Barbot de Gallon de *Villeneuve (1695–1755)

Françoise d'Issembourg de *Graffigny (1695–1758)

Marie Huber (1695–1753)

Marie de Vichy-Chamrond *Du Deffand (1697–1780)

Marie-Thérèse Rodet *Geoffrin (1699–1777)

EIGHTEENTH CENTURY

Mme de *Beaumer (?–?)

Mme *Beccary (?–?)

Mme de Coicy (?–?)

Mme *Le Givre de Richebourg (?–?)

Mme *Laisse (?–?)

Marie-Louise Charlotte de Pelard de Givre de *Fontaines (?–1730)

Françoise-Thérèse Aumerle de *Saint-Phalier Dalibard (?–1757)

Marie-Antoniette *Fagnon (?–1770)

Charlotte-Antoinette de Bressey de *Lezay-Marnésia (?–1785)

Mlle Fontette de *Sommery (?–1790)

Lousie Cavelier *Lévesque (1703–1743/1745)

Marie-Anne Roumier *Robert (1705–1771)

Gabrielle Emilie du *Châtelet (1706–1749)

Anne-Marie Fiquet *du Bocage (1710–1802)

Charlotte-Marie-Anne Charbonnier de *La Guesnerie (1710?–1785)

Marie-Madeleine (Marguerite) de *Lubert (c. 1710–1779)

Jeanne-Marie* Leprince de Beaumont (1711–1780)

Marie-Jeanne *Riccoboni (1713–1792)

Charlotte Reynier *Bourette (1714–1784)

Octavie Guichard *Belot (1719–1804)

Marie-Agnès Pillement de *Fauques (c. 1720–1777)

Madeleine d'Arsant de *Puisieux (1720–1798)

Marie-Geneviève-Charlotte Darlus *Thiroux d'Arconville (1720–1805)

Claire Josèphe *Clairon (1723–1803)

Françoise *Benoist (1724–1809)

Marie Anne Carrelet de *Marron (1725–1778)

Louise Florence Tardieu d'*Epinay (1726–1783)

Marie Justine Cabaret du Ronceray *Favart (1727–1772)

Marie Prudence *Plisson (1727–1788)

Marquise de *Belvo (1728?–?)

Marie-Louise-Anne Bouvard de *Fourqueux (1728–?)

Anne Louise *Elie de Beaumont (1729/1730–1783)

Claire Marie de la Vieuville de *Saint-Chamond (1731–?)

Julie-Jeanne Eléanore de Lespinasse (1732–1776)

Charlotte Chaumet d'*Ormoy (1732–1791)

Anne d'Aubourg de la Bove de *Miremont (1735–1811)

Marie Emilie de *Montanclos (1736–1812)

Jacqueline-Aimée *Brohon (1737?–1778)

Charlotte-Jeanne Béraud de la Haye de Riou de *Montesson (1737–1806)

Fanny de *Beauharnais (1737–1813)

Marie-Catherine-Renée Darcel de *Maraise (1737–1823)

Françoise de Chaumont *Falconnet (1738–1819)

Suzanne Curchod *Necker (1739–1794)

Isabelle de *Charrière (1740–1805)

Marie-Madeleine *Jodin (1741–1790)

Marie-Anne *Bourdic-Viot (1746–1802)

Stéphanie-Félicité Ducrest de Saint-Aubin de *Genlis (1746–1830)

Olympe de *Gouges (1748–1793)

Marie Elisabeth Bouée de *La Fite (1750?–1794)

Marie-Joséphine *Monbart (c. 1750–?)

Isabelle de *Montolieu (1751–1832)

Marie Moreau *Monnet (1752–1798)

Jeanne Louise Henriette *Campan (1752–1822)

Marie-Armande Jeanne d'Humières *Gacon-Dufour (1753–1835)

Marie-Charlotte-Pauline Robert de *Lézardière (1754–1835)

Marie-Jeanne (Manon) Phlipon *Roland de la Platière (1754–1794)

Adélaïde-Edmée Prévost de *La Briche (1755–1844)

Anne Pauline *Léon (1758–?)

Louise-Félicité Guynement de *Kéralio-Robert (1758–1822)

Elisabeth Louise *Vigée-Lebrun (1755–1842)

Marguerite-Victoire *Babois (1760–1839)

Anne-Hyacinthe Geille de Saint-Leger de *Colleville (1761–1824)

Anne Josephe Théroigne de *Méricourt (1762–1817)

Marie-Adélaïde *Barthélémy-Hadot (1763–1821)

Barbara Juliane de *Krüdener (1764–1824)

Sophie de Grouchy de *Condorcet (1764–1822)

Béatrix-Stéphanie *Lage de Volude (1764–1842)

Adélaïde-Gillette Billet *Dufrénoy (1765–1825)

Anne-Félicité d'Ormoy *Mérard de Saint-Just (1765–1830)

Claire (Rose) *Lacombe (1765–?)

Sophie *Gay (1766–1852)

Anne-Louise-Germaine Necker de *Staël-Holstein (1766–1817)

Charlotte *Corday (1768–1793)

Marie-Louise-Rose Lévesque *Pétigny de Saint-Romain (1768–?)

Sophie *Cottin (1770–1807)

Louise-Marie Victoire *Chastenay de Lanty (1771–1855)

Elisabeth-Charlotte-Pauline de Meulan *Guizot (1773–1827)

Claire de *Duras (1777–1828)

Claire Elisabeth de Vergenne de *Rémusat (1780–1821)

Marceline *Desbodes-Valmore (1786–1859)

Louise d'*Estournelles (1792–1860)

Henriette d'*Angeville (1794–1871)

Eugénie *Foa (1796–1852)

Eugénie *Niboyet (1796–1883)

Marie *Dorval (1798–1849)

Amable *Tastu (1798–1885)

Angélique *Arnaud (1799–1884)

Sophie Rostopchine, comtesse de *Ségur (1799–1874)

NINETEENTH CENTURY

Claire *Démar (1800?–1833)

Laure *Surville (1800–1871)

Marie-Sophie *Leroyer de Chantepie (1800–1888)

Hortense *Allart (1801–1879)

Suzanne *Voilquin (1801–1877)

Flora *Tristan (1803–1844)

Delphine *Gay de Giardin (1804–1855)

George *Sand (1804–1876)

Marie d'*Agoult (1805–1876)

Jeanne *Deroin (1805–1894)

Eugénie de *Guérin (1805–1848)

Marie-Desirée Pauline *Roland (1805–1852)

Cristina Trivulzio di *Belgiojoso (1808–1871)

Pauline *Craven de la Ferronays (1808–1891)

Elisa *Mercoeur (1809–1835)

Jenny d'*Héricourt (1809–1875)

Louise *Colet (1810–1876)

Louise Victoire Choquet *Ackermann (1813–1890)

Adèle *Hommaire de Hell (1819–?)

Pauline *Viardot (1821–1910)

Julie Victoire *Daubié (1824–1874)

André *Léo (1824–1900)

Céleste *Mogador (1824–1909)

Maria *Deraismes (1828–1894)

Zénaïde *Fleuriot (1829–1889)

Olympe *Audouard (1830–1890)

Augustine-Adolphine-Malvina Souville *Blanchecotte (1830–1897)

Louise *Michel (1830–1905)

Marie-Louise *Gagneur (1832–1902)

Pauline *Caro (1835–1901)

Juliette *Adam (1836–1936)

Thérèse *Blanc (1840–1907)

Nina de *Villard (Callias) (1843–1884)

Louisa Pène *Siefert (1845–1877)

Judith *Gautier (1845–1917)

Hubertine *Auclert (1848–1914)

*Gyp (1849–1932)

Jane *Dieulafoy (1851–1916)

Jeanne *Marni (1854–1910)

*Séverine (1855–1929)

Marie *Krysinska (1857–1908)

*Rachilde (1860–1953)

Marguerite *Audoux (1863–1937)

Marguerite *Durand (1864–1936)

Liane de *Pougy (1869–1950)

Gabrielle *Reval (1870–1938)

*Harlor (1871–1970)

*Colette (1873–1954)

Jeanne *Landre (1874–1936)

Madeleine *Pelletier (1874–1939)

Lucie *Delarue-Mardrus (1874–1945)

Colette *Yver (1874–1953)

Gérard d'*Houville (1875–1963)

Natalie Clifford *Barney (1876–1972)

Anna de *Noailles (1876–1933)

Renée *Vivien (1877–1909)

Marcelle *Tinayre (1877–1948)

Nelly *Roussel (1878–1922)

Catherine *Pozzi (1882–1934)

Hélène *Brion (1882–1962)

Jeanne *Humbert (1890–1986)

Elsa *Triolet (1896/1897–1970)

Clara *Malraux (1897–1982)

Valerie Boué *Penrose (1898–1978)

TWENTIETH CENTURY

Christine *Angot (?–)

Catherine *Anne (?–)

Louise-Marie *Compain (?–?)

Christiane *Baroche (?–)

Simone *Benmussa (?–)

Denise *Bonal (?–)

Antoinette *Fouque (?–)

Isabelle *Hausser (?–)

Evelyne *Le Garrec (?–)

Kim *Lefèvre (?–)

Micheline *Maurel (?–)

Michèle *Montrelay (?–)

Michèle *Sarde (?–)

Janine *Teisson (?–)

Nathalie *Sarraute (1900–)

Marguerite *Yourcenar (1903–1987)

Violette *Leduc (1907–1972)

Simone de *Beauvoir (1908–1986)

Simone *Weil (1909–1943)

Edith *Thomas (1909–1970)

Thérèse *Plantier (1911–)

Lucie *Aubrac (1912–)

Eugénie *Lemoine-Luccioni (1912–)

Charlotte *Delbo (1913–1985)

Marie-Louise Taos *Amrouche (1913–1976)

Dominique *Rolin (1913–)

Jacqueline de *Romilly (1913–)

Béatrix *Beck (1914–)

Marguerite *Duras (1914–1996)

Hélène *Parmelin (1915–)

Geneviève *Serreau (1915–1981)

Françoise *Giroud (1916–)

Anne *Hébert (1916–)

Zoé *Oldenbourg (1916–)

Christiane *Rochefort (1917–1998)

Françoise *Parturier (1919–1995)

Andrée *Chedid (1920–)

Françoise d'*Eaubonne (1920–)

Geneviève *Gennari (1920–)

Benoîte *Groult (1920–)

Anna *Langfus (1920–1966)

Gisèle *Prassinos (1920–)

Suzanne *Prou (1920–1995)

Christine de *Rivoyre (1921–)

Jeanine *Worms (1923–)

Evelyne *Sullerot (1924–)

Loleh *Bellon (1925–)

Madeleine *Chapsal (1925–)

Claudine *Herrmann (1928–)

Gisèle *Halimi (1927–)

Frédérique *Hébrard (1927–)

Françoise *Collin (1928–)

Joyce *Mansour (1928–1986)

Marie *Cardinal (1929–)

Yvette *Roudy (1929–)

Christine *Arnothy (1930–)

Luce *Irigaray (1930–)

Françoise *Mallet-Joris (1930–)

Michèle *Perrein (1930–)

Liliane *Atlan (1932–)

Marie-Claire *Bancquart (1932–)

Geneviève *Dormann (1933–)

Jocelyne *François (1933–)

Claire *Etcherelli (1934–)

Colette *Guillaumin (1934–)

Sarah *Kofman (1934–)

Régine *Deforges (1935–)

Françoise *Sagan (1935–)

Monique *Wittig (1935–)

Josette *Alia (1936–)

Assia *Djebar (1936–)

Anne-Marie *Albiach (1937–)

Hélène *Cixous (1937–)

Elisabeth *Gille (1937–1996)

Albertine *Sarrazin (1937–1967)

Marie *Etienne (1938–)

Catherine *Clément (1939–)

Denise *Le Dantec (1939–)

Ariane *Mnouchkine (1939–)

Annie *Ernaux (1940–)

Marie-Thérèse *Humbert (1940–)

Arlette *Laguiller (1940–)

Annie *Leclerc (1940–)

Danièle *Sallenave (1940–)

Christine *Delphy (1941–)

Pierrette *Fleutiaux (1941–)

Michelle *Foucher (1941–)

Julia *Kristeva (1941–)

Leïla *Sebbar (1941–)

Marie *Chaix (1942–)

Xavière *Gauthier (1942–)

Myriam *Anissimov (1943–)

Chantal *Chawaf (1943–)

Paule *Constant (1944–)

Elisabeth *Badinter (1944–)

Fatima *Gallaire (1944–)

Madeleine *Laïk (1944–)

Marie-France *Pisier (1944–)

Jeanne *Hyvrard (1945–)

Anne *Delbée (1946–)

Marina *Yaguello (1947–)

Cathy *Bernheim (1948–)

Louise *Doutreligne (1948–)

Djanet *Lachmet (1948–)

Michèle *Le Doeuff (1948–)

Marie *Redonnet (1948–)

Marlène *Amar (1949–)

*Djura (1949–)

Malika *Mokeddem (1949–)

Josiane *Balasko (1950–)

Muriel *Cerf (1950–)

Raphaële *Billetdoux (1951–)

Geneviève *Brisac (1951–)

Françoise *Rey (1951–)

Denise *Chalem (1952–)

Louise *Lambrichs (1952–)

Sophie *Chauveau (1953–)

Nancy *Huston (1953–)

Dorothée *Letessier (1953–)

Sylvie *Germain (1954–)

Emanuelle *Bernheim (1956–)

Alina *Reyes (1956–)

Farida *Belghoul (1958–)

Tassadit *Imache (1958–)

Sakinna *Boukhedenna (1959–)

Calixthe *Beyala (1961–)

Anne *Garréta (1962–)
Linda *Lê (1963–)
Nina *Bouraoui (1967–)
Marie *Ndiaye (1967–)

Index

Note: Boldface numbers indicate location of main entries.

Contributors

Carmeta Abbott, University of Waterloo, CAN

Lisa G. Algazi, Hood College

Grace M. Armstrong, Bryn Mawr College

Dorothy Backer, Dickinson College

Jolene Barjasteh, St. Olaf College

Cathleen M. Bauschatz, University of Maine

Cecilia Beach, Alfred University

Faith E. Beasley, Dartmouth College

S. Pascale Bécel, Florida International Institute

Edith J. Benkov, San Diego State University

Neil B. Bishop, Memorial University of Newfoundland, CAN

Michèle Bissière, University of North Carolina, Charlotte

Renate Blumenfeld-Kosinski, University of Pittsburgh

Karen Bouwer, University of San Francisco

Francis T. Bright, University of Redlands

Roberta S. Brown, Pacific Lutheran University

Matilda Tomaryn Bruckner, Boston College

Raymonde A. Saliou Bulger, Graceland College

Thomas M. Carr, Jr., University of Nebraska, Lincoln

Roland A. Champagne, University of Missouri, St. Louis

Frédérique Chevillot, University of Denver

Michelle Chilcoat, Colby College

Patricia Francis Cholakian, Hamilton College

Mary Cisar, St. Olaf College

Clark Colahan, Whitman College

Marina Mazal Tov Compson, Whitman College

Katharine Conley, Dartmouth College

Verena Andermatt Conley, Harvard University

Susan P. Conner, Central Michigan University

Isabelle Constant, Western Oregon State College

Robert D. Cottrell, Ohio State University

Madeleine Cottenet-Hage, University of Maryland

Jane Couchman, York University, Toronto, CAN

Olga B. Cragg, University of British Columbia, CAN

Armelle Crouzières-Ingenthron, Middlebury College

Diane Griffin Crowder, Cornelle College

Michael Danahy, University of Mississippi

Charlotte Daniels, Connecticut College

Denise Z. Davidson, University of Pennsylvania

Rosena Davison, Simon Fraser University, Burnaby, CAN

Julia K. DePree, Agnes Scott College

Sarah Harrell DeSmet, University of Georgia

S. Pascale Dewey, Kutztown University

Elyane Dezon-Jones, Washington University

Anne Donadey, University of Iowa

Lance K. Donaldson-Evans, University of Pennsylvania

Julia Douthwaite, University of Notre Dame

Sylvaine Egron-Sparrow, Wellesley College

Tama Lea Engelking, Cleveland State University

C. Frederick Farrell, Jr., University of Minnesota, Morris

Edith R. Farrell, University of Minnesota, Morris

Gary Ferguson, University of Delaware

Véronique Flambard-Weisbart, Loyola Marymount University

Yaël Simpson Fletcher, Emory University

Hannah Fournier, University of Waterloo, CAN

Christopher G. Fox, Rutgers University

Lucienne Frappier-Mazur, University of Pennsylvania

Jennifer L. Gardner, Rutgers University

Mary Anne Garnett, University of Arkansas, Little Rock

Nina Rattner Gelbart, Occidental College

Perry Gethner, Oklahoma State University

Nancy Sloan Goldberg, Middle Tennessee University

Elizabeth C. Goldsmith, Boston University

Elizabeth Fisher Goldsmith, Noble and Greenough School

Henriette Goldwyn, New York University

Susan Grayson, Occidental College

Susan Grayzel, University of Mississippi

Wendy Greenberg, Pennsylvania State University, Allentown

Melanie E. Gregg, Dickinson College

Jan Berkowitz Gross, Grinnell College

Madelyn Gutwirth, University of Pennsylvania

Jeanne Hageman, North Dakota State University

Colette T. Hall, Ursinus College

Sarah Hanley, University of Iowa

Patricia Hannon, Catholic University

Helynne H. Hansen, Western State College of Colorado

Margaret Harp, University of Nevada, Las Vegas

Melanie Hawthorne, Teaxas A&M University

Jeanette Marie Hecker, Georgia Southern University

Carla Hesse, University of California, Berkeley

Marie-France Hilgar, University of Nevada, Las Vegas

Susan Ireland, Grinnell College

Hélène Julien, Colgate University

Suzanne Kaufman, Loyola University of Chicago

Dorothy Kelly, Boston University

Angela Kimyongür, University of Hull, UK

Sharon Kinoshita, University of California at Santz Cruz

Nancy D. Klein, independent scholar

Bettina L. Knapp, Hunter College and the Graduate Center, City University of New York

Leonard R. Koos, Mary Washington College

Victoria B. Korzeniowska, University of Surrey, UK

April A. Knutson, University of Minnesota, Twin Cities

Pauline Kra, Yeshiva University

Donna Kuizenga, University of Vermont

Christine Lac, Carleton College

Norris J. Lacy, Pennsylvania State University

Bethany Ladimer, Middlebury College

Catherine Lafarge, Bryn Mawr College

Anne R. Larsen, Hope College

Valérie Lastinger, West Virginia University

Marie Lathers, Iowa State University

Patrick Laude, Georgetown University

Julia Lauer-Chéenne, Columbia College, Chicago

Marie-Pierre Le Hir, Case Western Reserve University

Gayle A. Levy, University of Missouri

Marie Liénard, University of Provence

Caryl L. Lloyd, University of West Georgia

Virginia Marino, National Council on Economic Education

Claire Marrone, Sacred Heart University

Florence Martin, Goucher College

Gita May, Columbia University

Sarah Maza, Northwestern University

Mary McAlpin, University of Tennessee

Jennifer McGonagle, Boston College

Mary B. McKinley, University of Virginia, Charlottesville

Mark McKinney, Miami University

Betty L. McLane-Iles, Truman State University

Heather McPherson, University of Alabama, Birmingham

Ana M. de Medeiros, University of Kent, Canterbury, UK

E. Nicole Meyer, University of Wisconsin, Green Bay

Judith G. Miller, University of Wisconsin

Bénédicte Monicat, Pennsylvania State University

Catherine Montfort, University of Santa Clara

Cheryl A. Morgan, Hamilton College

Martine Motard-Noar, Western Maryland College

Warren Motte, University of Colorado

Elisabeth-Christine Muelsch, Angelo State University

Jerry C. Nash, University of North Texas

Barbara Newman, Northwestern University

Pauline Newman-Gordon, Stanford University

Martha B. Nichols-Pecceu, Eckerd College

Anna Norris, Mary Baldwin College

Catherine O'Brien, Kingston University, UK

Sally O'Driscoll, Fairfield University

Adrianna M. Paliyenko, Colby College

Juliette Parnell-Smith, University of Nebraska, Omaha

Yolanda Astarita Patterson, California State University, Hayward

Velvet Pearson, University of Southern California, Los Angeles

Katrina Perry, University of Richmond

Marie-Pascale Pieretti, Drew University

Laurence M. Porter, Michigan State University

Eva Posfáy, Carleton College

Judith E. Preckshot, University of Minnesota, Twin Cities

Gerald Prince, University of Pennsylvania

Christine McCall Probes, University of South Florida

Patrice J. Proulx, University of Nebraska, Omaha

Annabelle M. Rea, Occidental College

Régine Reynolds-Cornell, Agnes Scott College

Mary Rice-DeFosse, Bates College

Sylvie L. F. Richards, Northwest Missouri State University

François Rigolot, Princeton University

Juliette M. Rogers, University of New Hampshire

Francis Ronsin, Université de Bourgogne

Marian Rothstein, Carthage College

Brigitte Roussel, Wichita State University

Mary Rowan, Brooklyn College, City University of New York

Monique Saigal, Pomona College

Tilde Sankovitch, Northwestern University

Miléna Santoro, Georgetown University

Jennifer I. Sartori, Emory University

Martine Sauret, Western Michigan University

Yaël Schlick, Queen's University, Kingston, CAN

Gretchen Schultz, Brown University

Lucy M. Schwartz, Buffalo State College

Lewis C. Seifert, Brown University

T. Denean Sharpley-Whiting, Purdue University

Constance Sherak, University of Hawaii

Carol Sherman, University of North Carolina, Chapel Hill

Catherine Slawy-Sutton, Davidson College

Annie Smart, Washington University

Antoinette Marie Sol, University of Texas, Arlington

Paula Sommers, University of Missouri, Columbia

Samia I. Spencer, Auburn University

Christie St. John, Vanderbilt University

Katherine Stephenson, University of North Carolina, Charlotte

Joan Hinde Stewart, North Carolina State University

Philip Stewart, Duke University

Felicia B. Sturzer, University of Tennessee, Chattanooga

Karyna Szmurlo, Clemson University

Ruth P. Thomas, Temple University

Suzanne C. Toczyski, Pacific Lutheran University

Holly Tucker, Vanderbilt University

Belle Stoddard Tuten, Juniata College

Frédérique Van de Poel-Knottnerus, Oklahoma State University

Gabrielle Verdier, University of Wisconsin, Milwaukee

Derk Visser, Ursinus College

Joëlle Vitiello, Macalester College

Lisa Walsh, University of Texas, Austin

Whitney Walton, Purdue University

Margaret Collins Weitz, Suffolk University

Marcelle Maistre Welch, Florida International University

Janet Whatley, University of Vermont

Charles G. S. Williams, Ohio State University

Renee Winegarten, Independent scholar

Colette H. Winn, Washington University, St. Louis

Mary Beth Winn, State University of New York, Albany

Margaret Wise, University of Pennsylvania

Aurora Wolfgang, California State University, San Bernardino

Monica L. Wright, Washington University, St. Louis

Catherine Yandell, Carleton College

Dorothy Wynne Zimmerman, University of Nebraska-Lincoln

Metka Zupančič, University of Guelph, CAN

ISBN 0-313-29651-0

9 780313 296512

HARDCOVER BAR CODE